solutions@syngress.com

With over 1,500,000 copies of our MCSE, MCSD, CompTIA, and Cisco study guides in print, we have come to know many of you personally. By listening, we've learned what you like and dislike about typical computer books. The most requested item has been for a web-based service that keeps you current on the topic of the book and related technologies. In response, we have created solutions@syngress.com, a service that includes the following features:

- A one-year warranty against content obsolescence that occurs as the result of vendor product upgrades. We will provide regular web updates for affected chapters.
- Monthly mailings that respond to customer FAQs and provide detailed explanations of the most difficult topics, written by content experts exclusively for solutions@syngress.com.
- Regularly updated links to sites that our editors have determined offer valuable additional information on key topics.
- Access to "Ask the Author"™ customer query forms that allow readers to post questions to be addressed by our authors and editors.

Once you've purchased this book, browse to

www.syngress.com/solutions.

To register, you will need to have the book handy to verify your purchase.

Thank you for giving us the opportunity to serve you.

SYNGRESS®

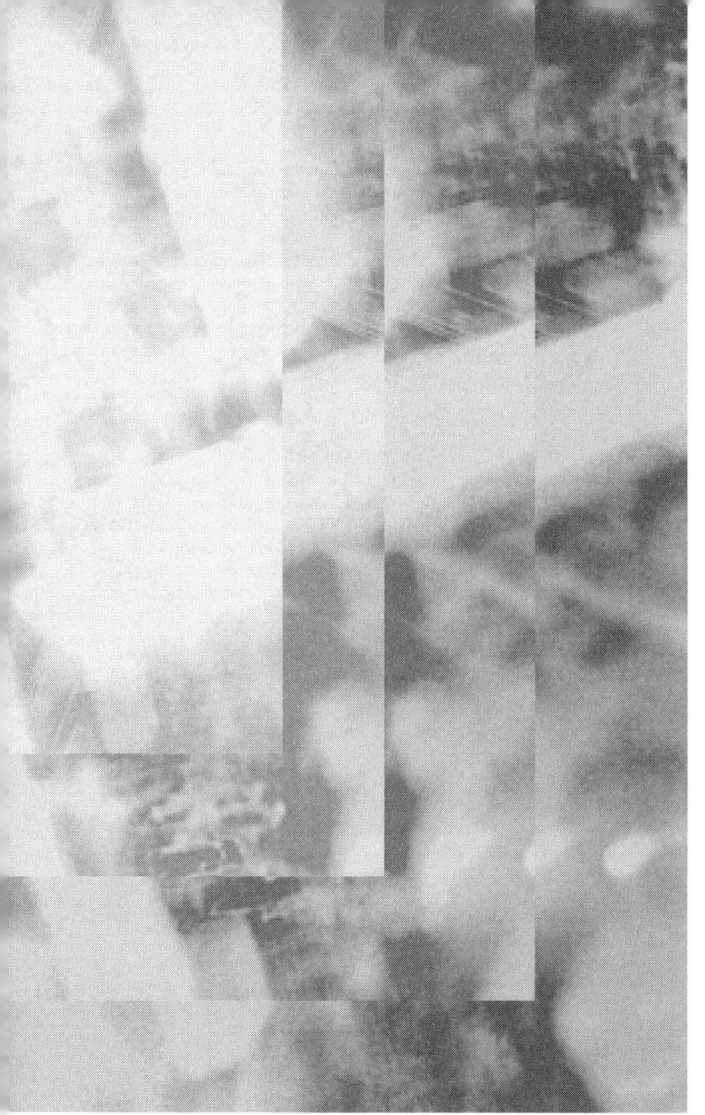

Alcanet International
Deutschland GmbH
Motorstraße 25
70499 Stuttgart
Deutschland

ADMINISTERING
CISCO QoS
FOR IP NETWORKS

SYNGRESS®

Syngress Publishing, Inc., the author(s), and any person or firm involved in the writing, editing, or production (collectively "Makers") of this book ("the Work") do not guarantee or warrant the results to be obtained from the Work.

There is no guarantee of any kind, expressed or implied, regarding the Work or its contents. The Work is sold AS IS and WITHOUT WARRANTY. You may have other legal rights, which vary from state to state.

In no event will Makers be liable to you for damages, including any loss of profits, lost savings, or other incidental or consequential damages arising out from the Work or its contents. Because some states do not allow the exclusion or limitation of liability for consequential or incidental damages, the above limitation may not apply to you.

You should always use reasonable case, including backup and other appropriate precautions, when working with computers, networks, data, and files.

Syngress Media® and Syngress® are registered trademarks of Syngress Media, Inc. "Career Advancement Through Skill Enhancement™," "Ask the Author™," "Ask the Author UPDATE™," "Mission Critical™," and "Hack Proofing™" are trademarks of Syngress Publishing, Inc. Brands and product names mentioned in this book are trademarks or service marks of their respective companies.

KEY	SERIAL NUMBER
001	ALKJD48753
002	LERQAR9T83
003	ERQ395E932
004	45BHSKERF3
005	SLDFAPW93V
006	LWE432532R
007	36FCBFGK454
008	NVCW5DGK43
009	FJA495G8N3
010	4U34BRA395

PUBLISHED BY
Syngress Publishing, Inc.
800 Hingham Street
Rockland, MA 02370

Administering Cisco QoS for IP Networks

Copyright © 2001 by Syngress Publishing, Inc. All rights reserved. Printed in the United States of America. Except as permitted under the Copyright Act of 1976, no part of this publication may be reproduced or distributed in any form or by any means, or stored in a database or retrieval system, without the prior written permission of the publisher, with the exception that the program listings may be entered, stored, and executed in a computer system, but they may not be reproduced for publication.

Printed in the United States of America

1 2 3 4 5 6 7 8 9 0

ISBN: 1-928994-21-0

Co-Publisher: Richard Kristof
Technical edit by: Michael E. Flannagan
Technical Review by: Mark Buchmann
Acquisitions Editor: Catherine B. Nolan

Freelance Editorial Manager: Maribeth Corona-Evans
Index by: Robert A. Saigh
Copy edit by: Beth Roberts and Juli Smith
Page Layout and Art by: Shannon Tozier

Distributed by Publishers Group West

Acknowledgments

We would like to acknowledge the following people for their kindness and support in making this book possible.

Richard Kristof, Duncan Anderson, David Marini, Jennifer Gould, Kevin Murray, Dale Leatherwood, Laura Cervoni, and Rhonda Harmon of Global Knowledge, for their generous access to the IT industry's best courses, instructors, and training facilities.

Ralph Troupe, Rhonda St. John, Emlyn Rhodes, and the team at Callisma for their invaluable insight into the challenges of designing, deploying and supporting world-class enterprise networks.

Karen Cross, Lance Tilford, Meaghan Cunningham, Kim Wylie, Harry Kirchner, Bill Richter, Kevin Votel, Brittin Clark, and Sarah MacLachlan of Publishers Group West for sharing their incredible marketing experience and expertise.

Mary Ging, Caroline Hird, Simon Beale, Caroline Wheeler, Victoria Fuller, Jonathan Bunkell, and Klaus Beran of Harcourt International for making certain that our vision remains worldwide in scope.

Anneke Baeten, Annabel Dent, and Laurie Giles of Harcourt Australia for all their help.

David Buckland, Wendi Wong, Daniel Loh, Marie Chieng, Lucy Chong, Leslie Lim, Audrey Gan, and Joseph Chan of Transquest Publishers for the enthusiasm with which they receive our books.

Kwon Sung June at Acorn Publishing for his support.

Ethan Atkin at Cranbury International for his help in expanding the Syngress program.

Joe Pisco, Helen Moyer, and the great folks at InterCity Press for all their help.

From Michael E. Flannagan, Technical Editor

A world of thanks to the Cisco RTP Routing Protocols Team for an unbelievable amount of knowledge, experience, assistance, and fun…you guys are the best! Thanks to Matt Carling (Cisco Systems, Australia) for his assistance with our MPLS chapter. Special thanks to Shannon Brown (Cisco Systems, TAC) for her knowledge and especially her patience back in the days when I could hardly spell "router." And, of course, I'll be disowned if I don't say…Hi mom!

From Global Knowledge

At Global Knowledge we strive to support the multiplicity of learning styles required by our students to achieve success as technical professionals. As the world's largest IT training company, Global Knowledge is uniquely positioned to offer these books. The expertise gained each year from providing instructor-led training to hundreds of thousands of students world-wide has been captured in book form to enhance your learning experience. We hope that the quality of these books demonstrates our commitment to your lifelong learning success. Whether you choose to learn through the written word, computer based training, Web delivery, or instructor-led training, Global Knowledge is committed to providing you with the very best in each of these categories. For those of you who know Global Knowledge, or those of you who have just found us for the first time, our goal is to be your lifelong competency partner.

Thank your for the opportunity to serve you. We look forward to serving your needs again in the future.

Warmest regards,

Duncan Anderson
President and Chief Executive Officer, Global Knowledge

Technical Editor

Michael E. Flannagan (CCNA, CCDA) is a Network Consulting Engineer in the Network Supported Accounts (NSA) Group at Cisco Systems and is a team lead for the MPLS/QoS Virtual Team. His experience includes extensive work with Routing Protocol and Quality of Service support for customer networks. Prior to joining Cisco Systems, he worked as an enterprise network architect and as a consultant specializing in Quality of Service. Mike's Quality of Service testing and research was used to recommend the implementation of various QoS mechanisms for one of the world's largest pharmaceutical companies and he has participated in large-scale QoS designs for several major US companies. In addition to holding various certifications from Cisco, 3Com, and Nortel Networks, Mike has passed both the CCIE Routing/Switching and the CCIE Design written exams and is currently preparing for his CCIE Lab exams. He lives in Morrisville, NC.

Technical Reviewer

Mark Buchmann (CCIE#3556, CCSI) is a Cisco Certified Internetworking Expert and has been a Certified Cisco Systems Instructor since 1995. He is the owner of MAB Enterprises, Inc., a company providing consulting, network support, training, and various other services. Mark is also a co-owner of www.CertaNet.com, a company providing on-line certification assistance for a variety of network career paths including all the various Cisco certifications. Mark is Series Editor for Syngress Media's Cisco Certification Study Guides.

In his free time he enjoys spending time with his family and boating. He currently lives in Raleigh, NC.

Contributors

Benoit Durand (CCIE #5754, CCNA, CCDA, CCNP, CCDP) is the Midwest Region Network Engineer for Tivoli Systems (www.tivoli.com) located in Indianapolis, IN. Ben designs and integrates high-end network solutions for Tivoli's worldwide operations while maintaining his own Cisco-powered network in Indianapolis. He has over 10 years of networking engineering experience in a wide range of environments. Prior to working at Tivoli, Ben worked on many high-profile military projects for the Canadian Air Force, deploying wide-area network solutions to peacekeeping forces in Kuwait, Yugoslavia, and other international locations. His latest projects involve Voice-over-ATM, Virtual Private Network solutions, and Wide-Area Network switching. Ben lives with his wife Dr. Christy Snider in Kingston, GA.

Ron Fuller (CCIE #5851, CCNP-ATM, CCNP-Voice, CCNP-Security, CCDP, MCNE) is a Senior Systems Engineer with 3X Corporation. He currently provides network design and implementation services to 3X Corporation clients in the Eastern United States. His specialties include Cisco LAN/WAN design, security consultation, and Novell network design. He has held senior engineer positions for two other network consulting companies in the past nine years. Ron also contributed to Syngress' *Building Cisco Remote Access Networks* (1-928994-13-X). He currently resides in Sunbury, OH with his wife, Julie, and his yet-to-be-born baby.

Jerry Sommerville (CCIE #1293) is a Senior Consultant for Callisma. His background includes network management, system management, system integration, network support and planning, user training, procedure automation, and program analysis. Jerry holds a Master of Science in Computer Aided Design & Computer Aided Manufacturing from Eastern Michigan University and a Bachelor of Science in Industrial Technology and Engineering from Texas A & M University.

James Placer (CCDP, CCNP Security, Voice Access, NNCDS, NNCSS, MCSE) is a Senior Network Design Engineer at Interactive Business Systems, Inc. in the Enterprise Networking Group (www.ibsentg.com). He designs, troubleshoots, and implements large-scale LAN and WAN networks based primarily on Cisco Systems and Nortel Networks platforms. James previously contributed to the Syngress *CCNP Support Study Guide for Exam 640-506* and has over 14 years of experience in the networking and computer systems field. He currently resides with his wife Kathy just outside the town of Allegan, MI.

Kevin Davis (CCNA, MCSE, MCP+I) is a Consultant with Callisma where he consults with Service Providers and enterprise clients on various networking issues. Formerly, Kevin was a consultant with International Network Services in Raleigh, NC working with Service Providers in the Research Triangle Park (RTP). He graduated with a degree in Computer Engineering from the Dwight Look College of Engineering at Texas A&M University in College Station, TX.
Kevin also contributed to Syngress' *Building Cisco Remote Access Networks* (1-928994-13-X) and has written several whitepapers on minimizing computer viruses in a network environment and browser security. He lives in McKinney, TX.

Paul Salas (CCNA, MCT, MCSE, Network+) is a Senior Network Engineer for Fleet Mortgage Corporation. Paul designs and manages Fleet's internetwork infrastructure, which consists of a wide variety of networking equipment from an assortment of vendors. He currently is involved in implementing a high-end Web network solution. He is also a part-time technical instructor for Microstaff Corporation where he delivers Microsoft Official Curriculum for the Windows 2000 track. Paul lives in Columbia, SC with his family. He would like to dedicate his writings to his wife, Margaret, for tolerating his "hair on fire" work pace and to his two children, Michael and Allison, *Mountains are conquered one step at a time.*

Jeff Corcoran (CCNA, MCSE, CNE) is a Senior Network Consultant for Siemens Enterprise Networks, Inc. where he is a network planner in the Ford Motor Company Advanced Network Technologies group. He is responsible for global network planning and testing of emerging network technologies and their application to the Ford Intranet. He has a special focus on VoIP, QoS, high availability architectures, and multicast. Jeff holds a Bachelors of Science in Physics and Applied Mathematics from the University of Toledo. He lives in Dearborn, MI.

Lisa Giebelhaus (CCNA) is a Senior Consultant with Callisma. She has been in the Telecommunications field for eight years. Her main focus has been designing, implementing, and managing projects for large-scale enterprise networks. Prior to joining Callisma, Lisa was a Senior Consultant for Lucent NetworkCare Professional Services (formerly INS) in Detroit, MI. She graduated from Michigan State University with a Bachelor of Science degree in Engineering Arts. She lives in Royal Oak, MI.

Richard Hamilton is a Senior Consultant with Callisma. He is currently responsible for leading engineering teams in the design and implementation of complex networks for service providers. Richard is industry recognized as a subject matter expert in MPLS, ATM, and Frame Relay switching. Richard has spent 14 years providing technical services in the financial and service provider industries for companies including NatWest Bank, Fleet Bank, International Network Services, Lucent Technologies, Cisco Systems, Sprint, WorldCom, South Western Bell, GTE, CapRock, CTC Communications, ILD Telecommunications, and Triton PCS. Richard also contributed to Syngress Publishing's *Building Cisco Remote Access Networks* (1-928994-13-X). He lives in Flower Mound, TX.

Robert Melancon is a Consultant with Callisma. His recent projects involve the maintenance of a 400+ site LAN/WAN implementing TCP/IP, Frame Relay, 3COM hubs, Cisco Catalyst 1900 series switches, and Cisco 2500 series routers. He has also worked on proof of concept and certification of xDSL and WAN technologies and vendor equipment including Promatory and Pairgain DSLAMs and Nortel and Lucent WAN switches. Robert has also developed many training programs and documentation. He has a degree in engineering from Southern Methodist University and lives in Dallas, TX.

Contents

Foreword	xxiii
Chapter 1 Cisco IOS Feature Review	**1**
Introduction	2
IP Address Classes and Classful IP Routing	2
Classes A, B, and C	5
Class D Addresses (Multicast)	8
RIPv1 and IGRP	10
RIPv1	11
IGRP	13
Variable-Length Subnet Mask (VLSM) Review	17
Why Do We Need VLSM?	19
Common Uses for Subnetting	20
Standard Access Control Lists (ACLs)	21
Filtering Traffic	24
Configuration Examples	25
Extended Access Control Lists (ACLs)	25
Benefits of Extended ACLs	30
Common Ports Used with Extended ACLs	30
Configuration Examples	32
Network Address Translation (NAT)	35
Controlling NAT with ACLs	39
Dynamic versus Static Translations	39
Configuration Example	40
Route Maps	40
Where to Use Route Maps	41
Controlling Traffic with Route Maps	41
Configuration Example	41
Summary	43
FAQs	44
Chapter 2 EIGRP A Detailed Guide	**47**
Introduction	48
Reviewing Basic Concepts of IGRP	48

How Does EIGRP Work?	50
Using Distance Vectors for Path Selection	50
Defining the Four Basic Components of EIGRP	57
Establishing Protocol-Dependent Modules	57
Establishing Neighbor Discovery/Recovery	58
Managing Reliable Transport Protocol	59
Establishing DUAL Finite State Machine	59
Implementing Packet Types	60
Configuring EIGRP's Distributed Update Algorithm (DUAL)	64
Choosing a Path Selection	64
Handling Failure and Recovery	72
Configuring Basic EIGRP	75
Verifying Configuration with Show Commands	84
Configuring Advanced EIGRP	87
Summarizing EIGRP Addresses	88
Redistributing EIGRP and OSPF	97
Unequal Cost Load Balancing	103
Recognizing Caveats	108
Stuck-in-Active	108
Auto-Summarization	109
Troubleshooting EIGRP	110
Troubleshooting Stuck-in-Active Routes	110
Troubleshooting Auto-Summarization	115
Troubleshooting not-on-common-subnet	117
Summary	119
FAQs	120
Chapter 3 Introduction to Quality of Service	**123**
Introduction	124
Defining Quality of Service	124
What Is Quality of Service?	125
Applications for Quality of Service	126
Three Levels of QoS	127
Understanding Congestion Management	129
Defining General Queuing Concepts	130
Leaky Bucket	131
Tail Drop	132
Token Bucket	133
First In First Out Queuing	134
Fair Queuing	136
Priority Queuing	138
Custom Queuing	139

Understanding Congestion Avoidance 141
   Congestion Avoidance in Action 142
      Pros and Cons of Congestion Avoidance 142
Introducing Policing and Traffic Shaping 143
   Traffic Shaping 144
      Generic Traffic Shaping 145
      Frame Relay Traffic Shaping 145
Summary 145
FAQs 146

Chapter 4 Traffic Classification Overview 147
Introduction 148
Introducing Type of Services (ToS) 148
   ToS Service Profile 150
   Defining the Seven Levels of IP Precedence 151
Explaining Integrated Services 152
Defining the Parameters of QoS 154
   Admission Requirements 155
      Resource Reservation Requirements 156
      Packet Classification 156
      Packet Scheduling 156
Introducing Resource Reservation Protocol (RSVP) 156
   RSVP Traffic Types 157
   RSVP Operation 157
   RSVP Messages 158
      Reservation-Request Messages 158
      Path Messages 158
      Error and Confirmation Messages 159
      Teardown Messages 159
Introducing Differentiated Service (DiffServ) 161
   The DiffServ Code Point (DSCP) 162
      Per Hop Behavior (PHB) 163
      Best Practice Network Design 165
Expanding QoS: Cisco Content Networking 168
   Application Aware Classification: Cisco NBAR 169
      HTTP Classification 169
      Citrix Classification 170
      Supported Protocols 170
   PDLM 174
      NBAR Supported QoS Services 174
      NBAR and Content Network Design Guidelines 175
Summary 176
FAQs 178

Chapter 5 Configuring Traffic Classification — 181
- Introduction — 182
- Configuring Policy-based Routing (PBR) — 182
  - Using PBR to Route Specific Packet Types — 184
- Defining Committed Access Rate (CAR) — 185
  - Configuring Distributed CAR (DCAR) — 188
- Marking and Transmitting Web Traffic — 188
  - Remarking the Precedence Bit and Transmitting Web Traffic — 189
  - Marking and Transmitting Multilevels of CAR — 190
- Marking and Rate Limiting ISPs — 191
  - Rate Limiting by Access List — 193
  - Using CAR to Match and Limit by MAC Address — 194
  - Monitoring CAR — 196
- Configuring Cisco Express Forwarding — 196
  - Enabling CEF — 197
  - Monitoring CEF — 198
  - Troubleshooting Cisco Express Forwarding Caveats and Bugs — 200
- Configuring Basic Network-based Application Recognition (NBAR) — 201
  - Creating an NABR Class Map — 202
  - Creating a Policy Map — 203
  - Applying the Policy Map to an Interface — 203
- Configuring Complex NBAR — 204
- Integrating NBAR with Class-based Weighted Fair Queuing — 206
  - Creating a Class Map to Identify NBAR — 207
  - Configuring Class Policy in the Policy Map — 207
  - Attaching the Policy to an Interface — 208
- Configuring NBAR with Random Early Detection — 209
- Configuring System Network Architecture Type of Service — 211
  - Mapping SNA CoS to IP ToS — 211
  - Prioritizing SNA Traffic — 212
- Summary — 213
- FAQs — 215

Chapter 6 Queuing and Congestion Avoidance Overview — 217
- Introduction — 218
- Using FIFO Queuing — 218
  - High Speed versus Low Speed Links — 220
    - When Should I Use FIFO? — 220
  - Using Priority Queuing — 221
    - How Does Priority Queuing Work? — 221

Queue Sizes	222
Why Do I Need Priority Queuing on My Network?	222
Using Custom Queuing	224
How Does Custom Queuing Work?	224
Queue Sizes	226
Protocol Interactions with Custom Queuing	226
Why Do I Need Custom Queuing on My Network?	227
Using Weighted Fair Queuing (WFQ)	228
How Does Weighted Fair Queuing Work?	228
Where Does the Weight Factor Come into Play?	230
Resource Reservation Protocol (RSVP)	231
Why Do I Need Weighted Fair Queuing on My Network?	231
Using Random Early Detection (RED)	232
How Does Random Early Detection Work?	232
TCP/IP Sliding Window	233
Why Do I Need Random Early Detection on My Network?	235
Summary	235
FAQs	236

Chapter 7 Configuring Queuing and Congestion Avoidance 239

Introduction	240
Configuring FIFO Queuing	240
Enabling FIFO	240
Verifying FIFO Operations	242
FIFO with RED	243
Configuring Priority Queuing	244
Enabling Priority Queuing	244
A Closer Look at the Protocol Classification	245
Applying Your Priority List to an Interface	247
Configuring the Queue Limits	247
Verifying Your Configuration	248
Troubleshooting Priority Queuing	250
Configuring Custom Queuing	252
Enabling Custom Queuing	252
Adjusting Byte Counts and Queue Sizes	254
Applying Your Configuration to an Interface	254
Verifying Your Configuration	255
Troubleshooting Custom Queuing	257
Configuring Weighted Fair Queuing	259
Enabling Weighted Fair Queuing	259
Verifying Your Configuration	260
Troubleshooting Weighted Fair Queuing	262

Configuring Random Early Detection 263
  Enabling Random Early Detection 263
    RED with Other Queuing Mechanisms 264
    Verifying Your Configuration 266
    Troubleshooting Random Early Detection 267
  Summary 267
  FAQs 268

Chapter 8 Advanced QoS Overview 271
Introduction 272
Using the Resource Reservation Protocol (RSVP) 272
  What Is RSVP? 273
  What RSVP Is Not 275
  How Does RSVP Work? 275
    Session Startup 276
    Session Maintenance and Tear-Down 278
    What Kind of QoS Can I Request with RSVP? 279
    Reservation Styles and Merging Flows 280
  Why Do I Need RSVP on My Network? 282
  Advantages of Using RSVP 283
  Disadvantages of Using RSVP 283
Using Class-Based Weighted Fair Queuing (CBWFQ) 284
  How Does CBWFQ Work? 284
  Why Do I Need CBWFQ on My Network? 286
  RSVP in Conjunction with CBWFQ 290
Using Low Latency Queuing (LLQ) 291
  How Does LLQ Work? 291
    Classifying Priority Traffic 292
    Allocating Bandwidth 292
    Limitations and Caveats 294
  Why Do I Need LLQ on My Network? 294
Using Weighted Random Early Detection (WRED) 295
  How Does WRED Work? 295
    WRED and IP Precedence 296
    WRED and RSVP 297
    WRED Algorithm 297
  Why Do I Need WRED on My Network? 298
Using Generic Traffic Shaping and Frame
Relay Traffic Shaping 299
  Token Bucket 299
  How Does GTS Work? 301
  Why Do I Need GTS on My Network? 301
  How Does FRTS Work? 303
  Why Do I Need FRTS on My Network? 305

Running in Distributed Mode	307
Features Supported in Distributed Mode	307
IOS Versions	308
Operational Differences	308
Restrictions	308
Using Link Fragmentation and Interleaving	309
How Does LFI Work?	311
LFI with Multilink Point-to-Point Protocol	312
How Can This Be Useful on My Network?	313
Understanding RTP Header Compression	313
How Does RTP Header Compression Work?	314
When Would I Need RTP Header Compression?	315
Summary	315
FAQs	318

Chapter 9 Configuring Advanced QoS   **321**

Introduction	322
Enabling, Verifying, and Troubleshooting	
Resource Reservation Protocol (RSVP)	322
Enabling RSVP	324
Verifying Your RSVP Configuration	324
Troubleshooting RSVP	327
Enabling, Verifying, and Troubleshooting	
Class-Based Weighted Fair Queuing (CBWFQ)	328
Enabling CBWFQ	328
Defining Class Maps	328
Creating Policies	330
Attaching Policies to Interfaces	334
Verifying Your CBWFQ Configuration	334
Troubleshooting CBWFQ	336
Configuring, Verifying, and Troubleshooting	
Low Latency Queuing (LLQ)	337
Configuring LLQ	337
Verifying Your LLQ Configuration	338
Troubleshooting LLQ	339
Configuring, Verifying, and Troubleshooting	
Weighted Random Early Detection (WRED)	340
Configuring WRED	340
Verifying Your WRED Configuration	343
Troubleshooting WRED	348
Configuring and Verifying Generic Traffic	
Shaping (GTS) and Frame	
Relay Traffic Shaping (FRTS)	349
Configuring GTS	351
Verifying Your GTS Configuration	352

Configuring FRTS	354
Enabling Frame Relay Traffic Shaping on the Interface	354
Configuring Traffic Shaping Parameters	354
Configuring Queuing for the VC	356
Applying Map Class to the Frame Relay Interface	357
Verifying Your FRTS Configuration	357
Understanding Distributed Technologies	359
DCEF	360
DWRED	360
Configuring, Verifying, and Troubleshooting Link Fragmentation and Interleaving (LFI)	362
Configuring LFI	362
Multilink PPP	362
LFI and Frame Relay	364
Verifying Your LFI Configuration	365
Troubleshooting MLP	366
Configuring, Verifying, and Troubleshooting RTP Header Compression	367
Configuring RTP Header Compression	368
Verifying Your RTP Header Configuration	368
Troubleshooting RTP Header Compression	369
Summary	370
FAQs	372

Chapter 10 Overview: Border Gateway Protocol (BGP) — 375

Introduction	376
The History of BGP	376
Exterior Gateway Protocol (EGP)	376
The Original Implementation	377
The Current RFC	378
Maximizing the Functionality of BGP	380
The BGP Routing Process	380
BGP Finite State Machine Logic	381
The Types of BGP Messages	384
The Format of BGP Packets	384
External BGP and the Internet	393
What Is an Autonomous System?	395
Does that Mean BGP Uses Hop Count?	397
Weight	397
How Do I Get There?	398
Multiexit Discriminator (MED), the BGP Metric	400
Local Preference	401
The BGP Path Selection Process	402
BGP Path Selection Example	403

Redistributing BGP into Your IGP	408
Redistributing the Default Route	409
BGP Synchronization	410
Defining Internal BGP, Route Reflectors, and Confederations	411
Internal BGP	412
Route Reflectors	412
Confederations	412
Advanced BGP Network Design	414
Building Network Redundancy	415
Common Design Methodologies	417
Summary	418
FAQs	419

Chapter 11 Configuring Border Gateway Protocol — 421

Introduction	422
Relevant RFCs	422
Enabling BGP Routing	423
Defining BGP for an Autonomous System	424
Defining the Remote AS	425
Public versus Private Autonomous Systems	426
Enabling BGP Routing	426
Configuring EBGP Neighbors	427
Defining the Remote Version	428
Removing Private AS Numbers	429
Configuring IBGP Neighbors	432
Peering to Loopback Interfaces	432
Configuring Route Reflectors	433
Configuring Confederations	436
When Do I Need Route Reflectors and Confederations?	438
Weight, MED, LOCAL PREF, and Other Advanced Options	439
Route-Map, Match, and Set Commands	441
Weight Attribute	442
Setting the Weight Attribute Using the Neighbor Statement	442
Setting the Weight Attribute Using Access Lists	443
Setting the Weight Attribute Using Route Maps	444
Multiexit Discriminate (MED) Attribute	444
Setting the MED Attribute Using the Set Metric Command	445
Setting the MED Attribute with the Default-Metric Command	446
Local Preference Attribute	446
Setting Local Preference with the Default Local-Preference Command	447

Setting the Local Preference Attribute with
the Set Local-Preference Command 448
AS_Path Attribute 448
Origin Attribute 449
Next_Hop Attribute 449
Other Advanced Options:
BGP Multiprotocol Extensions 450
Summary 454
FAQs 455

Chapter 12 Multiprotocol Label Switching (MPLS) 457
Introduction 458
Understanding MPLS 458
Label Switching Basics 460
That Sounds a Lot Like Routing! 463
Integrating MPLS into QoS 470
Ensuring MPLS Is Efficient and Reliable 470
Integrating ATM Classes of Service (CoS) with MPLS 471
Reducing Congestion with Traffic
Engineering and VPN 472
Standardizing MPLS for Maximum Efficiency 473
Deploying Link State Protocol Support 473
Integrating VPNs with BGP 474
Controlling MPLS Traffic Using Traffic Engineering 474
Deploying MPLS Using Cisco Express Forwarding 475
Unequal Cost Load Balancing 476
Configuring Loopback Interfaces 477
Integrating MPLS and Virtual Private Networking (VPN) 478
VPN Scalability 493
Reducing the Load on Network Cores 493
Summary 493
FAQs 494

Index 497

Foreword

Administering Cisco QoS in IP Networks discusses IP Quality of Service (QoS) and how it applies to Enterprise and Service Provider environments. It reviews routing protocols and quality of service mechanisms available today on Cisco network devices (routers, switches, etc.). This guide provides examples and exercises for a hands-on experience to give you the background and necessary details to implement these capabilities in your network today.

The business impact of QoS on major enterprises today ensures the delivery of the right information necessary to the bottom-line success of the business. QoS expedites the handling of mission-critical applications, while sharing network resources with non-critical applications. Today, with Cisco products, QoS has finally found its time by effectively providing algorithms to ensure delivery that was once only promised.

Over the past couple of years, the number of methods or protocols for setting quality of service (QoS) in network equipment has increased dramatically. Advanced queuing algorithms, traffic shaping, and access-list filtering, have made the process of choosing a QoS strategy a much more daunting task. All networks can take advantage of aspects of QoS for optimum efficiency, whether the network is for a small corporation, an enterprise, or an Internet Service Provider (ISP).

Through Callisma's skilled team of technology, operations, and project management professionals, we enable today's Enterprises and Service Providers to design and deploy networks that deliver business value. We help our clients compete effectively in the new e-business marketplace through strategic business planning, network design, and implementation services.

—Ralph Troupe, President and CEO
Callisma

Chapter 1

Cisco IOS Feature Review

Solutions in this chapter:

- IP Address Classes and Classful IP Routing
- Variable-Length Subnet Mask (VLSM) Review
- Standard Access Control Lists (ACLs)
- Extended Access Control Lists (ACLs)
- Network Address Translation (NAT)
- Route Maps

Introduction

In order to understand and configure Cisco IOS Quality of Service mechanisms, it is imperative that you have a full understanding of IP addressing, variable-length subnet masks, and all types of access lists. Most of the Quality of Service mechanisms that you will learn to deploy throughout this book will be matched against access lists, so it is highly recommended that even experienced network administrators pay close attention to the material in this chapter.

IP addressing seems like a very simple thing to do, but if you are considering Quality of Service on your network, you will want to pay close attention to your addressing scheme. This is especially important in making access lists to filter traffic or classify traffic based on source and destination IP addresses. You will find it easier to define traffic in granular detail if your IP addresses have been properly assigned.

Network Address Translation (NAT) is also reviewed in this chapter. Although it is a valuable tool, NAT can create difficulties when you are matching access lists in order to classify or queue traffic. There are many things to consider before deploying NAT, but armed with the proper information, you will be able to make the best design decisions.

IP Address Classes and Classful IP Routing

Much like a street address within a city, the TCP/IP address defines the location of a participating node within the network. Each node in a TCP/IP network must possess an address to be able to participate within the network. As with street addresses, TCP/IP addresses must be unique. Consider what would happen if two different houses had the same street address. This situation would make the mail carrier's job very difficult, and it would be unlikely that you would get your mail. This basic concept applies to networks varying from the simplest to the most complex internetworks, such as the Internet.

To understand TCP/IP addressing, you must first understand the binary concept. A data bit can have only one of two values, one or zero. One and zero (on and off, respectively) are the only two acceptable values in the binary system. It takes eight bits to make up a byte or octet. An octet may look similar to the following: 10111011. Notice that the octet consists of eight bits or positions.

Each bit or position within an octet has a specific value. To determine the total decimal value of an octet, you must first build a binary map. To do this, start with the left most bit, which has a value of 128. Moving to the right, each number is exactly half of the number to its left (See Table 1.1). Once you have completed this task of dividing each number in half to finish at one, you will notice that you have eight separate values. Each of these values is given to the bit in that respective position in the octet. For example, if an octet starts with a one and the rest of the values are zeros, then the value of that octet is 128. If the octet consists of all zeros except for the right most position, then that octet has a value of one.

Table 1.1 The Binary Conversion Map

128	64	32	16	8	4	2	1

To calculate the decimal value of an octet, you must add all the values together that have a binary position value of one. For example, if the two left-most bits have a value of one and the rest of the positions are zero, 11000000, then the value of that octet is 192 (128+64). If the octet in binary looked like 10101010, then the decimal value would be 170 (128+32+8+2). Table 1.2 gives several examples of binary to decimal conversion.

When learning the concept of binary to decimal conversion, it is best to practice the conversion until you feel thoroughly comfortable with it. Most scientific calculators have binary to decimal conversion capability, which will ensure your practice calculations are correct. This fundamental task must be mastered before you move on to more complex TCP/IP concepts.

Table 1.2 Binary to Decimal Conversion Examples

Binary Value	Decimal Value
11101010	234
00010010	18
00000101	5
01101001	105
11111111	255
00000000	0

The TCP/IP addressing scheme uses a four-octet value, represented in decimal format, to identify a host or network address. Each octet within this address has a binary value between 0 and 255 (See Table 1.3). Considering the address 120.89.234.23 for example, the following is what it would look like in binary:

```
01111000.01011001.11101010.00010111
```

The ability to convert TCP/IP addresses back and forth between decimal and binary is a critical skill. For instance, many subnetting problems may not be as obvious in decimal format, and observing the addresses in binary can make the solution clearer.

Table 1.3 Binary to TCP/IP Address Conversion Examples

Binary Value	TCP/IP Address
00000101.10100100.11110000.01010010	5.164.240.82
01010010.01000100.01000100.01101001	82.68.68.105
11101010.01000100.01010010.11111111	234.68.82.255
00000000.00000000.11111111.11111111	0.0.255.255

Two distinct portions make up TCP/IP addresses. The first portion defines the network in which the sought after host resides, whereas the second portion of the address defines the host. The subnet mask defines which portion of the address is for network identification and which portion is for host identification.

The process that defines whether an address resides on the local subnet or a remote network is known as ANDing. In binary, a logical ANDing relates the TCP/IP address with the subnet mask to determine the network identification. If both the TCP/IP address and the subnet mask have a value of one, then the subnet value is one. If the address, subnet mask, or both contain a value of zero, then the value is zero (See Table 1.4).

Table 1.4 ANDing Conversion Examples

Variable	Binary Value	Decimal Value
IP Address	00000101.10100100.11110100.01010010	5.164.244.82
Subnet Mask	11111111.11111111.11111100.00000000	255.255.252.0
Subnet	00000101.10100100.11110100.00000000	5.164.244.0
IP Address	11001000.10011110.00010000.00100011	200.158.16.35
Subnet Mask	11111111.11111111.11111111.00000000	255.255.255.0
Subnet	11001000.10011110.00010000.00000000	200.158.16.0

TCP/IP addressing is implemented by using either a classful or a classless scheme. Both methods have a purpose, and it is important that you understand the differences between them. Classful addressing consists of three different default classes of network addresses ranging from Class A to Class C. It also uses a default subnet mask related to each class of address (See Table 1.5). There are two other classes of addresses that are not used for normal traffic, Classes D and E. The Class D address range is reserved for multicasting, which will be discussed later in this chapter. The Class E address range is reserved for development and experimental use.

Classful addressing is a legacy implementation of IP addressing. In classful routing, routers do not advertise the mask with the network updates. This means that each router assumes the mask is the same as the ones assigned to their interfaces (see Table 1.5). In addition when advertising about one network address into another network address, the routers will automatically summarize on the class network boundary, not the subnet field.

Classful routing requires the same subnet mask be used throughout all subnetworks under the same network. This is a serious limitation to the flexibility of the network.

Classless addressing remedies this issue by including the subnet masks with routing advertisements. In classless addressing, no default subnet mask is assumed. Another benefit of classless addressing is that it supports Variable Length Subnet Masking (VLSM).

In VLSM, the subnet mask is manipulated so as to provide either more hosts or more networks for your network. Classless addressing gives you more flexibility to conform your network's addressing scheme to the logical or physical layout of your network. We discuss this further in the VLSM portion of this chapter.

Classes A, B, and C

As mentioned, classful addressing uses three different types of classes, Class A through C. These different classes offer varying numbers of hosts and networks and usually directly relate to your network needs.

Within the boundaries of a classful network address scheme, each class uses a different portion of the address to define the network, as well as the bits used for host addresses. Each class of address is assigned a default subnet mask (Table 1.5).

Table 1.5 The Class Range and Default Subnet Mask Table

Class	Range of 1st Octet	Subnet Mask
Class A	1-126*	255.0.0.0
Class B	128-191	255.255.0.0
Class C	192-223	255.255.255.0
Class D	224-239	255.255.255.255
Class E	240-254	255.255.255.255

* The 127.0.0.1 address is reserved for loopback and is not a valid range for networks.

A Class A address uses the first 8 bits to define the network. Class B addresses use the first 16 bits, and a Class C address uses the first 24 bits to define the network (See Figure 1.1).

Figure 1.1 IP Address Octet Representation

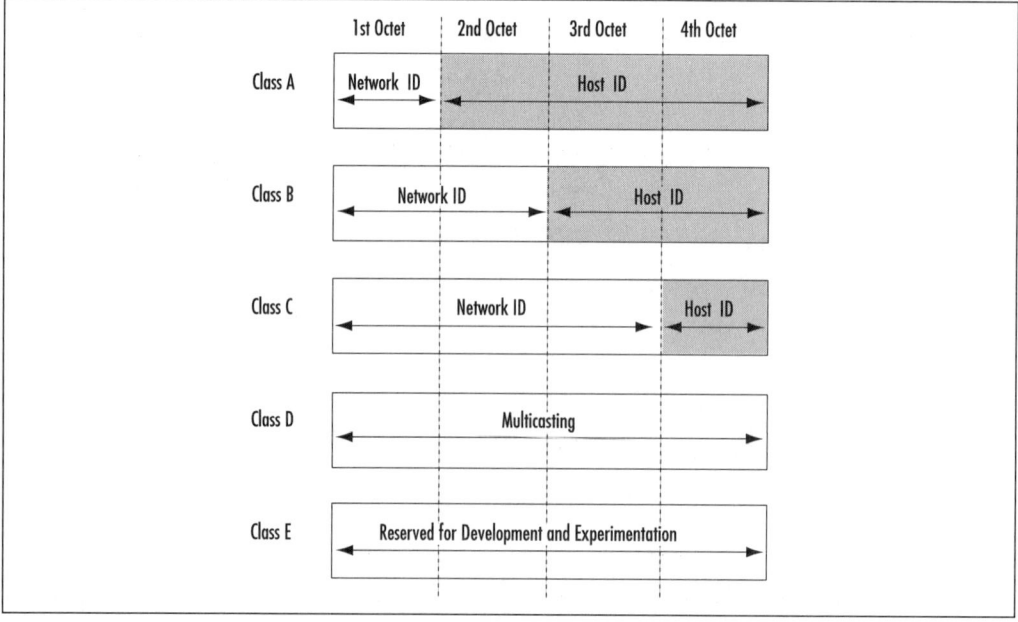

The 127.0.0.1 address is another exception to normal TCP/IP addressing. Although the whole range is reserved only 127.0.0.1 is normally used. This address is a special purpose address used when one machine is acting as both the client and the server. This address should not be used as a host address.

The idea of classes of addresses and default subnet masks does not apply to variable-length subnet masking (VLSM), which we will discuss later in this chapter. However, it will be very helpful to have a strong understanding of classful addressing before moving on to the more complex VLSM.

Although most Internet Class A, B, and C addresses have already been assigned, it is not uncommon to receive an address block within these classes from your address provider, which has already subnetted the addresses down to more economical portions.

The Internet uses a technology called Classless Interdomain Routing (CIDR), pronounced "cider." CIDR is a technique describing the aggregation of multiple networks, not subnets, which are then advertised with one routing table entry on the Internet (Figure 1.2). This reduces the size of the Internet routing tables which, as you can imagine, are massive. An easy way to think of this is that CIDR reduces the size of the network mask, while subnetting increases the size of the network mask. CIDR is also known as *supernetting*.

Figure 1.2 Classless Interdomain Routing (CIDR) Example

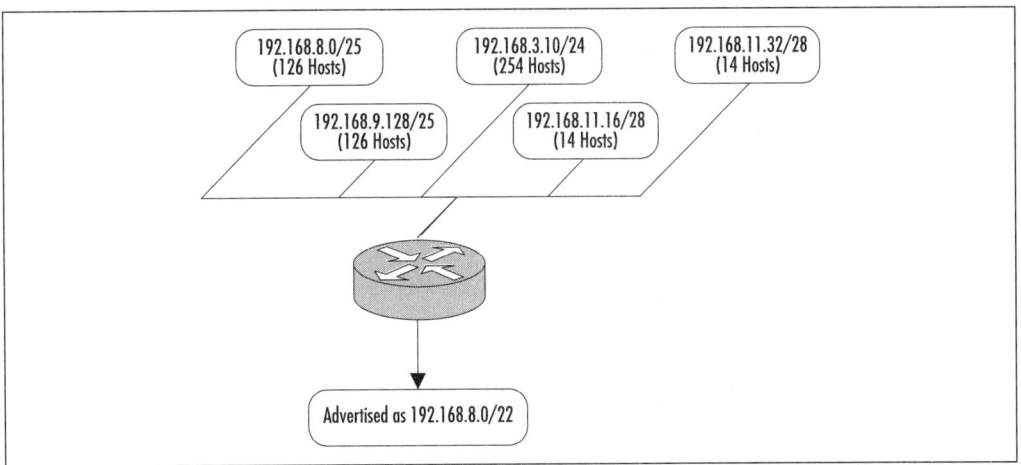

Networks that use VLSM or CIDR are often referred to as "slash x" networks. The number after the slash represents the number of bits that are masked, a topic discussed later in this chapter.

Different class networks require different numbers of bits for the network or host portion, and each network class provides different numbers of hosts as well as networks. The Class A address range provides 126 networks and 16,777,216 hosts per network. The Class A address, or /8, scheme is best used in a network where a large number of hosts and a small number of networks are required. The

Class B address scheme gives a total of 65,384 networks and hosts per network. The Class C address scheme gives a total of 16,777,216 networks, which give 254 hosts per network.

> **TIP**
>
> Remember that the number of host addresses you have directly relates to the number of hosts you can have. For example, the more host addresses you have per network, the fewer network addresses you will have to work with. It is a good practice to consider extra room for growth and expandability.

Class D Addresses (Multicast)

The Class D address range is reserved for multicasting. Multicasting is used to send packets from one server to many participating hosts (one-to-many). This concept is illustrated in Figure 1.3. In contrast, broadcasts are used to send packets from one server to all the users on a network, regardless of participation (one-to-all).

Figure 1.3 Multicasting Example

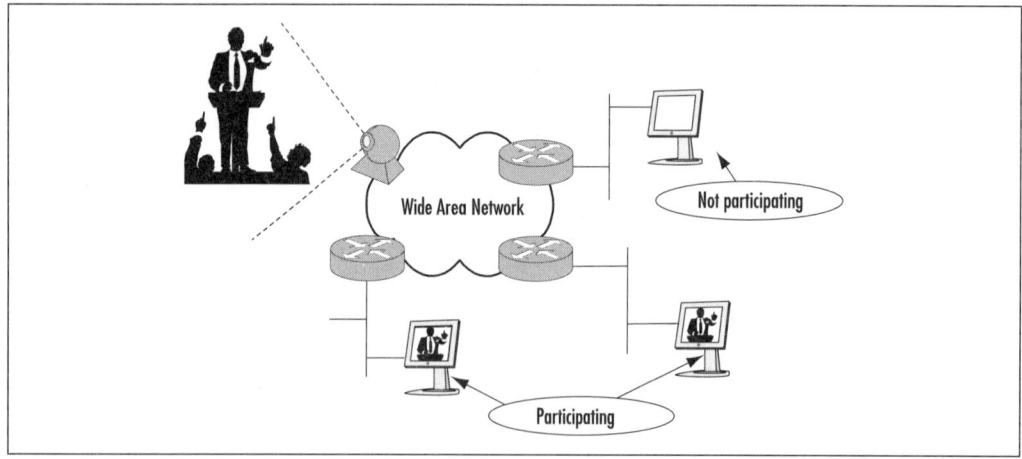

Hosts participating in a multicast begin receiving the data stream as soon as they join the group, and they stop receiving the stream when they leave. In addition, clients or end-stations can join and leave dynamically with little or no impact on the multicast or the network.

Multicasting can be used to deliver audio and video in real time, which is gaining popularity in corporations as well as with vendors. Multicasting is also used with a wide variety of computer-imaging tools since the technology does not flood the entire network like broadcasting.

Class D ranges from 224.0.0.0 through 239.255.255.255. In binary, an address beginning with 1110 is a multicast address, which allows the last 28 bits to be used for the group address of the specific multicast.

In an Ethernet environment, only devices participating in the same multicast group will listen for and process packets destined for that group. Non-participating computers within the same broadcast domain will see the packets but will not generate an interrupt to the CPU for processing. A multicast is thus more efficient than a broadcast, because a broadcast requires every computer in the broadcast domain not only to see the packets but also to process them.

Multicasts are similar to broadcasts in several ways. Like broadcasts, most multicasts provide a connectionless transmission, meaning that the multicast server makes its best effort for you to receive the packet, but it does not confirm receipt. Neither broadcasts nor multicasts require acknowledgements from the destination hosts.

Although multicasts are similar to broadcasts, some features are unique to multicasting. As mentioned, only participating end stations will listen for and process multicast packets. Each multicast application uses a different address, which allows end stations to participate in a number of different multicasts simultaneously.

The Internet Assigned Numbers Authority (IANA) assigns multicast addresses to vendors that require multicast applications to run over the Internet. More specifically, the IANA assigns *registered* multicast addresses.

There are two basic types of multicast routing protocols from which to choose: dense and sparse mode. Dense mode is used in environments where most or all of the routers located in the network will participate in multicasting. Sparse mode protocol does not assume that all routers will be participating in multicasting, but rather it uses join messages to build a tree of participating routers.

The two most common types of dense mode multicasting protocols are Distance Vector Multicast Routing Protocol (DVMRP) and Multicast Open Shortest Path First (MOSPF). DVMRP was the first multicasting protocol and actually is derived from the RIP routing protocol. Like RIP, DVMRP uses hop count to make its decisions, which makes this protocol not scalable. MOSPF is based on the Open Shortest Path First (OSPF) protocol and thus works very well in environments that have already applied OSPF as their routing protocol.

Core-Based Tree Protocol (CBT) currently is the most popular sparse mode multicasting protocol. CBT is an open standard that is governed by RFC 2201.

As a sparse mode protocol, CBT builds a single distribution tree, which uses very little overhead on the network. In CBT, a rendezvous point is identified to which all other branches can pass traffic. Sparse mode protocols scale much better than dense mode protocols.

There is one other type of multicasting protocol. Protocol Independent Multicast (PIM) is a new protocol that has not been clearly standardized by the IETF. PIM is unique because it supports both sparse and dense mode protocols. PIM is not protocol dependent, which makes it very flexible.

RIPv1 and IGRP

Distance vector protocols were the first dynamic routing protocols. The most common distance vector protocols are RIPv1 (Routing Information Protocol) and IGRP (Interior Gateway Routing Protocol). Although these two protocols are very similar, they handle routing quite differently.

It is important to note that both RIPv1 and IGRP are classful protocols, meaning that they do not send the subnet mask along with the TCP/IP address. By using the first octet in the address to identify the class of network, the protocol assumes the address is classful and uses the default subnet mask shown in Table 1.5.

It is important to understand what makes RIPv1 and IGRP distance vector protocols. A good analogy to help understand how a distance vector protocol works is to imagine that you are standing in a line within a very dark tunnel. The only way you can figure out what position you hold in the line is to ask the person in front of you, and then he would ask the person in front of him, and so on. This would continue until the message got to the front of the line, and then the reply would come back, counting each step in the process. This is the principle behind distance vector protocols (See Figure 1.4).

The only way a router knows its position in a network is by what its neighbors tell it about their own positions. Another name for distance vectoring is thus *"routing by rumor."*

Distance vector protocols are also defined by the way they update one anothers' routing tables, a process of sharing information known as convergence. Distance vector protocols send their entire routing tables at regular intervals. These updates are sent only to routers that are direct neighbors. A router's view of the network is limited because it is based on what its neighbors see and pass along.

Figure 1.4 Distance Vector Protocol Illustration

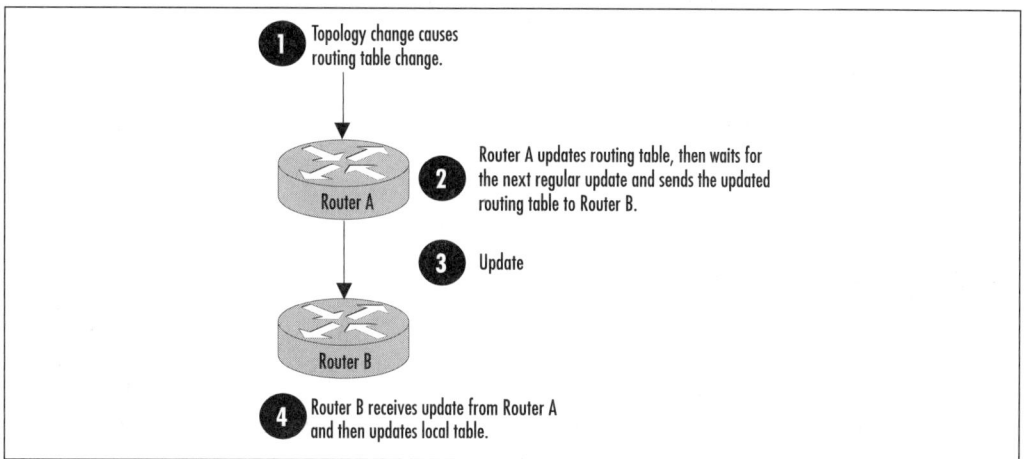

RIPv1

The RIPv1 protocol is an open standard protocol, meaning that it is not vendor specific. Because RIPv1 is an open standard, RFC 1058 and 1723 govern this protocol standard. Most router vendors support RIPv1 in one fashion or another and probably will continue to in the future.

RIPv1 uses a very simple measure, based exclusively on hop count, of how far the source is from the destination. Consequently, RIPv1 tends be easy to administer and troubleshoot.

After the router makes an update to its routing tables, it waits for the next regular interval (30 seconds) to expire before it sends the update to all of its neighboring routers. This creates a time lapse between when the router learns of a change and when it sends the update to other routers. If a change happens on the network, the neighboring routers will not be informed of the change until the next regular update.

If a change occurs in a RIP network, a flash update is sent from the router detecting the change to its adjacent neighbors. Upon receipt, the neighbors will send a poison reverse back to the advertising router confirming the change to the network. In addition, those neighbors will not relay these updates, but will wait for the normal 30-second interval before sending the update which will not contain the network entry.

When RIPv1 receives an update of a new network, it automatically installs the new route into its local routing table. If the router learns of a lower hop count for a route, it overwrites the existing route with the new route. RIPv1 keeps only the best routes (the lowest hop count) and flushes all other route updates for that destination.

If a network were to fail, the downstream router would no longer receive updates about that specific route. After 180 seconds (six updates) without receiving an update on a route, RIPv1 would designate the route as being down by giving it a value of 16. Once 240 seconds pass without an update (eight updates), RIPv1 would remove the entry from its routing tables.

RIPv1 thus possesses its share of drawbacks. Because it does not take into account any other variable besides hop count, RIPv1 quite often does not dynamically make the most logical decisions on its path selection through a network and, therefore, does not make it particularly scalable. RIPv1 uses regular scheduled updates to notify other routers of topology changes, thus creating a time lapse and possibly causing routing loops. Since RIPv1 is a distance vector protocol, it sends the entire routing table to update neighboring routers, thus using a large portion of the network's bandwidth. RIP is also limited to a maximum of 15 hops. Each hop represents a router, which the traffic will have to go through to get to the destination network. Paths with a hop count of 16 or greater are considered unreachable.

To enable RIPv1 on a Cisco router, you use the following command at the global configuration prompt.

```
Router1(config)#router rip
```

Once you have enabled the router for RIP configuration, the prompt changes to the following.

```
Router1(config-router)#
```

At this prompt, you input the network in which you want RIP to be enabled. The syntax for the command looks like this.

```
Router1(config-router)#network network-number
```

Here is an example.

```
Router1(config-router)#network 10.0.0.0
Router1(config-router)#network 20.0.0.0
```

After you have enabled RIP on all the networks you want, you now need to confirm your entries. To do this you run the following command.

```
Router1#show running-config
```

Browsing down to the RIP portion of the running configuration, you will notice an entry similar to this one.

```
router rip
 network 10.0.0.0
 network 20.0.0.0
```

Once you find this entry in your configuration, you can be confident that the configuration changes have occurred in your router. It is good practice at this time to save your running configuration file to your startup configuration file in case you lose power. To do this, type in the following command.

`Router1#`**`copy running-config startup-config`**

IGRP

Interior Gateway Routing Protocol (IGRP) is a proprietary protocol to Cisco Systems. This means the IGRP can be implemented only on Cisco routers. The IGRP protocol is a distance vector protocol like RIPv1, but IGRP has a more thorough metric that uses a variety of different variables to make its routing decisions.

Developed to replace RIPv1, IGRP had to be a faster and more scalable routing protocol. Cisco Systems developed IGRP with the following five distinct variables on which to base its routing decisions. By default, IGRP uses only bandwidth and network delays, but it can be configured to utilize all five variables.

- Bandwidth
- Delay
- Load
- Reliability
- Smallest MTU (maximum transmission unit)

IGRP works within an autonomous system (AS). Cisco defines an autonomous system as "a group of networks that has a consistent policy for routing purposes." This means that routers participating within the same routing domain must use the same autonomous system number. If you are running IGRP with different AS numbers per router, they will not communicate with each other.

The IGRP protocol does permit multiple autonomous systems to participate on the same router, but this requires the routers to run multiple instances of

IGRP. For all practical purposes, most administrators implement only one IGRP AS on the network.

Updates in IGRP occur every 90 seconds, which produces less network traffic then RIPv1's 30-second updateinterval. However, this also increases the time it takes for routers within the same network to converge. This longer convergence is remedied by IGRP's execution of flash updates.

In developing IGRP, Cisco Systems made numerous improvements compared to the RIPv1 protocol, thus making IGRP more scalable and robust. Routers not receiving a route update from the failed route for 270 seconds (three updates) identify the network as invalid. If the router receives an update within 280 seconds (three updates plus ten seconds), it can redeem the route. If 630 seconds (seven missed updates) pass since the router was last updated, the router deletes the route from its routing tables. IGRP has a default limit of no more than 100 hops to a single destination network. This value can me modified to 255 if necessary, but this is rarely done. In addition, keep in mind that hops are not part of the metric calculation for determining the best path, but a limiter to ensure against looping and sub-optimal routing.

> **TIP**
>
> Distance vector protocols are inadequate in really large network models. Although IGRP implements a stronger metric then RIPv1, it is still a distance vector protocol, which may be substandard for larger networks.

To configure IGRP, use the following syntax at the global configuration prompt on the router that you want to configure.

```
Router1(config)#router igrp autonomous-system-number
```

Here is an example.

```
Router1(config)#router igrp 1
```

This command enables IGRP on the router and advances you to the protocol configuration prompt, which should look like this.

```
Router1(config-router)#
```

This prompt enables you to enter the networks that you want to participate in the autonomous system. To enter the participating networks, type them in as you would in RIPv1 using the following syntax.

```
Router1(config-router)#network network-number
```

Here is the example.

```
Router1(config-router)#network 10.0.0.0
Router1(config-router)#network 20.0.0.0
```

Once you have entered all the networks that you would like to participate in the IGRP Autonomous System, you need to confirm your changes have taken place in the running-config file. To do this, you use the **show running-config** command. Browse down to the IGRP section of your configuration file to confirm the changes have been accepted.

```
router igrp 1
 network 10.0.0.0
 network 20.0.0.0
```

After confirming that there were no mistyped commands and that the configuration is indeed correct, you then save the file to your startup configuration by using the following command.

```
Router1#copy running-config startup-config
```

Routing loops can occur on a network because of slow convergence times or inconsistent routing entries. Consider Figure 1.5 when working through the following routing loop example.

Figure 1.5 Routing Loop Example

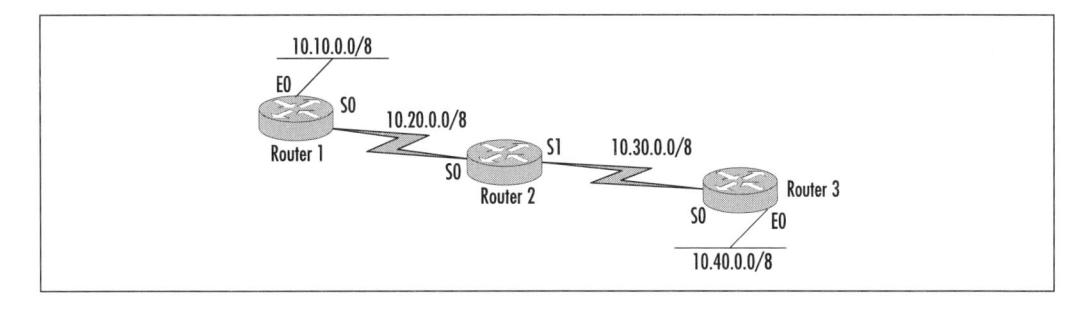

For simplicity, hop count is the metric that will be used, and each hop is a value of one. Before the failure of 10.10.0.0, routers 1, 2, and 3 all have consistent routing tables. As shown in Figure 1.5, Router 1's E0 interface is directly connected to the 10.10.0.0 network. Router 2 is one hop away from the 10.10.0.0 network, and Router 3 is two hops away through Router 2.

Router 1 detects a failure on network 10.10.0.0 and updates its local routing table. Router 2 still contains a path to 10.10.0.0 through Router 1 (1 hop) in its local routing table and continues to update Router 1 and Router 3 at regular intervals. At the same time, Router 3 has not received any notification of the down network and still holds the pathway to network 10.10.0.0 as two hops away through Router 2.

Router 1 is notified that Router 2 knows how to get to the 10.10.0.0 network and thus begins routing packets destined for the 10.10.0.0 network to Router 2. Router 3 continues to believe that the path to the 10.10.0.0 network is through Router 2, with a hop count of two.

Router 1 receives the update from Router 2 and recalculates its distance from the network as a hop count of two.

Routers 1, 2, and 3 all believe that the best path to network 10.10.0.0 is through one another. These inconsistencies cause packets destined for the 10.10.0.0 network to bounce between routers, creating a routing loop.

As seen in this example, routing loops can be very detrimental to a network and can actually bring a network to a complete halt. Precautionary measures have been implemented in distance vector protocols to help prevent these loops.

A repercussion of routing loops is a state called "count to infinity." Count to infinity occurs when an invalid routing update continues to loop, causing the hop count to increase by one each time the update passes through a router. Without preventative measures, the packets will continue to loop indefinitely.

Defining infinity prevents this loop from occurring indefinitely. For example, RIPv1 by default defines infinity as a hop count of 16. Once this maximum is reached, the packet will be killed and the network will be deemed unreachable.

"Split–horizon updates" are another tactic to stop routing loops from occurring. The logic behind split-horizon updates is that they will not send updates learned from a particular direction back in the direction from which they were learned. Split-horizon updates will not allow information to go out the same interface it was learned on.

A variation of split-horizon updates is "poison reverse." Poison reverse updates implement holddown timers to ensure that the entire network has converged after making a change, and thus a router will not learn incorrect information from another router that has not been updated. Poison reverse causes the routers to advertise the failed route, and this causes all routers to flush the route. The routing tables thus remain consistent throughout the network.

More complex protocols utilize triggered updates, which take a more proactive role in stopping routing loops. Triggered, or flash, updates allow immediate updates when a topology change occurs in the network. Instead of waiting for the normal update to send out changes, the protocol sends the updates immediately so that other routers can update their routing tables.

Variable-Length Subnet Mask (VLSM) Review

Variable-length subnet masks (VLSMs) give network engineers the ability to use IP addresses more efficiently than with classful addressing. As we learned, a subnet mask is a value that defines whether a host is on the local subnet or a remote subnet by using the "ANDing" process. Through manipulating this subnet mask, you can "borrow" bits from the host portion of the IP address and use them to make more subnets. The section that is "borrowed" from the host portion is used for the subnet. The number of subnets that is needed and the number of host addresses that will be on each subnet will determine the VLSM that is required.

When a source computer looks at its own IP address and subnet mask, it then determines whether a destination address is on the local subnet or on a different network. If the destination host were on a different network, the source host would send its packets to the local gateway address. If the destination host were on the same subnet as the source host, the source host would send the packet directly.

When using classless addresses, you represent the subnet mask with a /x following the TCP/IP address. The slash x represents the bits that have a value of one in the subnet mask. You must be able to translate subnet masks represented in decimal to binary in order to be able to figure out this value. If only the first octet (eight bits) is masked, this would be represented as /8. Taking this process a little further, if the subnet mask represented in decimal were 255.240.0.0, in binary it would look like 11111111.11110000.00000000.00000000. Considering the number of bits that are masked (have a value of one), the subnet mask would be represented as /12.

Creating a subnet mask table eases the translation from a binary subnet mask to a decimal format. To create the map, begin with the same mapping as in Table 1.1. Underneath this map, begin with the 128 value. Now, add this value to the value above and one step right (128+64), and place the sum of these two numbers in the next position to the right. Use this same pattern to finish the map (See Table 1.6).

In order to use this table you have to remember to count eight for each previous masked octet. In the octet that is subnetted, you find the subnet mask that is being used and count how many spaces are to the left including the mask value. Using the above example of 255.240.0.0, we know the first octet is completely masked, so we count eight for that octet. Since the second octet is where the address is subnetted at a value of 240, we can look in the table to find that there are four spaces to the left of 240, including the value 240. The /x value for 255.240.0.0 is thus /12 (8+4=12).

Table 1.6 Subnet Mask Map

128	64	32	16	8	4	2	1
128	192	224	240	248	252	254	255

To understand how a packet traverses networks, consider Figure 1.6. The network address of Network A is 10.1.1.0 with a subnet mask of 255.255.255.240 (or 28 bits). The network address of Network B is 10.1.1.16 with the same subnet mask as Network A.

If host A wanted to send a packet to host F, then host A, through the ANDing process, would determine whether or not host F was on the local subnet. Host F is not on the same subnet, so host A will send its packet to the default gateway, which then sends it on to the destination host address (Figure1.6).

Figure 1.6 Inter-Subnet Communication

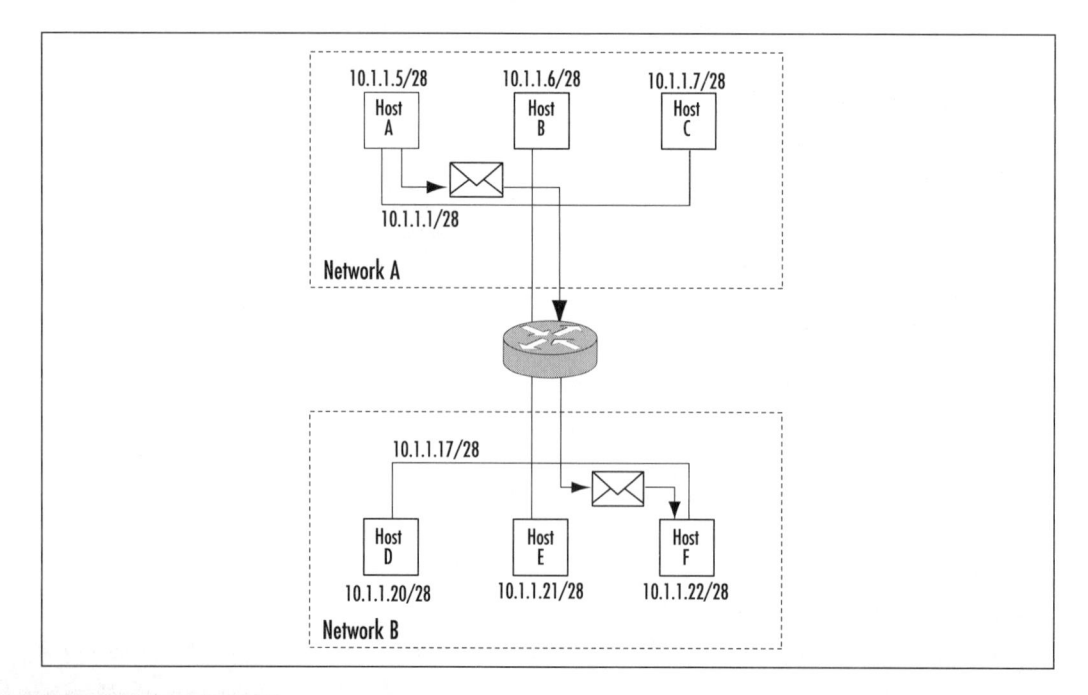

Why Do We Need VLSM?

VLSM has become a very important part of networks. Public IP addresses are in short supply because of Internet population increases in the last ten years. VLSM gives us a way around the TCP/IP address shortage by breaking down classful addresses into more efficient and manageable blocks.

Consider the example of a company that requires a minimum of 30 addresses per Ethernet and 2 address per serial link. Based on classful addressing, all subnets would have the same subnet mask. As we have learned, a Class C address has an 8-bit host field. Using VLSM we can take these 8-bits and create our network.

Given an IP address of 192.168.12.0/24, we can now start our process of VLSM. First, we know we have an 8 bit field we can manipulate. The other 24 bits are for our network. Using the 2(x)-2 to determine our number of host bits we come up with 5 bits required. This only leaves us 3 bits for subnetting for our Ethernets.

The binary of the last byte is shown below (Table 1.7). This gives us subnets:

Table 1.7 Binary Conversion of the last bytes of 192.168NNNHHHHH/27

000HHHHH	192.168.12.0/27	Reserved for Serial Links	
001HHHHH	192.168.12.32/27	Hosts 192.168.12.33 – 62 192.168.12.63	Broadcast
010HHHHH	192.168.12.64/27	Hosts 192.168.12.65 – 94 192.168.12.95	Broadcast
011HHHHH	192.168.12.96/27	Hosts 192.168.12.97 - 126 192.168.12.127	Broadcast
100HHHHH	192.168.12.128/27	Hosts 192.168.12. 129 - 158 192.168.12.159	Broadcast
101HHHHH	192.168.12.160/27	Hosts 192.168.12.161 - 190 192.168.12.191	Broadcast
110HHHHH	192.168.12.192/27	Hosts 192.168.12.193 - 222 192.168.12.223	Broadcast
111HHHHH	192.168.12.224/27	Hosts 192.168.12.225 – 254 192.168.12.255	Broadcast

* It is important to note that Cisco supports subnet zero and a subnet of all ones

If we take subnets 192.168.12.32/27 thru 192.168.12.224/27 and use them for our Ethernets, we can identify 7 unique Ethernet segments. Notice we did not use the 192.168.12.0/27 subnet. We will use this subnet to create our /30 subnets for our serial links.

VLSM is subnetting a prexisting subnet. What if we took 192.168.12.0/27 and expanded the subnet field? That would be subnetting a prexisting subnet, or VLSM.

192.168.12.0/27. The binary of the last byte is shown below (Table 1.8). Assuming that the first 3 bits of the fourth byte are "000" then we can look further into the remaining bits up to the last 2.

Table 1.8 Binary Conversion of the Last Byte of 000XXXHH

000000HH	192.168.12.0/30	hosts 192.168.12.1 and 2	Broadcast 192.168.12.3
000001HH	192.168.12.4/30	hosts 192.168.12.5 and 6	Broadcast 192.168.12.7
000010HH	192.168.12.8/30	hosts 192.168.12.9 and 10	Broadcast 192.168.12.11
000011HH	192.168.12.12/30	hosts 192.168.12.13 and 14	Broadcast 192.168.12.15
000100HH	192.168.12.16/30	hosts 192.168.12.17 and 18	Broadcast 192.168.12.19
000101HH	192.168.12.20/30	hosts 192.168.12.21 and 22	Broadcast 192.168.12.23
000110HH	192.168.12.24/30	hosts 192.168.12.25 and 26	Broadcast 192.168.12.27
000111HH	192.168.12.28/30	hosts 192.168.12.29 and 30	Broadcast 192.168.12.31

Keep in mind that you cannot do anything to the bits already used. Classful protocols do not support this, but Classless protocols can. Notice that no IP addresses have been wasted and all segments are addressable. This is the value of VLSM, and why more and more network designers are migrating away from IGRP and RIPv1. The Classless protocols that support VLSM are OSPF, EIGRP, RIPv2, IS-IS, and BGP.

Common Uses for Subnetting

Beyond making a contribution to saving IP addresses, there are other useful reasons to implement subnetting on your network. Subnetting can help you manage your network in a variety of ways.

In a point-to-point connection, you would want only the two end interfaces to be on that subnet. This is an excellent place to implement VLSM, because by manipulating the subnet mask, you can ensure that there are only two addresses on the subnet. Implementing a /30 (255.255.255.252) subnet mask would create this desired result. It would enable you to use a subnet for only two host addresses, leaving other bits for other networks and hosts.

Just as common and no less important, small offices are also good places to implement subnetting owing to their inability to use an entire classful address range. This saves wasted TCP/IP addresses that could be used elsewhere, either in that enterprise or on the Internet.

Let's refer back to the previous example of the company that needs only 70 addresses for their network. While not wasting an entire Class C address range on the 70 addresses, we can subnet that range down to a more efficient subnet range. The company's current TCP/IP network is 192.168.50.0. If we use a 27-bit or /27 subnet mask (255.255.255.224), that would allow 30 hosts per subnet. This arrangement allows for growth, at the same time as being resourceful with TCP/IP addresses. As a consequence, management is also easier.

Another useful management scheme using VLSM is to create a loopback interface on your router with an assigned IP address and a /32 mask. The router will accept this address and mask because it knows that the loopback is a logical interface and only the router can "connect" to it. An explicit /32 mask is OK. Use of the loopback interface eases management and monitoring within a network. Assuming we advertise these loopback networks within our routing protocol, we can then point our SNMP management servers to them, and use them for documentation. In addition loopback interfaces are used with certain routing protocols as router identifiers (RID's). We would be wasting IP addresses if we could not use a /32 mask.

Standard Access Control Lists (ACLs)

Network administrators have always faced the dilemma of allowing appropriate access while at the same time denying unwanted traffic. Access Control Lists (ACLs) enable administrators to shape and manage network traffic, prioritize queuing groups, route and service filtering, as well as heighten network security. All of these issues are critical when designing a network or administering an existing network.

There are many reasons that your network may experience latency or slow periods. Unwanted network traffic, such as meaningless broadcasts, only increases latency without bringing any real value to a network. Fortunately, Cisco routers equip you with the tools to manage this type of traffic.

Access Control Lists (ACLs), in their simplest form, test a packet against a set of rules. If the packet matches the rules, it is then either permitted or denied. It is critical to note that at the end of every ACL is an implied "deny all" statement. Therefore, if the packet does not match any rules, it is dropped. Table 1.9 illustrates number ranges for each type of access list.

ACLs are configured at the global configuration prompt and then applied to the desired interface. This is standard procedure for both standard and extended ACLs, regardless of which protocol is being used.

> **TIP**
>
> Implementing an Access Control List causes an implicit "deny all" statement at the end of the list. To enable all other traffic not identified in the ACL, you must enter a permit statement!

Table 1.9 ACL Number Ranges

Type	Range
Standard IP	1-99
Extended IP	100-199
Ethernet Type Code	200-299
DECnet	300-399
Xerox Network Systems (XNS)	400-499
Extended XNS	500-599
AppleTalk	600-699
Vendor Code	700-799
Standard IPX	800-899
Extended IPX	900-999
IPX SAP	1000-1099
Extended Transparent Bridging	1100-1199
NLSP Route Summary	1200-1299
Standard IP (Expanded Range)	1300-1999 (IOS 12.0 and higher)
Extended IP (Expanded Range)	2000-2699 (IOS 12.0 and higher)

Standard IP ACLs are based solely on the source address of the packet (See Figure 1.7). This is quite restrictive, but it makes administering Standard ACLs easy. Standard ACLs are not processor intensive, unlike extended ACLs.

Figure 1.7 Access Control List Illustration

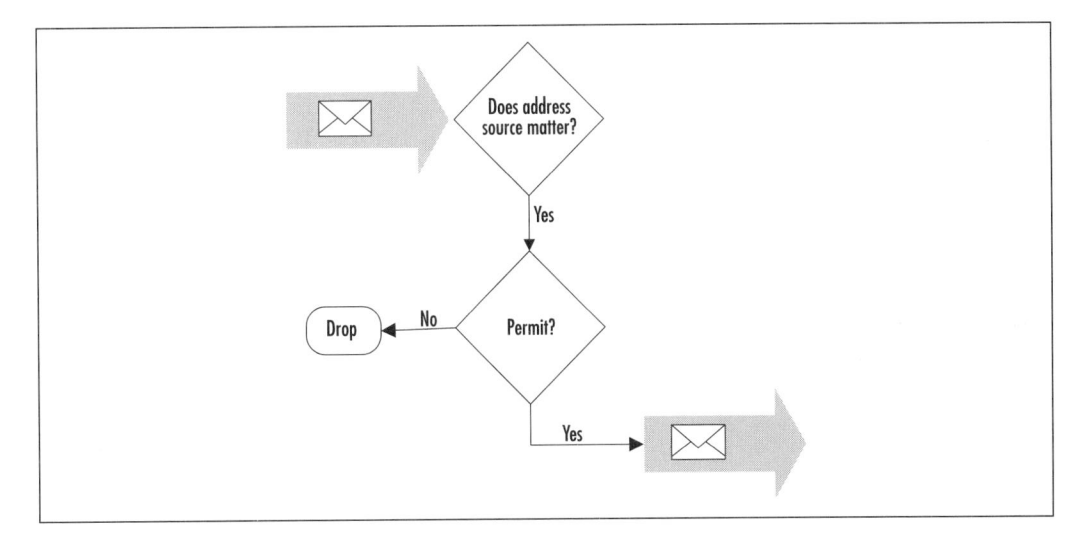

ACLs can be very specific or general depending on your needs. For a more general application, you can use wildcard masks to ease administration. The wildcard mask process is used to specify which address bits must match and which bits can be ignored (See Table 1.10). This is done for each octet in the network address. Unlike the ANDing process previously explained, ACLs use an exclusive OR operation. The Access Control List and the wildcard mask are compared to produce the result (See Table 1.11).

Table 1.10 ACL Wildcard Mask Translation

Address Bit	Mask Bit	Result	Translation
0	0	0	Must match
1	0	1	Must match
0	1	0	Does not matter
1	1	0	Does not matter

A wildcard mask bit with the value of 0 indicates you need to check the corresponding address bit for a match. A wildcard mask bit of 1 indicates you can ignore the corresponding address bit. When no wildcard mask is indicated, a mask of 0.0.0.0 is used. This mask requires the address to match each octet exactly. An access list entry is automatically appended to the end of the access list. This entry is known as an "Implicit Deny Any" entry. Network traffic not explicitly permitted in previously will be implicitly denied.

Table 1.11 ACL Wildcard Mask Example

Factor	Decimal Value	Binary Value
Address	138.125.21.54	10001010.01111101.00010101.00110110
Wildcard Mask	0.0.0.255	00000000.00000000.00000000.11111111
Conclusion	138.125.21.0	10001010.01111101.00010101.00000000
Address	192.23.56.0	11000000.00010111.00111000.00000000
Wildcard Mask	0.0.255.255	00000000.00000000.11111111.11111111
Conclusion	192.23.0.0	11000000.00010111.00000000.00000000

To configure a standard ACL, you would use the following syntax.

```
Router1(config)#access-list access-list-number permit source [source-wildcard]
```

Filtering Traffic

Traffic filtering is one of the reasons an administrator would implement Access Control Lists. For example, if there is a host on a specific network that has no need to traverse your network but is monopolizing your bandwidth, you can block this traffic by applying Access Control Lists.

Another example of using traffic filtering would be a situation where you wanted to allow traffic from Network A to go through serial interface 0 but not allow that traffic out of serial interface 1. You could do this by applying ACLs on the router to deny Netwkowk A's traffic on the serial 1 interface. Keep in mind, that if a packet from Network A was destined for a network and the exiting interface was Serial 1, the packet would be dropped – it would not be rerouted out of the interface without the ACL. This is an important consideration when implementing ACLs.

Configuration Examples

Figure 1.8 illustrates how the following configuration would impact the network.

```
Router1(config)#access-list 10 deny 127.56.25.0 0.0.0.255
Router1(config)#access-list 10 permit any
Router1(config)#interface serial 1
Router1(config-if)#ip access-group 10 in
Router1(config-if)#end
```

Figure 1.8 Standard Access Control List Example

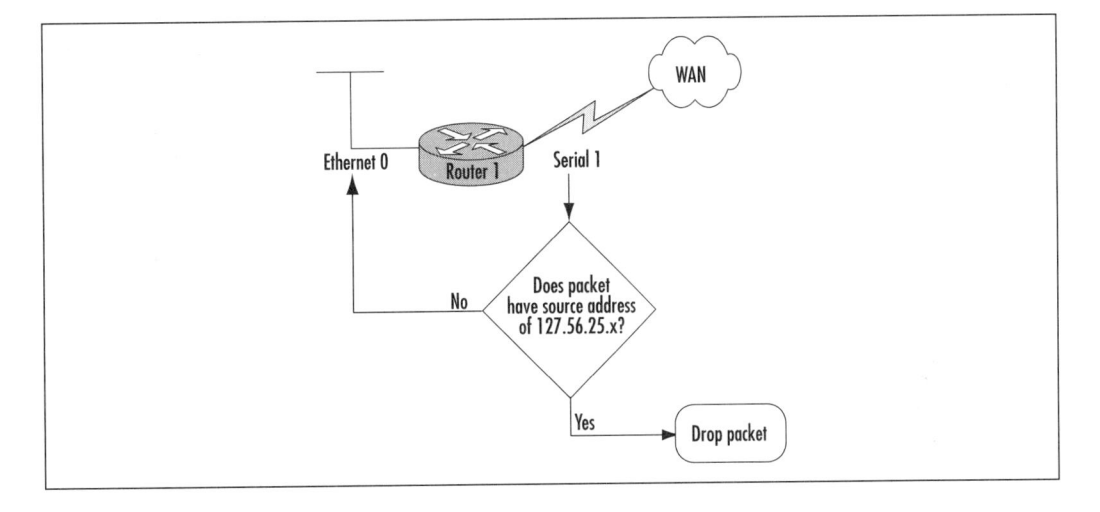

Notice that anything coming from the 127.56.25.0 network is dropped. Any other traffic is passed through the Access Control List and on to the destination host.

Extended Access Control Lists (ACLs)

When network requirements extend beyond the capabilities of standard Access Control Lists, you may need to implement extended Access Control Lists to meet the needs of your network. Extended Access Control Lists are more robust and granular than standard Access Control Lists, which permits network administrators to implement more jurisdictions over a network.

Extended Access Control Lists provide added capability by offering filtering of both source and destination addresses. In addition, extended IP Access Control Lists provide precise control over any IP protocol based traffic. Although extended ACLs provide more extensive filtering, they are similar in operation to standard ACLs.

Extended IP Access Control Lists support all of the network layer protocols (ARP, RARP, ICMP, etc.), which is made possible by specifying the protocol by either protocol number or a keyword when enabling the Access Control List. The protocol keywords are EIGRP, GRE, ICMP, IGMP, IGRP, IP, IPINIP, NOS, OSPF, TCP, OR UDP. Protocol numbers in the range 0 to 255 can also be used. Within each protocol all applications supported are filterable. This is accomplished by specifying the port number or application name. Port numbers range from 0 – 65535. Table 1.12 lists some common applications and their relative port numbers.

Table 1.12 Common Protocols and Port Numbers

Protocol	Port
FTP data port	20
FTP control port	21
Simple Network Management Protocol (SNMP)	161
Domain Name System (DNS)	53
Boot Protocol Server (BOOTPS)	67
Boot Protocol Client (BOOTPC)	68
Gopher	70
Post Office Protocol (POP3)	110
Network News Transport Protocol (NNTP)	119
Border Gateway Protocol (BGP)	179
Simple Mail Transport Protocol (SMTP)	25
Telnet	23
Trivial File Transport Protocol (SMTP)	69
World Wide WEB (WWW)	80

Extended Access Control Lists have a wide range of options available, which offers more control over specific types of network traffic. The following syntax is used when implementing extended ACLs.

```
access-list access-list-number [dynamic dynamic-name [timeout

    minutes]] {deny | permit} protocol source source-wildcard

    destination destination-wildcard [precedence precedence]

    [tos tos] [log | log-input]
```

Extended Access Control Lists are extensively more complex than standard ACLs. Table 1.13 defines each portion of the extended Access Control List command.

Table 1.13 Extended Access Control List Variable Definitions

Keyword	Description
access-list-number	This number identifies the access list as an extended ACL to the router.
dynamic	An actual name to use to identify the particular extended ACL.
timeout	Defines how long a temporary access list is good for on the interface.
deny|permit	Sets the condition that is applied to the access list.
protocol	Name or number of an IP protocol. The following protocols are valid in this field: **EIGRP**, **GRE**, **ICMP** (Table 1.12), **IGMP**, **IGRP**, **IP**, **IpinIP**, **NOS**, **OSPF**, **TCP** (Table 1.13 and Table 1.14), and **UDP** (Table 1.15).
source	Network or host address from which the packet is being sent.
source-wildcard	Wildcard value to be applied to the source address.
destination	Network or host address of where the packet is destined.
destination-wildcard	Wildcard value to be applied to the destination address.
precedence	Specifies a packet's precedence level by name or a number between 1 and 7.
tos	Specifies the type of service by either name or a number between 1 and 15.
log|log –input	Causes a logging message to be created and sent to the console.

When using the keyword **ICMP** in conjunction with the Access Control List, the following options become available.

Table 1.14 ICMP Options in Extended Access Control Lists

Keyword	Description
<0-255>	ICMP message type
administratively-prohibited	Administratively prohibited
alternate-address	Alternate address
conversion-error	Datagram conversion
dod-host-prohibited	Host prohibited
dod-net-prohibited	Net prohibited
Echo	Ping
echo-reply	Ping reply
General-parameter-problem	Parameter problem
host-isolated	Host isolated
host-precedence-unreachable	Host unreachable for precedence
host-redirect	Host redirect
host-tos-unreachable	Host unreachable for type of service
host-tos-redirect	Host redirect for type of service
host-unknown	Host is unknown
host-unreachable	Host is unreachable
information-reply	Information replies
information-request	Information requests
Log	Log entries
mask-reply	Mask replies
mask-request	Mask requests
mobile-redirect	Mobile host redirect
net-redirect	Network redirect
net-tos-redirect	Net redirect for type of service
net-tos-unreachable	Network unreachable for type of service
net-unreachable	Net unreachable
Network-unknown	Network is unknown
no-room-for-option	Parameter is required but there is no room
option-missing	Parameter is required but missing
packet-too-big	Fragmentation required and DF set

Continued

Table 1.14 Continued

Keyword	Description
parameter-problem	Parameter problem
port-unreachable	Port is unreachable
Precedence	Match packets with this precedence value
precedence-unreachable	Precedence cutoff
protocol-unreachable	Protocol is unreachable
reassembly-timeout	Reassembly timeout
Redirect	Redirect
router-advertisement	Router advertisement
router-solicitation	Router solicitation
source-quench	Source quenches
source-route-failed	Source route has failed
time-exceeded	Time has been exceeded
timestamp-reply	Timestamp reply
timestamp-request	Timestamp request
Tos	Type of service value match
traceroute	Traceroute
ttl-exceeded	Time-to-live has exceeded
unreachable	Unreachable

When using the keyword **TCP**, the following options become available.

Table 1.15 TCP Options in Extended Access Control Lists

Keyword	Description
Eq	Match packets by port
established	Match established connections
Gt	Match packets with a greater port number
Log	Log matches
Lt	Match packets with a lower port number
neq	Match packets not on a given port number
precedence	Match packets with a specific precedence

Continued

Table 1.15 Continued

Keyword	Description
Range	Match packets within a range
Tos	Match packets with a specific type of service
<cr>	Carriage return

After creating the extended Access Control List, you must apply it to an interface. This procedure is identical to the way you would implement a standard Access Control List to an interface. The following is the syntax for applying an extended Access Control List, as well as a standard Access Control List, to an interface. If you forget to specify whether the list is applied on the inbound or the outbound of the interface, the router will default to outbound "out."

```
ip access-group {access-list-number | name}{in | out}
```

Benefits of Extended ACLs

Extended Access Control Lists provide many benefits that make life easier for a network administrator. Extended ACLs give administrators the ability to shape network data flow, protect the network from malicious attacks, and log traffic.

Because extended ACLs have so many different types and combinations of control, they provide enough flexibility to be used in virtually all network environments and situations. The use of these types of access lists is limited only by the imagination of the administrator.

Common Ports Used with Extended ACLs

The following tables provide extensive lists of all the options you can implement to give you more granular control if you use the **eq** option in the **TCP** variable of this command.

Table 1.16 Options When Using the eq Switch with the TCP Variable

Keyword	Port	Protocol
<0-65535>		
Bgp	179	Border Gateway Protocol
Chargen	19	Character generator
Cmd	514	Remote commands
Daytime	13	Daytime

Continued

Table 1.16 Continued

Keyword	Port	Protocol
Discard	9	Discard
Domain	53	Domain Name System
Echo	7	Ping
Exec	512	Exec
Finger	79	Finger
ftp	21	File Transfer Protocol
ftp-data	20	File Transfer Protocol data connections
Gopher	70	Gopher
Hostname	101	Hostname server
Ident	113	Indent Protocol
Irc	194	Internet Relay Chats
Klogin	543	Kerberos login
Kshell	544	Kerberos shell
Login	513	Rlogin
Lpd	515	Print service
nntp	119	Network News Transport Protocol
pop3	110	Post Office Protocol 3
Smtp	25	Simple Mail Transfer Protocol
telnet	23	Telnet
Time	37	Time
www	80	World Wide Web

The following options are available if the **UDP** keyword is used within the access list 100-199 command (Table 1.17).

Table 1.17 UDP Options in Extended Access Control Lists

Keyword	Port	Protocol
<0-65535>		
Biff	512	Biff Mail Notification
Bootpc	68	Bootstrap protocol client
Bootps	67	Bootstrap protocol server
Discard	9	Discard

Continued

Table 1.17 UDP Options in Extended Access Control Lists

Keyword	Port	Protocol
Dnsix	195	DNSIX security protocol auditing
Domain	53	Domain Name System
Echo	7	Ping
Mobile-ip	434	Mobile IP registration
Nameserver	42	IEN116 name service
Netbios-dgm	138	NetBIOS datagram service
Netbios-ns	137	NetBIOS name service
Ntp	123	Network Time Protocol
Rip	520	Routing Information Protocol
Snmp	161	Simple Network Management Protocol
Snmptrap	162	Simple Network Management Protocol traps
Sunrpc	111	Sun remote-procedure call
Syslog	514	System log
Tacacs	49	TAC Access Control System
Talk	517	Talk
Tftp	69	Trivial File Transfer Protocol
Time	37	Time
Who	513	Who service
Xdmcp	177	X Display Manager Control Protocol

Configuration Examples

It is apparent after reviewing Tables 1.16 and 1.17 that extended Access Control Lists can be very granular and give very specific control over a variety of network traffic. However, in implementing this level of control, you must consider that the additional processor load will increase the possibility of network slowdown. You must be selective when implementing extended Access Control Lists.

The following entry is an example of an extended ACL that denies and logs all TCP traffic on port 80 that is destined for the 10.10.0.0 network, then permits everything else:

```
Router1(config)#access-list 101 deny tcp any 10.10.0.0 0.0.255.255 eq
    www log

Router1config#access-list 101 permit ip any any
```

To apply this control to a specific interface, you would go into the related interface configuration mode and use the access-group command. For example, to apply the above example to all inbound packets on Serial interface 1, you would use the following set of commands.

`Router1(config)#`**`interface serial 1`**
`Router1(config-if)#`**`ip access-group 101 in`**

The following example would deny Telnet traffic destined for a router with an address of 200.125.12.1. The extra option of logging is enabled to make it easier to track which users are trying to complete this action.

`Router1(config)# #`**`access-list 110 deny 23 any host 200.125.12.1 log`**
`Router1(config)# #`**`access-list 110 permit ip any any`**
`Router1(config)#`**`interface serial 1`**
`Router1(config-if)#`**`ip access-group 110`**

> **NOTE**
>
> The "out" keyword is not required, since that is the default it is included here for clarity.

This example shows that port 23 is denied access to the TCP/IP address 200.125.12.1, and any traffic matching this criteria will be logged. Applying this list to the Serial 1 interface with the **out** option will stop any traffic from going out this interface.

Extended ACLs can also be useful tools when trying to prevent malicious denial of service (DoS) attacks against your network. If, using network sniffing or some other means, the type of attack can be identified by what port it is attacking, it makes implementing extended ACLs considerably easier. At the end of this section on DoS attacksis a "catch-all" statement that makes this task a bit easier.

It is important to understand what a DoS attack is before we attempt to minimize its impact. A DoS attack is an attack on a network that monopolizes the network and server resources so that no other host can participate on the network, or, if they do, the network or service becomes very slow.

There are three general types of DoS attacks : Smurf, SYN floods, and Fraggle. A Smurf attack happens when the attacker uses a flood of ICMP packets to tie up the servers and the network. A SYN flood uses TCP connection requests to monopolize the network. The Fraggle attack uses a flood of broadcasts, like a Smurf attack, but it uses UDP echo requests instead of ICMP echo requests. Extended ACLs can both track and deny each of these attacks.

The following example would enable you to track a Smurf attack if you believed one was occurring on your network.

```
Router1(config)#access-list 102 permit icmp any any echo-reply
Router1(config)#access-list 102 permit ip any any
Router1(config)#interface serial 1
Router1(config-if)#ip access-group 102 in
```

Once the extended ACL has been applied to the serial interface, the **show access-list** command enables you to see if an attack is occurring. This would be evident if there were an outstanding number of matches on this access list.

To gather more information on this attack, you can alter the access list to log the matches. The following command enables you to see the source address.

```
Router1(config)#interface serial 1
Router1(config-if)#no ip access-group 102 in
Router1(config-if)#exit
Router1(config)#no access-list 102 permit icmp any any echo-reply
Router1(config)#access-list 102 permit icmp any any echo-reply log
Router1(config)#interface serial 1
Router1(config-if)#ip access-group 102 in
```

Only pings were allowed in the above example. It was shown as a general "how to," and is not intended to be complete due to the access list denying all other traffic from entering the serial interface. Obviously, you would want to make this list more robust in a production network. Applying a new access-group command will overwrite the existing access-group command, but for the sake of clarity we first removed the existing access group and extended ACL. Once that taks has been completed, we created the new Extended ACL and then re-applied it to the serial interface. Your system will begin logging each match, which you will be able to view with the **show log** command. After finding the network address from which this attack is originating, you can look up the administrator in the appropriate "who is" database on the Internet and contact them to help you stop the attacks. It is important to remember that the source address of a DoS attack is usually also a victim, because the real attacker will usually hide his identity behind this victim's address.

You would use the same technique in tracking the other two kinds of DoS attacks. The only difference in implementation is that in a Fraggle attack you would track UDP echo requests, and in a SYN flood you would track TCP establish connection requests. Many network engineers implement "catch-all" ACLs as a first line warning system to help minimize DoS attacks. The following is an example of a "catch-all" ACL configuration.

```
Router1(config)#access-list 101 permit icmp any any echo-reply
Router1(config)#access-list 101 permit udp any any eq echo
Router1(config)#access-list 101 permit udp any eq echo any
Router1(config)#access-list 101 permit tcp any any established
Router1(config)#access-list 101 permit ip any any
Router1(config)#interface serial 1
Router1(config-if)#ip access-group 101 in
```

This configuration would be used if a suspected DoS attack were occurring on your network. During the attack, if a **show access-list** command were issued, it would show the matches per list. This would indicate what kind of DoS attack was occurring by showing the matches for certain types of traffic. For instance, it there were a disproportional amount of established TCP connection requests occurring, that would indicate that the network was under a DoS SYN flood attack.

Network Address Translation (NAT)

Network Address Translation (NAT) is a technology that enables administrators to hide an unregistered TCP/IP address on the internal network behind a registered external address. This can be manipulated to hide many "private" addresses behind one registered public address, or many private addresses behind many public addresses.

Enabling Network Address Translation conserves the TCP/IP address pool because several Internet users can use one registered TCP/IP address, thus minimizing the requirement for valid Internet addresses.

NAT also provides increased security for the internal network. When users send traffic out to the Internet, they are not using their actual TCP/IP addresses. This makes malicious attacks on your internal network more difficult, which may be enough to turn the predator onto easier prey.

Because of the recent explosion of TCP/IP connectivity in the last ten years, as responsible administrators, we must conserve public TCP/IP addresses. Not only are public TCP/IP addresses in short supply, but they are also costly.

To understand Network Address Translation, it is critical to understand Request For Comments (RFC) 1918, developed by the Internet Engineering Task Force (IETF), and the reasons that network engineers worldwide are implementing this standard. The standards can be researched on the IETF's Web page at www.ietf.org.

RFC 1918 addresses are reserved blocks of addresses designated as internal, or private, addresses. This means that RFC 1918 addresses should not be routed onto the Internet, and border routers should be implementing NAT to translate these private addresses into registered public addresses. Table 1.18 illustrates the different classes of RFC 1918 address blocks.

Table 1.18 RFC 1918 Reserved Private Address Blocks

Network	Mask	Address Block
10.0.0.0	255.0.0.0	1 Class A Networks
172.16.0.0–172.31.0.0	255.255.0.0	16 Contiguous Class B Networks
192.168.0.0–192.168.255.0	255.255.255.0	256 Contiguous Class C Networks

There are four features of Cisco's implementation of Network Address Translation:

- Static Address Translation
- Dynamic Source Address Translation
- Port Address Translation (PAT)
- Destination Address Rotary Translation

Static Address Translation is a one-to-one mapping from a private internal address to a registered public address. Static Address Translation does create administrative overhead, because each addition, deletion, or change to the NAT must be done manually by the administrator. On the other hand, you do maintain more control with Static Address Translation because of this overhead. To configure a Static Address Translation, you would use the following command.

```
ip nat inside source static <local-ip><global-ip>
```

Here is an example.

```
Router1(config)#ip nat inside source static 192.168.20.1 30.20.10.1
```

Dynamic Source Address Translation associates an internal host automatically with a public address from a pool of addresses. This would be implemented in an environment where there is a group of public addresses to be used for Network Address Translation and numerous users may be on the Internet at any one time. This feature is dynamic, which eases administrative burden. The command to establish a NAT pool is as follows.

```
ip nat pool <name> <start-ip> <end-ip> { netmask <netmask> | prefix-
   length
<prefix-length> } [ type { rotary } ]
```

Consider this example.

```
Router1(config)#ip nat pool Syngress 30.20.10.1 30.20.10.254 prefix-
   length 24
```

Port Address Translation gives the administrator the option to conserve public addresses in the address pool by enabling source ports in TCP or UDP connections to be translated. This provides the opportunity for numerous different private addresses to be associated with one public address by using port translation for the proper distinctiveness. When more detailed translation is required, the new port number is assigned from the same pool as the original, following Berkley Standard Distribution (BSD) conventions (Table 1.17). The keyword **overload** enables UDP and TCP port translation. To configure a Port Address Translation, use the following command.

```
ip nat inside source list <acl> pool <name> [overload]
```

Here is an example.

```
Router1(config)#ip nat inside source list 1 pool Syngress overload
```

Destination Address Rotary Translation provides public address connectivity to private addresses. Once the relationship has been established, a destination private address matching an access list is replaced with an address from a pool using a round-robin procedure. A switch is made when every new TCP connection is made from the outside. All traffic that is not TCP will not be translated when passed.

This technique is used for protocol translation load distribution. This is low-level load distribution, so if a server were to go down, the rotary translation would still send inbound network traffic to the down server.

```
ip nat pool <name> <start-ip> <end-ip> { netmask <netmask> | prefix-
length <prefix-length> } [ type { rotary } ]
```

Here is a more concrete example.

```
Router1 (config)#ip nat pool Syngress 30.20.10.1 30.20.10.254 prefix-
length 24 type rotary
```

Table 1.19 Berkley Standard Distribution

Beginning of Range	End of Range
1	511
512	1023
1024	4999
5000	65535

Table 1.20 defines what traffic is supported by Cisco's Network Address Translation solution.

Table 1.20 Supported Traffic Types

TCP/UPD*	NetBIOS	ICMP	FTP	DNS
H.323	NetMeeting	HTTP	TFTP	Telnet
Archie	Finger	NTP	NFS	rlogin, rsh, rcp

* TCP/UDP traffic that does not have a source/destination address in the data stream

To enable a NAT on the interface, you would use the following basic command.

```
ip nat { inside | outside }
```

Here is an example.

```
Router1(config-if)#ip nat inside
```

The above command applies the NAT to the interface and designates that interface to be an "inside" interface. The "Inside" keyword in the command means that this interface is using private addresses, which need to be translated to "outside" or public addresses.

Controlling NAT with ACLs

In order to control which hosts apply to the established Network Address Translation, you have to implement Access Control Lists. Fortunately, you usually do not require the detailed scope of extended Access Control Lists, and most NAT requirements can be met with standard Access Control Lists.

When a translation entry has been made using an Access Control List, the NAT will create a "simple" translation entry. This entry will contain only the related private and public addresses for either the inside or the outside, depending on whether the "ip nat inside" or "ip nat outside" is configured, respectively.

To assign an Access Control List to a NAT configuration, you first need to establish the NAT and the ACL. Once you have done this, you are able to relate the Access Control List to the NAT. Identifying the Access Control List by utilizing the list portion of the ip nat command does this.

```
Router1(config)#ip nat pool Syngress 30.20.10.1 30.20.10.254 prefix-length 24
Router1(config)#access-list 1 permit 192.168.20.0 0.0.0.255

Router1(config)#ip nat inside source list 1 pool Syngress
```

In this example, the ip nat pool "Syngress" and Access Control List 1 were established. Once that was completed, the list variable was used within the ip nat command to connect the Syngress NAT to Access Control List 1. In this case, only hosts from network 192.168.20.0 can be translated from the 30.20.10.x NAT pool.

Dynamic versus Static Translations

When applying Network Address Translation to your network, you need to decide whether you want to utilize dynamic or static NAT. There are benefits to each that you need to consider before making your choice. It is possible to mix the two if you have different requirements for two different portions of your network, or if the severity of control differs between two networks or hosts.

Dynamic Network Address Translation uses a pool from which to draw source TCP/IP addresses. Generally, dynamic NAT is easier to administer, since address translation relationships are completed automatically. However, this also means that dynamic Network Address Translation does not allow as much control of the NAT process.

Configuration Example

In the example shown in Figure 1.9, Host A on the internal network would like to send a message to an external host on the Internet, namely Host B. Enabling a NAT to allow connectivity between network 192.168.20.0 and the Internet could be accomplished as follows.

```
Router1(config)#ip nat pool Syngress 30.20.10.1 30.20.10.254 prefix-
    length 24
Router1(config)#access-list 1 permit 192.168.20.0 0.0.0.255
Router1(config)#ip nat inside source list 1 pool Syngress
Router1(config)#interface ethernet 1
Router1(config-if)#ip nat inside
Router1(config-if)#interface serial 1
Router1(config-if)#ip nat outside
Router1(config-if)#end
```

Figure 1.9 Example NAT Environment

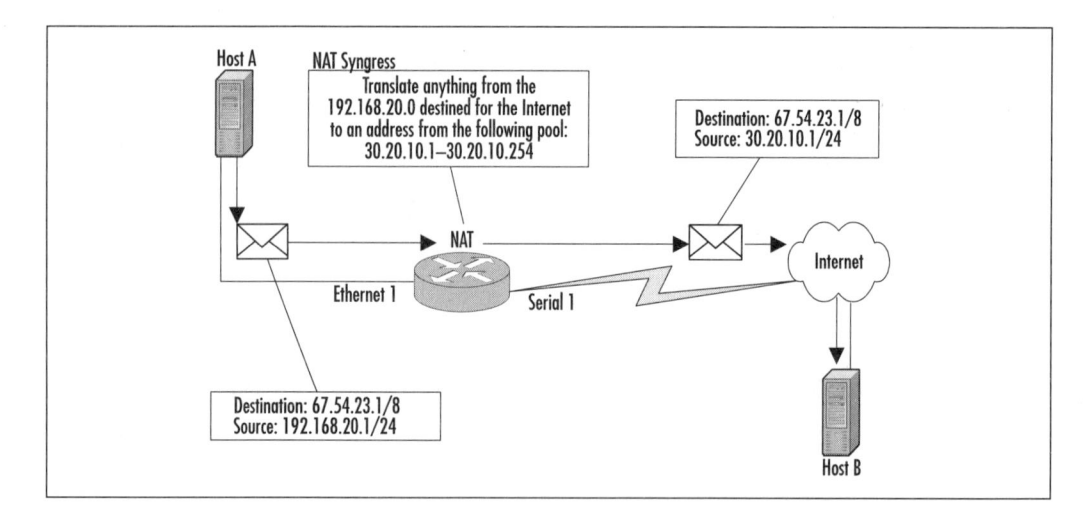

Route Maps

Route maps are intricate access lists. These access lists allow criteria to be tested against network traffic by using the **match** command. If the criterion is met then an action is taken against the traffic. This action is specified using the **set** command. By matching traffic against Access Control Lists, route maps allow granular control of how routes are redistributed among route processes. The **route-map** command enables the router to create a route-map in the router. The route-map command is used to define a criterion as well as the action to be taken once the criteria match is successful and can be used for redistribution, routing, policies, and traffic shaping.

When route maps are used for Network Address Translation, an entry is created for both the inside and the outside for both private and global addresses. Any TCP or UDP port information is included in the translation.

The benefit of route maps is they allow administrators to arrange any combination of access lists, output interface, and next-hop TCP/IP address to determine which NAT pool to use.

Where to Use Route Maps

In light of the fact that route maps provide more control by matching traffic against Access Control Lists, the applications are virtually limitless. Knowledge of route maps and the services they provide will enhance your ability to control the traffic on your network, thus increasing security and traffic flow.

Among other services, route maps allow administrators to combine access lists, output interface, and next-hop TCP/IP addresses to determine which NAT pool to use. Route maps are implemented when you have a variety of needs that you want your NAT tables to address. This gives administrators more control by providing detailed configuration and administration.

Controlling Traffic with Route Maps

The possibility of manipulating traffic a number of ways using route maps appeals to network administrators. With route maps, you can get the detail of multiple extended Access Control Lists in combination with a specific interface, or even the next-hop address, and then apply that route map to a NAT. You can produce a multitude of different combinationsto provide the specific control you want.

Configuration Example

Consider the following configuration on the router designated as NAT in Figure 1.10. This portion of the configuration defines the NAT pool and the associated route map.

```
Router1(config)#ip nat pool pool-110 120.110.187.1 120.110.187.254
    prefix-length 24
Router1(config)#ip nat inside source route-map MAP-110 pool pool-110
```

Figure 1.10 NAT Implementing RouteMaps

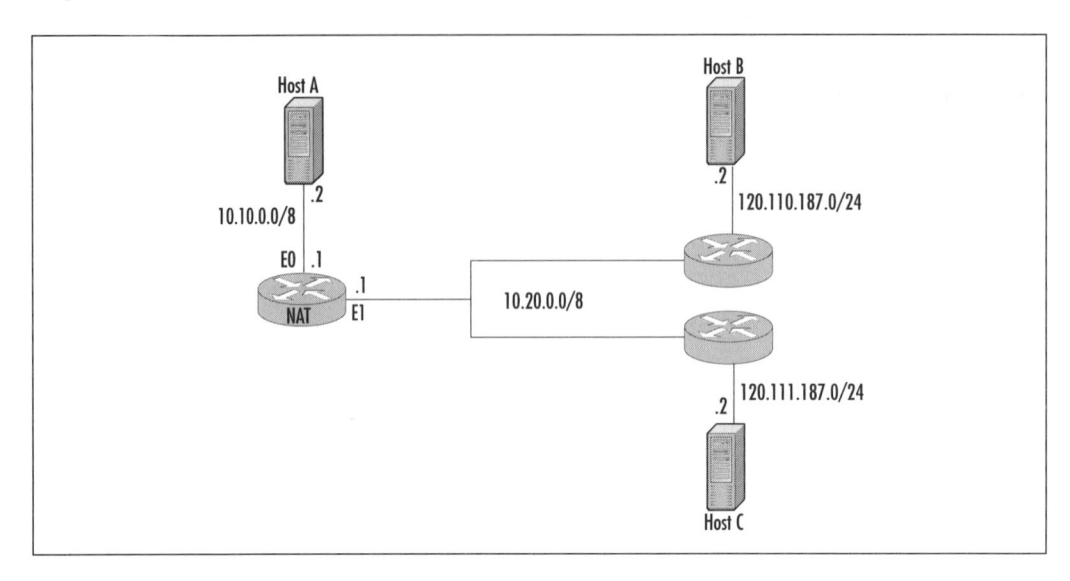

Once the pool has been defined, the NAT is assigned to an interface both on the inside and the outside, as seen in the next example.

```
Router1(config)#interface ethernet 0
Router1(config-if)#ip address 10.10.1.1 255.255.0.0
Router1(config-if)#ip nat inside

Router1(config-if)#interface ethernet 1
Router1(config-if)#ip address 10.10.2.1 255.255.0.0
Router1(config-if)#ip nat outside
Router1(config-if)#^z
```

After the pool has been established and has been assigned to an interface, an access list is used to define which traffic will be used.

```
Router1(config)#access-list 110 permit ip 10.10.0.0 0.0.255.255
       120.21.187.0 0.0.0.255
```

When these steps have been completed, the actual route map criteria are configured using the **match** command.

```
Router1(config)#route-map MAP-110 permit 10
Router1(config-route-map)#match ip address 110
```

In this example, if Host A sends traffic to Host B, an extended NAT will be created. On both the inside and outside interfaces, a NAT is created for translation.

Summary

In this chapter, we examined fundamental network skills, such as binary to decimal conversion, and explored new concepts that you may not as yet have had to implement, such as using route maps to help meet Network Address Translation requirements.

As networks continue to swell, TCP/IP subnet manipulation will become increasingly important. Classful TCP/IP addresses have three classes, namely, Classes A, B, and C. The first octet of the address defines the class of address, which defines the default subnet mask. All subnets within the network must have the same subnet mask, when advertised to another network, the default subnet will be used.

Class D and E ranges are reserved for special purposes. The Class E range is reserved for experimental and developmental purposes. The Class D range is reserved for multicasting. Unlike broadcasting, in multicasts, hosts do not have to process each packet. The only computers that process multicasts are computers that are actually participating in the multicast group. This technology dramatically saves bandwidth as well as nonmember computer processor cycles.

Classful protocols, such as RIPv1 and IGRP, do not include subnet masks with routing table updates.

RIPv1 bases its routing decisions solely on hop count, which is not always accurate, considering possible link congestion and reliability. Like all distance vector protocols, RIPv1 receives routing updates only from direct neighbors, and it sends and receives updates only at regular time intervals.

In order to make IGRP a more robust protocol than RIPv1, Cisco based IGRP's routing decisions on more network variables, thus making the protocol more "intelligent." The factors that IGRP takes into account when making its routing decisions are bandwidth, delay, load, and reliability. IGRP updates its routing table the same way as RIPv1, that is, by updating at regular time intervals and getting updates only from direct neighbors.

Variable-length subnet mask gives administrators the ability to break down addresses into more efficient and manageable pieces. This gives more control over the size of subnets and reduces the number of unused host addresses.

Access Control Lists enable you to shape your network traffic to make better use of the existing bandwidth. Standard ACLs allow you to control the network traffic based on the source of the network packets. Standard ACLs do not always isolate traffic enough to properly manage it, in which case, extended ACLs may be more appropriate. Extended ACLs have a wide range of flexibility, which usually gives you all the control that you need to manage network traffic in most environments.

Network Address Translation is used to hide private addresses behind a public address. While making your network more secure, NAT also minimizes public address needs, which lessens costs and contributes to the conservation of public TCP/IP addresses.

NAT's use of ACLs enables administrators the ability to isolate traffic that is to be translated to public addresses. You can also use route maps with Network Address Translation to combine any access lists, output interface, and next-hop TCP/IP address in order to determine which NAT pool to use.

As you continue to explore Cisco's Quality of Service, you will become more familiar with its tools and how they will help you control the data flow in your network.

FAQs

Visit **www.syngress.com/solutions** to have your questions about this chapter answered by the author.

Q: Should I implement a classful or a classless TCP/IP address scheme?

A: Most private networks implement a classless TCP/IP address scheme because VLSM enables you not only to conserve addresses but also to break networks down into more manageable pieces. If there is an existing network, you need to consider the routing protocol that is currently in place. If the protocol is a classful protocol, you need to either implement a classful address scheme or migrate to a classless routing protocol.

Q: You are a consultant to a small company that is implementing a network consisting of eight routers. The company's engineers would like to use either RIPv1 or IGRP. Which protocol should be used?

A: You first need to consider what types of routers are being used. If all of the routers are Cisco, then you should use IGRP since it is a more robust protocol. If the network consists of a mix of vendors, or perhaps has no Cisco routers at all, you would use RIPv1 because it is an open standard and most router manufacturers support this protocol.

Q: You have a requirement to filter traffic by source address. What type of Access Control List would you use?

A: If you are controlling only by source addresses, the preferred ACL would be standard Access Control List. Standard ACLs are great for this type of traffic and do not require more detailed configuration. If you need more granular control, such as filtering based on source address, destination address, or type of traffic, then your preference would be extended Access Control Lists. These types of ACLs require more configuration, but they enable an administrator to gain more thorough control over the network.

Q: A company that you work for has obtained ten registered TCP/IP addresses for Internet connectivity. You want to allow a portion of your one hundred users to access the Internet with these addresses. What would you need to use in order to make this possible?

A: Network Address Translation enables you to hide private addressing from the network behind actual registered addresses. You would first configure an address pool consisting of the ten registered addresses. You then need to filter which users you want to use the NAT by using an Access Control List. Finally, you would apply the NAT to the desired interface.

Chapter 2

EIGRP A Detailed Guide

Solutions in this chapter:

- Reviewing Basic Concepts of IGRP
- Defining the Four Basic Components of EIGRP
- Implementing Packet Types
- Configuring Basic EIGRP
- Configuring Advanced EIGRP
- Redistributing EIGRP and OSPF
- Recognizing Caveats
- Troubleshooting EIGRP

Introduction

Enhanced IGRP, or EIGRP, is one of the most versatile interior routing protocols available, and is often the protocol of choice in all-Cisco environments. Therefore, you should have a strong working knowledge of EIGRP. Whether you plan to implement QoS on your network today, in the future, or never, strongly consider EIGRP when choosing an interior routing protocol. EIGRP is Cisco's proprietary routing protocol, and you can rest assured that Cisco will continue to improve and grow this routing protocol. In addition, because there are no standards organizations with which to contend, Cisco can easily update and improve this protocol without compromise.

EIGRP is a very capable routing protocol with support for IP, IPX, and AppleTalk. With new enhancements, such as EIGRP Stubs, EIGRP is now more scalable than ever, and is becoming more viable every day. In fact, at Networks 2000 (Cisco's yearly convention) the person presenting the EIGRP session discussed the possibility that Cisco would soon greatly reduce the impact of the very nasty problem of Stuck-in-Active routes. It will be interesting to watch as this is implemented and deployed.

In the meantime, however, EIGRP remains one of the cleanest and easiest to configure of all the interior routing protocols available. In this chapter, you will learn some of the features and theories of EIGRP in the hope that you will have all of the information you need to make decisions about deploying EIGRP on your network. Additionally, you will see advanced EIGRP configuration examples to illustrate the best practices of configuring EIGRP.

Reviewing Basic Concepts of IGRP

Cisco's proprietary Interior Gateway Routing Protocol (IGRP) represented a leap forward in routing technologies over its distance-vector kid-brother, the Routing Information Protocol (RIP). While IGRP maintained the underlying distance-vector route establishment process, it redefined exactly what "distance" meant. RIP simply established the distance metric as the number of "hops" to the destination without considering the nature of the hops. IGRP, however, established the nature of the path to the destination as the distance metric. This allowed the routing process to consider bandwidth and delay (and optionally load, reliability, and MTU) as factors in establishing an efficient routing architecture. However, what IGRP failed to improve significantly was the efficiency of distributing routing information and the required self-healing aspect of a well-designed network.

Recognizing the need in modern, complex internetworks for rapid healing and efficient use of expensive bandwidth, Cisco designed EIGRP. While the name "enhanced" may lead you to believe that EIGRP is IGRP with a few functional modifications, it is actually a complete overhaul. In fact, the only significant similarity between the two protocols is the metric used to establish path cost. The processes used to share routing information and to reconverge after a failure are vastly different.

IGRP uses a system of periodic updates to inform directly connected routers, referred to as *neighbors*, of the routes that it knows. When the update period expires (every 90 seconds by default), the router broadcasts the entire routing table to its neighbors. This is a very inefficient way to share information. First, it is a waste of bandwidth. Second, bad things can happen in 90 seconds. EIGRP addresses these and other shortcomings with a very simple policy: "Don't talk to me unless something has changed, and if I need more information I will ask you for it." Not very neighborly I agree. However, do you tell your friends your telephone number on a daily basis, or do you tell them only when it has changed or if they have lost it?

Another major advantage that EIGRP has over IGRP is that it is a classless routing protocol. This allows us to use our address space much more efficiently using VLSM and CIDR, as well as streamlining the routing process through address summarization.

At its core, EIGRP remains a distance-vector routing protocol. As with RIP and IGRP, a route is selected as the optimum path using a distance metric and is placed in the routing table with a vector applied (the direction in which the specific traffic should flow). Unlike RIP and IGRP, however, alternative routes are not discarded. They are placed in a topology table and can be activated to replace the original route upon a topology change almost instantaneously. EIGRP maintains several other advances:

- **Efficient use of bandwidth** In a stable environment, only small hello packets will be exchanged.

- **Updates** Routing information is exchanged only when a topology change has occurred, and only the route in question is conversed.

- **Queries and replies** When a topology change occurs, a new route is established through a process of Q & A.

- **Scalability** Due to rapid convergence and efficient use of bandwidth, EIGRP is used in large all-Cisco networks (proprietary, remember!).

How Does EIGRP Work?

EIGRP has many mechanisms that must be fully understood before undertaking the design and successful implementation of an efficient, scalable, responsive network. To have a detailed discussion of these mechanisms first requires an overview discussion of distance-vector routing and the underpinnings of RIP and IGRP.

Using Distance Vectors for Path Selection

At the core of all routing protocols is the process of path selection. Any routing protocol's mechanism of path selection must meet two very important goals. First, the route selected to a destination must maintain some degree of advantage over alternative routes (with the exception of load balancing, discussed later). Second, the route must not create a loop in the network. Distance-vector protocols use several methods to achieve these goals.

Selecting the Optimum Path

Selecting the optimum path is quite simple in nature and is the responsibility of distance-vector routing algorithms known as Bellman-Ford or Ford-Fulkerson algorithms. Each router within the routing domain periodically broadcasts its routing table to neighbor routers through each interface participating in the routing process. When a router receives one of these periodic updates from a neighbor, it extracts the information it needs and updates its routing table. The update is not forwarded to the next upstream neighbor (*upstream* implies "in the opposite direction of the destination"). When the router's periodic update timer expires, it broadcasts an update of its own. The update period for RIP is 30 seconds; 90 seconds for IGRP. EIGRP does not use periodic updates, as you will soon see. This process of learning the topology of the network from the view of your neighbors is sometimes referred to as "routing by rumor."

If the process ended there, your network would be highly inefficient; in fact, it would completely fail. What if a router learned of a route to a destination from two or three or four different sources? Which route should be placed in the route table? This decision is made by applying a *metric* to the route and is illustrated in Figures 2.1 and 2.2. As you can see in Figure 2.1, RIP uses a very simple metric called *hop count*. Each router along the path increments the hop count by 1 as it places the route in its routing table and forwards the route to its upstream neighbors. Router B learns about network 172.16.0.0 from Router D and Router C. The route from Router C has a higher hop count, so it is discarded and is not forwarded to Router A. In this instance, RIP's simple metric failed to find the truly optimal route because the path selected traverses a 56 K link. Notice also that since RIP is a classful protocol, Router A only learns of the major network address 172.16.0.0, and not subnet 172.16.1.0.

Figure 2.1 The Route Selection Process

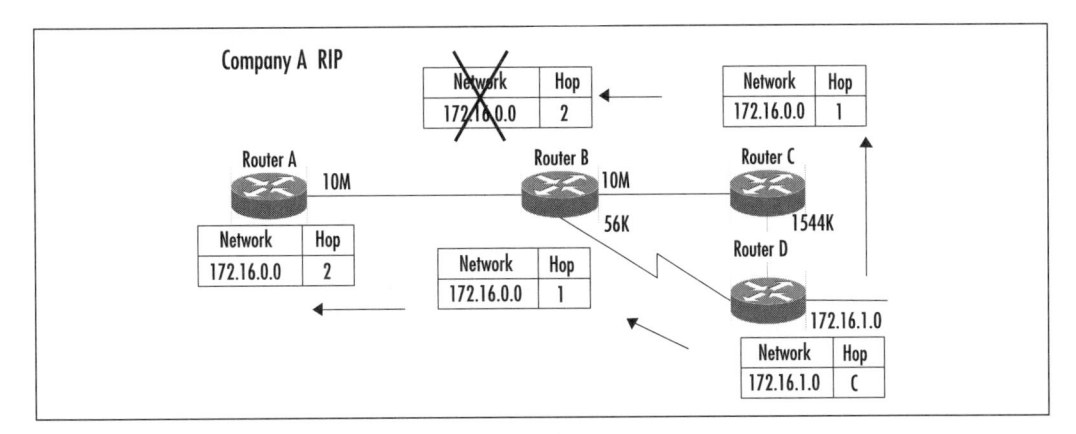

IGRP and EIGRP use a composite metric made up of bandwidth and delay by default, and optionally load, reliability and MTU. In Figure 2.2, Router B again learns about 172.16.0.0 from Routers D and C. However, using the composite metric, the path through Router C to Router D is selected due to the higher bandwidth of the link.

Figure 2.2 The Route Selection Process Continued

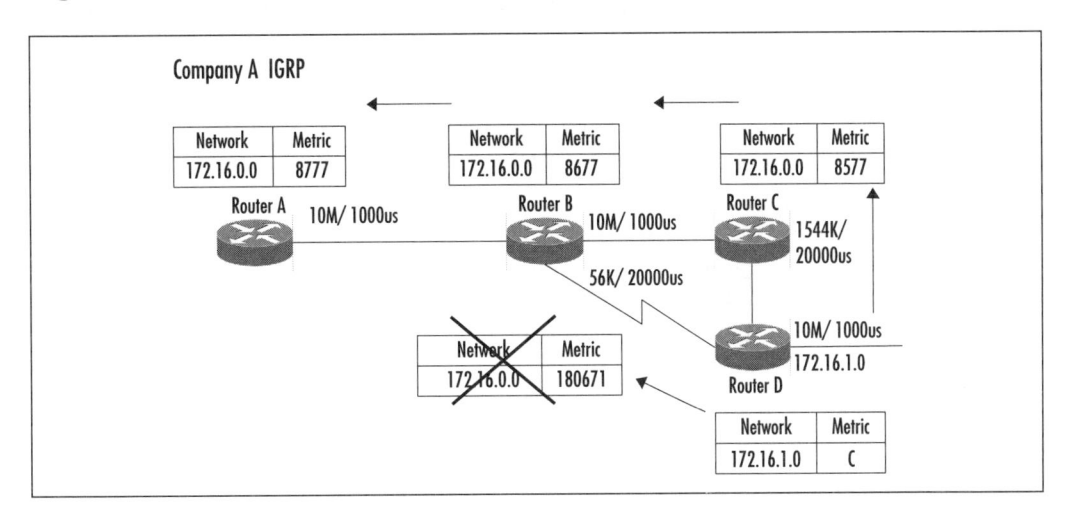

The actual formula used by IGRP and EIGRP to calculate the metric is:

Metric= [K1*10^7/BW+(K2*10^7/BW)/(256-LOAD)+K3*(DLY/10)]*[K5/(RELIABILITY+K4)]

where the default value for K1 and K3 is 1; and K2, K4, and K5 equal 0. BW is the minimum bandwidth along the path, and DLY is the cumulative delay along the path. Looking closely at the formula, you will notice that if K5 is 0, the resulting metric will always be 0. Therefore, as long as K5 is 0, the [K5/(RELIABILITY+K4)] portion of the formula is dropped. You will also notice that as long as K2 is 0, the (K2*10^7/BW)/(256-LOAD) portion can also be dropped. The resulting equation, if the default values for K1 through K5 are used, becomes:

Metric = 10^7/BW + DELAY/10

The only difference between IGRP and EIGRP is that EIGRP scales the resulting metric by 256 to provide a larger degree of granularity. Following this formula, we can calculate the metric from Router A to network 172.16.1.0 as:

Metric= [10^7/min BW] + [cumulative delay]/10

Metric = [10^7/1544] + [1000(A to B) + 1000(B to C) + 20000(C to D) + 1000 (segment D)]/10 = 6477 + 23000/10 = 6477 + 2300 = 8777 or 2246912 for EIGRP

The values of K1 through K5 can be adjusted using the **metric weights** tos k1 k2 k3 k4 k5 interface configuration command, where tos always equals 0 (*type of service* was planned but never implemented). Default bandwidth and delay values for certain interface types are listed in Table 2.1, and can be adjusted using the **bandwidth** and **delay** interface configuration commands. Use extreme caution when adjusting these values, as they can affect other processes running on the router and cause a cascade of reconvergence. EIGRP metric calculations are more fully explored in the *Configuring EIGRP's Distributed Update Algorithm* section later in this chapter.

Table 2.1 Bandwidth and Delay for Various Types of Interfaces

	Bandwidth	Delay
Fast Ethernet	100000K	100us
Ethernet	10000K	1000us
Token Ring	16000K	630us
FDDI	100000K	100us

Continued

Table 2.1 Continued

	Bandwidth	Delay
HSSI	45045K	20000us
T1	1544K	20000us
56K	56K	20000us
Loopback	8000000K	5000us

> **NOTE**
>
> It should be noted that while hop count is not used in calculating the metric, it is tracked. The maximum hop count in an IGRP or EIGRP network is by default 100, and can be changed to a value from 1 to 255 using the **metric maximum-hop** command.

Now let's look at how EIGRP would handle this same network. As with the previous two examples, we will focus our attention on establishing a path from Router A to network 172.16.1.0. As you can see in Figure 2.3, Router B again receives two advertised routes to 172.16.1.0, selects the path with the lowest metric, and advertises the metric for that path to Router A. On the surface, the outcome does not appear any different from IGRP. The default behavior of selecting the lowest-cost path remains the same. Beneath the surface, however, there are two major differences.

Figure 2.3 EIGRP Path Selection

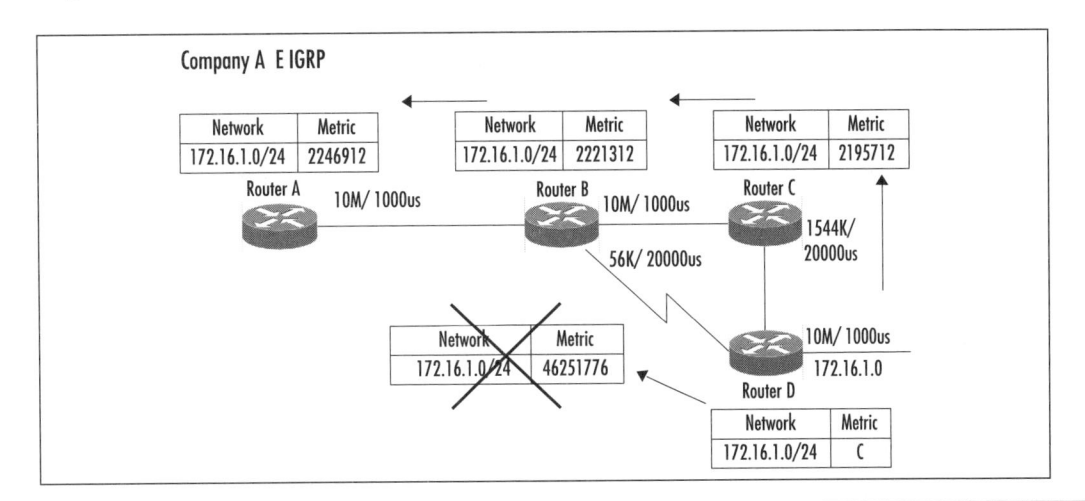

First, where IGRP dropped the route advertised across the 56 K link from Router D, Router B running EIGRP places the route in a *topology* table that lists routes and their associated metrics. Only the route with the best metric is placed in the routing table. The advantage of doing this is that, for example, if the link between C and D fails. the router already has another route in the topology table that can be placed in its routing table: B to D. It does not have to wait for another router's update period to expire to learn of an alternative route.

Second, you will notice that since EIGRP is a classless protocol, the subnet mask is passed along with the network address, and Router A learns of *subnet* 172.16.1.0. This is a distinct advantage. Using IGRP, Router A learned that network 172.16.0.0 is available through Router B. If we added another router to our network connected to Router A that needed to advertise a route to another 172.16.0.0 subnet—for example, 172.16.28.0—it again could only advertise 172.16.0.0. Router A's classfull behavior would be to believe that all subnets of 172.16.0.0 are available in either direction, and the direction with the lowest metric would be selected. One of these subnets would not get traffic intended for it.

EIGRP would allow Router D to advertise 172.16.1.0, and the new router to advertise 172.16.28.0. Router A would learn in which direction each subnet lies, and traffic would be routed properly.

Configuring Loop Avoidance

The second portion of the process, *loop avoidance*, is handled by IGRP by employing several basic rules and a series of timers that are designed to prevent routers from inadvertently advertising routes that create loops, and to prevent routers from accepting a new less favorable route while the network is reconverging.

The first rule, *split horizon,* is very simple: Do not send route information back through the interface from which it was learned. The philosophy behind the rule is very simple as well: "Why do I need to tell you what you just told me?"

Since distance-vector protocols select the direction from which they learned of a route as its vector, advertising that route back in that same direction could produce a routing loop. If there is a failure downstream (*downstream* implies "between you and the destination") and a router violates the split horizon rule by advertising the route back to the router from which it learned the route, downstream routers that have learned of the failure will believe that the violating router is now the vector for the failed route. This is because distance-vector protocols only advertise their distance to a location and not the vector.

Let's look at an example of a network that is not using split horizon. We can see in Figure 2.4 that network 172.16.1.0 has failed. Router D informs Routers B and C of this failure. It is now Router B's responsibility to inform Router A of the failure. However, before Router B's update period expires (every 90 seconds), it receives an update from Router A advertising a route to 172.16.0.0 with a metric of 8777. Router B would originally have ignored this update because the metric advertised by A is higher than the route that Router B was using. However, since the original route failed Router B now believes that there is a legitimate path to 172.16.1.0 through Router A! When Router B's update period finally arrives, it informs Routers C and D of this new route, and now they believe that 172.16.1.0 is accessible through Router B. When Router A receives an update from Router B, it simply increases the metric for the route, and vice versa. Router A never learns of the failure.

Figure 2.4 A Network Failure without Split Horizon

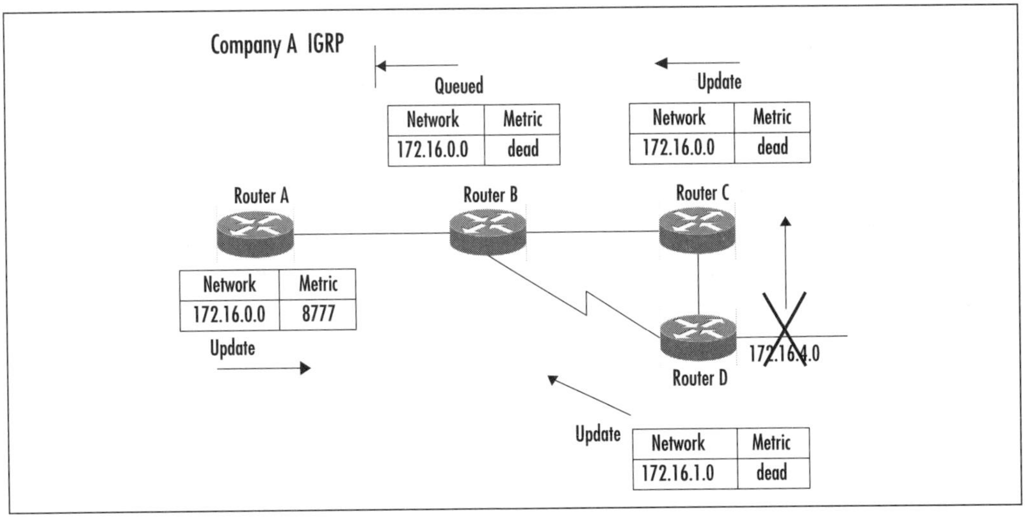

In Figure 2.5, we can see what happens when traffic destined for 172.16.1.0 enters the network at Router C. According to Router C, 172.16.1.0 is available through Router B. Router B believes that 172.16.1.0 is available through Router A. Router A believes it is available through Router B. The loop is formed.

This situation can be resolved through a system of *triggered updates, route poisoning,* and *hold-down timers.* The process again starts with a failure at 172.16.1.0. Instead of waiting for its update period to expire to inform its neighbors of the failure, Router D broadcasts a triggered update, thereby poisoning the route by setting the metric to infinity. Routers B and C receive this update, broadcast a triggered update to their neighbors in all directions (including back to Router D), and mark the route as possibly down (traffic is still forwarded). They also start a hold-down timer. During the hold-down period, any updates coming from a different direction that contain a higher metric than the original route are ignored. If an update received has a lower metric than the original, the route is marked accessible and the hold-down timer is disabled. After the hold-down period expires, the router will accept routing information from any source with any metric. The hold-down timer is by default three times the update period plus 10 seconds, and is used to allow enough time for word of the failure to reach all routers in the network.

Figure 2.5 A Routing Loop

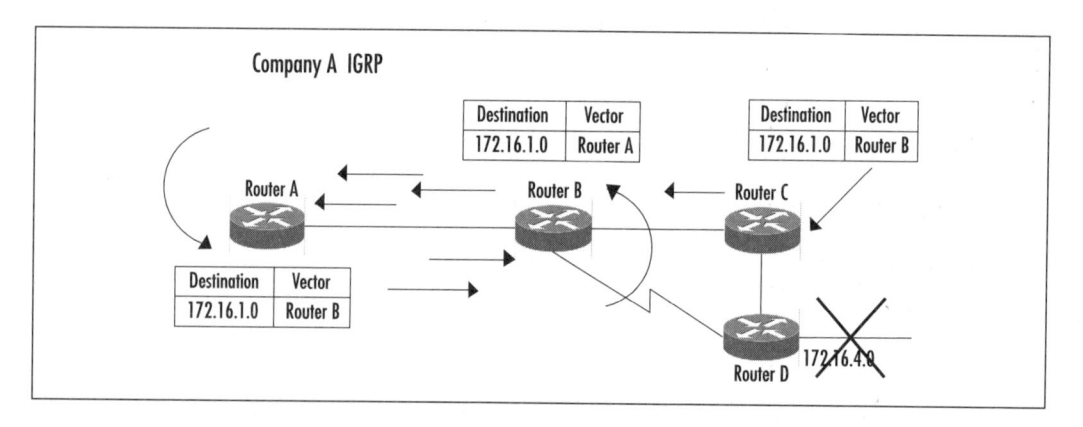

One final timer should be mentioned. When a route is placed in the routing table, a *flush timer* is set. The flush timer is seven times the update period and is reset each time the router receives an update containing the route. In previous the example, if a new route is never learned, the route will be removed from the routing table after the flush timer expires. The flush timer is also used to learn of a failed neighbor. When a neighbor fails, no triggered update is sent. If the flush timer expires for a route (or routes), the downstream neighbor from which the route(s) was learned is considered dead, and triggered updates are broadcast poisoning the route(s). The problem here is that it could take *630 seconds* to learn of a failed neighbor and to start the reconvergence process!

EIGRP handles this neighbor loss in a much more efficient manner. As stated previously, EIGRP does not implement an update period for broadcasting routing information. Small hello packets are exchanged to ensure that a neighbor is alive, and once route information is exchanged between routers, it is considered valid until informed otherwise by a triggered update. In most cases, on interfaces above T1 speeds, hellos are exchanged every 5 seconds. If a hello is not received within three times the hello period, a neighbor is declared dead and the topology table is parsed for an alternate route. This means that a failed neighbor can be discovered in 15 seconds as opposed to the 630 seconds that can expire in IGRP networks!

This, of course, is a very simplistic view of EIGRP. If the link between C and D did fail, Router C would not have an alternate route to Router D, and a process of Query and Reply to find a new route would begin. The reason Router C does not have an alternative route is because the only other possible way to reach Router D is through Router B. If Router C received an update from Router B advertising the route to Router D, the metric would be so much higher than its own directly connected route that the advertisement would be ignored. The basic behavior of EIGRP is that if an alternate route with a higher metric than the route in use to a destination is advertised, it will not be used as an alternative because the advertising router is farther from the destination. If a router is farther from a destination, the route that it is advertising could potentially pass back through the closer router, thereby forming a loop.

If this rule is employed throughout the network as a path to a destination is established, the potential of a loop forming is greatly reduced. This is still routing by rumor, because each router is taking on faith that the downstream routers have made the correct choice. When this policy is combined with split horizon, the chances are good that they have.

Defining the Four Basic Components of EIGRP

Before we can begin an in-depth discovery of EIGRP, we need to define the four basic components that define what EIGRP is and how it functions.

Establishing Protocol-Dependent Modules

EIGRP has been designed for implementation in IP, IPX, and AppleTalk environments. EIGRP uses protocol-dependent modules that are responsible for establishing and maintaining protocol-specific routing information. IPX and AppleTalk are outside of the scope of this book.

> ## EIGRP and Legacy Networks
>
> EIGRP was designed to coexist with legacy IP, IPX, and AppleTalk networks to allow an easy path of migration to EIGRP. EIGRP will automatically redistribute with legacy protocols in the following manner:
>
> - IP EIGRP automatically redistributes with IGRP if they are configured with the same Autonomous System number.
> - IPX EIGRP automatically redistributes with IPX RIP and NLSP.
> - AppleTalk EIGRP automatically redistributes with RTMP.
>
> With these redistribution capabilities, it becomes much easier to migrate your network segment by segment to EIGRP, or to interconnect a legacy network to a newer EIGRP network.

Establishing Neighbor Discovery/Recovery

Unlike other distance-vector protocols, EIGRP routers establish and maintain *adjacencies* with directly connected neighbors through a process of Neighbor Discovery/Recovery. Periodically, small hello packets are multicast identifying themselves to their neighbors to form the adjacencies. Only after the adjacency is established will the routers exchange routing information. Moreover, since EIGRP does not broadcast periodic updates, hello packets are also used to determine if a neighbor (and, therefore, any route through that neighbor) is still active.

The Hello Protocol controls this process. Hellos are multicast every *hello interval*. The hello interval is 5 seconds by default with the exception of multipoint WAN connections of speeds slower than T1, which unicast hellos every 60 seconds. When a router receives a hello packet, the information about the neighbor is extracted and placed in a *neighbor* table. When two routers learn of each other through this process and update their neighbor tables, they are said to have established an adjacency and can now share routing information. The hello packet also includes a *hold timer* that tells an adjacent router how long to wait for additional hello packets before declaring the neighbor dead. The hold timer is typically three times the hello interval; 15 seconds and 180 seconds, respectively. These two values can be adjusted using the **ip hello-interval eigrp** and **ip hold-time eigrp** commands.

It should also be mentioned that hello packets are used to acknowledge packets that have been sent reliably. This hello packet contains no data and is unicast to the destination requiring acknowledgment.

Managing Reliable Transport Protocol

Reliable Transport Protocol (RTP) is a proprietary transport protocol used to manage EIGRP communications. EIGRP relies heavily on guaranteed, ordered delivery of information to ensure efficient and accurate delivery of data. This is necessary because information (other than hello packets) is not exchanged unless there has been a change in the topology of the network. RTP allows for sequencing, acknowledgment, and retransmission, as well as concurrent multicast and unicast delivery.

RTP and Hello use the reserved multicast address 224.0.0.10. When guaranteed delivery is required, a Cisco proprietary algorithm called *reliable multicast* is used. When a router receives a reliable multicast, a unicast acknowledgment is sent. If a neighbor fails to respond to a reliable multicast within a finite time called the *multicast flow timer*, a unicast is sent to the nonresponding neighbor. The unicast will be retransmitted every *retransmission timeout* (RTO) period until the neighbor responds or until 16 retries have elapsed. The period between unicast retransmissions is called the *smooth round-trip time* (SRTT). The RTO and SRTT are calculated using a Cisco proprietary formula beyond the scope of this book. The neighbor is declared dead after 16 unsuccessful retries.

Packet sequencing is guaranteed by including sequence and acknowledgment fields in the packet headers. Examples of RTP packet headers are shown in the next section.

Establishing DUAL Finite State Machine

Diffusing Update Algorithm (DUAL) is the heart of EIGRP. While IGRP and RIP use a simple method of broadcasting their routing table to share information, EIGRP relies on a *diffused* decision-making process that involves updates, queries, and replies. If topology changes occur in the network, updates, queries, and replies ripple outward creating a near communal decision-making process. The result is a loop-free routing environment that responds rapidly to change, on scale with more complex link-state protocols such as OSPF.

When the network has fully converged, all routes are said to be in the *passive* state. If a topology change occurs at a router such as an increased metric and for which there exists an acceptable alternate route in the topology table, the new route is placed in the routing table and an update is sent to all neighbors. This is considered a *local computation* and the route remains in a passive state.

If a topology change occurs for which there is no acceptable alternate route in the topology table, the router places the route in the *active* state and sends a query to all neighbors asking for a new route. This is considered a *diffusing computation*, and spreads away from the source of the query until an acceptable alternative is found.

There is a serious drawback to diffused computations. When a router initiates this process, it sets a *reply status flag* and a timer for 3 minutes, by default, to track outstanding queries. The diffusing computation cannot be completed until a reply has been received from all adjacent neighbors that were queried. If a neighbor fails to respond and the computation cannot be completed, the route is said to be *stuck in active* (SIA). To allow the computation to complete, the router must declare the nonresponding neighbor dead and remove it from the neighbor table. It then continues with the computation as if the now dead router responded with an infinite metric. This is not a good situation in which to be.

Imagine for a moment that the two routers in question are core routers connecting two buildings on your campus. The moment that the nonresponding neighbor was declared dead, all routes between the two buildings entered the active state and the network was segmented. The result can be a network meltdown lasting several minutes. It should be noted that, as of 12.1(5a), this mechanism has been adjusted such that the effect of SIA routes is limited to the immediate area of the failure that caused a router not to respond. This change is a significant improvement to EIGRP.

Implementing Packet Types

Now that we have explored the basic components of EIGRP, let's take a moment to discuss the packet types that establish the communications between EIGRP-speaking routers.

EIGRP implements five packet types:

- **Hellos** Used for neighbor discovery/recovery and to acknowledge reliably sent information.

- **Updates** Used to inform neighbors of topology changes, or to convey routing information to a newly discovered neighbor.

- **Queries** Used to request routing information from neighbors when a route has become active.

- **Replies** Used to respond to queries.
- **Requests** Unused. Originally intended for use in route server applications.

All of these packets share the same packet header format shown in Figure 2.6.

Figure 2.6 EIGRP Packet Header

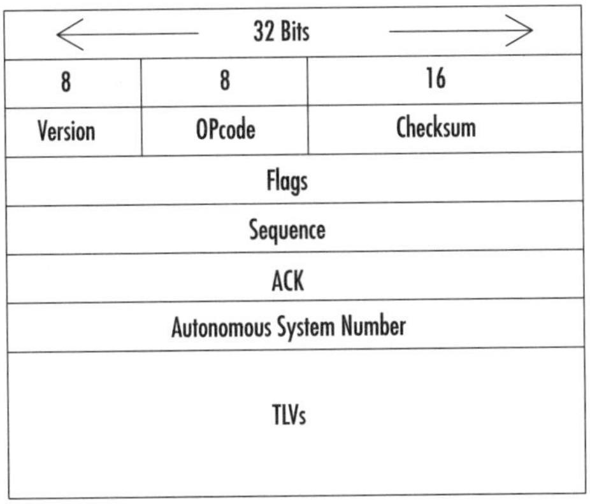

```
          <----- 32 Bits ----->
          8        8        16
       Version  OPcode    Checksum
              Flags
             Sequence
               ACK
       Autonomous System Number
               TLVs
```

The particular packet type is specified in the OPcode field following the rules in Table 2.2.

Table 2.2 EIGRP Packet Types

OPcode	Type
1	Update
3	Query
4	Reply
5	Hello
6	IPX SAP

TLV stands for Type/Length/Value and contains the information used to share routing information. Type is specified as one of the two octet values listed in Table 2.3.

Table 2.3 Type Values

Number	TLV Type
General TLV Types	
0x0001	EIGRP Parameters
0x0003	Sequence
0x0004	Software Version
0x0005	Next Multicast Sequence
IP-Specific TLV Types	
0x0102	IP Internal Routes
0x0103	IP External Routes
AppleTalk-Specific TLV Types	
0x0202	AppleTalk Internal Routes
0x0203	AppleTalk External Routes
0x0204	AppleTalk Cable Configuration
IPX-Specific TLV Types	
0x0302	IPX Internal Routes
0x0303	IPX External Routes

Figure 2.7 gives the format of a General TLV. As you can see, this is how management information is conveyed, including K values and the hold time.

Figure 2.7 The Format of a TLV

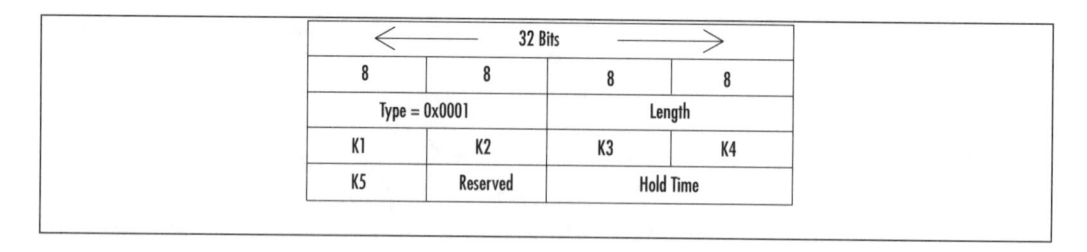

32 Bits			
8	8	8	8
Type = 0x0001		Length	
K1	K2	K3	K4
K5	Reserved	Hold Time	

Looking at the header format in Figure 2.6 and the General TLV format in Figure 2.7, it is important to note that neighbors will not form adjacencies unless the Autonomous System number and the K values match. In addition, the interface receiving the packet must be addressed in the same subnet as the source of the packet. EIGRP sources all packets from the primary ip address configured on an interface. When a router receives an EIGRP packet, it looks to see if the source of the packet is on the same network as the interface on which the packet was received. Thus, if you are using secondary addresses to allow the two routers to communicate, the receiving router must have a secondary interface that is on the same network as the sending router's primary interface. Otherwise, a neighbor relationship will not be formed. It is a common misconception that both routers' primary addresses must be on the same network.

Figure 2.8 is an example of an IP Internal Route TLV. Internal routes are routes that are learned from within the EIGRP autonomous system.

Figure 2.8 IP Internal Route TLV

32 Bits			
8	8	8	8
Type = 0x0102		Length	
Next Hop			
Delay			
Bandwidth			
MTU			Hop Count
Reliability	Load	Reserved	
Prefix Length	Destination		

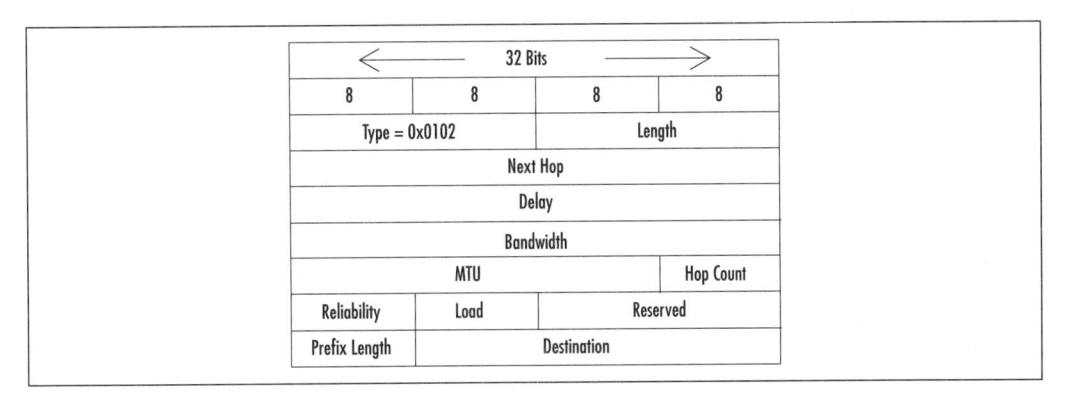

Figure 2.9 is an example of an IP External Route TLV. External routes are routes that have been redistributed into the EIGRP process from another routing process such as IGRP.

Figure 2.9 IP External Route TLV

32 Bits			
8	8	8	8
Type = 0x0103		Length	
Next Hop			
Originating Router			
Originating Autonomous System Number			
Arbitrary Tag			
External Protocol Metric			
Reserved		External Protocol ID	Flags
Delay			
Bandwidth			
MTU			Hop Count
Reliability	Load	Reserved	
Prefix Length	Destination		

Configuring EIGRP's Distributed Update Algorithm

EIGRP's Distributed Update Algorithm (DUAL) is loosely based on the Dijkstra algorithm used by *shortest path first* routing protocols such as OSPF. The intent is that a distributed decision-making process assists in the establishment of optimal routes and avoids routing loops at all times. The easiest way to understand this process is to see it in action.

Choosing a Path Selection

We begin the process by observing what happens when a new router is added to Company A's network. In Figure 2.10, we can see that Router E has been added and has a direct connection to Router D. The first step required to converge Router E with the rest of the network and to inform the existing routers of the two new subnets 172.16.2.0 and 172.16.3.0 is to create an adjacency between Routers D and E.

Figure 2.10 EIGRP Best Path Selection at Startup

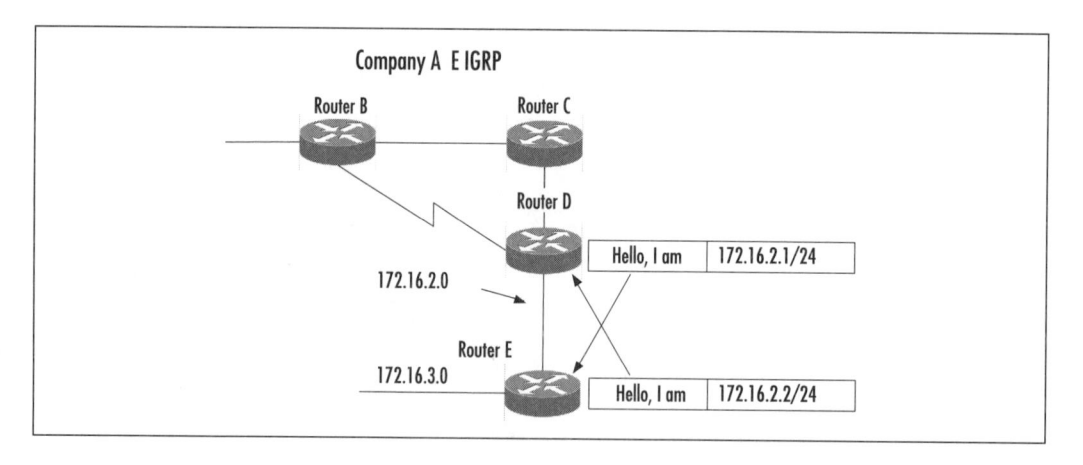

When interface 172.16.2.2 is brought up, Router E *unreliably multicasts* a hello packet to address 224.0.0.10. Router D is configured for EIGRP and is listening to this multicast address. When Router D receives this hello, it checks the neighbor table and determines that this is a new neighbor. The hello is parsed to determine if these two neighbors can form an adjacency by ensuring that the IP addresses are in the same subnet and in the same autonomous system, and that the K values listed in the packet match Router D's K values. When this has been accomplished, Router E is added to the neighbor table.

Router D also unreliably multicasts a hello of its own. Router E performs the same verification and adds Router D to the neighbor table. The routers have now formed an adjacency, and can exchange routing information. EIGRP does not confirm the adjacency between the routers. As soon as a new neighbor is added to the neighbor table, updates are sent. If the receiving router has not yet established the adjacency, the update is dropped and goes unacknowledged. The update will be retransmitted until the adjacency is formed and the update is acknowledged

Routing information is exchanged using RTP. Immediately upon discovering Router E as a new neighbor, Router D *reliably unicasts* an update containing information from its topology table. The update packet header contains an INIT flag that has been set to 1 to indicate that it is the first packet in the exchange. The header also contains a sequence number and an acknowledgment (ACK) number. Since this is the first packet in the exchange, the ACK is set to 0. Each update packet is queued until the update is acknowledged. If Router E fails to acknowledge the packet, it will be retransmitted up to 16 times. If Router E never responds, it will be removed from the neighbor table and the process will begin again as soon as Router D receives another hello from Router E.

When Router E receives a reliably sent update, it must be acknowledged. Generally, updates are acknowledged with a hello packet. However, if a router has an update packet queued for a neighbor that is awaiting an acknowledgment, it can be inserted into the queued update instead of sending a separate hello acknowledgment. In this instance, Router E sends an update packet with the INIT flag set to 1, establishes a sequence number of its own, and acknowledges the packet from Router D by setting the ACK value equal to the sequence value received from Router D. Figure 2.11 illustrates this process.

Figure 2.11 INITs and ACKs

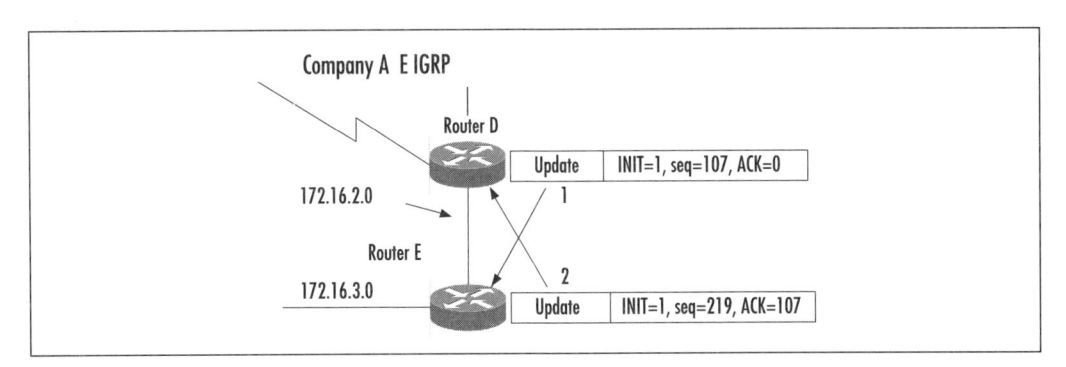

Subsequent updates are sent with the INIT flag set to 0, and the sequence and ACK numbers build. When all required information has been exchanged, the final update packets are acknowledged with a hello packet with the sequence number set to 0, and the ACK set to the last sequence value received. Figure 2.12 illustrates this process.

Figure 2.12 All Required Information Has Been Exchanged

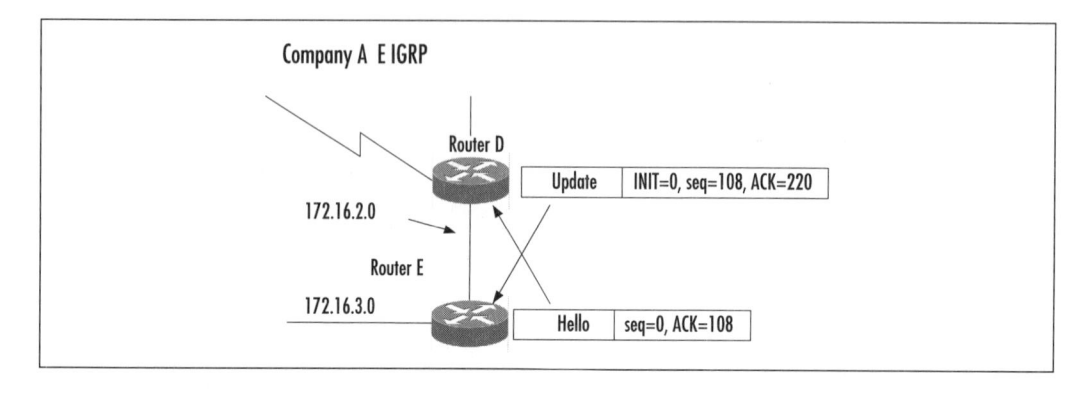

```
Company A EIGRP

                    Router D
                      [X]——— Update | INIT=0, seq=108, ACK=220
     172.16.2.0      ↑  ╲╱
                        ╱╲
           Router E  ↓ ╱  ╲
     172.16.3.0      [X]——— Hello  | seq=0, ACK=108
```

Routers D and E are now adjacent and converged. We need to look at how routing tables are built from the topology table information received from a neighbor. To do this, let's look at what happens when Router D informs Routers B and C of the new networks that were created when Router E was added to Company A.

From the perspective of Routers B and C, this is merely a topology change. They are not directly connected to Router E, so adjacencies do not need to be established. The responsibility falls to Router D to update Routers B and C of the change. To do this, Router D parses the neighbor table and creates update packets that are addressed to all neighbors except Router E. Each of these packets is queued to the interface through which each neighbor resides. If there is more than one neighbor through an interface, a packet is queued for each neighbor. The packets will remain in the queue and retransmitted every RTO period until the packet is acknowledged. In Figure 2.13, Router D has queued and *reliably unicast* update packets to Routers B and C. The amount of information exchanged is minimal, and only a single update is needed. Routers B and C reply with a hello acknowledging the sequence number, and the queued packets are removed.

Routers B and C add this information to their topology tables and route tables. For the time being, this route is considered the best because they have not learned of any alternatives.

Figure 2.13 Updates Are Sent via Reliable Unicast

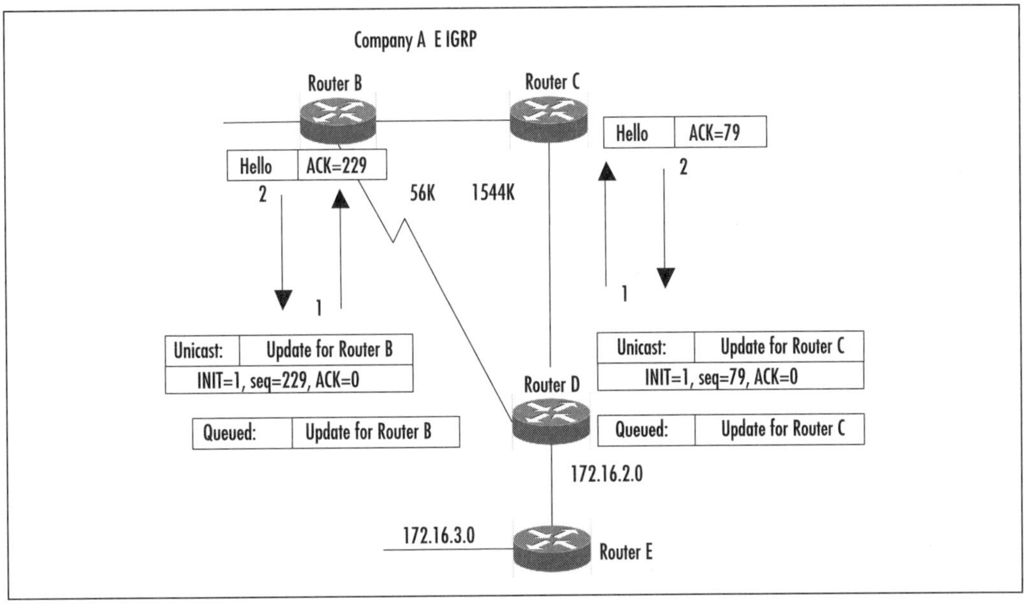
Company A E IGRP
Router B
Router C
Hello
ACK=79
Hello
ACK=229
2
2
56K
1544K
1
1
Unicast:
Update for Router B
INIT=1, seq=229, ACK=0
Unicast:
Update for Router C
INIT=1, seq=79, ACK=0
Router D
Queued:
Update for Router B
Queued:
Update for Router C
172.16.2.0
172.16.3.0
Router E

On the surface, this appears to be the same as the exchange between Routers D and E; in fact, it is. However, where DUAL begins to take effect is in the fact that Routers B and C will update each other regarding the new topology. Following the rule of forwarding new topology information to all neighbors except the neighbor from which the information was learned (split horizon), Router C forwards an update to Router B, and vice versa.

When Router C receives the update from Router B, it is disregarded. As stated previously, any advertisements of routes with a higher metric than what is currently being used is considered a loop potential.

NOTE

While I use the term *disregarded*, the information is not actually thrown away. It is placed in the topology table but is never considered a viable alternative to the current route. To view this information in the topology table, use the command **show ip eigrp topology all-links**.

Router B receives the update from Router C and is faced with a decision. A determination needs to be made regarding what information should be stored in the topology and routing tables. To see how Router B determines this, we need to revisit the process of metric calculation, starting from the source of the original update, Router E, and moving upstream to Router B.

As you recall from our earlier discussion, a route metric is passed to neighbor routers in the update packet. The metric received from a neighbor is called a *vector* metric (commonly known as Reported Distance (RD)) and is the metric that the originating router is using as the path cost from itself to the destination and is advertised to upstream routers. The vector metric does not contain any information regarding the link between the two directly connected neighbors. The vector metric element values are combined with the local interface metric values to generate a composite metric before a decision is made as to what information is placed in the topology and routing tables. The vector metric is not advertised to neighbors as an integer; it is advertised as a series of six values made up of bandwidth, delay, reliability, load, MTU, and hop count. Figure 2.14 shows the update packet that was sent from Router E to Router D.

Figure 2.14 An EIGRP Update Packet

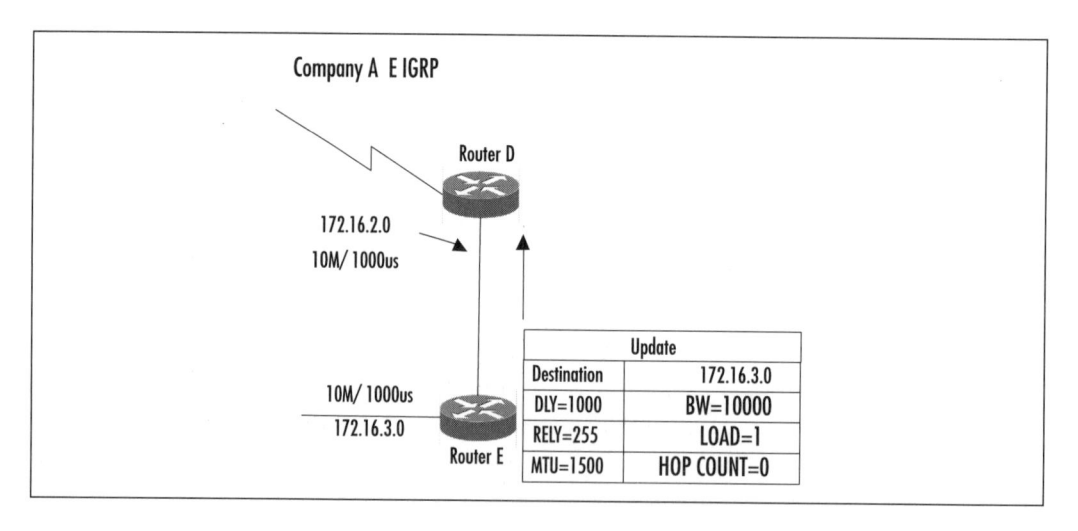

Note that BW is the minimum bandwidth along the path to the destination, and DLY is the aggregate delay along the path. Here we are dealing with a directly connected subnet, so these values are taken from the interface itself. If the vector metric were advertised as an integer, it would be impossible to know the minimum bandwidth to the destination. You will see this graphically demonstrated when we move upstream to router B.

When Router D receives the update, it plugs these values into the metric formula:

Vector Metric=[K1*10^7/10000+K3*1000/10]*256

Vector Metric=1000+100=1100*256=**281600**

> **NOTE**
>
> The complete metric formula is:
>
> Metric=[K1*10^7/BW+K2*(10^7/BW)/(256-LOAD)+K3*(DLY/10)]*[K5/(RELY+K4)]
>
> Where K1=K3=1, and K2=K4=K5=0, and that sections of the formula involving K2, K4, and K5 can be dropped.

This is the advertised cost from Router E. Router D must now combine this metric with its local metric values to calculate the composite metric. The composite metric is taken from the same elements that are used in the vector metric, with their values garnered from the downstream interface at Router D. To combine the values, Router D simply takes the minimum of either the local interface bandwidth or the bandwidth that was advertised by Router E. In this case, they are the same; therefore, BW remains 10000. Next, it adds the value of delay on the local interface to the value that was advertised by Router E. The result is:

DLY=1000 + 1000=2000

Plugging these values into our formula results in:

Metric= K1*10^7/10000+K3*2000/10=1000+200=1200*256=**307200**

This is the final metric that is placed in the topology table used to describe the route. All routing decisions are based on this calculation. If Router D were to receive an update describing this same route from another source, it would perform this same calculation for that update and compare the two results. The route with the lowest metric value would be considered the optimal route and would be placed in the routing table.

With that said, let's take a moment to learn some terminology that is at the heart of DUAL. When a route is selected as the optimum route based on having the lowest calculated metric, the downstream neighbor that advertised the path is referred to as the *successor*. The metric of the path through the successor is known as the *feasible distance (FD)* to the destination. If the router learns of an alternate path to the destination that is not superior to the successor, the metric advertised by the downstream neighbor for the new route is checked for its *feasibility condition (FC)*. FC is a condition whereby a reported distance is lower than the feasible distance (RD > FD) to the destination. In other words, the router advertising the new path has a lower cost to the destination than you do, implying that it is closer. If this condition is met, the downstream router advertising the new route is called a *feasible successor,* and the route is placed in the topology table and can be upgraded to successor if the current successor fails.

To fully understand this let's move back upstream to Router B which has received an update from both Router D and Router C. In Figure 2.15, you can observe both advertised vector metrics that Router B has received.

Figure 2.15 The Feasibility Process

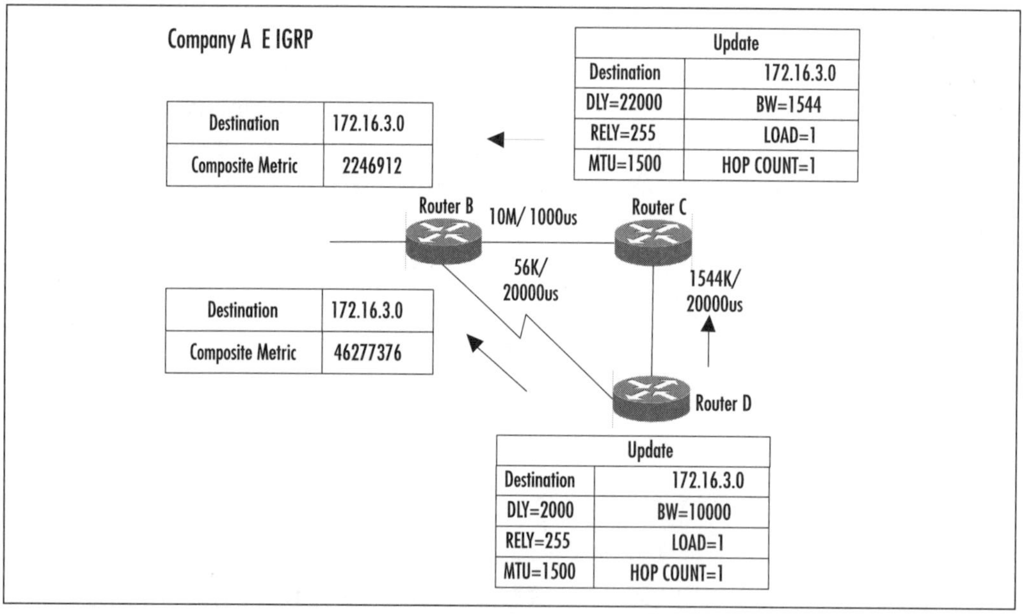

Company A E IGRP			Update	
			Destination	172.16.3.0
			DLY=22000	BW=1544
Destination	172.16.3.0		RELY=255	LOAD=1
Composite Metric	2246912		MTU=1500	HOP COUNT=1

Router B 10M/1000us Router C
56K/20000us
1544K/20000us

Destination	172.16.3.0
Composite Metric	46277376

Router D

Update	
Destination	172.16.3.0
DLY=2000	BW=10000
RELY=255	LOAD=1
MTU=1500	HOP COUNT=1

Looking at the bandwidth values that are advertised, it becomes clear why the vector metric cannot be passed as an integer. If it were, Router B would have no way of knowing what the minimum bandwidth is along the path from itself to Router C to Router D to Router E.

Let's look at how Router B calculated the composite metric.

First, the path through Router D:

Advertised Metric= $K1*10^7/10000+K3*2000/10=1000+200=1200*256=307200$

The minimum bandwidth along the path is 56K, and the aggregate delay is 22000us. Plugging these numbers into our formula, we get:

Composite Metric=

K1*10^7/56+K3*22000/10=178571+2200=180771*256=46277376

Second, the path through Router C:

Advertised Metric=

K1*10^7/1544+K3*22000/10=6477+2200=8677*256=2221312

The minimum bandwidth is 1544K, and the aggregate delay is 23000us. The result is:

Composite Metric=

K1*10^7/1544+K3*23000/10=6477+2300=8777*256=2246912

As you can see, the optimum route is the path through Router C. This path is the *successor* and is placed in the topology table with the complete metric (2246912) tagged as the *feasible distance*. Router B now checks the path through Router D for its *feasible condition*. To meet the feasible condition, the metric advertised by Router D must be lower than the feasible distance; in this case, the advertised distance is 307200, and the feasible distance is 2246912. The feasibility condition is met and the path through Router D is placed in the topology table as a *feasible successor* that can become the successor if the path through Router C fails.

The following output can been seen in the topology table on Router B dealing with 172.16.3.0.

```
Router B# show ip eigrp topology
IP-EIGRP Topology Table for process 100

Codes: P - Passive, A - Active, U - Update, Q - Query, R - Reply,
       r - Reply status

P 172.16.3.0 255.255.255.0, 1 successors, FD is 2246912
        via Router C (2246912/2221312), Ethernet0
        via Router D (46277376/307200), Serial1
```

> **NOTE**
>
> In the previous output, on the last two lines the host names of the downstream routers C and D are substituted for their IP addresses. We have not discussed the addressing scheme of the network; therefore, for the sake of clarity, the host names were substituted.

The "P" to the left of 172.16.3.0 indicates that a successor has been found and placed in the routing table, and that there are no calculations ongoing looking for a better route. The next line describes the successor route. The next-hop (see note) neighbor is listed along with the composite metric and then the vector metric advertised by Router C. Finally, the interface through which the neighbor is accessible is listed.

Handling Failure and Recovery

Now that we have an understanding of how adjacencies are formed and how DUAL builds neighbor, topology, and routing tables, let's look at how DUAL handles a failure. Let's break the connection between Routers C and D and focus on reestablishing a route from all routers to 172.16.3.0.

The most interesting place to start is at Router C. Router C forwarded its known route to 172.16.3.0 upstream to Router B. Following the split horizon rule, this means that Router B cannot send information regarding 172.16.3.0 back to Router C. Therefore, Router C would not have an alternate route to 172.16.3.0. Even if Router B violated split horizon or had simply been disabled (don't do that), Router C would still not have an alternate route. If you look back at our metric calculations in Figure 2.15, Router C is advertising a vector metric of 2221312. The advertised vector metric is always the feasible distance that a router is using. If Router B advertised a route to 172.16.3.0 for the path through Router D, the advertised metric would be 46277376. This would not meet the feasibility condition on Router C, and the route would not become a feasible successor.

Router C is now required to find an alternate route. It does this by placing the original route to 172.16.3.0 in an active state and reliably multicasting a query to all neighbors in the neighbor table (in this case, only Router B). This multicast query is an IP internal TLV that has the delay metric set to infinity (0xFFFFFFFF or 4294967295).

Figure 2.16 displays the current state of the network.

Figure 2.16 The Active Query Process

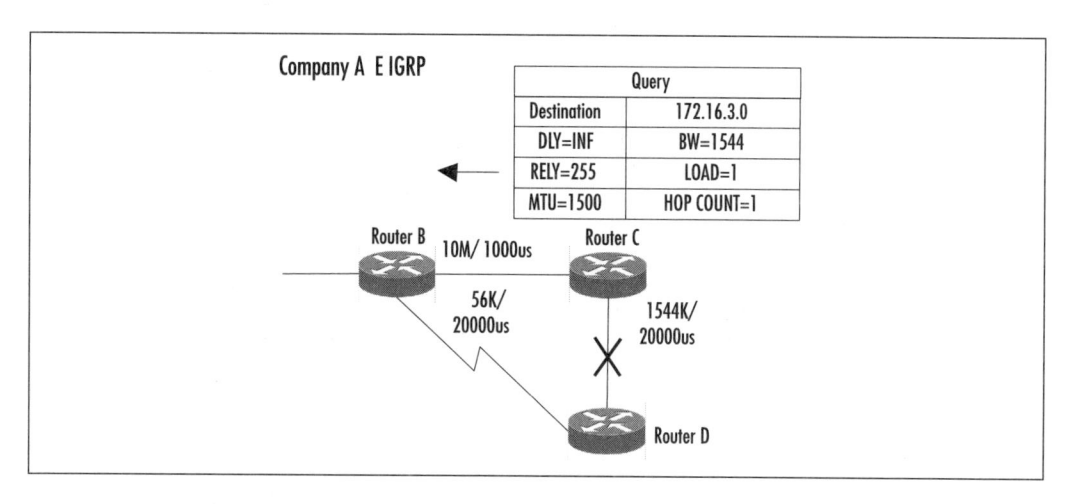

Query	
Destination	172.16.3.0
DLY=INF	BW=1544
RELY=255	LOAD=1
MTU=1500	HOP COUNT=1

The following output can be seen in Router C's topology table showing that the route to 172.16.3.0 is in an active state.

```
Router C# show ip eigrp topology
IP-EIGRP Topology Table for process 100

Codes: P - Passive, A - Active, U - Update, Q - Query, R - Reply,
       r - Reply status

A 172.16.3.0 255.255.255.0, 0 successors, FD is 2221312
        via Router D (2221312/307200), Serial0
```

When Router B receives the update from Router C, it parses the information contained in the packet and determines that the update affects the successor route to 172.16.3.0. This causes Router B to perform a local computation to determine if it has a feasible successor in the topology table. As we just discussed, Router B has a feasible successor to 172.16.3.0 through Router D. This allows the router to immediately promote Router D to successor and update the route in the routing table. The following shows the new topology table.

```
Router# show ip eigrp topology
```

```
IP-EIGRP Topology Table for process 100

Codes: P - Passive, A - Active, U - Update, Q - Query, R - Reply,
       r - Reply status

P 172.16.3.0 255.255.255.0, 0 successors, FD is 46277376
        via Router D (46277376/307200), Serial1
```

Router B now replies to the query advertising the distance to 172.16.3.0 through Router D as shown in Figure 2.17.

Figure 2.17 A Query Reply

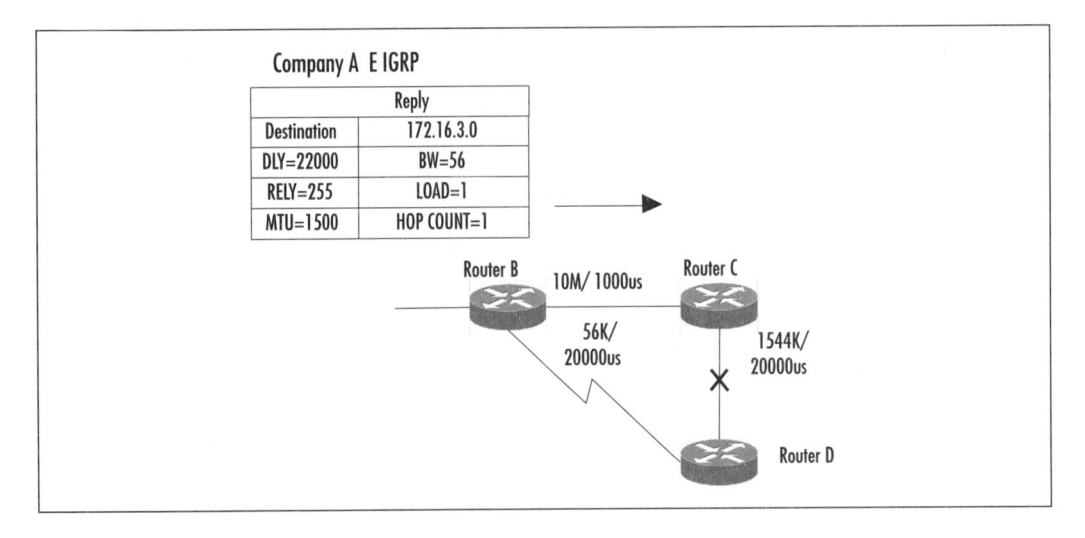

Company A EIGRP	
	Reply
Destination	172.16.3.0
DLY=22000	BW=56
RELY=255	LOAD=1
MTU=1500	HOP COUNT=1

Router B —— 10M/1000us —— Router C
Router B —— 56K/20000us —— Router D
Router C —X— 1544K/20000us —— Router D

When Router C receives the reply, it stores the information about the new route in the topology table. Router B now becomes the new successor, and the new feasible distance to 172.16.3.0 becomes:

Metric= $K1*10^7/56 + K3*23000/10 = 178571 + 2300 = 180871*256 = 46302976$

Router B must also send an update to all upstream neighbors (in this case, Router A) informing them of the metric increase. This step is vital to the efficiency of EIGRP. If an upstream neighbor had a feasible successor with a lower metric than the new metric, it would promote the feasible successor to successor. This ensures that optimum routes are always used. Since Router A is already using Router B as the successor and there are no feasible successors, it is not necessary for Router A to perform a feasibility check. It simply increases the metric to 172.16.3.0 and the route remains passive.

As you can see, the processes that EIGRP employs to determine optimal routes and to recover from failure are much more complex than IGRP. The result is a more efficient network that responds to failure very rapidly. In the next section, we begin the process of developing a comprehensive EIGRP network by starting with basic EIGRP configurations and moving into more advanced topics such as redistribution, route summarization, and bandwidth management.

Configuring Basic EIGRP

Configuring EIGRP on small to medium-sized networks can be simple and straightforward. This often leads to the incorrect conclusion that EIGRP is a simple protocol—as you have seen, this is not true. EIGRP processes are complex and must be kept in mind as your network is designed and ultimately implemented. In the next two sections, we discuss and design a increasingly complex network and see what design principals we should follow to allow an EIGRP network to adhere successfully to some basic tenants of routing:

- No routing protocol can overcome a poorly designed IP addressing scheme.
- Redundancy is key to your peace of mind (and peaceful nights and weekends).
- Know that your network will grow.

EIGRP was designed with several key features to allow for these and several other principles to greatly improve network reliability and efficiency. While a comprehensive design guide full of case studies would occupy the complete volume of this text, we will attempt to demonstrate the most common implementations that are encountered in today's networks. The end result will hopefully allow you to use these examples in your successful design and implementation.

Enabling EIGRP is as straightforward as IGRP and RIP. The process is started with the **router** command, and participating networks are added with the **network** command. Figure 2.18 shows a three-router network that will function under the same EIGRP process.

This simple network can be found as a piece of many networks. Router A could be functioning as a collapsed backbone or as a distribution node. Routers B and C may be access nodes servicing end-user segments. In our circumstances, let's assume that this is an accounting department, the server farm contains our mainframes, and Routers B and C provide access to end users. Enabling EIGRP here is very simple. We will start with Router A.

```
router eigrp 100
  network 172.16.0.0
```

Figure 2.18 A Working Example of an EIGRP Network

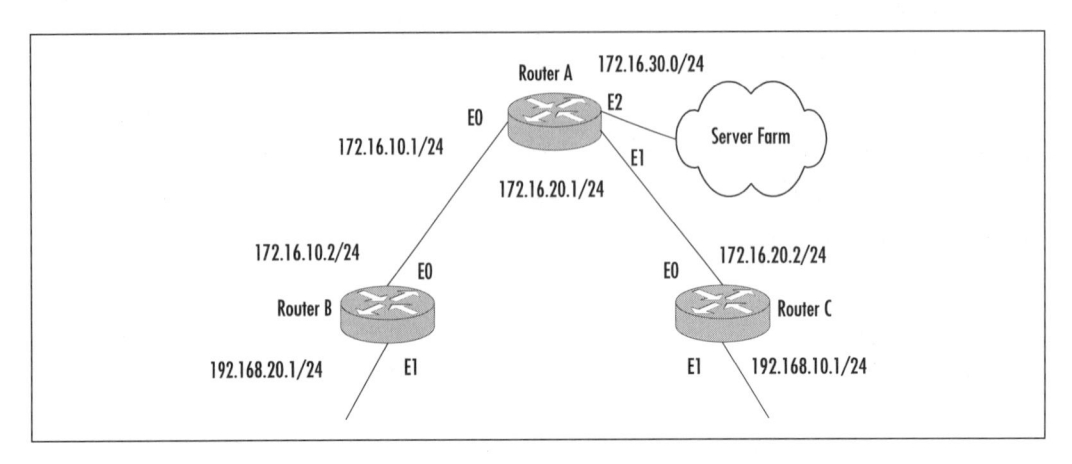

[Figure 2.18: Network diagram showing Router A (E0: 172.16.10.1/24, E1: 172.16.20.1/24, E2 to Server Farm 172.16.30.0/24), Router B (E0: 172.16.10.2/24, E1: 192.168.20.1/24), and Router C (E0: 172.16.20.2/24, E1: 192.168.10.1/24)]

Enabling EIGRP begins with the command **router eigrp** *process-id*. The process id is any number between 1 and 65535. This number can be selected at random, but it must be the same for all routers that are to participate in this EIGRP process. The **network** command is used to specify which networks will participate in the routing process, and specifies the major network address. It is typically believed that you are specifying the interfaces that will participate in the routing process. While it is absolutely true that only interfaces belonging to the major networks specified would participate, it is possible and sometimes necessary to specify a network that is not configured on the router at all. This implies that you are enabling the network, not the interface. This is a function of address summarization and is demonstrated in *Advanced Configuration*. In this scenario, interfaces E0, E1, and E2 will all participate.

Routers B and C require an additional network statement to enable their subnets in the private address space of network 192.168.0.0.

Router B

```
router eigrp 100
  network 172.16.0.0
  network 192.168.20.0
  no auto-summary
```

Router C

```
router eigrp 100
    network 172.16.0.0
    network 192.168.10.0
    no auto-summary
```

The *no auto-summary* command is explained later in this chapter. Our network is now up and running. After a few seconds of convergence, we can look at the route table for Router A and see that it has routes for all networks.

```
Router A#show ip route
Codes:
C - connected, S - static, I - IGRP, R - RIP, M - mobile, B - BGP
D - EIGRP, EX - EIGRP external, O - OSPF, IA - OSPF inter area
N1 - OSPF NSSA external type 1, N2 - OSPF NSSA external type 2
E1 - OSPF external type 1, E2 - OSPF external type 2, E - EGP
i - IS-IS, L1 - ISIS level-1, L2 - ISIS level-2,
* - candidate default, U - per-user static route, o - ODR

Gateway of last resort is not set

D    192.168.20.0/24 [90/307200] via 172.16.10.2, 00:01:27, Ethernet0
D    192.168.10.0/24 [90/307200] via 172.16.20.2, 00:01:27, Ethernet1
     172.16.0.0/24 is subnetted, 3 subnets
C       172.16.10.0 is directly connected, Ethernet0
C       172.16.20.0 is directly connected, Ethernet1
C       172.16.30.0 is directly connected, Ethernet2
```

At first glance, all appears well. Router A has established paths to all networks with their associated costs. However, to get a feel for EIGRP and to find any caveats in your design, you must examine the topology table.

```
Router A# show ip eigrp topology
IP-EIGRP Topology Table for process 100

Codes: P - Passive, A - Active, U - Update, Q - Query, R - Reply,
       r - Reply status
```

```
P 172.16.10.0 255.255.255.0, 1 successors, FD is 281600
        via Connected, Ethernet0
P 192.168.20.0/24 255.255.255.0, 1 successors, FD is 307200
        via 172.16.10.2(307200/281600), Ethernet0
P 172.16.20.0 255.255.255.0, 1 successors, FD is 281600
        via Connected, Ethernet1
P 172.16.30.0 255.255.255.0, 1 successors, FD is 281600
        via Connected, Ethernet2
P 192.168.10.0/24 255.255.255.0, 1 successors, FD is 307200
        via 172.16.20.2(307200/281600), Ethernet1
```

The first thing that should jump out at you is the lack of feasible successors to networks 192.168.10.0 and 192.168.20.0. A link failure between Routers A and B or Routers A and C will segment users from the server farm. This was obvious when looking at the network diagram. The easiest solution to this problem is to add a new segment between Routers B and C. While it is not always as easy as pulling a little Cat 5 to create redundancy as it is in our case, it should be a goal of a strong network design to eliminate single-link failures that can segment the network. Figure 2.19 illustrates the new segment.

Figure 2.19 Physical Redundancy Eliminated Single Points of Failure

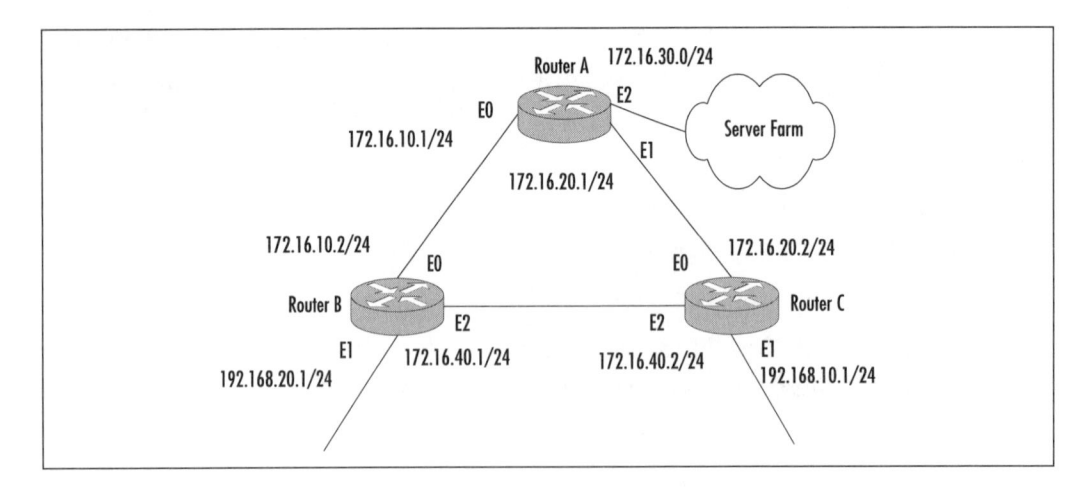

After adding this segment, the route table for Router A now changes to reflect the new segment. Notice that two routes for destination 172.16.40.0 exist in the route table. EIGRP, as with IGRP and RIP, will automatically load balance over equal-cost paths.

```
Router A#show ip route
Codes:
C - connected, S - static, I - IGRP, R - RIP, M - mobile, B - BGP
D - EIGRP, EX - EIGRP external, O - OSPF, IA - OSPF inter area
N1 - OSPF NSSA external type 1, N2 - OSPF NSSA external type 2
E1 - OSPF external type 1, E2 - OSPF external type 2, E - EGP
i - IS-IS, L1 - ISIS level-1, L2 - ISIS level-2,
* - candidate default
U - per-user static route, o - ODR

Gateway of last resort is not set

D     192.168.20.0/24 [90/307200] via 172.16.10.2, 00:02:17,
      Ethernet0
D     192.168.10.0/24 [90/307200] via 172.16.20.2, 00:02:17,
      Ethernet1
      172.16.0.0/24 is subnetted, 4 subnets
D        172.16.40.0/24 [90/307200] via 172.16.10.2, 00:00:21,
         Ethernet0
                        [90/307200] via 172.16.20.2, 00:00:21, Ethernet1
C        172.16.10.0 is directly connected, Ethernet0
C        172.16.20.0 is directly connected, Ethernet1
C        172.16.30.0 is directly connected, Ethernet2
```

Now lets take a look at the new topology table:

```
Router A# show ip eigrp topology
IP-EIGRP Topology Table for process 100

Codes: P - Passive, A - Active, U - Update, Q - Query, R - Reply,
       r - Reply status

P 172.16.10.0 255.255.255.0, 1 successors, FD is 281600
         via Connected, Ethernet0
P 172.16.40.0/24 255.255.255.0, 2 successors, FD is 307200
         via 172.16.10.2(307200/281600), Ethernet0
```

```
              via 172.16.20.2(307200/281600), Ethernet1
P 192.168.20.0/24 255.255.255.0, 2 successors, FD is 307200
              via 172.16.10.2(307200/281600), Ethernet0
              via 172.16.20.2(332800/307200), Ethernet1
P 172.16.20.0 255.255.255.0, 1 successors, FD is 281600
              via Connected, Ethernet1
P 172.16.30.0 255.255.255.0, 1 successors, FD is 281600
              via Connected, Ethernet2
P 192.168.10.0/24 255.255.255.0, 2 successors, FD is 307200
              via 172.16.20.2(307200/281600), Ethernet1
              via 172.16.10.2(332800/307200), Ethernet0
```

As you can see, we now have redundancy to our end-user segments. This leaves us with one more serious flaw in our design that must be addressed before moving on to more advanced topics. While we have removed single-link failure to our end users, we have left the server farm hanging out there off Router A. Regardless of the amount of redundancy we create between end users and the core, if the destination of the vast majority of network activity remains vulnerable, we have disarmed our network. Since this is an accounting department, count on Ethernet 2 on Router A failing the next time payroll is processed.

Creating redundancy to the server farm is not as easy as it might look. Following Cisco's design recommendation of implementing tiered, hierarchical networks, adding a link between Router C and the server farm would not be fundamentally sound. The theory is something like: Every router has a place, and every router in its place. Cisco's recommendation is to create three layers of routing responsibility: Core, Distribution, and Access. The Access layer is intended to provide end users with connectivity to the network and shared access to often-used network devices such as printers and storage servers. The Distribution layer is intended to perform such responsibilities as address summarization and policy routing, and to provide redundant access to the core. The Core layer should focus simply on high-speed data transport. Policy decisions should not be made here. Wasting processing cycles on ACLs, for example, is detrimental to the efficiency of core routers and should be left to the Distribution and Access layers.

Our network is currently a little less complex and does not require three tiers at this time. However, connecting Router C to the server farm would essentially place it in both the Access and Distribution layers, and the likelihood of it being overrun is high. Our network needs another distribution router. In Figure 2.20, we have added that router, Router D. It will now share the responsibility of feeding traffic into and out of the server farm with Router A.

Figure 2.20 Sharing the Load of Getting Traffic to the Server Farm

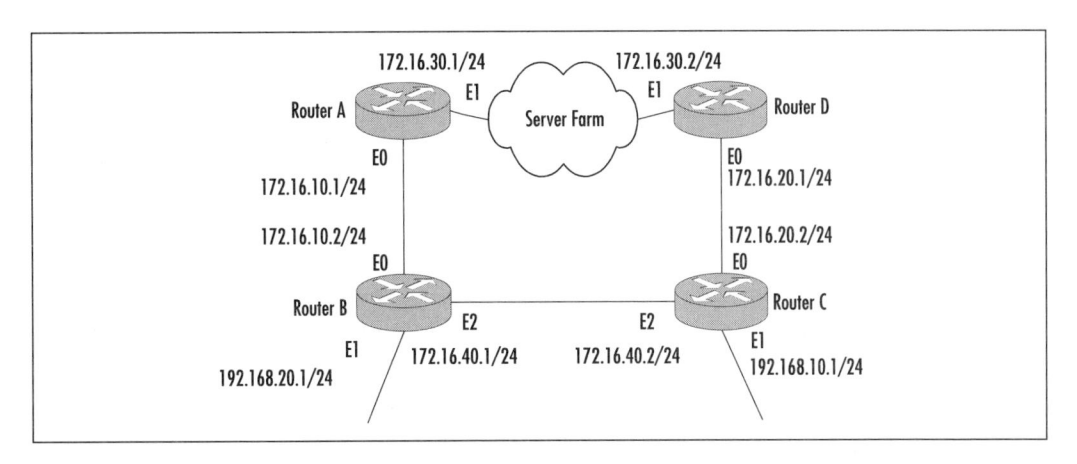

Adding this router is a fairly simple process. The EIGRP configurations on Router A, B, and C do not change. Although Router A lost interface Ethernet 2, it is still only running the process for network 172.16.0.0. This means that we can simply add Router D to the network with the following configuration:

```
router eigrp 100
  network 172.16.0.0
```

After our network has converged, we can see what Router D's route table looks like.

```
Router D#show ip route
Codes:
C - connected, S - static, I - IGRP, R - RIP, M - mobile, B - BGP
D - EIGRP, EX - EIGRP external, O - OSPF, IA - OSPF inter area
N1 - OSPF NSSA external type 1, N2 - OSPF NSSA external type 2
E1 - OSPF external type 1, E2 - OSPF external type 2, E - EGP
i - IS-IS, L1 - ISIS level-1, L2 - ISIS level-2, * - candidate default
U - per-user static route, o - ODR

Gateway of last resort is not set

D   192.168.20.0/24 [90/332800] via 172.16.30.1, 00:00:39,
```

```
                Ethernet1
                         [90/332800] via 172.16.20.2, 00:00:39, Ethernet0
D       192.168.10.0/24 [90/307200] via 172.16.20.2, 00:00:39,
        Ethernet0
        172.16.0.0/24 is subnetted, 4 subnets
D       172.16.40.0/24 [90/307200] via 172.16.20.2, 00:00:41,
        Ethernet0
D       172.16.10.0/24 [90/307200] via 172.16.30.1, 00:00:41,
        Ethernet1
C       172.16.20.0 is directly connected, Ethernet0
C       172.16.30.0 is directly connected, Ethernet1
```

As you can see, Router D has fully converged and has routes to all networks. It is load balancing between Routers A and C to access 192.168.20.0. While this sounds like a good thing, it actually is not. We do not want user traffic that is not destined for the server farm passing through that segment. We can remedy this situation using one of several methods.

One potential solution is to add a single configuration command, **passive-interface** *interface*, to Routers A and D. Their EIGRP configurations become:

Router A

```
router eigrp 100
  network 172.16.0.0
  passive-interface ethernet1
```

Router D

```
router eigrp 100
  network 172.16.0.0
  passive-interface ethernet1
```

This command blocks EIGRP traffic on the specified interfaces. The result is that Router D will not learn routes from Router A, and vice versa. If you were to look at Router D's route table, you would see that the redundant route is gone, and find that the route to 172.16.10.0 now has a vector of Router C.

There is a major drawback to this configuration: we have lost a layer of redundancy. If the link between Routers D and C were to fail, and Router D received traffic, it would simply drop the traffic because it would no longer know of any routes—Router C was its only neighbor. One potential solution to this problem is to add a *default route* pointing to Router A. Default routes are special static routes labeled as the "Gateway of last resort" in the routing table. They are added using the command **ip route 0.0.0.0 0.0.0.0 <*next hop router address*>**. This command tells the router that if it can find no other route to any destination in its routing table to forward the traffic to the router specified. In our case, this would be Router A.

The highs and lows of this solution can be debated. I follow a simple policy: If you are forced to use a static route within your meshed dynamic routing environment, you have done something wrong. This is not to say that static routes do not have their place—they do. They can be very useful in a hub-and-spoke network over slow links. However, that is not our situation—we need to dig a little deeper.

Recall from our earlier discussion that one of the greatest advantages of EIGRP is its efficient use of bandwidth. Our concern here is not that EIGRP traffic will clog our server farm segment, but that user traffic will. I believe that the better policy here would be to convince EIGRP not to use the segment unless absolutely necessary. This way, we leave the dynamic process in place and maintain our level of redundancy.

A method for resolving this entire situation that meets all of our needs without seriously affecting our network down the line is to adjust either the bandwidth or delay values on the link between Routers A and D to increase the metric. Once the paths are no longer equal, load balancing will not automatically occur, and the higher-cost route between the two routers will only be used if the other route fails. Adjusting the bandwidth can introduce serious problems, since EIGRP uses the bandwidth statement to determine how much bandwidth it can consume for EIGRP traffic (50 percent, by default). Adjusting the bandwidth statement up or down can also cause issues with Quality of Service (QoS) mechanisms, network management, and other problems. As such, it is preferable to adjust delay.

We will adjust the delay value on both Routers A and D with the following commands:

Router A

```
interface Ethernet1
    delay 1100
```

Router D

```
interface Ethernet1
    delay 1100
```

Looking at the topology table on Router D, we can observe the effect of this change.

```
Router D# show ip eigrp topology
IP-EIGRP Topology Table for process 100

Codes: P - Passive, A - Active, U - Update, Q - Query, R - Reply,
       r - Reply status

P 172.16.10.0 255.255.255.0, 2 successors, FD is 309760
        via 172.16.30.1(309760/281600), Ethernet1
        via 172.16.20.2(332800/307200), Ethernet0
P 172.16.40.0/24 255.255.255.0, 2 successors, FD is 307200
        via 172.16.20.2(307200/281600), Ethernet0
        via 172.16.30.1(335360/307200), Ethernet1
P 192.168.20.0/24 255.255.255.0, 2 successors, FD is 332800
        via 172.16.20.2(332800/281600), Ethernet0
        via 172.16.30.1(335360/307200), Ethernet1
P 172.16.20.0 255.255.255.0, 1 successors, FD is 281600
        via Connected, Ethernet0
P 172.16.30.0 255.255.255.0, 1 successors, FD is 281600
        via Connected, Ethernet1
P 192.168.10.0/24 255.255.255.0, 1 successors, FD is 307200
        via 172.16.20.2(307200/281600), Ethernet0
```

As you can see, the level of redundancy that we wanted to achieve has been successfully implemented, and the routes away from the server farm have been selected as the successors due to the adjustment that we made to our delay metric.

Our basic network is now up and running with a high degree of redundancy, and traffic is routed efficiently. Before we move on to more advanced configurations, let's take a moment to look at some more detailed show commands that can be useful in verifying your configuration and troubleshooting any problems that may arise.

Verifying Configuration with Show Commands

Let's start by looking at Router D's neighbor table—a very good starting point for all EIGRP verification. Adjacencies must be formed before routers will share information.

```
Router D#show ip eigrp neighbor
IP-EIGRP neighbors for process 100
H   Address       Interface    Hold Uptime    SRTT    RTO    Q    Seq
                               (sec)          (ms)                Cnt  Num
1   172.16.30.1   Ethernet1    13   00:01:23  12      30     0    620
0   172.16.20.2   Ethernet0     8   00:01:19  17      20     0    645
```

Both Routers A and C appear in the routing table, indicating that Router D has accepted them as neighbors and will attempt to share routing information.

```
Router D#show ip eigrp neighbor detail
IP-EIGRP neighbors for process 100
H   Address       Interface    Hold Uptime    SRTT    RTO    Q    Seq
                               (sec)          (ms)                Cnt  Num
1   172.16.30.1   Ethernet1    13   00:01:23  12      30     0    620
    Version 12.0, Retrans:    0, Retries:   0
0   172.16.20.2   Ethernet0     8   00:01:19  17      20     0    645
    Version 12.0, Retrans:    0, Retries:   0
```

This output displays the number of retransmissions and retries that have been attempted when communicating with a neighbor. Any outstanding unacknowledged queries or updates would be displayed beneath the neighbor that has yet to respond. One of the most important fields in both output examples is the Q Cnt field. If a neighbor does not acknowledge a reliably sent packet, the packet will remain in the queue and the number of retransmissions will rise. This output will be come very useful when troubleshooting SIA routes.

Another useful command for viewing queue information for nonresponding or slow to respond neighbors is **show ip eigrp interfaces**.

```
Router D#show ip eigrp interfaces
IP EIGRP interfaces for process 100
                  Xmit Queue    Mean  Pacing Time   Multicast   Pending
Interface  Peers  Un/Reliable   SRTT  Un/Reliable   Flow Timer  Routes
Et1        1      0/0           10    11/434        0           0
Et0        1      0/0           10    0/10          0           0
```

The Xmit Queue Un/Reliable is a running total of packets that are in the transmit queue. The number of routes that are affected by the queries or updates that are in the queue is displayed as Pending Routes.

Use the **show ip eigrp traffic** command to view the number of packets and their types that have been sent and received on an EIGRP neighbor.

```
Router# show ip eigrp traffic
IP-EIGRP Traffic Statistics for process 100
  Hellos sent/received: 508/619
  Updates sent/received: 21/18
  Queries sent/received: 6/0
  Replies sent/received: 0/6
  Acks sent/received: 17/13
```

The number of queries that have been sent or received should correlate to the number of replies sent or received. If these numbers do not match, you either have a currently outstanding query indicating that a diffused computation is in progress, or a neighbor failed to respond to a query sometime in the past. You can use the **show eigrp topology** command to determine if a route is currently active. The route will be coded with an A indicating that the route is active.

One final command we would like to look at is a more detailed view of a specific network in the topology table.

```
Router D#show ip eigrp topology 192.168.10.0 255.255.255.0
IP-EIGRP topology entry for 192.168.10.0/24
  State is Passive, Query origin flag is 1, 1 Successor(s), FD is 307200
  Routing Descriptor Blocks:
  172.16.20.2 (Ethernet0), from 172.16.20.2, Send flag is 0x0
      Composite metric is (307200/281600), Route is Internal
      Vector metric:
        Minimum bandwidth is 10000 Kbit
        Total delay is 2000 microseconds
        Reliability is 255/255
        Load is 1/255
        Minimum MTU is 1500
        Hop count is 2
```

As you can see, this output can be very useful in gleaning detailed information about a particular network. The composite metric is broken down into the individual elements that can be useful in troubleshooting unexpected routes in the routing table.

Configuring Advanced EIGRP

While our small network has several strong points such as high levels of redundancy, it has begun to develop several problems. First, our addressing scheme is not very hierarchical and wastes high numbers of host addresses on the point-to-point links.

Second, without a dedicated Distribution layer, our Access and Core layer routers are going to be forced to share the duties that should be restricted to the Distribution layer. This will become more evident when we connect our accounting network to the rest of the corporate office and to remote sites.

Resolving the addressing issues is our most pressing need. We know that the network will grow rapidly, and if we allow the problem to continue it will quickly become unmanageable. When core routers are aware of all network segments, any flapping routes down at the Access layer will cause diffused computations that will spread to the core. We do not want our core routers wasting processing cycles attempting to recalculate routes that they really did not need to know about to begin with. To illustrate this point, we are going to add two more Access layer routers and complete our accounting department by adding a core router that will connect to the corporate office network. In Figure 2.21, we have added the new routers and cleaned up our router-naming scheme.

Figure 2.21 A Slightly Larger EIGRP Network

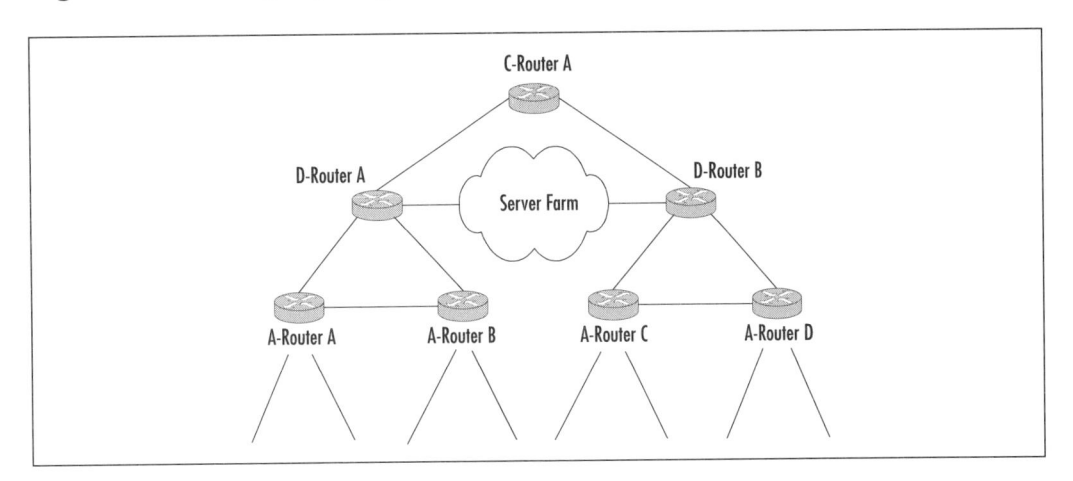

Routers that are designated as Core will begin with C-, Distribution routers will begin with D-, and Access routers will begin with A-. Our next task is to decide on a IP addressing scheme that is more efficient, conserves addresses, and is hierarchical in nature assisting EIGRP with address summarization. We decide that we will implement VLSM on the inter-router segments using 172.16.0.0. We also decided that the original addressing scheme sort of circled around between the Distribution and Access routers. That is not hierarchical. To overcome this issue, we implement a top-down addressing scheme that starts at the core and, using VLSM, continues down to the Access routers.

Summarizing EIGRP Addresses

EIGRP has a default behavior called *auto-summarization* and states that any router in an EIGRP process connected to two different major networks will not advertise subnets of either network into the other network. Only a summary address that encompasses all of the subnets will be advertised. To see what effect, if any, this rule has on our network, we need to look at an example of auto-summarization.

In Figure 2.22, the router sits on the boundary of both major networks 10.0.0.0 and 27.0.0.0. Following the rule of summarization, the networks are advertised as illustrated.

Figure 2.22 The EIGRP Auto-Summarization Process

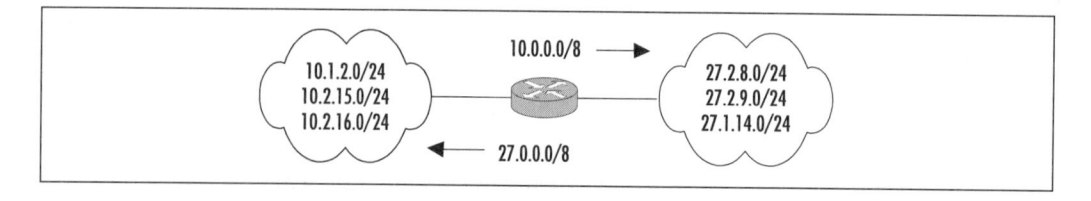

```
                10.0.0.0/8  →
 10.1.2.0/24                        27.2.8.0/24
 10.2.15.0/24      ⟩⟨                27.2.9.0/24
 10.2.16.0/24                       27.1.14.0/24
                ←  27.0.0.0/8
```

A positive impact that this behavior can have on the network is that if one of the networks such as 10.1.2.0 fails, that failure is not advertised to network 27.0.0.0. The result is what is referred to as a *query boundary*. When a diffusing computation begins in an attempt to discover a new route to the failed segment, routers in the 27.0.0.0 network are not queried. The network can reconverge in less time, and routers that do not need to waste processing cycles participating in the computation are left out.

The principal of boundaries needs to be considered as we begin to address our network. Another way to accomplish query boundaries is through address aggregation. Aggregation is similar in nature to address summarization, with the exception that you can work within the same major network. Aggregation is accomplished by shortening the mask of the advertised network as you move up through the hierarchy. As an example, in Figure 2.23 each progressive step yields a shorter address mask that aggregates all of the subnets below.

Figure 2.23 Address Aggregation Can Limit Query Range

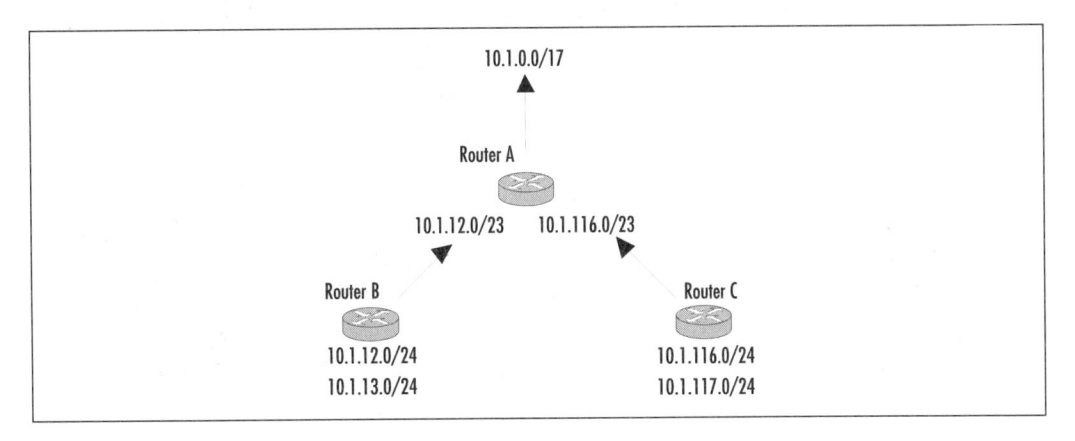

```
                        10.1.0.0/17
                            ▲
                            │
                         Router A
                            ⊗
             10.1.12.0/23      10.1.116.0/23
                 ▲                    ▲
                 │                    │
              Router B             Router C
                 ⊗                    ⊗
             10.1.12.0/24         10.1.116.0/24
             10.1.13.0/24         10.1.117.0/24
```

To see how this works, we need to look at our addresses in binary. In Table 2.2, we have laid out our addresses and highlighted the most significant common bits. You then mask the common bits to derive the aggregate address.

Table 2.2 Addresses and Significant Common Bits

Summarization at Router B

00001010	00000001	00001100	00000000	10.1.12.0/24
00001010	00000001	00001101	00000000	10.1.13.0/24
11111111	11111111	11111110	00000000	10.1.12.0/23

Summarization at Router C

00001010	00000001	01110100	00000000	10.1.116.0/24
00001010	00000001	01110101	00000000	10.1.117.0/24
11111111	11111111	11111110	00000000	10.1.116.0/23

Summarization at Router A

00001010	00000001	00001100	00000000	10.1.12.0/23
00001010	00000001	01110100	00000000	10.1.116.0/23
11111111	11111111	10000000	00000000	10.1.0.0/17

We need to perform this exercise at each layer in our hierarchy to ensure aggregation. With our current network design, only the server farm and access segments require more than two IP addresses. All other segments are point to point; therefore, our address conservation efforts will benefit greatly from the use of VLSM. We decide that we would like to reserve at least 50 addresses for the server farm segment, and 50 addresses for each access segment. We determine that we will have to reserve 6 bits in the last octet for host addresses. This is calculated using the formula

2^x-2=usable host addresses

where X is the number of bits you will need to reserve. Since we selected 50 host addresses, our formula becomes $2^x-2=50$. This formula cannot be resolved without X becoming a fraction of a whole number. We can either round up or round down—since we are planning for growth, we will round up. Where $2^5-2=30$ and $2^6-2=62$ we will use 6, resulting in 62 host addresses.

We only need two addresses for the point-to-point segments. Our formula becomes $2^x-2=2$, and X can be solved for directly resulting in X=2. Since we require a high number of host addresses, we are not going to be able to use a single octet to address all of the hosts. The total number of host addresses we need is nine segments of 62 addresses plus eight segments of 2, for a total of 574 host addresses. Plugging this total into our formula results in $2^x-2=574$. Where $2^9-2=510$ and $2^{10}-2=1022$, we would need a minimum of 10 bits for host addresses. However, we must take into account that this will only work in a flat address space. For each subnet we create, we lose two host addresses. When you are using VLSM, that value is compounded for each sub-subnet you create. We also need to consider that our address space will be hierarchical. When we apply addresses to our server farm, 192 host addresses will go unused because there are no other hosts at that level in the hierarchy. In addition, each of the access routers will need an individual network to divide between the two access segments that it serves, resulting in the reservation of another 128 hosts per access router. (This is not a loss of address space. The addresses can be used at any time in the future when additional network segments are added to the Access routers.) To allow room for these anomalies, we will use 11 bits for our address space.

It will serve us well to work with our addresses at the bit level now to determine our hierarchy. If you try to start applying addresses at the top or at the bottom before you have done the work to ensure summarization, you will meet with severe difficulty.

Since we know that we will need 11 bits for our address space, we can safely say that at the 21st bit will be our highest level of summarization. We will make this bit a 1 in all of our addresses to set a delimiter for our network. We also know that the first two octets will always be 172.16, and we can begin a chart for our bit-level addressing. In Table 2.3, with the 21st bit set to 1 and the remaining bits reserved for hosts, we see that we can begin our addressing with network 172.16.8.0/21. As long as we do not change any bits below 22 (1–21), our network can be summarized at Core Router A with this address.

Table 2.3 Bit-Level Addressing Table for Core Router A

Summarized Network

1 2 3 4 5 6 7 8	9 10 11 12 13 14 15 16	17 18 19 20 21 22 23 24	25 26 27 28 29 30 31 32
172	16	8	X
1 0 1 0 1 1 0 0	0 0 0 1 0 0 0 0	0 0 0 0 1 X X X	X X X X X X X X

At this point, it would be easiest to split the network in half at Core Router A. On the left side, we have Distribution Router A and Access Routers A and B. On the right, we have Distribution Router B and Access Routers C and D. We can distinguish between the two sides by toggling the 22nd bit. For all routes through Distribution Router A, bit 22 will be 0. For all routes through Distribution Router B, bit 22 will be 1. Table 2.4 shows this addition.

Table 2.4 Addition of Distribution Router B

Routes through Distribution Router A

1 2 3 4 5 6 7 8	9 10 11 12 13 14 15 16	17 18 19 20 21 22 23 24	25 26 27 28 29 30 31 32
172	16	8	X
1 0 1 0 1 1 0 0	0 0 0 1 0 0 0 0	0 0 0 0 1 0 X X	X X X X X X X X

Routes through Distribution Router B

172	16	12	X
1 0 1 0 1 1 0 0	0 0 0 1 0 0 0 0	0 0 0 0 1 1 X X	X X X X X X X X

Looking at the left side of our network, the total number of hosts needed is four segments of 62 addresses and three segments of 2, for a total of 254 host addresses. Again, due to the hierarchical structure of our network, we must account for the unused address space, 128 hosts per access router, plus the loss of 2 hosts per subnet. The result is approximately 524 host addresses. Inserting this number into our formula, we get $2^x=524$. Where $2^9=512$ and $2^{10}=1024$, we will use 10 bits for our address space on this segment. As this is the same number of host addresses that we will need on the right side of our network, we can make the decision to set the 23rd bit to 1 as the delimiter for host addresses below the Distribution layer. Again, it will be useful to split the network into halves, this time below the Distribution routers. Focusing on the two halves below Distribution Router A, we can distinguish between the two sides by toggling bit 24. For all routes through Access Router A, bit 24 will be 0; for routes through Access Router B, bit 24 will be 1. Table 2.5 establishes the summary addressing for the two sides of the network following this same rule for the routes through Access Routers C and D.

Table 2.5 Summary Addressing for Two Sides of the Network

1 2 3 4 5 6 7 8	9 10 11 12 13 14 15 16	17 18 19 20 21 22 23 24	25 26 27 28 29 30 31 32

Below Distribution Router A

Routes through Access Router A

172	16	10	X
1 0 1 0 1 1 0 0	0 0 0 1 0 0 0 0	0 0 0 0 1 0 1 0	X X X X X X X X

Routes through Access Router B

172	16	11	X
1 0 1 0 1 1 0 0	0 0 0 1 0 0 0 0	0 0 0 0 1 0 1 1	X X X X X X X X

Below Distribution Router B

Routes through Access Router C

172	16	14	X
1 0 1 0 1 1 0 0	0 0 0 1 0 0 0 0	0 0 0 0 1 1 1 0	X X X X X X X X

Routes through Access Router D

172	16	15	X
1 0 1 0 1 1 0 0	0 0 0 1 0 0 0 0	0 0 0 0 1 1 1 1	X X X X X X X X

Moving down to Access Router A, the number of host addresses needed is two segments of 62 addresses for each half plus the unused address space of 128 hosts, and an additional two hosts for the subnet space, for a total of 254 addresses. Inserting this number into our formula, we get $2^x=254$. Where $2^8=254$, we will use the 25th bit to delimit below the Access routers, and we can distinguish between the two sides by toggling bit 26. Table 2.6 establishes the summary addressing at the Access layer.

Table 2.6 Summary Addressing at the Access Layer

1 2 3 4 5 6 7 8	9 10 11 12 13 14 15 16	17 18 19 20 21 22 23 24	25 26 27 28 29 30 31 32

Below Access Router A

Segment One

172	16	10	128
1 0 1 0 1 1 0 0	0 0 0 1 0 0 0 0	0 0 0 0 1 0 1 0	1 0 X X X X X X

Segment Two

172	16	10	192
1 0 1 0 1 1 0 0	0 0 0 1 0 0 0 0	0 0 0 0 1 0 1 0	1 1 X X X X X X

Below Access Router B

Segment One

172	16	11	128
1 0 1 0 1 1 0 0	0 0 0 1 0 0 0 0	0 0 0 0 1 0 1 1	1 0 X X X X X X

Segment Two

172	16	11	192
1 0 1 0 1 1 0 0	0 0 0 1 0 0 0 0	0 0 0 0 1 0 1 1	1 1 X X X X X X

Below Access Router C

Segment One

172	16	14	128
1 0 1 0 1 1 0 0	0 0 0 1 0 0 0 0	0 0 0 0 1 1 1 0	1 0 X X X X X X

Segment Two

172	16	14	192
1 0 1 0 1 1 0 0	0 0 0 1 0 0 0 0	0 0 0 0 1 1 1 0	1 1 X X X X X X

Continued

Table 2.6 Continued

1 2 3 4 5 6 7 8	9 10 11 12 13 14 15 16	17 18 19 20 21 22 23 24	25 26 27 28 29 30 31 32
Below Access Router D			
Segment One			
172	16	15	128
1 0 1 0 1 1 0 0	0 0 0 1 0 0 0 0	0 0 0 0 1 1 1 1	1 0 X X X X X X
Segment Two			
172	16	15	192
1 0 1 0 1 1 0 0	0 0 0 1 0 0 0 0	0 0 0 0 1 1 1 1	1 1 X X X X X X

To see how this summarization will work, we need to group our addresses and find the common bits. Table 2.7 shows the summarization from the bottom to the top.

Table 2.7 Address Summarization from Bottom to Top

Summarization at Access Router A			
172	16	10	128
10101100	00010000	00001010	10000000
172	16	10	192
10101100	00010000	00001010	11000000
11111111	11111111	11111111	10000000=172.16.10.128/25 (Advertised to Distribution Router A)
Summarization at Access Router B			
172	16	11	128
10101100	00010000	00001011	10000000
172	16	11	192
10101100	00010000	00001011	11000000
11111111	11111111	11111111	10000000=172.16.11.128/25 (Advertised to Distribution Router A)
Summarization at Distribution Router A			
172	16	10	128/25
10101100	00010000	00001010	10000000

Continued

Table 2.7 Continued

172 10101100 11111111	16 00010000 11111111	11 00001011 11111110	128/25 10000000 00000000=172.16.10.0/23 (Advertised to Core Router A)

Summarization at Access Router C

172 10101100	16 00010000	14 00001110	128 10000000
172 10101100 11111111	16 00010000 11111111	14 00001110 11111111	192 11000000 10000000=172.16.14.128/25 (Advertised to Distribution Router B)

Summarization at Access Router D

172 10101100	16 00010000	15 00001111	128 10000000
172 10101100 11111111	16 00010000 11111111	15 00001111 11111111	192 11000000 10000000=172.16.15.128/25 (Advertised to Distribution Router B)

Summarization at Distribution Router B

172 10101100	16 00010000	14 00001110	128/25 10000000
172 10101100 11111111	16 00010000 11111111	15 00001111 11111110	128/25 10000000 00000000=172.16.14.0/23 (Advertised to Core Router A)

Summarization at Core Router A

172 10101100	16 00010000	10 00001010	0/23 00000000
172 10101100 11111111	16 00010000 11111111	14 00001110 11111000	0/23 00000000 00000000=172.16.8.0/21 (Advertised to Corporate Network)

Figure 2.24 graphically illustrates this aggregation.

Figure 2.24 The Aggregation of Routes in a Sample Network

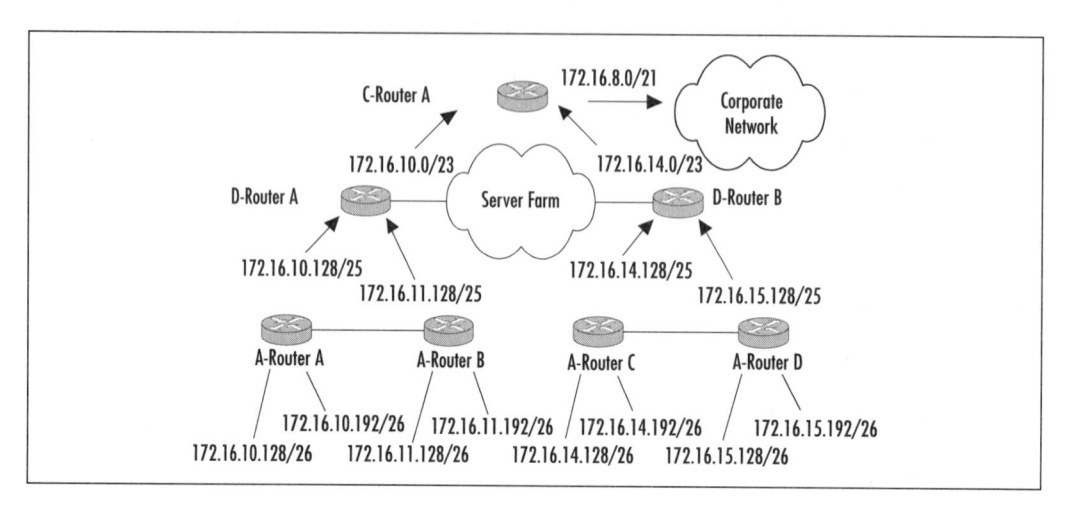

Now we have to implement our IP addressing scheme and address summarization. EIGRP does not perform this type of summarization automatically. Auto-summary only occurs at major network boundaries. We must manually configure summarization within a major network address space. This is done with the command **ip summary-address eigrp** *<process id> <network> <mask>*. This command is an interface configuration level command that tells EIGRP to suppress advertisements of more specific routes.

To configure Access Router A to advertise 172.16.10.128/25, use the following interface configuration where Ethernet 0 connects to Distribution Router A:

A-Router A

```
interface ethernet0
  ip summary-address eigrp 100 172.16.10.128 255.255.255.128
```

The remaining configurations are as follows, where the interface specified is connected to the upstream neighbor:

A-Router B

```
interface ethernet0
  ip summary-address eigrp 100 172.16.11.128 255.255.255.128
```

A-Router C
```
interface ethernet0
  ip summary-address eigrp 100 172.16.14.128 255.255.255.128
```

A-Router D
```
interface ethernet0
  ip summary-address eigrp 100 172.16.15.128 255.255.255.128
```

D-Router A
```
interface ethernet1
  ip summary-address eigrp 100 172.16.10.0 255.255.254.0
```

D-Router B
```
interface ethernet1
  ip summary-address eigrp 100 172.16.14.0 255.255.254.0
```

C-Router A
```
interface ethernet1
  ip summary-address eigrp 100 172.16.8.0 255.255.248.0
```

Configuring ip summary-address on the Core router assumes that the corporate office is also using 172.16.0.0. If this were not the case, it would not be necessary to manually configure summarization at Core Router A because it would automatically advertise 172.16.0.0/16 following the rules of auto-summarization.

Redistributing EIGRP and OSPF

It is quite common to find yourself in the position of needing to manage two routing protocols within the same network. This can be due to a merger between two companies or because you are migrating from one protocol to another. EIGRP has built-in mechanisms that allow you to easily translate route information from one protocol to another.

In the example that follows, we have two companies that are merging. In this instance, the new company is running OSPF and we need to insert routes from our EIGRP network into their network. We also need to receive route information from the OSPF process. However, there are certain routes that we do not want to inject into their network. We will use a *route filter* to prevent these routes from being propagated. Figure 2.25 show the two networks and the link used to connect them.

Figure 2.25 Redistributing between EIGRP and OSPF

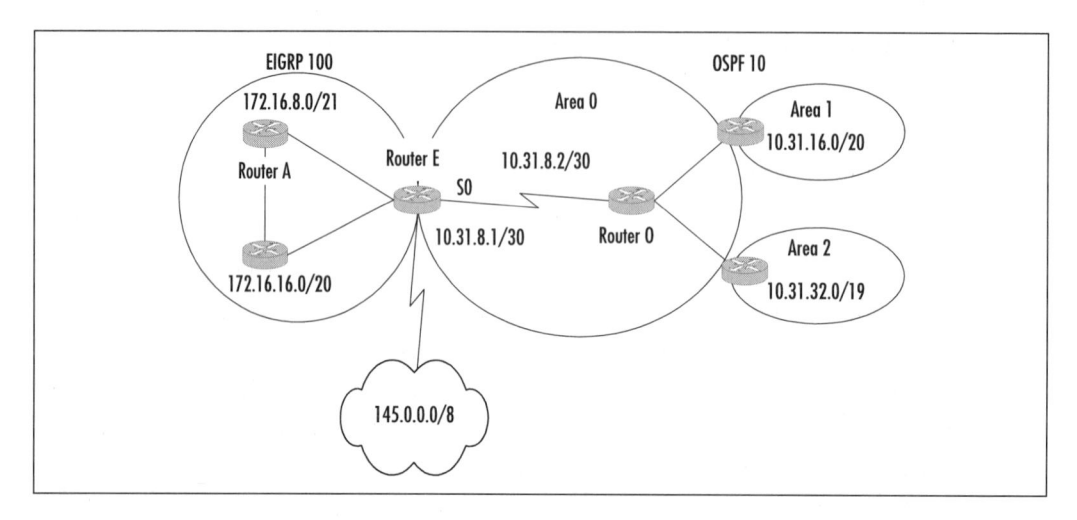

We will focus our attention on Router E. It will function both as an EIGRP Core router and an OSPF ASBR (Autonomous System Boundary Router), and we can control the redistribution process entirely from there. The first objective is to modify the original EIGRP-only configuration at Router E to add it to the OSPF 10 process. The original OSPF network is using the address space 10.31.0.0/16. We could enable OSPF on Router E using 10.0.0.0, but that would prevent us from ever using the 10.0.0.0 address space anywhere else in our network. Therefore, the configuration at Router E is:

```
interface serial0
   ip address 10.31.8.1 255.255.255.254

router eigrp 100
   network 172.16.0.0

router OSPF 10
   network 10.31.0.0 0.0.255.255 area 0
```

Router E will now fully converge with both networks. At this point, though, it will not advertise the routes from OSPF to the neighbor EIGRP routers, nor will it advertise the routes form EIGRP into area 0. We must use the **redistribute** command to inject the routes from each process. The configuration becomes:

```
router eigrp 100
  network 172.16.0.0
  redistribute ospf 10 metric 512 10000 255 1 1500


router ospf 10
  network 10.31.0.0 0.0.255.255 area 0
  redistribute eigrp 100 metric 195
```

Router E will now inject routes in both directions. The **metric** portion of the **redistribute** command allows each process to convert the other protocols metric to whatever you dictate in the command. For EIGRP, these are the familiar bandwidth, delay, reliability, load, and MTU. For OSPF, the metric is an administratively assigned *cost* for the path. The default values for OSPF metric are generated by the formula 10^8/Bandwidth. In this circumstance, the link is 512 kbps, so the value is 195. If there were redundant links between the two networks, it would be important to set this value correctly so that the correct route is chosen. In our situation, we could have selected an arbitrary value.

We could also choose to use the **default-metric** command in both the OSPF and EIGRP processes. If we were redistributing more than one routing protocol or a static route, applying a default metric to the routing process would eliminate the need for the **metric** keyword in the **redistribute** command. Previously, there was a connection from Router E on interface serial1 to 145.0.0.0/8. This connection can be added as a static route and redistributed to both the EIGRP and OSPF processes. The configuration at Router E becomes:

```
ip route 145.0.0.0 255.0.0.0 serial1

router eigrp 100
   network 172.16.0.0
   default-metric 512 10000 255 1 1500
   redistribute ospf 10
   reditribute static


router ospf 10
   network 10.31.0.0 0.0.255.255 area 0
```

```
default-metric 195
redistribute eigrp 100
redistribute static
```

If we look at the route table on Router O, we see that only network 172.16.0.0 is injected along with the route to 145.0.0.0. One of our design goals is to prevent network 172.16.8.0/21 from being advertised into OSPF. If only the major network address is advertised, we will not be able to block access to an individual subnet of network 172.16.0.0 without blocking the entire network. Fortunately, OSPF allows you to insert the keyword **subnets** at the end of the **redistribute** command to advertise the individual subnets.

```
Router O#show ip route
Codes:
C - connected, S - static, I - IGRP, R - RIP, M - mobile, B - BGP
D - EIGRP, EX - EIGRP external, O - OSPF, IA - OSPF inter area
N1 - OSPF NSSA external type 1, N2 - OSPF NSSA external type 2
E1 - OSPF external type 1, E2 - OSPF external type 2, E - EGP
i - IS-IS, L1 - ISIS level-1, L2 - ISIS level-2, * - candidate
    default
U - per-user static route, o - ODR

Gateway of last resort is not set

O E2 172.16.0.0/16 [110/195] via 10.31.8.1, 00:02:29, Serial0
O E2 145.0.0.0/8 [110/195] via 10.31.8.1, 00:00:09, Serial0
     10.31.0.0/16 is variably subnetted, 4 subnets, 3 masks
C       10.31.8.0/30 is directly connected, Serial0
```

Having made the subnets modification, we need to prevent the advertisement of 172.16.8.0/21 using a route filter. We can filter this route in two ways: we can use a *distribute-list* attached to an ip access list to deny the advertisement, or we can use a *route map*. Since we are going to block only a single advertisement, we have selected to use a distribute list.

The **distribute-list** command is applied to the EIGRP process and can limit routes advertised or accepted. The format of the command is **distribute-list**

<access list number> **in/out.** We will apply our **distribute-list** command to Router E and block the advertisement of network 172.16.8.0.

Our configuration becomes:

```
router eigrp 100
  network 172.16.0.0
  default-metric 512 10000 255 1 1500
  redistribute ospf 10
  reditribute static
  distribute-list 10 out

router ospf 10
  network 10.31.0.0 0.0.255.255 area 0
  default-metric 195
  redistribute eigrp 100
  redistribute static

access-list 10 deny 17.16.8.0 0.0.0.255
access-list 10 permit any
```

The following shows the final route table on Router O. We can see that it does not have a route to 172.16.8.0, and that all of the injected routes are External Type 2 routes. E2 routes simply mean that OSPF will only use the metric learned from the redistributed route. It will not increase the metric to account for the cost of the internal paths. If we wanted OSPF to include the cost of the internal paths, we would need to specify the routes as External Type 1 routes by adding the keyword **metric-type 1** to the **redistribution** or **default-metric** commands.

```
Router O#show ip route
Codes:
C - connected, S - static, I - IGRP, R - RIP, M - mobile, B - BGP
D - EIGRP, EX - EIGRP external, O - OSPF, IA - OSPF inter area
N1 - OSPF NSSA external type 1, N2 - OSPF NSSA external type 2
E1 - OSPF external type 1, E2 - OSPF external type 2, E - EGP
i - IS-IS, L1 - ISIS level-1, L2 - ISIS level-2, * - candidate default
U - per-user static route, o - ODR
```

```
Gateway of last resort is not set


     172.16.0.0/16 is subnetted, 1 subnet
O E2    172.16.16.0/20 [110/195] via 10.31.8.1, 00:02:44, Serial0
O E2 145.0.0.0/8 [110/195] via 10.31.8.1, 00:00:17, Serial0
     10.31.0.0/16 is variably subnetted, 4 subnets, 3 masks
C       10.31.8.0/30 is directly connected, Serial0
        ................
```

We can also look at the route table on Router A and see that EIGRP has learned the routes from the OSPF redistribution and tagged them as D EX routes.

```
Router A#show ip route
Codes:
C - connected, S - static, I - IGRP, R - RIP, M - mobile, B - BGP
D - EIGRP, EX - EIGRP external, O - OSPF, IA - OSPF inter area
N1 - OSPF NSSA external type 1, N2 - OSPF NSSA external type 2
E1 - OSPF external type 1, E2 - OSPF external type 2, E - EGP
i - IS-IS, L1 - ISIS level-1, L2 - ISIS level-2, * - candidate default
U - per-user static route, o - ODR

Gateway of last resort is not set

D EX 145.0.0.0/8 [170/5281536] via 172.16.4.193, 00:00:17,
     Ethernet1
     10.31.0.0/16 is variably subnetted, 3 subnets, 3 masks
D EX    10.31.8.0/30 [170/5281536] via 172.16.4.193, 00:00:42,
     Ethernet1
D EX    10.31.16.0/20 [170/5332736] via 172.16.4.193, 00:00:42,
     Ethernet1
D EX    10.31.32.0/19 [170/5332736] via 172.16.4.193, 00:00:42,
     Ethernet1
     172.16.0.0/16 is variably subnetted, 2 subnets, 2 masks
C       172.16.8.0/30 is directly connected, Ethernet0
        ................
```

Unequal Cost Load Balancing

You will often find yourself in a situation in which there exist two or more paths to the same destination. EIGRP will automatically balance traffic over the paths if the cost for each is the same. If the paths are not equal, EIGRP will allow you to proportionally divide the traffic over both links. This situation can occur when there are multiple WAN links between two routers, but it is more common to see this situation when there are paths through multiple neighbors to a destination.

In Figure 2.26, we want to create traffic distribution over the two WAN links to connect to the Internet. The command to generate load balancing is **variance** <*multiplier*>, where the multiplier tells the EIGRP process how many times larger the feasible successor total metric (including local interface cost) can be over the feasible distance and still load balance. Table 2.8 shows the metrics of both routes.

Table 2.8 Metrics of Both Routes

Metric over the 56 K link

Metric= $K1*10^7/56+K3*22000/10=178571+2200=180771*256=46277376$

Metric over the 128 K link (FD)

Metric= $K1*10^7/128+K3*22000/10=78125+2200=80425*256=20588800$

Figure 2.26 Efficient Use of Existing Links with the Variance Command

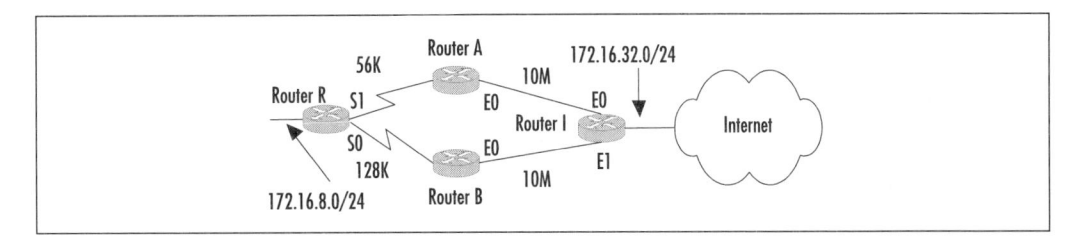

If we divide 46277376 by 20588800, we discover that it is 2.25 times the value of the feasible distance. Therefore, we need to use a variance multiplier of 3. Our configuration at Router R is:

```
router eigrp 100
  network 172.6.0.0
  variance 3
```

The default behavior of EIGRP is to distribute traffic over the paths that meet the variance requirement inversely proportional to their metric. In our circumstance, approximately one-third of the traffic will traverse the slower link.

There is an important rule regarding unequal-cost load balancing: The higher-cost path or paths must be feasible successors of the lower-cost path. Due to the nature of selecting feasible successors, you may discover that your load balancing is only working in one direction. In Figure 2.26, we have created load balancing from Router R through the two WAN links and to the Internet. We discover that the 128K link is becoming saturated during high periods of activity. This is the opposite behavior of what we would have expected.

When we begin to examine the metrics for our routes, we discover that the connection from Router I to Router R has only one successor, through Router B. The path through Router A does not meet the feasibility condition and is not in the topology table. Looking at the metric calculations in Table 2.8, we can see the problem.

Table 2.8 Metric Calculations for Routers A and B

Metric Advertised by Router A
Metric= K1*10^7/56+K3*20000/10=178571+2000=180571*256=46226176
Feasible Distance through Router B
Metric= K1*10^7/128+K3*21000/10=78125+2100=80225*256=20537600

There are two ways to resolve this problem. The first solution is to increase the physical bandwidth on the 56K link to 128K. You cannot deny the fact that during peak periods there is enough traffic to saturate the slow WAN links. However, if raising the bandwidth between the two sites were an option, we would have done that originally. The second solution is to tinker with the EIGRP metrics between Routers A and R until it becomes a feasible successor.

Do not be too quick to walk over to Router A and raise the bandwidth configuration until the route meets the feasibility condition. In doing so, you can adversely affect other routes, and the solution may not produce the expected results. As an example, if you raise the bandwidth metric at Router A to 128K to lower the metric below 20537600, you will end up with something close to equal-cost load balancing, and you will oversubscribe the 56K link. If you change the delay metric on Router B to increase the feasible distance, the result will be the same.

In many situations, we would simply be at a standstill and have to wait for the budget to increase to add physical bandwidth on the WAN links. In our simple network, though, we can perform one additional step to get the desired result.

We can achieve the desired result if we increase the delay over the link between Router B and Router R until the route through Router A becomes a feasible successor, and then increase the delay between Router A and Router I. This is not a generally recommended approach unless you very carefully examine all of the routes that will be affected. Influencing these metrics can result in sub-optimal path selection and is only given here as an example. In our network, this is the only path that will be affected so we are safe in moving forward.

We need to perform some calculations to determine the exact values of delay over the links. The first goal is to achieve feasible successor status for the link between Router A and Router R. To do this, we must raise the feasible distance to a value greater than 46226176, which is a factor of 2.251. To arrive at the delay value, we need to work through our formula backwards:

20537600*2.251=256(78125+Delay/10)

46230138/256=78125+Delay/10

1024615=Delay

Inserting this into our formula in Table 2.9 as our total delay between Router I and Router R through Router B, we can see that the feasibility condition is met and we have not increased the metric so high that the route through Router A becomes the successor.

Table 2.9 Total Delay between Router I and Router R

Metric Advertised by Router A
Metric= K1*10^7/56+K3*20000/10=178571+2000=180571*256=46226176

Feasible Distance through Router B
Metric= K1*10^7/128+K3*1024615/10=78125+102462=180587*256=46230272

Now we must determine how high to raise the delay value on the link between Router A and Router I. To get the appropriate balance, the total metric through Router A should be twice the metric through Router B. Currently, the total metric is:

Metric= K1*10^7/56+K3*21000/10=178571+2100=180671*256=46251776

Again, we need to work backwards for our solution:

2*46251776=256(178571+Delay/10)

92503552 /256=178571+Delay/10

1827710=Delay

Inserting this into our formula in Table 2.10, we can see that we have achieved the desired result:

Table 2.10 Continued Calculations of Metrics

Feasible Successor through Router A

Metric=
K1*107/56+K3*1827710/10=178571+182771=361342*256=92503552

Feasible Distance through Router B

Metric=
K1*107/128+K3*1024615/10=78125+102462=180587*256=46230272

The final configurations on our routers become:

Router R

```
router eigrp 101
  network 172.16.0.0
  variance 3
```

Router A

```
router eigrp 100
  network 172.16.0.0
```

Router B

```
router eigrp 100
  network 172.16.0.0
interface serial0
  delay 1023615
```

Router I

```
router eigrp 100
  network 172.16.0.0
```

```
variance 3
interface ethernet0
  delay 1807710
```

If we look at the route tables for Router R and Router I, we can see that both routes are entered in the route table.

```
Router R#show ip route
Codes:
C - connected, S - static, I - IGRP, R - RIP, M - mobile, B - BGP
D - EIGRP, EX - EIGRP external, O - OSPF, IA - OSPF inter area
N1 - OSPF NSSA external type 1, N2 - OSPF NSSA external type 2
E1 - OSPF external type 1, E2 - OSPF external type 2, E - EGP
i - IS-IS, L1 - ISIS level-1, L2 - ISIS level-2, * -
candidate default
U - per-user static route, o - ODR


Gateway of last resort is not set


D     172.16.32.0/24 [90/20588800] via 172.16.10.2, 00:00:39,
       Serial0
                     [90/46277376] via 172.16.11.1, 00:00:39,
       Serial1
              ...............


Router I#show ip route
Codes:
C - connected, S - static, I - IGRP, R - RIP, M - mobile, B - BGP
D - EIGRP, EX - EIGRP external, O - OSPF, IA - OSPF inter area
N1 - OSPF NSSA external type 1, N2 - OSPF NSSA external type 2
E1 - OSPF external type 1, E2 - OSPF external type 2, E - EGP
i - IS-IS, L1 - ISIS level-1, L2 - ISIS level-2, * -
candidate default
U - per-user static route, o - ODR


Gateway of last resort is not set
```

```
D      172.16.8.0/24 [90/92503552] via 172.16.16.2, 00:01:03,
       Ethernet0
                     [90/46230272] via 172.16.17.1, 00:01:03,
       Ethernet1
```

Recognizing Caveats

While EIGRP is a relatively mature protocol, it maintains several very important caveats that you must be aware of when designing and implementing an EIGRP network. I will briefly discuss the nature of these caveats and then provide troubleshooting examples in the next section.

Stuck-in-Active

One of the most common and well-known caveats of EIGRP is the Stuck-in-Active (SIA) route. While one of the main design goals of EIGRP was to create a fast converging protocol, it was realized that a diffused computation could be delayed indefinitely due to factors outside the protocol's own mechanisms. If the best decision is to be made, it must be made from all available information. Therefore, when a route needs to be selected or recalculated, a router must attempt to gather the best information available from its neighbors.

The architects of EIGRP designed it in such a way that no routing decisions will be made until all neighbors have had a chance to participate in the decision-making process. What should happen if a neighbor fails to respond to a query? The decision was made to declare the neighbor dead after an *active timer* expires, approximately 3 minutes. It could be argued that only the loss of hellos should cause a neighbor to be declared dead. After all, if the router does not respond to a query, won't it have stopped sending hellos? Simply stated: No.

To understand why a router may still be able to send hellos but not respond to a query, we need to take a quick look at the diffused computation process. When a router receives a query, it examines the route in question to determine if it is affected. If it does not have a route to this destination and is not affected by the change in state, it responds to the query with an infinite metric to the location. This tells the querying router that the path is not accessible through the responding router.

If the route in the query affects the router, it checks to see if the querying router is currently the successor for this route. If it is, the neighbor then checks to see if there is a feasible successor. In a perfect world, there will always be a feasible successor. If there is, the neighbor immediately promotes the FS to successor and responds to the query with the new successor's information. The querying router can then install this route as the new successor, and the diffused computation can end.

The problem begins when the queried neighbor does not have a feasible successor. It has just been told that the successor route is bad and has then discovered that there is no alternative. It begins a diffused computation of its own, and until it has information to pass along to the querying router, it never responds to the query. In large or small networks with slow WAN links or incorrect configurations, this process of cascading computations can exceed the 3-minute active timer on the originating router.

What should the originating router do? Since the computation cannot be completed until a response is received from all neighbors, the originating router creates a false response with an infinite metric so that the computation can be completed, the nonresponding neighbor is declared dead, all routes through that neighbor enter the active state, and a shower of queries may begin.

As you can see, although a neighbor may still be sending hellos, the failure to respond to a query can wreak havoc on your network. It is very important when designing you network that you pay very close attention to the distance that a diffused computation can travel from the source of the original query. The best way to prevent this situation is to create a hierarchical, summarized addressing scheme that creates query boundaries.

Auto-Summarization

When EIGRP was being designed, the architects wanted to ensure ease of interoperation with the most commonly deployed protocols at the time: classful protocols such as RIP and IGRP. It became necessary for EIGRP to send a summary address of one major network into another major network. To understand the problems that this behavior can generate, we need to take a look at how classful protocols deal with routes advertised form another major network.

The first and most important thing to realize is that classful protocols do not include subnet masks in routing updates. Therefore, when RIP or IGRP receives an update, it performs a series of checks to determine what to do with the information. If the update contains information about a network that is configured on the receiving interface, the mask on that interface is applied to the update. If the update contains information about a network that is not configured on the router, the classful network mask is applied to the update.

If EIGRP were to send subnet information into a RIP or IGRP process, the information would be dropped and only the major network would be placed in the routing table. This behavior works perfectly until you begin to try to implement classless behavior in your hybrid network. In classful behavior, a major network is expected to exist in only one direction. In classless environments, it becomes possible to create discontiguous networks by locating elements of the same major network in different locations throughout your design. If you attempt this with EIGRP, you will discover that segments of your network will become unreachable without manual intervention.

This dual nature of EIGRP to exhibit both classless and classful behavior is demonstrated in the *Troubleshooting EIGRP* section. It is quite common for an administrator to forget about this behavior and find him or herself searching for the lost route information.

Troubleshooting EIGRP

Troubleshooting EIGRP can be a complex process. This due to the fact that while EIGRP remains a hop-by-hop protocol, routing decisions are diffused through neighbors away from the source. This means that tracing a problem that originates in one portion of the network can lead you into other areas of the network that you would not have assumed to be involved at all. This is most commonly seen when troubleshooting SIA routes where a query has propagated away from the originator and never returned. As previously mentioned, 12.1(5a) introduced a mechanism that limits the effects of SIAs.

EIGRP was designed with many built-in show commands that are extremely useful troubleshooting tools. We have already used most of these commands, and we will now see how to use them to conduct step-by-step problem resolution.

Troubleshooting Stuck-in-Active Routes

As stated previously, SIA routes are generated when a query has not been replied to within the active timer period. The important thing to remember about SIAs (and the reason that they're so difficult to troubleshoot) is that an SIA isn't caused by just one problem—it's caused by two separate problems. The first is that something caused a route to be unavailable to a router that didn't have a feasible successor for that route. The cause of SIA routes can vary from an incorrect configuration to oversubscribed WAN links. The second problem is that, once that route became active and queries were sent out, something caused a router that received a query to be unable to reply to that query. Another flapping link, high CPU usage, or several other factors can cause this type of situation. Regardless of the cause, the process for troubleshooting SIA routes is generally the same: You must start at the router reporting the SIA route and, using the topology and neighbor tables, follow the direction of the query until the source of the error is discovered.

If you are lucky enough to be sitting in front of a router when a route becomes SIA, you will see the following error message:

```
JAN 27 11:28:32: %DUAL-3-SIA: Route 10.5.1.0/24 stuck-in-active
                state in IP-EIGRP 100.
Cleaning up
```

It is not typical that you would be sitting there when this happens. It is more common that a connectivity problem has occurred and you have been alerted. By the time you arrive, the route has been flushed and the network has reconverged. If the problem is intermittent, you will have a very difficult time locating the cause of an SIA route, although logging to a syslog server does provide you with a better frame of reference to help track down the problem. The reason for this is that the SIA is not caused by the failed route, but by a neighbor that failed to reply to a query. When you sit down and start troubleshooting the failed link, you may notice that other routes away from the original problem are missing as well, and after a brief period of time, the routes start to reappear. This is the first indication that an SIA event has occurred.

The reason for the missing and reappearing routes is that when a route becomes SIA, the neighbor that failed to respond is flushed from the neighbor table along with any routes learned from that neighbor. When hellos are received from the neighbor that was flushed, the adjacency is reformed and the routes are relearned.

In Figure 2.27, network 10.5.1.0 has failed. The failure is called to your attention and you head for Router A. When you get there, you observe the situation just mentioned. As the routes reappear, you check the neighbor table to see what is happening with Router B, and at first, you see nothing out of the ordinary.

You scratch your head and look a little closer, and the problem jumps out at you. The following will show that the uptime for Router B is at 19 seconds and you realize that the adjacency with Router B has been reset. This is the final piece of evidence that you need to convince yourself that an SIA event has occurred, and the task at hand shifts from determining why 10.5.1.0 failed to the much larger problem of determining why Router B failed to respond to Router A's query.

Figure 2.27 SIAs Aren't Always Easy to Find

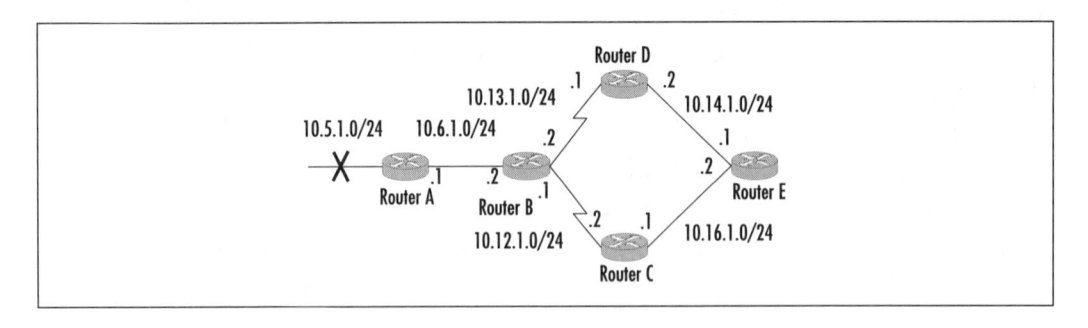

```
Router A#show ip eigrp neighbor
IP-EIGRP neighbors for process 100
H   Address         Interface    Hold  Uptime     SRTT   RTO    Q    Seq
                                 (sec)            (ms)               Cnt Num
0   10.6.1.2        Ethernet0     8   00:00:19    17     20     0    645
```

The next logical step is to move upstream to Router B and follow the problem. At Router B, you display the neighbor table and observe the following output:

```
Router B#show ip eigrp neighbor
IP-EIGRP neighbors for process 100
H   Address         Interface    Hold  Uptime     SRTT   RTO    Q    Seq
                                 (sec)            (ms)               Cnt Num
1   10.13.1.1       Serial1      13   00:00:23    12     30     0    620
0   10.12.1.2       Serial0       8   07:21:45    17     20     0    645
```

You notice that the uptime for Router D is only 23 seconds, while the uptime for Router C has not been reset. You are now hot on this problem's trail and continue upstream to Router D. The output from Router D's neighbor table pinpoints the link between Routers B and D as the source of the problem.

```
Router D#show ip eigrp neighbor
IP-EIGRP neighbors for process 100
H   Address         Interface    Hold  Uptime     SRTT   RTO    Q    Seq
                                 (sec)            (ms)               Cnt Num
1   10.13.1.2       Serial0       9   00:00:33    12     30     0    620
0   10.14.1.1       Serial1      12   09:11:15    17     20     0    645
```

Looking at the entry for Router C we can see that the uptime is very small, which could have been predicted due to the reset we already knew occurred. However, the difference here is that the adjacency with Router E did not reset. This means that if a query was received at Router D, it was forwarded to Router E and a response was received.

At this point, you should begin troubleshooting the connection between Routers B and D. In this circumstance, the problem reveals itself in a **show run** command. Examining the EIGRP configuration and interface configurations, we see that the bandwidth on the link between the two routers has been manipulated at Router D.

```
!
router eigrp 100
   network 10.0.0.0
!
interface serial0
   ip address 10.13.1.1 255.255.255.0
   bandwidth 18
```

Thinking back you remember that you changed this metric to convince Router E to use the path through Router C to reach across the WAN links. The problem arises because the default behavior of EIGRP is to limit its use of configured bandwidth to 50 percent. This means that the available bandwidth for EIGRP is a mere 9 K. The result is that the connection was too choked for Router D to ever receive the query or to reply to the query. This is a prime example of why it is never a good idea to manipulate the bandwidth of a link outside of what it actually is.

This problem can be resolved in two ways: the bandwidth could be set to its correct value (recommended), or you can tell EIGRP to use more than the default 50 percent. The interface configuration command **ip bandwidth-percent eigrp** *<process id>* *<percent of bandwidth>* is used to instruct EIGRP to use additional bandwidth.

This has been a best-case scenario for troubleshooting an SIA route. We would like to take a moment to examine how things could have been different. The point at which neighbor resets stop is not always the point where the problem exists. Let's take, for example, what may occur if the query has reached the edge of the network and the replies have begun to cascade back in toward the source but do not reach the originator of the query within the default 3-minute active time.

While this is uncommon, it can occur. If, because of high CPU utilization, it takes several minutes for the query from Router B to be processed by Router D, and then another moment for Router D to successfully reply to Router B, the original 3 minutes on Router A may have expired. In this circumstance, the adjacency between Routers A and B is reset, but not the adjacency to Router D. Even though Router D is the problem, there will be no indication pointing to the incorrect configuration once the SIA event is over. It becomes virtually impossible to locate the problem in a situation such as this.

If this happens, you may get lucky and the original problem, the failure of segment 10.5.1.0, may reoccur while you are observing the routers. If it does not, you may want to select a maintenance window within which to manually recreate the situation.

However the event reoccurs, you have about 3 minutes to locate the problem. The following output shows that you have caught the route in an active state on Router B.

```
Router B#show ip eigrp topology active
IP-EIGRP Topology Table for process 100
Codes: P - Passive, A - Active, U - Update, Q -
Query, R - Reply,
       r - Reply status
A 10.5.1.0 255.255.255.0, 1 successors, FD is
281600 1 replies,
     active 0:01:38,
                                  query-origin:
Successor Origin
       via 10.13.1.1 (Infinity/Infinity), r, Serial0, serno 1232
       via 10.12.1.2 (Infinity/Infinity), Serial1, serno 1227
```

The first thing to notice in this output is that the route has been active for 1:38 minutes. Any routes that are active for longer than 1 minute indicate a problem. Looking at the last two lines, we can see which neighbor has not responded. The lowercase r preceding the *via 10.13.1.1* statement indicates that the router is still waiting for a reply from Router D. You can now begin the process of moving downstream toward the problem.

> **NOTE**
>
> By default, changes in neighbor state are not logged. When the active timer expires and the adjacency with a neighbor is reset, you will not see any output unless you have enabled logging of neighbor changes. The command to enable this feature is **eigrp log-neighbor-changes**. Once enabled, any change in the state of an adjacency will be logged. The following is a sample output from a reset.
>
> ```
> JAN 27 11:38:32: %DUAL-5-NBRCHANGE: IP-EIGRP 1: Neighbor
>                  10.6.1.2 (Ethernet0)
>                  is down: retry limit exceeded
> ```

Troubleshooting Auto-Summarization

A classic problem in EIGRP networks occurs when administrators forget that EIGRP auto-summarizes at major network boundaries. The result can be that the administrator may create an addressing scheme that is well suited to a truly classless protocol that does not summarize at boundaries but generates routing black holes in an EIGRP network.

This situation can be easily demonstrated. In Figure 2.28 we have created redundant connections into the 10.0.0.0 network. On the surface, everything looks okay. However, as soon as connectivity is tested, it is realized that connectivity is intermittent at best.

Figure 2.28 Auto-Summarization Is One of the Most Common EIGRP Configuration Mistakes

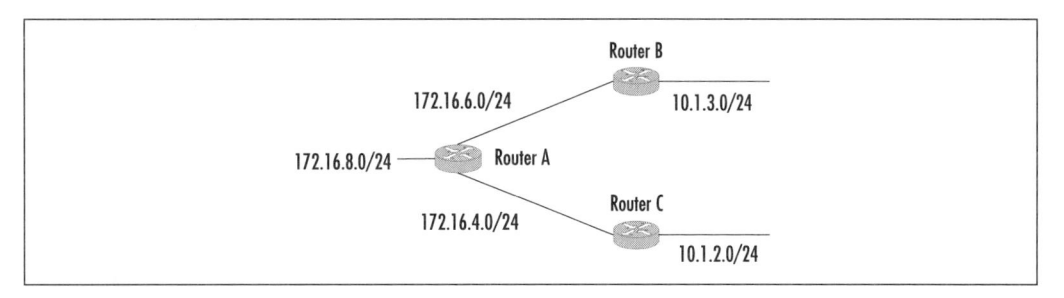

Observing the route table for Router A reveals the problem. Two equal-cost paths to the 10.0.0.0 network have been entered into the route table. Router A will load balance over the two links, regardless of which subnet you are trying to reach.

```
Router A#show ip route
Codes:
C - connected, S - static, I - IGRP, R - RIP, M - mobile, B - BGP
D - EIGRP, EX - EIGRP external, O - OSPF, IA - OSPF inter area
N1 - OSPF NSSA external type 1, N2 - OSPF NSSA external type 2
E1 - OSPF external type 1, E2 - OSPF external type 2, E - EGP
i - IS-IS, L1 - ISIS level-1, L2 - ISIS level-2, * -
candidate default
U - per-user static route, o - ODR

Gateway of last resort is not set

D    10.0.0.0/24 [90/281600] via 172.16.6.2, 00:01:27, Ethernet1
                 [90/281600] via 172.16.4.2, 00:01:27, Ethernet2
     172.16.0.0/24 is subnetted, 3 subnets
C       172.16.8.0 is directly connected, Ethernet0
C       172.16.6.0 is directly connected, Ethernet1
C       172.16.4.0 is directly connected, Ethernet2
```

This situation can be remedied by disabling auto-summarization on Routers B and C. This will enable them to advertise subnet information into network 172.16.0.0. The command to disable auto-summarization is **no auto-summary**. Generally speaking, there is no reason **not** to disable auto-summarization, unless you know the effects of leaving it enabled and desire those effects. In this example, the router configurations become:

Router A

```
router eigrp 100
  network 172.16.0.0
  network 10.0.0.0
  no auto-summary
```

Router B

```
router eigrp 100
  network 172.16.0.0
  network 10.0.0.0
  no auto-summary
```

It is not necessary to make this same change on Router A because this is currently the only connection to network 172.16.0.0 and the summarization is actually a beneficial behavior. The preferred method to avoid trouble with auto-summarization in the future would be to disable auto-summarization and configure manual summarization. Looking at the following route table for Router A, we can see that the problem has been corrected.

```
Router A#show ip route
Codes:
C - connected, S - static, I - IGRP, R - RIP, M - mobile, B - BGP
D - EIGRP, EX - EIGRP external, O - OSPF, IA - OSPF inter area
N1 - OSPF NSSA external type 1, N2 - OSPF NSSA external type 2
E1 - OSPF external type 1, E2 - OSPF external type 2, E - EGP
i - IS-IS, L1 - ISIS level-1, L2 - ISIS level-2, * -
candidate default
U - per-user static route, o - ODR

Gateway of last resort is not set

     10.0.0.0/24 is subnetted, 2 subnets
D       10.1.3.0/24 [90/281600] via 172.16.6.2, 00:00:07,
        Ethernet1
D       10.1.2.0/24 [90/281600] via 172.16.4.2, 00:00:33,
        Ethernet2
     172.16.0.0/24 is subnetted, 3 subnets
C       172.16.8.0 is directly connected, Ethernet0
C       172.16.6.0 is directly connected, Ethernet1
C       172.16.4.0 is directly connected, Ethernet2
```

Troubleshooting not-on-common-subnet

The not-on-common-subnet error message is generated when two EIGRP neighbors exchange hellos and their IP addresses are not configured for the same subnet. This can happen due to an accidental configuration or when implementing secondary IP addresses. The error message takes the form:

```
JAN 27 15:18:22: IP-EIGRP: Neighbor 10.1.2.1 not on common subnet
             for Ethernet2
```

When the two neighbor interfaces are brought up, the routers will begin exchanging hellos. When the hellos are parsed for information about the neighbor, the routers will examine the source IP address to determine if it is on the same subnet as the interface on which the hello was received. If it is not, you will see this error on both routers. This situation is easy to troubleshoot and resolve. When implementing secondary IP addresses, you may need to look a little more closely.

In Figure 2.29, Router A and Router B have been configured for EIGRP, but for some reason, they are not exchanging route information. When observing the situation at Router A, there are no error messages being logged.

Figure 2.29 Secondary IP Addresses Need to Be Carefully Planned

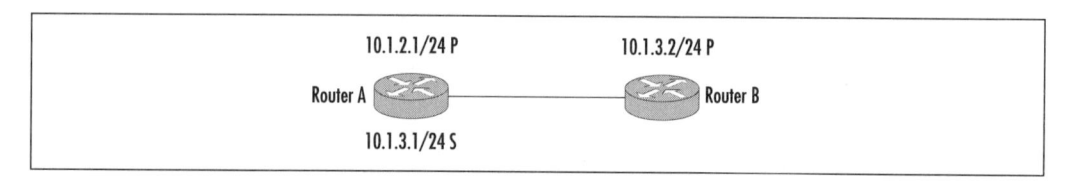

```
                    10.1.2.1/24 P         10.1.3.2/24 P
            Router A                                   Router B
                    10.1.3.1/24 S
```

We begin our troubleshooting by viewing Router A's neighbor table. As you can see in the following example, there does not appear to be any problems. We expect Router A to begin receiving updates from Router B, but no routes appear in the topology or route tables.

```
Router A#show ip eigrp neighbor
IP-EIGRP neighbors for process 100
H    Address          Interface    Hold   Uptime     SRTT    RTO   Q    Seq
                                   (sec)             (ms)          Cnt  Num
1    10.3.1.2         Ethernet0     9     00:00:33    12      30   0    620
```

If we move to Router B, believing that the problem resides there, and view the neighbor table, we see that Router B has no neighbors.

```
Router B#show ip eigrp neighbor
IP-EIGRP neighbors for process 100
```

A second later, a not-on-common-subnet error appears, indicating that neighbor 10.1.2.1 is not on the same subnet. Viewing the IP address information on both routers, the problem appears: Router A's secondary address is on the same subnet as Router B, but its primary address is not. EIGRP sources all hello packets from the primary IP address, but will match that address to any address configured on the receiving interface, primary or secondary.

Router A receives a hello from Router B with source address 10.1.3.2/24. It looks at the configuration on the receiving interfaces, sees that it has a secondary interface configured for that subnet, and adds Router B to the neighbor table. When Router B receives a hello from Router A, they are sourced from the primary address 10.1.2.1. Router B does not have an address configured for that subnet on the receiving interface and the hello is dropped. The error message is logged and no adjacency is formed. Router B will not send updates to Router A, even though the adjacency has formed at Router A. Reversing the secondary and primary addresses on Router A resolves this situation. Adding a secondary address to Router B that is on the same subnet as the primary IP address of Router A will also resolve this situation.

Summary

EIGRP is a distance-vector protocol that can be extremely easy to implement in small to medium networks, yet can be designed to manage large-scale complex internetworks with many of the same advantages of more complex link-state protocols. Its proprietary nature, belonging exclusively to Cisco, means that improvements can continuously flow without the impedance of standards bodies. What is the joke? A camel is a horse designed by committee.

The underlying complexity of the protocol needs very careful consideration, but also allows an administrator to trust that the network is stable and robust and easily recovers from many abusive situations. Implementing a diffused computation method of best-path selection and the Hello Protocol to eliminate the need for periodic updates allows EIGRP to be implemented in environments where bandwidth is at a premium and yet remain fully converged for long periods of time. The resulting loop-free topology and alternate-path redundancy greatly reduces the demand on an administrator's time.

As you have seen, EIGRP is by no means a small protocol. With the ability to support VLSM and hierarchical summary addressing, the efficiency of the protocol is limited more by the administrator's ability than by its own design. Planning your network growth and redundancy will pay heavy dividends in the long run.

FAQs

Visit www.syngress.com/solutions to have your questions about this chapter answered by the author.

Q: Is EIGRP as simple to implement as IGRP?

A: No. I have read that EIGRP is IGRP with an "E". This is absolutely not true. The underlying mechanisms of EIGRP are vastly different and must be considered when designing an EIGRP network. As stated earlier, the only similarity between the two protocols is their use of the composite metric. If EIGRP is implemented in the same manner in which IGRP would be used on the same network, many of the advantages of EIGRP are tossed out.

Q: Why is a diffused computation better than simple routing by rumor? Seems like a lot of extra work for the same result.

A: The result is not the same. While IGRP and EIGRP may select the same path, the guarantee of a loop-free topology created by a diffused computation outweighs the burden of understanding the complexity of the protocol. An IGRP process can never guarantee a loop-free topology; it can only attempt to prevent loops.

Q: If such things as stuck-in-active (SIA) routes are so difficult to troubleshoot, why not use another protocol?

A: In a well-designed and well-thought-out network, SIA events should not occur. If hierarchical summary addressing is implemented, query boundaries can be created that limit the propagation of diffused computations to only the routers that could possibly know another route. Congested, slow WAN links that are used to pass routing information will wreak even more havoc on protocols that are less efficient.

Q: Much of our legacy network is made up of non-Cisco equipment. Can I still use EIGRP?

A: EIGRP is Cisco proprietary and can only be implemented on Cisco gear. However, the answer to your question may be "yes." EIGRP can redistribute with any of the standard protocols such as OSPF and IS-IS. If it is your desire to move to an all-Cisco network using EIGRP, the migration can occur in phases, slowly isolating the legacy network. With the redistribution capabilities of EIGRP and the standard protocols, this can be done without segmenting the network.

Q: We still have older Novell servers and clients using bindery services. Does EIGRP integrate with IPX SAP?

A: EIGRP was designed to fully integrate with the IPX protocol stack. In fact, Cisco created a built-in reliability to IPX EIGRP that allows for the suppression of SAP updates, thereby conserving bandwidth on WAN links. EIGRP is every bit as suited to IPX as it is to IP.

Chapter 3

Introduction to Quality of Service

Solutions in this chapter:

- Defining Quality of Service
- Understanding Congestion Management
- Defining General Queuing Concepts
- Understanding Congestion Avoidance
- Introducing Policing and Traffic Shaping

Introduction

In this chapter, we will discuss the basic concepts behind Quality of Service (QoS), the need for it, and we will introduce you to several of the types of QoS mechanisms available. Quality of Service itself is not something that you configure on a Cisco router, rather it is an overall term that refers to a wide variety of mechanisms used to influence traffic patterns on a network.

Congestion Management is a collection of QoS mechanisms that will deal with network congestion as it occurs and will perform various actions on the traffic that is congesting the network. There are several congestion management mechanisms and each behaves differently. This chapter will introduce you to the overall concept of congestion management and some of the congestion management mechanisms that are available on Cisco routers.

Congestion avoidance is another classification within the larger umbrella of QoS mechanisms that focuses on preventing congestion, rather than dealing with it as it happens. This does not mean that congestion avoidance is any better or worse than congestion management, it is simply different. This chapter will discuss the theory behind congestion avoidance and present some possible scenarios where it may be preferable to use congestion avoidance, rather than congestion management.

Policing and Traffic Shaping are other groups of mechanisms that may help with network congestion and provide QoS to your network traffic. This chapter will introduce concepts and theories surrounding policing and shaping and will discuss where these may be preferable to other QoS mechanisms.

Defining Quality of Service

Quality of Service (QoS) is the term used to define the ability of a network to provide different levels of service assurances to the various forms of traffic. It enables network administrators to assign certain traffic priority over others or actual levels of quality with respect to network bandwidth or end-to-en delay. A typical network may have one or many of the following data link layer technologies for which can be QoS enabled:

- Frame Relay
- Ethernet
- Token Ring
- Point-to-Point Protocol (PPP)

- HDLC
- X.25
- ATM
- SONET

Each of these underlying technologies has different characteristics that need to be considered when implementing QoS. QoS can be implemented in congestion management or congestion avoidance situations. Congestion management techniques are used to manage and prioritize traffic in a network where applications request more bandwidth than the network is able to provide. By prioritizing certain classes of traffic, congestion management techniques enable business critical or delay sensitive applications to operate properly in a congested network environment. Conversely, collision avoidance techniques make use of the underlying technologies' mechanisms to try and avoid congestive situations.

Implementing QoS in a network can be a complicated undertaking for even the most seasoned network administrator. There are many different components of QoS, which this book will address on an individual basis to provide you with better understanding of each component. Enabling QoS on a network, when finished, will allow you as the network administrator, a very high level of flexibility to control the flow and actions of the traffic on the network.

What Is Quality of Service?

Quality of Service is simply a set of tools available to network administrators to enforce certain assurances that a minimum level of services will be provided to certain traffic. Many protocols and applications are not critically sensitive to network congestion. File Transfer Protocol (FTP), for example, has a rather large tolerance for network delay or bandwidth limitation. To the user, FTP simply takes longer to download a file to the target system. Although annoying to the user, this slowness does not normally impede the operation of the application. On the other hand, new applications such as Voice and Video are particularly sensitive to network delay. If voice packets take too long to reach their destination, the resulting speech sounds choppy or distorted. QoS can be used to provide assured services to these applications. Critical business applications can also make use of QoS. Companies whose main business focus relies on SNA-based network traffic can feel the pressures of network congestion. SNA is very sensitive to its handshake protocol and normally terminates a session when it does not receive an acknowledgement in time. Unlike TCP/IP, which recovers well from a bad handshake, SNA does not operate well in a congested environment. In these cases, prioritizing SNA traffic over all other protocols could be a proper approach to QoS.

Applications for Quality of Service

When would a network engineer consider designing quality of service into a network? Here are a few reasons to deploy QoS in a network topology:

- To give priority to certain mission critical applications in the network
- To maximize the use of the current network investment in infrastructure
- Better performance for delay sensitive applications such as Voice and Video
- To respond to changes in network traffic flows

The last bullet may seem like a trivial one. After all, traffic flow cannot dramatically change overnight can it? Naptser©. PointCast©. World-Wide-Web. These are all examples of "self-deployed" applications that cause network administrators nightmares. No one ever planned for Web browsing to take off the way it did, yet today, most of the traffic flowing through the Internet carries the prefix "http." In order to adapt to these changes in bandwidth requests, QoS can be used to ensure that users listening to radio stations over the Internet do not smother the network traffic vital to the company.

Often we find that the simplest method for achieving better performance on a network is to throw more bandwidth at the problem. In this day and age of Gigabit Ethernet and Optical Networking, higher capacities are readily available. More bandwidth does not, however, always guarantee a certain level of performance. It may well be that the very protocols that cause the congestion in the first place will simply eat up the additional bandwidth, leading to the same congestion issues experienced before the bandwidth upgrade. A more judicious approach is to analyze the traffic flowing through the bottleneck, determining the importance of each protocol and application, and determine a strategy to prioritize the access to the bandwidth. QoS allows the network administrator to have control over bandwidth, latency, and jitter, and minimize packet loss within the network by prioritizing various protocols. Bandwidth is the measure of capacity on the network or a specific link. Latency is the delay of a packet traversing the network and jitter is the change of latency over a given period of time. Deploying certain types of quality of service techniques can control these three parameters.

www.syngress.com

Currently within many corporate networks, QoS is not widely deployed. But with the push for applications such as multicast, streaming multimedia, and Voice over IP (VoIP) the need for certain quality levels is more inherent. Especially because these types of applications are susceptible to jitter and delay and poor performance is immediately noticed by the end-user. End-users experiencing poor performance typically generate trouble tickets and the network administrator is left troubleshooting the performance problem. A network administrator can proactively manage new sensitive applications by applying QoS techniques to the network. It is important to realize that QoS is not the magic solution to every congestion problem. It may very well be that upgrading the bandwidth of a congested link is the proper solution to the problem. However, by knowing the options available, you will be in a better position to make the proper decision to solve congestion issues.

Three Levels of QoS

QoS can be broken down into three different levels, also referred to as service models. These service models describe a set of end-to-end QoS capabilities. End-to-end QoS is the ability of the network to provide a specific level of service to network traffic from one end of the network to the other. The three service levels are best-effort service, integrated service, and differentiated service. We'll examine each service model in greater detail.

Best-Effort Service

Best-effort service, as its name implies, is when the network will make every possible attempt to deliver a packet to its destination. With best-effort service there are no guarantees that the packet will ever reach its intended destination. An application can send data in any amount, whenever it needs to, without requesting permission or notifying the network. Certain applications can thrive under this model. FTP and HTTP, for example, can support best-effort service without much hardship. This is, however, not an optimal service model for applications which are sensitive to network delays, bandwidth fluctuations, and other changing network conditions. Network telephony applications, for example, may require a more consistent amount of bandwidth in order to function properly. The results of best-effort service for these applications could result in failed telephone calls or interrupted speech during the call.

Integrated Service

The integrated service model provides applications with a guaranteed level of service by negotiating network parameters end-to-end. Applications request the level of service necessary for them to operate properly and rely on the QoS mechanism to reserve the necessary network resources prior to the application beginning its transmission. It is important to note that the application will not send the traffic until it receives a signal from the network stating that the network can handle the load and provide the requested QoS end-to-end.

To accomplish this, the network uses a process called admission control. Admission control is the mechanism that prevents the network from being overloaded. The network will not send a signal to the application to start transmitting the data if the requested QoS cannot be delivered. Once the application begins the transmission of data, the network resources reserved for the application are maintained end-to-end until the application is done or until the bandwidth reservation exceeds what is allowable for this application. The network will perform its tasks of maintaining the per-flow state, classification, policing, and intelligent queuing per packet to meet the required QoS.

Cisco IOS has two features to provide integrated service in the form of controlled load services. They are Resource Reservation Protocol (RSVP) and intelligent queuing. RSVP is currently in the process of being standardized by the Internet Engineering Task Force (IETF) in one of their working groups. Intelligent queuing includes technologies such as Weighted Fair Queuing (WFQ) and Weighted Random Early Detection (WRED).

RSVP is a Cisco proprietary protocol used to signal the network of the QoS requirements of an application. It is important to note that RSVP is not a routing protocol. RSVP works in conjunction with the routing protocols to determine the best path through the network that will provide the QoS required. RSVP enabled routers actually create dynamic access lists to provide the QoS requested and ensure that packets are delivered at the prescribed minimum quality parameters. RSVP will be covered in greater details later in this book.

Differentiated Service

The last model for QoS is the differentiated service model. Differentiated service includes a set of classification tools and queuing mechanisms to provide certain protocols or applications with a certain priority over other network traffic. Differentiated services rely on the edge routers to perform the classification of the different types of packets traversing a network. Network traffic can be classified by network address, protocols and ports, ingress interfaces or whatever classification that can be accomplished through the use of a standard or extended access list.

Understanding Congestion Management

Congestion management is a general term that encompasses different types of queuing strategies used to manage situations where the bandwidth demands of network applications exceed the total bandwidth that can be provided by the network. Congestion management does not control congestion before it occurs. It controls the injection of traffic into the network so that certain network flows have priority over others. In this section, the most basic of the congestion management queuing techniques will be discussed at a high level. A more detailed explanation will follow in later chapters in the book. We will examine the following congestion management techniques:

- First in First Out Queuing
- Priority Queuing
- Custom Queuing
- Weighted Fair Queuing (WFQ)

Many of these queuing strategies are applied in a situation where the traffic exiting an interface on the router exceeds the bandwidth on the egress port and needs to be prioritized. Priority and Custom Queuing require some basic planning and forethought by the network administration to implement and configure correctly on the router. The network administrator must have a good understanding of the traffic flows and how the traffic should be prioritized in order to engineer an efficient queuing strategy. Poorly planned prioritization can lead to situations worse that the congestive state itself. FIFO and WFQ, on the other hand, require very little configuration in order to work properly. In the Cisco IOS, WFQ is enabled by default on links of E1 speed (2.048 Mbps) or slower. Conversely, FIFO is enabled by default on links faster than E1 speeds. We will cover these default behaviors in greater details later in this chapter.

Queuing on Interfaces

Router interfaces can only be configured with one type of queuing. If a second queuing technique is applied to the interface, the router will either replace the old queuing process with the newly configured one, or report an error message informing the network administrator that a certain queuing process is in operation and needs to be removed before a new one can be applied. The following shows an error reported when custom queuing is applied over priority queuing:

```
Christy#
Christy#conf t
Enter configuration commands, one per line.  End with CNTL/Z.
Christy(config)#interface serial 0/0
Christy(config-if)#priority-group 1
Christy(config-if)#
Christy(config-if)#custom-queue-list 1
Must remove priority-group configuration first.
Christy(config-if)#end
Christy#
```

Defining General Queuing Concepts

Before we begin discussing different forms of queuing and QoS strategies, it is important to understand the basics of the queuing process itself. In this section, we will discuss the concepts of packet queues and the key concepts of leaky bucket and tail drops.

Queues exist within a router in order to hold packets until there are enough resources to forward the packets out the egress port. If there is no congestion in the router, the packets will be forwarded immediately. A network queue can be compared to a waiting line at a carnival attraction. If no one is waiting for the ride, people just walk through the line without waiting. This represents the state of a queue when the network is not experiencing congestion. When a busload of people arrives to try the new roller coaster, there may not me enough seats to handle everyone on the first ride. People then wait in line in the order they arrived in until it is their turn to ride the coaster. Network queues are used to handle traffic bursts arriving faster than the egress interface can handle. For example, a router connecting an FastEthernet LAN interface to a T1 WAN circuit will often see chunks of traffic arriving on the LAN interface faster than it can send it out to the WAN. In this case, the queue places the traffic in a waiting line so that the T1 circuit can process the packets at its own pace. Speed mismatches and queues filling up do not necessarily indicate an unacceptable congestion situation. It is a normal network operation necessary to handle traffic going in and out of an interface.

Leaky Bucket

The leaky bucket is a key concept in understanding queuing theory. A network queue can be compared to a bucket into which network packets are poured. The bucket has a hole at the bottom that lets packets drip out at a constant rate. In a network environment, the drip rate would be the speed of the interface serviced by that queue or bucket. If packets drop in the bucket faster than the hole can let them drip out, the bucket slowly fills up. If too many packets drop in the bucket, the bucket may eventually overflow. Those packets are lost since they do not drip out of the bucket. Figure 3.1 depicts the leaky bucket analogy.

Figure 3.1 The Leaky Bucket Analogy

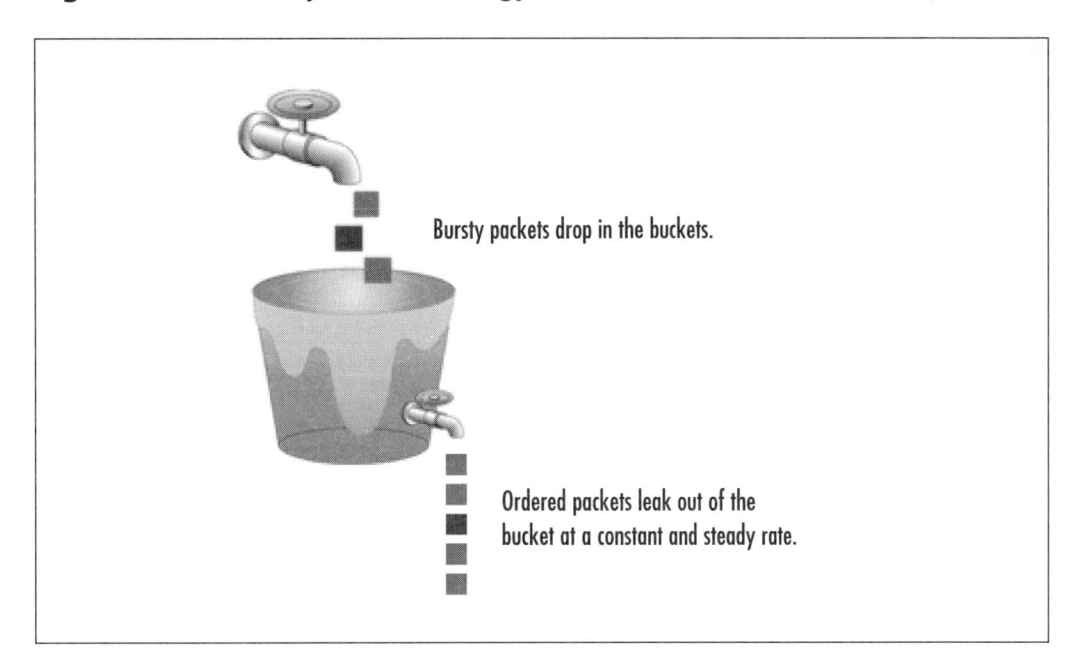

This mechanism is well suited to handle network traffic that is too large in nature. If packets drop in the bucket in bunches, the bucket simply fills up and slowly leaks out at its constant rate. This way, it doesn't really matter how fast the packets drop in the bucket, as long as the bucket itself can still contain them. This analogy is used when describing network queues. Packets enter a queue at any given rate, but exit the queue at a constant rate, which cannot exceed the speed of the egress interface.

Tail Drop

What happens when the bucket fills up? It spills over, of course. When dealing with network queues, these buckets are allocated a certain amount of the router's memory. This means that these queues are not infinite. They can only hold a pre-determined amount of information. Network administrators can normally configure the queue sizes if necessary, but the Cisco Internetwork Operating System (IOS) normally allows for pretty balanced default queue size values. When a queue fills up, packets are placed in the queue in the order that they were received. When the amount of packets that enter the queue exceed the queue's capacity to hold them, the bucket spills over. In queuing terminology, the queue experiences a tail drop. These tail drops represent packets that never entered the queue. They are instead simply discarded by the router. Upper layer protocols use their acknowledgement and retransmission process to detect these dropped packets and retransmits them. Tail drops are not a direct indication that there is something wrong with the network. For example, it is normal for a 100 Mbps FastEthernet interface to send too much information too fast to a 1.544 Mbps T1 interface. These dropped packets often are used by upper layer protocols to throttle down the rate at which they send information to the router. Some QoS mechanisms such as Random Early Detection (RED) and Weighted Random Early Detection (WRED) make use of these principles to control the level of congestion on the network.

Tail drops can obviously impact user response. Dropped packets mean requests for retransmissions. With more and more applications riding on the TCP/IP protocol, tail drops can also introduce another phenomenon known as *global synchronization*. Global synchronization comes from the interaction of an upper layer mechanism of TCP/IP called the *sliding window*. Simply put, the transmission window of a single TPC/IP communication represents the number of packets that the sender can transmit in each transmission block. If the block is successfully sent without errors, the window size "slides" upwards, allowing the sender to transmit more packets per interval. If an error occurs in the transmission, the window size slides down to a lower value and starts creeping up again. When many TCP/IP conversations occur simultaneously, each conversation increases its window size as packets are successfully transmitted. Eventually, these conversations use up all the available bandwidth, which causes the interface's queue to drop packets. These dropped packets are interpreted as transmission errors for all of the conversations, which simultaneously reduces their window sizes to send fewer packets per interval. This global synchronization causes the fluctuating network usage that can be seen in Figure 3.2.

Figure 3.2 Global Synchronization

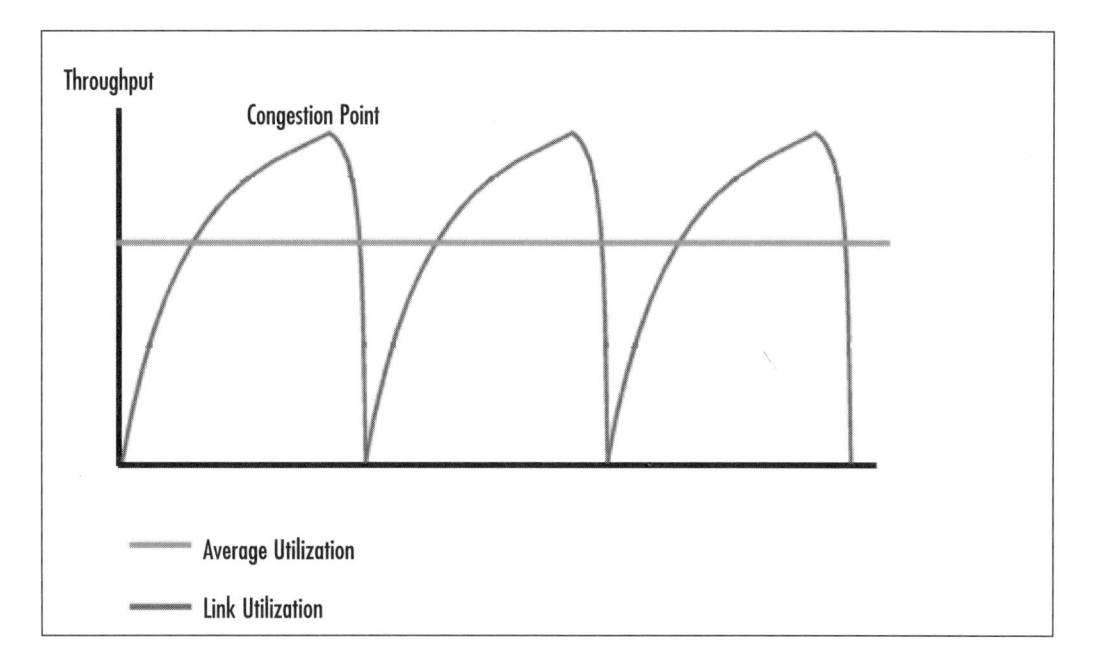

We can clearly see that the average utilization of the link over time is much less than the total available bandwidth. Later in this book, we will cover congestion avoidance methods which use the sliding window characteristics of TCP/IP to maximize the average throughput of a link by attempting to keep the link out of a congestive state.

Token Bucket

The token bucket is another mechanism used in QoS. It represents a pool of resources that can be used by a service whenever it needs it. Unlike the leaky bucket, the token bucket does not let anything drip from the bottom. What goes in the bucket must come out from the top. As time passes, tokens are added to the bucket by the network. When an application needs to send something out to the network, it must remove the amount of tokens equal to the amount of data it needs to transmit. If there are not enough tokens in the bucket, the application must wait until the network adds more tokens to the bucket. If the application does not make use of its tokens, the token bucket may eventually spill over. The spilled tokens are then lost and the application cannot make use of them. This means that each token bucket has a clearly defined maximum token capacity. Token buckets are used in traffic shaping and other applications where traffic occurs in bursts. The token bucket permits bursts by letting the application remove a large number of token from its bucket to send information, but limits the size of these bursts by only allowing a certain number of tokens in the bucket.

First In First Out Queuing

First in first out (FIFO) queuing is the simplest type. FIFO queuing simply states that the first packet entering the interface will be the first packet to exit the interface. No special packet classification is made. The mechanism is comprised on one single leaky bucket which handles all the traffic for the egress interface. Figure 3.3 shows FIFO queuing in action.

Figure 3.3 FIFO Queuing

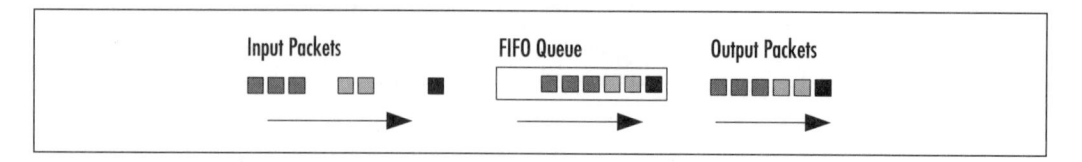

The main purpose of a FIFO queue is to handle inbound packets to an interface, place them in the queue in the order that they were received, and feed them out to the egress interface at a constant rate that the interface can handle. If the rate at which the packets enter the queue is slower than the rate at which the queue services them, FIFO queuing becomes a mechanism that is transparent to the packets flowing through the interface. The packets simply flow through the queue as if it wasn't there, similarly to an empty waiting line at a carnival ride.

FIFO Queuing

FIFO is the default queuing mechanism for all interfaces operating at speeds faster than E1 speed (2.048 Mbps). Interfaces at E1 speed or slower default to Weighted Fair Queuing (WFQ) in versions 11.2 and later. WFQ is not available in IOS prior to version 11.2. The following code output shows FIFO queuing in operation on a serial interface:

```
Christy#show interfaces serial 0/0
Serial0/0 is up, line protocol is up
  Hardware is PowerQUICC Serial
  Internet address is 192.168.10.1/24
  MTU 1500 bytes, BW 4096 Kbit, DLY 20000 usec,
     reliability 255/255, txload 1/255, rxload 1/255
  Encapsulation HDLC, loopback not set
  Keepalive set (10 sec)
  Last input 00:00:00, output 00:00:00, output hang never
  Last clearing of "show interface" counters never
  Queueing strategy: fifo
  Output queue 0/40, 0 drops; input queue 0/75, 0 drops
  5 minute input rate 0 bits/sec, 0 packets/sec
  5 minute output rate 0 bits/sec, 0 packets/sec
     144320 packets input, 8763937 bytes, 0 no buffer
     Received 141128 broadcasts, 0 runts, 0 giants, 0 throttles
     4 input errors, 0 CRC, 4 frame, 0 overrun, 0 ignored, 0
     abort
     144390 packets output, 8931257 bytes, 0 underruns
     0 output errors, 0 collisions, 13 interface resets
     0 output buffer failures, 0 output buffers swapped out
     4 carrier transitions
     DCD=up  DSR=up  DTR=up  RTS=up  CTS=up

Christy#
```

Fair Queuing

Fair queuing is another form of congestion management. Fair queuing, generally referred to as Weighted Fair Queuing (WFQ), is the default queuing strategy for slow speed interfaces. WFQ is an automated method providing fair bandwidth allocation to all network traffic. WFQ sorts network traffic into flows that make up a conversation on a network by using a combination of parameters. For example, individual TCP/IP conversations are identified using the following parameters:

- IP Protocol
- Source IP address
- Destination IP address
- Source port
- Destination port
- Type of Service (ToS) field

Other protocols or technologies use parameters that are appropriate to their characteristics. Chapter 6 will cover the characteristics of each protocol in greater details. By tracking the various flows, the router can determine which flows are bandwidth intensive, such as FTP, and others, which are more, delay sensitive, such as Telnet. The router then prioritizes those flows and ensures that the high-volume flows are pushed to the back of the queue and the low-volume delay sensitive flows are given priority over other conversations. There are 256 queues available by default when WFQ is enabled.

So why is this called *Weighted* Fair Queuing? So far we haven't seen anything which assigns priority to certain conversations other than the bandwidth requirement. The weighted factor of WFQ comes into play when packets have different levels of IP precedence. There are eight levels of precedence with the higher value providing the greater priority. There are as follows:

- Network control precedence (7)
- Internet control precedence (6)
- Critical precedence (5)
- Flash-override precedence (4)
- Flash precedence (3)

- Immediate precedence (2)
- Priority precedence (1)
- Routine precedence (0)

Weighted Fair Queuing

When designing a network with WFQ, some limitations and considerations must be respected. Here are some of the characteristics of WFQ to keep in mind prior to deploying it in a production network:

- SNA and DLSw+ traffic cannot be broken into separate flows due to the way the TCP/IP sessions are established within the flows. Because the conversations share a single TCP/IP session, there appears to be a single flow even if multiple conversations exist within that flow.
- It is not recommended to use WFQ for SNA sessions using DLSw+ IP encapsulation as well as APPN.
- Also, WFQ does not always scale well for heavy increases in traffic and is not available on high speed interfaces such as ATM.
- WFQ is not supported with tunneling or encryption.

When the IP Precedence bits in the ToS byte are in play, WFQ adjusts by processing more packets from the queues of higher precedence flows than those with a lower precedence. More packets are let out of their leaky bucket. The sequence in which the queues are serviced by WFQ remains the same, but the amount of information processed from each queue now depends on the weight of that queue.

The weight factor is inversely proportional to the precedence of the packet. Therefore, WFQ conversations with lower weights will be provided with better service than flows with higher weights.

Priority Queuing

Priority Queuing (PQ) is a powerful and strict form of congestion management. PQ allows the network administrator to define up to four queues for network traffic. These queues are the High, Medium, Normal, and Low priority queues. The router processes the queues strictly based on their priority. If there are packets in the high priority queue, this queue will be processed until it is empty, independently of the state of the other queues. Once the high priority queue is empty, the router moves to the medium queue and dispatches a single packet. Immediately the router checks the high queue to ensure it is still empty. If it is, it will go to the medium queue, then the normal, then the low. All three, high, medium, and normal, must be completely empty before a single packet is dispatched out of the low queue. Every time a packet is dispatched the router checks the high queue. Figure 3.4 shows PQ in operation.

Figure 3.4 Priority Queuing

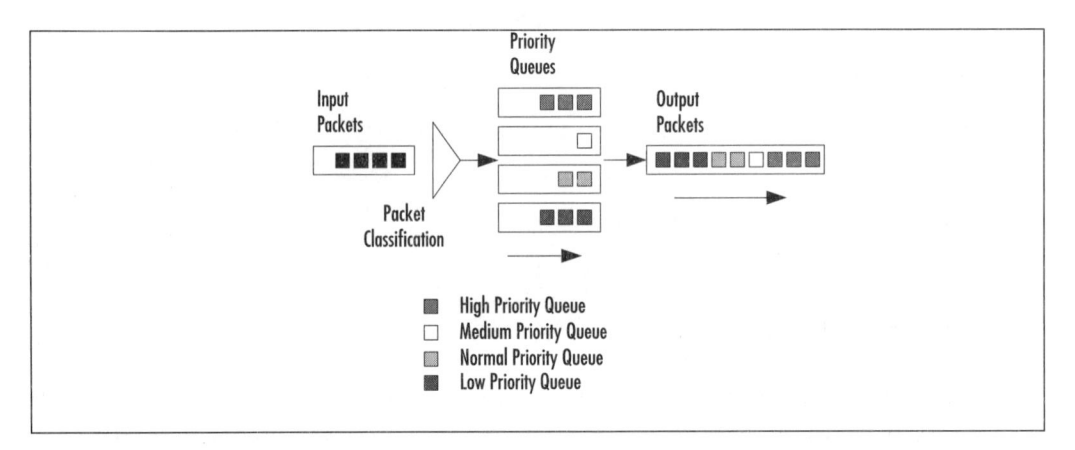

Priority queuing gives network administrators tremendous control over network traffic. However, it also gives the network administrator enough power to deny low priority traffic the chance to be transmitted at all. When a lower priority queue's traffic is not serviced because there is too much traffic in higher priority queues, a condition called *queue starvation* is said to have happened. Queue starvation is a serious pitfall of Priority Queuing, and the ability to completely starve lower priority traffic is something that you should carefully consider before designing your Priority Queuing strategy. Typically, PQ is used when delay-sensitive applications encounter problems on the network. A good example is IBM mainframe traffic, Systems Network Architecture (SNA). PQ can be an excellent tool to provide protocols such as Serial Tunneling (STUN), Data Link

Switching (DLSW), or Remote Source Route Bridging (RSRB) with the network resources they require to operate successfully. Particular care must be given to the traffic prioritization plan. If, for example, a network administrator configures http traffic as having high priority in a network where Web traffic is extensive, it is very likely that all other protocols will never get serviced since there would always have Web traffic in the high priority queue. All other queues would fill up and drop packets when they reach capacity. It is, therefore, important to understand the priority queuing mechanism and to engineer a proper prioritization plan before implementing it. PQ can classify network traffic using the characteristics shown below. Packets that are not classified by PQ are automatically placed in the Normal priority queue.

- Protocol type (IP, Appletalk, IPX, etc.)
- Packet size in bytes
- TCP or UDP Port Number for TCP/IP traffic
- Interface on which the packet arrived
- Whether or not the packet is an IP fragment
- Anything that can be described in a standard or extended access list

In priority queuing, the default queue is the normal queue; however, it can be moved to any queue. Additionally, the system queue is in fact higher than the high queue. We cannot use it, but it is there.

Custom Queuing

To overcome the rigidity of Priority Queuing (PQ), a network administrator can choose to implement Custom Queuing (CQ) instead. CQ allows the network administrator to prioritize traffic without the side effects of starving lower priority queues as seen in PQ. With CQ, the network administrator can create up to 16 queues to categorize traffic. Each of the queues is emptied in a round-robin fashion. Where the prioritization comes into play with CQ is in the amount of data that is serviced out of each queue during a cycle. The default about of data processed by CQ is 1500 bytes per cycle. However, CQ cannot fragment packets to enforce its byte count limitation. This means that if CQ processes a 1000 byte packet, leaving 500 available bytes, a 1500 byte packet following the first one will be entirely processed out of the queue, for a total of 2500 bytes being processed. This is an important factor to be remembered when engineering a CQ plan. It is also important to note that, while queue starvation in its true form is not possible with Custom Queuing, it is still possible to set the per cycle amount on some queue so high that other queues will not get the bandwidth that they need in a timely manner. When this happens, the applications with data in those smaller queues may time out. While this is not true queue starvation, the effects are similar in the sense that the application will be unable to function properly. Figure 3.5 shows CQ in operation.

Figure 3.5 Custom Queuing

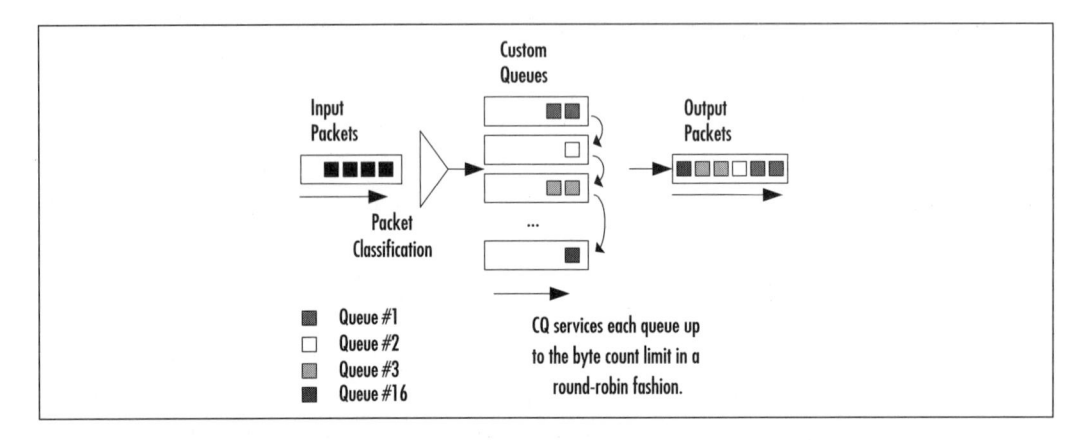

Custom queuing uses the same mechanisms as priority queuing to classify network packets. One of the CQ queues can be configured as a default queue in order to handle traffic that is not specifically identified by the classification process. If no default queue is defined, IOS will use queue #1 as the default queue. The classification process assigns the traffic to one of the 16 configurable queues acting as independent leaky buckets. There is also a queue 0, the system queue, which is reserved for network maintenance packets (routing protocol hellos, etc.). This system queue is serviced before all other queues. It is important to note that Cisco permits use of queue 0, but does not recommend it. If the byte count of the queues is left to their default values, the allocation of bandwidth remains evenly distributed among all of the queues. Note that by adjusting the byte count values of individual queues, network administrators can give certain protocols or applications preferential service, without the threat of queue starvation that is seen in priority queuing. This does not mean that tail drop does not occur. The depth of each queue can be too low to handle the amount of traffic assigned to that queue. This would cause the leaky bucket to spill some of the inbound packets. Conversely, if another queue is assigned a byte count value excessively high, CQ may spend a lot of time servicing that queue, during which time other queues may overflow from accumulating packets while waiting to be serviced. A good balance between byte count, queue depth, and traffic classification is required for the successful operation of custom queuing. Chapters 6 and 7 will cover congestion management techniques in greater detail. These techniques are used in situations where congestion is inevitable and certain traffic must be given a greater priority over other applications. The following section will cover techniques used to try and avoid the congestive state altogether. If congestion can be avoided, congestion management may not be necessary.

Understanding Congestion Avoidance

The queuing mechanisms described so far in this chapter do not solve the congestion problem. They merely put rules in place in order for more important or more sensitive traffic to be given a certain priority over other traffic. The circuit itself remains in a congestive state. Congestion avoidance techniques, on the other hand, make use of the way protocols operate to try and avoid the congestive state altogether. Random Early Detection (RED) and Weighted Random Early Detection (WRED) are some of the methods used for this purpose.

As discussed earlier in this chapter, TCP conversations are subject to a process called *global synchronization*, whereby multiple TCP flows are dropped within a router due to congestion and then start up again simultaneously. This leads to a cycle of throughput increase followed by a throttle back by all conversations when the congestion point is reached. As we saw in Figure 3.2, this leads to a suboptimal use of the link's bandwidth. Congestion avoidance techniques attempt to eliminate this global synchronization by dropping packets from TCP conversations at random as the link approaches the congestive state. By dropping packets from a conversation, RED forces that conversation to reduce the size of its transmission window and therefore throttle back the amount of information sent. By applying this principle randomly at scattered intervals, RED can maximize link utilization by keeping the link out of the congestive state. As the link approaches saturation, RED may increase the rate at which it drops packets. The allocation of these drops is still done randomly. *Weighted* Random Early Detection, on the other hand, uses a calculated weight to make selective packet dropping decisions. Once again, IP precedence is used to calculate a packet's weight. This allows network administrators to impact the WRED algorithm to provide preferential service to certain applications.

RED and WRED functions are performed by the router's CPU. Some high-end router platforms such as Cisco's 7100, 7200, and 7500 series routers offer interface modules which incorporate the smarts required to offload some of the tasks from the main CPU. These Virtual Interface Processor (VIP) cards can be configured to perform many functions normally assigned to the router's main processing engine. WRED is one of the functions that can be performed by the VIP card. When the VIP card performs WRED functions, the process is called *Distributed* Weighted RED (DWRED). This provides relief for the main processor and enables it to dedicate its resources to other tasks.

Congestion Avoidance in Action

In a network controlled by RED or WRED, the congestion avoidance mechanism starts discarding packets randomly as the link approaches a pre-configured threshold value. As conversations throttle back their transmission rates, the overall bandwidth usage of the link can be kept near an optimal value. This results in a better utilization of network resources and increased total throughput over time. Figure 3.6 shows the results of congestion avoidance compared to the global synchronization process shown earlier in Figure 3.2.

Figure 3.6 Congestion Management in Action

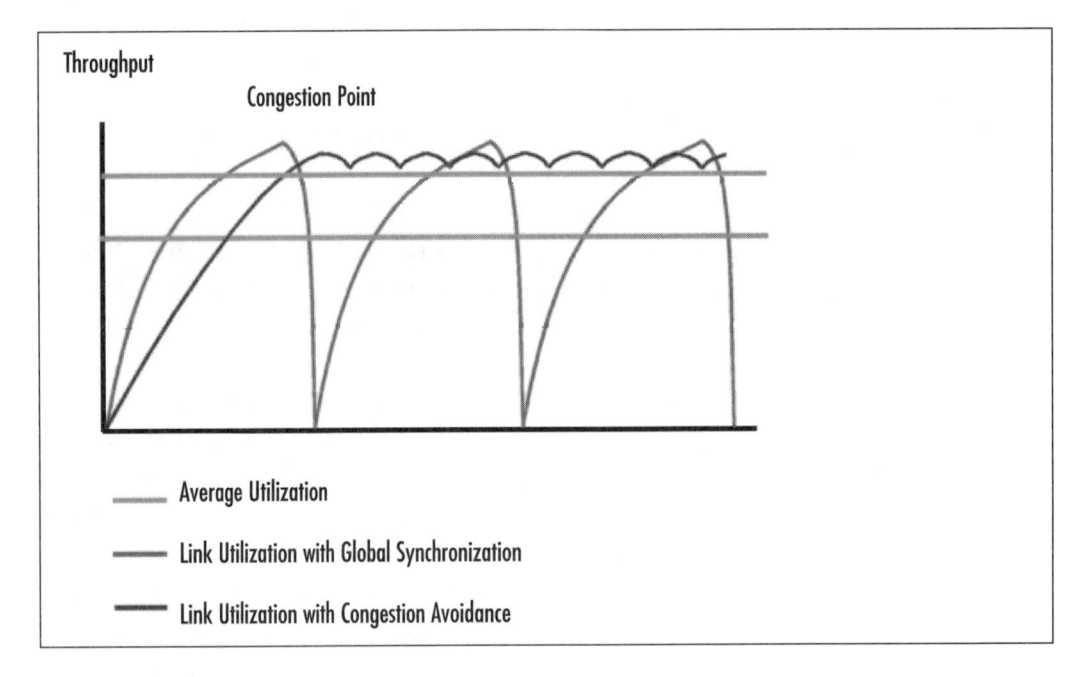

Pros and Cons of Congestion Avoidance

Congestion avoidance techniques such as RED and WRED may seem like the magic solution to everything. Why use congestion management techniques at all if we can avoid congestion altogether? Well, there are advantages and disadvantages to using congestion avoidance techniques. Here are some of them:

Advantages

- It prevents congestion from happening in some environments.
- It maximizes the utilization of a link.
- It can provide a level of priority through packet precedence.

Disadvantages

- It only works with TCP-based conversations. Other protocols such as IPX do not use the concept of a sliding window. When faced with a packet discard, these protocols simply retransmit at the same rate as before. RED and WRED are inefficient in a network mostly based on non-TCP protocols.
- It cannot be used in conjunction with congestion management techniques. The egress interface on which congestion avoidance is configured cannot handle a congestion management mechanism at the same time.
- Packets are dropped, not simply queued.

Introducing Policing and Traffic Shaping

So far we have seen the tools to manage specific traffic in a congestive state or try to avoid congestion altogether in TCP-based environments. Other mechanisms are available to network administrators that enforce a set of rules to adapt the outgoing traffic of an interface to the specific rate that interface can carry. Congestion management or congestion avoidance techniques do not operate differently whether they control a 1.544 Mbps T1 link or a 45 Mbps T3. They simply apply their regular algorithm as usual. Policing and shaping techniques are available to make use of what we know about the circuits to try and make sure that the network does not become congested. Imagine, for example, a frame relay WAN circuit going from New York to London UK. The New York router connects to a T1 access circuit (1.544 Mbps) while the London access circuit connects to the European E1 standard (2.048). The maximum throughput of this link is 1.544 Mbps, the speed of the New York interface. Congestion avoidance techniques on the London router would not prevent congestion since the London router, 1.544 Mbps out of 2.048 Mbps is not a congestive state. Since congestion management operates on traffic leaving an interface, not entering it, they are inefficient in these conditions. Policing and shaping techniques overcome this limitation. Both use the token bucket principle explained earlier in this chapter to regulate the amount of information that can be sent over the link. The principle difference between the two techniques is as follows:

- **Policing Techniques** Policing techniques make use of the token bucket to strictly limit the transmission to a predetermined rate. Conversations that exceed the capacity of their token bucket see their traffic being dropped by the policing agent or have their ToS field rewritten to a lesser precedence. Cisco's Committed Access Rate (CAR) performs this type of function.

- **Shaping Techniques** Shaping techniques are a little more diplomatic in the way that they operate. Instead of strictly discarding traffic that exceeds a certain predetermined rate, shaping techniques delay exceeding traffic through buffering or queuing in order to "shape" it into a rate that the remote interface can handle. This means that shaping techniques take into account additional parameters such as burst sizes to calculate a debt value for a conversation. The conversation can basically "borrow" tokens from the bank when its token bucket is empty.

Traffic Shaping

Traffic shaping (TS) splits into two different variants. Generic Traffic Shaping (GTS) and Frame Relay Traffic Shaping (FRTS). Both techniques operate under the same principles, but their implementation and interaction with other congestion control processes are different. Traffic shaping is an excellent tool in situations where outbound traffic must respect a certain maximum transmission rate. This is done independently of the actual total bandwidth of the circuit. This is especially useful in frame relay circuits where the access rates of the source and target circuits are different. An access circuit may have a rate of 1.544 Mbps, but it may be necessary to enforce a 256k average rate in order to match the access rate of the remote target circuit that has a 256k access rate. It is also possible to apply traffic shaping to large circuits like a 45 Mbps T3 circuit and create multiple T1 rate traffic flows through traffic shaping. We could, therefore, traffic shape the rate of Web traffic to a T1 equivalent speed, FTP traffic to a rate of 2 x T1, and the rest of the traffic to consume the remainder of the T3 bandwidth. TS can use access lists to classify traffic flows and can apply traffic shaping policies to each flow. By using these classified groups and applying traffic shaping restrictions, network managers can manage the flow of traffic leaving an interface and make sure that it respects the capabilities of the network. The design and implementation of traffic shaping will be covered in greater detail later in Chapter 8 of this book.

Generic Traffic Shaping

Generic traffic shaping uses the token bucket process to limit the amount of traffic that can leave the egress interface. It can be applied on a per-interface basis and make use of extended access lists to further classify network traffic into different traffic shaping policies. On frame relay subinterfaces, GTS can be configured to respond to Backward Explicit Congestion Notification (BECN) signals coming from the frame relay network to adjust its maximum transfer rate. This way, GTS can traffic shape network traffic to the rate that the frame relay network itself is capable of supporting. As we mentioned before, traffic shaping can operate in conjunction with a congestion management technique. GTS is only compatible with WFQ. Once GTS has performed its network classification and shaped the traffic through the token bucket process, GTS sends the traffic to WFQ to be queued out of the interface.

Frame Relay Traffic Shaping

Frame relay traffic shaping uses the same mechanisms as GTS to shape traffic on the network. FRTS, however, can perform traffic shaping functions for each frame relay Data Link Channel Identifier (DLCI). In frame relay design, a single interface can carry multiple DLCIs. GTS can only be applied at the interface or subinterface level. In this case, GTS would not be able to discriminate between the multiple DLCIs carried by a single interface. This limitation is overcome by using FRTS. Like GTS, FRTS works in conjunction with a queuing mechanism. FRTS can work in conjunction with FIFO, custom queuing, or priority queuing. FRTS is not compatible with WFQ. As for the selected rate, FRTS can be configured to use a specifically configured rate or to follow the circuit's Committed Information Rate (CIR) for each virtual circuit.

Summary

In this chapter, we have introduced some basic Quality of Service techniques available to network administrators that provide certain guarantees of service to the applications which flow through the network. We have seen how Random Early Detection and Weighted Random Early Detection are Congestion Avoidance techniques used to try and avoid the congestive state altogether. It is important to remember that these techniques only work on TCP-based traffic.

When congestion is inevitable, congestion management techniques such as Weighted Fair Queuing, Priority Queuing, and Custom Queuing can be used to prioritize the traffic through the bottleneck. Remember that the crucial part of deploying these techniques is to design a solid and comprehensive prioritization plan. We have seen how poor planning can actually lead to a degradation of network services worse than the bottleneck situation itself. Finally, we have discussed Policing and Traffic Shaping techniques such as Committed Access Rate, Generic Traffic Shaping, and Frame Relay Traffic Shaping. These tools are used to mold network traffic into a stream that meets the transmission characteristics of the circuit itself. The operation and configuration of all of these techniques will be covered in greater details in later chapters.

FAQs

Visit www.syngress.com/solutions to have your questions about this chapter answered by the author.

Q: Why would I want to use QoS?

A: QoS is designed to allow network administrators to define the different types of traffic on their network and prioritize them accordingly. This is especially beneficial for networks running delay sensitive data.

Q: Will QoS hurt my network?

A: Queuing technologies such as Custom Queuing and Priority Queuing CAN make a network behave in unexpected ways. Always use caution when implementing QoS.

Q: What queuing mechanism should I use?

A: The queuing method used will vary from network to network and will depend on the applications in use.

Q: Do I have to use QoS?

A: No, you do not have to use QoS on your network. However, with the introduction of new-world applications such as streaming Video and Voice over IP, your network may require QoS to operate properly. Of course, WFQ is a QoS mechanism that is probably in use on most of your lower speed interfaces already.

Chapter 4

Traffic Classification Overview

Solutions in this chapter:

- Introducing Type of Services (ToS)
- Explaining Integrated Services
- Defining the Parameters of QoS
- Introducing the Resource Reservation Protocol (RSVP)
- Introducing Differentiated Services
- Expanding QoS: Cisco Content Networking

Introduction

Sometimes, in a network, there is the need to classify traffic. The reasons for classifying traffic vary from network to network but can range from marking packets with a "flag" to make them relatively more or less important than other packets on the network to identifying which packets to drop. This chapter will introduce you to several different theories of traffic classification and will discuss the mechanics of how these "flags" are set on a packet.

There are several different ways in which these flags are set, and the levels of classification depend on which method is used. Pay particular attention to the ideas covered in this chapter because the marking of packets will be a recurring theme throughout this book since many QoS mechanisms use these markings to classify traffic and perform QoS on the packets that have them.

Classification may be viewed as infusing data packets with a directive intelligence in regard to network devices. The use of prioritization schemes such as Random Early Detection (RED) and Adaptive Bit Rate (ABR) force the router to analyze data streams and congestion characteristics and then apply congestion controls to the data streams. These applications may involve the utilization of the TCP sliding window or back-off algorithms, the utilization of leaky or token bucket queuing mechanisms, or a number of other strategies. The use of traffic classification flags within the packet removes decision functionality from the router and establishes what service levels are required for the packet's particular traffic flow. The router then attempts to provide the packet with the requested quality of service.

This chapter will examine in detail the original IP standard for classifying service levels, the Type of Service (ToS) bit, the current replacement standard, the Diffserv Code Point (DSCP), the use of integrated reservation services such as RSVP, and finally delve into integrated application aware networks using Cisco Network Based Application Recognition (NBAR). This chapter will not deal with configurations or product types, rather it will deal with a general understanding of the theories and issues surrounding these differing QoS architectures.

Introducing Type of Services (ToS)

The ToS bit was implemented within the original IP design group as an 8-bit field composed of a 3-bit IP precedence value and a 4-bit service provided indicator. The desired function of this field was to modify per-hop queuing and forwarding behaviors based on the field bit settings. In this manner, packets with differing ToS settings could be managed with differing service levels within a network. This may seem to be an extremely useful functionality, but due to a number of issues, the ToS has not been widely used. The main reason being it can be traced to the definition ambiguity of the ToS field in RFC791 with the ensuing difficulty of constructing consistent control mechanisms. However, the ToS field does provide the key foundation for the beginning of packet service classification schemes. Figure 4.1 illustrates the location, general breakdown, and arrangement of the ToS field within the original IP header packet standard.

Figure 4.1 IP Header ToS Field Location

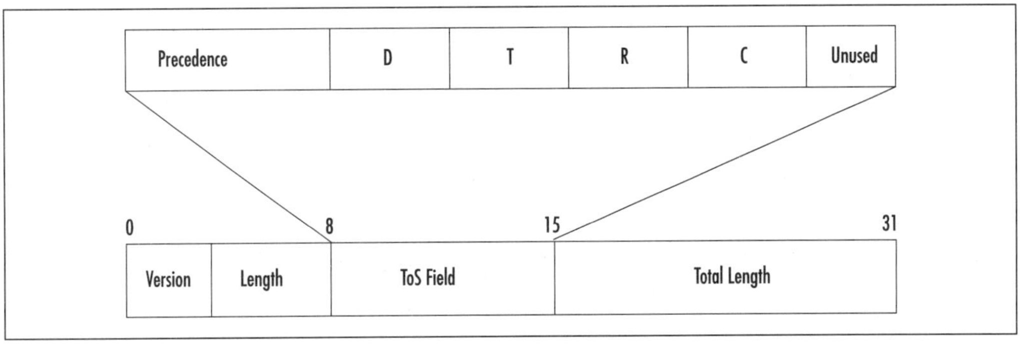

| Precedence | D | T | R | C | Unused |

| Version | Length | ToS Field | Total Length |

0   8   15   31

RFC791

RFC791 defines the ToS bit objective as:
"The Type of Service provides an indication of the abstract parameters of the quality of service desired. These parameters are to be used to guide the selection of the actual service parameters when transmitting a datagram through a particular network. Several networks offer service precedence, which somehow treats high precedence traffic as more important than other traffic."

To achieve what is defined in this rather ambiguous statement the ToS field is defined by RFC791 as being composed of two specific sub fields, the Service Profile and the Precedence Field.

ToS Service Profile

The Service Profile Field represents bits 3, 4, and 5 of the ToS field. Table 4.1 illustrates the bit meanings of the Service Profile bit. This field was intended to provide a generalized set of parameters which characterize the service choices provided in the networks that make up the Internet.

Table 4.1 Service Profile Bit Parameters, RFC791

0	1	2	3	4	5	6	7
Precedence			D	T	R	O	O

Bit 3: 0 = Normal Delay,   1 = Low Delay.
Bit 4: 0 = Normal Throughput, 1 = High Throughput.
Bit 5: 0 = Normal Reliability, 1 = High Reliability

The issues that prevented the adoption of the service profile as a usable means of providing QoS are related to the definitions provided by RFC791. No definition is provided for reliability, delay, or throughput. RFC791 acknowledges such a case by stating that the use of delay, throughput, or reliability indications may increase the cost of the service. The RFC states that no more than two of these bits should be used except in highly unusual cases. The need for network designers and router architects to arbitrarily interpret these values led to a significant failure to adopt this field as a defining feature of network data streams.

The original specification for this field was to be modified and refined by RFC1349. RFC1349 modified the service field by expanding it to 4 bits instead of the 3, specified in RFC791. This allowed the retention of the 3 levels matching the single bit selectors of RFC791, but also allowed for a 4th value of minimizing monetary cost. The exact meanings and bit configurations are illustrated in Table 4.2.

If the total number of bits is considered it can be noted that there do exist 16 possible values for this field, however, only the 4 shown in Table 4.3 are defined. The 5th value of 0 0 0 0 is considered normal best effort service and as such is not considered a service profile. The RFC stated that any selection of a service profile was to be considered a form of premium service that may involve queuing or path optimization. However, the exact relation of these mechanisms was undefined. As such this ambiguity has prevented almost any form of adoption of the service profile bits as a form of differentiating service for the last 20 years.

Table 4.2 Service Profile Bit Parameters and Bit String Meanings, RFC1349

0	1	2	3	4	5	6	7
Precedence			X	X	X	X	0

Service Field Bit Configurations
1000 — Minimize Delay
0100 — Maximize Throughput
0010 — Maximize Reliability
Service Field Bits
0001 — Minimize Monetary Cost
0000 — Normal Service

Defining the Seven Levels of IP Precedence

RFC791 defined the first 3 bits of the ToS field to be what is known as the precedence subfield. The primary purpose of the precedence subfield is to indicate to the router the level of packet drop preference for queuing delay avoidance. The precedence bit was intended to provide a fairly detailed level of packet service differentiation as shown in Table 4.3.

Table 4.3 Precedence Bit Parameters, RFC791

0	1	2	3	4	5	6	7
Precedence Bits			D	T	R	0	0

Precedence Bit Setting Definitions
111 — Network Control
110 — Internetwork Control
101 — CRITIC/ECP
100 — Flash Override
011 — Flash
010 — Immediate
001 — Priority
000 — Routine

The 3 bits are intended to be the service level selector indicator requirement. The packet can be provisioned with characteristics that minimize delay, maximize throughput, or maximize reliability. However, as with the service profile field, no attempt was made to define what is meant by each of these terms. A generalized rule of thumb can be stated that a packet with higher priority should be routed before one with a lower prioritized setting. In the case of the routine 000 precedence setting, this was to correspond to normal best effort delivery service that is the standard for IP networks. 111 was for critical network control messages.

As with the service profile setting, the use of the original precedence subfield settings has never been significantly deployed in the networking world. These settings may have significance in a local environment, but should not be used to assign required service levels outside of that local network.

The precedence subfield was redefined significantly for inclusion in the integrated and differentiated services working groups to control and provide QoS within those settings. We will be discussing the changes in this field with respect to those architectures later in this chapter.

Explaining Integrated Services

The nature of IP is that of a best-effort delivery protocol with any error correction and re-broadcast requests handled by higher-level protocols over primarily low speed links (less than T1/E1 speeds). This structure may be adequate for primarily character based or data transition applications, but is inadequate for time and delay sensitive applications such as Voice and Video that are now becoming mission critical to the networking world. Integrated Services (Intserv) is one of the primary attempts to bring QoS to IP networks. The Intserv architecture as defined in RFC1633 and the Internet Engineering Task Force (IETF) 1994b is an attempt to create a set of extensions to extend IP's best-effort delivery system to provide the QoS that is required by Voice and other delay sensitive applications.

Before we discuss Intserv in detail, two points that are frequently stated must be addressed, they are the assumption that Intserv is complex and that Intserv does not scale well. Intserv will seem very familiar to people that are used to Asynchronous Transfer Mode (ATM). In fact, Intserv attempts to provide the same QoS services at layer 3 that ATM provides at layer 2. ATM may seem complex if a person is only familiar the Ethernet or the minimal configuration that Frame-Relay requires.

With regards to scalability, Intserv scales in the same manner as ATM. This is not surprising if one considers the mechanics of Intserv. Using a reservation system, flows of traffic are established between endpoints. These flows are given reservations that obtain a guaranteed data rate and delay rate. This is analogous to the negotiation of Virtual Circuits that occurs in ATM or circuit switched architectures. As such, the link must have sufficient bandwidth available to accommodate all of the required flows and the routers or switches must have sufficient resources to enforce the reservations. Again, to data professionals that are used to working with low speed links such as Frame-Relay, X25, ISDN, or any sub full T1/E1 links, this can pose a significant issue. Intserv was architecture to be used only on high speed (faster that T1/E1) links and should not be used on slower links. In terms of processing, routers and switches that are required to process higher speed links (such as multiple T1s or T3s) should have sufficient resources to handle Intserv.

The Integrated services model was designed to overcome the basic design issues that can prevent timely data delivery, such as those that are found on the Internet. The key being that the Internet is a best-effort architecture with no inherent guarantee of service or delivery. While this allows for considerable economies within the Internet, it does not meet the needs of real-time applications such as Voice, Video Conferencing, and Virtual reality applications. With Intserv the aim is to use a reservation system (to be discussed later in this chapter) to assure that sufficient network resources exist within the best-effort structure of the Internet.

The basics can be thought of as very host centric. The end host is responsible for setting the network service requirements and the intervening network can either accept those requirements along the entire path or reject the request, but it cannot negotiate with the host. A prime example of this would be a Voice over IP call. The reservation protocol from the end host may request a dedicated data flow of 16k with an allowable delay of 100ms. The network can either accept or reject this requirement based on existing network conditions, but cannot negotiate any variance from these requirements. (This is very similar to the VC concept in circuit switched or ATM networks.) This commitment from the network continues until one of the parties terminates the call. The key concept to remember with Intserv is that Intserv is concerned first and foremost with per-packet delay or time of delivery. Bandwidth is of less concern than is delay. This is not to say the Intserv does not guarantee bandwidth, it does provide a minimum bandwidth as required by the data flow. Rather the architecture of Intserv is predicated to provide for a jitter free (and hence minimally delay specific) service level for data flows such as voice and video. In other words Intserv was designed to service low bandwidth, low latency requirement applications.

The basic Intserv architecture can be defined as having five key points:

- QoS or control parameters to set the level of service
- Admission requirements
- Classification

- Scheduling
- RSVP

Defining the Parameters of QoS

Intserv defines data flow into two primarily kinds: tolerant and intolerant applications. Tolerant applications can handle delays in packet sequence, variable length delays, or other network events that may interrupt a smooth, constant flow of data. FTP, Telnet, and HTTP traffic are classic examples of what may be considered tolerant traffic. Such traffic is assigned to what is considered the controlled load service class. This class is consistent with better than normal delivery functioning of IP networks. Intolerant applications and data flows require a precise sequence of packets delivered in a prescribed and predictable manner with a fixed delay interval. Examples of such intolerant applications are interactive media, Voice and Video. Such applications are afforded a guaranteed level of service with a defined data pipe and an upper guaranteed bound on end-to-end delay.

For guaranteed service classes it is of prime importance that the resources of each node be known during the initial setup of the data flow. Full details of this process are available in the IETF1997G draft. We will only cover the basic parameters to provide a general idea of the Intserv QoS functioning.

- **AVAILABLE_PATH_BANDWIDTH** This is a locally significant variable that provides information about the available bandwidth available to the data flow. This value can range from 1 byte per second to up to the theoretical maximum bandwidth available on a fiber strand, currently in the neighborhood of 40 terabytes a second.

- **MINIMUM_PATH_LATENCY** This is a locally significant value that represents the latency associated with the current node. This value is critically important in real-time applications such as voice and video that require a 200ms or less round trip latency for acceptable quality. Knowing the upper and lower limits of this value allow the receiving node to properly adjust its QoS reservation requirements and buffer requirements to yield acceptable service.

- **NON_IS_HOP** This is also known as a break bit. It provides information about any node on the data flow that does not provide QoS services. The presence of such nodes can have a severe impact on the functioning of Intserv end-to-end. It must be stated that a number of manufacturers of extreme performance or terabit routers do not include any form of QoS in their devices. The reasoning is that the processing required by QoS causes unnecessary delays in packet processing. Such devices are primarily found in long haul backbone connections and are becoming more prevalent with the advent of 10 Gb and higher DWDM connections.

- **NUMBER_OF_IS_HOPS** This is simply a counter that represents the number of Intserv aware hops that a packet takes. This value is limited for all practical purposes by the IP packet hop count.

- **PATH_MTU** This value informs the end point of the maximum packet size that can transverse the internetwork. QoS mechanisms require this value to establish the strict packet delay guarantees that are integral to Intserv functionality.

- **TOKEN_BUCKET_TSPEC** The token bucket spec describes the exact traffic parameters using a simple token bucket filter. While queuing mechanisms may use what is known as a leaky bucket, Intserv relies on the more exact controls that are found in the Token Bucket approach. Essentially in a Token Bucket methodology each packet can only proceed through the internetwork if it is allowed by an accompanying token from the Token Bucket. The token bucket spec is composed several values including:

    - **Token Rate** This is measured in IP data grams per second.
    - **Toke Bucket Depth** In effect, a queue depth.
    - **Peak Available Data Rate** This is measured in IP data grams per second.
    - **Minimum Policed Unit** This is measured in bytes and allows an estimate of the minimum per-packet resources found in a data flow.
    - **Maximum Packet Size** This is a measure that determines the maximum packet size that will be subject to QoS services.

Admission Requirements

Intserv deals with administering QoS on a per flow basis because each flow must share the available resources on a network. Some form of admission control or resource sharing criteria must be established to determine which data flows get access to the network. The initial step is to determine which flows are to be delivered as standard IP best-effort and which are to be delivered as dedicated Intserv flows with a corresponding QoS requirement. Priority queuing mechanisms can be used to segregate the Intserv traffic from the normal best-effort traffic. It is assumed that there exists enough resources in the data link to service the best effort flow, but in low speed highly utilized links this may not be the case. From this determination and allocation to a priority usage queue acceptance of a flow reservation request can be confirmed. In short, the admission requirements determine if the data flow can be admitted without disrupting the current data streams in progress.

Resource Reservation Requirements

Intserv delivers quality of service via a reservation process that allocates a fixed bandwidth and delay condition to a data flow. This reservation is performed using the Resource Reservation Protocol (RSVP). RSVP will be discussed in detail in a following section, but what must be noted here is that RSVP is the ONLY protocol currently available to make QoS reservations on an end-to-end flow basis for IP based traffic.

Packet Classification

Each packet must be mapped to a corresponding data flow and the accompanying class of service, the packet classifier then sets each class to be acted upon as an individual data flow subject to the negotiated QoS for that flow.

Packet Scheduling

To ensure correct sequential delivery of packets in a minimally disruptive fashion proper queuing mechanisms must be enacted. The simplest way to consider the packet scheduler is to view it as a form of high-level queuing mechanism that takes advantage of the token bucket model. This assumes the role of traffic policing because it determines not just the queuing requirements, but rather if a data flow can be admitted to the link at all. This admission is above and beyond what is enacted by the admission requirements.

Introducing Resource Reservation Protocol (RSVP)

RSVP is of prime importance to Intserv, and in effect, any IP QoS model, as it is the only currently available means to reserve network resources for a data stream end-to-end. RSVP is defined in IETF1997F as a logical separation between QoS control services and the signaling protocol. This allows RSVP to be used by a number of differing QoS mechanisms in addition to Intserv. RSVP is simply the signaling mechanism by which QoS-aware devices configure required parameters. In this sense, RSVP is analogous to many other IP based control protocols such as the Internet Group Management Protocol (ICMP) or many other routing protocols.

RSVP Traffic Types

RSVP is provisioned for three differing traffic types: best effort, rate sensitive, and delay sensitive. Best effort is simply the familiar normal IP connectionless traffic class. No attempt is made to guarantee delivery of the traffic and all error and flow controls are left to upper level protocols. This is referred to as best-effort service.

Rate sensitive traffic is traffic that requires a guarantee of a constant data flow pipe size such as 100K or 200K. In return for having such a guaranteed pipe, the application is willing to accept queuing delays or timeliness in delivery. The service class that supports this is known as guaranteed bit-rate service.

Delay sensitive traffic is traffic that is highly susceptible to jitter or queuing delays and may have a variable data stream size. Voice and streaming Video are prime examples of such traffic. RSVP defines two types of service in this area: controlled delay service (for non-real-time applications) and predicative service for real-time applications such as Video teleconferencing or Voice communications.

RSVP Operation

The key requirement to remember with RSVP is that the RECIEVER is the node that requests the specified QoS resources, not the sender. The procedure of RSVP is that the sender sends a Path message downstream to the receiver node. This path message collects information on the QoS capabilities and parameters of each node in the traffic path. Each intermediate node maintains the path characterization for the senders flow in the senders Tspec parameter. The receiver then processes the request in conjunction with the QoS abilities of the intermediate nodes and then sends a calculated Reservation Request (Resv) back upstream to the sender along the same hop path. This return message specifies the desired QoS parameters that are to be assigned to that data flow by each node. Only after the sender receives the successful Resv message from the intended receiver does a data flow commence.

RSVP Messages

RSVP messages are special raw IP data grams that use protocol number 46. Within RSVP there exist 7 distinct messages that may be classified as 4 general types of informational exchanges.

Reservation-Request Messages

The Reservation Request Message is sent by each receiver host to the sending node. This message is responsible for setting up the appropriate QoS parameters along the reverse hop path. The Resv message contains information that defines the reservation style, the filter spec that identifies the sender, and the flow spec object. Combined these are referred to as the flow descriptor. The flow spec is used to set a node's packet classifier process and the filter spec is used to control the packet classifier. Resv messages are sent periodically to maintain a reservation state along the path of a data flow. Unlike a switched circuit, the data flow is what is known as a soft state circuit and may be altered during the period of communication.

The flow spec parameter differs depending upon the type of reservation that is being requested. If only a controlled load service is being requested, the flow spec will only contain a receiver Tspec. However, if guaranteed service is requested, the flow spec contains both the Tspec and Rspec elements.

Path Messages

The path message contains three informational elements: the sender template, the sender Tspec, and the Adspec.

The sender's template contains information that defines the type of data traffic that the sender will be sending. This template is composed of a filter specification that uniquely identifies the sender's data flow from others. The sender Tspec defines the properties of the data flow that the sender expects to generate. Neither of these parameters are modified by intermediate nodes in the flow but rather serve as unique identifiers.

The adspec contains unique, node significant, information that is passed to each individual nodes control processes. Each node bases its QoS and packet handling characteristics on the Adspec and updates this field with relevant control information to be passed on to upstream nodes as required. The adspec also carries flag bits that are used to determine if the non-Intserv or non-RSVP node is in the data plow path. If such a bit is set, then all further information in the adspec is considered unreliable and best-effort class delivery may result.

Error and Confirmation Messages

Three error and confirmation message types exist: path error messages (Patherr), reservation request error message (Resverr), and reservation request acknowledgment messages (Resvconf).

Patherr and Reserr messages are simply sent upstream to the sender that created the error, but they do not modify the path state in any of the nodes that they pass through. Patherr messages indicate an error in the processing of path statements and are sent back to the data sender. Reserr messages indicate an error in the processing of reservation messages and are sent to the receivers. (Remember that in RSVP it is the receiver only that can set up a RSVP data flow.)

Error messages that can be included are:

- Admission failure
- Ambiguous path
- Bandwidth unavailable
- Bad flow specification
- Service not supported

Confirmation messages can be sent by each node in a data flow path if a RSVP reservation from the receiving node is received that contains an optional reservation confirmation object.

Teardown Messages

Teardown messages are used to remove the reservation state and path from all RSVP enabled nodes in a data flow path without waiting for a timeout. The teardown can be initiated by either the sender or receiving node or by an intervening transit node if it has reached a timeout state. There are two types of teardown messages supported by RSVP: path teardown and reservation request teardown. The path teardown deletes the path state and all associated reservation states in the data flow path. It effectively marks the termination of that individual data flow and releases the network resources. Reservation request teardown messages delete the QoS reservation state but maintain the fixed path flow. These are used primarily if the type of communication between end points qualitatively changes and requires differing QoS parameters.

RSVP Scaling

On of the key issues of Inserv and RSVP is scaling, or increasing the number of data flows. Each data flow must be assigned a fixed amount of bandwidth and processor resources at each router along the data flow path. If a core router is required to service a large number of data flows processor or buffer capability could rapidly become exhausted resulting in a severe degradation of service. If the routers processor and memory resources are consumed with attending to RSVP/Inserv flows then there will be a severe drop in service of any and all remaining traffic.

Along with the router resource requirements of RSVP there are also significant bandwidth constraints to be considered. Both Intserv and RSVP were not designed for use on low speed links. Currently significant amount of data traffic is carried over fractional T1 frame relay or ISDN connections. The provisioning of even a single or a few multiples of streams of voice or video traffic (at either 128K or 16 to64K of bandwidth) can have a severe impact on performance. Consider this classic case, a company with 50 branch offices has a full T1 line back to its corporate headquarters. They decide to provision Voice over their IP network with a codex that allows for 16K voice streams. Their network, which was running fine with normal Web traffic and mainframe TN3270 traffic, comes to a screeching halt due to the RSVP. With a T1 line they can only accommodate about 96 streams of voice with no room left for anything else on the circuit. Intserv with RSVP, because of the fact that it requires dedicated bandwidth, has more in common with the provisioning of voice telecommunications than with the shared queue access of data. Performance and scale analysis is of prime importance if you wish to deploy RSVP and Intserv in your network to avoid network saturation.

Intserv and RSVP Scaling

RSVP is the protocol used to set up Voice over IP telephony calls. To address the scaling issue, let's take a typical example from an enterprise that is deploying IP telephony. In a closet they have a standard Cisco 6509 switch with 48 port powered line cards. There are 7 of these cards in the unit for a total of 336 ports. Let's assume that each of those ports

Continued

> has an IP phone attached, and we want 50 percent of these people to be on the phone at the same time. If we want near toll quality voice, we give them a 16k codec. This means that for all of the reserved data flows by RSVP, we would have committed a total of 2688K of bandwidth. This is not much on a 100base or 1000 base LAN. But is almost 100 percent of the capacity of two full external T1 circuits. If we had only 2 T1 circuits going outside to the adjacent location, and all of these people were making calls, no further data traffic could flow along that link until some of the Voice call data flows were terminated. This is the important issue to remember with Intserv and RSVP. We are not sharing the bandwidth and using queuing to dole it out while everyone slows down. We are locking down a data pipe so no one else can use it. Be very careful that you do a capacity analysis before implementing Intserv or RSVP. If you do implement RSVP or Intserv, keep a close watch on your buffer drops and processor utilization. A high utilization and/or significant increase in buffer overflows are indications that your routers do not have the capacity to support your requirements, and you should either examine another QoS method, or look for increasing your hardware.

Introducing Differentiated Service (DiffServ)

When the Integrated Services Model with RSVP was completed in 1997, many Internet service providers voiced issues with implementing this model due to its complexity and inability to run effectively over lower speed links. It was determined that, due to the nature of the Internet and provider/enterprise interconnections, it made bad business sense and was overly expensive to implement a design that would only allow for limited flow service to ensure QoS. What was needed was a simpler differentiation of traffic that could be handled by queuing mechanisms without the dedicated bandwidth and associated limitations on use at lower connection speeds.

The basics of DiffServ are fairly simple. A fairly coarse number of service classes are defined within Diffserv and individual data flows are grouped together within each individual service class and treated identically. Each service class is entitled to certain queuing and priority mechanisms within the entire network. Marking, classifying, and admittance to a Diffserv network occur only at the network edge or points of ingress. Interior routers are only concerned with Per Hop Behaviors (PHB) as marked in the packet header. This architecture allows Diffserv to perform far better on low bandwidth links and provide for a greater capacity than would a corresponding Intserv architecture.

This is not to say that Diffserv can only be marked at network ingress points. From a network efficiency standpoint it should only be marked at the ingress points with your core set up as high speed switching only. Note that Diffserv values can be marked at any point within a network. Also, the Diffserv meanings can be re-written and different meanings can be assigned at any point within the internetwork. This will impact the efficiency of the network and as such must be carefully considered.

The DiffServ Code Point (DSCP)

DiffServ uses, as its packet marker, Differentiated Services Code Point or DSCP. Originally defined in RFC2474 and RFC2475, the DSCP is found within the Differentiated Services (DS) field, which is a replacement for the ToS field of RFC791. The DS field is based on reclaiming the seldom-used ToS field that has existed since the inception of IP packets. The 8-bit ToS field is repartitioned into a 6-bit DSCP field and a 2-bit unused portion that may have future use as a congestion notification field. The DS field is incompatible with the older ToS field. This is not to say that an IP precedence aware router will not use the DSCP field. The structure in terms of bits is identical for both IP precedence and DSCP. However, the meanings of the bit structures varies. An IP precedence aware router will interpret the first 3 bits based on IP precedence definitions. The meaning inferred as to how the packets are to handled may be considerably different to what is intended by DSCP definitions. Table 4.4 illustrates the DSCP field structure. Compare this to the ToS field structure and you will see the physical similarities.

Table 4.4 Differentiated Code Point

0	1	2	3	4	5	6	7
DSCP						CU	

DSCP: differentiated services code point
CU: currently unused

The DSCP field maps to a provisioned Per Hop Behavior (PHB) that is not necessarily one to one or consistent across service providers or networks. Remember that the DS field should only be marked at the ingress point of a network, by the network ingress device for best performance. However, it may be marked, as needed, anywhere within the network with a corresponding efficiency penalty.

This is significantly different from both the old ToS field and from the Intserv model in which the end host marked the packet. This marker was carried unaltered throughout the network. In Diffserv, the DS field may be remarked every time a packet crosses a network boundary to represent the current settings of that service provider or network. No fixed meanings are attributed to the DS field. Interpretation and application are reserved for the network administrator or service provider to determine based on negotiated service level agreements (SLA) with the customers or other criteria.

Per Hop Behavior (PHB)

The key aspect of the DSCP is that it maps to PHBs as provisioned by the Network Administrator. RFC2744 defines four suggested code points and their recommended corresponding behaviors. The Diffserv specification does attempt to maintain some of the semantics of the old ToS field and, as such, specifies that a packet header that contains the bit structure of xxx000 is to be defined as a reserved dscp value.

The default PHB corresponds to a value of 000000 and states that the packet shall receive the traditional best-effort based delivery with no special characteristics or behaviors. This is the default packet behavior. This PHB is defined in RFC2474

The Class Selector Code Points utilize the old ToS field and as such are defined as being up to 8 values of corresponding PHBs. There is no defined value to these code points; however, in a general statement, RFC2474 states that packets with a higher class selector code point and PHB must be treated in a priority manner over ones with a lower value. It also states that every network that makes use of this field must map at least two distinct classes of PHBs. These values are only locally significant within the particular network.

The Express Forwarding PHB is the highest level of service possible in a Diffserv network. It utilizes RSVP to assure low loss, low jitter, and guaranteed bandwidth priority connections through a Diffserv enabled network (RFC2598). This traffic is defined as having minimal, if any, queuing delays throughout the network. Note that this is analogous to a data flow (or micro flow in Diffserv) in the Intserv architecture and care must be taken to provide sufficient resources for this class. Extreme importance is assigned to admission controls for this class of service. Even a priority queue will give poor service if it is allowed to become saturated. Essentially this level of service emulates a dedicated circuit within a

Diffserv network. In terms of traffic that would utilize such a conduit, Voice data traffic would be one of the prime data types. However, scaling issues with this again occur as they did in Intserv.

Assured forwarding (AF) PHB is the most common usage of the Diffserv architecture. Within this PHB are 4 AF groups (called class 1,2,3, and 4 by Cisco) that are further divided into three Olympics groups, gold, silver, and bronze, to represent differing packet drop allowances. Table 4.5 illustrates the bit structure and corresponding precedence and class values.

RFC2597 states that each packet will be delivered in each service class as long as the traffic conforms to a specific traffic profile. Any excess traffic will be accepted by the network, but will have a higher probability of being dropped based on its service class and group. The Diffserv specification does not lay out drop rates but states that class 4 is preferentially treated to class 3 and that within each AF, each class gets preferential treatment over other classes. The individual values are left to the network administrator to assign as desired based on their existing service level agreements and network requirements.

Table 4.5 Assured Forwarding Bit Drop Precedence Values

	Class 1	Class 2	Class 3	Class 4
Low Drop Precedence	001010	010010	011010	100010
Medium Drop Precedence	001100	010100	011100	100100
High Drop Precedence	001110	0101110	011110	100110

To support the assured forwarding functionality, each node in a Diffserv network must implement some form of bandwidth allocation to each AF class and some form of priority queuing mechanism to allow for policing of this categorization. Cisco IOS would use one of several queuing mechanisms such as Weighted Random Early Detection (WRED), weighted round robin, priority queuing, or one of several other available methods that are supported by the Cisco IOS.

Diffserv Functionality

For traffic to flow in a Diffserv enabled network, several steps must sequentially occur. First, the edge device classifies the traffic. In this process, the individual data flows are marked according to their precedence in a manner predetermined by the network administrator. This classification can be either on the value present in the DSCP value if available, or a more general set of conditions including, but not limited to, IP address, port numbers, destination address, or even the ingress port. Once traffic has been classified within the Diffserv service provider definitions, it is then passed to an admission filter that shapes or conditions the traffic to meet existing network traffic streams and behavioral aggregates. This includes measuring each stream against relative token bucket burst rates and buffer capacities to determine if ingress will be allowed or if packets should be differentially dropped or delayed. If the packet is admitted into the Diffserv network, its DSCP field is either written or rewritten (if it already existed) and passed as an aggregate stream through the network. The DSCP field then triggers a pre-configured PHB at each node along the Diffserv network.

Best Practice Network Design

Integrated services, by their functioning definition, require that the end nodes in a data flow mark the packets with the required QoS characteristics. The internetwork then provides the required data flow up to the limit of available resources. In the Diffserv architecture, differentiated services, by design, mark and classify packets only at the network ingress points. The core network then simply imposes the Per Hop Behaviors as defined by the service provider in response to information contained within the DSCP. This form of architecture is at the core of network design and implementation of Diffserv, and it is what is responsible for the scalability of this architecture. The core of network consists of a large number of high-speed connections and data flows. Speeds of T3, OC3, and higher are common for node interconnects. For every data flow that must be monitored by a node, significant resources are allocated. The amount of resources required to control data flows at core backbone speeds would require significant investments and configurations and impose undue switching latency. The Cisco design model of Core, Distribution, and Access stipulates that the core network should be non-blocking with minimal or no impediments to data flow and solely devoted to high speed switching of data. If a node in the core must make decisions based on ingress and queuing characteristics such a model is compromised. The best architectures classify traffic at the ingress edges of the network. That way each router has to only deal with a small volume of manageable traffic. This allows for maximum response, utilization, and minimal latency from all network components concerned. As the number of data streams decreases, the amount of classification and queuing is less at the edge which means that delay and jitter are minimized, thus the chances of exhausting resources is reduced and over all costs are lowered as less expensive hardware can be utilized.

Classification Falls Short

Both Integrated services and differentiated services fall short of the current requirements for high quality of service delivery over varied conditions in today's networks. An integrated service model has each end node request a reserved set of network resources for its exclusive use. While this is required for jitter and delay sensitive applications, this precludes use for all protocols and places a significant load on network resources, especially on core network nodes. Differentiated services, while resolving a number of the resource issues, fail to address the basic differentiation of service levels that is required by today's multiservice networks. Traditional queuing and differentiation methods rely on gross categories such as start or destination address, protocols, fixed application port numbers, or initiating ports as classification markers. This has been adequate when data was the sole network traffic. When TN3270 or telnet traffic, HTTP, or otherwise fixed port traffic was concerned, with applications being run locally, no further classification was needed. However, the current network traffic has changed considerably. Client server traffic can have applications that communicate over variable port numbers. Critical applications are being served remotely from an application service provider or via a thin client procedure, streaming voice and video are contending at the same time. Customers are requesting service level agreements that specify not only traffic from a specific address, but also that traffic for specific applications is delivered with priority. Classification schemes that rely on fixed addresses, protocols, or port definitions are inadequate to serve the needs of the current network environment.

To meet these demands networks are becoming application aware and differentiating with service levels between not just data streams but the individual applications that compose those very streams. In other words, networks are becoming aware not only of the data streams but also of the content of those streams and how that content must be serviced.

ATM: The Original QoS

Much of what we have and will be discussing concerns the IP world. If you want to start the equivalent to a severely heated discussion about QoS, just talk to a person that works with ATM. They will almost always

Continued

state that only ATM can provide true QoS and any other form of communication, be it Ethernet, frame relay, X25, or long haul gigabit Ethernet is simply a Class of Service (CoS) but not a true QUALITY of service.

In a sense this is correct. The ATM forum is what defined QoS and the differentiated levels that are required for fixed quality levels. They also defined QoS equivalencies and functionalities. ATM was designed to provide circuit level guarantees of service at higher speeds and with easier implementation. As such, quality of service was deemed to be based on circuit switched technology that creates a dedicated end-to-end circuit for each data stream. Until the recently, introduction of long haul gigabit Ethernet and 10Gb Ethernet using dense wave division multiplexing (DWDM) ATM, was the only option to reaching speeds of 155Mb (OC3) or faster on long haul WAN links. ATM defines 4 QoS classes.

- **QoS Class1** Also called Service Class A. This has the same characteristics as a dedicated end-t- end digital private line.
- **QoS Class 2** Also called service Class B. This provides performance acceptable for packetized video and audio in teleconferencing or multimedia applications.
- **QoS Class 3** Also called Service Class 3. This provides acceptable performance for connection-oriented protocols such as frame relay that may be mapped to ATM.
- **QoS Class 4** Also called Service Class 4. This is the equivalent of the best-effort delivery of IP with no guarantees of delivery or available bandwidth.

ATM engineers may argue that any attempt to impose QoS on IP is an attempt to create a stable guaranteed environment on an inherently unstable best-effort delivery system of IP. In a sense, this is correct. Any form of layer 3 QoS will never match the rich level of controls available within a layer 2 protocol such as ATM. By use of a fixed 53-bit cell length, ATM avoids long packet queuing delays that can occur in IP based networks. As such, jitter is kept to a bare minimum in an ATM network. The fundamental issue is that ATM can and does emulate a circuit based environment. Virtual circuits are constructed and torn down for the length of a data transition. While with upper layer protocol's packet loss is expected to occur to indicate traffic congestion issues, such indicators are excess baggage to an ATM based network. In fact, the mapping of significant QoS parameters in IP based traffic that is being tunneled over an ATM backbone can seriously affect the 53-bit cell pay-

Continued

> load capacity. The best question for QoS in ATM is one of design. If the network is properly dimensioned to handle burst loads, QoS will be inherent within an ATM network with no further IP controls being needed. Thus, as ATM has an inherent QoS, we must address the role of capacity engineering. Give a big enough pipe for the expected streams and your data will be jitter free and prioritized. This is very similar to what was said of Intserv.

Expanding QoS: Cisco Content Networking

In response to the new network requirements posed by the rapidly changing and unifying network service requirements, Cisco has expanded their network service and QoS offerings to include Content Networking classification and differentiation. Cisco Content Networking is an intelligent networking architecture that uses active classification and identification of complex and critical application streams and applying defined QoS parameters to these streams to ensure timely and economical delivery of the requested services. This architecture is composed of three key components:

- The ability to use intelligent network classification and network services utilizing IOS software features.
- Intelligent network devices that integrate applications with network services.
- Intelligent policy management for configuration, accounting, and monitoring.

Networks have become increasingly complex and are carrying more and more data types. In the past, it was sufficient to allow priority to or from a particular address or for a particular protocol, but this is no longer sufficient. The ubiquity of IP and client server applications has rendered such a model sorely inadequate. A single user using IP may at the same time be sending Voice over IP, be obtaining an application served by an application service provider, be running a thin client session while getting their email and surfing the Web, all from a single IP address using a single protocol. Clearly each of these tasks does not have the same importance. Voice requires a premium service to be of acceptable near toll quality, the client may be paying for the application served by the ASP and, as such, wants the greatest return on their investment, while Web traffic may not be productive at all. Content Networking, by looking at the application level inside the data stream allows us to differentiate the application requirements and assign appropriate levels of service for each. Classification has developed from a fairly coarse network based differentiation to a fine application layer classification and service.

Application Aware Classification: Cisco NBAR

A key to content enabled networks is the ability to classify traffic based on more detailed information than static port numbers or addresses. Cisco addresses this requirement by the development of a new classification engine called Network Based Application Recognition or NBAR. NBAR is a new classification engine that looks within a packet and performs a stateful analysis of the information contained within the packet. While NBAR can classify static port protocols, its usefulness is far greater in recognizing applications that use dynamically assigned port numbers, detailed classification of HTTP traffic, and classification of Citrix ICA traffic by published applications. Before we proceed, it must be noted that there are two significant issues with NBAR classification. First, NBAR only functions with IP traffic; therefore, if you have any SNA or legacy traffic other classification and queuing schemes must be used. The second issue is that NBAR will only function with traffic that can be switched via Cisco Express forwarding (CEF).

HTTP Classification

NBAR can classify HTTP traffic not just on address or port number but can classify on any detailed information within the URL up to a depth of 400 bytes. The code is actually written such that NBAR will look at a total of 512 bytes; however, once you deduct the L2 Header, L3 Header, L4 Header, and HTTP Header, 400 bytes is a safe estimate of how much URL you can actually match on. HTTP subport classification is really the only subport classficiation mechanism with NBAR today that is pushing the potential to go this deep into the packet.

NBAR can classify all HTTP traffic by the mime type, or get request destination packets. The limitations of NBAR with regards to Web traffic are that there can be no more than 24 concurrent URL host or mime type matches classified by NBAR. Pipeline persistent HTTP requests cannot be classified nor can any classification by url/host or mime type if the traffic is protected by secure HTTP.

> **Using NBAR and Policing to Protect Scarce Bandwidth**
>
> Normally we would not think of a classification tool as a form of security. In fact, security is probably a bad term, bandwidth abuse might be a better one. The ability of NBAR to look up to 400 bytes into a URL header and the ability to classify on mime types can make NBAR a powerful tool to prevent network abuse. High utilization of network capacity can occur in a number of cases, but very few are as deleterious as large .mp3 files or .mov and .mpeg files being transferred between users. We could filter on the Napster protocol, but that would not prevent users from simply trading these files on your local private LAN or expensive WAN circuits directly. It is rare to have firewalls on private WAN circuits to act as controls for such traffic. This is exactly where NBAR's application classification can come in handy. We can filter on recognized mime types to classify any traffic that may involve mp3's or other form of unauthorized multimedia files. Once these packets are classified they can then be assigned to a very low priority queue or provisioned to be dropped altogether. In this manner, we prevent these recreational uses of our network from being propagated past our router boundaries.

Citrix Classification

With the advent of thin client services led by Citrix winframe and metaframe NBAR provides the ability to classify certain types of Citrix Independent Computing Architecture Traffic. If the Citrix client uses published application requests to a Citrix Master browser, NBAR can differentiate between the application types and allow application of QoS features. NBAR cannot distinguish among Citrix applications in Published Desktop mode or for Seamless mode clients that operate in session sharing mode. In either of these cases only a single TCP stream is used for data communication and as such differentiation is impossible. For NBAR to be utilized on Citrix flows traffic must be in published application mode or for clients in Seamless non-sharing mode. In these cases, each client has a unique TCP stream for each request and as such these streams can be differentiated by NBAR.

Supported Protocols

NBAR is capable of classifying a TCP and UDP protocols that use fixed port numbers as well as Non-UDP and Non-TCP protocols. Tables 4.6, 4.7, and 4.8

list some of the supported protocols, as well as their associated port numbers, that may be classified by NBAR.

Table 4.6 NBAR Supported Non-TCP, Non-UDP Protocols

Protocol	Type	Port Number	Description	Command
EGP	IP	8	Exterior Gateway Protocol	egp
GRE	IP	47	Generic Routing Encapsulation	gre
ICMP	IP	1	Internet Control Message Protocol	icmp
IPINIP	IP	4	IP in IP	ipinip
IPSec	IP	50, 51	IP Encapsulating Security Payload/ Authentication Header	ipsec
EIGRP	IP	88	Enhanced Interior Gateway Routing Protocol	eigrp

Table 4.7 NBAR Supported Static TCP UDP Protocols

Protocol	Type	Port Number	Description	Command
BGP	TCP/UDP	179	Border Gateway Protocol	bgp
CU-SeeMe	TCP/UDP	7648, 7649	Desktop Videoconferencing	cuseeme
CU-SeeMe	UDP	24032	Desktop Videoconferencing	cuseeme
DHCP/ BOOTP	UDP	67, 68	Dynamic Host Configuration Protocol/ Bootstrap Protocol	dhcp
DNS	TCP/UDP	53	Domain Name System	dns
Finger	TCP	79	Finger User Information Protocol	finger
Gopher	TCP/UDP	70	Internet Gopher Protocol	gopher
HTTP	TCP	80	Hypertext Transfer Protocol	http
HTTPS	TCP	443	Secured HTTP	secure-http
IMAP	TCP/UDP	143, 220	Internet Message Access Protocol	imap
IRC	TCP/UDP	194	Internet Relay Chat	irc
Kerberos	TCP/UDP	88, 749	Kerberos Network Authentication Service	kerberos

Continued

Table 4.7 Continued

Protocol	Type	Port Number	Description	Command
L2TP	UDP	1701	L2F/L2TP Tunnel	l2tp
LDAP	TCP/UDP	389	Lightweight Directory Access Protocol	ldap
MS-PPTP	TCP	1723	Microsoft Point-to-Point Tunneling Protocol for VPN	pptp
MS-SQLServer	TCP	1433	Microsoft SQL Server Desktop Videoconferencing	sqlserver
NetBIOS	TCP	137, 139	NetBIOS over IP (MS Windows)	netbios
NetBIOS	UDP	137, 138	NetBIOS over IP (MS Windows)	netbios
NFS	TCP/UDP	2049	Network File System	nfs
NNTP	TCP/UDP	119	Network News Transfer Protocol	nntp
Notes	TCP/UDP	1352	Lotus Notes	notes
Novadigm	TCP/UDP	3460-3465	Novadigm Enterprise Desktop Manager (EDM)	novadigm
NTP	TCP/UDP	123	Network Time Protocol	ntp
PCAnywhere	TCP	5631, 65301	Symantec PCAnywhere	pcanywhere
PCAnywhere	UDP	22, 5632	Symantec PCAnywhere	pcanywhere
POP3	TCP/UDP	110	Post Office Protocol	pop3
Printer	TCP/UDP	515	Printer	printer
RIP	UDP	520	Routing Information Protocol	rip
RSVP	UDP	1698, 1699	Resource Reservation Protocol	rsvp
SFTP	TCP	990	Secure FTP	secure-ftp
SHTTP	TCP	443	Secure HTTP	secure-http
SIMAP	TCP/UDP	585, 993	Secure IMAP	secure-imap
SIRC	TCP/UDP	994	Secure IRC	secure-irc
SLDAP	TCP/UDP	636	Secure LDAP	secure-ldap
SNNTP	TCP/UDP	563	Secure NNTP	secure-nntp

Continued

Table 4.7 Continued

Protocol	Type	Port Number	Description	Command
SMTP	TCP	25	Simple Mail Transfer Protocol	smtp
SNMP	TCP/UDP	161, 162	Simple Network Management Protocol	snmp
SOCKS	TCP	1080	Firewall security protocol	socks
SPOP3	TCP/UDP	995	Secure POP3	secure-pop3
SSH	TCP	22	Secured Shell	ssh
STELNET	TCP	992	Secure Telnet	secure-telnet
Syslog	UDP	514	System Logging Utility	syslog
Telnet	TCP	23	Telnet Protocol	telnet
X Windows	TCP	6000-6003	X11, X Windows	xwindows

Table 4.8 NBAR Supported TCP UDP Dynamic Protocols

Protocol	Type	Description	Command
FTP	TCP	File Transfer Protocol	ftp
Exchange	TCP	MS-RPC for Exchange	exchange
HTTP	TCP	HTTP with URL, MIME, or Host Classification	http
Netshow	TCP/UDP	Microsoft Netshow	netshow
Realaudio	TCP/UDP	RealAudio Streaming Protocol	realaudio
r-commands	TCP	rsh, rlogin, rexec	rcmd
StreamWorks	UDP	Xing Technology Stream Works Audio and Video	streamwork
SQL*NET	TCP/UDP	SQL*NET for Oracle	sqlnet
SunRPC	TCP/UDP	Sun Remote Procedure Call	sunrpc
TFTP	UDP	Trivial File Transfer Protocol	tftp
VDOLive	TCP/UDP	VDOLive Streaming Video	Vdolive

> **NOTE**
>
> You could also add Citrix and Napster into the lists above, as they will soon be moved from PDLM format and incorporated natively.

PDLM

One of the key aspects of NBAR is that new classification templates can be loaded at any time without disrupting operation of the router. This is accomplished by use of a Packet Description Language Module (PDLM). The PDLM is copied to flash memory and loaded from the router console or existing configuration to add additional protocol support for NBAR. No down time is needed to enable new protocol classification. Currently PDLMs (as of this writing) are available to classify Napster, Citrix, and Novadigm protocols. Note that this list is updated frequently and should be checked on a regular basis.

NBAR Supported QoS Services

A key concept to remember is that NBAR is for classification only. It does not apply QoS but provides a means of defining classes for application of QoS based on application information rather than the normal fixed port or network information. Once traffic has been classified by NBAR, there are several QoS mechanisms and services that can be utilized to enforce levels of required service. These available services can include:

- Minimum Guaranteed bandwidth using Class based Weighted Fair Queuing (CBWFQ)
- Low Latency Queuing (LLQ)
- Traffic Policing to limit rates
- Traffic Shaping to avoid congestion
- Congestion Avoidance using Weighted Random Early Detection (WRED)
- Packet Marking/Coloring for use in DiffServ or IntServ architectures
- Flow-Based Weighted Fair Queuing (traditionally known as WFQ)

NBAR and Content Network Design Guidelines

While the concept of NBAR and Content Networking is instantly appealing based on the current network requirements care must be taken in its architecture and implementation. Significant hardware and architectural limits do exist and must be carefully considered. NBAR was originally availably only for the 7200 and 7100 series routers;

However, as of IOS 12.15T release, NBAR functionality is available on the 2600 and 3600 series routers as well. This allows NBAR functionality to be on the majority of newly purchased branch office and hub routers, as well as a majority of small to medium enterprise core routers.

> **NOTE**
>
> Distributed NBAR (DNBAR) will be available on the FLEXWAN and 7500 Series in 12.1.6E and 12.2(1)T and on the 1700 Series in 12.2(2)T.

Deployment of NBAR must be carefully considered. The ability to classify IP based traffic without an investment in network probes or sniffers can be extremely beneficial in a significant number of networks. Content Networking and NBAR is extremely well suited to thin client or winframe traffic or to serve any of a wide range of client server applications or ASP served traffic. In these cases, the ability to classify based on application levels will provide a greatly enhanced network response provided that available network hardware resources are considered and allowed for.

The use of NBAR itself will result in the allocation of 1MB of memory to support up to 500 classification streams. On lower end routers such as the 2600 this can have severe effects. NBAR can also increase router processor utilization by 15 percent. This increase is in excess of any that will result from activation of QoS and queuing mechanisms that can also consume significant resources.

NBAR can only classify traffic that can be switched by the use of Cisco Express Forwarding (CEF). In fact, CEF must be enabled on the router for NBAR to function. The use of CEF can again impact available router resources and certain traffic types cannot be handled by CEF. The primary concerns are unicast and multicast traffic. This can be a problem if an attempt is made to use NBAR to classify and guarantee resources to streaming multicast traffic such as broad range video distribution.

NBAR does not support non-IP traffic, so if your network is composed of a significant amount of legacy traffic such as SNA or IPX, NBAR will be of very limited use. But this is less and less of a concern as networks migrate from a mixed protocol environment to a pure IP solution.

NBAR cannot be used on any form of logical interface, including VLANs, channeled interfaces, (etherchannel), or on dialer or multilink PPP interfaces. If any form of tunneling or encryption is used on an interface NBAR will not function. This is because the encryption or tunnel encapsulates and encrypts the original packet and as such prevents NBAR from looking into the packet header. In such a case NBAR would have to classify on the LAN interface rather that the WAN interface.

These may appear on the surface to be significant; however, NBAR is a relatively new technology and some growing pains are to be expected. If the network is running pure IP, NBAR can provide a significant ability to classify and streamline data delivery in a network, significantly increasing efficiencies and service response. The ability to provide this detailed look into your network without the purchase of expensive probes (i.e., Cisco NetScout) can be of significant help to any network administrator.

Summary

Quality of Service is a requirement of today's multi-service networks. Quality of service may be viewed as an enforced set of capabilities that allow you to differentiate between differing traffic types on a network and assign priority service as required to high demand and high value applications or data flows. With today's integration of Voice and Video, along with the resurgence of client/server application bandwidth constraints are becoming critical. It is imperative that enterprises allow traffic that requires priority service the dedicated bandwidth and low delay characteristics that are needed. The standard best-effort delivery of IP networks is unable to keep up with these demand requirements. To meet these requirements several service level architectures have been created that allow the creation of class of service on the connectionless IP network.

Integrated Services represent the highest level of dedicated Quality of Service. By use of RSVP this level of service emulates the connection oriented end-to-end circuit based nature of dedicated private lines for each data flow. While this may provide the highest possible level of service, it does have significant scaling and implementation issues and is not recommended for link speeds of less than T1 or E1. Note that RSVP, as originally defined for Integrated

Services, is the only protocol available at this time that is capable of guaranteeing a reservation across an IP network. For specific applications such as Voice traffic, Intserv with RSVP may be the architecture of choice.

In contrast to and as a response to the limited low bandwidth capabilities of Integrated Services, the Differentiated Services model was created. The Diffserv model does not attempt to provide the same per data flow dedication of resources as is seen in the Intserv model. Rather Diffserv primarily acts as a coarse classification scheme. Traffic is aggregated into one of a number of coarse flows and then each flow receives a provided per hop behavior. Exact definitions of queuing, drop behaviors, and per hop behaviors are not defined by the Diffserv architecture and are left to the individual service providers to define based on the customer negotiated service level agreements. By classifying and aggregating data flows at the network edge, Diffserv results in networks that can scale to considerably larger size than the fixed data flows of Intserv networks. As no classification is required to be performed on the packets by intervening routers, hardware requirements are significantly reduced and per hop latencies may be significantly lower.

Diffserv does not provide the same level of dedicated service that is available with Intserv and, as such, may suffer if significant Voice or other low latency traffic is sent across a Diffserv network. Also, as the Per Hop Behaviors and classification are defined by each service provider, there is no way to guarantee service across differing service provider networks.

With current growth of application service providers and the spread of pay per use applications corporations are looking for a way to classify and prioritize network traffic based on layer 4 to 7 information. Content Networking facilitates this by looking within a packet and extracting the application information. By the use if intelligent classification tools such as Cisco NBAR, network administrators can precisely control which applications get the premium service required. However, this degree of control does come at a cost. Significant resources are used on classification edge routers to accomplish this task and network analysis must be performed to ensure that network response is not compromised.

We have presented several differing QoS architectures in an overview manner in this chapter. QoS is not a uniform requirement in every network. There is significant strength in the argument that if networks were engineered with enough burst capacity there would be no need for QoS services. QoS will never replace proper and thorough network design. Until unlimited fiber bandwidth becomes economically and readily available to every location in the networking world, network engineers and managers will continue to struggle with providing premium service to a limited number of applications and services. Many differing architectures exist to meet current quality of service needs. No one architecture type can provide the perfect fit for each and every need. Only after a careful and thorough evaluation of a network's QoS needs will a decision as to which architecture or combination of architectures can meet your individual performance needs.

FAQs

Visit **www.syngress.com/solutions** to have your questions about this chapter answered by the author.

Q: I want to implement Content Networking using NBAR on my existing infrastructure. On what hardware platforms can I implement NBAR?

A: NBAR will run on any current Cisco 2600, 3600, 7200, or 7100 platform router as of IOS 12.1.5T. However, CEF must be enabled on the device otherwise NBAR will not function. NBAR will soon be available on the 1700 series routers and dNBAR will soon be available for the 7500 series.

Q: If I am architecting a Diffserv network, where should the classification occur?

A: All classification and aggregation of network traffic should occur as far out on the edges of your network as possible. In the Cisco Networking model, classification should occur at the Access layer only.

Q: I have been tasked with implementing Voice over our data network, what QoS architecture would I be using and are there any special concerns I need to be aware of?

A: Voice is the showstopper in today's network. It is extremely dependent on low delay round trip times. It must be treated as priority traffic. The overall bandwidth requirements for Voice are low (16K per data flow for near toll quality). As Voice will primarily use either premium service in Diffserv, or more likely RSVP based Intserv proper capacity, planning must be performed to ensure that the summation of all the voice streams leaves enough traffic room in the pipe for other traffic and vice versa. Also, Voice requires a careful token bucket queuing system, as large packet sizes from other applications can be extremely destructive to voice quality.

Q: I have enabled using the precedence bit on my routers for QoS. Can I still use this with Diffserv?

A: Maybe. The ToS bit and the DSCP use entirely different bit codings even though the header is the same. They are not compatible. Your precedence enabled routers will process the ToS bit field with the RFC791 meanings which may not be the same service level as you expect from your DSCP definitions. You should run either precedence or Diffserv only in your network, not a mixture of both.

Q: We plan to move to IP V6 shortly, what QoS tagging method can I use?

A: The DSCP format is the default for IP6. The ToS field definitions are not valid and there is no precedence definition for IPV6 routers. IP V6 routers will only use DSCP definitions.

Q: I have mulilinked a number of analog dialup connections for a remote site using multilink PPP, and I want to use NBAR to speed up some winframe applications.

A: No, you cannot use NBAR because NBAR will not work on virtual interfaces such as PPP multilink, ether channel, encrypted or tunneled interfaces, or on VLAN interfaces.

Q: Can I use Cisco Content Networking and NBAR on my mixed protocol network to prioritize the IPX and SNA legacy traffic over IP Web traffic?

A: No. NBAR only functions with IP traffic. However, you could use Diffserv or Intserv to prioritize the non-IP traffic and then classify the remaining IP traffic using NBAR.

Chapter 5
Configuring Traffic Classification

Solutions in this chapter:

- Configuring Policy-based Routing (PBR)
- Defining and Configuring Committed Access Rate (CAR)
- Marking and Transmitting Web Traffic
- Marking and Rate Limiting ISPs
- Configuring Cisco Express Forwarding (CEF)
- Configuring Basic Network-based Application Recognition (NBAR)
- Configuring Complex NBAR
- Integrating NBAR with Class-based Weighted Fair Queuing (CBWFQ)
- Configuring System Network Architecture Type of Service (SNA ToS)

Introduction

Enough with theory, I suppose. Now it is time to show you how to configure all of the things that we discussed in the last chapter. This chapter shows you how to put into practice all of the theories that were introduced in the last chapter, how you would implement these technologies in your network.

This chapter contains many configuration examples, but is by no means a complete listing of all possible uses for the technologies presented.

The configurations presented center on the Quality of Service (QoS) configuration steps required. Basic configuration of interfaces and devices is not discussed. Remember that the classification examples we show are only one part of the equation. After a packet is classified, an appropriate queuing mechanism must be configured on the devices to provide the required QoS. For details on configuring the queuing mechanisms required, please see the relevant chapters in this text.

We strongly encourage you to visit the Cisco Web site at www.cisco.com to view more configuration examples, as new uses for these mechanisms are constantly being developed. Cisco's Web site has one of the best collections of configuration examples available.

What we hope that we have done here is provide you with excellent examples for the most popular uses of these technologies. By doing so, it is our hope that you will use this book as a reference when you are configuring these mechanisms on your network.

Configuring Policy-based Routing (PBR)

Policy-based routing is one of the original methods of providing QoS marking within networks. It provides a method of marking packets not by destination, but rather by originating source, be this address or port, and applying defined policy meanings to these packets. This functionality is the key to understanding PBR. It acts and makes decisions based on the SOURCE address or port number, not the destination address or port as is most common in routing or QoS situations.

PBR works in conjunction with access control lists (ACLs) to first select the traffic to be marked. After the traffic is selected, PBR can either direct all of the traffic to certain networks or interfaces, or selectively mark the (Type of Service) ToS bit to indicate levels of service to be provided to that traffic. As PBR works by the use of ACLs, any traffic that can be differentiated by ACLs can be subjected to PBR. This includes, but is not limited to:

- Source system address
- Application
- Protocol
- Size of packet

PBR has a fairly straightforward configuration that is based on the concept of route maps. A route map is a list of accept or deny clauses against which every packet that enters an interface is matched. If a packet meets the accept clause (which is defined via ACLs), a set command is performed against the packet. The set command specifies the routing behavior or QoS tagging that will be performed on the packet. A key difference to remember is that in a normal ACL, if a packet is not matched it is dropped and not passed through the interface. In a PBR route map ACL, the packet is not dropped; rather, it will not be subjected to the PBR defined actions and will instead be forwarded by the normal destination-based best effort routing procedure.

An important caveat with PBR is to ensure that you are using at least IOS 12.0. Prior to 12.0, all PBR was process switched, which limited the packet response rate to levels that may cause some applications to quit responding. As of 12.0 and later, PBR is fast switched with a correspondingly significant increase in packet rates.

Beginning in global config mode, first define a route map and enter the route map configuration mode using the following command:

route-map map-tag [**permit** | **deny**]

Then, match a defined access list for an IP address or protocol on which the eroute map is to act.

match ip address (access-list-number)

Next, you should set the action to be performed on the packet:

set ip precedence (number or name)

or

set ip next-hop ip-address

Either of these commands routes the packet to a defined address or sets the precedence bit to a predetermined level. Then we will specify the interface on which the PBR is to be applied.

interface interface-type interface-number

Finally, apply the route map to the interface.

`ip policy route-map` *map tag*

Using PBR to Route Specific Packet Types

PBR can be used to specifically direct certain traffic types to required destinations. This example network (Figure 5.1) is composed of a core 6509 with an MSFC doing core layer-three switching. There are two WAN connections. One is via the firewall out to the Internet. The second is to a corporate network. The requirement is that all HTTP traffic, which is proxied as port 8080, is to be directed to the firewall. In addition, all RDP traffic (port 1330) is to be assigned a higher priority level for premium service levels.

Figure 5.1 PBR Network Configuration

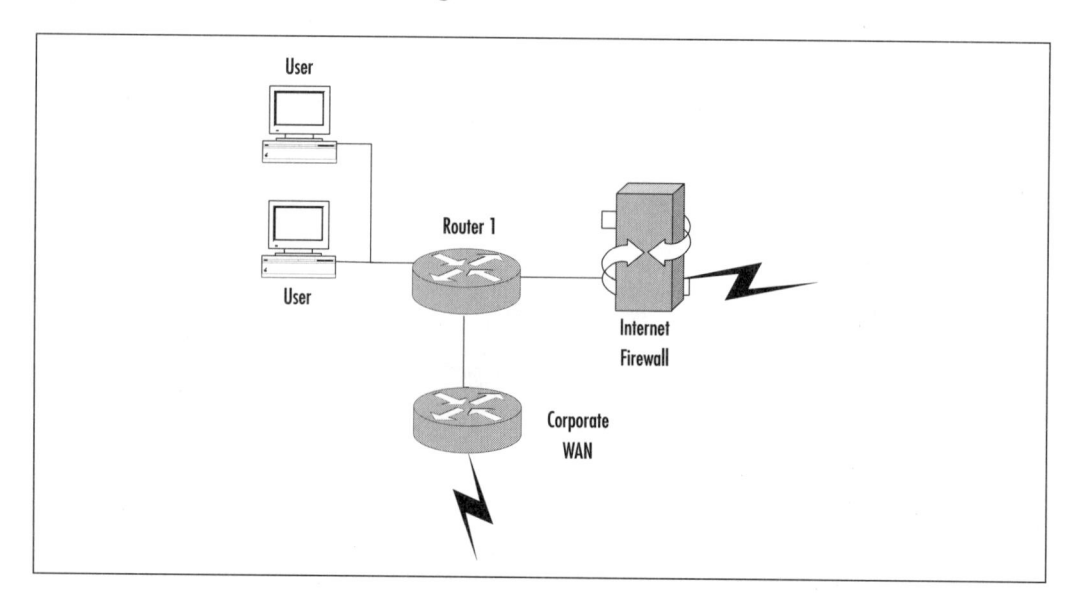

The following shows the MSFC configuration to send all HTTP traffic on port 8080 to the firewall, which has an internal IP address of 10.20.218.17. All RDP traffic on port 1330 is being increased in precedence to a level of 5 to allow for priority service.

```
version 12.15
no service pad
service timestamps debug datetime
```

```
service timestamps log datetime
no service password-encryption
!
hostname router1
!
ip route-cache policy
!
interface Vlan1
   ip address 10.20.10.1 255.255.255.0
   ip policy route-map outgoing
!
route-map outgoing permit 10
match ip address 101
set ip next-hop 10.20.218.17
!
route-map outgoing permit 20
match ip address 102
set ip precedence priority
!
access-list 101 permit tcp any any eq 8080
access-list 102 permit tcp any any eq 1330
```

In this example, the **ip route-cache policy** statement enables PBR fast cache processing. Any traffic that matches access list 101 that specifies traffic on port 8080 (this network is using translation to hide the inside addresses and ports) will be directed to IP address 10.20.218.17 by the **outgoing** route map statement. Any RDP traffic on port 1330 will have its precedence bit set to priority to ensure proper QoS processing within the network.

Defining Committed Access Rate (CAR)

CAR is the most widely used method in a Cisco environment to mark packets at the network edge ingress and egress points. CAR can perform, in general terms, one of two functions: rate limiting, and packet classification through IP precedence and QoS group setting.

With CAR's rate limiting mechanism, you can control the base rate of traffic received or transmitted on an interface. Typically, classification and marking occur on the ingress, and rate limiting occurs on the egress. CAR defines traffic for rate limitation in one of three ways.

- **Average rate** Average rate determines long-term average transition rate. Any traffic that falls under this parameter is transmitted.

- **Normal burst** This determines how large a burst can be before some of the traffic exceeds the rate limit.

- **Excess burst size** This determines how large bursts can be before all traffic exceeds the rate limit.

Concerning bursts, it is important to note that CAR does no traffic shaping or smoothing. It has no burst buffer capabilities. Because of this, CAR does add to interpacket delay; however, this also means that CAR's greatest benefits occur on high-speed links of DS3 speed or greater. Low-speed links that must contend with a significant amount of buffering to deal with bursty traffic will not see the benefits of CAR as would higher-speed links.

CAR's rate limiting feature works on the principle of a token bucket. The bucket depth is indicative of the burst size that is configured for the link. Traffic rate capabilities can be configured in 8 k segments up to the physical capacity of the link. If a packet arrives and there exists enough tokens within the bucket, the packet is allowed to pass. If, however, there is a shortage of tokens, the packet is allowed to borrow tokens up to the Excess burst size. This Excess packet depth is a loan against future traffic and must be rebuilt from periods of low traffic. The idea is to allow for a gradual reduction in packet traffic using a WRED-type procedure rather than a tail drop in packets that may occur. If the cumulative burst size exceeds the excess burst size, packets will be dropped. When traffic has been classified as belonging to a specific rate, one of several actions will occur, depending on how the network administrator has configured the response.

- Transmit the packet.

- Drop the packet.

- Set precedence and transmit. The packet may have a lower precedence set and be transmitted with a lower QoS.

- Continue. If there are further CAR statements, the packet will continue to be processed. At the end of the chain, it will be transmitted.

If the router is a VIP-based platform (7000 series or better), there are two other options available.

- Set QoS group and transmit. The packet is assigned to a specific QoS group and transmitted.

- Set QoS Group and continue. The packet is assigned a QoS group and further processing is continued. If no further rate policies exist, the packet is transmitted.

It is important to note that, for rate limiting procedures, only packets that are in burst mode are subjected to changes in the precedence or QoS. Packets that are within the average rate are not modified and transmitted as specified by their QoS parameters.

Concerning QoS, the marking capabilities of CAR are of prime importance. CAR has the ability to mark packets by setting the IP Precedence bits. While there do exist eight differing possible levels of IP Precedence (0–7) it is strongly recommended that the network administer only use the first six levels. The two highest levels are to be reserved for critical network control and routing protocols that must pass from device to device to ensure proper internetwork functioning.

CAR can mark traffic based on physical port, source or destination IP address, MAC address, IP protocol type, or any other differentiation that can be specified by normal or extended IP access lists. The key is that CAR will only function on IP-based traffic. Non-IP traffic is switched normally and is unaffected by CAR rate limiting or marking features.

As of IOS 12.04, CAR is available on all Cisco router platforms from the 1720 series and up. However, CAR does require that Cisco Express Forwarding (CEF) is enabled, and not all line cards support CEF. It is recommended that you check the exact model number of all interface cards to ensure that CEF, and correspondingly CAR, can be deployed.

CAR does have a number of significant limitations in design and implementation of network services.

- CAR will only affect IP traffic. Non-IP traffic is not rate limited or marked. This may cause issues on a legacy network; however, as most networks are being migrated to pure IP, this will become less of a concern.

- CAR is not supported on EtherChannel, Tunnel, or ISDN PRI interfaces.

- On ATM interfaces, CAR only supports aal5snap, aal5mux, or aal5nlpid interfaces.

- There is no support for BECN or FECN in Frame Relay (backward and forward express congestion notification).

Configuring Distributed CAR (DCAR)

DCAR is found on the Cisco 7500 or 12000 series router platforms. In these routers, each card has the ability to handle processing by maintaining an individual copy of the routing database and thereby offloading processor load from the central processor. The VIPs serve as unique processors for all packets. In this manner, with DCEF enabled, DCAR is enabled and functions autonomously on each VIP, rather than being a processor-based operation. This architecture provides significant improvements in base efficiencies compared to the standard processor bounded CAR functionality.

To configure CAR, follow these steps in order. First, enter the interface configuration mode.

`interface` *interface-type interface-number*

Next, specify the rate policy for each class of traffic and the action to be taken if the rate is exceeded.

`rate-limit {input | output} [access-group [rate-limit]` *acl-index]bps burst-norma lburst max 3)* `conform action` *action* `exceed-action` *action*

Valid actions include continue, drop, set-prec-con (Set the precedence bit and continue), set-prec-trans (set the precedence bit and transmit), and transmit. Then we can use the optional command to specify a rate limited access list.

`access-list rate-limit`

Finally, we should use another optional command that specifies a standard or extended access list to be used.

`access-list` *acl-index* `{deny | permit}`

Marking and Transmitting Web Traffic

In this initial example, Web traffic is allowed access to a network via a token ring interface on a 7513 router. This Web traffic is to be assigned a precedence of 5 up to a bandwidth of 4MB. Anything over 4MB is to be assigned to a best-effort delivery class. Enter the incoming token ring interface and configuration mode.

```
Int Tok 2/0
```

Next, use the following command to define that all traffic that meets access list 101 will have a precedence setting of 5 if has 4MB or under in bandwidth. Anything over 4MB will be delivered, but will be only best-effort QoS.

```
Rate-limit input access-group 101 16000000 4000 4000
    conform-action set prec-transmit 5 exceed action
    set-prec-transmit 0
```

Now, enable the access list that will define that we will be matching on Web traffic only.

```
Access-list 101 permit tcp any any eq www
```

The following illustrates the exact router interface configuration for this configuration.

```
router#Show run
!
interface TokenRing2/0
 description web in
 ip address 207.48.198.1 255.255.255.0
Rate-limit input access-group 101 16000000 4000 4000 conform-
     action set prec-transmit 5 exceed action set-prec-transmit 0
 no ip directed-broadcast
 ring-speed 16
 hold-queue 500 in
!
Access-list 101 permit tcp any any eq www
```

Remarking the Precedence Bit and Transmitting Web Traffic

CAR provides the ability to sort on the precedence bit of packets and reassign this precedence bit to better fit the current network model. In this example, we will be using the same token ring interface as we did previously, but will remark all precedence level 0,1, and 2 bits as precedence level 4.

First, enter the configuration mode and input the incoming token ring.

```
Int Tok 2/0
```

Next, set the rate command to set any packets that match our rate limited access list to have their precedence level reset to 4.

`rate-limit input access-group rate-limit 25 conform-action set prec-transmit 4:`

The following access list uses a binary mask to match the precedence levels 0, 1, and 2 only.

`access-list rate-limit 25 mask 07`

The following illustrates the interface configuration for this required configuration.

```
router#Show run
!
interface TokenRing2/0
 description web in
 ip address 207.48.198.1 255.255.255.0
Rate-limit input access-group  conform-action set prec-transmit 4
 no ip directed-broadcast
 ring-speed 16
 hold-queue 500 in
!
Access-list   rate-limit 25 mask 07
```

The access-list command that is used is different from that of the standard access list. CAR defines the access-list rate-limit special format access list. This list has the format **access-list rate-limit** *acl-index* {*precedence* | *mac-address* | **mask prec-mask**}. While normal access lists and extended access lists allow us to permit by port numbers, services, and source and destination addresses, this format allows filtering on specific properties of the ToS bit. Specifically, this will filter by existing precedence bit; if the mask is used, it will filter on a range of precedence bits that are converted to binary, or it will filter on individual MAC addresses. This addition provides for further fine-tuning and granularity in CAR.

Marking and Transmitting Multilevels of CAR

CAR allows for up to 100 levels of precedence marking and action per interface or subinterface. As such, extremely fine differentiation can be achieved with minimal delay and processor utilization. In this configuration, we are using a three-level marking and transmitting differentiation on a 12MB IMA connection. RDP traffic is allowed 8MB with a burst capacity of 10MB. If traffic conforms, the Precedence bit is to be set to 5. If traffic does not conform, it is delivered as best effort only.

FTP traffic is to be allowed 4MB of the bandwidth with a precedence of 5. It can burst to 5MB, but exceeding traffic will be delivered only with best effort.

Any remaining traffic is to be serviced as best effort only. The configuration of this interface follows exactly in pattern the configuration used in the previous two examples. The Final interface and access list configuration is shown here:

```
interface ATM1/IMA0
 ip address 192.168.160.2 255.255.255.0
 ip directed-broadcast
 no ip route-cache
 no ip mroute-cache
 no atm oversubscribe
 no atm ilmi-keepalive
pvc ip1/42
   protocol ip 192.168.160.1 broadcast
   encapsulation aal5snap
rate-limit output access-group 101 8000000 8000 10000 conform-
     action set-prec-
transmit 5 exceed-action set-prec-transmit 0
rate-limit output access-group 102 4000000 5000 5000 conform-
     action
set-prec-transmit 5 exceed-action set-prec-transmit 0
rate-limit output 4000000 4000 4000 conform-action set-prec-
     transmit 5
exceed-action drop
!
access-list 101 permit tcp any any eq RDP
access-list 102 permit tcp any any eq ftp
```

Marking and Rate Limiting ISPs

In this example, an ATM OC3 connection joins the two remote sites. The routers are managed and the customer has paid for an OC0 (25MB) connection. The ISP has implemented CAR with a drop all service action when the maximum contracted bandwidth is reached. However, the customer is allowed to burst up to 30MB if needed. Figure 5.2 illustrates this concept.

Figure 5.2 CAR Rate Limiting Network Configuration

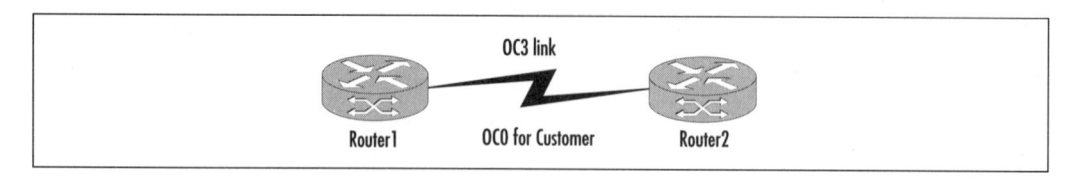

Enter the ATM interface configuration mode.

`Interface atm2/0`

Next, enter the PVC to be configured; in this case:

`Pvc 1/42`

Limit the inbound traffic so that it drops all traffic bursts over 30MB.

`Rate-limit input 25000000 30000 30000 conform-action transmit`
    `exceed-action drop`

We will also need to limit the outbound traffic so that it drops all traffic over 30MB.

`Rate-limit output 25000000 30000 30000 conform-action transmit`
    `exceed-action drop`

The interface configuration on the router is shown here:

```
!
 interface ATM2/0
 ip address 192.168.160.2 255.255.255.0
 no ip mroute-cache
 no atm ilmi-keepalive
 pvc 1/42
   protocol ip 192.168.160.1 broadcast
     encapsulation aal5snap
     Rate-limit input 25000000 30000 30000 conform-action transmit
       exceed-action drop
```

```
Rate-limit output 25000000 30000 30000 conform-action
    transmit exceed-action drop
```

Rate Limiting by Access List

In this example, a 12MB IMA connection joins two 3640s. FTP traffic is to be allowed up to 4MB of the link with a priority of 6. Any FTP traffic in excess of 4MB is to be assigned a priority of 1. All HTTP traffic is to have a precedence of 3 for the second policy. If it exceeds this, it will be dropped. The router orientation is shown in Figure 5.3.

Figure 5.3 Rate Limiting by Access List Network Configuration

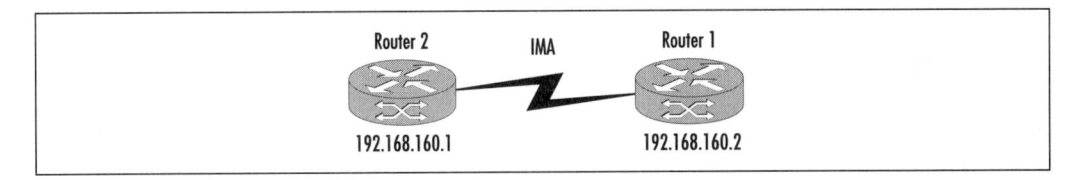

Enter the interface configuration mode.

```
interface atm1/ima0
```

Next, we will need to enter the PVC configuration mode.

```
pvc ip 1/42
```

Then, set the FTP traffic to have a capacity of 4MB and a precedence level of 6 if in bound. Any traffic over 4MB has a precedence value set to 1.

```
rate-limit output access-group 101 12000000 4000 4000 conform
    -action set-prec-transmit 6 exceed action set-prec-transmit 1
```

Next, set the HTTP traffic to have 3 MB of capacity and a precedence level of 3 if inbound. Any traffic over 3MB is dropped.

```
rate-limit output access-group 102 6000000 3000 3000 conform-
    action set-prec-transmit 3 exceed action drop
```

Use the following FTP protocol access list:

```
access-list 101 permit tcp any any eq ftp
```

Finally, enter the following to enable the HTTP access list:

```
access-list 102 permit tcp any any eq www
```

The following is the actual Router1 configuration for the interface and access list.

```
!
interface ATM1/IMA0
 ip address 192.168.160.2 255.255.255.0
 ip directed-broadcast
 no ip route-cache
 no ip mroute-cache
 no atm oversubscribe
 no atm ilmi-keepalive
 pvc ip /42
    protocol ip 192.168.160.1 broadcast
    encapsulation aal5snap
    rate-limit output access-group 101 12000000 4000 4000
      conform-action set-prec-   transmit 6 exceed action set-
      prec-transmit 1
    rate-limit output access-group 102 6000000 3000 3000 conform-
      action set-prec-transmit 3 exceed action drop
!
access-list 101 permit tcp any any eq ftp
access-list 102 permit tcp any any eq www
```

Using CAR to Match and Limit by MAC Address

CAR also has the ability to match by MAC Address. In this example, all packets that are from the MAC address 0090.27d1.2917 on the FDDI ring are to be dropped by the CAR interface. This type of network is illustrated in Figure 5.4.

Enter the interface configuration mode for the FDDI interface.

```
Int FDDI11/0
```

Then, define that all traffic that meets the access list MAC will be dropped.

```
rate-limit input access-group rate-limit 100 conform-action
    drop
```

Figure 5.4 Car Packet MAC Match Network Diagram

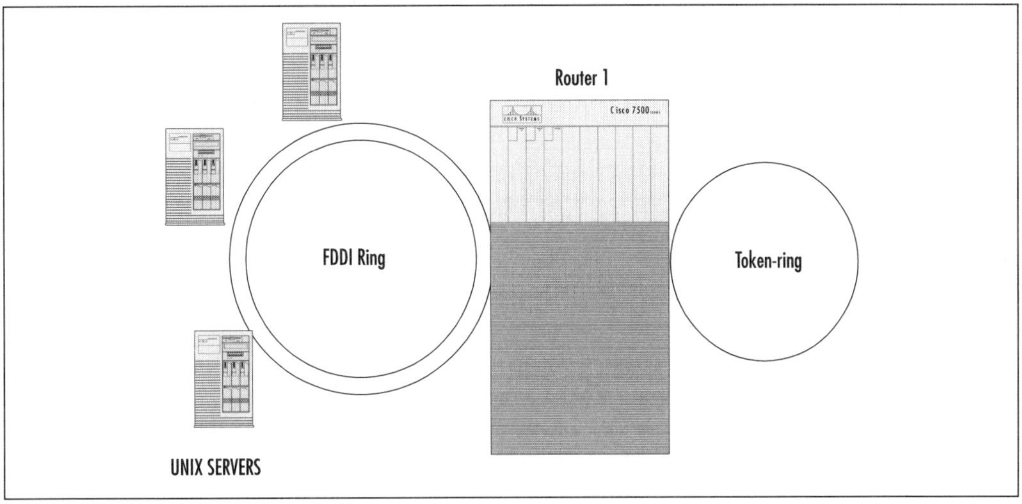

Next, specify that all traffic matching the MAC will be matched.

```
access-list rate-limit 100   0090.27d1.2917
```

The following output is the Final Interface configuration on the 7513. All traffic that matches the MAC address configured will be dropped. All other traffic receives the standard best-effort delivery service.

```
!
interface Fddi11/0
 description FDDI Backbone
 ip address 207.48.199.3 255.255.255.0
 no ip directed-broadcast
 no ip route-cache
 no ip mroute-cache
 no keepalive
 hold-queue 3000 in
 hold-queue 3000 out
   rate-limit input access-group rate-limit 100 conform-action
     drop
!
access-list rate-limit 100   0090.27d1.2917
```

Monitoring CAR

To monitor CAR, the primary command within the Cisco IOS is **show interfaces rate-limit**. This command shows all of the rate limiting interfaces and the current packet drop and match/exceed statistics. The following output shows this command applied to a 7513 router running rate limiting on one interface. In this example, nine packets exceeded the Web rate limit of 10MB and were dropped.

```
7513#show int rate-limit
TokenRing1/0 remote
  Input
    matches: access-group 102
      params:  6000000 bps, 8000 limit, 10000 extended limit
      conformed 81751 packets, 10713419 bytes; action: set-prec-
         transmit 3
      exceeded 9 packets, 5030 bytes; action: drop
      last packet: 313748ms ago, current burst: 0 bytes
      last cleared 00:08:34 ago, conformed 166000 bps, exceeded
         0 bps
```

Configuring Cisco Express Forwarding

CAR (and other functions such as NBAR, to be discussed later) requires that CEF be enabled on the router. Therefore, before we get into CAR configurations, we must have a firm knowledge of CEF functionality.

CEF is, as of IOS 12.0, the default switching mode in Cisco 7500 routers. In fact, in the 8500 and 12000 series, it is the only available mode. CEF uses what is known as a fast cache that is composed of two basic structures, the CEF table and the adjacency table.

The CEF table can be best viewed as a stripped down version of the route table that is implemented as a 256-way mtrie data structure. This is known as a Forwarding Information Base (FIB). This means that each node in the structure can have up to 256 children. In the CEF table, each child represents one octet in an IP address. Each final node in the CEF table contains a pointer to a unique entry in the adjacency table. The adjacency table is what actually contains the MAC information needed to switch the packet. The CEF table is built from the routing table; the adjacency table is constructed from the ARP table, Frame Relay map table, or other table types.

In comparison to fast switching, where the first packet must be routed to establish a path, in CEF the tables are constructed before any packets are switched. This allows for a considerable increase in efficiency. Therefore, every packet can be routed via a known route and can be switched using IOS interrupts rather than process switching. This can significantly improve router processor utilization.

The other major advantage of CEF is that as of IOS 12.0, CEF load sharing is enabled by default in the Cisco 7500 series. This allows for a network with multiple paths to implement automatic load-sharing capabilities over those equal or unequal path links.

CEF entries never age. As they are linked directly to their routing table, any changes in the dynamic routing tables are immediately propagated to the CEF tables.

> **NOTE**
>
> IF you are running a 7500, 8500, or 12000 series router, CEF is the default (in two of these cases the only mode), so no configuration is needed. However, CEF must be enabled manually on all other routers. If you wish to use NBAR or CAR, CEF must be enabled.

Enabling CEF

Use the **IP CEF** command at the global configuration prompt to enable CEF on a router. The effect of CEF on a router's processor load can be significant. The following outputs show processor utilization before CEF and after CEF is enabled for the same traffic load on a 7513 router with an RSP4. Five-second utilization dropped from 54 percent to 16 percent, with a corresponding decrease in peak utilization. CEF is extremely useful even with the caveats that must be observed.

```
7513#show proc
CPU utilization for five seconds: 80%/54%; one minute: 27%; five
    minutes: 18%
PID QTy        PC Runtime (ms)  Invoked  uSecs  Stacks       TTY Process
1   Csp 602E87D8 896             30142    2      2600/3000    0   Load Meter

2   M*  0        9508            1690     5626   9804/12000   2   Virtual Exec

3   Lst 602CCA50 115592          18056    6401   5636/6000    0   Check heaps

4   Cwe 602C4248 0               1        0      5568/6000    0   Chunk Manage
```

The following is the processor utilization with IP CEF-enabled output.

```
7513#show proc
CPU utilization for five seconds: 18%/16%; one minute: 39%; five
    minutes: 24%
PID QTy        PC Runtime (ms)  Invoked  uSecs  Stacks       TTY Process
1   Csp 602E87D8 896             30153    29     2600/3000    0   Load Meter

2   M*  0        11128           1802     6175   9804/12000   2   Virtual Exec

3   Lst 602CCA50 115644          18063    6402   5636/6000    0   Check heaps

4   Cwe 602C4248 0               1        0      5568/6000    0   Chunk Manage
```

Monitoring CEF

Use the **show IP cef** command on the router to monitor the current CEF database for general details on which routes are formed via which destination interface. The following shows a partial output of this command on a Cisco 7513 router. This result is essentially a mirror of the current router table.

```
7513#show ip cef
Prefix              Next Hop            Interface
0.0.0.0/0           10.20.10.5          GigabitEthernet8/0/0
0.0.0.0/32          receive
```

```
10.0.0.0/8              0.0.0.0            Null0
10.0.0.0/23             10.20.10.2         GigabitEthernet8/0/0
                        10.20.10.3         GigabitEthernet8/0/0
10.0.0.101/32           10.20.10.2         GigabitEthernet8/0/0
                        10.20.10.3         GigabitEthernet8/0/0
10.0.0.105/32           10.20.10.2         GigabitEthernet8/0/0
                        10.20.10.3         GigabitEthernet8/0/0
10.0.0.109/32           10.20.10.2         GigabitEthernet8/0/0
                        10.20.10.3         GigabitEthernet8/0/0
10.0.0.122/32           10.20.10.2         GigabitEthernet8/0/0
                        10.20.10.3         GigabitEthernet8/0/0
10.0.0.126/32           10.20.10.2         GigabitEthernet8/0/0
                        10.20.10.3         GigabitEthernet8/0/0
10.0.0.162/32           10.20.10.2         GigabitEthernet8/0/0
```

You can obtain detailed CEF FIB information by using the show ip cef detailed command from enable mode. This result can be extremely lengthy, so be warned that you may have a significant amount of detail to look through. The following shows the output of a show IP CEF detailed.

```
7513#show ip cef detail
IP CEF with switching (Table Version 2083), flags=0x0
  1974 routes, 0 reresolve, 0 unresolved (0 old, 0 new)
  1974 leaves, 244 nodes, 531688 bytes, 2086 inserts, 112
     invalidations
  733 load sharing elements, 240424 bytes, 750 references
  3 CEF resets, 24 revisions of existing leaves
  refcounts:   66423 leaf, 62720 node

Adjacency Table has 1026 adjacencies
0.0.0.0/0, version 1960, cached adjacency 10.20.10.5
0 packets, 0 bytes
  via 10.20.10.5, GigabitEthernet8/0/0, 0 dependencies
    next hop 10.20.10.5, GigabitEthernet8/0/0
    valid cached adjacency
0.0.0.0/32, version 0, receive
```

```
10.0.0.0/8, version 1468
0 packets, 0 bytes
  via 0.0.0.0, Null0, 0 dependencies
    next hop 0.0.0.0, Null0
    valid null adjacency
10.0.0.0/23, version 1471, per-destination sharing
0 packets, 0 bytes
  via 10.20.10.2, GigabitEthernet8/0/0, 0 dependencies
    traffic share 1
 —More—
```

Troubleshooting Cisco Express Forwarding Caveats and Bugs

While CEF does significantly reduce router utilization and improve packet switching efficiency, there are several bugs and caveats that one must be aware of before using CEF (and the corresponding dependent QoS services). The more severe ones are listed next. Remember that CEF is a fairly new technology, and as such is constantly being improved. If you wish to use QoS services in your network, you will be required to use CEF on your routers. Keeping up to date with current code revisions will mediate much, if not all, of the issues that are currently found in CEF implementations. The load reduction on core routers is considerable with IP CEF enabled. As such, this alone makes this technology extremely worth considering on supported hardware, as long as the caveats are considered regarding current network traffic and configurations.

CSCdr56112 Voice traffic is dropped when you use compression, and a call cannot be resumed. If an error appears at the decompressor when you use Voice over IP over Frame Relay (VoIPoFR) and fast switching or CEF switching, all subsequent packets in the flow are dropped, and voice connection is never regained.

CSCdr68372 When Multilink PPP and fast switching or CEF switching are configured, Real Time Protocol (RTP) packets are not compressed. When you use Multilink PPP for link fragmentation and interleaving (LFI) in a voice and data environment, the **ip rtp header-compression** command has no effect on most platforms and may cause a Cisco 7200 series router to reload.

CSCdr97427 A Cisco 7500 series router that runs on the r7k processor (RSP8 and possibly others) may reload if all of the following conditions are true:

- It is configured as a Multiprotocol Label Switching (MPLS) Router.
- It is running Cisco IOS Release 12.1(3)T or later.
- It has serial/hssi interfaces that are either VIP (Versatile Interface Processors) or non-VIP, but the router is running the **ip cef** command in non-distributed mode.
- The serial/hssi links receive MPLS packets.

CSCds21333 Some Quality of Service (QoS) features may not perform as expected when CEF is enabled.

CSCds53550 When rate limiting with CAR, Cisco CEF does not drop packets as intended.

Configuring Basic Network-based Application Recognition (NBAR)

NBAR was discussed in considerable detail in Chapter 4, so we will not be discussing the inner workings of NBAR at this point. Rather, we will be concentrating on configuration of NBAR, and its interaction with Random Early Detection (RED) and Class-based Weighted Fair Queuing (CBWFQ) to provide QoS within the network. Remember that NBAR is a protocol discovery tool and a classification engine only. While it can provide the intelligence to look into a network to discern what is occurring at a packet load level, it requires other tools to create and enforce a QoS policy.

The first step in NBAR configuration is to enable NBAR protocol discovery on an interface or interfaces that will be used to monitor traffic. The caveat is that the use of NBAR will increase CPU utilization by up to 15 percent, so it should not be used on heavily loaded routers. Be sure to check your CPU utilization using the **show proc** command before implementing NBAR. The discovery feature supports any protocol supported by NBAR. To enable NBAR on a port:

```
7206(config)#int faste0/0
7206(config-if)#ip nbar protocol-discovery
```

To view the results of the NBAR discovery on a specific interface, the show **ip nbar protocol-discovery** interface is given from enable mode. The following is partial output of this command for the interface.

```
7206#show ip nbar protocol-discovery int Fast0/0
!
FastEthernet0/0
Input            Output
Protocol    Packet Count              Packet Count
            Byte Count                Byte Count
            5 minute bit rate (bps)   5 minute bit rate (bps)
-----------------------------------------------------------
http        1765473                   0
            18739887                  0
            9832477                   0

.
.
.

Total       9875462282                989836234
            7465873457                768236287
            6726362252                8876545
```

Three basic tasks must be sequentially performed to apply NBAR to an interface. First, a class map command must be used to define one or more traffic classes by specifying the criteria on which traffic is to be classified. The second step is to create a policy map to define a QoS apply to the traffic class. The final step is to use a service-policy command to attach the policy to a specific interface on a router. Each of these steps is required for basic NBAR functionality.

Creating an NABR Class Map

The class-map command is used to define a matching traffic class and define all identifiers that will be used to classify traffic as belonging to the class. For NBAR classification, the matching parameter must be a protocol supported by NBAR. The following illustrates the structure of this command as applied to a 7206 router for matching on PcAnywhere traffic.

```
7206(config)#class-map PCanywhere
7206(config-cmap)#match protocol pcanywhere
```

Creating a Policy Map

The Policy-Map configuration command is used to define what QoS are to be applied to a traffic class that was defined by the class-map statement. To accomplish this, first create a policy name, then define the class to which this policy is to be applied, and finally, define the QoS features that will be used. The exact commands are shown next. In this command, we are defining our policy to allow PCAnywhere traffic 50 percent of the available bandwidth. However, while this uses a simple rate limiting bandwidth statement, the QoS can be any CAR configured statement, weighted fair queuing, random early detection, or precedence modification as required.

```
7206(config)#policy-map traffic
7206(config-pmap)#class PCanywhere
7206(config-pmap-c)#bandwidth percent 50
```

Applying the Policy Map to an Interface

The final step is to apply the defined policy map to a specific interface so that rate controlling can occur. This is done by using the service-policy command to attach a policy to a specific interface and specify the direction of the traffic control. The following shows the Service Policy applied in the input direction.

```
7206(config)#int faste0/0
7206(config-if)#service-policy input PCAnywhere
7206(config-if)#exit
```

The preceding configuration is the bare minimum to configure NBAR on an interface. Next will be the configuration of complex NBAR settings that are more likely to be encountered in commercial settings. Remember that NBAR is a logical extension of CAR and uses much the same principles. While CAR and PBR use access lists and rate limited lists that must define specific protocols, NBAR is not bounded by simple port definitions or IP addresses. Rather, NBAR allows the network administrator to detect and configure on a broad range of defined IP- and not IP-based protocols by use of a simple work definition. This feature alleviates the need for expense and complex network probes, and allows flexibility and intelligence to be built into each network routing device.

Configuring Complex NBAR

In real-world scenarios, simple situations such as the one illustrated previously would not be used. Rather, NBAR would be deployed to provide mission-critical levels of service to a wide range of applications in disparate environments. The next scenario involves using NBAR on an ATM OC0 WAN interface of a 7206 VXR router. Citrix traffic is priority, as is Cu-SEEME for video conferencing. X Windows is used for remote work, and SQL*NET is used. All Web traffic on port 8080 is to be directed to the Internet firewall with an IP address of 10.20.218.17.

The first step is to classify all of the differing traffic types using individual class-map commands.

To classify Citrix traffic:

7206(config)#**class-map match-all Citrix**
7206(config-cmap)#**match protocol Citrix**

To classify Cu-SEEME traffic:

7206(config)#**class-map match-all Video**
7206(config-cmap)#**match protocol Cu-SeeMe**

To classify X Windows traffic:

7206(config)#**class-map match-all Xwindows**
7206(config-cmap)#**match protocol X Windows**

To classify SQL traffic:

7206(config)#**class-map match-all SQL**
7206(config-cmap)#**match protocol SQL.Net**

To classify Web proxy traffic:

7206(config)#**class-map match-all Internet**
7206(config-cmap)#**match protocol 8080**

The next step is to configure the policies to be used to assign QoS. Citrix is to be assigned 20 percent of the available bandwidth; video is to have 30 percent; X Windows will receive 20 percent; and SQL will receive 20 percent. All Internet traffic is allowed 2MB of bandwidth; any exceeding this is to be dropped.

7206(config)#**policy-map WAN**
7206(config-pmap)#**class Citrix**

```
7206(config-pmap-c)#bandwidth 20
7206(config-pmap-c)#class Video
7206(config-pmap-c)#bandwidth 30
7206(config-pmap-c)#class Xwindows
7206(config-pmap-c)#bandwidth 20
7206(config-pmap-c)#class SQL
7206(config-pmap-c)#bandwidth 20
7206(config-pmap-c)#class internet
7206(config-pmap-c)#police 2000000 conform transmit exceed drop
```

The last step is to attach this policy to the provisioned WAN link.

```
7206(config)#interface ATM2/0
 7206(Config-if)# pvc 1/42   ip
7206(config-if-atm-vc)#service-policy output wan
```

The final router configuration is summarized in the following output.

```
Current configuration:
!
version 12.15
service timestamps debug uptime
service timestamps log uptime
!
hostname 7206
!
ip cef
!
class-map match-all Citrix
 match protocol Citrix
!
class-map match-all Video
match protocol Cu-SeeMe
!
class-map match-all Xwindows
 match protocol X Windows
!
```

```
class-map match-all SQL
match protocol SQL.Net
!
class-map match-all Internet
match protocol 8080
!
policy-map WAN
 class Citrix
 bandwidth 20
 class Video
 bandwidth 30
 class Xwindows
 bandwidth 20
 class SQL
 bandwidth 20
 class internet
 police 2000000 conform transmit exceed drop
!

interface ATM2/0
 ip address 192.168.160.2 255.255.255.0
 no atm ilmi-keepalive
 pvc 1/42
  protocol ip 192.168.160.1 broadcast
  service-policy output wan
  encapsulation aal5snap
 !
```

Integrating NBAR with Class-based Weighted Fair Queuing

Class-based Weighted Fair Queuing (CBWFQ) is an extension of normal weighted fair queuing to allow for user-defined classes of protocols. In this functionality, the integration of NBAR, which is a classification mechanism, with CBWFQ provides for an extremely flexible and configurable QoS mechanism.

NBAR provides the classification steps that would normally be using ACL ports, or IP addresses. However, these classification procedures are not exclusionary. You can still use NBAR with ACLs or interface classifications if needed. By the use of weighted fair queuing mechanisms, it is possible to accommodate the bursty nature of current network traffic, while still providing adequate network resources and response for required services. The configuration of CBWFQ with NBAR is very similar to normal queuing configuration, with the difference being conceptually that NBAR is performing the classification instead of manually entering the required classifications.

Creating a Class Map to Identify NBAR

The initial configuration is to define a class map that will identify the NBAR specific protocol or protocols that will be subject to CBWFQ. This is done with the **class-map** command. In normal CBWFQ, we would be using ACL interfaces or port protocols to perform the matching. With NBAR, we use the NBAR defined protocol settings to establish matching criteria.

```
7206(config)#class-map match-any  Priority
7206(config-cmap)#match protocol FTP
7206(config-cmap)#match protocol Telnet


7206(config)#class-map match-all Citrix
7206(config-cmap)#match protocol Citrix
```

Configuring Class Policy in the Policy Map

This configuration step defines the service policy that will be used to service the classes that were defined in the first step. A combination of queuing and bandwidth limitation may be used here to define levels of expected service. The maximum number of policies that may be configured on the router is equivalent to the number of class maps that were defined, up to a maximum level of 64. In the following policy map configuration, the policy map has been named "quality." The Citrix class is assigned a bandwidth of 6000 Kbps (6MB) with a serviced queue depth of 100 packets to allow for burst. The priority class is assigned a bandwidth of 3000 Kbps (3MB). Remember that CBFWQ is a tail-drop functionality, as it limits the packets available in the token buffer via the queue-limit command. Any traffic that does not match a class map and a corresponding policy is treated as best-effort delivery by the router and is required to use only the available non-allocated link bandwidth.

```
7206(config)#policy-map Quality
7206(config-pmap)#class Citrix
7206(config-pmap-c)#bandwidth 6000
7206(config-pmap-c)#queue-limit 100
7206(config-pmap)#exit
7206(config-pmap)#class priority
7206(config-pmap-c)#bandwidth 3000
7206(config-pmap)#exit
```

Attaching the Policy to an Interface

The final step involves attaching a policy to an interface. This process activates CBWFQ for either inbound or outbound traffic as defined for that interface. While you can assign the same policy to multiple interfaces, each interface can have only one policy assigned at the inbound and outbound directions.

```
7206(config)#interface Tok2/1
7206(config-if)#service input Quality
7206(config-if)#exit
7206(config)#interface Tok2/2
7206(config-if)#service output Quality
7206(config-if)#exit
```

The following illustrates the relevant final router configuration for the NBAR configured with CBWFQ in the previous steps.

```
Current configuration:
!
hostname 7206
!
ip cef
!
class-map match-any  Priority
match protocol FTP
match protocol Telnet
!
class-map match-all citrix
match protocol citrix
```

```
!
policy-map Quality
class Citrix
bandwidth 6000
queue-limit 100
class priority
bandwidth 3000
!
interface TokenRing2/1
 ip address 10.20.198.1 255.255.255.0
 service input quality
 custom-queue-list 2
 ring-speed 16
!
interface TokenRing2/2
 ip address 10.20.202.1 255.255.255.0
 service output quality
 ring-speed 16
```

Configuring NBAR with Random Early Detection

Configuring Random Early Detection (RED) and Weighted Random Early Detection (WRED) with NBAR follows the same steps as configuring NBAR with CBWFQ. The only differences are in the construction and structure of the policy map statements. RED uses a packet drop model as opposed to the tail drop of CBFWQ. Using the previous configuration used CBWFQ, we will reconfigure the class policy to act as WRED. Note that WRED has a default class that must be defined. This default class services any packets that do not fit into the class map classification. There are no queue-limit commands with WRED and RED as there are in CBFWQ. Rather, RED uses a random detect constant to calculate packet drops.

```
7206(config)#policy-map Quality
7206(config-pmap)#class Citrix
7206(config-pmap-c)#bandwidth 6000
```

```
7206(config-pmap)#exit
7206(config-pmap)#class priority
7206(config-pmap-c)#bandwidth 3000
7206(config-pmap)#exit
7206(config)#random-detect exponential-weighting-constant 10
7206(config-pmap)#class class-default
7206(config-pmap-c)#fair-queue 20
7206(config)#queue-limit 100
```

The following output is similar to the previous example, except that NBAR is configured with WRED instead of CBFWQ.

```
Current configuration:
!
hostname 7206
!
ip cef
!
random-detect exponential-weighting-constant 10
queue-limit 100
class-map match-any  Priority
match protocol FTP
match protocol Telnet
!
class-map match-all citrix
match protocol citrix
!
policy-map Quality
class Citrix
bandwidth 6000
class priority
bandwidth 3000
!
interface TokenRing2/1
  ip address 10.20.198.1 255.255.255.0
  service input quality
```

```
  custom-queue-list 2
  ring-speed 16
!
interface TokenRing2/2
  ip address 10.20.202.1 255.255.255.0
  service output quality
  ring-speed 16
```

Configuring System Network Architecture Type of Service

Many corporations rely on large, high-powered background mainframes to provide the database powered needed to properly run their enterprise. This environment has primarily used Systems Network Architecture (SNA) as its main communications protocol. SNA is optimized for low-speed dedicated connections. On the front, this may not seem to be an issue; after all, SNA applications have been running quite well over dedicated 9.6 K low-speed serial lines. However, the issue is that SNA is a connection-oriented protocol. SNA may not require much bandwidth, but what it does require must be there in a constant, low latency, guaranteed, and invariant manner. This is at significant odds with the connectionless model of the normal TCP/IP network. (however, it fits in with the new demands being placed on IP networks by applications such as voice). SNA is characterized by true class of service (CoS) functionality that is used to differentiate between interactive and batch mode traffic. The key is to be able provide the low latency service that is expected by SNA. Cisco developed DLSw+ to address the need to carry SNA traffic across today's predominantly IP networks. DLSw+ encapsulates the SNA packet within an IP packet by adding a 56-bit header to the SNA packet. The key benefit of DSLw+ is that it provides for SNA to automatically receive the required level of service from the IP network.

Mapping SNA CoS to IP ToS

So, how does DLSw+ maintain the connection-oriented nature of SNA traffic across an IP network? APPN is the prime method for setting COS within the SNA world. DSLw+ automatically creates four TCP port values that are mapped to respective APPN values. This mapping is seen in Table 5.1.

Table 5.1 Port to APPN to IP Precedence Values

TCP Ports	Priority Queue Level	IP Precedence APPN Value	IP Precedence DLSw+ Value
2065	High	Network	Network control
1981	Medium	High	Internetwork control
1982	Normal	Medium	Critical
1983	Low	Low	Flash override

DSLw+ will automatically map APPN marked COS values to the corresponding ports and set the IP ToS bit to represent the required IP service requirement. In the absence of APPN and DLSw+ on the same router, DSLw+ will assign all SNA traffic to port 2065 with a network control ToS field. This may pose a problem if you are running an IP precedence aware network, as network control traffic is treated before all other traffic. If a significant amount of SNA traffic exists, starvation for all other traffic types may occur.

Prioritizing SNA Traffic

The key is how to prioritize SNA traffic over other kinds. There are several solutions. The first and simplest if you have a ToS precedence enabled network is to do nothing and let DSLw+ take care of it. DSLw+ automatically will set the ToS precedence bit to network control, thereby guaranteeing that SNA traffic will be serviced before any other traffic. The downside of this is that bandwidth starvation could occur if a significant amount of SNA traffic exists, as the network control precedence level is serviced before all others.

The second way is to use access lists and prioritize all traffic on port 2065 as a high queue. Priority queuing allows for four queuing levels with the high queue receiving priority treatment over all others. This solution itself is not that sufficient, as the same bandwidth starvation scenarios as were seen in using the precedence bit can occur. However, the best method for most interfaces is to configure no traffic shaping for SNA traffic. Weighted Fair Queuing (WFQ) is enabled by default on all Cisco WAN interfaces. WFQ will use the precedence bit that is set automatically by DLSw+ to compute the packet scheduling order as a function of the frame length of the packet and its place within the conversational queue. With the ToS precedence bit set to network, SNA packets will receive priority service without starving existing network resources.

This leaves the LAN and high-speed interfaces having the default configurations as providing the best differentiation and service for SNA. This is not to say that various methods such as WRED could not be used to guarantee service for SNA traffic. However, a significant amount of SNA traffic is being asked to traverse WAN links; specifically, lower-speed Frame Relay connections that may account for up to 90 percent of current WAN capabilities. It is specifically on such connections with their slower propagation and entry times that SNA traffic can encounter significant issues. The best way to provision SNA DSLw+ traffic is to direct it using PBR to a separate Frame Relay DLCI. In this manner, the environment is mimicking the natural service environment of SNA with minimal queuing delays. Actual QoS is then left to negotiated parameters within the Frame Relay switch and service provider. The following is a simple PBR configuration to send all DLSw+_ traffic out a subinterface.

```
Interface serial 2/0
      Encap frame-relay
      Frame-relay lmi-type ansi
Interface ser1/0.1 point-to-point
      ip address 20.23.32.1 255.255.255.0
      frame-relay interface-dlci 10

access-list 101 permit tcp any nay eq 2065
access-list 101 permit tcp any eq 2065 any

route-map sna permit 10
 match ip address 101
set next-interface serial1/0.1
```

Summary

In an ideal network world, everything would be connected via high-speed fiber connections with unlimited bandwidth and router processing capacity. Unfortunately, this case doesn't exist in most networks. Unfettered demands and competing applications can frequently cause network response issues. Users complain about choppy video and voice transfers, and productivity can suffer from these issues. The explosive growth of the Web and the bursty, unpredictable nature of its core traffic makes providing a guaranteed level of service extremely difficult in today's environment.

Various queuing and classification schemes were developed to provide a level of guaranteed service for mission-critical applications. Normal destination-based routing parameters are frequently insufficient to meet today's needs. Policy-based routing (PBR) provides a means of differentiating traffic by source port or IP address, and directing such traffic to particular service interfaces or modify the service level of these packets if they are deemed to be of lower priority. This feature has been extremely useful when corporations are providing lower-speed links for nonessential Web traffic while wishing to maintain higher-speed dedicated links for mission-critical Citrix or other applications.

To optimize both netowek and router resources, packets should be marked as close as possible to the ingress points of a network. CAR was created to meet this need. CAR provides a guaranteed level of bandwidth and classification for packets at the network ingress points (ideally, but can be anywhere). CAR provides the ability to limit the bandwidth that a data flow can have, and sets exception behaviors for burst characteristics. As such, while CAR will not shape traffic, it does provide a useful tool to guarantee bandwidth for mission-critical applications and prevent network saturation.

NBAR provides a ready-made tool that can quickly and easily provide for differentiation and classification of traffic within a network. When used in conjunction with queuing mechanisms, NBAR provides a simple and efficient method to maintain optimal network application response times. It provides the network administrator a new tool to maintain and extend network services while maximizing current investments in infrastructure.

The field of classification within network hardware and routers may be fairly recent—as is the use of new technologies to improve efficiencies, such as CEF—and does have a number of caveats and issues that must be closely monitored. However, the benefits that are gained from the use of these mechanisms and tools far outweigh the cost at this time. Even with legacy protocols, such as SNA, the use of recent advances such as DLSw+ allows for excellent traffic flows with minimal configuration.

FAQs Visit www.syngress.com/solutions to have your questions about this chapter answered by the author.

Q: What platforms support NBAR?

A: The 2600, 3600, and 7100, 7200 series router platforms support NBAR. However, 12.2 IOS promises to support NBAR for the 1700 series, and dNBAR will soon be available for the 7500 series.

Q: How much of a performance penalty is there with NBAR?

A: NBAR can have as much as a 15-percent processor hit, so make sure that you have enough processor capacity.

Q: I want to send all proxy Web traffic to a lower-speed dedicated link, while allowing all other traffic to use my higher-speed link. What is the best procedure to use?

A: Policy-based Routing (PBR) ideal for such a situation.

Q: I enabled PBR, but I have extremely slow response time. What can I do?

A: Enable fast switching using the IP route-cache policy command.

Q: My core routers are showing constant high processor utilization. What can I do to reduce this without buying new hardware?

A: Try enabling IP CEF on the core devices (but mind the caveats); you may see significant processor utilization drops.

Q: Can I use NBAR on all protocols?

A: No. NBAR, like CAR and CEF, will only function on IP-based traffic.

Chapter 6

Queuing and Congestion Avoidance Overview

Solutions in this chapter:

- Using FIFO Queuing
- Using Priority Queuing
- Using Custom Queuing
- Using Weighted Fair Queuing
- Using Random Early Detection

Introduction

In this chapter, we introduce the default queuing mechanisms used on interfaces of various speeds and examine the reasons for using different queuing mechanisms on different types of interfaces. You should pay particular attention to the fact that the choice of different queuing methods as the default behavior for an interface is based on bandwidth.

This chapter also introduces some basic types of queuing, such as priority and custom queuing. We will investigate, in detail, the benefits and drawbacks of these methods, and thereby provide the basis for making a decision as to whether these queuing methods are appropriate for implementation on your network.

This chapter also introduces the theory of random discard congestion avoidance. We discuss where this might be used, where it may or may not be needed, and what the benefits and drawbacks of the random discard method of congestion avoidance are. This discussion will be continued in later chapters, as some of these technologies are the foundation of other, more advanced, methods.

Using FIFO Queuing

As network traffic reaches an ingress or egress point, such as a router interface, network devices, such as a router, must be able to adequately process this traffic as it is being received. FIFO (first in/first out) queuing is the most basic approach to ordering traffic for proper communication. Like a line at a carnival ride, a FIFO queue places all packets in a single line as they enter the interface.

Packets are processed by the router in the same order they enter the interface. No priority is assigned to any packet. This approach is often referred to using the "leaky bucket" analogy. Packets are placed in the bucket from the top and "leak" out of the bucket from a controlled opening at the bottom. Why then is a FIFO queue necessary, if no priority or packet control is applied? Why not just let packets flow as they come in to the interface? The reason is simple. During the routing process, when a packet goes from one router interface to another, it often changes interface type and speed. Consider, for example, a single communication stream going from a 10BaseT Ethernet segment to a 256 Kbps serial connection. Figure 6.1 shows the FIFO queuing process for this stream. The stream encounters a speed mismatch. The Ethernet segment feeds the stream to the router at 10 Mbps, whereas the outbound serial connection sends the stream out at 256 Kbps. The FIFO queue is used to order the packets and hold them until the serial link can properly process them.

Figure 6.1 FIFO Queue in Operation

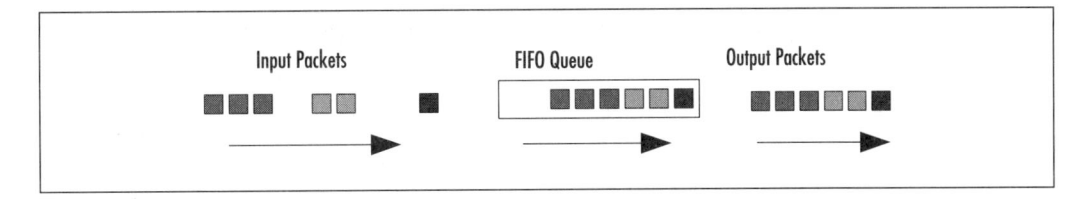

The FIFO queue enables the router to process higher speed communications exiting through a slower speed medium. In cases where the Ethernet communication is comprised of short bursts, the FIFO queue handles all the packets without difficulty. However, an increased amount of higher speed traffic coming from the Ethernet interface can often cause the FIFO queue to overflow. This situation is called "tail drop," because packets are dropped from the tail of the queue. The queue will continue to drop packets at the tail until it processes packets from the head, thus freeing space within the queue to accommodate new packets inbound from the tail end. Figure 6.2 shows a tail end drop situation.

Figure 6.2 FIFO Tail End Drop

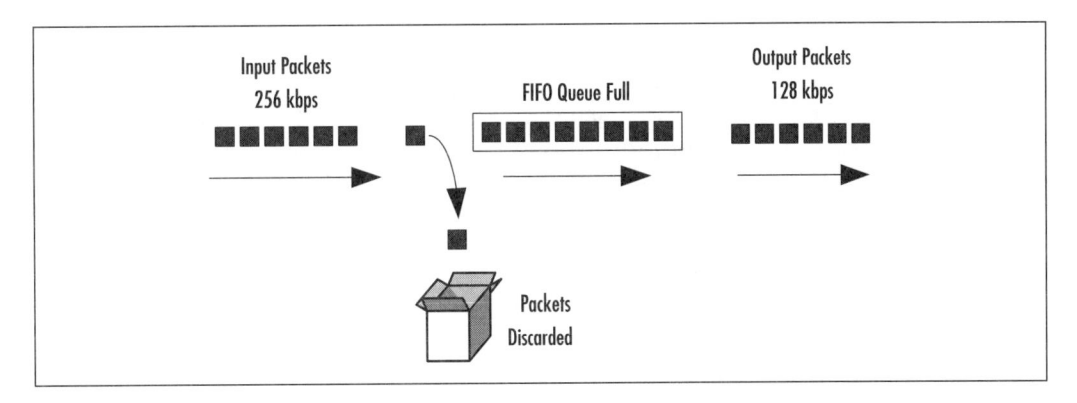

The disadvantage of FIFO queuing comes from its simplicity. Since it does not have a mechanism to distinguish the packets that it handles, it has no way to ensure that it processes the packets fairly and equally. It simply processes them in the same order that they enter the queue. This means that high traffic protocols, such as FTP (File Transfer Protocol), can use significant portions of the FIFO queue, leaving time sensitive protocols such as Telnet with little bandwidth to operate. In such a case, the Telnet session would seem interrupted and unresponsive, since the greater share of the queue is used by the FTP transfer.

It is thus apparent that FIFO is a very basic queuing mechanism that allows the router to order and process packets as they compete to exit an interface. These packets may come from one or multiple other interfaces connected to the router. For example, if a router has one serial interface connected to a wide area network and two Ethernet interfaces connected into two different local IP networks, packets from both Ethernet interfaces would compete for a spot in the outgoing FIFO queue running on the serial interface.

This single queue principle is the base of all other queuing mechanisms offered by the Cisco Internet Operating System (IOS). All other queuing mechanisms build on this single queue principle to offer better quality of service (QoS), depending on the traffic requirements.

High Speed versus Low Speed Links

By default, the Cisco IOS has Weighted Fair Queuing (WFQ) for any link having a speed of E1 (2.048 Mbps) or lower. This is an "invisible" feature of IOS, as it does not show up in the configurations. If you want to use FIFO queuing on an interface of E1 speed or lower, WFQ must be manually disabled through the IOS configurations. This feature first appeared in version 11.0 of the IOS.

> **TIP**
>
> Cisco has good reason for placing these default settings within the IOS configuration. FIFO queuing normally is not the preferred queuing method on slow speed links. If you use FIFO on these links, you must be aware of the consequences.

When Should I Use FIFO?

FIFO may not seem like a very sophisticated, or even desirable, queuing method, considering the rich features of other queuing mechanisms offered by the Cisco IOS. However, FIFO can be a very efficient queuing method in certain circumstances. Imagine, for example, a 10BasetT Ethernet segment connected to a router that in turn connects to a wide area network (WAN) through a T3 segment (45 Mbps, approximately). In this case, there is no chance that the inbound 10 Mbps communication can overwhelm the 45 Mbps outbound pipe. The router still requires the FIFO queue to order the packets into a single line in order to feed them to the T3 interface for processing. Using a simple queuing mechanism reduces the delay experienced by the packets as the router processes them. In delay-sensitive applications such as voice or video, this can be an important factor.

QoS with FIFO

One negative consequence of packets being tail dropped is that retransmissions are required at the upper layers of the OSI model. With TCP/IP for example, the Session layer would detect a break in the communication through the acknowledgement process. The Session layer would then adjust the transmission window size and start sending packets in smaller numbers. This retransmission process can be controlled for our purposes through techniques such as random early detection (RED) and weighted random early detection (WRED). These techniques are used in conjunction with FIFO queuing to maximize the throughput on congested links. They will be discussed in detail later in this chapter.

Using Priority Queuing

Priority queuing (PQ) enables network administrators to prioritize traffic based on specific criteria. These criteria include protocol or sub-protocol types, source interface, packet size, fragments, or any parameter identifiable through a standard or extended access list. PQ offers four different queues:

- low priority
- normal priority
- medium priority
- high priority

Through the proper configuration of PQ, each packet is assigned to one of these queues. If no classification is assigned to a packet, it is placed in the normal priority queue.

How Does Priority Queuing Work?

The priority of each queue is absolute. As packets are processed, PQ examines the state of each queue, always servicing higher priority queues before lower priority queues. This means that as long as there is traffic in a higher priority queue, lower priority queues will not be processed. PQ, therefore, does not use a fair allocation of resources among its queues. It services them strictly on the basis of the priority classifications configured by the network administrator. Figure 6.3 shows PQ in action.

Figure 6.3 Priority Queuing in Operation

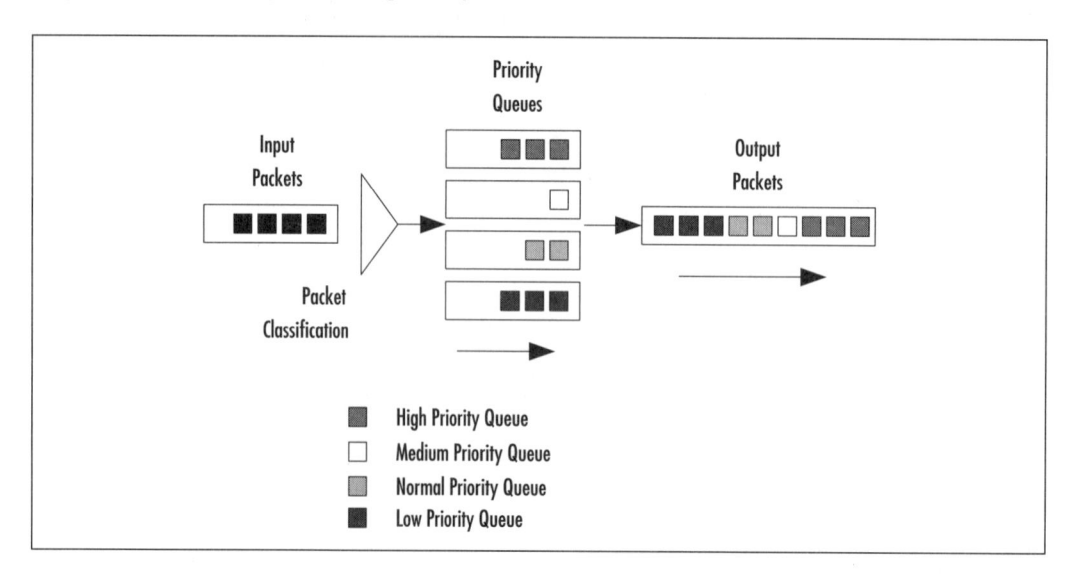

Queue Sizes

Each of these queues acts as an individual "leaky bucket" which is prone to tail discards. The default queue sizes for PQ are shown in Table 6.1. These queue sizes can be manually adjusted from 0 to 32,767 packets.

Table 6.1 Priority Queuing Default Queue Sizes

Limit	Size
High priority queue limit	20 packets
Medium priority queue limit	40 packets
Normal priority queue limit	60 packets
Low priority queue limit	80 packets

Why Do I Need Priority Queuing on My Network?

Priority queuing can seem like a coarse or "brute force" approach to traffic prioritization, but it allows you to give certain traffic classes absolute priority over others. For example, many legacy systems such as mainframes use Systems Network Architecture (SNA) as their method of transport. SNA is very susceptible to delays and so would be an excellent candidate for a high priority queue. If Telnet is the core business of an enterprise, it could also be given high priority over all other traffic. This ensures that high volume protocols such as FTP or HTTP do not negatively impact business-critical applications.

Remember that the configuration of PQ dictates how the queuing process will operate on that link. If new applications using new protocols are deployed within the networking environment, PQ will simply place these unaccounted for protocols in the normal priority queue. The configuration of PQ should therefore be periodically reviewed to ensure the validity of the queuing configuration.

Queue Starvation

When using PQ, you must give serious consideration to your traffic prioritization. If the traffic assigned to the high priority queue is heavy, lower priority queues will never be serviced. This leads to the traffic in these queues never being transmitted and additional traffic assigned to these queues being tail dropped . Figure 6.4 depicts such a situation.

Figure 6.4 Queue Starvation in Priority Queuing

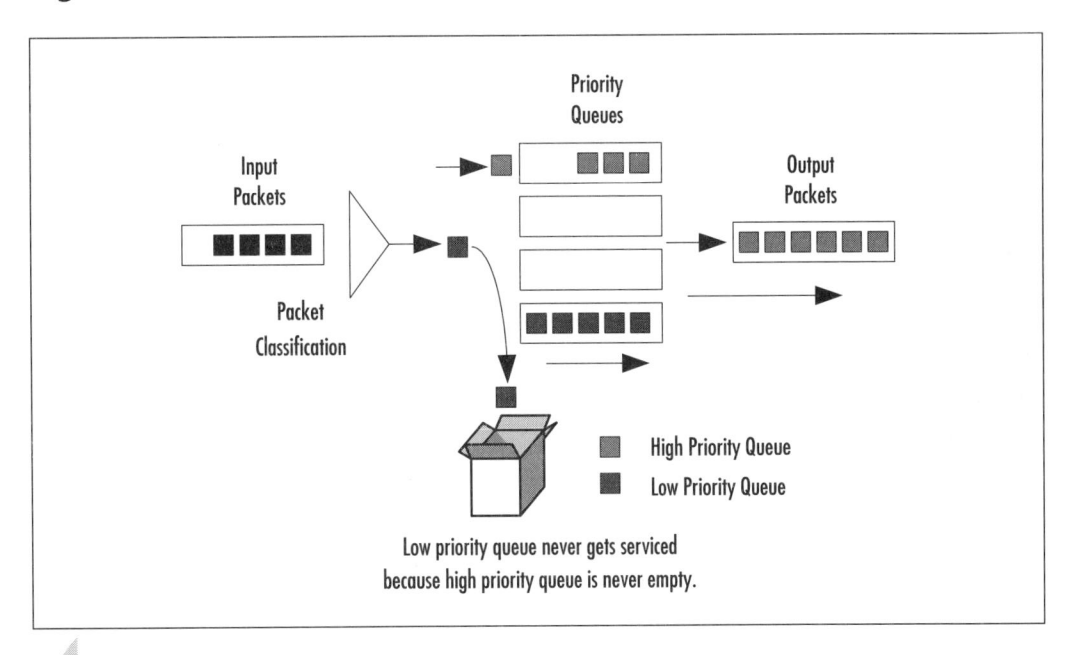

> **NOTE**
>
> Priority queuing does not work with any type of tunnel interface. Make sure you remember this fact when engineering QoS in a network that includes tunnels.

Using Custom Queuing

We have seen how priority queuing allows us to assign traffic to different queues, each queue being serviced depending strictly on its priority. Custom queuing (CQ) shifts the service of queues from an absolute mechanism based on priority to a round-robin approach, servicing each queue sequentially. CQ allows the creation of up to 16 user queues, each queue being serviced in succession by the CQ process. There is also one additional queue, called queue 0, which is created automatically by the CQ process. This queue is user configurable, but is not recommended. We will discuss this queue in greater detail later in this section. Each of the user-configurable queues, and even queue 0, represents an individual "leaky bucket" which is also susceptible to tail drops. Unlike priority queuing, however, custom queuing ensures that each queue gets serviced, thereby avoiding the potential situation in which a certain queue never gets processed. Custom queuing gets its name from the fact that network administrators can control the number of queues in the queuing process. In addition, the amount of bytes, or "byte count" for each queue can be adjusted in order for the CQ process to spend more time on certain queues. CQ can therefore offer a more refined queuing mechanism, but it cannot ensure absolute priority like PQ.

How Does Custom Queuing Work?

Custom queuing operates by servicing the user-configured queues individually and sequentially for a specific amount of bytes. The default byte count for each queue is 1500 bytes, so without any customization, CQ would process 1500 bytes from queue 1, then 1500 bytes from queue 2, then 1500 bytes from queue 3, and so on. Traffic can be classified and assigned to any queue through the same methods as priority queuing, namely, protocol or sub-protocol types, source interface, packet size, fragments, or any parameter identifiable through a standard or extended access list. Figure 6.5 shows CQ in action.

Through a judicious use of the byte count of each queue, it is possible to perform bandwidth allocation using custom queuing. Imagine, for example, an enterprise wanting to restrict Web traffic to 25 percent of the total bandwidth, Telnet traffic to 25 percent of the total bandwidth, and the remaining 50 percent for all other traffic. They could configure custom queuing with three queues. Queue 1 would handle all Web traffic with a default byte count of 1500 bytes. Queue 2 would handle all Telnet traffic, also with a default byte count of 1500 bytes. Queue 3 would handle all remaining traffic, but it would be manually assigned a byte value of 3000 bytes. Figure 6.6 shows this CQ configuration.

Figure 6.5 Custom Queuing in Action

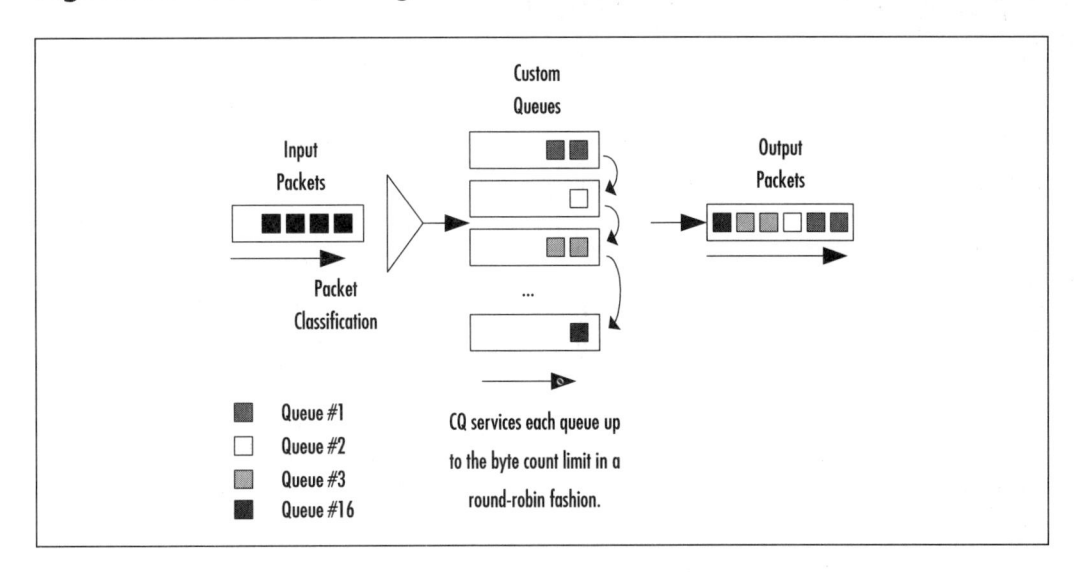

In this case, CQ would process 1500 bytes of Web traffic, then 1500 bytes of Telnet traffic, and finally 3000 bytes of remaining traffic, giving us the 25 percent, 25 percent, 50 percent allocation desired. If more bandwidth is available towing to a light network traffic load, CQ can actually process more information from each queue. In Figure 6.6, if only queues 1 and 2 had traffic in them, they would each be allocated 50 percent of the total bandwidth. The byte count values indicate the bandwidth allocation in a congested situation.

Figure 6.6 CQ with Custom Byte Count

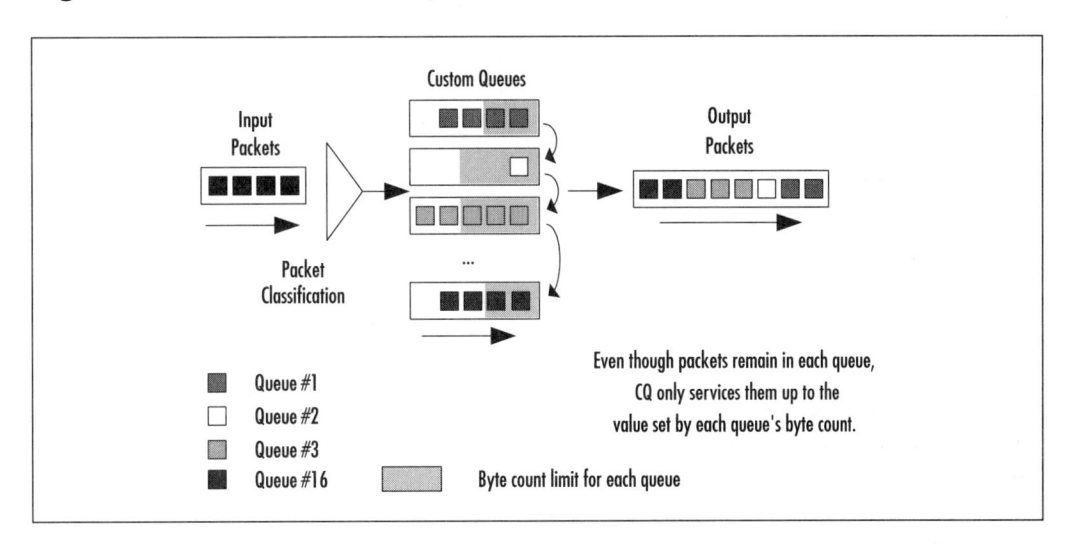

> **WARNING**
>
> Custom queuing does not perform packet fragmentation. If a packet is larger than the total byte count allocation of that queue, CQ processes the entire packet anyway. This means that a 1500-byte queue will service a 3000-byte packet in its 1500-byte interval. In an Ethernet or HDLC environment where the maximum transmission unit (MTU) size is 1500, the default byte count value of CQ is appropriate. In other environments, such as Token Ring, where the MTU can climb to 4098 bytes, using 1500-byte queues to allocate bandwidth can lead to inaccurate allocation of resources. In the previous example, increasing the byte count ratio to 4098/4098/8196 would be more appropriate. Be aware of your environment.

This warning is necessary in a variety of situations. We have seen that if an interface is allowed to send 1500 bytes and the first packet in the queue is 1501 bytes or more, the entire packet will be sent. However, it is also true that if the first packet is 1499 bytes and the second packet is 1500 bytes or more, the entire first packet will be sent, and because an additional 1 byte is allowed to be transmitted, the entire second packet will also be sent.

The disadvantage of custom queuing is that, like priority queuing, you must create policy statements on the interface to classify the traffic to the queues. If you do not create custom queuing policies on the custom queuing interface, all traffic is placed in a single queue (the default queue) and is processed on a first in/first out basis, in the same manner as a FIFO queuing interface.

Queue Sizes

As with priority queuing, each custom queue is an individual "leaky bucket." The default queue size for each CQ queue is 20 packets. Individual queue sizes can be manually adjusted from 0 to 32,767 packets.

Protocol Interactions with Custom Queuing

It is important to understand that custom queuing does not provide absolute guarantees with respect to bandwidth allocation. CQ supports network protocols, but it is also dependent on their operation. For example, consider the windowing mechanism of TCP/IP. On an Ethernet segment (MTU of 1500 bytes), if the TCP/IP transmission window is set to 1, the Session layer will send one packet and wait for an acknowledgement (ACK) before sending another packet. If the byte count of the queue configured to handle TCP/IP is set to 3000 bytes, the queue will always remain half empty when serviced by CQ, since TCP/IP will not send more than 1500 bytes at a time (one packet). Therefore, doubling the byte count value of the TCP/IP queue will not increase the throughput of that queue.

Why Do I Need Custom Queuing on My Network?

Custom queuing is an excellent mechanism to perform bandwidth allocation on a high traffic link. It allows network administrators to control the flow of packets and provide assured throughput to preferred services. Unlike priority queuing, the custom queuing mechanism ensures that each queue is serviced sequentially. However, as with priority queuing, custom queuing does not automatically adapt to a changing network environment. All new protocols that are not defined in the custom queuing configuration will be allocated to the default queue for processing.

Complicated Cores

Junior network administrators dealing with small routers such as Cisco's 2500 series often wonder what it is like to work at the core of a large WAN using high caliber routers such as Cisco's 7500 series engines. They imagine complex routing schemes working in conjunction with exotic queuing processes and other extravagant services, when in fact; these routers are much less interesting than devices located at the edge of a network. Normally, core routers are not used for time consuming tasks such as tunnel encapsulation, encryption, traffic classification, or queuing mechanisms other than FIFO. The single command that should be found on these routers is "route!"

Mechanisms such as priority queuing and custom queuing should be placed near the edge of the network. Border routers connecting a site to a company WAN, for example, can be an excellent location to enforce traffic prioritization.

What Is Queue 0?

Queue 0 is a special queue used by the system to pass "network control packets," such as keepalive packets, signaling packets, and so forth. It is user-configurable, but is not recommended. Queue 0 has priority over all other queues and so is emptied before any user-defined queues.

Using Weighted Fair Queuing (WFQ)

As of IOS version 11.0, weighted fair queuing is turned on by default on links of 2.048 Mbps (E1) or below. WFQ dynamically classifies network traffic into individual flows and assigns each flow a fair share of the total bandwidth. Each flow is classified as a high bandwidth or low bandwidth flow. Low bandwidth flows, such as Telnet, get priority over high bandwidth flows such as FTP. If multiple high bandwidth flows occur simultaneously, they share the remaining bandwidth evenly once low bandwidth flows have been serviced. Each of these flows is placed into an individual queue that follows the leaky bucket analogy. If packets from a specific flow exceed the capacity of the queue to which it is allocated, that queue is subject to tail drops like all other queues.

Routers equipped with Versatile Interface Processor (VIP) cards can offload the WFQ process to these VIP cards. In this case, the process is referred to as distributed weighted fair queuing (DWFQ). A VIP card is, in essence, a "router within a router." VIP cards have the brains and computing power necessary to perform certain functions that would normally be sent to the main processor. Delegating the WFQ process to the VIP card thus makes additional memory and CPU cycles from the main router processor available. This distributed architecture enables high-powered routers to perform a large number of concurrent tasks without overtaxing the router's processor. These functions will be described in greater detail in another chapter.

How Does Weighted Fair Queuing Work?

WFQ first identifies each individual flow and classifies it as a high or low bandwidth flow. Each flow is characterized using the information in Table 6.2.

Table 6.2 Weighted Fair Queuing Flow Identification Fields

Protocol	WFQ Flow Identification Fields
TCP/IP	IP Protocol Source IP address Destination IP address Source port Destination port Type of service (ToS) field
Appletalk	Source network, node and socket Destination network, node and socket Protocol type
IPX	Source network, host and socket Destination network, host and socket Level 2 protocol type
DECnet	Source address Destination address
Frame relay	DLCI value
Transparent Bridging	Source and destination MAC address
CLNS	Source NSAP Destination NSAP
Banyan VINES	Source network and host Destination network and host Level 2 protocol type
Apollo	Source network, host and socket Destination network, host and socket Level 2 protocol type
All others	Control protocols (one per queue)

Once classified, the flows are placed in a fair queue. The default number of dynamic queues is 256. Each queue is serviced in a round-robin fashion, like custom queuing, with service priority being given to low bandwidth queues. Each queue is configured with a default congestive discard threshold that limits the number of messages in each queue. The default congestive discard value for each queue is 64 packets. For high bandwidth flows, messages attempting to enter the queue once the discard threshold is reached are discarded. Low bandwidth messages, however, can still enter the queue even though the congestive discard threshold is exceeded for that queue. The limits for dynamic queues and the congestive discard threshold can both be adjusted up to a value of 4096 packets. So far, the process described shows an equal treatment of all the conversations occurring on an outbound interface. Aside from the differentiation between low- and high-speed flows, these conversations are not given any priority or weight over one another. This process would thus be better referred to as "fair queuing." The next section addresses the "weighted" aspect of WFQ.

> **NOTE**
>
> Weighted fair queuing is not compatible with the technologies listed below. Priority queuing and custom queuing can, however, be used to provide QoS on these circuits.
>
> - X.25
> - Synchronous Data Link Control (SDLC)
> - Link Access Procedure, Balanced (LAPB)
> - Tunnel, loopback, dialer, bridged, and virtual interfaces

Tunnel interfaces are virtual conduits across an existing internetwork. Different kinds of tunnels use different kinds of technologies. Generic routing encapsulation protocol (GRE), Cayman TunnelTalk AppleTalk encapsulation, and IP over IP encapsulation are some of the protocols available to encapsulate tunnel traffic. GRE tunneling is the default encapsulation on Cisco routers. This is important because tunnel interfaces are not physical interfaces on a router. They make use of a physical interface such as a serial or Ethernet interface for transport to their final destination or exit point. Consequently, the tunnel traffic can be classified in the queuing process of the physical interface. For example, if a CQ process on a serial interface allocates 50 percent of the bandwidth to a GRE tunnel, applying a different CQ process to the tunnel to control bandwidth would be pointless, since the tunnel is controlled by another queuing mechanism. In the case of WFQ, the tunnel would be considered as one single flow, since the protocol type (GRE), source address, and destination address remain the same, independent of the traffic carried inside the tunnel. Applying queuing mechanisms to a tunnel interface other than FIFO, therefore, would not provide any congestion control, since the tunnel is subject to control by another mechanism running on the physical interface.

Where Does the Weight Factor Come into Play?

Up to this point, it appears that WFQ classifies flows only in terms of high or low bandwidth. Where, then, does the "weighted" factor start affecting the queuing process? The answer is, when the ToS field, or IP precedence field, is different. WFQ takes into account IP precedence and gives preferential treatment to higher precedence flows by adjusting their weight. If all packets have the same default precedence value, then the "weighted" factor does not affect the WFQ process.

The weight of flows when different ToS values are present is calculated by adding 1 to the packet's precedence. The total weight of all flows represents the total bandwidth to be divided amongst the individual flows. For example, if three flows all use the default IP precedence of 0, they are each given a weight of 1 (0 + 1). The weight of the total bandwidth is 3 (1 + 1 + 1), and each flow is given one-third of the total bandwidth. On the other hand, if two flows have an IP precedence of 0, and a third flow has a precedence of 5, the total weight is 8 (1 + 1 + 6). The first two flows are each given one-eighth of the bandwidth, whereas the third flow receives six-eighths of the total bandwidth.

Resource Reservation Protocol (RSVP)

RSVP is a Cisco proprietary protocol used to guarantee timely delivery of network traffic. It allows applications to make bandwidth reservations across the entire network. When WFQ is configured on a link, RSVP makes use of different queues within the WFQ process in order to ensure that the QoS requirements of RSVP conversations are respected. The default number of RSVP reservable queues is 0. This means that in order for WFQ to adequately support RSVP, it must be manually configured to a value other than its default.

Why Do I Need Weighted Fair Queuing on My Network?

WFQ is a simple to implement, dynamic queuing mechanism which ensures that every conversation in the network gets a fair share of the bandwidth. Unlike PQ and CQ, which need to be manually configured, WFQ dynamically adapts to changes in the network, including new protocols and applications. If there is no mission-critical traffic that must be given priority over other traffic, WFQ is an easy and efficient method to provide the best level of service to every network user. Be aware of the technology limitations of WFQ, however. Even though traffic flow considerations would seem to make WFQ an excellent choice, the underlying technology may prevent WFQ from being used.

What Does "Flow Based" Mean?

The term "flow based" refers to a method of identifying streams of communications. This is how WFQ allocates traffic to different queues. Priority queuing and custom queuing use a static, pigeonhole method of traffic classification. Packets entering the queuing process are classified by protocol, port, network address, or other factors determined by the network administrator. For example, if Telnet traffic is assigned to the high priority queue in PQ, all Telnet traffic, regardless of source and destination, will be allocated to the high priority queue. PQ would treat all Telnet traffic the same. Consequently, if one host had more Telnet traffic than another host, priority queuing could not ensure any sort of fairness within that high priority queue. WFQ, on the other hand, classifies traffic using a combination of all the parameters listed in Table 6.2. This means that Telnet traffic from host A to host B would be considered as one flow, and Telnet traffic from host A to host C would be considered as a separate flow.

> **NOTE**
>
> When dealing with flows, bear in mind the mechanisms that protocols and applications use to communicate. For example, one visit to a Web page can initiate multiple connections from the same source host to the same destination host. Downloading the page, the graphics, and other information can generate multiple connections, each of which will be interpreted by WFQ as an individual flow.

Using Random Early Detection (RED)

RED is a mechanism that prevents congestion situations by dealing with network communications as the link starts showing the early signs of congestion. Consequently, with RED enabled, a link should never reach the point of congestion because the RED mechanism will restrict the flow of packets before this happens. This also has the effect of normalizing the bandwidth usage of a link and maintaining it at peak capacity.

How Does Random Early Detection Work?

RED works by randomly discarding packets from different conversations. It uses TCP/IP's sliding window and rapid recovery mechanisms to force the communication to reduce the speed at which it is transmitting packets, thus reducing the bandwidth usage of that particular conversation. By applying this principle randomly to various ongoing communications, RED can slow things down as it detects that a link approaches a congestive state. RED is not appropriate in situations where UDP traffic is predominant, because RED has no appreciable effects on it. We will see why later in this section.

TCP/IP Sliding Window

In order to fully understand how RED operates, it is important to understand the underlying mechanism that RED uses to reduce communications. Figure 6.7 shows the sliding window mechanism of TCP in action.

Figure 6.7 TCP Sliding Window

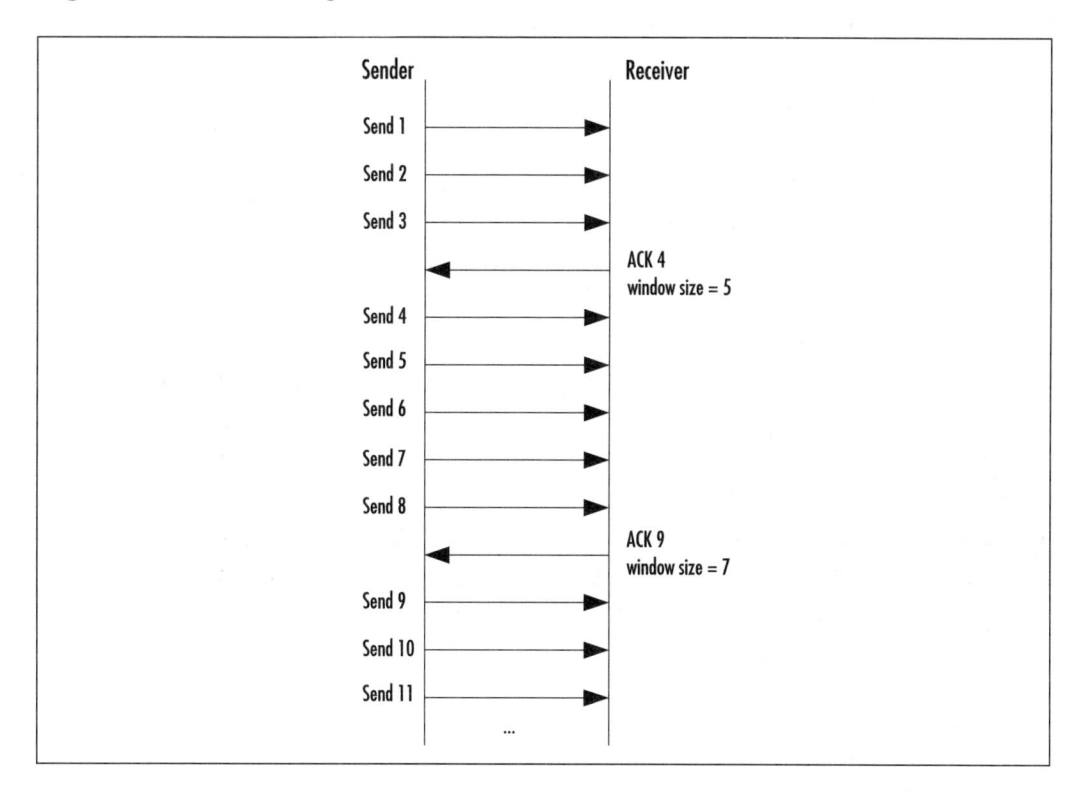

```
Sender                          Receiver

Send 1       ──────────────▶
Send 2       ──────────────▶
Send 3       ──────────────▶
             ◀──────────────    ACK 4
                                window size = 5
Send 4       ──────────────▶
Send 5       ──────────────▶
Send 6       ──────────────▶
Send 7       ──────────────▶
Send 8       ──────────────▶
             ◀──────────────    ACK 9
                                window size = 7
Send 9       ──────────────▶
Send 10      ──────────────▶
Send 11      ──────────────▶
                  ...
```

As the sender sends trains of packets, the receiver acknowledges the last packet of the train and informs the sender that the transmission was successful. Furthermore, it instructs the sender that it may increase the number of packets per train, or window size, in its next transmission. In Figure 6.7, the window size of the transmission increases from 3 to 5 to 7 packets. If left unchecked, TCP sessions will increase their window size until a packet is dropped and a NAK is sent by the receiver, or until an out of sequence ACK is received by the sender. At that point, TCP recovers at the last successful ACK sequence and reduces the window size in an attempt to achieve successful communication.

When multiple TCP connections operate on a common link, they will all increase the size of their sliding windows as successful ACKs are received. This synchronized progression gradually consumes the bandwidth of the link until the link is congested. At that point, all TCP communications experience a transmission error, resulting in a sizeable drop in bandwidth usage as all the TCP connections move to smaller sliding window sizes simultaneously. This process is called "global synchronization," and it creates problems on the link owing to the fact that all the streams will then start ramping back up simultaneously, leading to another congestion situation. This cycle continues over and over, creating peaks and valleys of bandwidth utilization on the link.

RED tries to prevent this fluctuation in bandwidth by randomly dropping packets from various connections as the link approaches a congestive state. Consequently, the windows of TCP connections are throttled back one by one as the random algorithm of RED discards packets from their connections. This results in a normalization of network traffic close to the congestion point of the link, rather than having massive backoffs as all TCP connections drop packets when they hit the congestion point of the link. Figure 6.8 shows the effect of

Figure 6.8 The Effect of RED on a TCP Sliding Window Size

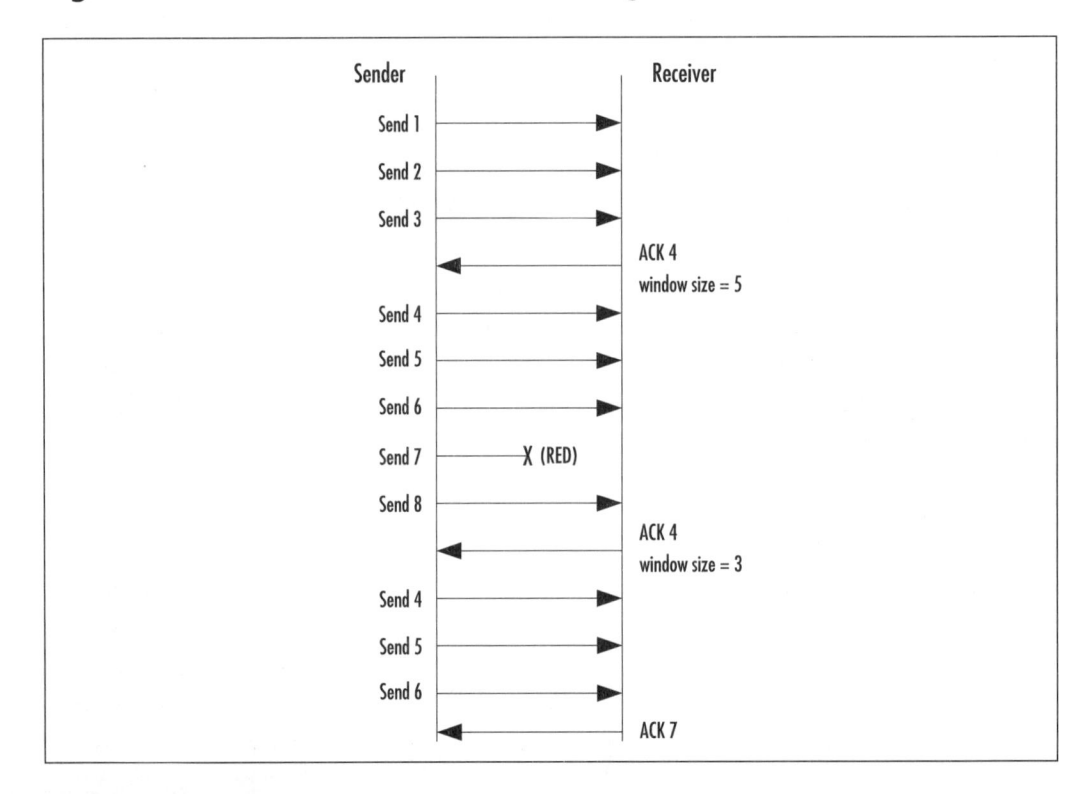

```
Sender                          Receiver
Send 1    ────────────▶
Send 2    ────────────▶
Send 3    ────────────▶
          ◀────────────   ACK 4
                          window size = 5
Send 4    ────────────▶
Send 5    ────────────▶
Send 6    ────────────▶
Send 7    ─────X (RED)
Send 8    ────────────▶
          ◀────────────   ACK 4
                          window size = 3
Send 4    ────────────▶
Send 5    ────────────▶
Send 6    ────────────▶
          ◀────────────   ACK 7
```

RED on a TCP sliding window size when it drops a packet at random from that connection. In this example, when RED drops packet 7, the next packet received by the receiver is packet 8, which is out of sequence. The receiver sends back a second ACK for the last valid packet train received and decreases the sliding window size for the sender to use.

Why Do I Need Random Early Detection on My Network?

RED is useful on links where TCP/IP traffic congestion is expected. It uses no traffic classification or prioritization in relation to the random discards, but rather indiscriminately drops packets as it senses impending link congestion. The benefit of RED is that link utilization will normalize close to its maximum capacity. Without RED, the average utilization will actually be lower, with the actual usage fluctuating as the link reaches the congestion point and then all the TCP sessions back off simultaneously.

This fair distribution of discards does not take into account other factors such as a packet's IP precedence. As with "fair queuing," RED can make use of a mechanism that takes into account the IP precedence of a packet. It would thus schedule discards less randomly by providing fewer discards for high precedence packets. This process is called Weighted Random Early Detection (WRED) and will be discussed in another chapter.

What If I Run AppleTalk or IPX?

RED makes use of TCP's sliding window mechanism. Other protocols such as IPX or Appletalk have the same retransmission mechanisms as TCP/IP, but they do not use the same sliding window process. This means that when faced with a random discard or an actual packet drop, they simply retransmit at the same rate as the previous packet train. Unlike TCP/IP, there is no mechanism to throttle back the speed at which these protocols transmit. Therefore, the use of RED should be restricted to TCP/IP networks only.

Summary

In this chapter, we covered the basic mechanisms for congestion management and avoidance. Techniques such as priority queuing, custom queuing, and weighted fair queuing are all valid techniques used to prioritize the processing of network traffic over high contention links. They allow network managers to provide preferential treatment to certain classes of protocols, ports, and other classification attributes. It is important to understand the mechanics behind each queuing process in order to select the one that best suits your environment. Typical use of these techniques gives priority to delay-sensitive applications such as voice and video, business-critical traffic, traffic that is dependant on timely handshakes such as legacy SNA, or application traffic such as Telnet, where delays in communication result in a poor performance of the user interface. High volume traffic such as FTP rarely receives preferential treatment, since a reduction in total throughput does not normally affect end users. If a large file transfer takes 85 minutes when queuing is in place, instead of 80 minutes without QoS for the other users, that normally does not cause additional hardship to the FTP user. The performance improvement for the remaining users may, however, be sizeable if the proper queuing rules are applied.

Queuing normally involves giving someone priority over someone else in order to provide the best overall service. However, in cases where all traffic should be considered equal, queuing would not be an appropriate choice. For example, on a site dedicated solely to anonymous FTP transfers, all traffic will be high volume file transfers. In this case, congestion avoidance mechanisms, such as random early detection, are better suited to improving overall network performance. RED can improve the overall average throughput by avoiding collective TCP backoffs and enabling the link to operate continuously at or near its maximum capacity. The following chapter will describe how to configure the queuing and congestion avoidance techniques covered in this chapter.

FAQs

Visit www.syngress.com/solutions to have your questions about this chapter answered by the author.

Q: I have placed a simple priority queuing process on my fast Ethernet interface, but this has resulted in degraded service rather than an improvement for my users. Why?

A: Priority queuing is not suitable for high-speed links, since the additional processing involved may not be completed fast enough to keep up with the speed of incoming packets.

Q: I have a mainframe connected to the network on a Token Ring interface, and the remainder of my network is connected to an Ethernet interface. I have created two custom queues, each using the default 1500 byte count, to handle this traffic. Queue 1 handles strictly SNA traffic, whereas queue 2 takes care of all the Ethernet traffic. I would expect a 50/50 distribution, but traffic analysis shows my SNA traffic is taking much more than that. Why?

A: Custom queuing does not fragment packets. If a packet larger than the total byte count of a queue is transmitted, custom queuing will transmit the entire packet even though the byte count for that queue is lower than the number of bytes it transmits. In this case, the SNA traffic comes from a Token Ring segment, which normally has a maximum transmission unit size of 4098 bytes. This means that many packets from the Token Ring segment will enter the queue with a packet size greater than the byte count of that queue. These packets will be transmitted in their entirety, skewing the bandwidth distribution you have put in place.

Q: I do not see any configurations related to weighted fair queuing on my router. Is it really happening? If so, where?

A: WFQ is enabled by default on links having a speed of E1 (2.048 Mbps) or lower. On these links, the absence of any WFQ configuration indicates that the network administrator has not manually disabled it. On links faster than E1, the absence of WFQ configurations indicates that the network administrator has not enabled WFQ, and the interface would resort to simple FIFO queuing. The commands "show interface" and "show queuing" can be used to view the queuing mechanism on each interface.

Q: FIFO seems like a very basic and ineffective queuing mechanism. Should I make sure I use at least WFQ everywhere in my network to provide the best service to everyone?

A: No. FIFO is an essential mechanism to properly order and transmit packets from one interface to another. FIFO is also the queuing mechanism of choice at the core of a network where a high-speed router's function is not to classify traffic and make decisions, but rather to route traffic in from one interface and out through another. Mechanisms like PQ, CQ, and WFQ should be applied closer to the edge of the network.

Q: I have two sites connected through five routers, as shown in Figure 6.9. I want to give Telnet traffic priority over everything else by classifying Telnet into the high priority queue and having the remaining traffic flow through the normal priority queue. Do I need to configure PQ on every router or just the edge routers?

Figure 6.9 Priority Queuing Across Multiple Routers

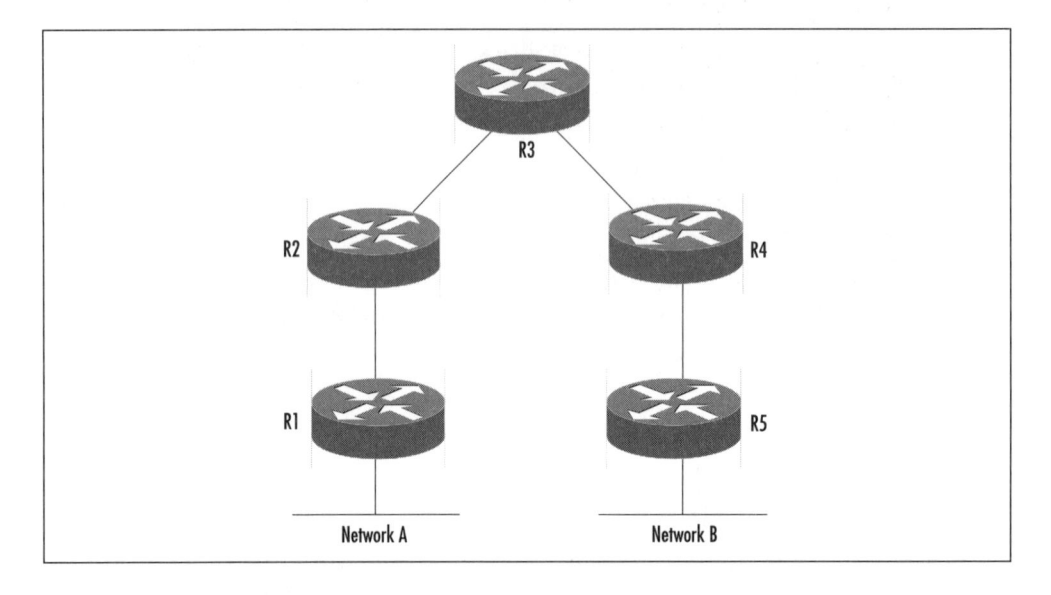

A: Priority queuing, custom queuing, and weighted fair queuing affect only outbound traffic from an interface. Assuming that the link speed between routers is identical, having R1 and R5 prioritize outbound traffic is all that is required. Routers R2, R3, and R4 will simply route traffic and will not experience any congestion. All of the prioritization and packet tail drops will have been performed by R1 and R5 at the edge of the network.

Q: I am not using IPX, Appletalk, or any protocol other than TCP/IP. Will random early detection properly throttle back conversations in every instance, ensuring that all my network links remain free of congestion and operate at peak efficiency?

A: No. RED is an excellent mechanism to help prevent congestion situations, but it will not work with all TCP/IP traffic. UDP, for example, can also carry high throughput applications like voice and video, but it does not use the sliding window mechanism used by TCP. In this case, discarding a packet from a UDP stream will not cause that stream to slow its pace of information transmission.

Chapter 7

Configuring Queuing and Congestion Avoidance

Solutions in this chapter:

- **Configuring FIFO Queuing**
- **Configuring Priority Queuing**
- **Configuring Custom Queuing**
- **Configuring Weighted Fair Queuing**
- **Configuring Random Early Detection**

Introduction

Now that we have an understanding of the basic queuing and congestion avoidance mechanisms, it is time to become familiar with how these mechanisms are configured. This chapter describes how to reset an interface to its default queuing method, change its queuing method, and configure the queuing methods introduced in Chapter 6.

FIFO and weighted fair queuing require very little configuration, whereas priority and custom queuing configurations can range from extremely simple to quite complex. The level of complexity is almost entirely related to the access lists that control the functions of the queuing mechanisms, so it is important that you review access lists in detail before configuring these mechanisms.

The configurations shown in this chapter do not represent every possible configuration scenario or configuration option. If you need more information about configurations not shown in this chapter, there are many excellent examples on Cisco's Web site (www.cisco.com).

Configuring FIFO Queuing

FIFO is the default queuing mechanism for links with a speed greater than E1 (2.048 Mbps). On these links, no special configuration is required. However, on links of E1 speed or lower, weighted fair queuing is the default queuing mechanism. Thus, in order to make FIFO the queuing mechanism for these slower links, WFQ must be manually disabled.

Enabling FIFO

The interface command "no fair-queue" is used to disable WFQ when it is the default queuing mechanism. The following code disables WFQ so that FIFO can act as the queuing mechanism for that link:

```
Rosa#show interface serial 0/0
Serial0/0 is up, line protocol is up
  Hardware is PowerQUICC Serial
  Internet address is 192.168.10.1/24
  MTU 1500 bytes, BW 1544 Kbit, DLY 20000 usec,
     reliability 255/255, txload 1/255, rxload 1/255
  Encapsulation HDLC, loopback not set
  Keepalive set (10 sec)
```

```
Last input 00:00:08, output 00:00:00, output hang never
Last clearing of "show interface" counters 5d05h
Input queue: 0/75/0 (size/max/drops); Total output drops: 0
Queueing strategy: weighted fair
Output queue: 0/1000/64/0 (size/max total/threshold/drops)
   Conversations  0/2/256 (active/max active/max total)
   Reserved Conversations 0/0 (allocated/max allocated)
5 minute input rate 0 bits/sec, 0 packets/sec
5 minute output rate 0 bits/sec, 0 packets/sec
   51061 packets input, 3102381 bytes, 0 no buffer
   Received 51046 broadcasts, 0 runts, 0 giants, 0 throttles
   1 input errors, 0 CRC, 1 frame, 0 overrun, 0 ignored, 0 abor
   51116 packets output, 3200654 bytes, 0 underruns
   0 output errors, 0 collisions, 132 interface resets
   0 output buffer failures, 0 output buffers swapped out
   29 carrier transitions
   DCD=up  DSR=up  DTR=up  RTS=up  CTS=up


Rosa#
Rosa#configure terminal
Enter configuration commands, one per line.  End with CNTL/Z.
Rosa(config)#interface serial 0/0
Rosa(config-if)#no fair-queue
Rosa(config-if)#end
Rosa#


Rosa#show interfaces serial 0/0
Serial0/0 is up, line protocol is up
  Hardware is PowerQUICC Serial
  Internet address is 192.168.10.1/24
  MTU 1500 bytes, BW 1544 Kbit, DLY 20000 usec,
     reliability 255/255, txload 1/255, rxload 1/255
  Encapsulation HDLC, loopback not set
  Keepalive set (10 sec)
  Last input 00:00:07, output 00:00:08, output hang never
```

```
Last clearing of "show interface" counters 5d05h
Queueing strategy: fifo
Output queue 0/40, 0 drops; input queue 0/75, 0 drops
5 minute input rate 0 bits/sec, 0 packets/sec
5 minute output rate 0 bits/sec, 0 packets/sec
    51075 packets input, 3103231 bytes, 0 no buffer
    Received 51060 broadcasts, 0 runts, 0 giants, 0 throttles
    1 input errors, 0 CRC, 1 frame, 0 overrun, 0 ignored, 0 abor
    51129 packets output, 3201506 bytes, 0 underruns
    0 output errors, 0 collisions, 133 interface resets
    0 output buffer failures, 0 output buffers swapped out
    29 carrier transitions
    DCD=up  DSR=up  DTR=up  RTS=up  CTS=up
```

Verifying FIFO Operations

In order to verify the operation of the FIFO queuing process on an interface, the command "show queueing" is used. This command has multiple optional parameters to guide IOS in showing only the appropriate information. The output of this command shows the status of the FIFO queue along with tail drop statistics and queue depth:

```
Rosa#show queueing?
  interface
  custom          custom queueing list configuration
  fair            fair queueing configuration
  priority        priority queueing list configuration
  random-detect   random early detection configuration
  |               Output modifiers
  <cr>

Rosa#show queueing interface serial 0/0
Interface Serial0/0 queueing strategy: fifo
  Queueing strategy: fifo
  Output queue 0/40, 0 drops; input queue 0/75, 0 drops
Rosa#
```

These results can also be observed in the previous example in the output following the "show interface" command.

FIFO with RED

Once FIFO has been successfully configured on an interface, it is possible to add random early detection as a congestion avoidance mechanism on that interface. Since RED is not a queuing or traffic prioritization process, it can work in conjunction with FIFO. The following code activates RED on an interface already configured with FIFO. The configuration of RED is explained in further detail later in this chapter.

```
Rosa#configure terminal
Enter configuration commands, one per line.  End with CNTL/Z.
Rosa(config)#interface serial 0/0
Rosa(config-if)#random-detect
Rosa(config-if)#end


Rosa#show interface serial 0/0
Serial0/0 is up, line protocol is up
  Hardware is PowerQUICC Serial
  Internet address is 192.168.10.1/24
  MTU 1500 bytes, BW 1544 Kbit, DLY 20000 usec,
     reliability 255/255, txload 1/255, rxload 1/255
  Encapsulation HDLC, loopback not set
  Keepalive set (10 sec)
  Last input 00:00:06, output 00:00:09, output hang never
  Last clearing of "show interface" counters 5d06h
  Input queue: 0/75/0 (size/max/drops); Total output drops: 0
  Queueing strategy: random early detection(RED)
  5 minute input rate 0 bits/sec, 0 packets/sec
  5 minute output rate 0 bits/sec, 0 packets/sec
     51159 packets input, 3108331 bytes, 0 no buffer
     Received 51144 broadcasts, 0 runts, 0 giants, 0 throttles
     2 input errors, 0 CRC, 2 frame, 0 overrun, 0 ignored, 0 abor
     51213 packets output, 3206762 bytes, 0 underruns
     0 output errors, 0 collisions, 134 interface resets
```

```
       0 output buffer failures, 0 output buffers swapped out
       29 carrier transitions
       DCD=up  DSR=up  DTR=up  RTS=up  CTS=up
```

Rosa#

Configuring Priority Queuing

The tasks involved in configuring priority queuing are as follows:

- Define a priority list
- Assign the priority list to an interface

Of the two tasks, defining the priority list is the most important because it is at this point that the packet classification is determined for the entire priority queuing process. The following discussion includes multiple ways to classify network traffic, which will help you apply the principles of priority queuing in your network.

Enabling Priority Queuing

The first step in configuring priority queuing is to define the priority list. The following code depicts the priority-list command and its parameters:

```
Rosa(config)#priority-list ?
  <1-16>   Priority list number


Rosa(config)#priority-list 1 ?
  default     Set priority queue for unspecified datagrams
  interface   Establish priorities for packets from an interface
  protocol    priority queueing by protocol
  queue-limit Set queue limits for priority queues
```

The command first requires us to select a priority list number between 1 and 16. This is necessary because multiple priority lists can be configured on a single router to control different interfaces using different priority queuing policies. Next, the command requires us to select what we want to prioritize. We can prioritize by inbound interface or by protocol type. The command also allows us to select the default priority of unclassified traffic and to set the queue limits in packets.

Consider the following sample requirements. All packets that enter the router from interface Ethernet 0/0 should be classified as medium priority. The default priority of all unclassified packets should be low. AppleTalk traffic should have priority over all other traffic, so we should assign it to the high priority queue. TCP/IP traffic should be placed in the normal queue. The code to set up this configuration is as follows:

```
Rosa#configure terminal
Enter configuration commands, one per line.  End with CNTL/Z.
Rosa(config)#priority-list 1 protocol appletalk high
Rosa(config)#priority-list 1 interface ethernet 0/0 medium
Rosa(config)#priority-list 1 protocol ip normal
Rosa(config)#priority-list 1 default low
Rosa(config)#end
Rosa#
```

> **NOTE**
>
> Not all versions of the IOS support protocols such as Appletalk, IPX, and DECnet. These restrictions also exist in the configuration of priority queuing and other queuing techniques. Consequently, when attempting to configure your priority list using the protocol parameter, you will find certain protocols may not be listed, depending on the feature set supported by your version of the IOS.

A Closer Look at the Protocol Classification

The sample configuration code above uses general protocol classifications such as "ip" and "appletalk" to classify traffic into certain priority queues. Unlike the default and interface priority list parameters, the protocol parameter allows you to design traffic configurations at an even more granular level using the features of each protocol, or even to make use of access lists to identify specific packets for classification. It is important to look at the IP protocol in greater detail, since it is the most common protocol.

```
Rosa(config)#priority-list 1 protocol ip medium ?
  fragments   Prioritize fragmented IP packets
```

```
gt             Prioritize packets greater than a specified size
list           To specify an access list
lt             Prioritize packets less than a specified size
tcp            Prioritize TCP packets 'to' or 'from' specified port
udp            Prioritize UDP packets 'to' or 'from' specified port
<cr>
```

As we see in this code output, TCP/IP allows us to classify traffic using parameters such as packet size, fragments, TCP or UDP port numbers, or using an access list.

Classification Process Considerations

It is important to reiterate that the configuration of the classification process is crucial to the proper operation of priority queuing. The following code is an example of a priority list configuration that can lead to queue starvation, causing Telnet to stop functioning across the network.

```
Rosa(config)#priority-list 3 protocol ipx high
Rosa(config)#priority-list 3 protocol ip low eq telnet
```

The intent of this priority list is to prioritize IPX traffic over Telnet traffic. However, although it is not evident in this example, the default value of unclassified protocols is normal priority, and consequently, all traffic other than IPX will have absolute priority over Telnet. Since this includes high throughput protocols such as FTP, it is possible that the router would be presented with so many packets in the normal priority queue that it never services the low priority queue where Telnet packets are held.

Consider a second example of defining a priority list using the following requirements. All unclassified traffic should have a low priority. All traffic from interface Ethernet 0/0 should have normal priority. All Telnet traffic should have high priority. All IP packets having a size greater than 1000 bytes should have a medium priority. All IP traffic from host 10.1.1.1 should have high priority. These requirements result in the following configuration code:

```
Rosa#configure terminal
Enter configuration commands, one per line.  End with CNTL/Z.
Rosa(config)#priority-list 2 protocol ip high tcp telnet
Rosa(config)#priority-list 2 protocol ip high list 101
Rosa(config)#priority-list 2 protocol ip medium gt 1000
Rosa(config)#priority-list 2 interface ethernet 0/0 normal
Rosa(config)#priority-list 2 default low
Rosa(config)#access-list 101 permit ip host 10.1.1.1 any
Rosa(config)#end
Rosa#
```

In this example, access list 101 was created to identify source host 10.1.1.1. This access list was then applied to the priority list by using the "list" keyword.

Applying Your Priority List to an Interface

The process of configuring priority queuing is similar to the process of defining and applying an access list using the "access-list" and "access-group" commands. First the priority-list is defined, and then the priority-group is applied to the interface. This second step, applying the priority list to an interface, is accomplished using the interface command "priority-group." In this example, we apply priority lists 1 and 2, defined earlier, to interfaces serial 0/0 and 0/1 respectively:

```
Rosa#configure terminal
Enter configuration commands, one per line.  End with CNTL/Z.
Rosa(config)#interface serial 0/0
Rosa(config-if)#priority-group 1
Rosa(config-if)#exit
Rosa(config)#interface serial 0/1
Rosa(config-if)#priority-group 2
Rosa(config-if)#end
Rosa#
```

Configuring the Queue Limits

The default queue size values are 20, 40, 60, and 80 packets for the high, medium, normal, and low priority queues, respectively. To modify these default values, the queue-limit parameter is used at the global configuration level. In the following code output, the high, medium, normal, and low priority queues are adjusted to values of 200, 400, 600, and 800 packets, respectively:

```
Rosa#configure terminal
Enter configuration commands, one per line.  End with CNTL/Z.
Rosa(config)#priority-list 4 queue-limit ?
  <0-32767>  High limit


Rosa(config)#priority-list 4 queue-limit 200 ?
  <0-32767>  Medium limit


Rosa(config)#priority-list 4 queue-limit 200 400 ?
  <0-32767>  Normal limit


Rosa(config)#priority-list 4 queue-limit 200 400 600 ?
  <0-32767>  Lower limit


Rosa(config)#priority-list 4 queue-limit 200 400 600 800
Rosa(config)#end
Rosa#
```

Be careful when changing these default values. Setting the queue sizes to larger values may have a negative impact on router operations because of the amount of memory used by the queuing process. Also, having larger high priority queues and funneling more traffic to them can cause the queuing process to spend too much time emptying those queues. The lower priority queues will thus not get serviced in time, and the upper layer protocols will start timing out. Conversely, reducing the queue sizes to values that are too small will result in unnecessary tails drops. This in turn will negatively impact the operation of the protocols flowing through the queues.

Verifying Your Configuration

As in the case of FIFO, the first step in verifying the priority queuing configuration is to determine if the queuing process runs properly on the interface. The command "show interface" is used for this purpose:

```
Rosa#show interface serial 0/0
```

```
Serial0/0 is up, line protocol is up
  Hardware is PowerQUICC Serial
  Internet address is 192.168.10.1/24
  MTU 1500 bytes, BW 1544 Kbit, DLY 20000 usec,
     reliability 255/255, txload 1/255, rxload 1/255
  Encapsulation HDLC, loopback not set, keepalive set (10 sec)
  Last input 00:00:04, output 00:00:00, output hang never
  Last clearing of "show interface" counters never
  Input queue: 0/75/0 (size/max/drops); Total output drops: 0
  Queueing strategy: priority-list 1
  Output queue (queue priority: size/max/drops):
     high: 0/20/0, medium: 0/40/0, normal 0/60/0, low 0/80/0
  5 minute input rate 0 bits/sec, 0 packets/sec
  5 minute output rate 0 bits/sec, 0 packets/sec
     937 packets input, 84028 bytes, 0 no buffer
     Received 937 broadcasts, 0 runts, 0 giants, 0 throttles
     1 input errors, 0 CRC, 1 frame, 0 overrun, 0 ignored, 0 abor
     820 packets output, 51295 bytes, 0 underruns
     0 output errors, 0 collisions, 15 interface resets
     0 output buffer failures, 0 output buffers swapped out
     0 carrier transitions
     DCD=up  DSR=up  DTR=up  RTS=up  CTS=up

Rosa#
```

This command also shows the present state of the queues, as well as the maximum size and tail drops for each queue. Next, you can verify the configuration of the priority lists using the command "show queueing priority."

```
Rosa#show queueing priority
Current priority queue configuration:

List    Queue   Args
1       low     default
1       medium  interface Serial0/0
1       high    protocol appletalk
1       normal  protocol ip
```

```
2       low     default
2       normal  interface Ethernet0/0
2       high    protocol ip         tcp port telnet
2       medium  protocol ip         gt 1000
2       high    protocol ip         list 101

Rosa#
```

This command shows the queuing process alphanumerically, then it shows the unique characteristics of the queuing policy alphanumerically, not the way it will be processed. To see how it will be processed, you would have to look at the configuration file.

Troubleshooting Priority Queuing

The first step in troubleshooting priority queuing is to examine the state of the queues and the number of tail drops experienced by each queue. In the following output, we can clearly see a problem with the low priority queue:

```
Rosa#show int
Rosa#show interface serial 0/0
Serial0/0 is up, line protocol is up
  Hardware is PowerQUICC Serial
  Internet address is 192.168.10.1/24
  MTU 1500 bytes, BW 1544 Kbit, DLY 20000 usec,
     reliability 255/255, txload 229/255, rxload 219/255
  Encapsulation HDLC, loopback not set, keepalive set (10 sec)
  Last input 00:00:00, output 00:00:00, output hang never
  Last clearing of "show interface" counters never
  Input queue: 0/75/0 (size/max/drops); Total output drops: 0
  Queueing strategy: priority-list 1
  Output queue (queue priority: size/max/drops):
     high: 17/20/0, medium: 1/40/0, normal 0/60/0, low 80/80/6933
  5 minute input rate 0 bits/sec, 0 packets/sec
  5 minute output rate 0 bits/sec, 0 packets/sec
     8932382 packets input, 21294686 bytes, 0 no buffer
     Received 7845 broadcasts, 0 runts, 0 giants, 0 throttles
     0 input errors, 0 CRC, 1 frame, 0 overrun, 0 ignored, 0 abor
```

```
     5433928 packets output, 23228392 bytes, 0 underruns
     0 output errors, 0 collisions, 1 interface resets
     0 output buffer failures, 0 output buffers swapped out
     0 carrier transitions
     DCD=up  DSR=up  DTR=up  RTS=up  CTS=up

Rosa#
```

This output indicates that the high priority queue is receiving most of the traffic on a congested link. Consequently, there is queue starvation in the low priority queue, indicated by the queue being full and having a high number of tail drops. It would be advisable to review the priority list of this process.

The second step in troubleshooting is to use the powerful "debug" feature of the Cisco IOS. For priority queuing, the syntax of the command is "debug priority."

```
Rosa#debug priority
02:05:38: PQ: Serial0/0: cdp (defaulting) -> low
02:05:38: PQ: Serial0/0 output (Pk size/Q 292/3)
```

In this output, we see that the router has processed a Cisco Discovery Protocol (CDP) packet out of the serial 0/0 interface. Since CDP was not specifically classified in the configuration of priority list 1, PQ classifies the packet under the default queue, which was configured to use the low priority queue. This is apparent in the debug output "cdp (defaulting) -> low." The output also shows the size of the packet and the queue number the packet was assigned. In this case, the CDP packet was 292 bytes long and was assigned to queue number 3. Pinging the next hop router will generate some IP traffic.

```
Rosa#ping 192.168.10.2

Type escape sequence to abort.
Sending 5, 100-byte ICMP Echos to 192.168.10.2, timeout is 2 seconds:
!!!!!
Success rate is 100 percent (5/5), round-trip min/avg/max = 28/30/32 ms
Rosa#
02:05:47: PQ: Serial0/0: ip -> normal
02:05:47: PQ: Serial0/0 output (Pk size/Q 104/2)
02:05:47: PQ: Serial0/0: ip -> normal
```

```
02:05:47: PQ: Serial0/0 output (Pk size/Q 104/2)
02:05:47: PQ: Serial0/0: ip -> normal
02:05:47: PQ: Serial0/0 output (Pk size/Q 104/2)
02:05:47: PQ: Serial0/0: ip -> normal
02:05:47: PQ: Serial0/0 output (Pk size/Q 104/2)
02:05:47: PQ: Serial0/0: ip -> normal
02:05:47: PQ: Serial0/0 output (Pk size/Q 104/2)
Rosa#undebug all
All possible debugging has been turned off
Rosa#
```

Queue numbering for the debug output is 0 = high, 1 = medium, 2 = normal, 4 = low. A ping to the directly connected router on serial 0/0 forced five IP packets to be forwarded out of the interface. Since IP was identified by the priority list as having a normal priority, PQ gave it the proper priority by assigning the 104-byte packets to queue number 2.

Configuring Custom Queuing

The tasks involved in configuring custom queuing are as follows:

- Define a custom queue list
- Assign the custom queue list to an interface

As with priority queuing, the definition of the custom queue list is vital to the proper operation of custom queuing. This section examines several examples of custom queuing and explains the potential pitfalls to be avoided when preparing a custom queue list.

Enabling Custom Queuing

The first task in configuring custom queuing is to declare a valid custom queue list. This is accomplished using the global configuration command "queue-list." As with priority queuing, custom queue lists are identified using a list number:

```
Rosa(config)#queue-list 1 ?
  default        Set custom queue for unspecified datagrams
  interface      Establish priority for packets from an interface
  lowest-custom  Set lowest number of queue to be treated as
                 custom
```

```
protocol            priority queueing by protocol
queue               Configure parameters for a particular queue
stun                Establish priorities for stun packets
```

This code output shows the various parameters used to configure priorities. As with priority queuing, custom queuing can prioritize by inbound interface or by protocols. The default keyword is used to define the queue that will handle all unclassified traffic.

Let us configure a custom queue list to meet the following requirements. All default traffic will be assigned to queue 1. All AppleTalk and IPX traffic will be assigned to queue 2. All Telnet traffic will be assigned to queue 3. All traffic from IPX host 3C.ABCD.ABCD.ABCD is to be assigned to queue 4. All traffic coming from interface Ethernet 0/0 is to be assigned to queue 5. Finally, all remaining IP traffic will be assigned to queue 6. Unlike priority queuing, the queue numbers used by custom queuing do not represent assigned priority levels. The following custom queue list configuration meets these requirements:

```
Rosa#configure terminal
Enter configuration commands, one per line.  End with CNTL/Z.
Rosa(config)#access-list 801 permit 3c.abcd.abcd.abcd -1
Rosa(config)#access-list 801 deny -1
Rosa(config)#
Rosa(config)#queue-list 1 default ?
  <0-16>   queue number

Rosa(config)#queue-list 1 protocol appletalk 2
Rosa(config)#queue-list 1 protocol ipx 2
Rosa(config)#queue-list 1 protocol ip 3 tcp telnet
Rosa(config)#queue-list 1 protocol ipx 4 list 801
Rosa(config)#queue-list 1 interface serial 0/0 5
Rosa(config)#queue-list 1 protocol ip 6
Rosa(config)#queue-list 1 default 1
Rosa(config)#end
Rosa#
```

The first part of the configuration identifies IPX host 3C.ABCD.ABCD.ABCD with the definition of an access list. This access list is later applied in the custom queue list to place IPX traffic from that host into custom queue 4. As shown in this example, the classification of custom queuing traffic can use the same level of granularity as priority queuing. So far, we have classified various protocols and interfaces into six different queues. Each of these queues has a default byte count of 1500 bytes and a default queue depth of 20 packets. This means that the custom queuing process should service an equal number of bytes among each queue. However, this does not always remain true when larger packets reach the custom queuing process.

Adjusting Byte Counts and Queue Sizes

In order to modify the byte count and queue size of each queue, the "queue" keyword of the queue-list command is used. Each queue is individually configured. In the following example, we change the byte count of queues 1, 2, and 3 to 3000 bytes, and the queue depth of queues 4, 5, and 6 to 60 packets:

```
Rosa#configure terminal
Enter configuration commands, one per line.  End with CNTL/Z.
Rosa(config)#queue-list 1 queue 1 ?
  byte-count  Specify size in bytes of a particular queue
  limit       Set queue entry limit of a particular queue

Rosa(config)#queue-list 1 queue 1 byte-count ?
  <0-16777215>  size in bytes

Rosa(config)#queue-list 1 queue 1 byte-count 3000
Rosa(config)#queue-list 1 queue 2 byte-count 3000
Rosa(config)#queue-list 1 queue 3 byte-count 3000
Rosa(config)#queue-list 1 queue 3 limit ?
  <0-32767>  number of queue entries

Rosa(config)#queue-list 1 queue 4 limit 60
Rosa(config)#queue-list 1 queue 5 limit 60
Rosa(config)#queue-list 1 queue 6 limit 60
Rosa(config)#end
Rosa#
```

Applying Your Configuration to an Interface

Once you have successfully configured your custom queue list, the second step is to apply the list against an interface. The interface command "custom-queue-list" is used to perform this function. In the following code, we apply the custom queue configuration defined above to interface serial 0/0.

```
Rosa#configure terminal
Enter configuration commands, one per line.  End with CNTL/Z.
Rosa(config)#interface serial 0/0
Rosa(config-if)#custom-queue-list 1
Rosa(config-if)#end
Rosa#
```

At this point, you should have a valid, operational custom queuing configuration. The following sections examine how to confirm the operation of custom queuing, and how to troubleshoot potential problems.

Verifying Your Configuration

As with FIFO and PQ, the first step is to verify that your configuration is properly applied to the interface. This is accomplished using the "show interface" command:

```
Rosa#show interface serial 0/0
Serial0/0 is up, line protocol is up
  Hardware is PowerQUICC Serial
  Internet address is 192.168.10.1/24
  MTU 1500 bytes, BW 1544 Kbit, DLY 20000 usec,
     reliability 255/255, txload 1/255, rxload 1/255
  Encapsulation HDLC, loopback not set, keepalive set (10 sec)
  Last input 00:00:07, output 00:00:08, output hang never
  Last clearing of "show interface" counters never
  Input queue: 0/75/0 (size/max/drops); Total output drops: 0
  Queueing strategy: custom-list 1
  Output queues: (queue #: size/max/drops)
     0: 0/20/0 1: 0/20/0 2: 0/20/0 3: 0/20/0 4: 0/60/0
     5: 0/60/0 6: 0/60/0 7: 0/20/0 8: 0/20/0 9: 0/20/0
     10: 0/20/0 11: 0/20/0 12: 0/20/0 13: 0/20/0 14: 0/20/0
     15: 0/20/0 16: 0/20/0
  5 minute input rate 0 bits/sec, 0 packets/sec
  5 minute output rate 0 bits/sec, 0 packets/sec
     17212 packets input, 1533621 bytes, 0 no buffer
```

```
            Received 16828 broadcasts, 0 runts, 0 giants, 0 throttles
            2 input errors, 0 CRC, 2 frame, 0 overrun, 0 ignored, 0 abor
            15098 packets output, 940003 bytes, 0 underruns
            0 output errors, 0 collisions, 15 interface resets
            0 output buffer failures, 0 output buffers swapped out
            0 carrier transitions
            DCD=up  DSR=up  DTR=up  RTS=up  CTS=up

     Rosa#
```

This output shows that custom queue list 1 was successfully applied to interface serial 0/0. The command also shows the state of each queue at the time the command was issued. We can see that the queue depths for queues 4, 5, and 6 were successfully adjusted to 60 packets. Notice that all sixteen custom queues are displayed. This means that the IOS allocated memory space for all possible configurable queues, even though we have used only six of them. We can also use the command "show queueing" to show the actual configuration of the custom queues:

```
Rosa#show queueing ?
   custom     custom queueing list configuration
   fair       fair queueing configuration
   priority   priority queueing list configuration
   red        random early detection configuration
   <cr>


Rosa#show queueing custom
Current custom queue configuration:

List    Queue   Args
1       2       protocol appletalk
1       2       protocol ipx
1       3       protocol ip              tcp port telnet
1       4       protocol ipx             list 801
1       5       interface Ethernet0/0
1       6       protocol ip
1       1       byte-count 3000
1       2       byte-count 3000
```

```
1       3       byte-count 3000
1       4       limit 60
1       5       limit 60
1       6       limit 60
Rosa#
```

Troubleshooting Custom Queuing

If the output of the "show interface" command displays an inordinate number of tail drops for a particular queue, it is advisable to verify the proper operation of the custom queuing process. The command "debug custom-queue" is used to monitor the activities of the custom queuing process:

```
Rosa#debug custom-queue
Custom output queueing debugging is on
Rosa#ping 192.168.10.2

Type escape sequence to abort.
Sending 5, 100-byte ICMP Echos to 192.168.10.2, timeout is 2 seconds:
!!!!!
Success rate is 100 percent (5/5), round-trip min/avg/max = 32/32/33 ms
Rosa#
1d11h: CQ: Serial0/0 output (Pk size/Q: 104/6) Q # was 1 now 6
1d11h: CQ: Serial0/0 output (Pk size/Q: 104/6) Q # was 6 now 6
1d11h: CQ: Serial0/0 output (Pk size/Q: 104/6) Q # was 6 now 6
1d11h: CQ: Serial0/0 output (Pk size/Q: 104/6) Q # was 6 now 6
1d11h: CQ: Serial0/0 output (Pk size/Q: 104/6) Q # was 6 now 6
Rosa#
1d11h: CQ: Serial0/0 output (Pk size/Q: 292/1) Q # was 6 now 1
```

In this example, we forced a ping to the next hop router in order to generate some IP traffic. You will notice that unlike priority queuing, custom queuing does not indicate the protocol type. We can verify that these are actually our ping packets by comparing them with the packet size found in the priority queuing example. In both cases, the packets are 104 bytes in length. Another method of ensuring that these are the correct packets would be to use the "debug ip packet detail" in conjunction with the "debug custom-queue" command. We can also see that the packets were assigned to queue 6, which is consistent with our custom queue list configurations.

```
Rosa#configure terminal
Enter configuration commands, one per line.  End with CNTL/Z.
Rosa(config)#access-list 100 permit tcp any any eq www
Rosa(config)#access-list 100 deny ip any any
Rosa(config)#end
Rosa#
Rosa#debug ip packet detail ?
  <1-199>      Access list
  <1300-2699>  Access list (expanded range)
  <cr>


Rosa#debug ip packet detail 100
IP packet debugging is on (detailed) for access list 100
Rosa#
```

> ### Be Careful with debug Commands!
>
> The output of the commands "debug ip packet detail" and "debug custom-queue" can severely impact the operation of the router by requiring it to process vast amounts of information through the console. Be ready to issue the "undebug all" command if this happens. One way to reduce the amount of information shown by the "debug ip packet detail" command is to use an access list to select specific traffic to be analyzed. For example, if you wanted to see the detailed IP packets for Web traffic only, the configuration would be as follows.

The debug output also shows the custom queuing process state by describing queue servicing. In the previous output, custom queuing went from servicing packets in queue 1 to those in queue 6. Subsequent ping packets also flow through queue 6, indicating that the router continues to service this queue since there are no other packets in the other queues. Let us now start a short Telnet session to our next hop router.

```
Rosa#
Rosa#telnet 192.168.10.2
Trying 192.168.10.2 ... Open


User Access Verification

Password:
1d12h: CQ: Serial0/0 output (Pk size/Q: 48/3) Q # was 6 now 3
1d12h: CQ: Serial0/0 output (Pk size/Q: 44/3) Q # was 3 now 3
1d12h: CQ: Serial0/0 output (Pk size/Q: 62/3) Q # was 3 now 3
1d12h: CQ: Serial0/0 output (Pk size/Q: 44/3) Q # was 3 now 3
1d12h: CQ: Serial0/0 output (Pk size/Q: 47/3) Q # was 3 now 3
1d12h: CQ: Serial0/0 output (Pk size/Q: 53/3) Q # was 3 now 3
1d12h: CQ: Serial0/0 output (Pk size/Q: 55/3) Q # was 3 now 3
1d12h: CQ: Serial0/0 output (Pk size/Q: 47/3) Q # was 3 now 3
1d12h: CQ: Serial0/0 output (Pk size/Q: 47/3) Q # was 3 now 3
1d12h: CQ: Serial0/0 output (Pk size/Q: 47/3) Q # was 3 now 3
```

Notice that Telnet traffic, although IP based, flows through queue 3 rather than queue 6. This is because the custom queue list has a more precise classification for Telnet traffic that forces it to queue 6. This again is consistent with our configuration. The queue service shifts from the last queue it serviced, queue 6, to the new queue, queue 3.

Configuring Weighted Fair Queuing

Configuring weighted fair queuing is fairly simple. It involves applying the weighed fair queuing configuration commands at the interface level. Keep in mind that WFQ is enabled by default on links of E1 speeds (2.048 Mbps) or less. These configurations will not show up in the router's configurations, but they are visible through the "show interface" command. You may want to modify these default configurations.

Enabling Weighted Fair Queuing

The interface command "fair-queue" is used to configure the weighted fair queuing process on an interface. The optional parameters are congestive discard threshold, the maximum number of dynamic conversation queues, and the maximum number of RSVP reservable queues. The number of conversation queues must be a power of 2 (16, 32, 64, 128, 256, 512, 1024); otherwise, the IOS will refuse the command. The following code configures serial interface 0/0 with a congestive discard threshold of 512 bytes, a maximum of 1024 dynamic conversation queues, and 10 reservable queues for RSVP:

```
Rosa#configure terminal
Enter configuration commands, one per line.  End with CNTL/Z.
Rosa(config)#interface serial 0/0
Rosa(config-if)#fair-queue 512 1048 10
Number of dynamic queues must be a power of 2 (16, 32, 64, 128, 256, 512, 1024)
Rosa(config-if)#fair-queue 512 1024 10
Rosa(config-if)#end
Rosa#
```

Verifying Your Configuration

As with the other queuing processes discussed, the first step in verifying the operation of WFQ is to use the "show interface" command to see if the queuing process is in operation on that interface:

```
Rosa#show interface serial 0/0
Serial0/0 is up, line protocol is up
  Hardware is PowerQUICC Serial
  Internet address is 192.168.10.1/24
  MTU 1500 bytes, BW 1544 Kbit, DLY 20000 usec,
     reliability 255/255, txload 1/255, rxload 1/255
  Encapsulation HDLC, loopback not set, keepalive set (10 sec)
  Last input 00:00:01, output 00:00:00, output hang never
  Last clearing of "show interface" counters never
  Input queue: 0/75/0 (size/max/drops); Total output drops: 0
  Queueing strategy: weighted fair
  Output queue: 0/1000/512/0 (size/max total/threshold/drops)
     Conversations  0/1/1024 (active/max active/max total)
     Reserved Conversations 0/0 (allocated/max allocated)
  5 minute input rate 0 bits/sec, 0 packets/sec
```

```
  5 minute output rate 0 bits/sec, 0 packets/sec
     341 packets input, 30537 bytes, 0 no buffer
     Received 341 broadcasts, 0 runts, 0 giants, 0 throttles
     4 input errors, 0 CRC, 4 frame, 0 overrun, 0 ignored, 0 abor
     298 packets output, 18667 bytes, 0 underruns
     0 output errors, 0 collisions, 16 interface resets
     0 output buffer failures, 0 output buffers swapped out
     2 carrier transitions
     DCD=up  DSR=up  DTR=up  RTS=up  CTS=up

Rosa#
```

The command indicates that WFQ is in operation on this interface. It also shows the status of the WFQ process when the command was issued. In this example, 0 packets were in the output queue. The queue itself has a maximum size of 1000 packets, and WFQ will start the congestive discard process as the queue reaches a depth of 512 packets. There have been 0 tail drops so far. We can also see the state of the conversations. Out of a total maximum of 1024 conversations, 0 conversations are presently active. Also, 0 of 10 RSVP reservable queues are in operation. The "show interface" command properly reflects the configuration we applied to the interface. We can also use the command "show queueing fair" to display the configuration of the WFQ process:

```
Rosa#show queueing fair
Current fair queue configuration:
```

Interface	Discard threshold	Dynamic queue count	Reserved queue count
BRI0/0	64	256	0
BRI0/0:1	64	256	0
BRI0/0:2	64	256	0
Serial0/0	512	1024	10
Serial0/1	64	256	0

```
Rosa#
```

We can see that the router has properly configured the WFQ process on interface serial 0/0 with the non-default values we entered.

Troubleshooting Weighted Fair Queuing

Since the operation of weighted fair queuing is completely dynamic, it is more difficult to troubleshoot problems than it would be with static queuing processes such as priority queuing or custom queuing. We cannot control the information coming into the router, nor can we control which queue this information is assigned to. These functions are under the control of the WFQ algorithm. There are also no debug commands specifically related to WFQ. The best indicators of what might be going wrong are the dynamic queue usage and the number of tail drops experienced by the WFQ process. Consider the following example of code output:

```
Rosa#show queueing fair
Current fair queue configuration:

   Interface         Discard        Dynamic         Reserved
                     threshold      queue count     queue count
   BRI0/0            64             256             0
   BRI0/0:1          64             256             0
   BRI0/0:2          64             256             0
   Serial0/0         1              16              0
   Serial0/1         1              16              0

Rosa#show interface serial 0/0
Serial0/0 is up, line protocol is up
  Hardware is PowerQUICC Serial
  Internet address is 192.168.10.1/24
  MTU 1500 bytes, BW 1544 Kbit, DLY 20000 usec,
     reliability 255/255, txload 183/255, rxload 127/255
  Encapsulation HDLC, loopback not set, keepalive set (10 sec)
  Last input 00:00:07, output 00:00:04, output hang never
  Last clearing of "show interface" counters never
  Input queue: 0/75/0 (size/max/drops); Total output drops: 0
  Queueing strategy: weighted fair
  Output queue: 257/1000/1/27 (size/max total/threshold/drops)
     Conversations  16/16/16 (active/max active/max total)
     Reserved Conversations 0/0 (allocated/max allocated)
```

```
5 minute input rate 0 bits/sec, 0 packets/sec
5 minute output rate 0 bits/sec, 0 packets/sec
    47602 packets input, 2954033 bytes, 0 no buffer
    Received 1597 broadcasts, 0 runts, 0 giants, 0 throttles
    0 input errors, 0 CRC, 0 frame, 0 overrun, 0 ignored, 0 abor
    52327 packets output, 3733139 bytes, 0 underruns
    0 output errors, 0 collisions, 1 interface resets
    0 output buffer failures, 0 output buffers swapped out
    1 carrier transitions
    DCD=up  DSR=up  DTR=up  RTS=up  CTS=up

Rosa#
```

We can see from this example that the WFQ configuration parameters have been adjusted on serial 0/0 to a congestive threshold value of 1 packet, a maximum of 16 conversations, and 0 reservable RSVP queues. These are the minimum values for WFQ. The consequences of these changes are indicated by the "show interface command." The low threshold value has caused the queue to discard 27 packets. We can also see that WFQ has reached its maximum of 16 concurrent conversations.

By continuously monitoring the output of this command, we can determine if this is a temporary problem caused by a burst of network activity or if it is a constant state, with the number of packet discards steadily increasing. The latter situation would require intervention by the network administrator to adjust the WFQ process using more appropriate values.

Configuring Random Early Detection

The process of configuring random early detection is simple. It involves applying only one command on the interface that is to participate in the RED process. Even though RED is a congestion avoidance mechanism rather than a congestion management mechanism, it is not compatible with all the queuing processes described in this chapter. We will first look at how to enable RED and then discuss its compatibility with other mechanisms.

Enabling Random Early Detection

RED is simple to configure. It involves applying the command "random-detect" to the interface that will participate in the RED process.

```
Rosa#configure terminal
Enter configuration commands, one per line.  End with CNTL/Z.
Rosa(config)#interface serial 0/0
Rosa(config-if)#random-detect
Rosa(config-if)#end
Rosa#
```

RED with Other Queuing Mechanisms

RED is not compatible with all the queuing mechanisms we have discussed so far. We have seen that RED is compatible with FIFO. Let us now explore RED's compatibility with PQ, CQ, and WFQ:

```
Rosa#configure terminal
Enter configuration commands, one per line.  End with CNTL/Z.
Rosa(config)#interface serial 0/0
Rosa(config-if)#priority-group 1
Rosa(config-if)#random-detect
Must remove priority-group configuration first.
Rosa(config-if)#
Rosa(config-if)#no priority-group 1
Rosa(config-if)#custom-queue-list 1
Rosa(config-if)#random-detect
Must remove custom-queue configuration first.
Rosa(config-if)#
Rosa(config-if)#no custom-queue-list 1
Rosa(config-if)#end
Rosa#
```

It is apparent that RED is not compatible with either PQ or CQ. In terms of its compatibility with WFQ, the following example shows that when RED is configured on an interface already configured with WFQ, RED replaces WFQ on that interface:

```
Rosa#show queueing fair
Current fair queue configuration:


    Interface           Discard     Dynamic     Reserved
```

	threshold	queue count	queue count
Serial0/0	**64**	**256**	**0**
BRI0/0	64	16	0
BRI0/0:1	64	16	0
BRI0/0:2	64	16	0
Serial0/1	64	256	0

```
Rosa#configure terminal
Enter configuration commands, one per line.  End with CNTL/Z.
Rosa(config)#interface serial 0/0
Rosa(config-if)#random-detect
Rosa(config-if)#end
Rosa#
01:37:16: %SYS-5-CONFIG_I: Configured from console by console
Rosa#
Rosa#show queueing fair
Current fair queue configuration:
```

Interface	Discard threshold	Dynamic queue count	Reserved queue count
BRI0/0	64	16	0
BRI0/0:1	64	16	0
BRI0/0:2	64	16	0
Serial0/1	64	256	0

```
Rosa#show interface serial 0/0
Serial0/0 is up, line protocol is up
  Hardware is PowerQUICC Serial
  Internet address is 192.168.10.1/24
  MTU 1500 bytes, BW 1544 Kbit, DLY 20000 usec,
     reliability 255/255, txload 1/255, rxload 1/255
  Encapsulation HDLC, loopback not set
  Keepalive set (10 sec)
  Last input 00:00:05, output 00:00:06, output hang never
  Last clearing of "show interface" counters never
```

```
Input queue: 0/75/0 (size/max/drops); Total output drops: 0
```
Queueing strategy: random early detection(RED)
```
5 minute input rate 0 bits/sec, 0 packets/sec
5 minute output rate 0 bits/sec, 0 packets/sec
   686 packets input, 42602 bytes, 0 no buffer
   Received 681 broadcasts, 0 runts, 0 giants, 0 throttles
   9 input errors, 0 CRC, 9 frame, 0 overrun, 0 ignored, 0 abor
   686 packets output, 44797 bytes, 0 underruns
   0 output errors, 0 collisions, 17 interface resets
   0 output buffer failures, 0 output buffers swapped out
   2 carrier transitions
   DCD=up  DSR=up  DTR=up  RTS=up  CTS=up

Rosa#
```

Verifying Your Configuration

As before, the first step in verifying your configuration is to see if the random early detection process was successfully applied to the desired interface. The "show interface" command is used for this purpose. In the previous example, the "show interface" command indicated that the interface is indeed configured for RED. The second step is to verify the RED process itself. This is done using the command "show queueing random-detect."

```
Rosa#show queueing random-detect
Current random-detect configuration:
  Serial0/0
    Queueing strategy: random early detection (WRED)
    Exp-weight-constant: 9 (1/512)
    Mean queue depth: 0

    Class   Random    Tail    Minimum    Maximum     Mark
             drop     drop   threshold  threshold  probability
              0        0         0         20         40       1/10
              1        0         0         22         40       1/10
              2        0         0         24         40       1/10
              3        0         0         26         40       1/10
```

4	0	0	28	40	1/10
5	0	0	31	40	1/10
6	0	0	33	40	1/10
7	0	0	35	40	1/10
rsvp	0	0	37	40	1/10

```
Rosa#
```

Here we see that RED is ready to operate on interface serial 0/0. The output of this command shows elements of weighted random early detection (WRED), which takes type of service (ToS) or IP precedence into account when discarding packets. WRED is discussed in more detail in another chapter.

Troubleshooting Random Early Detection

There is no debug command for monitoring the performance of RED. The best method of confirming the proper operation of RED is to monitor the RED process itself and the distribution of random drops, as opposed to tail drops, reported by the command "show queueing random-detect." The proper operation of RED is evidenced by an increase in the random drop numbers as the conversations are throttled back. This will be discussed in more detail in the section concerning WRED.

Summary

In this chapter, we discussed the proper steps for configuring priority queuing, custom queuing, weighted fair queuing, and random early detection. We also examined methods of ensuring that these mechanisms are properly configured and operating on the desired interfaces. Finally, we discussed the tools available in IOS to troubleshoot these processes and restore their proper operation.

Of all the topics covered in this chapter, the most important are the proper configuration of the priority list for priority queuing and the custom queue list of custom queuing. These are the sections that require the most planning and design.

FAQs

Visit www.syngress.com/solutions to have your questions about this chapter answered by the author.

Q: Are tail drops a strong indication that my queuing mechanism is poorly configured?

A: Not necessarily. On a link that is highly contended for, bursts of traffic are likely to overwhelm the queuing mechanism in place. The key is to have a properly configured queuing process so that less important traffic is discarded first.

Q: I do not see any weighted fair queuing configurations on my router. I know there is a speed marker under which WFQ is automatically configured, but I do not remember what it is. How can I tell whether WFQ is in operation?

A: You can issue the command "show queueing fair" to see all the interfaces that are running WFQ. You can also use the "show interface" command to individually examine each interface.

Q: How many priority lists and custom queue lists can I configure on a single router?

A: The maximum number of priority and custom queue lists is 16. Be careful when configuring this many queuing processes, as it may adversely affect the router's operation. Make sure you have ample memory and CPU power to accommodate these processes.

Q: I read that custom queuing services each custom queue one by one, but when I look at the output of the command "debug custom-queue," I see the queuing process jumping from queue to queue in an apparently random fashion. Why is this?

A: The output of the command "debug custom-queue" shows the queues as they are being serviced. If no packets are in a queue, custom queuing skips to the next queue and does not report anything about the empty queue to the console. If, for example, you see messages about queues 2 and 6 being serviced, it means that the custom queuing process serviced a packet in queue 2, went through empty queues 3, 4, and 5, and then serviced queue 6 which had packets waiting.

Q: I have typed "priority-list 1 protocol?", but I do not see many protocols in the list. I need AppleTalk and IPX. Where are they?

A: They are in a different feature set. These features are available in the Desktop feature set and later. Contact your Cisco Account Manager if you need a different version of IOS for your router.

Q: I tried a debug as suggested, but now the output is overwhelming my console, and I cannot type anything anymore. What can I do? This is a production router, and I cannot turn it off!

A: You can Telnet to the router from another workstation. As long as you do not have terminal monitoring turned on, the debug outputs will not be sent to your Telnet session. You will then be able to turn off debugging and regain control of your console terminal.

Chapter 8

Advanced QoS Overview

Solutions in this chapter:

- **Using the Resource Reservation Protocol**
- **Using Class-Based Weighted Fair Queuing**
- **Using Low Latency Queuing**
- **Using Weighted Random Early Detection**
- **Using Generic Traffic Shaping and Frame Relay Traffic Shaping**
- **Running in Distributed Mode**
- **Using Link Fragmentation and Interleaving**
- **Understanding RTP Header Compression**

Introduction

This chapter outlines some of the more cutting edge QoS mechanisms available at press time. Some of these technologies are just beginning to be widely deployed on production networks, and, though Quality of Service is constantly being improved and modified, these technologies will undoubtedly remain a significant factor in the Quality of Service marketplace for some time to come.

Several of these technologies, such as RSVP and LLQ, are currently being used mostly for voice applications, and you will find that these more advanced mechanisms are often used in conjunction with each other, rather than independently. These mechanisms, although powerful and useful in their own right, gain power and functionality when used along with other mechanisms.

Some of the benefits of more advanced queuing mechanisms are increased granular control of traffic behavior, and the ability to be far more specific when classifying and queuing or dropping traffic. However, this presents a potential problem. There is a trade-off between granular control and flexibility of use. LLQ, for example, is a very specific mechanism with a very specific purpose, but it not well suited for many things other than that purpose. It is particularly important in this chapter to pay attention to recommendations about where the deployment of these technologies is appropriate.

Using the Resource Reservation Protocol (RSVP)

The Resource Reservation Protocol (RSVP) is the first attempt at an industry standard implementation of the Internet Integrated Services (Intserv) model of QoS. Researchers at the Information Sciences Institute (ISI) at the University of Southern California (USC) and the Xerox Palo Alto Research Center first conceived of RSVP.

> **NOTE**
>
> In 1993, the Internet Engineering Task Force (IETF) started working toward standardization through an RSVP working group. Version 1 of this protocol is currently defined by RFC 2205. Interested readers may find the IETF Applicability Statement (RFC 2208) helpful in pointing out both the uses and current issues with an RSVP deployment. This chapter will illustrate both of these briefly.

The Intserv model is characterized by applications or end stations reserving resources across a network to guarantee a particular level of service. RSVP is a protocol that implements this signaling.

RSVP is independent of, yet complimentary to, Intserv. Whereas Intserv specifies the set of classes of service and the parameters to deliver QoS, RSVP requests this service level from network nodes and, in some cases, carries the Intserv parameters.

RSVP does not provide QoS directly to applications, but instead, coordinates an overall service level by making reservation requests with as many nodes as possible across the network. It is up to other QoS mechanisms to actually prevent and control congestion, provide efficient use of links, and classify and police traffic. A successful implementation of RSVP requires that it work in conjunction with these other mechanisms.

RSVP's popularity lies in its capacity to give guaranteed QoS to real-time applications that have either constant bandwidth requirements or low latency requirements. This is why its primary use today on networks is to deliver multimedia streams such as voice and video.

What Is RSVP?

RSVP is a signaling protocol that makes reservations of resources for client applications to guarantee a certain QoS. It is considered a signaling protocol because these reservations are negotiated by communication between end stations. Furthermore, it is an out-of-band signaling protocol. RSVP packets are not used to transmit bulk data; they coexist on the network with other packets and are used to reserve resources for typical IP packets or, more specifically, the IP packets that make up the flows that are to get specialized QoS.

RSVP makes reservations of resources for data flows across a network. These reserved flows are usually referred to as *sessions*. A session is defined as packets having the same destination address (unicast or multicast), IP protocol ID, and destination port. Resources could be considered such things as allocated bandwidth, CPU cycles, or queuing priority. Clients use RSVP to request a guarantee of QoS across the network. Routers participate in RSVP by allocating resources to particular flows, or denying resources if there are none available, and by forwarding RSVP information to other routers.

> **NOTE**
>
> A signaling protocol can be either in-band or out-of-band, depending on whether the signaling data flows over the same medium as the bulk data. In the telephony world, ISDN would be considered an out-of-band signaling protocol, because all information for setting up a call passes over a separate D- channel (*data*), whereas the actual telephone conversation flows over the Bchannels -(*bearer*). In a way, RSVP could be considered an in-band signaling protocol, since it flows over the same physical media, the same data-link layer, and even the same network as the bulk data. However, it is usually referred to as out-of-band because the packets are separate from the bulk data. A flow that was set up by RSVP would have nothing in its packets to indicate that it is participating in RSVP. The state of active reservations is stored in each routed node.

RSVP is an Internet Control Protocol that resides at Layer 4 of the OSI model, the transport layer. It is similar to other control protocols, such as Internet Control Message Protocol (ICMP) and Internet Group Management Protocol (IGMP). It is fully compliant with Internet Protocol version 4 (IPv4) and the emerging Internet Protocol version 6 (IPv6). It is not a routing protocol. The path that it takes across the network is the same as other IP packets and is determined by the underlying routing protocol (OSPF, EIGRP, BGP, and so forth)

Besides interoperating with routing protocols, RSVP also works with QoS implementation mechanisms. These are the mechanisms that provide QoS directly, such as weighted fair queuing (WFQ), weighted random early detection (WRED), and the like. What implementation mechanisms are used is not the direct concern of RSVP. It is up to the routers to determine how QoS will be implemented, based on their own particular capabilities. RSVP only makes the request and leaves it up to the intermediary nodes to deliver QoS.

Both unicast and multicast traffic are supported by RSVP. Support for multicast is fortuitous, since RSVP is currently used the most prevalently for voice and video traffic, much of which is characterized by multicast flows. We will see later how RSVP interoperates with the Internet Group Management Protocol (IGMP) and Protocol Independent Multicast (PIM) to reserve resources for multicast flows.

> **NOTE**
>
> It is not mandatory that RSVP be enabled everywhere on a network in order for a reservation to be made. RSVP has the built-in capability to tunnel over non-RSVP aware nodes (see the discussion later on the setup process). Though a guaranteed QoS may not be possible in this case, if the non-RSVP network has sufficient bandwidth, for example, tunneling over a Gigabit Ethernet or ATM core, it might be feasible for most applications. In addition, it is not even necessary for the clients to be RSVP capable. Cisco routers provide RSVP functionality for VoIP dial peers. In the next chapter, we configure RSVP in a test environment using RSVP proxy—a function that emulates clients sending RSVP Path and Resv messages.

What RSVP Is *Not*

RSVP is not a routing protocol. It relies on typical IP routing protocols to forward the RSVP packets. The next section shows how RSVP uses the routed path to create the setup messages that make the actual reservations.

Because of its protocol-based nature, RSVP does not monitor reservations. It is, therefore, not a resource manager. It is worth reiterating that it is simply a signaling protocol—client talking to client, router talking to router. It does not actually control what kinds of resources are reserved, either. That is up to the routers and their particular capabilities. You can imagine the benefit to a network administrator of knowing at any given moment how many reservations are made across the network. This would help for bandwidth planning and provisioning. Although it is possible to see what reservations are active in the routers, as we will see in chapter 9, the Resource Reservation Protocol has no capability of providing this information directly.

Although RSVP is an important QoS mechanism, it is not an implementation mechanism. It could be better thought of as a mechanism that requests QoS from other mechanisms. It is not a packet scheduler, link-efficiency mechanism, or traffic classifier. It does, however, necessarily work with these mechanisms. Otherwise, there would be no actual QoS—just a reservation!

How Does RSVP Work?

Now that we have a basic understanding of what RSVP is and is not, let us look at the mechanics of setting up a RSVP session. We leave the specifics of configuring RSVP for the next chapter and concentrate for now on the overall strategy.

Session Startup

RSVP is often set up between two clients in a point-to-point situation, or between multiple senders and multiple recipients (multicast). It is even possible for RSVP to negotiate a multipoint to single-point transmission. In any case, the RSVP session startup process reserves resources in a single direction only. To have full-duplex QoS guarantees, it is necessary for the session startup process to be performed twice, once in each direction. For example, in the case of setting up a VoIP call between two telephone users, it would usually be necessary to set up two reservations, one each way, to guarantee good QoS for both callers. On the other hand, a video stream would necessitate only a one-way reservation.

Let us step through the process of a RSVP session startup. In Figure 8.1 we have two clients across a RSVP-enabled network. At the top we have Client A, which we will designate as the sender, and at the bottom we have Client B, which we will consider the receiver. Thus, after the reservation is set up, the bulk data, whether it is voice, video, or something else, will flow from Client A to Client B in a downstream manner.

Figure 8.1 RSVP Session Startup, Path Messages

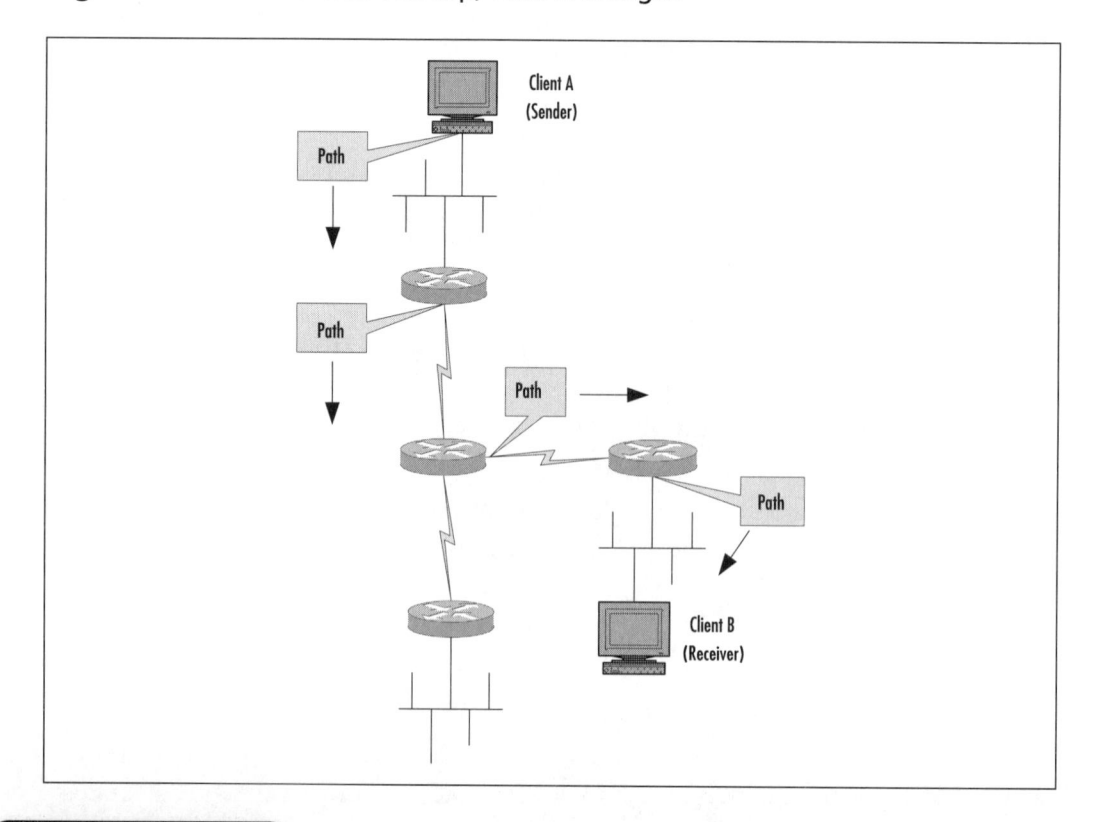

The first step is for Client A, the sender, to transmit a RSVP Path message to Client B, the receiver. This Path message travels across the network according to the underlying routing protocol. At each hop through the network, the Path message is modified to include the current hop. In this way, a history of the route taken across the network is built and passed to the receiver, Client B.

Now that Client B has the complete route from the Path message, a reservation (Resv) message is constructed and sent to Client A along the exact reverse path, as shown in Figure 8.2. At each hop, the router determines if the reservation can be made, based on available bandwidth, CPU cycles, and so on. If the reservation is possible, resources in the router are allocated, and the Resv packet is forwarded upstream to the previous hop, based on the information in the Resv packet.

Figure 8.2 RSVP Session Startup, Resv Messages

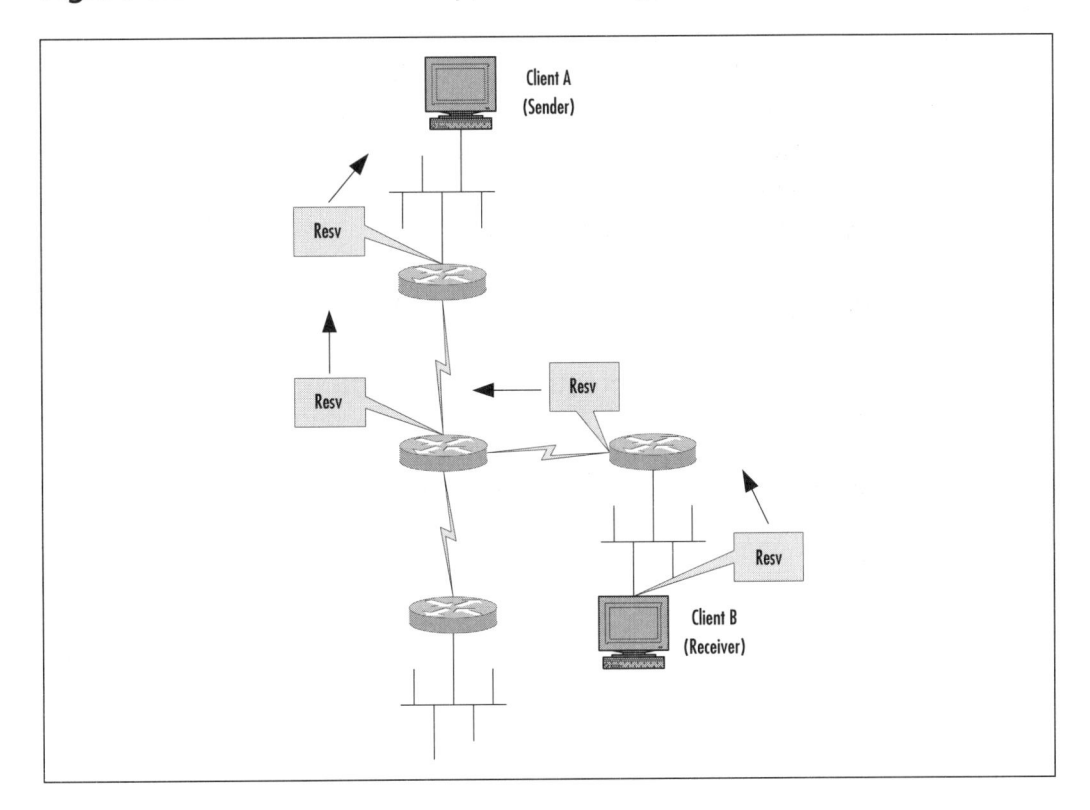

> **NOTE**
>
> In both the Path and Resv messages, the upstream hop is usually referred to as the *previous hop,* and the downstream hop is called the *next hop*. This terminology is derived from the reference point of the bulk data moving in a downstream direction, from sender to receiver.

If the reservation is declined, an error message is sent to the receiver, Client B, and the Resv packet is *not* forwarded. Only when Client A receives a Resv packet does it know that it can start sending data and guarantee a particular QoS to the downstream receiver, Client B.

You may think it is odd for the entire RSVP process to begin with the sender building the Path message to the receiver. This might be analogous to a television network deciding that it is time for you to watch your favorite show and automatically turning on the TV. However, there is usually some kind of non-RSVP request originating from the receiver to set up this flow. This might be an H.323 conversation between IP telephony applications, or an IGMP request to join a multicast group to watch a video clip.

> **NOTE**
>
> Though it is necessary for the sender to first transmit the Path message before the receiver can transmit the Resv message, RSVP is still considered receiver-oriented. That is, the receiver of the data flow initiates and maintains the actual resource reservation used for that flow.

Session Maintenance and Tear-Down

After a session is initiated, it is maintained on the routers as a "soft state." With a soft state session, the path connecting two end stations can be renegotiated without consultation with those end stations. This contrasts with a circuit-switched network, where the connection between two end stations is a hard connection, and when a failure occurs, the connection is broken.

This soft state session must be refreshed by periodic Path and Resv messages; otherwise, it will be terminated after a "cleanup timeout" interval. RSVP's default interval for this "cleanup timeout" is some multiple of the period of the Path and

Resv messages. Therefore, if the router misses a single Path or Resv refresh, it will not terminate the session. This kind of tolerance is necessary, since there is no preferential QoS treatment for RSVP messages inherent to the protocol. These messages are sent as best effort unless some provision has been made otherwise, such as DiffServ.

These "soft states" are dynamic in response to route changes in the network, changes in senders or receivers, or changes in the requested QoS. There is no real difference between the process of initiating a new reservation and refreshing an old one. In both cases, the Path message is built with the previous hop and next hop information, and the Resv statement is adjusted with any new QoS requirements.

> **NOTE**
>
> The refresh interval presents a potential problem when the routing changes across an IP network. If a route change causes any change to the shortest path for an active flow, packets will be forwarded over the new route as best effort until Path and Resv messages are sent along this new path. When this occurs, it is possible that there may not be the necessary resources to complete the RSVP session. In this case, it is up to the application to decide whether to terminate the session or continue best-effort delivery. Therefore, RSVP may not give the desired results in a network with unstable route paths.

Good implementations of RSVP will issue tear-down messages when the reservation is no longer needed, instead of waiting for the "cleanup timeout" to remove the session. There are two types of tear-down messages: PathTear and ResvTear. PathTear messages, like Path messages, flow in the downstream direction, whereas ResvTear messages, like Resv messages, flow upstream. In addition to clients issuing immediate requests for tear-downs, routers detecting a session timeout or a loss of resources will send their own tear-down messages to upstream (ResvTear) and downstream (PathTear) neighbors.

What Kind of QoS Can I Request with RSVP?

The types of QoS that can be reserved by RSVP are consistent with the Internet Integrated Services Model. These types are *controlled-load* and *guaranteed-rate*. According to the Intserv definition, controlled-load gives applications service as if they were traversing an unloaded network. Applications requesting controlled-load can expect low latency and a low number of packet drops. These applications are usually considered *tolerant real-time* applications. An example could be an adaptive real-time application like the playback of a recorded conference call. On Cisco routers, controlled-load services are implemented primarily with weighted random early detection (WRED). We will discuss WRED later in this chapter.

RSVP can also request guaranteed-rate services. According to the Intserv definition, guaranteed-rate delivers assured bandwidth with constant delay. Applications that require this service to function well are usually considered *intolerant real-time* applications. An example would be delay-sensitive applications like Voice over IP (VoIP). On Cisco routers, guaranteed-rate services are implemented primarily with weighted fair queuing (WFQ).

> **NOTE**
>
> AlthoughWFQ can provide guaranteed-rate services to applications, it alone may not be sufficient to assure low latency to delay-sensitive applications such as VoIP during periods of congestion. IOS version 12.1(3)T provides support for low latency queuing (LLQ) to RSVP.

Reservation Styles and Merging Flows

When a reservation is made, a set of options can be chosen that is collectively called the reservation "style." RSVP supports two classes of reservations, *shared* and *distinct*, and two scopes of reservations, *explicit* and *wildcard*. A *shared* reservation is a single reservation made for all packets from multiple upstream senders. A *distinct* reservation establishes a reservation for each sender. For the scope, an *explicit* list can be chosen for the senders, in which each sender is enumerated. The other scope option is to use a *wildcard* that implicitly selects all the senders.

These options give rise to three possible reservation styles (see Table 8.1). The combination of a distinct reservation with a wildcard scope is disallowed and is therefore not defined.

Table 8.1 RSVP Reservation Styles

Scope	Reservations	
	Distinct	Shared
Explicit	fixed-filter (FF) style	shared-explicit (SE) style
Wildcard	not defined	wildcard-filter (WF) style

These different styles are chosen based on the type of transmitted data that will comprise the reservation.

Wildcard-Filter (WF) Style

The combination of a shared reservation and a wildcard sender selection gives the wildcard-filter style. In this style, a single reservation is made and shared by *all* upstream senders. Reservations can be thought of as a shared pipe whose size is the largest of the resource requests from all receivers for that link, independent of the number of senders.

Shared-Explicit (SE) Style

The combination of a shared reservation and an explicit sender list gives rise to the shared-explicit style. The SE style creates a single reservation shared by a *list* of upstream senders. Both the WF and SE reservation styles are appropriate for data flows that are known not to interfere with each other. An example of this would be an audio conference where it could be assumed that the multiple senders would not typically talk at the same time. It might, however, be wise to make the reservation twice for an audio conference in order to allow for some over-talking while still retaining QoS.

Fixed-Filter (FF) Style

The combination of a distinct reservation and an explicit sender list gives rise to the fixed-filter style. In this style, a distinct reservation is created for data packets from a particular sender. This reservation is not shared with any other sender. However, if another receiver is added for that sender, the reservation is not doubled, but merged. This kind of style would be appropriate for video signals where the data from each sender are different.

An RSVP *flow descriptor* is the combination of a *flowspec* and a *filterspec*. A *flowspec* is the QoS requested, and the *filterspec* is the set of packets to receive this QoS. When new flows are added to the group of reservations in a node, they will often need to be merged into a common reservation. In the case of multicast traffic where the same data is going to multiple recipients, the recipients will still make a Resv request. It is up to RSVP to join this request with the active reservations. When this is done, the flows are referred to as "merged."

The RSVP rules do not allow the merging of distinct and shared reservations, nor the merging of explicit sender selection and wildcard sender selection. As a result, all three styles are mutually incompatible.

Subnetwork Bandwidth Manager

We have seen that RSVP is largely independent of the media it is running on with respect to the QoS mechanisms used to implement a particular reservation. With serial links, WFQ and WRED can be used to provide either a controlled-load or a guaranteed-rate to an application. These mechanisms are not appropriate on a shared medium like Ethernet that has multiple participants competing for the bandwidth. Because of its end-to-end signaling nature, without a common node to keep track of active reservations, a RSVP client on a shared medium would have no way of knowing if there are resources available for the new reservation.

Subnetwork Bandwidth Manager (SBM) was created to implement RSVP on IEEE 802-based networks (Ethernet/Token Ring). SBM acts very much like RSVP. On a shared medium, all SBM-enabled nodes elect a Designated SBM to manage the resources for that network. All RSVP requests by clients on this network are sent to the DSBM for verification. If the resources are available, the request is sent on to the destination address. If the resources are not available, the request is denied.

When using SBM, in order to guarantee that RSVP sessions are not overwhelmed by non-RSVP traffic, you must ensure that all nodes connected to the shared media are RSVP compliant. This might be difficult to put into practice.

Depending on the topology, SBM will not always be necessary to provide good end-to-end service for critical applications. Just because part of the journey that a packet takes includes a non-RSVP shared medium such as Ethernet, does not mean that QoS will be impossible. Consider the case of a switched 100BaseTX network connected to a WAN via a T1 on a serial interface of a local router. If it can be assumed that all RSVP requests are destined across the WAN, the bottleneck is clearly the T1. If there are available resources on the T1, there will probably be available resources on the Ethernet segment, assuming that non-RSVP flows do not overwhelm the RSVP sessions.

Why Do I Need RSVP on My Network?

RSVP is used primarily to guarantee QoS to real-time applications such as voice and video. RSVP-aware clients can make a reservation and be guaranteed a good QoS across the network for the length of the reservation.

Because RSVP takes the Intserv approach to QoS, all traffic in the network does not need to be classified in order to give proper QoS to RSVP sessions. On the other hand, for the same reason, a multifield classification must be performed on each packet at each node in the network to discover if it is part of the RSVP session for which resources have been reserved. This can lead to a consumption of network resources like memory and CPU cycles.

RSVP's open architecture and transparency allow for deployment on many platforms, and even tunneling across non-RSVP aware nodes. Despite this, RSVP has some distinct scaling issues that make it doubtful that it will ever be implemented successfully on a very large network, or on the Internet, in its current revision. These advantages and disadvantages, as well as others previously discussed, are summarized here.

Advantages of Using RSVP

- **Admissions Control** RSVP not only provides QoS, but also helps other applications by *not* transmitting when the network is busy.
- **Network Independence/Flexibility** RSVP is not dependent on a particular networking architecture.
- **Interoperability** RSVP works inside existing protocols and with other QoS mechanisms.
- **Distributed** RSVP is a distributed service and therefore has no central point of failure.
- **Transparency** RSVP can tunnel across an RSVP-unaware network.

Disadvantages of Using RSVP

- **Scaling Issues** Multifield classification and statefulness of reservations may consume memory and CPU resources.
- **Route Selection and Stability** The shortest path may not have available resources, and the active path may go down.
- **Setup Time** An application cannot start transmitting until the reservation has been completed.

Using Class-Based Weighted Fair Queuing (CBWFQ)

We saw in Chapter 6 that priority queuing and custom queuing can be used to give certain types of traffic preferential treatment when congestion occurs on a low-speed serial link. We also saw that weighted fair queuing (WFQ) accomplishes the same effect by automatically detecting conversations and guaranteeing that no one conversation monopolizes the link. But WFQ has some scaling limitations. The algorithm runs into problems as traffic increases or if it is stressed by many conversations. Additionally, it does not run on high-speed interfaces such as ATM. Class-based weighted fair queuing (CBWFQ) was developed to overcome these factors. CBWFQ carries the WFQ algorithm further by allowing user-defined classes, which allow greater control over traffic queuing and bandwidth allocation. CBWFQ provides the power and ease of configuration of WFQ, along with the flexibility of custom queuing. This advanced queuing mechanism also incorporates weighted random early detection (WRED). WRED is not necessary for the operation of CBWFQ but works in conjunction with it to provide more reliable QoS to user-defined classes. We discuss WRED in more detail later in this chapter.

CBWFQ is a very powerful congestion management mechanism that is offered by Cisco for its router platforms. Although it is still being developed to be even more robust and intelligent, its wide platform support and functionality warrants it for consideration as part of your overall QoS solution. Let us take a look at the inner workings of this mechanism.

How Does CBWFQ Work?

Chapter 6 showed that flow-based WFQ automatically detects flows based on characteristics of the third and fourth layers of the OSI model. Conversations are singled out into flows by source and destination IP address, port number, and IP precedence.

If a packet going out an interface needs to be queued because of congestion, the conversation it is part of is determined, and a weight is assigned based on the characteristic of the flow. Such weights are assigned to ensure that each flow gets its fair share of the bandwidth. The weight assigned also subsequently determines which queue the packet will enter and how it will be serviced.

The limitation of flow-based WFQ is that the flows are automatically determined, and each flow gets a fair share of the bandwidth. This "fair share" of the bandwidth is determined by the size of the flow and moderated by IP precedence. Packets with IP precedences set to values other than the default (zero) are placed into queues that are serviced more frequently, based on the level of IP precedence, and thus get a higher overall bandwidth. Specifically, a data stream's weighting is the result of some complex calculations, but the important thing to remember is that weight is a relative number and the lower the weight of a packet, the higher that packet's priority. The weight calculation results in a weight, but the most important thing isn't that number—it's the packet's specific handling. Thus, a data stream with a precedence of 1 is dealt with twice as fast as best-effort traffic. However, even with the action of IP Precedence on WFQ, sometimes a specific bandwidth needs to be guaranteed to a certain type of traffic. CBWFQ fulfills this requirement.

CBWFQ extends WFQ to include user-defined classes. These classes can be determined by protocol, Access Control Lists (ACLs), IP precedence, or input interfaces. Each class has a separate queue, and all packets found to match the criteria for a particular class are assigned to that queue.

Once the matching criteria are set for the classes, you can determine how packets belonging to that class will be handled. It may be tempting to think of classes as having priority over each other, but it is more accurate to think of each class having a certain guaranteed share of the bandwidth. Note that this bandwidth guarantee is not a reservation as with RSVP, which reserves bandwidth during the entire period of the reservation. It is, instead, a guarantee of bandwidth that is active only during periods of congestion. If a class is not using the bandwidth guaranteed to it, other traffic may use it. Similarly, if the class needs more bandwidth than the allocated amount, it may use any free bandwidth available on the circuit.

You can specifically configure the bandwidth and maximum packet limit (or queue depth) of each class. The weight that is assigned to the class's queue is calculated from the configured bandwidth of that class.

CBWFQ allows the creation of up to 64 individual classes plus a default class. The number and size of the classes are, of course, based on the bandwidth. By default, the maximum bandwidth that can be allocated to user-defined classes is 75 percent of the link speed. This maximum is set so that there is still some bandwidth for Layer 2 overhead, routing traffic (BGP, EIGRP, OSPF, and others), and best-effort traffic. Although not recommended, it is possible to change this maximum in aggressive situations in which you want to give more bandwidth to user-defined classes. In this case, caution must be exercised to ensure that you allow enough remaining bandwidth to support Layer 2 overhead, routing traffic, and best-effort traffic.

Each user-defined class is guaranteed a certain bandwidth, but classes that exceed that bandwidth are not necessarily dropped. Traffic in excess of the class's guaranteed bandwidth may use the "free" bandwidth on the link. "Free" is defined as the circuit bandwidth minus the portion of the guaranteed bandwidth currently being used by all user-defined classes. Within this "free" bandwidth, the packets are considered by fair queuing along with other packets, their weight being based on the proportion of the total bandwidth that was guaranteed to the class. For example, on a T1 circuit, if Class A and Class B were configured with 1000 Kbps and 10 Kbps, respectively, and if both were transmitting over their guaranteed bandwidths, the remaining 534 Kbps (1544 − 1010) would be shared between the two at a 100:1 ratio.

All packets not falling into one of the defined classes are considered part of the default class (or class-default, as it appears in the router configuration). The default class can be configured to have a set bandwidth like other user-defined classes, or configured to use flow-based WFQ in the remaining bandwidth and treated as best effort. The default configuration of the default class is dependent on the router platform and the IOS revision. Chapter 9 will discuss the user-defined classes and default class perform and how they are configured in more depth.

Even though packets that exceed bandwidth guarantees are given WFQ treatment, bandwidth is, of course, not unlimited. When the fair queuing buffers overflow, packets are dropped with tail drop unless WRED has been configured for the class's policy. In the latter case, packets are dropped randomly before buffers totally run out in order to signal the sender to throttle back the transmission speed. We will see in a later section how WRED interoperates with CBWFQ.

Why Do I Need CBWFQ on My Network?

You might ask yourself, "Why do I need *any* kind of special queuing?" Packet based networks drop packets by their very nature. IP network protocols are designed around the inevitability of dropped packets. The question therefore becomes, "If you had a choice, which packets would you prefer to keep and which would you prefer to drop?" This will help determine what type of queuing mechanism you choose.

WFQ is on by default on low-speed serial interfaces for good reason. It works well to overcome the limitations of first in/ first out (FIFO) queuing by not allowing large flows to dominate over smaller, interactive flows, and it is easy to implement. However, even with the extension of the weighting model by using IP precedence, flow-based fair queuing is still just that—fair. There are times when the fair slice of the bandwidth pie is less than you require for certain applications, or when you require more granular control over the QoS provided to your traffic. When you want a guaranteed bandwidth for particular types of traffic, you need CBWFQ.

The Battle of the Internet Protocols

Protocols can be categorized as either *congestion notification responsive* or *congestion notification unresponsive*. The *slow start* algorithm characterizes TCP as being responsive to congestion situations since when a TCP flow fails to get an acknowledgement that a packet was received, it throttles back its send rate and then slowly ramps up.

On the other hand, UDP is unresponsive to congestion notification. Unless there are acknowledgements at a higher layer, a UDP stream will continue to transmit at the same rate despite packet drops. If we think of the congested link as the battlefield, and the combatants as TCP and UDP, then TCP is polite and UDP is usually the spoiler. The unresponsiveness of UDP applications can be the detriment of not only other "impolite" UDP streams but also well-behaved TCP sessions.

NOTE

Advanced queuing mechanisms (basically, anything except FIFO) work to schedule which of the packets waiting in queue will be next to go out the interface. Thus, advanced queuing mechanisms really do not come into play unless there is congestion. If there are no packets waiting in queue, then as soon as a packet comes into the router, it goes directly out of the interface, and the queuing works essentially the same as FIFO. Therefore, CBWFQ does not "kick in" until congestion starts.

With CBWFQ, you can leverage the DiffServ model to divide all your traffic into distinct classes to which CBWFQ can subsequently give specialized bandwidth guarantees. The typical application of this is to mark traffic at the edge with IP precedence, and then let mechanisms like CBWFQ give differential treatment throughout the entire network according to the service levels defined. By placing important applications into a class to which CBWFQ can give a guaranteed bandwidth, you have effectively prevented other applications from stealing bandwidth from those critical applications. Let us examine a couple of illustrative cases.

Case Studies

1. Using a SQL Application on a Slow WAN Link

Problem: Imagine that Company A uses a SQL application for centralized inventory. It was originally used only at the corporate headquarters; however, it has now become critical to the core business, and its use has been extended to remote sites. Unfortunately, because it was developed in a LAN environment, it does not respond well to delays and packet loss. Assume that it needs 50 Kbps to function adequately, and that all the remote sites are connected with 256 Kbps serial links. In the absence of other traffic, the application functions perfectly. However, at peak times during the day, other applications such as bulk transfers from FTP, Telnet sessions to the corporate mainframe, Web browsing, and messaging are periodically filling the link to capacity. With WFQ enabled, some SQL packets may be dropped in a congestion situation because of the competing conversations. Remember that all traffic gets its fair share of the bandwidth and its fair share of packet drops. The drops would cause TCP retransmissions, which could slow down the SQL application considerably. Because of the SQL application's interactive nature, the user's productivity drops, and he or she comes to you requesting an upgrade of the link speed. A circuit upgrade might sound like a good idea if we could get the project funding. However, if we did this, we might quickly find out that even if we doubled the circuit speed, the company's critical application might still not achieve the performance it requires. IP networks work in bursts, and even the largest pipes can momentarily become saturated.

Solution: One solution would be to configure a class for the SQL application. The SQL traffic could be classified by the TCP port number of incoming packets. By applying a policy to the output of the serial interface allocating 50 Kbps to this class, we could guarantee that even in the busiest part of the day, this application would be given the amount of

Continued

bandwidth needed for good performance. In addition, all other traffic could be configured to function under flow-based WFQ so that all conversations would have fair access to the remaining bandwidth.

In effect we have carved out a slice of the serial bandwidth for the SQL application but also allowed it to use more than this amount, although its use above 50 Kbps would not be guaranteed. In addition, other applications can use the reserved 50 Kbps when SQL is not using it. Remember, CBWFQ does not function unless there is congestion.

2. Total Traffic Classification (CBWFQ in a DiffServ Model)

In the previous case study, we saw that we could effectively guarantee a certain amount of bandwidth to a mission-critical application. But what if there were many other applications that needed minimum bandwidth guarantees? We may need more granular control over how our applications behave under WFQ. CBWFQ allows us to configure up to 64 distinct classes. However, we probably would not want to put each application into a separate class. Not only would we be limited in the amount of bandwidth we could allocate to the class (the sum of all bandwidth cannot exceed the link speed), but it could also be confusing having this many classes.

A best-practice approach would be to define just a few of the classes, and categorize all applications into these classes based on expected bandwidth utilization and the application's tolerance of dropped packets. With this approach, applications would be sharing bandwidth with others within the same class, but a degree of granularity is added in addition to WFQ that would be adequate for most networks.

We saw in Chapter 4 that the IP ToS header allows us to enumerate packets into eight levels of IP precedence, two of them being reserved for network applications, leaving six levels for user applications. We can map these IP precedence levels directly into our network classes of service. Using a precious metal analogy, we would have six classes of service, as shown in Table 8.2.

In this example, we can realize the economy of using CBWFQ within the DiffServ model. Using packet classification at the edge of the network to mark IP precedence, we have effectively divided all of our applications into 5 classes of service plus a default class. Except for the edge devices, no other classification may be necessary to place a packet into the proper queue as it traverses the network. By marking applications at the edge and allowing internal routers to queue packets according to these classes, we not only assure consistent QoS for that application

Continued

across the entire network, but we also reduce the resource load on both the routers and the network administrator. The routers do not have to process lengthy ACLs at every hop, and the administrators have to worry about classification only at the edge of the network. Additionally, it is at these edge devices that packet rates are the smallest and processor utilization according to packet marking is manageable. To classify packets at the hub site where many circuits are being aggregated might be too much for the router to handle.

Table 8.2 An Example of a Class of Service Mapping

Class of Service	IP Precedence
Platinum	5
Gold	4
Silver	3
Bronze	2
Iron	1
Best-Effort (default)	0

> **NOTE**
>
> Remember that QoS is never a substitute for bandwidth. On the other hand, even a gigabit link can drop packets if the queues fill up. Congestion management rations the limited bandwidth to the most important applications, or in the case of CBWFQ, ensures that certain applications get at least the percentage of total bandwidth allocated.

RSVP in Conjunction with CBWFQ

CBWFQ and RSVP can be configured on the same interface. There is, in general, no specific interaction between the two. They are configured as if the other mechanism were not present. However, because RSVP reserves bandwidth for its clients and CBWFQ guarantees bandwidth for its classes, it is possible to configure the router to guarantee bandwidth to each of them in such a way that the total guaranteed bandwidth exceeds the circuit speed.

This constitutes a potential problem. In a congestion situation, if you have promised the majority of the circuit bandwidth to two mechanisms separately, which one will succeed in getting the bandwidth it needs? You cannot promise three-quarters of the bandwidth to CBWFQ and half the bandwidth to RSVP and expect that they would both have sufficient bandwidth in a congestion situation. In practice, if you need to guarantee bandwidth to classes as well as to RSVP sessions, you would avoid an overlapping bandwidth guarantee like this. Still, there is nothing in the IOS code to prevent you from making this configuration.

So, what exactly does happen if you over-subscribe the guaranteed bandwidth by promising it to both RSVP and CBWFQ? Because of the WFQ implementation in the routers, RSVP wins out in the end, taking as much bandwidth as it needs from all other classes equally.

Using Low Latency Queuing (LLQ)

The previous section demonstrated that CBWFQ can give bandwidth guarantees to different classes of traffic. Although CBWFQ can provide these bandwidth guarantees, low latency transmission may not be provided to packets in congestion situations, since all packets are transmitted fairly based on their weight. This can cause problems for applications like VoIP that are sensitive to delays, especially variations in delays. Variation in the delay time between individual packets that make up a voice stream is usually referred to as *jitter*. Although most voice applications can tolerate a certain amount of delay, jitter can cause choppiness in voice transmissions and quickly degrade overall voice quality. Low latency queuing (LLQ) extends CBWFQ to include the option of creating a strict priority queue. Strict priority queuing delivers low latency transmission to constant bit rate (CBR) applications such as voice.

How Does LLQ Work?

Once you know how CBWFQ works, LLQ is easy to understand. LLQ creates a strict priority queue that you might imagine as resting on top of all other queues. This priority queue is emptied before any other queue is serviced. A strict priority queue is often referred to as an exhaustive queue, since packets continue to be removed from the queue and transmitted until it is empty. Only after the strict priority queue is totally empty are the other queues serviced in the order determined by whatever weighting has been configured by the CBWFQ bandwidth statements.

> **NOTE**
>
> When LLQ was first created, it was referred to as PQCBWFQ, or priority queuing with class-based weighted fair queuing. Although this lengthy acronym was appropriate because it clearly described the combined functionality of PQ with CBWFQ, it has been changed in most documentation to simply LLQ.

If packets come into the priority queue while another queue is being serviced, the packets waiting in the priority queue will be the very next packets sent out the interface, after the current packet has been transmitted. In this way, the delay between packets sent from the priority queue is minimized, and low latency service is delivered. The maximum time between priority packets arriving at the far end would occur in the case in which a packet arrives in the previously empty priority queue as soon as the router starts to transmit a large packet. The largest possible packet is referred to as the maximum transmission unit (MTU), which is 1500 bytes on Ethernet. The priority packet will have to wait for the non-priority packet to finish transmitting. Thus, the longest delay possible between arriving priority packets is limited to the serialization time of the MTU plus the serialization time of the priority packet itself. The serialization time is calculated by dividing the size of the packet by the link speed (packet size/link speed). We discuss the implications of serialization delay and how to overcome it in more detail in a later section on Link Fragmentation and Interleaving (LFI).

Classifying Priority Traffic

The traffic placed into the priority queue under LLQ is determined by the same criteria available to any other user-defined class under CBWFQ. Specifically, these criteria include protocol, Access Control Lists (ACLs), IP precedence, and input interface.

Allocating Bandwidth

Bandwidth is allocated to the priority class a little differently than to other user-defined classes. Instead of specifying the guaranteed bandwidth of the class with the *bandwidth* command, the *priority* command is used. This gives a priority class that will deliver LLQ to all traffic falling under this classification. There is a particular distinction between how traffic metering is handled with the priority class as opposed to other user-defined classes. Unlike normal classes, with the priority class under congestion situations, bandwidth in excess of the limit configured with the priority command *is always dropped*. This is to prevent the priority queue from starving other traffic, both other user-defined classes and other important traffic like network routing updates. However, in non-congestion situations, the bandwidth allocated to the priority class may be exceeded.

It is important that you limit the bandwidth allocated to the priority class to a reasonable value. If you configure too much of your traffic as priority traffic, then it really is not priority at all. On an airplane, if everyone flies first class, can you really call it first class? Additionally, it is strongly recommended that packets classified into the priority class be limited to voice traffic alone. Voice streams are made of small packets of constant bit rate that are well behaved by nature. By classifying applications into the priority class that are prone to bursts or comprised of large packets, you essentially destroy the low latency provided to the small-packet CBR voice traffic also waiting in the priority queue.

The fact that bandwidth of the priority class under congestion situations creates a "hard upper limit" to voice traffic should not cause insurmountable problems. Voice planners are accustomed to providing for an exact number of voice calls on traditional voice networks. The same can be done on VoIP networks by multiplying the bandwidth of each voice call (determined by the codec) by the number of simultaneous calls in order to get the bandwidth necessary. It is important to note that a call admission control process for the voice calls is required. This guarantees that the number of calls supported by the bandwidth provisioned by the priority command is not exceeded. Exceeding this bandwidth would potentially lead to poor voice performance for *all* voice callers. Here is an example.

Consider that a remote site needs up to 24 simultaneous voice calls connected to the main hub site. The remote site is connected via a T1 serial link. When the G.729 codec is used with compressed RTP (CRTP), you can expect each call to use a maximum of 12 Kbps. This gives a provision of 288 Kbps for all 24 calls. This bandwidth is configured for the priority class with the priority command. In an uncongested situation, more than 24 calls could be completed and still have good quality. However, if congestion occurs in this overloaded call state, even for a moment, packets will be dropped from the priority queue. Since it can be assumed that the packets from the individual voice calls are interleaved with each other, some drops will occur across all connected voice calls, resulting in poor performance for everyone. To avoid this, some kind of admission control system is necessary to assure that no more than 24 calls are ever connected. This can be accomplished in a number of ways, including using gatekeeper technology available on the Cisco Call Manager, the Cisco AS5300, and Cisco 3640 routers (IOS 12.1(1)), or by limiting the number of active voice ports on communicating gateways. In either case, it would be preferable for a caller to get a busy signal indicating that the call could not be completed, rather than the quality of all connected callers being affected.

Note that it is possible to have multiple classes configured as priority classes. In this case, the classes are policed and rate-limited individually. That is, although a single policy map might contain multiple priority classes, all in a single priority queue, they are each treated as separate flows with separate bandwidth allocations and constraints.

Limitations and Caveats

A notable difference between the priority class and other user-defined classes under CBWFQ is that WRED is not available in the priority class. LLQ is to be used for CBR services, especially VoIP. Voice traffic is UDP-based and therefore not adaptive to the early packet drop characteristic of WRED. If a packet is dropped from a UDP stream, UDP will not react to this by reducing the send rate. Because WRED would be ineffective, configuration of this feature for a priority class using the **random-detect** command is disallowed.

Why Do I Need LLQ on My Network?

You should consider using LLQ if you need to provide good QoS to delay- and jitter-sensitive applications like VoIP. Because LLQ is an extension of CBWFQ, it complements network designs that are already using CBWFQ to give differential services to classes of applications. You have only to configure another class and designate it as "priority" with an appropriate bandwidth limitation to give low latency service to your real-time applications.

Because LLQ is an extension of CBWFQ, you also have access to all the matching criteria that is provided normally to CBWFQ. This is in contrast to RTP priority queuing, which limits match criteria to a UDP port range. Because one of these matching criteria is IP precedence, the DiffServ model can be leveraged to use packet marking at edge devices and allow CBWFQ with LLQ to give low latency service to designated packets without long Access Control Lists (ACLs). This speeds up packet processing time and overall performance. LLQ is also more flexible than RTP priority queuing in that it can be enabled on ATM virtual circuits (VCs) to allow timely dequeuing of delay sensitive traffic into ATM networks.

Finally, the "hard limit" of the bandwidth for priority classes acts as a sort of admission control that prevents starving other traffic classes of bandwidth in congested situations.

Using Weighted Random Early Detection (WRED)

In Chapter 6 we saw that Random Early Detection (RED) can be used as a congestion avoidance mechanism to prevent congestion problems at bandwidth bottlenecks on networks. WRED is the Cisco implementation of RED that combines the RED algorithm with weighting determined by IP precedence levels. This effectively gives higher precedence traffic lower drop rates and thus priority over lower precedence traffic in the network.

How Does WRED Work?

RED works on the basis of active queue management, and it addresses the shortcomings of tail drop. A RED enabled router signals congestion to TCP senders by dropping packets before the router is actually out of buffer space. Compliant TCP senders detecting the dropped packets will throttle back the send rate using the TCP slow start algorithm. RED drops arriving packets randomly so that the probability of a particular flow having packets dropped is in proportion to the flow's share of the bandwidth. Thus, flows using more bandwidth have a greater chance of dropped packets than flows using small amounts of the overall bandwidth.

RED operates by monitoring the buffer level and discarding packets probabilistically (see Figure 8.3) based on minimum and maximum threshold values. Below the minimum threshold, no packets are dropped; above the maximum threshold, all packets are dropped. When the buffer is between these two thresholds, the drop rate is calculated as a function of the average queue size. The average queue size is a running average over time. How responsive this average is to changes is reflected in the configurable weighting average (discussed later). Because of the randomness in which packets are dropped, packets across all flows are dropped at different times, thus preventing the phenomenon of *global synchronization* commonly associated with tail drop.

Figure 8.3 Weighted Random Early Detection (WRED)

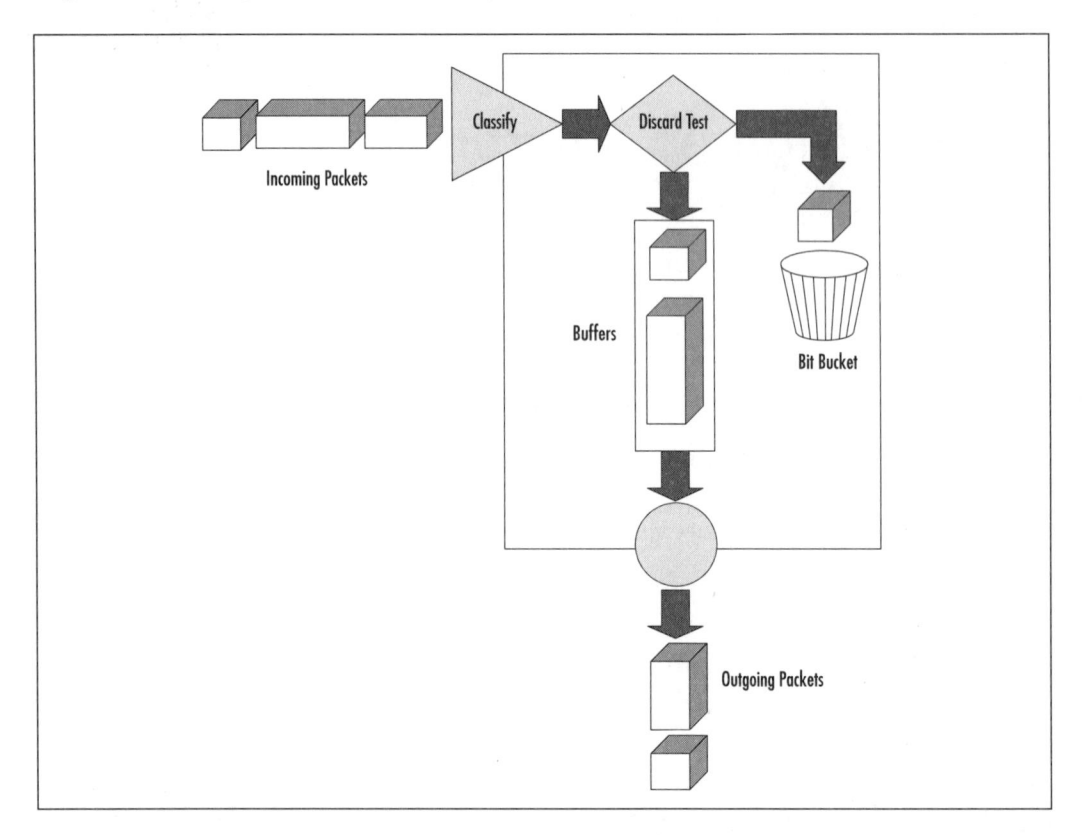

WRED and IP Precedence

Weighted random early detection (WRED) is the Cisco implementation of RED that combines the capabilities of the RED algorithm with IP precedence to provide lower drop rates for higher priority, or higher precedence, packets. The router attributing different minimum and maximum threshold levels to each precedence accomplishes this. By default, the minimum threshold in packets for IP precedence level 0 is one half the maximum. The values for the remaining precedences fall between half the maximum threshold and the maximum threshold at evenly spaced intervals. Table 8.3 shows the default values for both WRED and Distributed WRED (DWRED), which is available on the VIP-based RSP platform. See the discussion later in this chapter on "Running in Distributed Mode."

> **NOTE**
>
> Although WRED gives lower drop probabilities to higher IP precedence values, it can be configured to change the weighting of each precedence level, or even to ignore precedence altogether, and thus function as normal RED. By using the **random-detect precedence** command, you can set the minimum and maximum threshold levels to something other than the default values shown in Table 8.3. By making all the thresholds the same, you essentially make WRED function as normal RED.

Table 8.3 Default WRED and DWRED Threshold Values

IP Precedence	WRED Threshold Values Minimum	Maximum	DWRED Threshold Values Minimum	Maximum
0	20	40	95	190
1	22	40	106	190
2	24	40	117	190
3	26	40	128	190
4	28	40	139	190
5	31	40	150	190
6	33	40	161	190
7	35	40	172	190
RSVP	37	40	N/A	N/A

WRED and RSVP

WRED is the primary QoS mechanism responsible for providing *controlled-load* service to RSVP sessions. Remember from our RSVP discussion that Intserv defines *controlled-load* service as service across the network as if it were unloaded. By WRED keeping a link in an uncongested state by detecting impending congestion situations and preemptively dropping traffic, WRED can effectively grant services to RSVP flows *as if the network were unloaded*.

WRED Algorithm

The basic RED algorithm uses a calculated average queue size to determine when to drop packets and with what probability. This average is based on the previous average and the current queue size. It therefore can be considered a moving average with the following formula:

average = (old_average * (1-2 $^{-n}$)) + (current_queue_size * 2 $^{-n}$)

In this equation, *n* is the exponential weighting constant that affects how rapidly the average changes with respect to the current queue size. By changing this constant, WRED can be configured to be more or less adaptive to bursts in traffic. Cisco recommends using the default value of 9, but you can change this by using the **random-detect exponential-weighting-constant** command. Valid ranges are between 1 and 16. Higher values will make the moving average slower, which smooths out the peaks and lows in queue length at the expense of not reacting to congestion fast enough. Lower values will make WRED more adaptive but at the expense of possibly overreacting to temporary traffic bursts and dropping traffic unnecessarily.

Why Do I Need WRED on My Network?

WRED makes early detection of congestion possible and provides differentiated services for multiple classes of traffic. Like basic RED, it also protects against *global synchronization* as long as flows are compliant to congestion notification, like TCP. For these reasons, WRED is useful on any output interface where you expect congestion to occur. However, it is most effective in backbone networks that aggregate many paths from remote sites. If the routers at the edge are marking traffic into classes with IP precedence, WRED can act more intelligently in the backbone with its drop decisions.

WRED was primarily designed for use in IP networks dominated by TCP. You may not want to use WRED if your network has a large amount of UDP traffic. With TCP, dropped packets indicate congestion, so the packet source will reduce its transmission rate. With other protocols, like UDP, it is left to higher layer protocols, such as the application itself, to respond to dropped packets by slowing down transmission. With UDP, this usually does not happen. When packets are dropped from a UDP transmission, the source may continue to send packets at the same rate. Thus, dropping packets does not decrease congestion, and WRED is ineffective. Making sure that adaptive flows get their fair share of bandwidth in comparison to non-adaptive flows may be possible using flow-based RED (see sidebar).

Additionally if your network is not strictly IP, you may not gain the benefit of the IP precedence weighting of WRED. WRED treats non-IP traffic as precedence 0, the lowest precedence. Therefore, non-IP traffic, in general, is more likely to be dropped than IP traffic. This may cause problems if most of your important traffic is something other than IP. The case for QoS may encourage you to advocate transforming your network into a strictly IP network.

> ### Flow-based Random Early Detection
>
> Flow-based RED (FRED) is an extension to WRED that ensures that no single flow can monopolize all the buffer resources at the output interface queue. With normal WRED, a packet dropped from a TCP source causes the source to reduce its transmission, whereas a packet dropped from a non-compliant source, like UDP, does not. This may have the end effect of the "polite" flows being drowned out by the "impolite" flows. Flow-based RED prevents this by maintaining minimal information about the buffer occupancy of each flow. In this way, when a flow exceeds its share of the output buffer, it is dropped. This is in contrast to the more random buffer drops of normal WRED. This feature first became available in IOS version 12.0(3)T.

Using Generic Traffic Shaping and Frame Relay Traffic Shaping

Traffic shaping is a mechanism that restricts traffic going out an interface to a particular speed, at the same time attempting to buffer bursts in excess of this maximum speed. Traffic shaping thereby acts to smooth out or "shape" traffic into a stream that conforms to downstream requirements. Cisco offers two traffic shaping features, namely, Generic Traffic Shaping (GTS) and Frame Relay Traffic Shaping (FRTS). These two features are more similar than they are different. To understand traffic shaping in general, let us first look at the fundamental algorithm behind it.

Token Bucket

In Chapter 3 we discussed the leaky bucket algorithm in detail. Both GTS and FRTS use a construct called a token bucket to rate-limit traffic. A token bucket differs from a leaky bucket in that a token bucket should be thought of as being filled with tokens, not packets. You can think of tokens as permissions for a specific number of bits to be transmitted to the network. The token bucket is also commonly referred to as a *credit manager* that gives credits to traffic to be used for transmission. Before a packet is sent out the interface, a certain number of tokens need to be removed from the bucket. Tokens fill the token bucket at a constant rate, and the bucket is a certain size. After the bucket is full, newly arriving tokens are discarded. If the bucket is empty, an incoming packet has to wait for enough tokens to fill the bucket before it can be transferred. Thus, with the token bucket analogy, the burst size is roughly proportional to the size of the bucket. A depiction of a token bucket is shown in Figure 8.4.

Figure 8.4 Token Bucket Algorithm

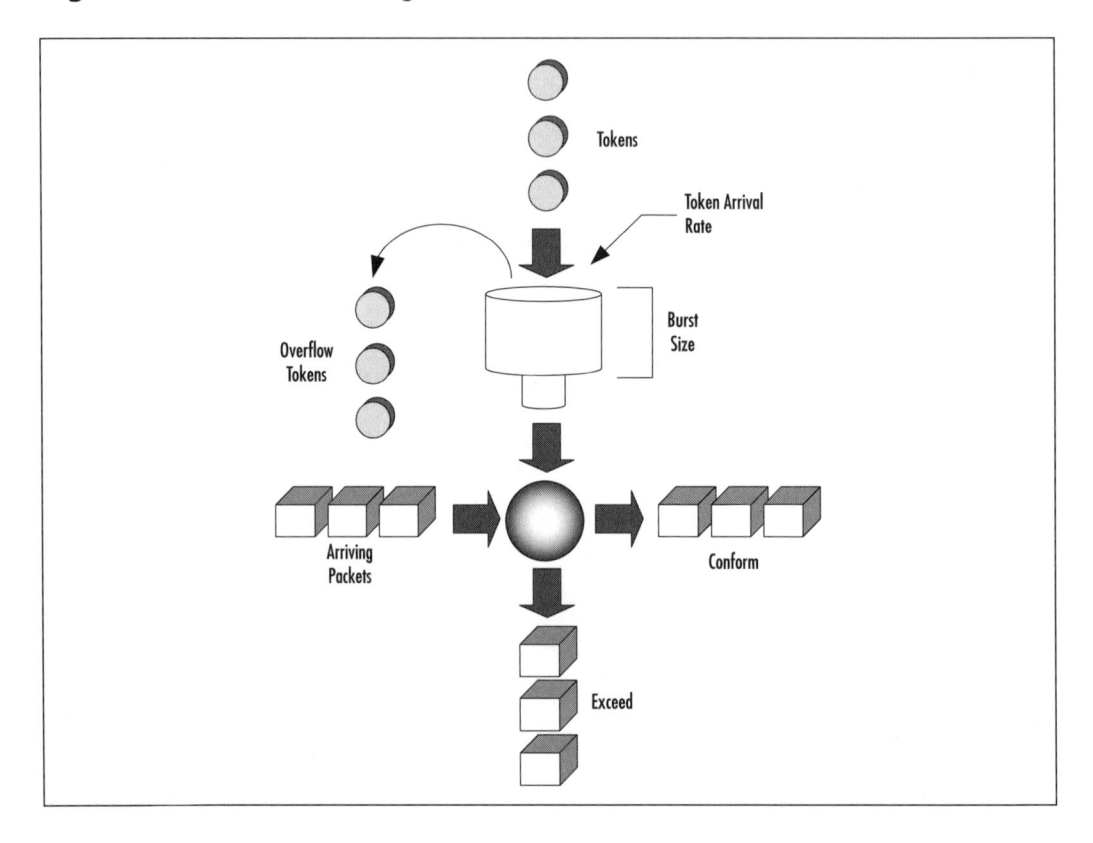

There are three primary variables associated with token bucket traffic shaping: burst size, mean rate, and time interval.

- **Mean Rate** Specifies how much data can be sent on average. This is also called the committed information rate (CIR).
- **Burst Size** Specifies how much data can be sent over a single time interval without causing scheduling problems. This is also called the Committed Burst size.
- **Time Interval** This is the time quantum for a single burst. This is also called the measurement interval.

The burst size is the amount of data that can be sent with the token bucket over a single time interval. The mean rate is the burst size divided by the time interval. Therefore, when a token bucket is regulating an output interface, its rate over an interval of time cannot exceed the mean rate. However, within that interval, the bit rate may be arbitrarily fast. In this way, large data flows are regulated down to what the network can actually handle, and momentary bursts are smoothed out by buffering, rather than being dropped.

How Does GTS Work?

GTS acts to limit packet rates sent out an interface to a mean rate, while allowing for buffering of momentary bursts. With GTS parameters configured to match the network architecture, downstream congestion can be avoided, eliminating bottlenecks in topologies with data-rate mismatches. GTS has the following characteristics:

- Rate enforcement on a per interface, or subinterface, basis—the mean rate can be set to match the circuit CIR or some other value.
- Traffic selection using Access Control Lists (ACLs).
- GTS works on many Layer 2 interface types, including Frame Relay, ATM, Switched Multimegabit Data Service (SMDS), and Ethernet.
- It supports BECN messages for bandwidth throttling.
- It supports WFQ per subinterface.

GTS works with the token bucket algorithm in the following way. When packets arrive at the router, an interrupt occurs. If the queue is empty, GTS consults the credit manager (token bucket) to see if there is enough credit to send the packet. If there is not, the packet is sent to the queue configured, in this case, WFQ. If there is credit available, the packet is sent to the output interface, and the associated credit value is deducted from the token bucket. Queued packets are serviced at regular time intervals. The credit manager is checked each time interval to determine if there is enough credit to transmit the next packet waiting in queue. If there is, the packet is sent to the output interface, and the VC is charged the appropriate number of credits.

Why Do I Need GTS on My Network?

Many times a situation exists in which a carrier provides a circuit with a committed information rate (CIR) less than the access rate of the physical interface.

For example, a Frame Relay service may be provisioned with a 1544 Kbps CIR, but the circuit is delivered on an E1 (2048 Kbps) interface. In the absence of traffic shaping, the router will send up to a rate of 2048 Kbps. This may cause problems, since the traffic in excess of the CIR could be dropped in the Frame Relay network. In this situation, you may get considerably more throughput than the CIR at times, but you are at the mercy of the Frame Relay network. During times when the network is not busy, you may get all your traffic through, but during congested times, many of your packets may be dropped. You may think that any amount of bandwidth over the CIR is a bonus, but when packets like TCP are dropped in large quantities, the retransmission can cause not only increased congestion, but *global synchronization* as well. Additionally, if you are transmitting real-time data, any dropped packets will immediately degrade performance. Depending on your network applications, it may be better to take the more conservative approach by using traffic shaping and sleep soundly knowing that you have a reliable service.

Although GTS is available on a variety of interfaces, it may not be that useful in light of other QoS mechanisms and modern technologies. For example, you would rarely want to limit traffic rates on a shared, private medium such as Ethernet, especially if it was switched Ethernet. Also, in the case of ATM, if a variable bit rate (VBR) service was ordered, the carrier would most likely tell you the sustainable cell rate (SCR), peak cell rate (PCR), and maximum burst size (MBS). By configuring an ATM VBR service on the router with these parameters, you have already enabled traffic shaping. Adding GTS on top of this would be redundant. Finally, for Frame Relay circuits, FRTS, not surprisingly, has features that are more suited to this medium.

How Do FECNs and BECNs Work?

Forward explicit congestion notification (FECN) and backwards explicit congestion notification (BECN) are used in networks by intermediary nodes to inform other nodes of congestion that was experienced as a packet traveled across the network. In Frame Relay, setting a specific bit in a normal Frame Relay packet indicates a FECN or BECN. Here's how it works.

Continued

> If device A is sending data to device B across a Frame Relay infrastructure, and one of the intermediary Frame Relay switches encounters congestion, congestion being full buffers, an over-subscribed port, overloaded resources, and so forth, it will set the BECN bit on packets being returned to the sending device (A), and the FECN bit on the packets being sent to the receiving device (B). This has the effect of informing the sending router to slow down and apply flow control, such as traffic shaping, and informing the receiving device that the flow is congested and that upper layer protocols should expect some delays.

How Does FRTS Work?

FRTS works essentially the same as GTS. It uses a token bucket, or credit manager, algorithm to service the main queuing mechanism and send packets out the interface. It also is commonly used to overcome data-rate mismatches. However, it does have these differing characteristics:

- Enhanced queuing support on a per VC basis—both PQ and CQ are available.
- Traffic selection using Access Control Lists (ACLs)
- Rate enforcement on a per VC basis—the mean rate can be set to match CIR or some other value.
- FRTS supports both BECN and Cisco Foresight congestion notification on a per VC basis.

Notice that WFQ is not available (see the following note for the IOS release in which it is available), but PQ and CQ are configurable on a per VC basis. This means that you are not limited to one queuing mechanism for the whole interface, but you can pick the queuing method that suits each VC the best. Additionally, by using ACLs, you can direct traffic to separate VCs, creating a virtual time-division multiplexing (TDM) network. This method may not make the most efficient use of your purchased bandwidth if you pay by CIR, since if there is no incoming traffic for a particular traffic type, the associated VC will be basically empty.

Another approach that would make more efficient use of bandwidth would be to divide your traffic into classes on a single VC. For example, suppose DECnet was a critical application across your Frame Relay network. Using PQ, you could classify all your DECnet traffic into the high priority queue, while classifying other traffic into lower ones. Since all the packets in the high priority queue would be serviced before the lower priority queues, you would ensure that DECnet packets would not be delayed unduly by other traffic.

Still another approach would be to divide your traffic into classes and use CQ to give each a guaranteed bandwidth percentage. This has the benefit over multiple VCs and the virtual TDM network of allowing a class's reserved bandwidth to be used by other classes when available.

> **NOTE**
>
> If you want to transmit voice over Frame Relay and ensure low latency, you may want to consider the combination of RTP priority, PQ or CQ, and FRF.12 for link fragmentation and interleaving (see the section on RTP priority and LFI for more information). However, this combination has been superceded in later releases of IOS code (12.1(2)T) by the more flexible feature, low latency queuing for frame relay, also called priority queuing/class-based weighted fair queuing (PQ/CBWFQ). Although this is not discussed in this book, the concept and configuration are very similar to general CBWFQ with LLQ covered earlier in this chapter.

FRTS will heed congestion notifications from both BECN and Cisco Foresight messages. The Foresight algorithm notifies switches of congestion situations on the Cisco StrataCom line of ATM switches. Whereas Cisco routers may be configured to listen to Foresight messages, BECN responsiveness is enabled by default with FRTS. To enable the router to respond to the ForeSight feature, you must enter the **frame-relay adaptive-shaping foresight** command within the VC's map class. Because BECNs are relayed within normal Frame Relay packets, there must be an occasional packet sent back to the transmitting router for BECNs to be received. Thus, when congestion occurs, the sending router might not be informed to throttle back immediately. One of the benefits of Foresight over BECN is that with Foresight, there is a special status packet that is sent on a regular basis (every 40 to 5000 ms), which guarantees that congestion information is relayed when it happens. Whether BECN or Foresight is used for congestion notification, the router will respond by adapting its rate downwards based on the number of notifications received. Specifically, for each time interval that one or more BECNs are received, the router's send rate will be decreased by 25 percent. This will continue as long as BECNs are received, or until the rate reaches the minimum CIR. This is an optional configurable parameter that we will look at in the next chapter. When congestion notifications stop for 16 time intervals, the router will slowly start stepping the data rate back up, much more slowly than it originally throttled down.

Why Do I Need FRTS on My Network?

The most common use for FRTS is to overcome data-rate mismatches. Earlier in our discussion of GTS, we saw that sometimes the allowed data rate for the network is lower than the port speed that the interface is delivered on. Beyond this data-rate mismatch that occurs at the router/switch interface, there is a situation that is almost as common that occurs when a site acts as the central hub that terminates many other Frame Relay connections. Consider the example shown in Figure 8.5.

Figure 8.5 Traffic Shaping on a Frame Relay Network

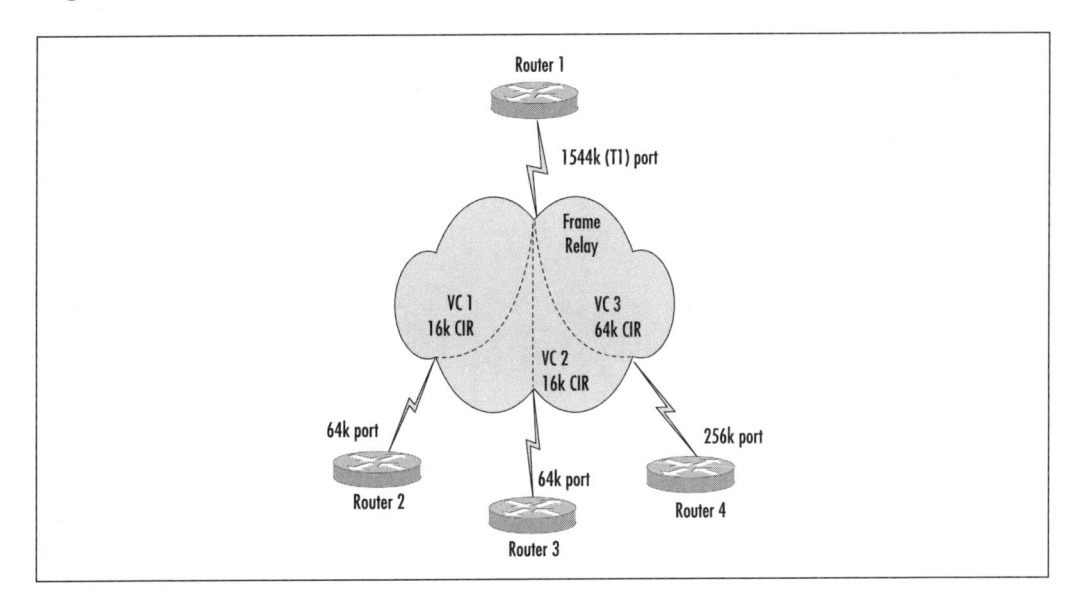

In this example, we see that Router 1 is connected to a Frame Relay switch network (shown as the cloud) via a T1 interface with three virtual circuits. Routers 2 and 3 are connected to different parts of the network, each with a 64 Kbps port speed and a CIR of 16 Kbps. Router 4 is connected with a port speed of 256 Kbps and a 64 Kbps CIR.

With this configuration, we have a separate virtual circuit (VC) going to each remote site in a point-to-multipoint configuration. Because of the unequal data rates, without traffic shaping, it is possible that the traffic flowing out of Router 1 might overload any one of the three other routers. Traffic could potentially travel across the majority of the Frame Relay network, only to be dropped at the egress of the network, right before the remote router. This does not make very efficient use of the network. You might consider simply lowering the port speed of the hub router to 64 Kbps to prevent this; however, not only would Router 4 then have the potential to overwhelm the hub router, but if Routers 2, 3, and 4 all transmitted at their port speed simultaneously (64 + 64 + 256 = 384), they definitely would.

FRTS can solve this problem. What is typically done is enable FRTS at the hub location and set the FRTS CIR parameter (not the carrier CIR) equal to the port speed at the far end of the VC. Thus, for the first VC from Router 1 to Router 2, we would have a CIR set to 64 Kbps. The same configuration would apply to the second VC. We would set the CIR of the third VC to 256 Kbps. This overcomes the data-rate mismatch, the traffic becomes well behaved, and unnecessary packet drops are eliminated. Enabling FRTS on the remote ends might be helpful if you wanted the routers to heed BECNs and throttle down when the network is congested, but by enabling FRTS on the hub site alone, we have eliminated the data-rate mismatch problem. Chapter 9 deals with the specifics of configuring FRTS.

Committed Access Rate (CAR)

CAR is another mechanism that provides policing of traffic to router platforms. It has the ability to rate-limit traffic based on certain matching criteria, such as incoming interface, IP precedence, QoS group, or ACLs. But unlike GTS and FRTS, besides being able to rate-limit outgoing traffic, it can also rate-limit traffic entering the router, as well as perform other actions. CAR provides configurable actions, such as transmit, drop, set precedence, or set QoS group when traffic conforms to, or exceeds, the rate limit. It could be the primary method used for marking IP precedence levels at the edge of a routed network in a DiffServ core.

Running in Distributed Mode

The Cisco 7500 Series Advanced Router System (ARS) is Cisco's high-performance distributed LAN/WAN services router. It follows its predecessor, the 7000 Series, which has been discontinued and will not support IOS revisions above version 11.2. The 7500 Series has architecture quite different from other Cisco router platforms. It is comprised of one Route/Switch Processor (RSP) and multiple Versatile Interface Processors (VIPs). Each VIP not only provides modular Port Adapter functionality that supports a wide range of interfaces, but also effectively offloads many tasks from the main RSP. This leads to scalability and an easy network upgrade path. When more capacity is required, additional VIPs can be installed. There are a few types of VIPs that differ in their processing power. In general, higher capacity circuits require faster processors. The true scalability of this platform is realized only when the VIP takes on tasks normally run by the RSP. When these services are run on the individual VIP, the service is said to be running in *distributed mode*. Let us look at some of the features supported in distributed mode.

Features Supported in Distributed Mode

There are many services that can run in distributed mode, including:

- Basic Switching (Cisco Express Forwarding, IP fragmentation, Fast EtherChannel)
- VPN (IP Security (IPSec), generic routing encapsulation (GRE) tunnels)
- QoS (NBAR, traffic shaping (DTS), policing (CAR), congestion avoidance (DWRED), weighted fair queuing (DWFQ), guaranteed minimum bandwidth (DCBWFQ), policy propagation via BGP)
- Multiservice (low latency queuing (LLQ), FRF 11/12, RTP header compression, Multilink PPP with link fragmentation and interleaving (MLP/LFI))
- Accounting (NetFlow export)
- Load Balancing (CEF load balancing)
- Caching (WCCP)
- Compression (hardware and software compression)
- Multicast (multicast distributed switching)

You may not be familiar with all of these features. Unfortunately, it is beyond the scope of this book to discuss all of them. We will discuss some of the major things you should be aware of when you are considering running a feature on the RSP platform in distributed mode, and we will also look at some examples.

IOS Versions

Because of the VIP architecture, when a new feature comes out for the core router platforms, the code needs significant rewriting to port it to the RSP platform. As a result, there may be a significant amount of time before the feature is available in distributed mode, if at all, on the RSP platform. An example is RTP header compression (CRTP). Although this functionality was originally released on most platforms with IOS version 11.1(15), it was not released as a distributed feature on the 7500 Series until version 12.1(5)T. RTP header compression is a very processor-intensive service that would not scale to many connections on the RSP platform without distributed support.

Operational Differences

Although the underlying concepts of each of these features are basically the same in the distributed versions, the exact implementation may differ significantly. To maximize the efficiency of the router, the inner workings of a particular feature may need revision when running in distributed mode. Consider Cisco express forwarding as an example. With distributed CEF (DCEF), a forwarding information base (FIB) is built on the RSP, which caches the outgoing interface corresponding to a route. This FIB is shared by the RSP with each VIP by downloading it directly to the VIPs. Changes are made to the FIB only when the routing table changes. Any change to the FIB is again shared with all VIPs. Since the RSP and each VIP use the same FIB, there is an efficiency gain by sharing it. This eliminates the per-flow overhead of route-cache maintenance. With DCEF, switching decisions are handled by the VIP whenever possible. However, if DCEF does not have the route cached, it will fall back to the next level of routing on the RSP, usually fast switching or process switching.

Restrictions

There may also be restrictions that you need to be aware of when implementing features in distributed mode. There may be other features that need to be enabled before a particular feature is turned on, or there may be features that are disabled necessarily when a distributed feature is used. Distributed WRED (DWRED) is an example. WRED is used to avoid congestion by dropping packets and thereby throttling back congestion notification compliant flows. Distributed WRED was designed for ISP providers who would be aggregating many smaller circuits into larger ones. Since WRED needs to monitor the current buffer state of interface output queues, and because interfaces reside on the VIP, it makes sense that the WRED process would run in distributed mode on the VIP. Otherwise, the RSP would have to continually poll the status of all buffers across all VIPs. By offloading this function to the VIP, the main processor is freed up to do other things. However, as at press time, there are some technical restrictions.

- You cannot configure DWRED on the same interface as RSP-based custom queuing, priority queuing, or weighted fair queuing (WFQ). However, you can configure both DWRED and DWFQ (or DCBWFQ) on the same interface.
- DWRED is available only on a per interface basis. You cannot configure DWRED on a subinterface.
- DWRED is not supported with the ATM encapsulations AAL5-MUX and AAL5-NLPID.
- DWRED is not supported on Fast EtherChannel or Tunnel interfaces.

Although the goal is to make these distributed feature differences transparent and the restrictions as few as possible, differences and restrictions do exist. If you have 7500 Series routers in your network, it is up to you to do a little research to make sure that the features you need can be extended to the RSP platform, and that they will scale by running them in distributed mode. There are many tools and a vast amount of documentation on Cisco's Web site that can help with this. The *IOS Feature Navigator* tool can help in determining if the feature you want is available on a particular platform, and it can tell you what IOS code and feature set you need to run. Additionally, IOS software release notes can give you detailed information on how to configure distributed features. Finally, you can always contact your Cisco representative for especially difficult queries.

Using Link Fragmentation and Interleaving

Real-time and interactive traffic like Telnet, voice, and video can be affected negatively by jitter created when a router must process large packets on low-speed interfaces. These real-time streams usually consist of small packets, and jitter is caused when the regularly timed transmission of these packets is interrupted by the serialization delay of sending a large packet. Serialization delay is the fundamental time it takes a packet to be sent out a serial interface. It is based on the simple function:

$$\text{SerializationDelay} = \frac{\text{PacketSize(bits)}}{\text{BitRate(bps)}}$$

Table 8.4 shows serialization delays tabulated for common circuit speeds.

Table 8.4 Serialization Delays

Link Speed	Number of Bytes and Transmission Time for Link Speed (in ms)				
	64	256	512	1024	1500
64	8	32	64	128	188
128	4	16	32	64	94
192	3	11	21	43	63
256	2	8	16	32	47
320	2	6	13	26	38
384	1	5	11	21	31
448	1	5	9	18	27
512	1	4	8	16	23
576	1	4	7	14	21
640	1	3	6	13	19
704	1	3	6	12	17
768	1	3	5	11	16
832	1	2	5	10	14
896	1	2	5	9	13
960	1	2	4	9	13
1024	1	2	4	8	12
1088	0	2	4	8	11
1152	0	2	4	7	10
1216	0	2	3	7	10
1280	0	2	3	6	9
1344	0	2	3	6	9

Continued

Table 8.4 Serialization Delays

Link Speed	Number of Bytes and Transmission Time for Link Speed (in ms)				
	64	256	512	1024	1500
1408	0	1	3	6	9
1472	0	1	3	6	8
1536	0	1	3	5	8

Using a feature like LLQ or PQ can significantly reduce delays on real-time traffic, but even with this enabled, the time a real-time packet may have to wait for even one large packet to be transmitted could be large enough to add jitter to the stream. What usually happens is that after the priority queue empties, a large packet is started out the interface. Shortly after this, another packet comes into the priority queue but now has to wait for the whole large packet to be transmitted. Meanwhile, other priority packets queue up behind the first one at regular intervals. When the packets finally go, they go in a little burst. For an application like VoIP, the dejitter buffer may have difficulty playing out all these packets smoothly with the delays and the bursts without dropping a packet or adding an unacceptably large amount of delay.

Link Fragmentation and Interleaving overcomes this by reducing the maximum packet size of all packets over a serial link to a size small enough that no single packet will significantly delay critical real-time data. These large packets that are broken up can now be interleaved with the real-time packets. LFI is superior to just changing the maximum transmission unit (MTU) size, because with LFI, fragmented packets are put back together at the other end of the serial link. With MTU fragmentation, the packets travel across the whole network to their destination before being reassembled. This causes unnecessary traffic and processor utilization caused by increased header information.

How Does LFI Work?

Figure 8.6 shows the basic process of LFI. LFI effectively chops up large datagrams into smaller fragments (F) so that they can be interleaved with real-time packets (R). These resulting smaller packets are then mixed in with other packets by whatever queuing mechanism has been configured (WFQ, LLQ, and so forth). When the packets arrive at the other end, they are reassembled into their original forms.

Figure 8.6 Link Fragmentation and Interleaving

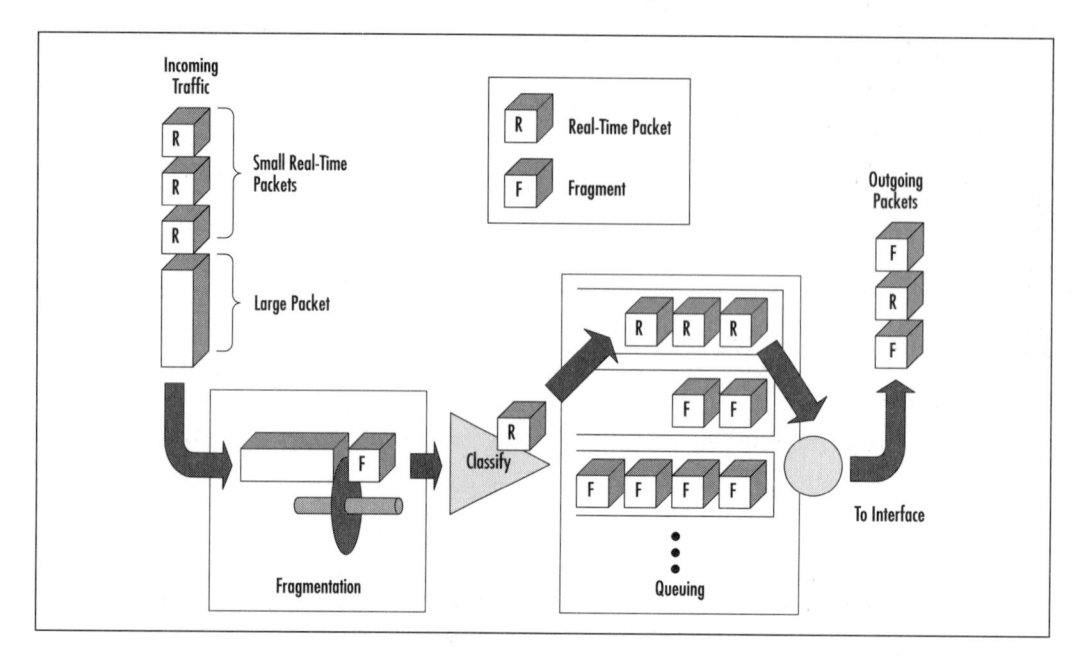

How is the fragmentation size chosen? A particular packet size corresponds to a serialization delay. We choose the serialization delay by considering the maximum delay tolerated by the critical application. From this delay, the fragmentation size can be calculated as the product of the link speed and the target delay. Let us illustrate this with an example.

Imagine that we have a VoIP application running in the company of other data on a 128 Kbps circuit. Ethernet has an MTU of 1500 bytes, so on a 128 Kbps circuit without LFI, it would take 94 ms to serialize the entire packet (see Table 8.4). Therefore, a VoIP packet could potentially wait 94 ms before it could begin to be transmitted. This delay is too long and would cause jitter in the playout stream of the listener. VoIP is usually sent with two 10-ms samples in each packet. Assume we want to set the target delay between each packet to 10 ms. The fragmentation size for this circuit is thus calculated to be 160 bytes (128 kbps * 10 ms). Therefore, to guarantee the target delay of 10 ms, each large packet needs to be fragmented into 160-byte pieces.

LFI with Multilink Point-to-Point Protocol

Multilink Point-to-Point Protocol (MLP) is an extension of PPP and is necessary for LFI to be used. It provides load balancing functionality over multiple WAN links. With LFI, it provides packet fragmentation and proper re-sequencing, according to RFV 1717. It treats multiple links as one circuit and gives load calculation on both inbound and outbound traffic. Although MLP is necessary for LFI to be used, it is not necessary to have more than one WAN link.

> ### FRF.12
>
> FRF.12 is the Frame Relay Forum standard for implementing LFI on Frame Relay. It was created with Voice over Frame Relay (VoFR) in mind, and like MLP with LFI, it must be used when voice packets are mixed with larger, non-voice packets. It is available on the 2600/3600/MC3810/7200 platforms with IOS 12.0(4)T and later.

How Can This Be Useful on My Network?

If you are planning to implement on VoIP on circuit speeds less than 768 Kbps, LFI is indispensable, that is, if your network is really a multiservice network and has other traffic besides voice packets. At speeds below this, the MTU of an IP/Ethernet packet (1500 bytes) will take more than 15 ms to serialize. If you are really interested in good quality voice transmissions, you need to use some kind of priority queuing like LLQ as well. If your link speed is small, you will also obtain significant gains by another link efficiency mechanism, RTP header compression. We will consider that next.

Understanding RTP Header Compression

The general functions of RTP can be described as follows:

- Provides end-to-end network transport functions for audio and video over multicast or unicast services.
- Supports real-time conferencing of groups.
- Supports source identification of gateways and multicast-to-unicast translators.
- Provides feedback from receivers on QoS.
- Synchronizes video and audio streams with time stamping.

There has been a growing interest in RTP because of its interoperability among different implementations of network audio and video applications. However, RTP has a header field of 12 bytes. This, combined with the encapsulated UDP and IP, increases the total overhead to 40 bytes. Because of the large amount of header information for the relatively small size of multimedia data payloads, extending RTP to slow links (dial-up modems, ISDN/BRI, subrate T1s) has been difficult. RTP Header Compression (CRTP) was created to offset the large header size associated with Real-Time Transport Protocol (RTP).

How Does RTP Header Compression Work?

RTP has two parts: a data portion and a header portion. The header can be much larger than the data portion and therefore can add quite a lot of overhead to media applications that use RTP. RTP is based on UDP, as opposed to TCP, since acknowledgements are not needed for real-time data streams. If a real-time data packet is lost, it does not usually make sense to resend it, since the time when it was needed would have already passed.

Since RTP encapsulates UDP and IP headers, the total amount of header information (RTP/UDP/IP) adds up to 40 bytes (see Figure 8.7). Considering the small packet size that usually comprises multimedia streams, this is a lot of overhead. Since most of the header information does not change very much from packet to packet, this lends to the idea of compressing it. RTP header compression can reduce this 40-byte header to about 5 bytes on a link-by-link basis.

Figure 8.7 RTP/UDP/IP Packet Headers

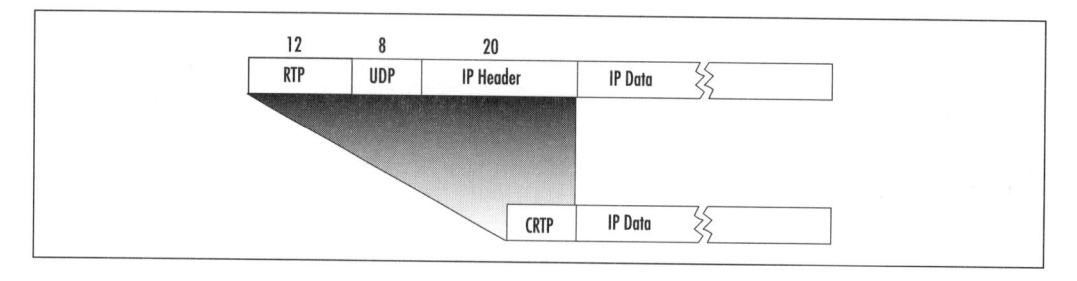

12	8	20		
RTP	UDP	IP Header	IP Data	
			CRTP	IP Data

The RTP compression process is shown in Figure 8.8. We can see that CRTP works to compress RTP packets after the configured queuing process. Only RTP packets are compressed by the engine. After the compression process, both CRTP and non-RTP packets go to the interface to be serialized.

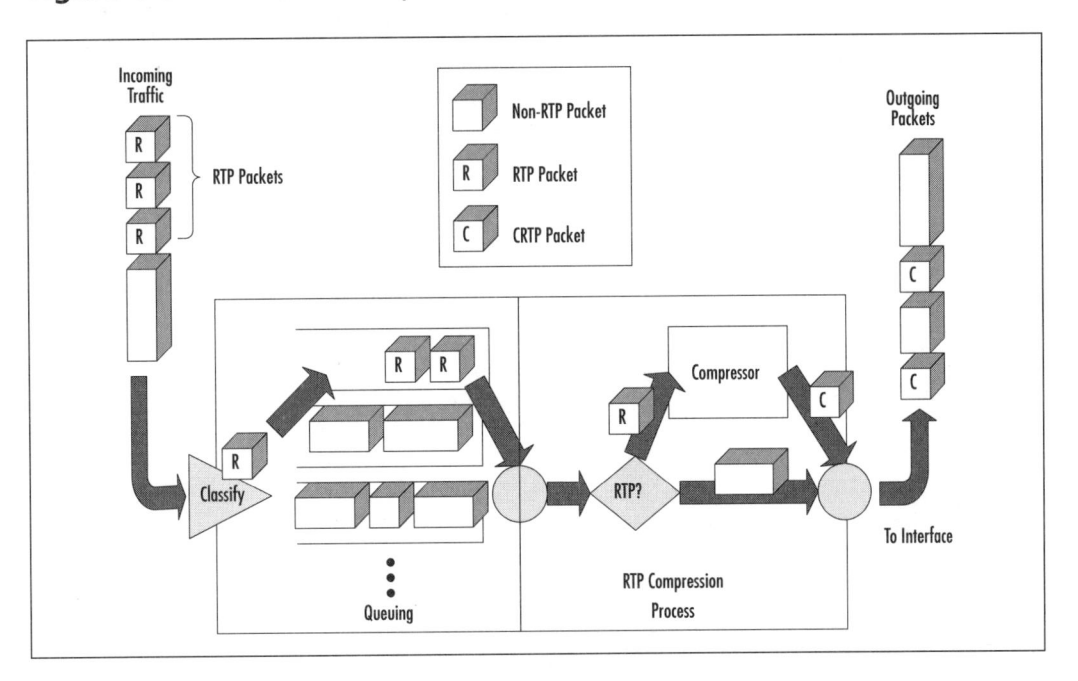

Figure 8.8 RTP Header Compression Process

When Would I Need RTP Header Compression?

RTP header compression can be useful on any narrowband link. Narrowband is usually defined by speeds less than T1, but in making your decision whether to use CRTP, you should consider not only your link speed, but also the available router resources (CPU) and your overall traffic patterns. Since CRTP is performed at the main processor, enabling it could cause your utilization to jump if you have high packet rates (lots of headers), many serial interfaces, or large serial interfaces.

Summary

In this chapter, we introduced a lot of QoS mechanisms of various natures. It is apparent that there is no single mechanism that is a cure-all for every situation. On the contrary, the power of these mechanisms lies in their capacity to work together. Each of the mechanisms has its own particular place in the network and its own particular function. *Classification*, simply put, can help to divide your traffic into classes of service, marking them so that other mechanisms can deliver differentiated QoS. With *congestion management* mechanisms, you can determine which packets get dropped and which ones get priority through the network.

Congestion avoidance works to prevent congestion by notifying senders to slow down when the network is busy. *Policing and shaping* techniques regulate traffic flow according to set parameters, dropping traffic that does not conform, to avoid congestion situations downstream. *Signaling* can be used by clients to request end-to-end QoS across a network. Finally, *link efficiency* mechanisms can make the most efficient use of available bandwidth by using compression techniques and by binding small links into one logical pipe. The following list arranges the mechanisms discussed in this chapter by type and usage. To help consolidate the information presented in this chapter, Figure 8.9 shows a small network indicating where each of these mechanisms would be applicable.

Figure 8.9 Advanced QoS Mechanisms in the Network

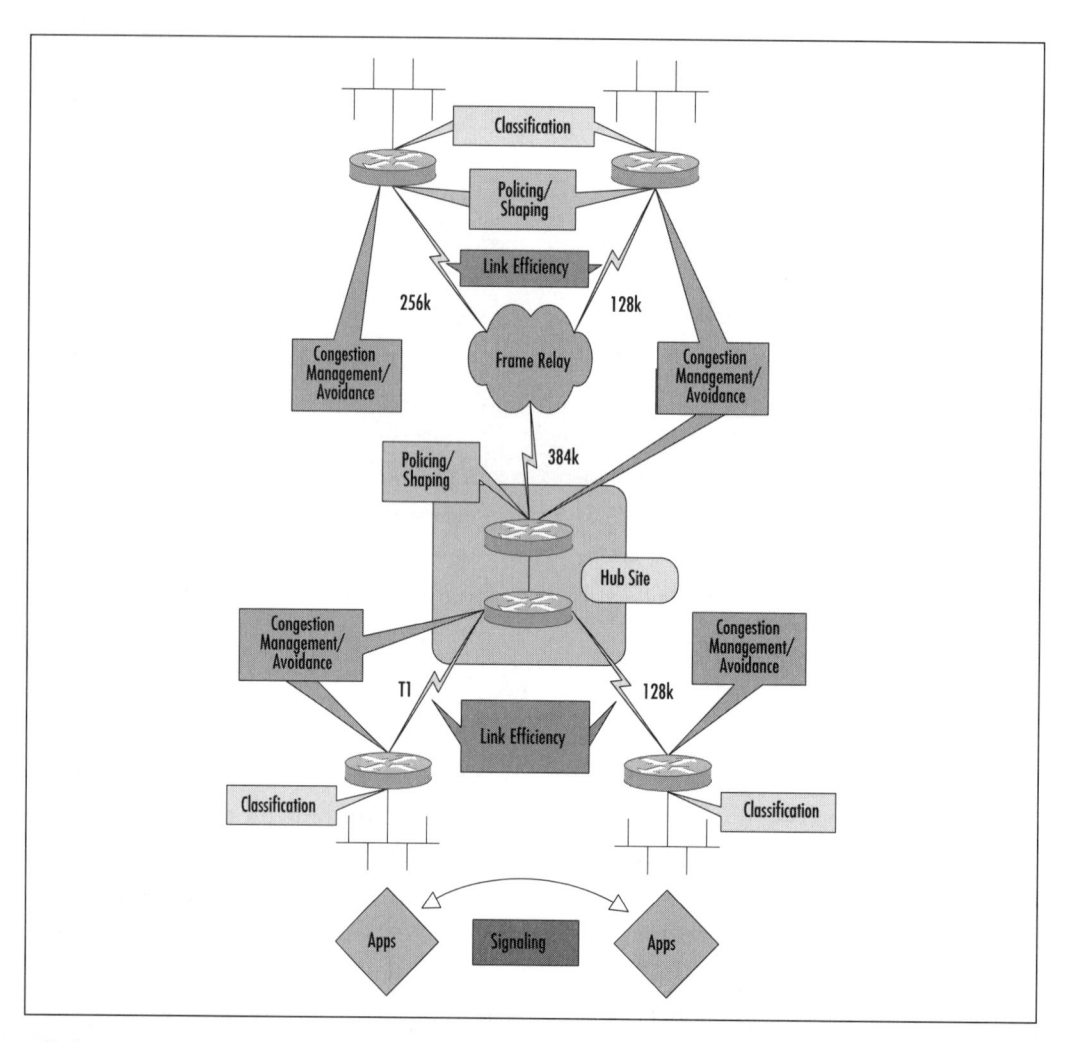

- **Classification/Marking** Used primarily at the edge of the network (ACLs, IP precedence)

- **Congestion Management** Used on serial interfaces (PQ, CQ, WFQ, CBWFQ, LLQ)

- **Congestion Avoidance** Used on Frame Relay interfaces and aggregating interfaces (RED, WRED, BECN, Foresight)

- **Policing and Shaping** Used on data-rate mismatched interfaces (GTS, FRTS, CAR)

- **Signaling** Used end-to-end between clients and on intermediate nodes (RSVP)

- **Link Efficiency** Used on low-speed and multilink interfaces (CRTP, MLP, LFI, FRF.12)

By classifying packets at the edge of the network into distinct classes, the network can provide differential services to the packets without having to examine each one in detail at every hop. After they are marked once with IP precedence, congestion management and avoidance mechanisms can act upon them as they travel to their destination. This is the essence of the DiffServ model of QoS. Since DiffServ does not employ end-to-end signaling between clients, it is basically a *connectionless* form of QoS. Although it may not be able to guarantee QoS totally, it will scale well and make efficient use of spare network resources.

On the other hand, we also looked at the Intserv model embodied by RSVP. Since RSVP is a signaling protocol between clients, it can be thought of as *connection-oriented* QoS model. Connection-oriented networks are traditionally good at providing QoS guarantees, but they do not make efficient use of spare bandwidth, and they have serious scaling problems.

So which approach should you take? There is no doubt that for most networks, DiffServ and IP precedence will be convenient and functional. Cisco's direction seems to indicate a growing trend towards creating and improving mechanisms that will heed class-marking bits such as IP precedence and Differentiated Services Code Point (DSCP). The lack of RSVP-enabled clients and other Intserv signaling mechanisms also points towards DiffServ. However, in future networks, the most effective QoS will probably be found by using a combination of the two models. One can imagine a large network (maybe even the Internet) with a DiffServ core, enhanced, perhaps, by technologies such as Multiprotocol Label Switching (MPLS), with an Intserv function like RSVP working at the client level. With technology changing as rapidly as it is, it is very difficult to predict.

FAQs

Visit **www.syngress.com/solutions** to have your questions about this chapter answered by the author.

Q: Is CBWFQ better than PQ, CQ, or basic WFQ?

A: WFQ is a great queuing mechanism when you want every packet flow to have fair use of the available link bandwidth. PQ can give better than fair treatment for particular classes, but at the risk of starving some traffic of bandwidth completely. CQ allows guarantees of bandwidth to particular types of traffic, but it may be too granular, since unclassified flows are all given the same treatment. CBWFQ works on top of WFQ to provide flow-based prioritization with bandwidth reservations for the classes you specify. Additionally, CBWFQ includes a strict priority queue for real-time packets (LLQ).

Q: Why should I use traffic shaping?

A: Traffic shaping is usually used to overcome data-rate mismatches. This happens when the port speed is greater than the speed at which the network can successfully transmit, or when the speed at the egress of the network is different from that of the ingress. It can also be used to rate-limit traffic of a particular classification.

Q: How do I use RSVP with non-RSVP enabled clients?

A: For the most part, you cannot. Because RSVP is end-to-end signaling between clients, the clients themselves must be able to send RSVP packets. However, if you are using Cisco routers as voice gateways, you can set up VoIP dial-peers to use RSVP in order to request *controlled-load* or *guaranteed-rate* service. It is also possible to set up a reservation for a non-RSVP client using the RSVP proxy function on Cisco routers, but this is mostly for testing purposes, since each reservation must be manually configured, and the reservation will stay in place until unconfigured.

Q: I have enabled LLQ in my network for VoIP traffic. To a particular remote site, I have reserved enough bandwidth to support 12 simultaneous calls. When more than 13 calls are connected, callers often experience poor performance. How do I resolve this?

A: The short answer to this is "Admission Control." When the strict priority queue that is behind low latency queuing reaches its configured bandwidth for priority packets, if congestion exists on the line, that is, the link is fully utilized, packets in excess of this configured bandwidth will be dropped. Because packets may be dropped from all voice streams, the quality of all calls can be affected. Admission control acts to limit the number of calls from one area to another, or across a link, to a particular number. In this way, the thirteenth simultaneous call would be refused by a busy signal. Admission Control can be implemented in a number of ways including using Cisco Call Manager and gatekeeper software on Cisco routers.

Q: When do I need LFI?

A: LFI is needed only on serial links below a speed of 768 Kbps when small, real-time packets such as voice are being transmitted with other large packets such as FTP.

Q: When should I use RTP header compression?

A: In general, RTP header compression should be used for links below T1/E1 speed where there is a reasonable number of RTP packets on the link. The more RTP traffic such as voice and video you have on the link, the more benefit you will get from CRTP. CRTP is processor intensive, so you will want to limit the number of RTP compressed links on a single router to a value appropriate for that router's processor speed.

Q: What are the best QoS mechanisms to use on my network?

A: There is no simple formula for determining the best mechanisms for a particular network. You will likely want to become familiar with the features of each mechanism and use a combination of some or all of them, depending on your network and your business requirements. These mechanisms each have their own place in the network and work together to provide QoS.

www.syngress.com

Chapter 9
Configuring Advanced QoS

Solutions in this chapter:

- Enabling, Verifying, and Troubleshooting RSVP
- Enabling, Verifying, and Troubleshooting CBWFQ
- Configuring, Verifying, and Troubleshooting LLQ
- Configuring, Verifying, and Troubleshooting WRED
- Configuring and Verifying GTS and FRTS
- Understanding Distributed Technologies
- Configuring, Verifying, and Troubleshooting Link Fragmentation and Interleaving
- Configuring, Verifying, and Troubleshooting RTP Header Compression

Introduction

This chapter demonstrates how to properly configure the advanced technologies introduced in chapter 8. It will become a great reference tool to use when you are ready to configure these technologies on your network, and thus, as far as possible, every effort has been made to afford complete coverage of advanced technologies configurations. It is not feasible, however, to show all of the options available with these mechanisms.

In the last chapter, we introduced these advanced mechanisms and mentioned that they are typically far more versatile when used in combination with other QoS techniques. In this chapter, we show you how these mechanisms can be used alone, as well as how powerful they can be when combined with other techniques.

There will be things that you want to do with these QoS mechanisms that we do not show you. Thus, you should become familiar with Cisco's Web site (www.cisco.com). The pages of CCO (Cisco Connection Online) contain more information than any book could ever hope to have, and this resource is kept up to date with the most cutting edge technologies and uses for existing technologies.

Enabling, Verifying, and Troubleshooting Resource Reservation Protocol (RSVP)

In Chapter 8, we learned that RSVP guarantees QoS to applications by reserving resources on the router. Specifically, two types of services can be guaranteed. To provide *controlled-load* service to applications, RSVP uses WRED on the output interface in the downstream direction of the reservation. To provide *guaranteed-rate* service, RSVP uses WFQ on the output interface in the downstream direction of the reservation. WRED helps to emulate an unloaded network by making sure that congestion never really starts. WFQ gives a rate guarantee and low packet drop rate to applications by giving the RSVP session priority over other flows.

It is important to remember that RSVP works in one direction only (simplex). If a two-way (full duplex) reservation is needed, RSVP reservations must be made in each direction independently. Figure 9.1 shows how reservations for the RSVP session are enforced on the output interfaces of the routers in the direction of the session stream. Though the router keeps a stateful database of all reservations, it is at these interfaces that WFQ, WRED, or both act to implement the reservation.

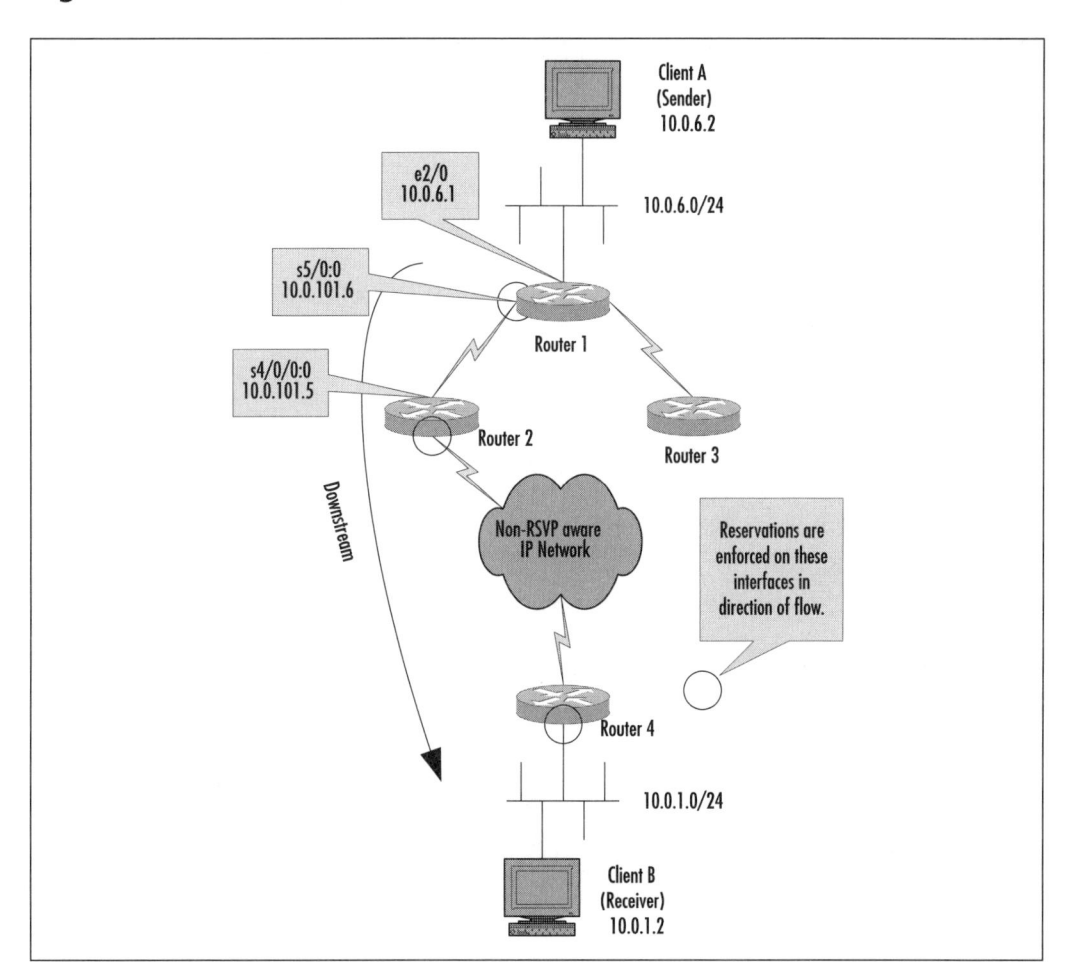

Figure 9.1 RSVP on the Network

[Figure 9.1: Network diagram showing Client A (Sender) 10.0.6.2 on subnet 10.0.6.0/24 connected via Router 1 (interfaces e2/0 10.0.6.1, s5/0:0 10.0.101.6). Router 2 (s4/0:0:0 10.0.101.5) connects downstream through a Non-RSVP aware IP Network cloud. Router 3 also connects from Router 1. Router 4 connects to Client B (Receiver) 10.0.1.2 on subnet 10.0.1.0/24. Callout: "Reservations are enforced on these interfaces in direction of flow."]

We also saw in Chapter 8 that RSVP is transparent to non-RSVP enabled nodes so that they can tunnel over non-RSVP aware networks (as shown in the Figure). However, notice that no reservations are made in the cloud or at its egress; therefore, there can be no bandwidth guarantees here.

Enabling RSVP is much easier than trying to explain the mechanics of how it works. However, even though it is simple to enable, do not be tempted to enable it carelessly on all interfaces in your router network. It does take planning to ensure that RSVP reservations do not run rampant and take bandwidth from other applications.

You will want to refer to Figure 9.1 throughout this section. We will reference it in relation to enabling RSVP, and to illustrate particular show commands.

Enabling RSVP

Because WRED and WFQ act to implement RSVP reservations on the output interfaces of routers, RSVP must be enabled on a per interface basis. To do this, use the **ip rsvp bandwidth** command in the interface configuration context:

```
Router1 #config t
Enter configuration commands, one per line.  End with CNTL/Z.
Router1 (config)#int s5:0/0
Router1 (config-if)#bandwidth 1152
Router1 (config-if)#ip rsvp bandwidth 768 128
```

The first argument on the **ip rsvp bandwidth** command is the total amount of bandwidth that can be reserved on the interface. The second argument is the maximum bandwidth of a single reservation. Thus, the interface can set aside no more than 768 Kbps for RSVP reservations, with each reservation being no larger than 128 Kbps.

Notice that the **bandwidth** command was entered first to tell the router the value of the total link speed. Many serial interfaces will default to 1544 Kbps unless otherwise specified. This is important since RSVP uses the bandwidth of the serial interface to calculate how much of the total can be reserved. RSVP will not allow more than 75 per cent of the total bandwidth to be reserved.

Remember that you have to enable RSVP on each interface that you would like to participate in RSVP. Specifically, enable it on interfaces on which you expect QoS implementation mechanisms like WRED and WFQ to act to deliver QoS.

Verifying Your RSVP Configuration

You can confirm that your RSVP configuration is entered properly with the **show run** command, but there are other commands that you will find useful to monitor the status of RSVP.

With the **show ip rsvp installed** command, all the current reservations can be displayed for each interface:

```
Router1#show ip rsvp installed
RSVP: Ethernet2/0 has no installed reservations
RSVP: Serial5/0:0
BPS   To         From       Protoc  DPort   Sport   Weight  Conversation
128K  10.0.1.2   10.0.6.2   TCP     0       0       6       271
64K   10.0.1.3   10.0.6.3   TCP     0       0       12      272
```

In this example, there are two reservations going out Serial5/0:0 from the senders 10.0.1.2 and 10.0.1.3 to the receivers 10.0.6.2 and 10.0.6.3 (the second pair of senders and receivers are not shown in Figure 9.1). The first reservation is for 128 Kbps, and the second is for 64 Kbps. The weight listed is the weighting factor used by WFQ. The conversation is the number assigned to that flow. Take a look at Figure 9.1 again, and remember that since the session flow is towards Client B from Client A, and because WFQ and WRED work on output interfaces, there is no reservation on the Ethernet 2/0, even though the session is flowing *in* to the router through this interface.

To see interface specific information, such as how much total bandwidth has been set aside for RSVP (i/f max) and the amount currently being used (allocated), issue the **show ip rsvp interface** command:

```
Router1#show ip rsvp interface
interface  allocated  i/f max  flow max  pct  UDP  IP  UDP_IP  UDP M/C
Et2/0      0M         7500K    7500K     0    0    2   0       0
Se5/0:0    192K       1152K    1152K     16   0    1   0       0
```

Sometimes it is helpful to see all neighboring nodes that are participating in RSVP. To do this, use the **show ip rsvp neighbor** command:

```
Router1#show ip rsvp neighbor
Interfac  Neighbor      Encapsulation
Et2/0     10.0.6.3      RSVP
Et2/0     10.0.6.2      RSVP
Se5/0:0   10.0.101.5    RSVP
```

This tells us that there are two RSVP neighbors out the Ethernet 2/0 interface and another one out the Se5/0:0 interface. These neighbors can be any nodes that are currently using RSVP. They could be end-stations (10.0.6.3 and 10.0.6.2) or RSVP participating router interfaces (10.0.101.5).

To display RSVP information such as requests flowing upstream and receiver and sender information currently in the database, use the following commands, respectively:

```
Router1#show ip rsvp request
To         From       Pro DPort Sport Next Hop   I/F    Fi   Serv  BPS   Bytes
10.0.1.2   10.0.6.2   TCP 0     0     10.0.6.2   Et2/0  FF   LOAD  128K  64K
10.0.1.3   10.0.6.3   TCP 0     0     10.0.6.3   Et2/0  FF   RATE  64K   1K
Router1#show ip rsvp reservation
To         From       Pro DPort Sport Next Hop   I/F    Fi   Serv  BPS   Bytes
10.0.1.2   10.0.6.2   TCP 0     0     10.0.101.5 Se5/0  FF   LOAD  128K  64K
10.0.1.3   10.0.6.3   TCP 0     0     10.0.101.5 Se5/0  FF   RATE  64K   1K
Router1#show ip rsvp sender
To         From       Pro  DPort  Sport  Prev Hop   I/F    BPS   Bytes
10.0.1.2   10.0.6.2   TCP  0      0      10.0.6.2   Et2/0  128K  1K
10.0.1.3   10.0.6.3   TCP  0      0      10.0.6.3   Et2/0  64K   1K
```

The request and reservation show commands also indicate the type of service desired, either controlled-load (LOAD) or guaranteed-rate (RATE).

RSVP Proxy

To capture the outputs shown above, a network similar to the one in Figure 9.1 can be set up in the lab. Because of the lack of RSVP-enabled clients, a feature called RSVP proxy is used to generate the Send and Resv messages. RSVP proxy is available on Cisco routers and allows the manual configuration of reservations. These are statically entered and remain in place until removed. Because they are not dynamic, it is not recommended that they be used for anything but testing, since the bandwidth remains "nailed-up" and cannot be used by packets outside of the reservation. Nonetheless, with these reservations up, QoS can be provided to packets matching the criteria set up with the proxy commands. For reference, here are the necessary commands.

Router1:

```
ip rsvp sender 10.0.1.2 10.0.6.2 TCP 0 0 10.0.6.2
  Ethernet2/0 128 1
ip rsvp sender 10.0.1.3 10.0.6.3 TCP 0 0 10.0.6.3
  Ethernet2/0 64 1
```

Continued

> Router4:
>
> ```
> ip rsvp reservation 10.0.1.2 10.0.6.2 TCP 0 0 10.0.1.2
>   Ethernet0/1 FF LOAD 128 64
> ip rsvp reservation 10.0.1.3 10.0.6.3 TCP 0 0 10.0.1.3
>   Ethernet0/1 FF RATE 64 1
> ```
>
> The **ip rsvp sender** command emulates a sender and generates RSVP Path packets. The **ip rsvp reservation** command emulates a receiver and generates RSVP Resv packets. Refer to Chapter 8 for a refresher on how these two packet types work to make a reservation, and see the Cisco documentation for the exact syntax of these commands if you want to use them to test your RSVP network.

Troubleshooting RSVP

The first step in troubleshooting an RSVP configuration is to use the show commands discussed. A good understanding of the session start-up process is required in order to determine where things might be going wrong. To help figure it out, you can use debugging commands. To turn on RSVP debugging, issue the **debug ip rsvp** command from the privileged exec command mode (enable mode). After enabling debugging, check your log with the **show log** command. Alternatively, you can enable terminal monitoring (if you are using Telnet) with **terminal monitor** to copy debug commands to the terminal window.

WARNING

Debugging is a privileged command that can be frustrating at times. If there is a lot of output from the debugging, you could swamp the processor and your terminal session, essentially locking you out of the router. If you expect large amounts of output, consider debugging with an access list. For example, use **debug ip rsvp 100 detail**, where 100 is an access list to select the addresses or protocols you are interested in.

Enabling, Verifying, and Troubleshooting Class-Based Weighted Fair Queuing (CBWFQ)

CBWFQ allows the guarantee of bandwidth to classes defined by criteria such as protocol, Access Control Lists (ACLs), IP precedence, or input interfaces. CBWFQ is available on most Cisco router platforms, starting with IOS code version 12.0(5)T.

To get up and running with CBWFQ, you first have to determine how many classes you need in order to categorize all your traffic. You also need to know what criteria you are going to use to map traffic into those classes, and what bandwidth guarantees you will give to each class. If you have already classified your traffic at the edge of the network, IP precedence may the only criterion you need. If you are configuring a more modest, point-to-point implementation of CBWFQ, you will probably use extended ACLs to categorize incoming traffic into classes.

Enabling CBWFQ

There are three major steps in configuring CBWFQ:

1. Defining class maps
2. Creating policy maps
3. Attaching policies to interfaces

Class maps determine what traffic goes into what class and can be used in one or more policy maps. Policy maps determine how that traffic is handled. But no QoS is delivered until the policy map is applied to the interfaces. Let us see how this is done.

Defining Class Maps

The **class-map** statements in the router configuration determine how traffic is classified. The configured class must have a name that you can reference later. Within the class map, you set your match criteria. Consider this example:

```
router1#config t
Enter configuration commands, one per line.  End with CNTL/Z.
router1(config)#class-map Gold
router1(config-cmap)#match access-group name Gold
```

In this example, we created a class map with the name Gold. This could be a premium service offered to applications that guarantees a certain bandwidth. Furthermore, while in the class-map (**config-cmap**) command mode, we entered a match criterion, namely, the ACL named Gold. Thus, all traffic that matches the ACL will be part of the Gold class map. We have used the same name, *Gold*, for both the class map and the ACL name for consistency. It is necessary to configure the ACLs if you want the class maps to use them. In this case, the ACL might be configured like this:

```
router1(config)#ip access-list extended Gold
router1(config-ext-nacl)#permit ip any any precedence flash-override
```

An extended access list is used so we can specify a match for any IP packet with a precedence of 4 (the fourth level of precedence is traditionally given the name *flash-override*). If it could not be expected that packets were marked at the edge of the network with IP precedence, then you would probably use an ACL that classifies traffic based on criteria like protocol and port number. If you are not already familiar with Access Control Lists, you should take some time to learn more about them. They are used frequently in many Cisco router features and are essential if you want fine control over what kinds of traffic end up in your QoS classes.

NOTE

In the previous example, we used an access list to specify the traffic. But if your match criteria are a little simpler, you may be able to match all your traffic with commands in the class map alone. With IOS 12.0(5)T, you can match all packets corresponding to a particular protocol with the **match protocol** command, or all packets arriving on a particular interface with the **match input-interface** command. With more recent versions of IOS, you can match according to criteria such as source address, destination address, protocol, IP precedence, and DSCP levels—all without using ACLs. Furthermore, you can place logical "AND" or "OR" statements between each of these criteria by specifying the class map with the **class-map match-all** or **class-map match-any** commands, respectively.

Now that the Gold class has been configured, we can configure more class maps the same way:

```
router1(config)#class-map Silver
router1(config-cmap)#match access-group name Silver
router1(config-cmap)#class-map Bronze
router1(config-cmap)#match access-group name Bronze
```

The extended access lists would be defined as follows:

```
router1(config)#ip access-list extended Bronze
router1(config-ext-nacl)#permit ip any any precedence immediate
router1(config-ext-nacl)#ip access-list extended Silver
router1(config-ext-nacl)#permit ip any any precedence flash
```

This gives us three classes, Gold, Bronze, and Silver, mapped to the IP precedence levels 4, 3, and 2, respectively.

Creating Policies

Now that we have defined class maps, we can continue on to the second step to create the policy maps that specify the QoS the classes will ultimately have. Let us configure the policy for the Gold class configured in the last example:

```
router1(config)#policy-map PPP-T1
router1(config-pmap)#class Gold
router1(config-pmap-c)#bandwidth 216
```

We have given the name "PPP-T1" to the policy-map. You should use a name that will be descriptive, such as what kind of circuit bandwidth it was meant to run on. This leads us into the policy map command context (config-pmap). We now enter the class that we want to specify parameters for, in this case, Gold. Under this new context (config-pmap-c), we specify the bandwidth reserved for this class in Kbps. You can enter the following commands to configure the QoS the class will be given:

- **bandwidth** Bandwidth (in Kbps)
- **queue-limit** Maximum queue threshold for tail drop
- **random-detect** Enable WRED as drop policy

The bandwidth is the rate guaranteed to this class in Kbps. By default, the sum of all bandwidth rates for a policy cannot exceed 75 percent of the interface's total bandwidth. This leaves room for Layer 2 keepalives, routing updates, and so on.

> **NOTE**
>
> The maximum value that you can allocate to all classes can be changed from the default value of 75 percent using the **max-reserved-bandwidth** command while in the interface configuration mode. Although Cisco discourages changing this value, you can increase it in aggressive situations if you know the composition of your traffic. It is even possible to raise it to 100 percent if you create an explicit class for IP precedence levels 6 and 7 (*internet* and *network*) and ensure that no other traffic gets marked into these precedence levels. In the case of routing protocols like EIGRP and OSPF, leave the router IP precedence set automatically.

You should choose the bandwidth for each class carefully, based on your needs. Remember that since the bandwidth you give to a class is measured at the interface, it must be large enough to accommodate Layer 2 overhead.

> **NOTE**
>
> In IOS version 12.1 and later, the **bandwidth** command for the class can be entered in Kbps or as a percentage of the total bandwidth. However, all classes must be configured consistently in either Kbps rates or percentages. The exception is for LLQ. The priority class inside LLQ can have bandwidth specified only in Kbps.

The last two configurable parameters, queue-limit and random-detect, specify the drop policy for the class. By default, the drop policy is tail drop with a queue limit of 64 for that class. You may use the **queue-limit** command to change it to a value between 1 and 64. A shorter queue will drop packets quicker in times of congestion. WRED can be configured with the **random-detect** command. Additionally the **random-detect exponential-weighting-constant** command can be used to adjust how adaptive WRED is to bursts. See the discussion on WRED in Chapter 8 for an overview and a later section in this chapter for configuration specifics.

Unclassified traffic, that is, traffic that is not matched into any of the user-defined classes, gets put into a special class called *class-default*. This class does not appear explicitly in the router configuration unless you configure it. By default, unclassified traffic will be flow-classified and queued by WFQ. However, if you configure this class specifically, you can give it a bandwidth guarantee too. Let us configure the default-class:

```
router1(config)#policy-map PPP-T1
router1(config-pmap)#class class-default
router1(config-pmap-c)#bandwidth 31
```

Treatment of the Default Class in CBWFQ

The treatment of the default class in CBWFQ varies depending on the IOS revision and platform. This is because of enhancements in the router code. For IOS releases before 12.1(2)E1 on the 7500 platform and all other platforms before release 12.1(5), if left unconfigured, the default class is flow-classified and given best-effort treatment by WFQ. If the user-defined classes exceed their bandwidth, they will use the non-guaranteed bandwidth proportionately among themselves, but at the detriment of the default class. This has the effect in high congestion situations of dropping default traffic if the link is filled with classified traffic.

To illustrate this, consider an example of two defined classes. Class A is guaranteed 20 percent of the bandwidth, and class B is guaranteed 10 percent of the bandwidth. The maximum reserved bandwidth is left at its default value of 75 percent of the link speed. In a congested situation, after the two classes get their guaranteed bandwidth, the remaining bandwidth (45 percent) is divided proportionately between these two classes at a 2:1 ratio. The default class will not receive any bandwidth if there is enough classified traffic to fill the remaining 45 percent.

After the router code levels listed above, the default class is treated exactly like the user-defined classes. Considering the same example, the default class gets a guarantee of 45 percent of the bandwidth. After all classes reach their guarantees, the remaining bandwidth (25 percent) is divided among Class A, Class B, and the default class with a 20:10:45 weighting, respectively.

Continued

> To make the earlier code revisions act like the new versions, you should configure the default class. That is, set the bandwidth statement in the default-class to the value you want to guarantee to unclassified traffic. Setting the bandwidth statement for the default class is not allowed under the newer code, because it is already guaranteed the remaining bandwidth.

Instead of being fair-queued, the default class, consisting of unclassified traffic, will now be guaranteed at least 31 Kbps of bandwidth.

We can thus configure the policy map (PPP-T1) with the other classes we are interested in so that the entire policy looks as follows in the router's configuration:

```
class-map Gold
   match access-group Gold
class-map Bronze
   match access-group Bronze
class-map Silver
   match access-group Silver
!
policy-map PPP-T1
   class Gold
     bandwidth 216
   class Silver
     bandwidth 169
   class Bronze
     bandwidth 108
   class class-default
     bandwidth 31
!
. . .
!
ip access-list extended Gold
 permit ip any any precedence flash-override
ip access-list extended Bronze
 permit ip any any precedence immediate
```

```
ip access-list extended Silver
 permit ip any any precedence flash
```

Attaching Policies to Interfaces

The final step required to enable CBWFQ is to attach the service policy to an interface:

```
router1(config)#interface serial 0/0
router1(config-if)#service-policy output PPP-T1
```

After a service policy is defined, it can be enabled on multiple interfaces, assuming the interface has enough bandwidth to support all the guarantees. In contrast to this, only one policy can be attached to a single interface. Furthermore, after the policy is attached, certain commands relating to queuing and WRED are disabled, since the policy now controls these functions.

The preceding three-step approach to enabling CBWFQ is a demonstration of Cisco's Modular QoS Command Line Interface. It is this modular approach that allows you not only to modify policies without disturbing interfaces and to attach policies to multiple interfaces, but also to copy a policy to like routers, thereby making network-wide configuration of QoS easier.

Verifying Your CBWFQ Configuration

The first step in assuring that your policies are configured correctly is to look at the configuration with the **show running-config** command. After that, you can view a particular policy with the **show policy-map** command:

```
router1#show policy-map
 Policy Map PPP-T1
  Weighted Fair Queueing
    Class Gold
      Bandwidth 216 (kbps) Max Thresh 64 (packets)
    Class Silver
      Bandwidth 169 (kbps) Max Thresh 64 (packets)
    Class Bronze
      Bandwidth 108 (kbps) Max Thresh 64 (packets)
    Class class-default
      Bandwidth 31 (kbps) Max Thresh 64 (packets)
```

This shows the configured bandwidth for each class within the policy, and the maximum threshold for the queue before tail drop is enacted. If you have multiple policies configured, you can specify the name of the policy with the same command **show policy-map** *policy-map-name*, and even the specific class within the policy:

```
router1#show policy-map PPP-T1 class Gold
    Class Gold
      Bandwidth 216 (kbps) Max Thresh 64 (packets)
```

To view the statistics of how the policy has been functioning on the interface, use the **show policy-map interface** command:

```
router1#show policy-map interface serial 0/0
 Serial0/0  output : PPP-T1
  Weighted Fair Queueing
    Class Gold
     Output Queue: Conversation 265
       Bandwidth 216 (kbps) Packets Matched 248318 Max Threshold 64
       (packets)
       (discards/tail drops) 95418/84680
    Class Silver
     Output Queue: Conversation 266
       Bandwidth 169 (kbps) Packets Matched 248305 Max Threshold 64
       (packets)
       (discards/tail drops) 119558/109829
    Class Bronze
     Output Queue: Conversation 267
       Bandwidth 108 (kbps) Packets Matched 248292 Max Threshold 64
       (packets)
       (discards/tail drops) 156598/148956
    Class class-default
     Output Queue: Conversation 268
       Bandwidth 31 (kbps) Packets Matched 428362 Max Threshold 64
       (packets)
       (discards/tail drops) 234720/222514
```

You can use this command to see what your class composition is with respect to the number of packets matched into the classes and the effect of tail drop (or WRED) on each class. You can always see the overall performance of the interface to which the policy is applied by using the **show interface** or **show queue** command:

```
router1#show queue serial 0/0
    Input queue: 0/75/0 (size/max/drops); Total output drops: 778978
    Queueing strategy: weighted fair
    Output queue: 0/1000/64/778978 (size/max total/threshold/drops)
        Conversations  0/4/256 (active/max active/max total)
        Reserved Conversations 4/4 (allocated/max allocated)
```

This shows the current state of the input and output queues, including current size, maximum size, and number of drops. It also shows the specifics of WFQ. As usual, the total number of conversations is 256. However, note that there are four reserved conversations corresponding to the four classes (including the default class) configured on the interface by the policy.

Troubleshooting CBWFQ

Because CBWFQ is not a network QoS mechanism per se, but rather a queuing mechanism that operates individually on a router, troubleshooting faulty configurations always starts with the router in question. If you have problems with CBWFQ, the first step is to use the show commands to verify that the policies are configured properly and attached to the appropriate interfaces.

Usually, the ultimate question with CBWFQ is, "Is it working?" Though you may be able to see from commands like **show policy interface** that it does seem to be working, the real test lies in your applications' performance. Are they getting the bandwidth guarantees that you expect? This is not always easy to answer. Besides the router show commands, you may want to consider doing some formalized testing of your applications in congestion situations, with and without the policy, to determine the effect. You can also use tools such as packet decoders and packet generators to emulate a production environment. A product such as Cisco Internetwork Performance Monitor (IPM) can also be of use in monitoring the status of your network.

Configuring, Verifying, and Troubleshooting Low Latency Queuing (LLQ)

As discussed in chapter 8, low latency queuing (LLQ) extends CBWFQ to include the option of creating a strict priority queue. Strict priority queuing delivers low latency transmission to constant bit rate (CBR) applications such as voice. It has wide platform availability starting with IOS release 12.0(7)T.

Configuring LLQ

After you understand how to configure CBWFQ, configuring LLQ is easy. A low latency class is configured very much like other user-defined classes. Let us add to the example in the last section and configure another class with a guarantee of bandwidth and low latency transmission. We first must define a class map:

```
router1(config)#class-map Platinum
router1(config-cmap)#match access-group name Platinum
```

Again, we use an ACL to match traffic into this class. If you imagine that, like the other classes in our example, we already have marked traffic into granular IP precedence levels, then our access list for this class might be configured like this:

```
router1(config)#ip access-list extended Platinum
router1(config-ext-nacl)#permit ip any any precedence critical
```

In this configuration, incoming packets matching IP precedence 5 (critical) are mapped into this priority class. IP precedence 5 is the normal level for VoIP traffic, which is what we can imagine would comprise this class exclusively.

Now we must add the class to a policy map:

```
router1(config)#policy-map PPP-T1
router1(config-pmap)#class Platinum
router1(config-pmap-c)#priority 384
```

This is where we denote that this class should have low latency queuing. By using the **priority** command, we have specified that the Platinum class will receive priority treatment in an exhaustive queue. The **priority** command is used instead of the **bandwidth** command to specify the guarantee of bandwidth. This is the only major difference in configuring LLQ.

After using the priority command on a class within a policy, the command to enable WRED, **random-detect,** is disabled. The priority queue does not support WRED because of the nature of the priority queue and the type of traffic that should be placed in it, notably voice. Voice packets are UDP-based and therefore not responsive to congestion notifications through packet drops. Furthermore, drops do not occur at the priority queue unless the bandwidth set with the priority command has been exceeded and there is congestion on the line. In the event of congestion, all packets in excess of the guaranteed bandwidth are dropped from the priority queue.

Verifying Your LLQ Configuration

We use the same commands to examine the function of LLQ as we used for CBWFQ. The output for the priority class does look a little different. Notice that the class shows that it is being given strict priority treatment:

```
router1#show policy PPP-T1 class Platinum
    Class Platinum
       Strict Priority
       Bandwidth 384 (kbps) Max Threshold 64 (packets)
```

Similarly, the policy statistics for the interface shows strict priority for the Platinum class:

```
router1#show policy-map interface serial 0/0
 Serial0/0   output : PPP-T1
  Weighted Fair Queueing
    Class Platinum
      Strict Priority
      Output Queue: Conversation 264
        Bandwidth 384 (kbps) Packets Matched 0 248368 Max Threshold 64
        (packets)
        (discards/tail drops) 0/0
    Class Gold
      Output Queue: Conversation 265
        Bandwidth 216 (kbps) Packets Matched 248318 Max Threshold 64
        (packets)
        (discards/tail drops) 95418/84680
    Class Silver
```

```
     Output Queue: Conversation 266
       Bandwidth 169 (kbps) Packets Matched 248305 Max Threshold 64
       (packets)
       (discards/tail drops) 119558/109829
     Class Bronze
       Output Queue: Conversation 267
       Bandwidth 108 (kbps) Packets Matched 248292 Max Threshold 64
       (packets)
       (discards/tail drops) 156598/148956
     Class class-default
       Output Queue: Conversation 268
       Bandwidth 31 (kbps) Packets Matched 428362 Max Threshold 64
       (packets)
       (discards/tail drops) 234720/222514
```

Troubleshooting LLQ

Like CBWFQ, troubleshooting LLQ starts with knowing what to expect from the router configuration and how your applications are performing. If it seems that your applications are not getting low latency priority queuing, you can use the **debug priority** command to troubleshoot. This command will notify you of drops in the priority queue, which should happen only when the subscribed bandwidth has been exceeded and the link is congested. Here is a sample output when a T1 link was filled to capacity and the priority queue was overflowing:

```
Jan 30 22:42:45: WFQ: dropping a packet from the priority queue 0
Jan 30 22:42:45: WFQ: dropping a packet from the priority queue 0
Jan 30 22:42:45: WFQ: dropping a packet from the priority queue 0
Jan 30 22:42:45: WFQ: dropping a packet from the priority queue 0
Jan 30 22:42:45: WFQ: dropping a packet from the priority queue 0
Jan 30 22:42:46: WFQ: dropping a packet from the priority queue 0
```

Each packet that is dropped is logged. This debug command also works with other priority queuing schemes besides LLQ, such as RTP priority queuing.

Configuring, Verifying, and Troubleshooting Weighted Random Early Detection (WRED)

In the last chapter, we saw that WRED is a congestion avoidance mechanism that takes advantage of TCP's congestion control by randomly dropping packets from flows before congestion occurs. It gives differential treatment to packets of different IP precedence levels by assigning different drop thresholds. Because of this, and because it can be enabled on a variety of interfaces, it is often used in high-speed backbones where packets are marked with IP precedence at the edge of the network. It is not necessary to have packets marked with different levels of IP precedence for WRED to function, but without differing levels of IP precedence, you are using regular RED, because all packets of a given weight (all packets have a weight of zero, by default) are treated equally.

Configuring WRED

To enable WRED on an interface, use the **random-detect** command while in interface configuration mode:

```
router1(config)#interface serial 0/0
router1(config-if)#random-detect
```

This is the typical way to configure WRED on an interface. The exception is, as we saw in a previous section, for CBWFQ policies. In this case, the random-detect command is issued in the policy itself, not the interface.

Using the random-detect command is all that is normally necessary to enable WRED on an interface. The default operation of WRED has been optimized for typical use. However, you can modify WRED from its default behavior in a couple of ways, as we will demonstrate.

The average queue length is the moving average used in the WRED algorithm to determine with what probability to drop packets (see chapter 8 for more information). Although Cisco does not recommend it, the weighting factor of this average can be changed from the default (9) to make WRED more or less adaptive to traffic bursts. To change this weighting factor, perform the following command while in interface configuration mode:

```
router1(config)#interface serial 0/0
router1(config-if)#random-detect exponential-weighting-constant 10
```

A higher factor will make the average queue length "heavier" and more resistant to changes in traffic speed, whereas a lower factor will make the queue length "lighter" and more sensitive to traffic changes. If the value is too high, the algorithm may not be reactive to congestion situations. If the value is too low, a burst of packets may be dropped unnecessarily.

Another aspect of WRED that you can configure away from the defaults is how each IP precedence level is weighted. Again, the default values are usually fine, but you can modify the configuration if you need to. By using the **random-detect precedence** command, you can set the following values for each precedence level:

- Minimum threshold
- Maximum threshold
- Mark probability denominator

Table 9.1 Default WRED and DWRED Threshold Values

IP Precedence	WRED Threshold Values Minimum	Maximum	DWRED Threshold Values Minimum	Maximum
0	20	40	95	190
1	22	40	106	190
2	24	40	117	190
3	26	40	128	190
4	28	40	139	190
5	31	40	150	190
6	33	40	161	190
7	35	40	172	190
RSVP	37	40	N/A	N/A

Table 9.1 shows the default values of the minimum and maximum thresholds for each precedence. The minimum threshold for IP precedence 0 is one half the maximum. The value of the minimum threshold for the remaining precedences falls between half the maximum threshold and the maximum threshold at evenly spaced intervals. The *mark probability denominator* is the fraction of packets dropped when the average queue depth is at the maximum threshold. By default, this value is set to 10 for all precedences. This means that when the average queue is at the maximum threshold, one out of every 10 packets is dropped. Over this maximum, all packets are dropped.

To change these values, use the following syntax while in interface configuration mode:

`random-detect precedence` precedence min-threshold max-threshold mark-prob-denominator

This configuration can be repeated for each precedence level. If the values are configured to be the same for each precedence, WRED essentially becomes RED (unweighted).

Flow-Based WRED

Flow-based WRED (FRED) was developed to overcome the problem occurring when non-adaptive flows such as UDP were taking bandwidth away from congestion-responsive flows like TCP. The problem occurs when the average queue depth rises above the maximum threshold for WRED. When this happens, packets are dropped across all flows, which discriminates unfairly against smaller congestion-responsive flows. FRED works by categorizing incoming data into flows, keeping track of the state of these flows, and dropping packets from non-responsive flows when they exceed a multiple of their average flow depth. In this way, FRED ensures that packets that reduce their transmission because of WRED packet drops are protected from flows that do not respond to WRED packet drops. It also guarantees that a non-responsive flow will not monopolize the entire link.

To enable FRED, after configuring WRED on the interface, use the **random-detect flow** command. You can change the default behavior by modifying the *flow threshold multiplier* and the *maximum flow count* using the **random-detect flow average-depth-factor** and **random-detect flow count** commands, respectively. By default, the *flow threshold multiplier* is 4, whereas the *maximum flow count* is 256. Increasing the *flow threshold multiplier* will configure FRED to tolerate higher amounts of non-responsive traffic.

Verifying Your WRED Configuration

After enabling WRED, check the configured parameters and the number of drops per class (IP precedence) using the **show queueing random-detect** command:

```
router2#show queueing random-detect
Current random-detect configuration:
  Serial5/0:0
    Queueing strategy: random early detection (WRED)
    Exp-weight-constant: 9 (1/512)
    Mean queue depth: 0

    Class  Random drop   Tail drop      Minimum    Maximum    Mark
           pkts/bytes    pkts/bytes     threshold  threshold  probability
    0      4914/560382   18964/2161896  20         40         1/10
    1      4786/545604   18834/2147076  22         40         1/10
    2      4705/536370   18853/2149242  24         40         1/10
    3      4700/535800   18938/2158932  26         40         1/10
    4      4612/525768   18830/2146620  28         40         1/10
    5      4543/517902   18857/2149698  31         40         1/10
    6      4494/512282   18928/2157622  33         40         1/10
    7      4380/499320   18851/2149014  35         40         1/10
    rsvp   0/0           0/0            37         40         1/10
```

This provides good information on what kind of traffic, with respect to IP precedence (or *Class*), is flowing through the router, and what kind of drop treatment it is getting—random drop or tail drop. We can see from this output that each IP precedence level (0 to 7) dropped approximately the same number of packets. For congestion notification responsive flows such as TCP traffic, you should not see a lot of tail drop. Tail drop occurs when the upper threshold has been exceeded. When this occurs, packets are dropped wholesale. In this example, there is a high amount of tail drop because the traffic was created with a packet generator that did not throttle down when packets were dropped.

The same information can be shown a little differently on the VIP-based RSP platform for DWRED by using the **show interfaces** [*interface-type interface-number*] **random-detect** command:

```
router3#show queueing random-detect
Current random-detect configuration:
```

```
Serial4/0/0:0
  Queueing strategy: fifo
  Packet drop strategy: VIP-based random early detection (DWRED)
  Exp-weight-constant: 9 (1/512)
  Mean queue depth: 192
  Queue size: 194     Maximum available buffers: 384
  Output packets: 150838  WRED drops: 10434  No buffer: 0
```

Class	Random drop	Tail drop	Minimum threshold	Maximum threshold	Mark probability	Output Packets
0	1067	543	96	192	1/10	21456
1	0	0	108	192	1/10	0
2	1054	546	120	192	1/10	21412
3	1049	535	132	192	1/10	21428
4	1042	530	144	192	1/10	21439
5	836	517	156	192	1/10	21658
6	831	531	168	192	1/10	21649
7	808	545	180	192	1/10	21658

Here we can see the number of packets of each precedence that were output from the interface, and the number of drops, both random and tail drop. The number of packets sent was approximately equal for each class, except that there were no packets sent with an IP precedence of 1.

If CBWFQ is configured with WRED, these commands will not work to show WRED statistics; however, the **show policy-map interface** command includes WRED information for each class. Take a look at the following output, paying special attention to the "random-detect" information:

```
router3#show policy int s4/0/0:0

Serial4/0/0:0

  service-policy output: PPP-T1

    queue stats for all priority classes:
      queue size 0, queue limit 96
      packets output 22418, packet drops 0
```

```
    tail/random drops 0, no buffer drops 0, other drops 0

class-map: Network (match-all)
  22751 packets, 11375500 bytes
  30 second offered rate 203000 bps, drop rate 0 bps
  match: access-group name Network
  queue size 0, queue limit 84
  packets output 22417, packet drops 1
  tail/random drops 1, no buffer drops 0, other drops 0
  bandwidth: kbps 338, weight 29
  random-detect:
    Exp-weight-constant: 10 (1/1024)
    Mean queue depth: 0
```

Class	Random drop	Tail drop	Minimum threshold	Maximum threshold	Mark probability	Output packets
0	0	0	21	42	1/10	0
1	0	0	23	42	1/10	0
2	0	0	25	42	1/10	0
3	0	0	27	42	1/10	0
4	0	0	29	42	1/10	0
5	0	0	31	42	1/10	0
6	0	0	33	42	1/10	0
7	0	1	35	42	1/10	22417

```
class-map: Internet (match-all)
  22751 packets, 11375500 bytes
  30 second offered rate 203000 bps, drop rate 0 bps
  match: access-group name Internet
  queue size 0, queue limit 69
  packets output 22099, packet drops 319
  tail/random drops 319, no buffer drops 0, other drops 0
  bandwidth: kbps 277, weight 24
  random-detect:
    Exp-weight-constant: 10 (1/1024)
    Mean queue depth: 0
```

Class	Random drop	Tail drop	Minimum threshold	Maximum threshold	Mark probability	Output packets
0	0	0	17	34	1/10	0
1	0	0	19	34	1/10	0
2	0	0	21	34	1/10	0
3	0	0	23	34	1/10	0
4	0	0	25	34	1/10	0
5	0	0	27	34	1/10	0
6	18	22	29	34	1/10	22099
7	0	0	31	34	1/10	0

```
class-map: Platinum (match-all)
  22751 packets, 11375500 bytes
  30 second offered rate 203000 bps, drop rate 0 bps
  match: access-group name Platinum
  Priority: kbps 384, burst bytes 9600, b/w exceed drops: 0

class-map: Gold (match-all)
  22751 packets, 11375500 bytes
  30 second offered rate 203000 bps, drop rate 0 bps
  match: access-group name Gold
  queue size 0, queue limit 54
  packets output 21096, packet drops 1322
  tail/random drops 1322, no buffer drops 0, other drops 0
  bandwidth: kbps 216, weight 18
  random-detect:
    Exp-weight-constant: 10 (1/1024)
    Mean queue depth: 3
```

Class	Random drop	Tail drop	Minimum threshold	Maximum threshold	Mark probability	Output packets
0	0	0	13	27	1/10	0
1	0	0	14	27	1/10	0
2	0	0	15	27	1/10	0
3	0	0	16	27	1/10	0
4	95	121	17	27	1/10	21429

5	0	0	18	27	1/10	0
6	0	0	19	27	1/10	0
7	0	0	20	27	1/10	0

```
class-map: Silver (match-all)
   22751 packets, 11375500 bytes
   30 second offered rate 203000 bps, drop rate 37000 bps
   match: access-group name Silver
   queue size 42, queue limit 42
   packets output 17610, packet drops 5141
   tail/random drops 5141, no buffer drops 0, other drops 0
   bandwidth: kbps 169, weight 14
   random-detect:
     Exp-weight-constant: 10 (1/1024)
     Mean queue depth: 8
```

Class	Random drop	Tail drop	Minimum threshold	Maximum threshold	Mark probability	Output packets
0	0	0	10	21	1/10	0
1	0	0	11	21	1/10	0
2	0	0	12	21	1/10	0
3	1359	1562	13	21	1/10	17610
4	0	0	14	21	1/10	0
5	0	0	15	21	1/10	0
6	0	0	16	21	1/10	0
7	0	0	17	21	1/10	0

```
class-map: Bronze (match-all)
   22752 packets, 11376000 bytes
   30 second offered rate 203000 bps, drop rate 104000 bps
   match: access-group name Bronze
   queue size 27, queue limit 27
   packets output 11227, packet drops 11524
   tail/random drops 11524, no buffer drops 0, other drops 0
   bandwidth: kbps 108, weight 9
   random-detect:
```

```
      Exp-weight-constant: 10 (1/1024)
      Mean queue depth: 6
   Class  Random  Tail    Minimum    Maximum    Mark         Output
          drop    drop    threshold  threshold  probability  packets
   0      0       0       6          13         1/10         0
   1      0       0       6          13         1/10         0
   2      909     6490    6          13         1/10         11227
   3      0       0       6          13         1/10         0
   4      0       0       6          13         1/10         0
   5      0       0       6          13         1/10         0
   6      0       0       6          13         1/10         0
   7      0       0       6          13         1/10         0

   class-map: class-default (match-any)
     22771 packets, 11377558 bytes
     30 second offered rate 203000 bps, drop rate 144000 bps
     match: any
       22771 packets, 11377558 bytes
       30 second rate 203000 bps
     queue size 9, queue limit 11
     packets output 7548, packet drops 15391
     tail/random drops 15391, no buffer drops 0, other drops 0
```

The fact that we have divided each CBWFQ class by IP precedence (using ACLs) is evident because each class map's random-detect information has statistics for only one particular *Class*, that is, precedence. For example, the Bronze class was defined as packets matching IP precedence 2, so within this user-defined class, only packets with a *Class* equal to 2 had any drops.

Troubleshooting WRED

The first step in troubleshooting routers running WRED is to understand the previous show commands. Assuming that you can trust the output of these commands, you can monitor how WRED is functioning on the router. It helps when looking at these statistics to have a good base line of how things look when the network is running well. That way, when you check back at a later time, you can ask yourself questions like the following:

- **Are the higher priority (precedence) classes getting a lower drop rate than the lower priority classes?** If not, it may be because you have changed the default operating parameters using **random-detect exponential-weighting-constant** or **random-detect precedence**. If the results are not what you want, you may have to reevaluate your settings or change back to the defaults.

- **Is there a higher amount of tail drop than usual?** If so, this could mean an increase in the presence of non-congestion responsive applications like UDP. You may want to consider using flow-based WRED (FRED) to increase the discrimination ability of WRED.

- **Is the critical traffic getting marked into IP precedence in the first place?** If all your traffic is IP precedence 0, it will all get the same treatment, and WRED essentially functions as unweighted RED. For the 7500 RSP platform and CBWFQ configurations, the show commands discussed display the number of packets output for each class. This can aid you in determining what portion of your overall traffic is of a particular precedence. Alternatively, you could use a packet decoder to capture some traffic and verify your IP precedence levels.

Configuring and Verifying Generic Traffic Shaping (GTS) and Frame Relay Traffic Shaping (FRTS)

Traffic shaping works to regulate the flow of packets out of an interface so that it matches the transmission speed of a remote interface. This is done to avoid downstream packet drops. It has the effect of limiting traffic to a particular rate while buffering burst traffic. It can also be used to provide subrated circuit service. For an overview of traffic shaping, see the discussion in Chapter 8.

Both GTS and FRTS use the token bucket analogy to rate-limit traffic and produce well-behaved packet flow. They also share some common parameters that configure how the token bucket (or credit manager) operates, as well as the resulting overall behavior. The following is a list of parameters using Frame Relay terminology. For GTS, the parameters function the same but have different names.

- **CIR** Committed Information Rate. The average bit rate to send out the interface.

- **Bc** Committed Burst. Number of bits to transmit in the specified time interval (Tc).

- **Be** Excess Burst. Number of bits to transmit in the first interval of active transmission, once credit is built up.

- **Mincir** Minimum amount of data to be sent during periods of congestion. This defaults to half of CIR. (Applicable only for FRTS.)

The Be value is the number of bits that can be sent in addition to the Bc value during the first interval of transmission. It can be set when it is known that the network has enough bandwidth and buffers to handle it. It is assumed that the network will be able to deal with this excess rate, since there was previously no data being sent. After there is an interval with no packets to send and the credit manager is built back up, the next transmission can burst again.

The last parameter is not configurable directly, but internally calculated from the above values:

- **Tc** Time interval. Bc/CIR

Tc has an internal maximum of 125 milliseconds (ms), or 1/8 of a second. Because the Committed Burst (Bc) is the number of bits than can be sent out the interface during time Tc, small values of Tc correspond to small values of Bc for a given CIR, which gives less leeway to burst traffic. The smaller the Tc value, the more the flow will approach a constant bit rate (CBR) service for incoming packets. Be aware that a smaller interval can result in higher CPU utilization. So be careful when using small Tc values on busy routers with lots of VCs, or on fast interfaces. We will demonstrate later how to determine what this time interval is set to, using show commands.

WARNING

Generic Traffic Shaping and Frame Relay Traffic Shaping are functional for only the fast switching and process switching paths. Other switching methods, such as CEF and Netflow, are not supported. The interface where GTS or FRTS is to be applied, as well as any interface that will be sending this interface traffic, must have the "ip route-cache flags" set to *fast* or *none* (*none* implying process switching only). The switching path of an interface can be checked with the **show ip interfaces** command.

Configuring GTS

Generic Traffic Shaping can be enabled on a variety of interfaces and subinterfaces. Exceptions to this are ISDN, tunnel, or dial-up interfaces. For GTS, the parameters CIR, Bc, and Be are named burst-rate, burst-size, and excess-burst-size, respectively.

To configure GTS to rate-limit all traffic outbound on an interface, use the **traffic-shape rate** command while in interface configuration mode. It has the following syntax:

`traffic-shape rate` bit-rate [burst-size[excess-burst-size [buffer limit]]]

Only the first argument is required. For an example, imagine that you want to rate limit all traffic out to a 10BaseT Ethernet interface. Here is what you would enter:

```
router1(config)#interface ethernet 0/1
router1(config-if)#traffic-shape rate 5000000
```

Only the first argument is entered in bits per second, and the others are entered automatically so that the full command in the router looks like this:

```
traffic-shape rate 5000000 125000 125000 1000
```

This specifies a sustainable bit rate, or target rate, of 5 Mbps, with a burst-size and excess-burst-size equal to 125,000 bits. From these parameters, we can calculate that the time interval (Tc = Bc/CIR) is 25 ms. Thus, there are 40 intervals per second. Because the excess-burst-size is 125,000, in the first interval (after credit has built up) the router may send (burst-size + excess-burst-size) 250,000 bits out the Ethernet interface. Therefore, by applying traffic shaping on this Ethernet interface, we have limited the traffic to 50 percent utilization, with an initial burst of 250,000 bits in the first 25 ms. The number 1000 is chosen by default for the maximum number of buffers for all queues.

GTS can also be enabled to limit a particular type of traffic specified with an ACL, using the **traffic-shape group** command:

```
router1(config)#access-list 101 permit udp any any
router1(config)#interface ethernet 0/1
router1(config-if)#traffic-shape group 101 2000000
```

This example will limit all UDP traffic going out Ethernet 0/1 to less than 2 Mbps.

Verifying Your GTS Configuration

In the following example, we configure GTS on an Ethernet interface as in the previous example, and configure traffic shaping on Serial 0/0 to limit traffic to rates of 64 Kbps. Here is a fragment of the total configuration:

```
interface Ethernet0/1
  ip address 10.0.4.1 255.255.255.0
  no ip directed-broadcast
  traffic-shape group 101 2000000 50000 50000 1000
end
!
interface Serial0/0
  ip address 10.0.101.10 255.255.255.252
  encapsulation ppp
  traffic-shape rate 64000 8000 8000 1000
  service-module t1 timeslots 1-24
end
!
access-list 101 permit udp any any
```

We can verify these configuration parameters with the **show traffic-shaping** command:

```
router1#show traffic-shape


Interface   Se0/0
     Access Target  Byte    Sustain    Excess     Interval Increment Adapt
VC   List   Rate    Limit   bits/int   bits/int   (ms)     (bytes)   Active
-           64000   2000    8000       8000       125      1000      -


Interface   Et0/1
     Access Target  Byte    Sustain    Excess     Interval Increment Adapt
VC   List   Rate    Limit   bits/int   bits/int   (ms)     (bytes)   Active
-    101    2000000 12500   50000      50000      25       6250      -
```

Notice that the interval for Serial 0/0 is 125 ms, and the interval for Ethernet 0/1 is 25 ms. This is the default on each of these interface types when only the bit-rate (CIR) is specified. Serial interfaces default to a larger time interval than Ethernet because they have a much lower bandwidth. A larger time interval will deal with bursts better. Again, this time interval value (Tc) can be adjusted indirectly by modifying the bit-rate (CIR) and burst-size (Bc). A larger Tc value for the Ethernet port would make it more tolerant of bursts, and a smaller value of Tc for the serial port would make it more like a CBR service. We can also see in this example that Ethernet 0/1 has access list 101 attached to it to classify packets that should be shaped.

With this configuration active and data flowing through the Serial interface, we can see the immediate status of the traffic-shaping queues:

```
router1#show traffic-shape queue
Traffic queued in shaping queue on Serial0/0
   Queueing strategy: weighted fair
   Queueing Stats: 17/1000/64/0 (size/max total/threshold/drops)
      Conversations   2/4/256 (active/max active/max total)
      Reserved Conversations 0/0 (allocated/max allocated)

   (depth/weight/discards/tail drops/interleaves) 1/4626/0/0/0
   Conversation 238, linktype: ip, length: 46
   source: 10.0.101.10, destination: 10.0.101.9, id: 0x0740, ttl: 255,
   TOS: 192 prot: 6, source port 23, destination port 29186

   (depth/weight/discards/tail drops/interleaves) 16/32384/0/0/0
   Conversation 58, linktype: ip, length: 600
   source: 10.0.101.10, destination: 10.0.112.51, id: 0x010B, ttl: 255,
   TOS: 0 prot: 6, source port 29239, destination port 41559


Traffic queued in shaping queue on Ethernet0/1
  Traffic shape group: 101
   Queueing strategy: weighted fair
   Queueing Stats: 0/1000/64/0 (size/max total/threshold/drops)
      Conversations   0/0/256 (active/max active/max total)
      Reserved Conversations 0/0 (allocated/max allocated)
```

Here we see that Serial 0/0 is using WFQ and has 17 packets in queue with two active conversations. The two active conversations (238 and 58) are shown with their source and destination addresses.

To show the statistics over time, use the **show traffic-shape statistics** command:

```
router1#show traffic-shape statistics
        Access  Queue   Packets  Bytes   Packets  Bytes    Shaping
I/F     List    Depth                    Delayed  Delayed  Active
Se0/0   16      92179   9784808  1386    661558            yes
Et0/1   101     0       28       13968   0        0        no
```

From this output, we note that Serial 0/0 has a current queue depth of 16 packets and that 92,179 packets have been sent since the last clearing of the counters. Also, 1386 packets were delayed in the queue because of traffic shaping. Traffic shaping is configured for both of these interfaces; however, the *Shaping Active* flag is set to "yes" only when packets are in queue and traffic shaping is working to regulate the flow.

Configuring FRTS

To configure FRTS, you must, at minimum, complete these steps:

1. Enable FRTS on the interface.
2. Create a map class defining the FRTS parameters, including queuing method.
3. Attach the map class to the interface.

Enabling Frame Relay Traffic Shaping on the Interface

Before you can get started with FRTS on an interface, it must be enabled. To enable FRTS, while in interface configuration mode, issue this command:

```
router1(config-if)#frame-relay traffic-shaping
```

This enables traffic shaping on a per VC basis.

Configuring Traffic Shaping Parameters

The second step is to create a Frame Relay map class to specify traffic shaping parameters. The map class can then be attached to one or more interfaces to indicate the QoS. Let us start by configuring a Frame Relay circuit with a 128 Kbps CIR and a port speed of 256 Kbps. Then we will explain each of the parameters.

```
router1(config)#map-class frame-relay Data
router1(config-map-class)#frame-relay traffic-rate 256000
router1(config-map-class)#frame-relay adaptive-shaping becn
router1(config-map-class)#frame-relay mincir 128000
```

After defining the name of the class map, *Data*, we use the **frame-relay traffic-rate** command to set the CIR parameter. The syntax of the command is like this:

```
frame-relay traffic-rate average [peak]
```

The *peak* argument is optional and defaults to the same value as the average, if not entered. If the peak value is entered, it indirectly sets the excess-burst-rate (Be), as follows:

peak = CIR + Be/Tc

Since we set the CIR to the port speed, it is impossible to burst over this, so we leave the *peak* set to the same value as the *average*. Why did we set the *average* rate to the port speed (256 Kbps) instead of the carrier's CIR (128 Kbps)? Frame Relay services are provided with a Committed Information Rate (CIR), which is the rate at which the carrier guarantees that you can transmit without experiencing packet drops. However, in general practice, you want to set the FRTS CIR parameter to the port speed, unless the port speed is very much greater than the CIR, or if the carrier will not allow you to burst above the CIR. Because we are assuming that this VC is for data that can tolerate packet drops, we set CIR to port speed to maximize throughput.

> **WARNING**
>
> You may not want to set the CIR parameter higher than the carrier CIR if you are carrying real-time traffic on the virtual circuit. Real-time traffic, such as voice, is intolerant of packet drops. By transmitting at the carrier CIR or lower, you are unlikely to experience packet drops in the carrier network. With the use of other configuration techniques, such as isolating your voice traffic on a separate VC or using queuing mechanisms such as IP RTP priority queuing, you can also guarantee low latency transmission.

To make the VC responsive to congestion notifications, we use the **frame-relay adaptive-shaping** command, which has this syntax:

```
frame-relay adaptive-shaping {becn | foresight}
```

Here, two choices exist for the type of notification: BECN or Foresight. BECN is the standard congestion notification method for Frame Relay, whereas Foresight can be used only when connecting to a Cisco switch. Foresight offers more responsive congestion notification by sending frames in both directions at regular intervals to monitor congestion. When either notification is received within an interval of time (Tc), the rate is throttled back by 25 percent. See Chapter 8 for more information.

Finally, we set the **frame-relay mincir** value to the actual carrier CIR, since this is the lowest rate to which traffic shaping will slow the flow as a result of receiving BECNs.

> **NOTE**
>
> We used the **frame-relay traffic-rate** command to set the FRTS parameters while configuring the map class. This command is basically a shortcut for setting the CIR, Bc, and Be all at once. Equivalently, we could specify the CIR, Bc, and Be parameters independently using the **frame-relay CIR**, **frame-relay Bc**, and **frame-relay Be** commands, respectively. This second method gives a little more control, allowing us to indirectly specify a different time interval Tc by explicitly configuring a Bc value.

Configuring Queuing for the VC

FRTS supports the application of FIFO, PQ, and CQ on a per VC basis. Each VC will default to FIFO unless a map class associated with it specifies a different queuing mechanism. If you have a priority list defined, you can apply it to the map class with this command:

```
frame-relay priority-list list-number
```

Similarly, if you have a custom queuing list defined, it can be applied to the map class:

```
frame-relay custom-queue-list list-number
```

To specify a particular type of traffic that is transmitted out a Frame Relay VC, it is necessary to configure PQ or CQ with an Access Control List to denote the specific traffic to match. To see how to configure priority queuing or custom queuing, see Chapter 7.

Applying Map Class to the Frame Relay Interface

Now that we have the map class *Data* defined, we can apply it to the interface:

```
router1(config)#int s0/0.1 point-to-point
router1(config-subif)#frame-relay class Data
```

This class map can be applied to the parent interface or to the subinterface, as demonstrated here. In the first case, the parameters of the map class will be applied by default to all subinterfaces of the parent. In the latter case, the class will apply to the single subinterface, possibly overriding parameters if they were set at the parent interface.

Verifying Your FRTS Configuration

You can use the same set of show commands to verify the configuration of FRTS that you use to verify GTS. The following is a fragment of a FRTS configuration for a serial port with a CIR of 128 Kbps and a port speed of 256 Kbps:

```
interface Serial0/0
 no ip address
 no ip directed-broadcast
 encapsulation frame-relay
 no ip mroute-cache
 no fair-queue
 service-module t1 timeslots 1-4
 frame-relay traffic-shaping
!
interface Serial0/0.1 point-to-point
 ip address 10.0.101.10 255.255.255.252
 no ip directed-broadcast
 frame-relay class Data
 frame-relay interface-dlci 1000
!
map-class frame-relay Data
```

```
frame-relay traffic-rate 256000 256000
frame-relay adaptive-shaping becn
frame-relay mincir 128000
```

We can see the traffic-shaping parameters as they are configured for the VC, as follows:

```
router1#show traffic-shape

Interface   Se0/0.1
        Access  Target  Byte    Sustain     Excess      Interval  Increment  Adapt
VC      List    Rate    Limit   bits/int    bits/int    (ms)      (bytes)    Active
1000            256000  4000    256000      0           125       4000       BECN
```

Here are the statistics:

```
router1#show traffic-shape statistics
            Access  Queue   Packets   Bytes      Packets  Bytes     Shaping
I/F         List    Depth                        Delayed  Delayed   Active
Se0/0.1             13      25259     6206586    3415     1740015   yes
```

And finally, here is the queue. Some packets have been omitted from the output for brevity:

```
router1#show traffic-shape queue
Traffic queued in shaping queue on Serial0/0.1 dlci 1000
   Queueing strategy: fcfs
   Queueing Stats: 19/40/0 (size/max total/drops)
Packet 1, linktype: ip, length: 600, flags: 0x10000008
   source: 10.0.101.10, destination: 10.0.112.51, id: 0x0BD0, ttl: 255,
   TOS: 0 prot: 6, source port 36622, destination port 46138
      data: 0x8F0E 0xB43A 0x9302 0x7DC7 0xEC0E 0xF46B 0x5010
            0x4000 0x9357 0x0000 0x6E78 0xDF82 0x7BAA 0xB86E

Packet 2, linktype: ip, length: 45, flags: 0x10000008
   source: 10.0.101.10, destination: 19.12.224.31, id: 0x0654, ttl: 255,
   TOS: 192 prot: 6, source port 23, destination port 1103
      data: 0x0017 0x044F 0x8D5C 0x3F2A 0x4546 0xF595 0x5018
            0x0F3D 0x0863 0x0000 0x2169 0xE29B 0xD177 0xEC41
```

```
.  .  .
Packet 19, linktype: ip, length: 46, flags: 0x10000008
    source: 10.0.101.10, destination: 10.0.101.1, id: 0x01A4, ttl: 255,
    TOS: 192 prot: 6, source port 23, destination port 17923
      data: 0x0017 0x4603 0x71DC 0x85C3 0x71DC 0x2B88 0x5018
            0x0E30 0xC90C 0x0000 0x0D0A 0x5DD5 0xE139 0x23AD
```

Understanding Distributed Technologies

In Chapter 8, we discussed the wide variety of features that can be run in distributed mode on the 7500 RSP platform. For the most part, on the RSP, QoS mechanisms such as CBWFQ, LLQ, and RSVP are configured the same way as on other router platforms. However, when you configure any feature on a distributed architecture like the 7500 RSP, it is important that you know whether it is running in distributed mode. With any large capacity router, features that are handled by the main processor exclusively may have scaling problems. In addition, there may be differences in what features can operate together in distributed mode, as well as differences in the output of certain show commands.

The Cisco 12000 series router, also called the Gigabit Switch Router (GSR), is another distributed router platform. The GSR was designed to aggregate high traffic volumes at the core of networks. Therefore, the QoS mechanisms supported are tailored to meet the needs of a core switch router. Additionally, some of the QoS mechanisms that we have covered are not supported because they would not be appropriate for the high-speed interfaces of the GSR.

The following QoS mechanisms are supported on the GSR:

- Deficit Round Robin (DRR)
- Modified Deficit Round Robin (MDRR)
- Weighted Random Early Detection (WRED)
- Committed Access Rate (CAR)
- Per Interface Rate Control (PIRC)

DRR is the queuing mechanism provided on the GSR. It provides a packet scheduling service analogous to WFQ. MDRR extends DRR with a priority queue for voice and video traffic. The GSR also supports implementation of the

WRED and CAR mechanisms for congestion avoidance and rate limiting. PIRC is a trimmed-down version of CAR. Other QoS mechanisms such as WFQ, CBWFQ, and CRTP are not supported.

DCEF

In the last chapter, we saw that distributed CEF operates by the Route/Switch Processor (RSP), sending each VIP an identical copy of the Forwarding Information Base (FIB) and adjacency tables. Let us see how to configure distributed CEF and distributed WRED on the 7500 Series router.

> **NOTE**
>
> On the Cisco 12000 series router (GSR), DCEF is not an option, but mandatory—it cannot be turned off. A GSR always operates with distributed CEF switching.

To enable distributed CEF on the 7500 series router, use the following global configuration command:

```
router3(config)#ip cef distributed
```

This will enable DCEF on all interfaces by default. Distributed CEF can be toggled on or off for each interface with the interface configuration commands **ip route-cache distributed** and **no ip route-cache distributed**, respectively. To view the current switching path of an interface, use the **show ip interface** command.

DWRED

DWRED is enabled just like regular WRED, with the **random-detect** interface command. Consider the following interface configuration:

```
interface Serial4/0/1:0
 ip address 10.0.101.13 255.255.255.252
 encapsulation ppp
 ip route-cache distributed
  random-detect
end
```

In this case, VIP-based fair queuing is enabled by default, but in addition, we have VIP-based DWRED enabled. When we look at the interface, we see that both fair queuing and WRED are running in distributed mode:

```
router3#show interfaces serial 4/0/1:0
Serial4/0/1:0 is up, line protocol is up
  Hardware is Multichannel T1
  Description: Connection to router4 s0/1
  Internet address is 10.0.101.13/30
  MTU 1500 bytes, BW 1536 Kbit, DLY 20000 usec,
     reliability 255/255, txload 1/255, rxload 206/255
  Encapsulation PPP, crc 16, CRC 16, Data non-inverted
  Keepalive set (10 sec)
  LCP Open
  Open: IPCP, CDPCP
  Last input 00:00:00, output 00:00:01, output hang never
  Last clearing of "show interface" counters 1d00h
  Queueing strategy: VIP-based fair queuing
  Packet Drop strategy: VIP-based random early detection (DWRED)
  Output queue 0/40, 198 drops; input queue 0/75, 0 drops
  30 second input rate 1245000 bits/sec, 104 packets/sec
  30 second output rate 0 bits/sec, 0 packets/sec
     10934723 packets input, 3387288221 bytes, 0 no buffer
     Received 0 broadcasts, 0 runts, 0 giants, 0 throttles
     0 input errors, 0 CRC, 0 frame, 0 overrun, 0 ignored, 0 abort
     35262 packets output, 2359859 bytes, 0 underruns
     0 output errors, 0 collisions, 4 interface resets
     0 output buffer failures, 0 output buffers swapped out
     5 carrier transitions no alarm present
  Timeslot(s) Used:1-24, subrate: 64Kb/s, transmit delay is 0 flags
  Transmit queue length 60
```

Notice that *VIP-based fair queuing* is designated as the queuing mechanism, whereas *VIP-based random early detection* is shown as the "packet drop strategy." On non-distributed router platforms, WRED and WFQ are mutually exclusive, except when using CBWFQ. You would see the same interface output when CBWFQ is enabled with a service policy, instead of using WFQ.

Configuring, Verifying, and Troubleshooting Link Fragmentation and Interleaving (LFI)

Real-time data packets, like VoIP, are susceptible to delay and jitter when transmitted over low-speed serial links with other large packets. LFI is the process of reducing packet size on low-speed serial connections by fragmenting large packets so that they may be mixed with smaller real-time data packets. The fragments are then reassembled at the other end of the serial link and continue to travel through the network in their original form. LFI is usually configured on serial interfaces below 768 Kbps.

> **NOTE**
>
> LFI usually goes hand in hand with a priority queuing mechanism like LLQ or RTP priority queuing to give real-time traffic the delay requirements it needs for good QoS. A primary reason is that WFQ works on the packet level, not the level of fragmented packets. Therefore, without a priority queue set aside for real-time packets, a large packet, even though fragmented, might be entirely transmitted while a real-time packet waits in queue.

Configuring LFI

LFI is available on PPP encapsulated links, as well as on Frame Relay encapsulated links. The configuration is different, depending on the Layer 2 protocol. LFI is delivered to PPP links by the Multilink PPP technology, whereas the Frame Relay Forum's standard FRF.12 outlines the method for providing LFI to Frame Relay.

Multilink PPP

Even though the Multilink Point-to-Point Protocol (MLP) is used primarily to bundle two or more circuits (dialer interface, BRI interface, PRI interface, or virtual interface template) into one logical interface, it can be used on a single interface to take advantage of its LFI capabilities.

In this case, a parent serial interface can be linked to a child multilink interface. In order to use MLP, we first need to configure the virtual multilink interface:

```
router1(config)#interface multilink 1
router1(config-if)#ip address 10.0.101.10 255.255.255.252
router1(config-if)#ppp multilink interleave
router1(config-if)#fair-queue
```

Here we have created a new interface called "multilink 1," the "1" being arbitrarily chosen to designate this multilink interface. The IP address assigned here will eventually become the IP address of the link itself when we bind this multilink interface to the parent serial interface in a later step. To avoid an IP address conflict, if the parent serial interface has an IP address assigned, you would normally remove it with the **no ip address** command before creating the multilink interface.

Interleaving is enabled by the **ppp multilink interleave** command. Fair queuing also needs to be enabled for interleaving to be functional; hence, the **fair-queue** command. If we wanted to specify that real-time packets have a particular upper boundary on serialization delay, we could also enter an optional command to set the fragmentation delay, as follows:

```
router1(config-if)#ppp multilink fragment-delay 20
```

This sets an upper boundary on delay of 20 ms. This time value is converted internally to a fragmentation size in bytes by figuring the product of the fragment delay and the circuit speed. If this parameter is left unconfigured, the fragment delay defaults to 30 ms. For VoIP applications, a fragment delay between 10 and 20 ms is desirable, since the voice sample size per packet is usually 20 ms.

The next step is to enable the multilink group on the parent serial interface:

```
router1(config-if)#interface serial 0/0
router1(config-if)#ppp multilink
router1(config-if)#multilink-group 1
```

This effectively turns over most of the interface control to the multilink interface. If a priority queue is desired, it is enabled on the multilink interface. LLQ could be used by applying a service policy to the interface, like this:

```
router1(config)#interface multilink 1
router1(config-if)#service-policy output PPP-T1
```

Or alternatively, here is what it would look like for RTP priority queuing:

```
router1(config-if)#ip rtp priority 16384 16383 288
```

Here, the first argument is the starting UDP port, and the second argument is the port range. This marks all UDP ports in the range from 16384 to 32767 into the RTP priority queue, with a guaranteed bandwidth of 288 Kbps. RTP priority queuing functions very much like any other priority queuing mechanism such as LLQ or PQ; therefore, it is important not to oversubscribe the bandwidth guaranteed to this queue in order to prevent bandwidth starvation of other queues.

> **WARNING**
>
> Because MLP fragments and multilink-encapsulates large packets, the other side of the serial link must be configured with MLP as well; otherwise, the line protocol will not come up, and communication will not be possible. Consequently, you must be careful when configuring MLP over WAN connections not to cut yourself off from the router.

LFI and Frame Relay

LFI is available on Frame Relay circuits with IOS 12.0(7)XK1. It is specified by the Frame Relay Forum standard FRF.12 and is enabled on the map class with this command:

```
frame-relay fragment fragment_size
```

Because we specify the *fragment_size* in bytes instead of the fragmentation time (as in MLP), we have to compute the fragmentation size manually by multiplying the link capacity by the target fragmentation time. Thus, for a 128 Kbps circuit, a 20 ms fragmentation delay would be equivalent to a 320-byte fragment size.

> **NOTE**
>
> Though not discussed here, LFI over Frame Relay and ATM virtual circuits is possible via Multilink PPP in IOS revisions 12.1(5)T.

Verifying Your LFI Configuration

After configuring PPP multilink, to view the status, use the **show ppp multilink** command:

```
router1#show ppp multilink

Multilink1, bundle name is router2
 0 lost fragments, 0 reordered, 0 unassigned, sequence 0x2BF/0x524 rcvd/sent
 0 discarded, 0 lost received, 1/255 load
 Member links: 1 active, 0 inactive (max not set, min not set)
   Serial0/0 1920 weight
```

Even though we are using only one serial interface, multilink still shows as a bundle, with the bundle name being the host name of the far router. If there are any problems with multilink encapsulation, you will see it manifested here as fragments or reordered, unassigned, discarded, or lost packets.

Also, since we now have the multilink interface as a virtual interface, we can display the interface statistics with the **show interfaces** command:

```
router1#show interfaces multilink 1
Multilink1 is up, line protocol is up
 Hardware is multilink group interface
 Internet address is 10.0.101.10/30
 MTU 1500 bytes, BW 1536 Kbit, DLY 100000 usec,
    reliability 255/255, txload 43/255, rxload 1/255
 Encapsulation PPP, loopback not set
 Keepalive set (10 sec)
 DTR is pulsed for 2 seconds on reset
 LCP Open, multilink Open
 Open: IPCP, CDPCP
 Last input 00:00:00, output never, output hang never
 Last clearing of "show interface" counters 5d21h
 Input queue: 2/75/0 (size/max/drops); Total output drops: 0
 Queueing strategy: weighted fair
 Output queue: 6/1000/64/0 (size/max total/threshold/drops)
    Conversations 1/3/256 (active/max active/max total)
```

```
   Reserved Conversations 0/0 (allocated/max allocated)
5 minute input rate 3000 bits/sec, 10 packets/sec
5 minute output rate 264000 bits/sec, 35 packets/sec
   1003558 packets input, 128454537 bytes, 0 no buffer
   Received 0 broadcasts, 0 runts, 0 giants, 0 throttles
   0 input errors, 0 CRC, 0 frame, 0 overrun, 0 ignored, 0 abort
   35573 packets output, 24346968 bytes, 0 underruns
   0 output errors, 0 collisions, 0 interface resets
   0 output buffer failures, 0 output buffers swapped out
   0 carrier transitions
```

Troubleshooting MLP

There are a couple of debug commands that are useful if you run into problems configuring MLP. The first, **debug ppp multilink event**, allows you to see any important event that occurs with MLP. In the following debug trace, the multilink interface was reset using shutdown/no shutdown, with the following output:

```
Jan 30 16:15:55: Mu1 MLP: Bundle 'router2' reset
Jan 30 16:15:55: Se5/1:0 MLP: Multilink down event pending
Jan 30 16:15:55: Se5/1:0 MLP: Multilink down event pending
Jan 30 16:15:55: Se5/1:0 MLP: Removing link from router1
Jan 30 16:15:55: Mu1 MLP: Removing bundle 'router2'
Jan 30 16:15:56: %LINEPROTO-5-UPDOWN: Line protocol on Interface
 Multilink1, changed state to down
Jan 30 16:15:56: %LINEPROTO-5-UPDOWN: Line protocol on Interface
 Serial5/1:0, changed state to down
Jan 30 16:15:56: %LINK-3-UPDOWN: Interface Multilink1, changed state to
 down
Jan 30 16:15:59: Se5/1:0 MLP: Multilink up event pending
Jan 30 16:15:59: Se5/1:0 MLP: router1, multilink up, first link
Jan 30 16:15:59: %LINK-3-UPDOWN: Interface Multilink1, changed state to
 up
Jan 30 16:16:00: %LINEPROTO-5-UPDOWN: Line protocol on Interface
 Serial5/1:0, changed state to up
Jan 30 16:16:00: %LINEPROTO-5-UPDOWN: Line protocol on Interface
 Multilink1, changed state to up
```

In this output, we see the step-by-step process of downing the interface and the associated MLP bundle named "router2," and subsequently bringing it back up. Notice that the console messages for the interface's line protocol and link state are also part of this trace.

Another possible trace can be done using the **debug ppp multilink fragment** command. Be very careful with this command, as it can use a lot of memory, produce a lot of output, and therefore, potentially lock you out of the router, especially if you are using Telnet. The following is a small sample of the output:

```
Jan 30 16:14:19: Se5/1:0 MLP: O seq C000210C size 166
Jan 30 16:14:19: Se5/1:0 MLP-FS: O seq C000210D size 51
Jan 30 16:14:19: Se5/1:0 MLP-FS: I seq C0002114 size 52
Jan 30 16:14:19: Se5/1:0 MLP-FS: I seq C0002115 size 57
Jan 30 16:14:19: Se5/1:0 MLP-FS: O seq C000210E size 50
Jan 30 16:14:19: Se5/1:0 MLP-FS: O seq C000210F size 51
Jan 30 16:14:19: Se5/1:0 MLP-FS: I seq C0002116 size 52
Jan 30 16:14:19: Se5/1:0 MLP-FS: I seq C0002117 size 57
```

In this case, we can see each fragment byte size, sequence number, and the associated interface. The "O" designates output, and the "I" designates input.

Configuring, Verifying, and Troubleshooting RTP Header Compression

Multimedia applications such as voice and video often use Real-Time Transport Protocol (RTP) to send stateful information between communicating clients in order to provide features like gateway support and time synchronization. RTP packets usually have relatively small payloads because of their real-time nature, but the RTP/UDP/IP headers can be, in comparison, quite large. Thus, quite a lot of bandwidth can be devoted to overhead. RTP header compression (CRTP) can reduce the overall bandwidth necessary to transmit RTP packets by decreasing the RTP/UDP/IP header from 40 bytes to about 4 bytes. It is usually used on low-speed serial interfaces only (speeds less than T1), because on high-speed interfaces, the compression process could be too intensive for the CPU to handle.

CRTP is available on serial interfaces with HDLC, PPP, and Frame Relay encapsulation. It is also available on ISDN interfaces and the virtual multilink interface created by the use of Multilink PPP.

Configuring RTP Header Compression

RTP header compression can be enabled on HDLC or PPP encapsulated serial interfaces by applying the **ip rtp header-compression** command to the interface. RTP header compression must be enabled on each end of a serial link in order to function. However, if the *passive* argument is used, the router will send RTP compressed packets only if the other side is sending RTP compressed packets.

To enable CRTP on a Frame Relay connection when using subinterfaces, issue the following command while in the subinterface configuration context:

```
frame-relay ip rtp header-compression [passive]
```

If using Frame Relay map commands rather than subinterfaces, use the following:

```
frame-relay map ip ip-address dlci [broadcast] rtp header-compression [active | passive]
```

Verifying Your RTP Header Configuration

With the **show ip rtp header-compression** command, you can view statistics of how CRTP is performing, including the number of RTP packets received and sent, and the compression efficiency status. The following output was created after a single VoIP had been connected for a couple of minutes:

```
router2#show ip rtp header-compression
RTP/UDP/IP header compression statistics:
  Interface Serial0/0:
    Rcvd:    7639 total, 7529 compressed, 3 errors
             0 dropped, 0 buffer copies, 0 buffer failures
    Sent:    3512 total, 3511 compressed,
             133213 bytes saved, 568987 bytes sent
             1.23 efficiency improvement factor
    Connect: 16 rx slots, 16 tx slots, 1 long searches, 1 misses
             99% hit ratio, five minute miss rate 0 misses/sec, 0 max
```

One of the most beneficial statistics in this output is the *efficiency improvement factor*. This factor is calculated using the following formula:

$$\frac{BytesSaved}{BytesSent} + 1$$

By viewing these statistics, you can tell if there are problems such as excessive errors or a poor *efficiency improvement factor* (a value not significantly higher than 1). Note that these packet values are for RTP packets only. If there are no RTP packets, these counters will be zero, and the *efficiency improvement factor* cannot be calculated.

When you look at CRTP statistics on a Frame Relay interface, the information is the same but also includes DLCI information and link protocol information:

```
router1#show ip rtp header-compression
RTP/UDP/IP header compression statistics:
  DLCI 1000       Link/Destination info: ip 10.0.101.9
    Interface Serial0/0:
      Rcvd:     38818 total, 38816 compressed, 0 errors
                0 dropped, 0 buffer copies, 0 buffer failures
      Sent:     44831 total, 44829 compressed,
                1703063 bytes saved, 7262737 bytes sent
                1.23 efficiency improvement factor
   Connect: 256 rx slots, 256 tx slots, 1683 long searches, 2 misses
            99% hit ratio, five minute miss rate 0 misses/sec, 0 max
```

Troubleshooting RTP Header Compression

There are a few debug commands that can be used to monitor the RTP packets through the router. To debug RTP errors, use the **debug ip rtp errors** command. If you are using CRTP and you suspect a problem, you may want to use the **debug ip rtp header-compression**. To see a detailed output of the contents of the RTP/UDP/IP packet headers, such as source and destination address, source and destination port, and RTP sequence and timestamp information, use the **debug ip rtp packets** command. The following sample output shows three packets from an RTP stream:

```
Jan 30 20:59:48:    RTP packet dump:
```

```
    IP:  source: 10.0.112.44, destination: 10.0.101.10,
         id: 0x6254, ttl: 252,
         TOS: 176 prot: 17,
    UDP: source port: 23724, destination port: 18890, checksum:
         0x0000,len: 180
    RTP: version: 2, padding: 0, extension: 0, marker: 0,
         payload: 0, ssrc 834388628,
         sequence: 44951, timestamp: 9456768, csrc count: 0
Jan 30 20:59:48:    RTP packet dump:
    IP:  source: 10.0.112.44, destination: 10.0.101.10,
         id: 0x6254, ttl: 252,
         TOS: 176 prot: 17,
    UDP: source port: 23724, destination port: 18890, checksum:
         0x0000,len: 180
    RTP: version: 2, padding: 0, extension: 0, marker: 0,
         payload: 0, ssrc 834388628,
         sequence: 44997, timestamp: 9464128, csrc count: 0
Jan 30 20:59:48:    RTP packet dump:
    IP:  source: 10.0.112.44, destination: 10.0.101.10,
         id: 0x6254, ttl: 252,
         TOS: 176 prot: 17,
    UDP: source port: 23724, destination port: 18890, checksum:
         0x0000,len: 180
    RTP: version: 2, padding: 0, extension: 0, marker: 0,
         payload: 0, ssrc 834388628,
         sequence: 44998, timestamp: 9464288, csrc count: 0
```

Summary

In this chapter, we configured a number of advanced QoS mechanisms. Many of these were developed to accommodate the move to convergent networks, where data and multimedia coexist. Very few of these mechanisms are exclusive of one another, but instead, they work in combination to deliver comprehensive, network-wide QoS to applications.

RSVP can be used to provide end-to-end QoS by signaling for a reservation across a network configured to participate in RSVP. WRED and WFQ are the implementation mechanisms that allow RSVP to deliver *controlled-load* and *guaranteed-rate services*, respectively.

Although RSVP is simple to configure, implementing it across an entire network requires a thorough knowledge of network traffic patterns, and extensive bandwidth planning. Special attention must be paid to scaling considerations, because the reservations are kept in a stateful database, and because of the multifield classification necessary to identify packets belonging to an RSVP reservation. Although RSVP can tunnel through non-RSVP enabled networks, only clients that are RSVP aware can participate in RSVP.

Some amount of congestion and packet drops are unavoidable in most IP networks. When congestion occurs, network interface queues can fill up and overflow. CBWFQ gives you greater control over these queues and over what kind of traffic gets dropped. CBWFQ is a specialized queuing technique that can deliver guaranteed bandwidth to packets belonging to user-defined classes. LLQ extends the CBWFQ algorithm to add a strict priority queue to deliver not only low packet drop rates, but also low latency transmission, especially crucial for real-time applications like voice. We saw how CBWFQ is configured with a three-step approach. Its modular and policy-based nature allows easy extension to multiple interfaces, and even multiple routers and router platforms.

You can prevent congestion from occurring in the first place with WRED. This is especially useful in the backbone of a network where many circuits are being aggregated.

WRED was designed to work with TCP's congestion adaptation algorithm by signaling applications to reduce transmission speed by dropping packets. The "weighted" aspect of WRED is controlled by IP precedence. When IP precedence is marked at the edge of the network, WRED works intelligently to give higher drop probabilities to lower precedence packets. WRED is easily configured on each interface and works well with the default parameters.

Traffic shaping is used to buffer and shape traffic transmitted out of an interface. It is especially useful on Frame Relay networks to overcome data-rate mismatches, or to keep transmission rates below the carrier CIR to avoid packet drops. Avoiding packet drops is important for real-time applications. Traffic shaping works with common queuing mechanisms: GTS works with WFQ, and FRTS works with FIFO, PQ, or CQ. Configuring traffic shaping is not trivial; however, after reading this chapter, hopefully you have a better understanding of it and how it can be used to maximize traffic and limit packet drops.

Although most QoS mechanisms have been successfully ported over to the distributed 7500 series router, there are some minor differences in feature availability and functionality. The 12000 Series (GSR) has a different set of QoS mechanisms because of the high-speed line cards that it supports.

It is important to know which QoS features are available in a particular IOS revision, and if or how they run in distributed mode. The best source of this information is the Cisco documentation. Look for the platforms supported to see if the feature you want is available.

LFI is used on low-speed serial links to fragment large packets so that they can be interleaved with smaller, real-time packets. It is a point-to-point protocol, in that fragmented packets are reassembled on the far end and traverse the rest of the network in their original form. In conjunction with a priority queue, such as LLQ or RTP priority queuing, it can be very effective in giving low latency, low drop treatment to traffic such as VoIP. We discussed configuring LFI on a PPP interface using MLP.

CRTP is a compression algorithm that can significantly reduce the overall packet size of RTP packets. It is most practically used on narrowband circuits (less than T1) that have a large amount of RTP traffic, such as voice or multimedia. We demonstrated how easily we could configure CRTP on HDLC, PPP, and Frame Relay encapsulated serial interfaces in just a single command. Care must be exercised in its application, however, because of its CPU-intensive nature.

FAQs

Visit **www.syngress.com/solutions** to have your questions about this chapter answered by the author.

Q: I would like to carry VoIP over Frame Relay. What are the minimum QoS mechanisms needed for a good implementation?

A: For VoIP over Frame Relay, you want to provide low latency to voice packets and ensure a low packet drop rate. To provide this, you could use a separate VC just for voice, or you could use a combination of FRTS and PQ or CQ. In either case, you would want to set your FRTS CIR value equal to the carrier CIR in order to avoid packet drops. Additionally, LFI would be important on CIRs less than 768 Kbps if the voice were going to be mixed with larger data packets.

Q: Does LFI work on ATM?

A: Cisco provides support for LFI on ATM by using Multilink PPP in IOS version 12.1(5)T and later. The same MLP mechanism in this IOS revision can also deliver LFI to Frame Relay.

Q: The QoS feature that I have configured does not seem to work properly. What am I doing wrong?

A: The first thing to do is review your configuration and use the show and debug commands to try to figure out what might be wrong. Also, return to the Cisco documentation and try to understand all aspects of the feature. If this fails, you might have encountered a genuine bug. Even though it is not normally necessary to reload the router after making configuration changes, it could fix the problem. Also, sometimes an easy test is to upgrade to a more recent IOS, if you can. The Cisco Web site has a bug navigation tool, which allows you to search for outstanding bugs in the software version you are running. If all these steps fail, consult the Cisco Technical Assistance Center (TAC) to get expert help.

Q: What is the best method to classify my traffic?

A: To provide differentiated services, it is necessary to divide your traffic into classes. Many mechanisms require classification, such as CBWFQ or LLQ, whereas some are enhanced by classification, such as GTS and FRTS. If you can mark traffic into IP precedence levels, some mechanisms function more intelligently with this approach (WFQ and WRED). How you do it depends on your network and overall business needs. If you are interested only in providing QoS on a couple of congested links, you can use access lists on the routers to feed mechanisms like queuing and traffic shaping. If you are more interested in moving towards end-to-end QoS following the DiffServ model, using a mechanism such as CAR at the edge of your network and marking traffic into classes with IP precedence would be highly beneficial. If you are not sure how to classify your important traffic, you can start by building ACLs using a list of "well-known ports." These lists are quite common and can be found in numerous places on the Internet. This way, you will know what TCP or UDP ports your applications use and can then match them with Access Control Lists.

Q: If WRED can avoid congestion, why do I need anything else?

A: First of all, WRED works only for TCP traffic. Although it adds weights to packet drop thresholds by examining IP precedence, it cannot guarantee low latency to applications, or guarantee that no critical packets will be dropped. Furthermore, on low-speed serial interfaces, it is overshadowed by other more useful technologies such as LFI, CRTP, and traffic shaping.

Q: Does CBWFQ work on Frame Relay?

A: Not until IOS version 12.1(2)T. After this revision, not only is CBWFQ available, but LLQ and WRED are as well. They are configured the same way as discussed in this chapter.

Chapter 10

Overview: Border Gateway Protocol (BGP)

Solutions in this chapter:

- The History of BGP
- Maximizing the Functionality of BGP
- External BGP and the Internet
- The BGP Path Selection Process
- Redistributing BGP into Your IGP
- Defining Internal BGP, Route Reflectors, and Confederations
- Advanced BGP Network Design

Introduction

As at press time, the Internet holds well over 90,000 routes, which is far more than Interior Gateway Protocols (IGPs) such as EIGRP or OSPF were designed to handle. Additionally, whereas private internetworks generally have only a few possible paths, with the Internet, there could literally be thousands of ways to arrive at the same destination. EIGRP or OSPF would have major problems under these circumstances.

Clearly, another protocol is needed to deal with the complex routing issues on the public Internet. The answer to this problem is BGP, or, more precisely, BGP 4. Unlike OSPF or EIGRP, which were designed to be intra-AS (autonomous system), BGP was specifically designed to route traffic between autonomous systems, and is therefore called an Inter-AS routing protocol.

This chapter gives some background on the development of this protocol, explains the difference between EBGP and IBGP, explores some of the most popular design concepts, and discusses more complex issues such as route reflectors and confederations.

The History of BGP

Border Gateway Protocol 4 (BGP 4) was preceded by BGP 1, BGP 2, and BGP 3 as standards for use in exchanging TCP/IP routing information between domains. Furthermore, all BGP versions were preceded by the Exterior Gateway Protocol (EGP) as both a standard and a protocol for interdomain routing. The Internet and most of the backbone providers were using EGP exclusively until the mid 1990's. There was limited use of BGP 3 on any production network, primarily because of the stability of EGP and the lack of significant differences in features available in BGP 3.

However, BGP 4 was developed to fix several major problems with EGP, and it led to the widespread use of BGP that exists today. Specifically, BGP 4 provided for the use of classless interdomain routing (CIDR), it provided for a more open topology structure between BGP speakers, and it could coexist with EGP on a router. These features provided a means of minimizing the routing tables and easily moving to this new standard.

Exterior Gateway Protocol (EGP)

The Exterior Gateway Protocol dates back to the early 1980's. Its implementation assumed an engineered tree topology throughout the Internet. Since there was no overall network architect authority for the Internet and connecting regional networks, this limitation was the root cause of many problems associated with full mesh peering. The full mesh network configuration created backdoor routes between regional networks that resulted in "suboptimal routing," "routing loops," or "black holes" that prevented IP packets from traversing the Internet efficiently.

Suboptimal routing can best be described as routing that does not use the best path between the source and destination systems. A "routing loop" is a situation that exists when two systems both see each other as an appropriate next hop to forward packets for a given network. The forwarding decision is determined by the routing table, derived from the routing protocol. In this situation, both systems will forward packets to each other until the time-to-live (TTL) for the packets is exhausted. A "black hole" occurs when a collection of routers believes that the best forwarding path to a destination network is via a router that does not have a route to the destination network. Supposing we refer to this router as Router A, when other routers send packets destined for the unknown network to Router A, and it does not know how to reach this destination, Router A simply discards the packets. Since it appears that the packets disappeared for no apparent reason, they are spoken of as having disappeared into a "black hole." This is how the term "black hole" came to be used. EGP could not prevent the propagation of false routing information between regional networks and the backbone Internet that created these situations.

RFC 1092, "EGP and Policy Based Routing in the New NSFNET Backbone," addressed these problems in relation to the NSFNET. This RFC acknowledged that because the processes proposed were interim measures and did not scale for a global Internet, they should be used only until a better routing algorithm could be developed and put into use.

The Original Implementation

RFC 1267 established the standards for the original implementation of BGP. This implementation is also referred to as BGP 3. It built upon lessons learned with EGP and began the transition process. However, there is no evidence of wide-scale use of this protocol in the Internet, and it was simply relegated to labs and test networks for test purposes. Since this implementation of BGP did not solve the most pressing needs of backbone providers, namely, the classful routing dilemma, there was no incentive to go through the trouble of conversion.

BGP was introduced as an inter-autonomous system (AS) routing protocol. An AS is defined as a collection of routers under a common administration. Furthermore, within the AS you can have multiple Interior Gateway Protocols

(IGPs) that are used to exchange network routing information. A BGP speaker's primary function is to exchange network reachability information with other BGP systems. Since the BGP speaker sees the Internet as a collection of autonomous systems (AS), the network reachability information includes the full AS path that traffic must travel to reach these networks. This information allows the BGP system to construct a graph of AS connectivity. This graph is used to prune routing loops, and it permits policy decisions by the system. Thus, BGP is best described as a hop-by-hop protocol in which each system advertises only the network reachability information that it uses.

The implementation of BGP 3 introduced the foundation elements that are still in use today. First of all, BGP systems establish a connection upon initialization over TCP using port 179. Next, the systems exchange the complete routing table and send incremental updates only as necessary. Since there is no provision to periodically refresh the complete BGP database, all systems keep track of a version of one another's table.

Once the BGP speakers enter the established state, the BGP scanner process on each system ensures consistency among the BGP database, the IGP database, and the IP routing table. If you issue the exec command **show process cpu,** you will see this process in the list identified as BGP Scanner. It is important to note that this process is different from the BGP Router process, which is used to establish and maintain the BGP session.

Finally, the session will remain up unless the connection experiences an error condition. When this situation occurs, the initialization process begins and will continue until the BGP session is reestablished. This procedure is fairly straightforward and depends on the reliability provided with a TCP connection. The fundamental elements of BGP 3 provided a stable basis on which to make the improvements that were eventually released as BGP 4.

The Current RFC

The current RFC standard actually consists of two documents: RFC 1771, "A Border Gateway Protocol 4 (BGP 4)," and the companion document, RFC 1772, "Application of the Border Gateway Protocol in the Internet." Both documents define the inter-autonomoussystem routing protocol in use today. Fundamentally, BGP 4 is simply a new and improved version of its predecessor. The foundation elements of BGP 4, such as BGP connection, messages, peer establishment, and error correction mechanisms, are essentially the same as in BGP 3.

However, BGP-4 provides a new set of mechanisms to support both Classless Interdomain Routing (CIDR) and Variable Length Subnet Mask (VLSM).

BGP 4 also introduces mechanisms to aggregate routes and AS paths. These additions make supernetting possible and serve as a solution to database growth on the Internet, as well as a means to address the IP, version 4, address space depletion problem. This concept is called classless interdomain routing (CIDR) and is explained in the CIDR sidebar in this chapter.

This implementation of BGP 4 also provides support for multiple network protocols, such as IPv4, IPv6, and IPX, which allows it to carry network information for these protocols. In this form, BGP is known as Multiprotocol BGP (MBGP). RFC 2283 outlines the specifications for all protocols supported, and the mechanisms to exchange reachability information between BGP speakers. In general, the individual network layer protocols are identified by an Address Family (AF), defined in RFC 1700. Through the multiprotocol extensions, BGP peers can, with a single peering session, exchange reachability information on multiple AFs, such as IPv4, IPv6, and IPX, ,as well as subAFs, for instance, unicast and multicast.

Finally, BGP4 provides an easy means to work with EGP that facilitates a transition path to this new standard. This probably is what finally served to make BGP 4 the preferred interdomain routing protocol compared to EGP and all previous versions of BGP.

Classless Interdomain Routing (CIDR) and the Current RFC

The specifications of CIDR are listed in RFC 1519. These standards were adopted to curb the routing table growth on the backbone Internet routers in the early 1990's. Between 1991 and 1995, the Internet routing tables doubled every 10 months. If CIDR had not been standardized and implemented, we could have had hundreds of thousands of Internet routes in the routing tables today.

CIDR, simply stated, provides a means to view a network and mask combination that will summarize a group of consecutively numbered networks into a single advertisement. This summarized group of networks is known as a supernet. Consider the Class C network

Continued

> 192.168.3.0 and natural mask of 255.255.255.0. In this example, we know the network identifier is 192.168.3.0. In CIDR terminology, this network-mask pair is represented as 192.168.3.0/24. The /24 indicates the masking length in bits for the network identifier. In this case, 24 bits of network mask are used to identify the network bit boundary. If we attempt to summarize a group of Class C networks into a supernet that includes the network 192.168.3.0, we only need to reduce the number of bits that indicates the network mask. Thus, a supernet of 192.168.0.0/16 indicates a CIDR block of contiguous networks with 16 bits identifying the network boundary. In this example, the address range is 192.168.0.0 to 192.168.255.255. You can see just from this example how CIDR has helped slow down the growth of the routing table size for Internet routers.
>
> Today, the use of CIDR and supernetting has spread to the enterprise network for the same reasons that it was used in the Internet. However, you must remember that using CIDR and supernets requires a routing protocol that can pass along network and mask combinations in the routing advertisement. For example, BGP 4, OSPF, and EIGRP are examples that can be used in this environment.

Maximizing the Functionality of BGP

BGP works like any other routing protocol by maintaining routing tables, exchanging routing updates with peer routers, and making routing decisions based on BGP and neighbor parameters.

Each BGP speaker exchanges network reachability information that includes the AS path list to permit the building of an AS graph for all network prefixes. This graph, or tree, is used to prune routing loops, and it determines the best forwarding path to place into the forwarding database or routing table. All routing information is retained by the BGP speakers until an update message withdraws the network prefix, changes the AS path, or modifies a metric.

The BGP Routing Process

The BGP routing process begins with the establishment of a connection. Once this connection is created and both BGP speakers agree on the parameters to use for the session, a complete BGP database is sent by each system. The systems keep the session alive with periodic KEEPALIVE messages and will send a BGP UPDATE message only if a network prefix is modified with a different AS path or metric. In this case, the network prefix entry is updated in all BGP tables, as appropriate. If a network prefix disappears, then a BGP UPDATE message is sent out that withdraws the network prefix or prefixes from all BGP tables. In such a case, the prefixes are removed from the BGP tables until a BGP UPDATE message is received that specifically adds the networks back.

The BGP system keeps track of the current database version for all BGP speakers, and it can determine the reliability of the data in updates and KEEPALIVE messages. Since all BGP speakers track one another's database versions, they can use this to detect missed updates and determine the reliability of information from their respective neighbors. This mechanism enables the various BGP neighbors to simply send out incremental updates to the BGP database as necessary, and avoids the need to periodically resend the complete BGP database.

This process that BGP systems cycle through is called the BGP Finite State Machine. Figure 10.1 depicts the movement through this cycle and identifies the decision points in the cycle.

BGP Finite State Machine Logic

The following information summarizes the various transitional states that a BGP speaker goes through with the BGP Finite State Machine. Refer back to Figure 10.1 for clarification.

- **1 Idle** This is the first state in the BGP Finite State Machine cycle. At this stage, the BGP speaker is waiting for a Start event. A Start event can be caused by an Administrator establishing a new BGP router configuration peer statement or resetting an existing BGP peer session. In this state, the BGP speaker initiates the TCP session with the BGP peer.

- **2 Connect** At this stage, the BGP speaker is waiting for the TCP connection to establish. When this occurs, it moves to the OpenSent state. If the TCP transport fails, the state becomes Active. If the ConnectRetry timer expires, the state remains in the Connect phase. Any other events initiated by the system or operator cause the state to return to Idle.

- **3 Active** In this stage, the BGP system attempts to establish a TCP session. Once the TCP session is established, the BGP session is in the OpenSent state. If the TCP session fails to establish and the ConnectRetry timer expires, the BGP session returns to the Connect state. If the system or operator causes a Stop event, the session will revert to the Idle state.

- **4 OpenSent** In this state, BGP is waiting for a BGP OPEN message. Once the OPEN message is received, it is checked for errors. If errors are detected, such as a bad version number or unacceptable AS, a NOTIFICATION message is sent out and the system returns to the Idle state. If no errors are detected, the system starts sending out BGP KEEPALIVE messages, the two systems negotiate a BGP hold time value, and the state advances to OpenConfirm. In the hold time negotiation, the smallest value of either system is selected. As with the other states, if a TCP disconnect or problem occurs, the system goes back to the Active state. If the hold time expires, a NOTIFICATION message is sent out and the system moves to the Idle state.

- **5 OpenConfirm** BGP waits to receive a KEEPALIVE message in this phase. Once the KEEPALIVE message is received, the system moves on to the Established state and the hold timer is initialized. If any errors occur at this point, a NOTIFICATION message is sent out and the system returns to the Idle state.

- **6 Established** This is the state that you want to see all BGP systems in. At this phase, UPDATE and KEEPALIVE messages are exchanged as necessary, and you can see the prefixes that each BGP system is sending out. If any errors occur while in this state, a NOTIFICATION message is sent out and the system returns to the Idle state.

- **Prefix Exceeded** This is a "Cisco Only" state. It indicates that the BGP system is operational but is limiting the total number of prefixes in the database to a quantity less than has been received by an adjacent neighbor. Issuing the exec command **clear ip bgp** will reset all BGP neighbors and return the system to an Idle state.

- **Shutdown** This is also a "Cisco Only" state and indicates an administrative state for a given system. It is used when a BGP neighbor is configured in the router and is administratively shut down. Once a Start event is issued, the system will move to the Idle state.

> **NOTE**
>
> A BGP session that oscillates between the Connect and Active states indicates there is a problem with the TCP transport layer for the two systems. Check the definition in the configuration lines carefully, and verify reachability with a ping and a traceroute.

Figure 10.1 BGP Finite State Machine Logic Cycle

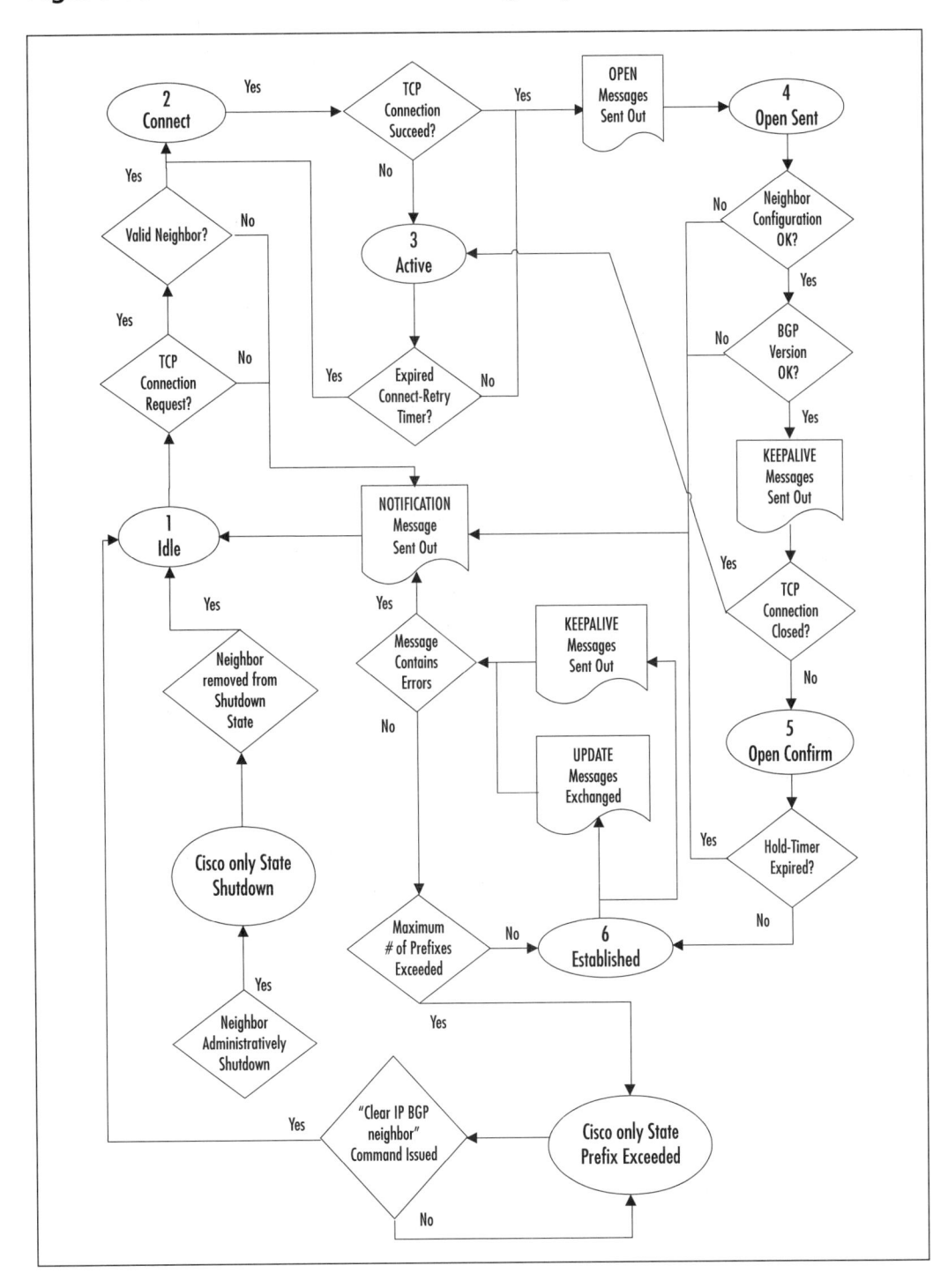

The Types of BGP Messages

There are four BGP message types used to establish and maintain BGP connections.

- **OPEN** This message establishes BGP communications between speakers and is the first message sent once a TCP session is established between the two BGP speakers.

- **UPDATE** This message is used to notify BGP peers about network prefixes and their associated BGP attributes.

- **NOTIFICATION** This message is used to notify a speaker that a protocol error condition has occurred and the active session is being closed.

- **KEEPALIVE** This message is used to prevent the TCP session from expiring by notifying the BGP peer that a device is active. Such messages are exchanged if the keepalive period is exceeded and an UPDATE message has not been exchanged.

The Format of BGP Packets

All BGP messages start with a BGP header. The OPEN, UPDATE, and NOTIFICATION messages all contain additional fields that are explained in the following sections. The BGP header is 19 bytes in length, has three fields, and is also used as a KEEPALIVE message. A complete BGP message can range in size from a minimum of 19 bytes for a KEEPALIVE message, to a maximum of 4096 bytes for a large UPDATE message containing multiple network layer reachability information (NLRI) entries. However, the BGP speaker will evaluate the Maximum Transmission Unit (MTU) value of the outgoing interface before building the packet to send out on the interface. Thus, if an interface supports only a MTU of 1500 bytes the BGP packet will also have a maximum size of 1500 bytes. Figure 10.2 illustrates the fields and layout of the BGP header.

- **Marker** This 16-byte field contains a sequence that is predictable by a BGP peer. Being predictable means that the remote system can process the information based on a common algorithm used by both systems. Given this capability, the systems can utilize this field for authentication or synchronization. Furthermore, the standards specify the use of this field in the routing protocols, and, based on the values, each system should calculate the same resulting value.

- **Length** This 2-byte field indicates the total length of the complete BGP message, including header.
- **Type** This single-byte field indicates the message data type following the header in the complete message. The four possibilities are:
  - OPEN
  - UPDATE
  - NOTIFICATION
  - KEEPALIVE

Figure 10.2 BGP 4 Packet Header Fields

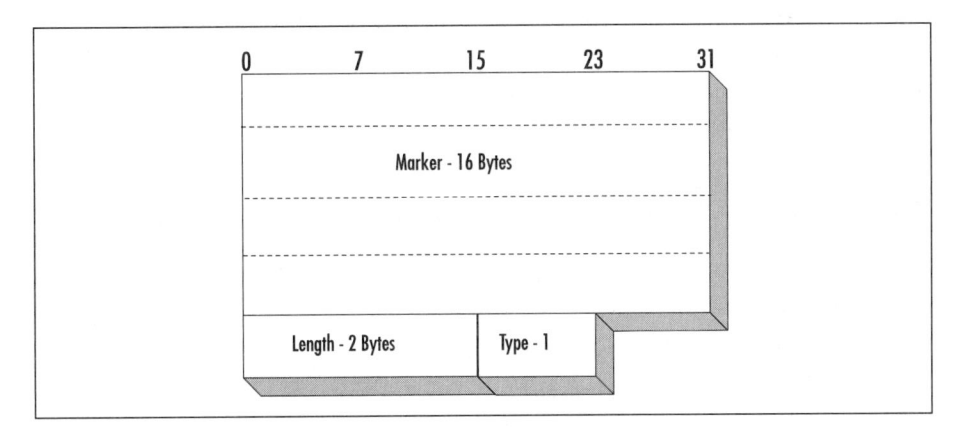

> **NOTE**
>
> With the Cisco BGP implementation, the Marker field is set to all ones if it is not used for authentication or synchronization. Thus, this implementation assumes that authentication is being performed at the TCP layer.

BGP 4 OPEN Message

The BGP 4 OPEN message is a variable-length packet containing 6 fields. The maximum message length including the BGP header is 4096 bytes. Figure 10.3 depicts the field layout for this message.

Figure 10.3 BGP 4 OPEN Message Fields

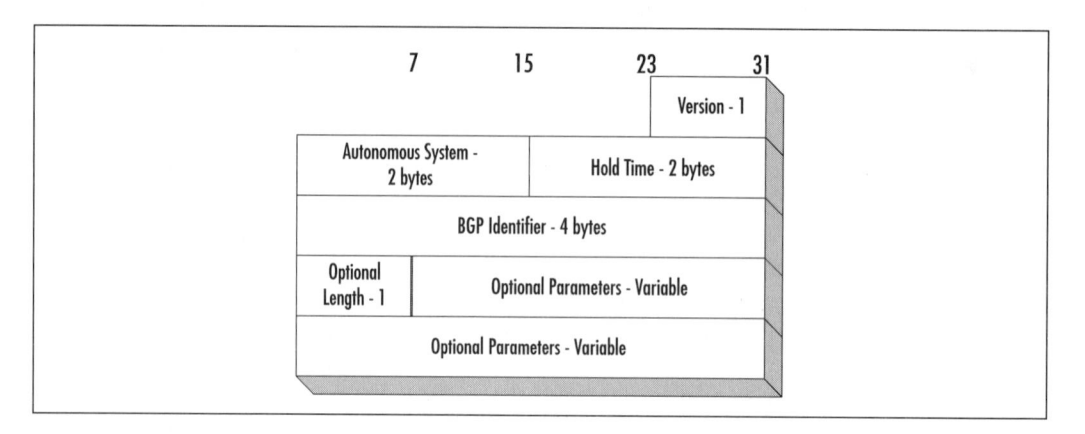

```
         7              15              23              31
                                                  Version - 1
         Autonomous System -           Hold Time - 2 bytes
             2 bytes
                        BGP Identifier - 4 bytes
         Optional
         Length - 1     Optional Parameters - Variable
                        Optional Parameters - Variable
```

- **Version** This is a single-byte field that identifies the BGP version being used. This value is usually version four. However, Cisco routers will automatically negotiate between version two and version four.

- **Autonomous System** This 2-byte field identifies the AS of the remote neighbor. If the AS value does not correspond to the AS value set in the router's BGP configuration line, the local router sends out a NOTIFICATION message and closes the session.

- **Hold Time** This 2-byte field is used to specify the amount of time the session will be paused if a KEEPALIVE, UPDATE, or NOTIFICATION message is not received. This value is negotiated between the two BGP peers and will be the lowest value sent by either router. Thus, the routers do not have to agree initially on this value.

- **BGP Identifier** This 4-byte field is the identifier by which all information is known about the particular BGP speaker. In essence, this is the router's name. The BGP can be manually set using the **bgp router-id** *ip-address* BGP router configuration command. If this value is not set manually, the router will select the highest IP address as the BGP identity. Loopback interfaces are considered before using any physical interface address for this value.

- **Optional Length** This single-byte field indicates the total length of the Optional Parameters field. Thus, if this value is zero, no Optional Parameters are used.

- **Optional Parameters** This variable-length field contains a list of optional parameters. The optional parameters may be encoded as a triplet of Parameter Type, Parameter Length, and Parameter Value. The format for this field is depicted in Figure 10.4.

Figure 10.4 Optional Parameters Field Layout in the BGP OPEN Message

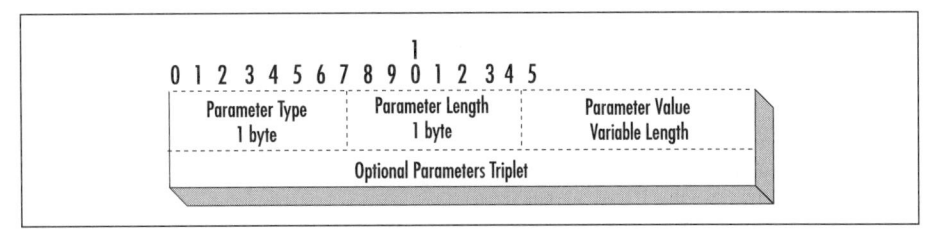

```
                           1
   0 1 2 3 4 5 6 7 8 9 0 1 2 3 4 5
   +---------------+---------------+------------------+
   | Parameter Type| Parameter Length| Parameter Value|
   |    1 byte     |     1 byte      | Variable Length|
   +---------------+---------------+------------------+
              Optional Parameters Triplet
```

Parameter Type This is a single-byte field that identifies the parameter type being used. There are two common types in use:

- Type 1 indicates that the BGP authentication is using MD5. The Cisco implementation does not use this method of BGP session authentication. In a Cisco implementation, authentication can be accomplished at the TCP level and enabled using the **neighbor** *(ip address/ peer-group-name)* **password** *string* subcommand.
- Type 2 is used for capability negotiation. This facilitates the introduction of new capabilities into a BGP network, and permits BGP peers to negotiate these capabilities without closing the BGP session.

Parameter Length This is a single-byte field that contains the length of the Parameter Value field.

Parameter Value This is a variable-length field that is interpreted according to the value in the Parameter Type field. Thus, if the Parameter Type were Type 1, the Parameter Value would contain the authentication information necessary to understand the message. Since Cisco does not use this mechanism, this information is included for explanation only.

BGP 4 UPDATE Message

The BGP 4 UPDATE message is a variable-length packet containing a BGP header and five fields. This message is used to advertise routes, withdraw routes, or a combination of the two. The total length of an UPDATE message cannot exceed 4096 bytes. Figure 10.5 depicts the field layout for this message type.

Figure 10.5 BGP 5 UPDATE Message Fields

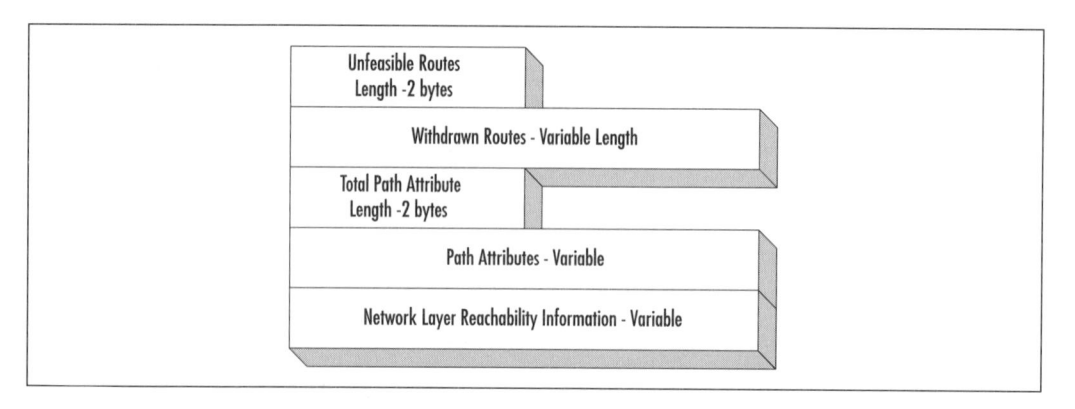

```
Unfeasible Routes
Length -2 bytes
Withdrawn Routes - Variable Length
Total Path Attribute
Length -2 bytes
Path Attributes - Variable
Network Layer Reachability Information - Variable
```

- **Unfeasible Routes Length** This 2-byte field indicates the total length of the Withdrawn Routes field. If this value is zero, then no routes were withdrawn.

- **Withdrawn Routes** If the Unfeasible Routes Length field is greater than zero, then this variable-length field contains a list of routes that are not feasible to use and need to be withdrawn. The withdrawn list takes a 2-tuple <length, prefix> format. In this case, the length value indicates the network mask size. For example, a tuple like <18, 200.200.64.0> would indicate that the supernet 200.200.64.0 /18 is being withdrawn.

- **Total Path Attribute Length** This 2-byte field indicates the total length in bytes of all network paths contained within the Path Attribute field and the Network Layer Reachability Information (NLRI) field. If no NLRI information is present, the length is zero.

- **Path Attributes** This is a variable-length field that depicts the Attribute Type, Attribute Length, and Attribute Value in a triple format <attribute type, attribute length, attribute value>. The Attribute Type field is 2-bytes and includes Attribute Flags and the Attribute Type Code. Figure 10.6 depicts the layout of the Attribute Type field. Table 10.1 lists possible values for the four high-order bits (bits 0 to 3) used in the Attribute Flags field, and Table 10.2 lists the appropriate values for the Attribute Type Code.

Figure 10.6 Attribute Type Field Layout

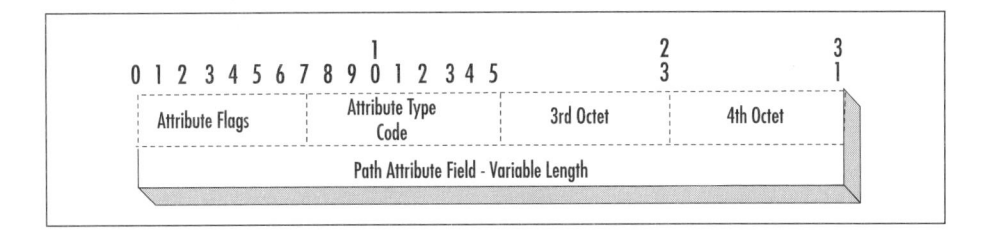

```
 0 1 2 3 4 5 6 7 8 9 0 1 2 3 4 5        2 3                3 1
 |Attribute Flags|Attribute Type Code|   3rd Octet    |    4th Octet    |
 |              Path Attribute Field - Variable Length                  |
```

- **Network Layer Reachability Information** This is a variable-length field that contains a list of IP address prefixes. The information is encoded as 2-tuples in the format <length, prefix>. The length field is a single byte that indicates the length in bits of the IP prefix. A length of zero means match all IP addresses.

- **Attribute Flags** This single-byte field uses only the high-order bits 0 to 3. Table 10.1 identifies the meanings of, and interactions among, the four flags.

- **Attribute Type Code** This single-byte field contains the Attribute Type Codes explained in Table 10.2.

- **3rd and 4th Octets** These two bytes contain the length of the Attribute data in bytes. If the Extended Length Bit flag is set to 0, only the 3rd Octet is used. If the Extended Length Bit flag is set to 1, both the 3rd and 4th bytes are used to identify the length of the Path Attribute data.

Table 10.1 Attribute Flag Field Values

High-order Bit	Flag Name	Value and Meaning	Value and Meaning	Notes
Bit 0	Optional Bit	0 – well-known attribute	1 – optional attribute	
Bit 1	Transitive Bit	0 – attribute is non-transitive	1 – attribute is transitive	Transitive bit (bit 1) must be 1 for well-known attributes (bit 0)

Continued

Table 10.1 Continued

High-order Bit	Flag Name	Value and Meaning	Value and Meaning	Notes
Bit 2	Partial Bit	0 – optional transitive information is complete	1 - optional transitive information is partial	Partial bit (bit 2) must be 0 for well-known attributes (bit 0 = 0) and non-transitive attributes (bit 1 = 0)
Bit 3	Extended Length Bit	0 – attribute length is 1 byte	1 – attribute length is 2 bytes	
Bits 4 to 7	Not Used	0 –	N/A	Must be set to 0

Table 10.2 Attribute Type Codes

Type Code	Name / Related RFC	Value	Meaning
1	ORIGIN / RFC 1771	0	IGP – NLRI is interior to the originating AS
		1	EGP – NLRI is learned via EGP
		2	INCOMPLETE – NLRI is learned by other means
2	AS_PATH / RFC 1771	1	AS_SET – unordered set of ASs in UPDATE
		2	AS_SEQUENCE – ordered set of ASs in UPDATE
3	NEXT_HOP / RFC 1771		IP address of the border router to be used
4	MULTI_EXIT_DISC / RFC 1771		Also known as MED or BGP metric. Used by EBGP to determine the best entry point to a destination in a neighboring AS when multiple connections exist. A lower value is preferred.

Continued

Table 10.2 Continued

Type Code	Name / Related RFC	Value	Meaning
5	LOCAL_PREF / RFC 1771		Used by IBGP to determine the best exit path to a neighboring AS prefix. A higher value is preferred.
6	ATOMIC_AGGREGATE / RFC 1771		Once set, it indicates a loss of AS path information.
7	AGGREGATOR / RFC 1771		Used to identify the AS and router ID that is generating an aggregate route.
8	COMMUNITY / RFC 1997		Used to identify communities of interest and determine if routes can be advertised beyond the local AS.
9	ORIGINATOR_ID / RFC 1966		Router ID of a route reflector that injects a route of a client into an AS.
10	Cluster List / RFC 1966		Used to identify the CLUSTER_IDs of the reflection path as a network prefix. It can aid in debugging problems and route reflector problems, and it is used for automatic loop detection.
14	Multiprotocol Reachable NLRI / RFC 2283		Used by BGP to describe the multiprotocol extensions and routes available.
15	Multiprotocol Unreachable NLRI / RFC 2283		Used by BGP to withdraw multiprotocol routes.
255			Reserved

BGP 4 NOTIFICATION Message

The NOTIFICATION message is a variable-length packet consisting of a BGP header and three data fields. This message is sent if errors are encountered and the BGP connection is closed, and the peers begin to reestablish the session. Figure 10.7 depicts the field layout for these messages, and Table 10.3 lists the error codes with possible subcodes.

Figure 10.7 BGP 4 Notification Message Fields

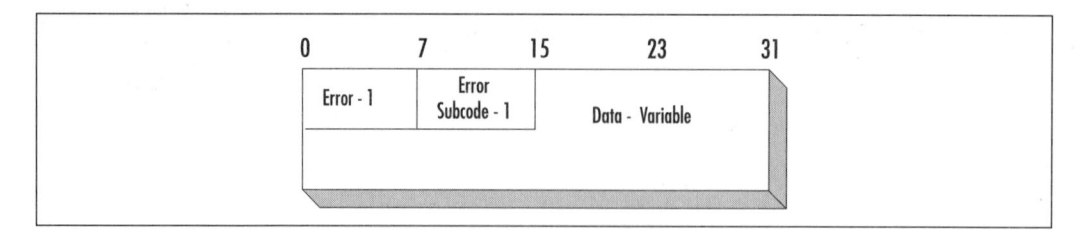

```
0           7    15                23              31
       Error - 1   Error         Data - Variable
                   Subcode - 1
```

- **Error** This single-byte field is used to indicate the type of notification.
- **Error Subcode** This single-byte field provides additional information about the nature of the error condition.
- **Data** This variable-length field contains data relevant to the specific error, such as a bad header, an improper AS number, and so forth.

Table 10.3 Notification Error Codes and Error Subcodes

Error Code	Error Subcode
1 – Message header error	1 - Connection Not Synchronized 2 - Bad Message Length 3 - Bad Message Type
2 – OPEN message error	1 – Unsupported Version Number 2 – Bad Peer AS 3 – Bad BGP Identifier 4 – Unsupported Optional Parameter 5 – Authentication Failure 6 – Unacceptable Hold Timer 7 – Unsupported Capability
3 – UPDATE message error	1 – Malformed Attribute List 2 – Unrecognized Well-Known Attribute 3 – Missing Well-Known Attribute 4 – Attribute Flags Error 5 – Attribute Length Error 6 - Invalid Origin Update 7 – AS Routing Loop 8 – Invalid NEXT_HOP Attribute 9 – Optional Attribute Error 10 - Invalid Network Field 11 – Malformed AS_PATH

Continued

Table 10.3 continued

Error Code	Error Subcode
4 – Hold Timer expired	N/A
5 – Finite State Machine error (FSM error)	N/A
6 – Cease (other fatal errors)	N/A

BGP 4 KEEPALIVE Message

The BGP 4 KEEPALIVE message is essentially the BGP 4 header with no data and a message type code of 4 (KEEPALIVE). These messages are sent only after the hold timer has expired and there is no UPDATE message to send. Thus, this message prevents the session from expiring. All Fields are the same as the BGP 4 header. The only valid value for the Type field is a type code of 4. Figure 10.8 depicts the field layout for the BGP 4 KEEPALIVE message.

Figure 10.8 BGP 4 KEEPALIVE Message Fields

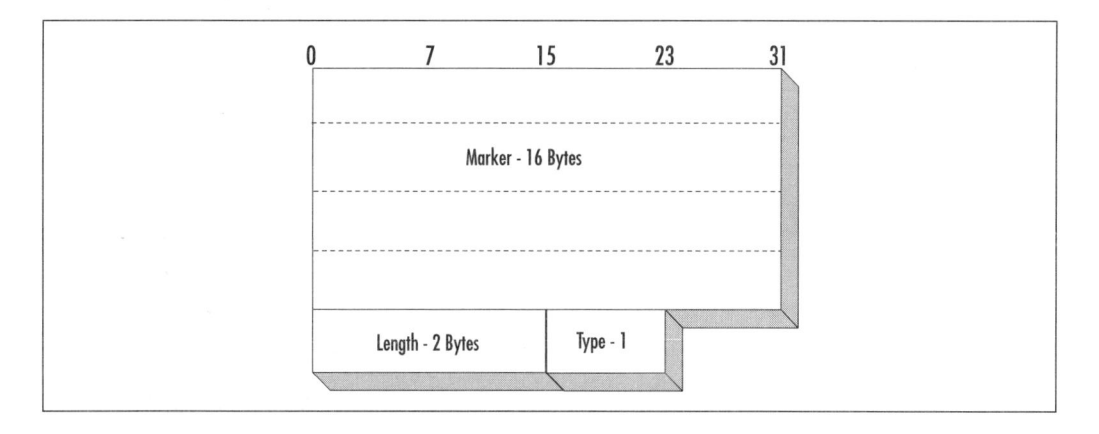

External BGP and the Internet

The introduction to this chapter indicated that there are over 90,000 routes on the Internet. In Figure 10.9, which we will use as an example for this discussion, you can see that there are actually 93,861 network entries derived from five different BGP sources.

We can also see from this screen capture in Figure 10.9 the memory requirements for the BGP database. For this particular router, the requirements are listed

Figure 10.9 Internet BGP Table Summary Information

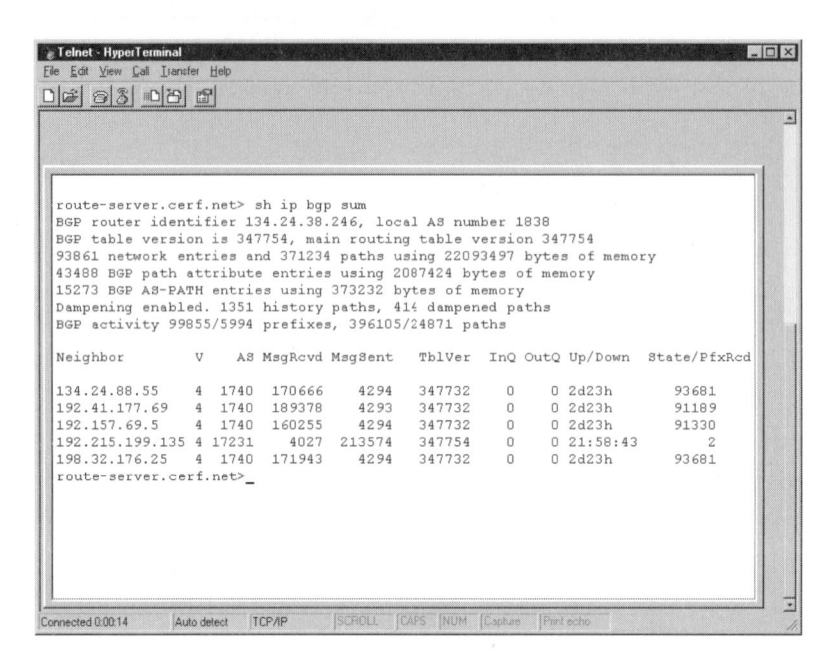

```
route-server.cerf.net> sh ip bgp sum
BGP router identifier 134.24.38.246, local AS number 1838
BGP table version is 347754, main routing table version 347754
93861 network entries and 371234 paths using 22093497 bytes of memory
43488 BGP path attribute entries using 2087424 bytes of memory
15273 BGP AS-PATH entries using 373232 bytes of memory
Dampening enabled. 1351 history paths, 414 dampened paths
BGP activity 99855/5994 prefixes, 396105/24871 paths

Neighbor          V    AS  MsgRcvd MsgSent   TblVer  InQ OutQ Up/Down  State/PfxRcd
134.24.88.55      4  1740   170666    4294   347732    0    0 2d23h          93681
192.41.177.69     4  1740   189378    4293   347732    0    0 2d23h          91189
192.157.69.5      4  1740   160255    4294   347732    0    0 2d23h          91330
192.215.199.135   4 17231     4027  213574   347754    0    0 21:58:43           2
198.32.176.25     4  1740   171943    4294   347732    0    0 2d23h          93681
route-server.cerf.net>
```

in Table 10.4. Analyzing the memory requirements for BGP indicates that we need a minimum of 24.6 megabytes of memory. When we add in the Cisco IOS that also runs from memory, as well as other processes that will require memory, we see that this router needs a minimum of 50 megabytes of memory. If we assume a worst case scenario and plan for a two-fold increase in BGP database requirements over two years, we need close to 100 megabytes of memory for a router that will get two to three years of use. Is this a realistic estimate? We know it is if we recall the PCs in use three years ago. They were slower and had less memory than the ones we use today. IOS requirements, database requirements, and features all have a similar impact on the memory requirements for routers. At one time, a Cisco 7000 with a 16MB Route Processor (RP) and a Silicon Switch Processor (SSP) with 2MB of memory was plenty to run a network for five years. However, with network growth and additional features being used, router CPU and memory must be reassessed to enable these features every 18 months. Therefore, maximum memory and processor capability are key components to putting together the specifications for your next generation network routers. Furthermore, this identifies a key learning experience for network administration staff. When you develop the specifications for your core network elements, plan for the impact of all additions and new features that you will use over the next two to three years. Then this configuration becomes the benchmark when evaluating a request for a feature that was not included in the plan.

Table 10.4 BGP 4 Database Memory Requirements for a Full Internet BGP Table

Purpose	Bytes
Network Entries and Paths	22,093,497
BGP Path Attributes	2,087,424
BGP AS_PATH entries	373,232
Total	24,554,153

What Is an Autonomous System?

The Internet is generally thought of as a collection of autonomous systems (ASs) which uses an interdomain routing protocol to share network layer reachability information (NLRI). More generally speaking, an AS is a network that falls under a common administrative control and is identified by a two-byte number that is either allocated by the InterNIC (1 to 64511) or private (64512 to 65535). Private AS identifiers are not allowed across the Internet and must be translated to a public AS before advertising this information to the Internet.

Systems that share BGP information among different ASs use External BGP (EBGP) to exchange network reachability information. These systems usually reside on a connected network that is common to both systems. Thus, no IGP is needed for the two systems to communicate. BGP systems that reside within an AS use Internal BGP (IBGP) to exchange network reachability information. IBGP assumes that an IGP is used to facilitate network connectivity between the systems.

An AS can be further classified as transit, multihomed, or stub. A transit AS provides connectivity between other ASs, such as between a stub AS and a multihomed AS. Thus, a transit AS is similar to the inter-exchange carriers (IXCs) that provide long distance connections among local phone companies.

A multihomed network has multiple connections to the Internet using different ISPs. A stub AS is connected to only one transit AS and can have multiple links to this transit AS. Figure 10.10 depicts an example of a simple AS arrangement .

In this example, Stub AS 101 has a single connection to Transit AS 1. Therefore, to ensure global connectivity to any other AS, the transit AS must connect to a peer level transit AS or to a higher level transit AS. Currently,

Figure 10.10 Simple AS Example

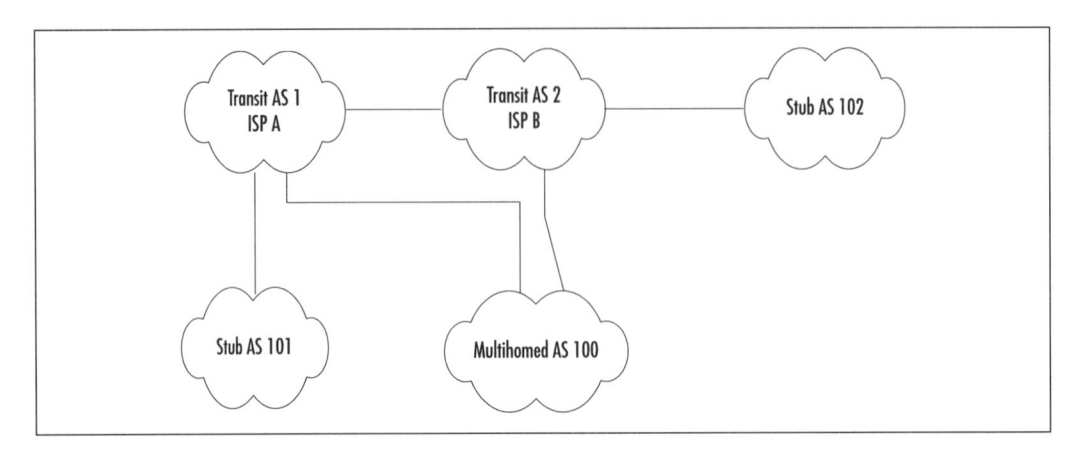

regional transit AS and global transit AS classifications are given to ISPs. Since this diagram depicts peer level transit AS connections, Stub AS 101 has connectivity to Stub AS 102 only through Transit AS 1 and Transit AS 2. Note that the Multihomed AS 100 is not an alternative to transit AS connectivity for Stub AS 101 and Stub AS 102. This network is multihomed for redundancy purposes and will not facilitate routing between Stub AS 101 and Stub AS 102 unless the multihomed AS is reconfigured to become a transit AS. A look at the specific BGP database information on the two stub ASs and the multihomed AS would reveal the information in Table 10.5.

Table 10.5 Pseudo AS Path List for Figure 10.10

Local AS	Remote AS	AS Path
Stub AS 101	Stub AS 102	AS1 AS2 AS102
Stub AS 101	Multihomed AS 100	AS1 AS100 or AS1 AS2 AS100
Multihomed AS 100	Stub AS 101	AS1 AS101 or AS2 AS1 AS101
Multihomed AS 100	Stub AS 102	AS2 AS102 or AS1 AS2 AS102

Does that Mean BGP Uses Hop Count?

BGP uses six of the path attributes to determine the best path for any given network prefix. These attributes are all considered in order, and, as with an access list, the first match for selection wins. The process is discussed in detail in a later section of this chapter titled, "The BGP Path Selection Process." However, before covering the selection process, we need to discuss details about the key AS path attributes and how they influence the path selection. The term "hop count" has no relevance in determining a BGP path. Our traditional understanding of this term is that we count router hops between a source and destination IP address. With IGP's, the path with the fewest hops usually calculates out to be the best. As with IGPs, BGP generally also selects a network path that has the fewest number of AS hops, and thus we get the idea that BGP uses only hop count to determine the best path for a network. However, the mechanism BGP uses to select the best path uses several variables.

Does BGP Use Only AS Paths to Make Routing Decisions?

In an ideal world where all preceding AS path attributes and variables are equal, the answer to this question is "yes." However, it is also true that we need some other means to differentiate possible paths. Since this is a theoretical question, there is only one shortest path. But if all paths were of equal length, then we must use another AS path attribute to determine the best BGP route.

Weight

BGP Weight is a Cisco proprietary parameter that is used only by the local router. This parameter is applied to the routing source and concerns all prefixes advertised by a particular BGP neighbor. It is applied on a per neighbor basis, and we should be extremely careful when configuring weight in relation to a BGP speaker's network advertisement. Since this value overrides all other BGP parameters, the path selection process is abbreviated to consider only the NEXT_HOP reachability and the Weight. Because the Weight parameter has this effect, it can be very useful in resolving routing problems associated with redundant configurations. Weight is set on a perneighbor basis by using the BGP router configuration command **neighbor** {*ip-address* *peer-group-name*} **weight** *weight* . We can verify the use of this parameter by issuing the **show ip protocol** exec command on the local router. In Figure 10.11, we see that no Weight is configured for any of the BGP neighbors of this particular router.

Figure 10.11 BGP Neighbor Configuration

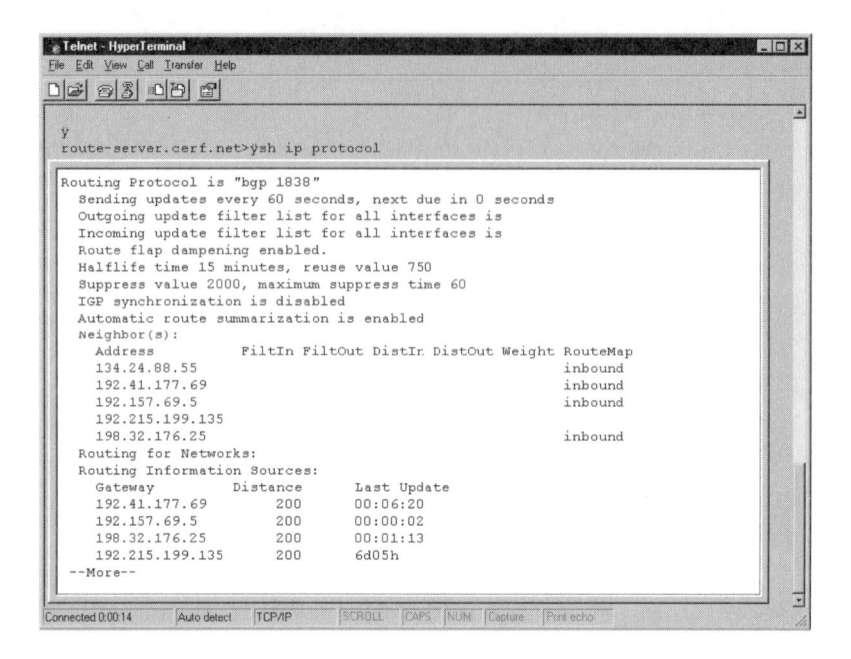

```
y
route-server.cerf.net>ysh ip protocol
Routing Protocol is "bgp 1838"
  Sending updates every 60 seconds, next due in 0 seconds
  Outgoing update filter list for all interfaces is
  Incoming update filter list for all interfaces is
  Route flap dampening enabled.
  Halflife time 15 minutes, reuse value 750
  Suppress value 2000, maximum suppress time 60
  IGP synchronization is disabled
  Automatic route summarization is enabled
  Neighbor(s):
    Address          FiltIn FiltOut DistIn DistOut Weight RouteMap
    134.24.88.55                                          inbound
    192.41.177.69                                         inbound
    192.157.69.5                                          inbound
    192.215.199.135
    198.32.176.25                                         inbound
  Routing for Networks:
  Routing Information Sources:
    Gateway         Distance    Last Update
    192.41.177.69      200      00:06:20
    192.157.69.5       200      00:00:02
    198.32.176.25      200      00:01:13
    192.215.199.135    200      6d05h
--More--
```

How Do I Get There?

BGP refers to the method of getting to a destination as the "NEXT_HOP" path attribute. The value of this attribute is the IP address of the BGP system that can facilitate a connection out of the local AS to the destination network. Thus, for any network path to be valid, the BGP system must have a route that it can use to get to the NEXT_HOP IP address. Otherwise, the route is ignored and fails to meet the criteria to be installed in the IP routing table, or to be advertised to other BGP routers. Furthermore, when an EBGP-learned route is advertised into IBGP, this NEXT_HOP value is not changed. Therefore, IBGP speakers must have a route to the next hop address of EBGP derived routes.

Figure 10.12 depicts the two NEXT_HOP scenarios that you will see in EBGP and IBGP peering configurations. Using these scenarios we will develop a foundation for understanding how the next hop value is set. This foundational understanding can then be applied to any future scenario encountered.

First, consider the EBGP scenario. When Router 1 needs to advertise Network A to Router 2 and Router 3, it will set the NEXT_HOP value for this network to the IP address of the outgoing interface on the peering subnet. In this case, the NEXT_HOP value would be 200.200.200.33 for the network prefix 198.160.1.0/24. When Router 2 and Router 3 receive the advertisement, they will know the NEXT_HOP information and will have a viable route to the NEXT_HOP via a connected interface.

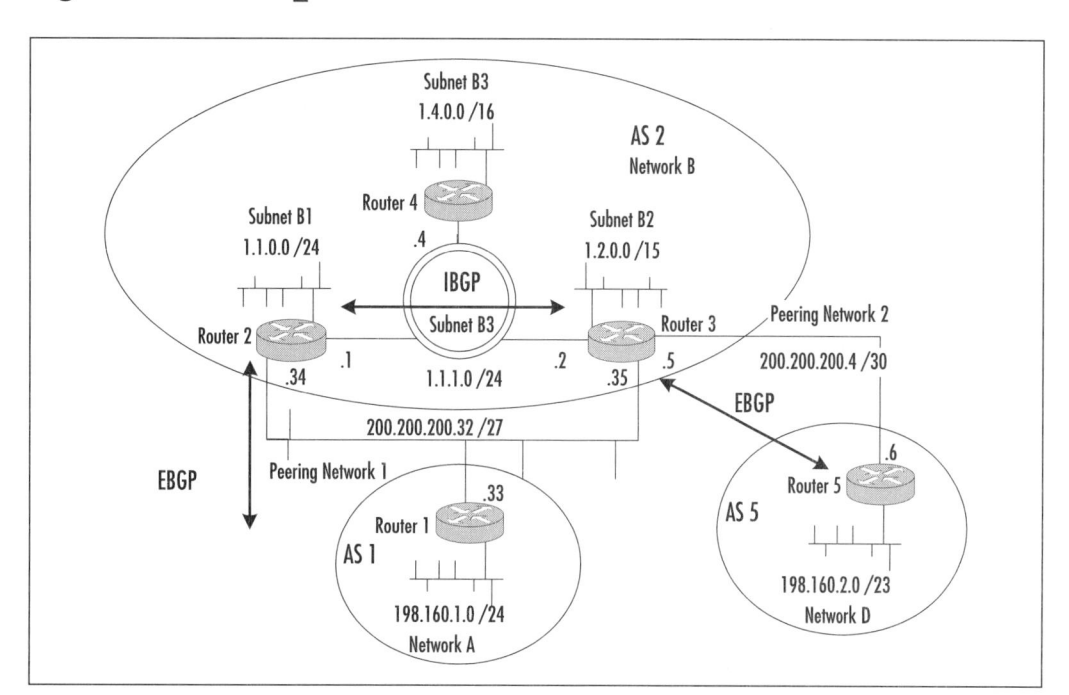

Figure 10.12 NEXT_HOP Information for EBGP and IBGP

By default, IBGP does not make any changes to the NEXT_HOP value. Thus, if Router 1 peers only with Router 2, then Router 3 will learn the appropriate forwarding path through an IBGP advertisement. In this scenario, Router 3 will still see Router 1's IP address as the NEXT_HOP value and will forward packets directly to Router 1 for Network A destinations. Furthermore, Router 4 will need to forward packets to Network A and must also have a route to the NEXT_HOP, or Peering Network 1. This scenario also depicts the situation that exists among Router 5, Router 3, Router 2, and Router 4. If the router does not have a route to the NEXT_HOP network, the BGP prefix is not installed into the forwarding database or routing table. This default behavior can be modified through the **next-hop-self** router configuration command or the **set-next-hop** route-map command. In this example, if Router 2 applies the **next-hop-self** command to the IBGP session with Router 3, the packets destined for Network A will be routed through Router 2.

Multiexit Discriminator (MED), the BGP Metric

This optional non-transitive parameter is used to indicate the best entry point to reach a destination in a neighboring AS. The MED is a four-byte variable with a valid range of 0 to 4,294,967,295. In the Cisco implementation, an update without a MED is assumed to have a value of zero. RFC 1771 specifies that an update without a MED value should be assumed to have a MED of infinity. Since the lowest value is better in the decision process, we should be very careful when peering with non–Cisco BGP routers. Otherwise, we may have some challenges in relation to BGP path selection and MED. Figure 10.13 is an example of how MED is used in a network configuration.

Figure 10.13 MED Example

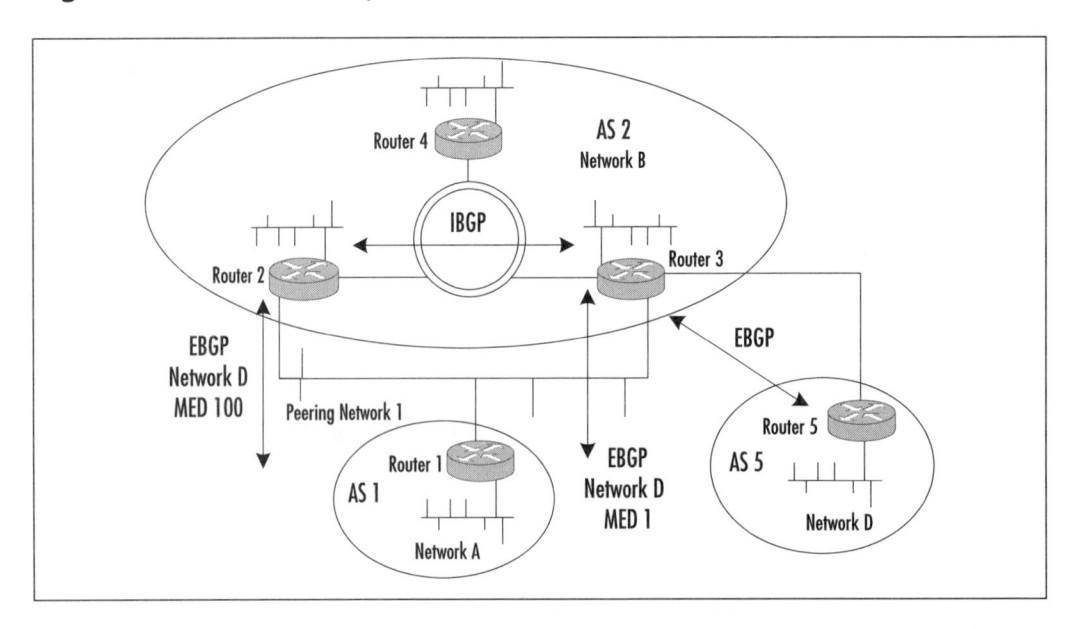

In this example, MED influences Router1's path selection of Network D. Assuming AS 2 is a transit AS, and assuming all other path selection variables are equal and the BGP ID of Router 3 is less than the BGP ID of Router 2, we can tell AS 1 that the most direct path to Network D is via Router 3.. To guarantee that Router 1 will use a path through Router 3, we must set the MED value for the Network D prefix on Router 2 and Router 3 as indicated in the diagram. In this case, Router 3 sets the MED to a value of one, and Router 2 sets this value to 100. Since the lowest MED is preferred, Router 1 will use a path through Router 3 for Network D addresses.

Local Preference

Local preference (LOCAL_PREF) is used only in IBGP updates and is ignored in EBGP updates. This is the highest ranked AS path attribute used in the path selection process, and it influences local decisions only. The LOCAL_PREF attribute is used to influence AS path decisions within an AS, primarily to differentiate a higher capacity AS path that has more AS hops from a low capacity backup path that has the fewest number of AS hops. The default value for local preference is 100 and can be modified with the BGP router configuration command **bgp default local-preference**. Figure 10.14 shows an example.

Figure 10.14 Local Preference Example

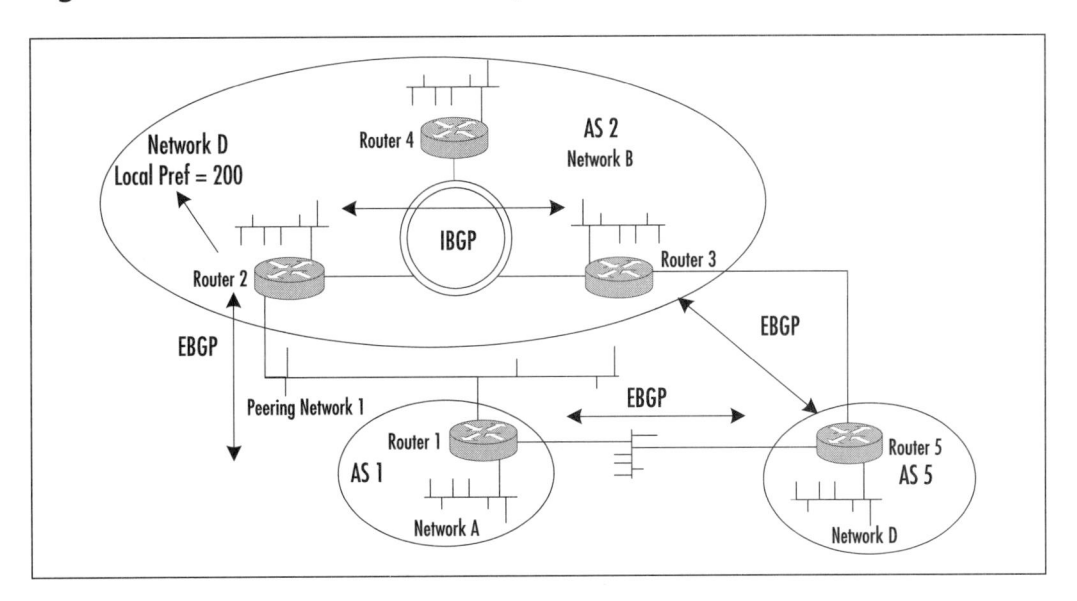

In this example, we can assume that the connection between Router 1 and Router 5 is a high bandwidth connection, such as Ethernet or T3, and the connection between Router 3 and Router 5 is a low bandwidth connection (T1s). Also, we can assume that AS 1 will serve as a transit AS for Network D, and that AS 5 will serve as a transit AS for Network A. This might be a common scenario in a merger or acquisition. In this example, if Router 2 sets the local preference for Network D to 200, then the best exit path for AS 2 to reach Network D will be through Router 2. Thus, Router 3 and Router 4 will forward packets through Router 2 for Network D. AS 2 will use the connection between Router 3 and Router 5 only if a failure occurs at Router 1 or Router 2.

The BGP Path Selection Process

BGP uses a hierarchical process to evaluate multiple sources for the same network prefix. This process determines the best source path to use in reaching a given network prefix. BGP 4 can support multiple parallel paths that have the same path parameters. If the BGP speaker is configured to support multiple paths, the router will load balance connections across all paths. The selection process evaluates the neighbor advertising a route and the AS path attributes for a particular network prefix to determine the best path to use in the local routing table and the forwarding database.

This process is outlined in Table 10.6 with a brief explanation of the decision criteria used at each step, as well as the analysis performed by the BGP system. The variables involved in this process, and their use, was explained in the previous section. The selection process flows from one step to the next to determine the best value for a given parameter. The selection process can exit at any point to determine the best path.

Table 10.6 BGP Path Selection Process

Path Selection Step	Path Selection Criteria
1. Next Hop Comparison	Next hop destination must be reachable from the local routing table.
2. Synchronization Comparison	If synchronization is enabled, the route must be in the IGP. This applies only to IBGP derived routes.
3. Weight Comparison	Highest value is better.
4. Local Preference Comparison	Highest value is better.
5. Local Origination Comparison	Prefer routes that are locally originated with the **network** *n.n.n.n* or **aggregate** *n.n.n.n* BGP commands to IGP redistribution.
6. AS Path Comparison	Prefer the fewest number of AS hops (AS_PATH).
7. Origin Comparison	Prefer the route with the best origin type. Order of preference: 1 – IGP 2 – EGP 3 – Incomplete

Continued

Table 10.6 Continued

Path Selection Step	Path Selection Criteria
8. Multiexit Discriminator Comparison	Select the path with the lowest MED value. This applies only when the neighboring AS is the same, that is, two connections between different ASs.
9. BGP Source Comparison	Select an EBGP path versus an IBGP path. Select confederation EBGP versus confederation IBGP.
10. IGP Metric to Next_Hop Comparison	Select the shortest IGP path to the BGP NEXT_HOP (lowest IGP metric).
11. BGP Multipath support	"N" paths will be installed for load balancing if this feature is enabled. The paths are external and originate from the same AS.
12. ROUTER_ID Comparison	Select the path from the BGP speaker with the highest ROUTER_ID value.

BGP Path Selection Example

The best way to understand the BGP path selection process is to use an actual BGP network prefix and follow the decision process used to determine the best path. For example, we can look at a screen capture from the BGP speaker "route-server.cerf.net" and follow the path selection process for the network prefix 208.188.42.0 (see Figure 10.15). We will need to refer back to Figure 10.11 to see the parameters for this BGP speaker and the BGP neighbors. Figure 10.16 depicts the routing table to the NEXT_HOP sources for this network prefix. Table 10.7 lists all path selection values from the four sources of this network prefix, and identifies the best path selected.

Figure 10.15 gives the AS_PATH, origin, IGP metric value, local preference value, NEXT_HOP identifier, ROUTER_ID, and the path that this router believes is the best source. The BGP speaker sees the network 208.188.42.0 as a supernet of 208.188.0.0. As discussed in the CIDR sidebar, a supernet is several consecutively numbered networks that are advertised as a CIDR block using a network and mask. In this case, the network is 208.188.0.0 and the mask is 255.255.192.0, or, in CIDR terminology, this is a /18 block of addresses.

Table 10.7 BGP Path Selection Process for 208.188.0.0

Path Selection Step	Source 134.24.88.55	Source 198.32.176.25	Source 192.41.177.69	Source 192.157.69.5	Evaluation Result
1. Next_Hop Comparison	Reachable	Reachable	Reachable	Reachable	All reachable via static routes (Fig. 10.16)
2. Synchronization Comparison	N/A	N/A	N/A	N/A	N/A with EBGP
3. Weight Comparison	N/A	N/A	N/A	N/A	None (Fig. 10.11)
4. Local Preference Comparison	100	100	100	100	All equal (Fig. 10.15)
5. Local Origination Comparison	IGP	IGP	IGP	IGP	All equal (Fig. 10.15)
6. AS Path Comparison	1740 2548 7132	1740 2548 7132	1740 2548 7132	1740 2548 7132	All have 3 AS hops (Fig. 10.15)
7. Origin Comparison	IGP	IGP	IGP	IGP	All equal (Fig. 10.15)
8. Multiexit Discriminator Comparison	N/A	N/A	N/A	N/A	None (Fig. 10.15)
9. BGP Source Comparison	EBGP	EBGP	EBGP	EBGP	All equal (Fig. 10.15)

Continued

Table 10.7 Continued

Path Selection Step	Source 134.24.88.55	Source 198.32.176.25	Source 192.41.177.69	Source 192.157.69.5	Evaluation Result
10. IGP Metric to Next_Hop Comparison	0	0	0	0	All equal (Fig. 10.16)
11. BGP Multipath Support	N/A	N/A	N/A	N/A	None (Fig. 10.11)
12. ROUTER_ID Comparison	134.24.88.55	198.32.176.25	192.41.177.69	192.157.69.5	Largest ID 198.32.176.25 (Fig. 10.15)
Best Path		*			

Figure 10.15 BGP Route Information for 208.188.42.0

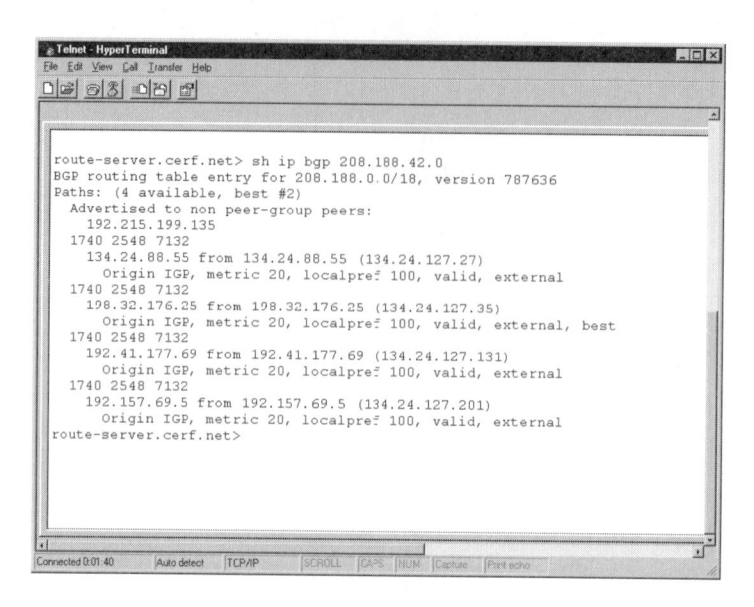

```
route-server.cerf.net> sh ip bgp 208.188.42.0
BGP routing table entry for 208.188.0.0/18, version 787636
Paths: (4 available, best #2)
  Advertised to non peer-group peers:
    192.215.199.135
  1740 2548 7132
    134.24.88.55 from 134.24.88.55 (134.24.127.27)
      Origin IGP, metric 20, localpref 100, valid, external
  1740 2548 7132
    198.32.176.25 from 198.32.176.25 (134.24.127.35)
      Origin IGP, metric 20, localpref 100, valid, external, best
  1740 2548 7132
    192.41.177.69 from 192.41.177.69 (134.24.127.131)
      Origin IGP, metric 20, localpref 100, valid, external
  1740 2548 7132
    192.157.69.5 from 192.157.69.5 (134.24.127.201)
      Origin IGP, metric 20, localpref 100, valid, external
route-server.cerf.net>
```

Figure 10.16 Routing Table Entry for NEXT_HOP Sources for 208.188.42.0

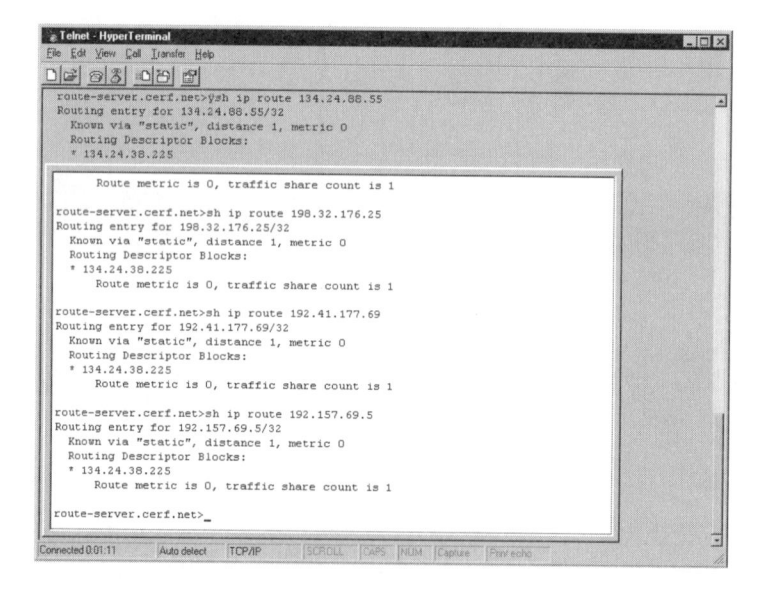

```
route-server.cerf.net>sh ip route 134.24.88.55
Routing entry for 134.24.88.55/32
  Known via "static", distance 1, metric 0
  Routing Descriptor Blocks:
  * 134.24.38.225
      Route metric is 0, traffic share count is 1
route-server.cerf.net>sh ip route 198.32.176.25
Routing entry for 198.32.176.25/32
  Known via "static", distance 1, metric 0
  Routing Descriptor Blocks:
  * 134.24.38.225
      Route metric is 0, traffic share count is 1
route-server.cerf.net>sh ip route 192.41.177.69
Routing entry for 192.41.177.69/32
  Known via "static", distance 1, metric 0
  Routing Descriptor Blocks:
  * 134.24.38.225
      Route metric is 0, traffic share count is 1
route-server.cerf.net>sh ip route 192.157.69.5
Routing entry for 192.157.69.5/32
  Known via "static", distance 1, metric 0
  Routing Descriptor Blocks:
  * 134.24.38.225
      Route metric is 0, traffic share count is 1
route-server.cerf.net>
```

Figure 10.16 depicts the routing information used to reach the NEXT_HOP sources for the network 208.188.0.0. In this case, we can use router 134.24.88.25, 198.32.176.25, 192.41.177.69, or 192.157.69.5 to get to the network 208.188.0.0. The route to all sources is known via static IP routing, and all metrics are identical.

Following the path selection process for the network prefix 208.188.0.0, we find that all selection parameters are identical among the four BGP speakers except for the ROUTER_ID. In this case, the ROUTER_ID 198.32.176.25 is the highest value and thus the best path to use for forwarding packets. Figure 10.17 confirms the next-hop forwarding destination for packets destined for the network 208.188.0.0 /18.

Figure 10.17 Routing Table Entry for 208.188.42.0

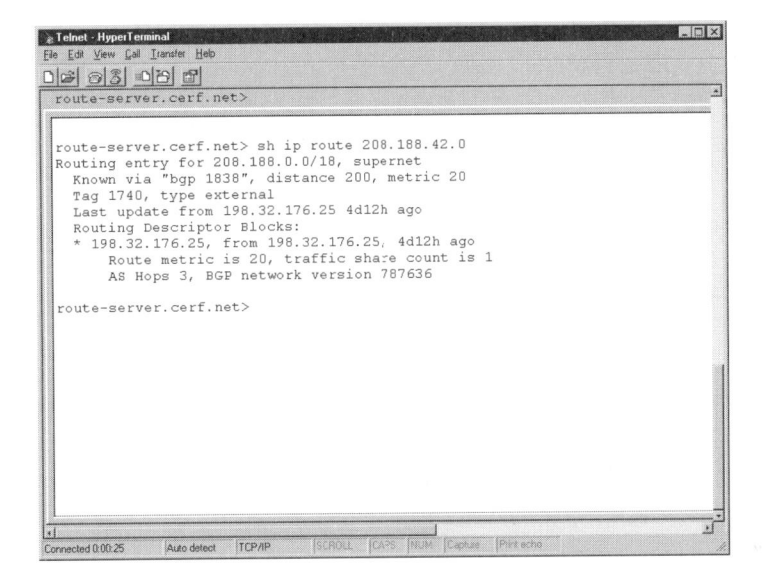

```
route-server.cerf.net> sh ip route 208.188.42.0
Routing entry for 208.188.0.0/18, supernet
  Known via "bgp 1838", distance 200, metric 20
  Tag 1740, type external
  Last update from 198.32.176.25 4d12h ago
  Routing Descriptor Blocks:
  * 198.32.176.25, from 198.32.176.25, 4d12h ago
      Route metric is 20, traffic share count is 1
      AS Hops 3, BGP network version 787636

route-server.cerf.net>
```

Figure 10.17 depicts the information as it appears in the IP routing table, which will be used to develop the forwarding information to advertise to other BGP speakers. It also depicts the router 198.32.176.25 as the next hop along the IP path to reach 208.188.0.0/18 IP addresses.

Internet Information Sources for External BGP and the Internet

There are several relevant sources of information that can be accessed by anyone connected to the Internet.

www.rsng.net This is the location of the Route Server Next Generation Project (RSng), which has a wealth of information

Continued

about the evolution from the NFSNET and the Routing Arbiter Project.

www.mae.net This location has everything you want to know about the MAE Internet Exchange Points operated by MCI Worldcom.

http://nanog.org This is the North American Network Operators Group site, which serves as a link between the academic community and technical communities.

http://nitrous.digex.net/mae/mae-lg.html This link provides a Web-enabled link to get BGP information from the MAE East Looking Glass server.

Also, there are several route servers available for general information about Internet routes and BGP tables. These servers are essentially Cisco routers running standard IOS that allow user access without a logging on, and they permit the user to issue a subset of available commands. Simply Telnet to one of the following route servers and issue an IOS command.

```
route-server.ip.att.net
route-views.oregon-ix.net
route-server-eu.exodus.net
route-server.cerf.net
route-server.exodus.net
```

Redistributing BGP into Your IGP

BGP was developed to handle large numbers of routes. This feature remedied the IGP limitations in relation to large databases. Therefore, we should be extremely cautious about redistributing any BGP derived routes into an IGP. The backbone of the Internet has over 90,000 routing entries. If we have a BGP peering session with an ISP, the ISP will send all, or a subset, of the complete Internet BGP table. Furthermore, we can ask our ISP to inject a default route for us to use in making our routing policies.

We should never consider redistributing a complete BGP table into an IGP of any sort. Doing this will lead to network instability and an IGP that will probably never converge in a failure. Also, it is unlikely that the resources are available to upgrade the processor and memory on every router in the IGP to accommodate this policy. It is always best to try to make all IP routing work using the simplest method possible. One method is to use only a default route to attract traffic out of an AS. To make this work effectively, you must have a well-thought-out IP network plan that summarizes IP address space from the access layer up to the core network layer. A thorough network plan that summarizes IP network prefixes along these boundaries provides the flexibility needed for implementation, and avoids instability associated with IGPs and large IP databases. Finally, the plan and routing policy should be flexible enough to allow for exceptions. An exception can be described as a network prefix that is not located in an area where it can be summarized into a CIDR block.

Redistributing the Default Route

We should use the default network like a magnet to attract IP traffic out of an AS. A routing policy that injects only a default network "0.0.0.0" limits the routing table size and makes trouble-shooting somewhat easier. Trouble-shooting is easier in that we know that the IP traffic should always flow towards the autonomous system boundary router (ASBR) for destinations that are not within the AS. The IGP used within an AS must also support classless routing; otherwise, we may need to inject a network default for the major net of our IP address space, for example, 172.20.0.0 for a Class B, or 10.0.0.0 for a Class A. This can be turned on in the Cisco IOS by using the exec command **IP Classless** on every router in the network.

Figure 10.18 gives a graphical representation of a typical IP routing policy for injecting a default route and summarizing an IP network towards the Internet that uses both public and private ASs. In this example, Router 1 sends to Router 2 via EBGP a complete Internet IP database and a default route of 0.0.0.0. This means that Router 2 must have the processing power and memory to handle a complete Internet BGP database to avoid network failure. Router 2 sends to Router 1 only the CIDR block 208.188.0.0/16 that resides within or beyond AS 10001, and strips off all private ASs in the AS_PATH. This is a Cisco unique feature that enables the public AS to serve as a proxy advertisement to the Internet for all private AS networks that reside behind the public AS.

Router 2 then advertises via EBGP to Routers 3 and 4 a default route only. Router 3 and Router 4 will advertise via EBGP to Router 2 the network prefixes that they can reach. In this case, Router 3 advertises the network 208.188.0.0/17, and Router 4 advertises the Network 208.188.128.0/17. They will also advertise these prefixes to each other. Assuming BGP synchronization is disabled, we do not need to redistribute the network prefixes 208.188.0.0/17 or 208.188.128.0/17 into the OSPF 1 process. Synchronization is discussed in detail in the next section. Therefore, the OSPF 1 database contains only the NEXT_HOP routing information necessary for IBGP.

Figure 10.18 Redistribution Plan

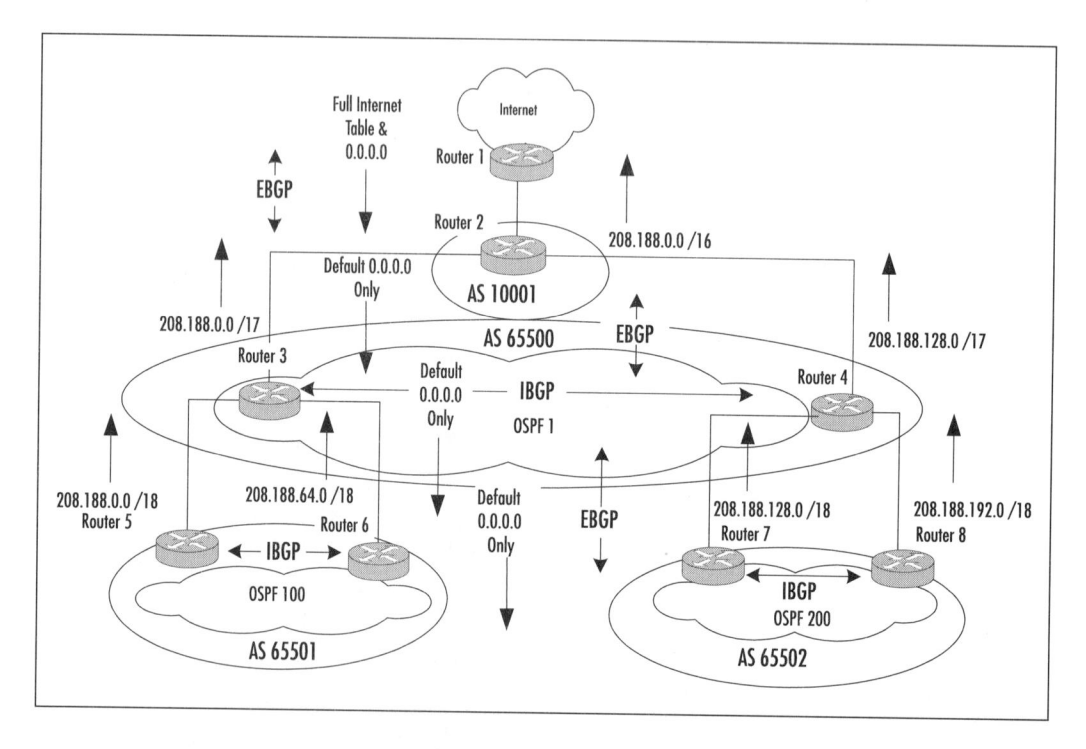

Routers 3 and 4 now advertise to Router 5, Router 6, Router 7, and Router 8 a default network. If desired, these routers can also advertise one another's network prefixes into the neighboring ASs. However, Figure 10.18 does not depict this scenario. Router 5, Router 6, Router 7, and Router 8 will advertise to Router 3 and Router 4 their respective network prefixes. Thus, we can see how advertising only a default network into an AS, and summarizing network prefixes into CIDR blocks, works in an ideal network.

BGP Synchronization

BGP synchronization applies only to IBGP network configurations, and it is enabled by default in the Cisco IOS. If you want to disable this feature, you should have a clear understanding of the routing policy for the network. Synchronization prevents an AS from flooding network prefix information to an external AS where no route exists within the IGP for the prefix in question. Therefore, routes learned via IBGP are not advertised to EBGP neighbors unless a corresponding prefix also exists within the IGP. The primary reason for this feature is depicted in Figure 10.19.

Figure 10.19 Synchronization and IBGP

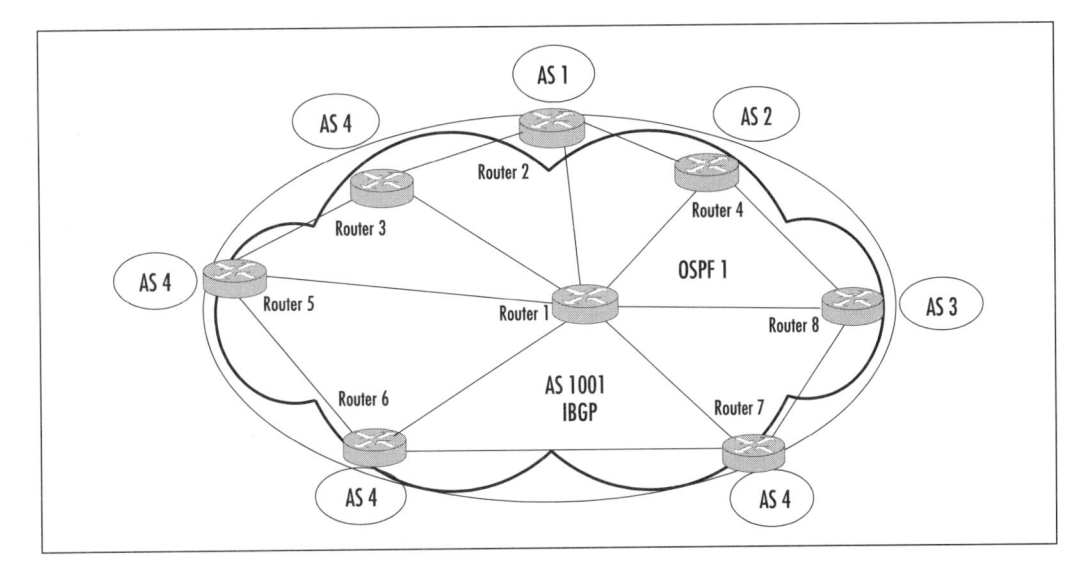

In this diagram, you can see that Router 1 is in the middle of the network and is not running a BGP process. Thus, if we disable synchronization on all IBGP routers, they will pass along the network prefixes that each learns from its neighboring AS, even though there is no route in the IGP. Connections will fail in this configuration, because Router 1 will discard the packets. To avoid this problem, do not use a topology that looks like Figure 10.19. An alternative to this would be either to have each router connect to three IBGP neighbors, or to enable synchronization and redistribute the network prefixes into the IGP.

Defining Internal BGP, Route Reflectors, and Confederations

We have touched on several aspects of Internal BGP (IBGP) in the preceding sections. IBGP is not a separate BGP process that you enable on a BGP speaker. Instead, IBGP is the term used to refer to all BGP speakers within the same AS. Since all BGP speakers are under the same administrative authority and are running a common IGP, we use the term IBGP to refer to the relationship each speaker has with the others. IBGP requires a full mesh of peering, which may become difficult to manage in a large network. Cisco provides two features to resolve the complexities of a full BGP mesh. These features operate by either grouping a collection of routers with common policies into a common AS using a Route Reflector (RR) and Route Reflector Client (RRC) configuration, or by establishing a Confederation among all BGP speakers in the AS.

Internal BGP

Internal BGP (IBGP) is the term given to BGP speakers within the same AS. IBGP requires that all BGP speakers in an AS share the same information regarding network prefixes that reside within the AS, and regarding network prefixes learned from neighboring ASs. Furthermore, a BGP speaker will not pass information it learns from IBGP to an EBGP neighbor unless a corresponding prefix exists in the IGP database. This is called synchronization and was discussed in the previous section.

Route Reflectors

We can use Route Reflectors (RR) in a network to assist with the full mesh peering required with IBGP. This concept involves grouping BGP speakers into logical clusters or groups. You should plan your groups along a hierarchical boundary, and this hierarchy should follow the physical topology. If it does not, routing loops can occur because of conflicting information. Therefore, you need to pay close attention to how the Route Reflector Clients (RRC) will get information from the Route Reflectors. We can think of this as a consistent information flow from the RRs down to the RRCs. In all cases, consider the redundant links in the network as both an asset and a problem.

Figure 10.20 depicts an IBGP network with twelve routers. The full mesh rule indicates that each of these BGP speakers will have eleven neighbors. In this diagram, there are two peer groups that are each served by two Route Reflectors. The four Route Reflectors have a full mesh peering to ensure consistent information by all RRs. In this case, we are using OSPF as the IGP, and the Route Reflector sessions follow the physical topology. Thus, Routers 3 to 6 have a connection to Router 1 and Router 2, and Routers 9 to 12 have a connection to Router 7 and Router 8.

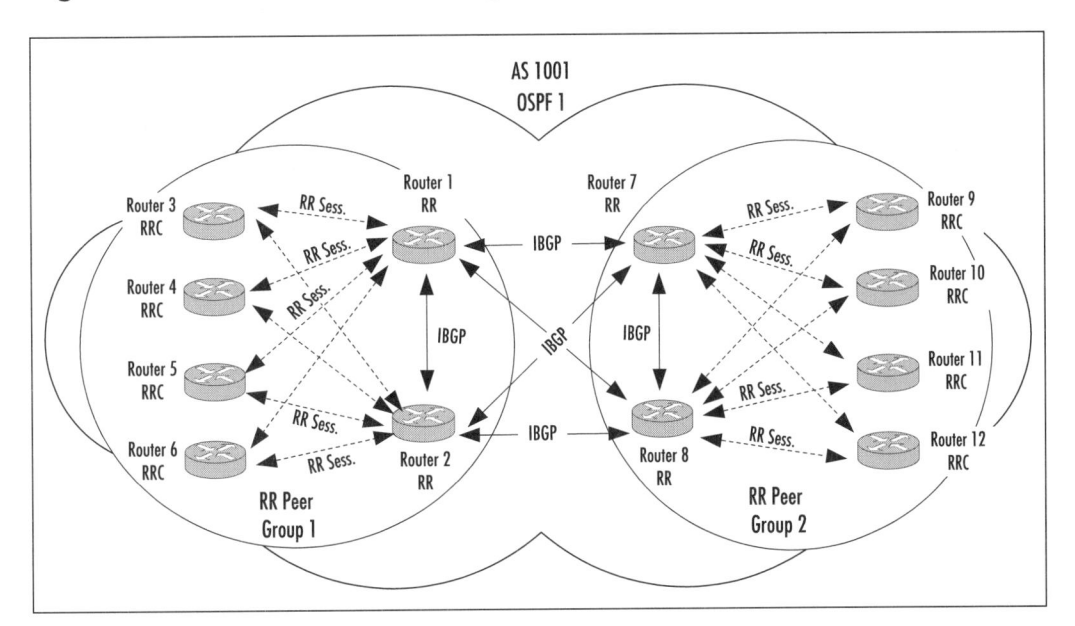

Figure 10.20 Route Reflector Design and Function

Confederations

Confederations are used like Route Reflectors to solve the problem of full meshing within a large AS. However, a BGP Confederation does not have the physical topology requirements that exist with Route Reflectors. Confederations divide an AS into subASs and reduce the IBGP peering sessions of each BGP speaker to a manageable number. Within each subAS, a full mesh of IBGP peering is required, and the subAS appears as another AS within the BGP Confederation. The outside world will not see the subASs that reside within the BGP Confederation in the AS_PATH information of a network prefix. Thus, to the outside world, a Confederation is seen as one AS. For this reason, we can implement private AS numbers fairly easily within the Confederation, and use a public registered AS for peering with the Internet or other corporations. The outside world will see only a public AS in the AS_PATH information for all network prefixes that originate from within the Confederation.

The subASs communicate using EBGP peering sessions. However, routing within the Confederation behaves like IBGP, since the NEXT_HOP, MED, and LOCAL_PREF values are preserved when crossing a subAS boundary. It should be noted that migrating from a non-BGP Confederation configuration to a Confederation network requires major reconfiguration. Therefore, the implementation should be carefully planned in an existing BGP network. Also, routing through the Confederation often takes less than optimal network paths. Therefore, you should make a careful review of the IP flow through the network and perhaps set some BGP policies to prevent this situation.

Figure 10.21 depicts a simple Confederation configuration. In this example, AS 1001 is split into two subASs, namely, AS 65500 and AS 65501, respectively. Routing within AS 65500 and AS 65501 follows the rules of IBGP with a full mesh. Since the NEXT_HOP value is not modified between subASs, the IGP must provide an appropriate route. With this network, we have two peering connections to the Internet via a single Service Provider (SP). In the future, we can add connections to a different SP using Router 2 and Router 8. We would then have SP redundancy to the Internet.

Figure 10.21 Confederation Design and Function

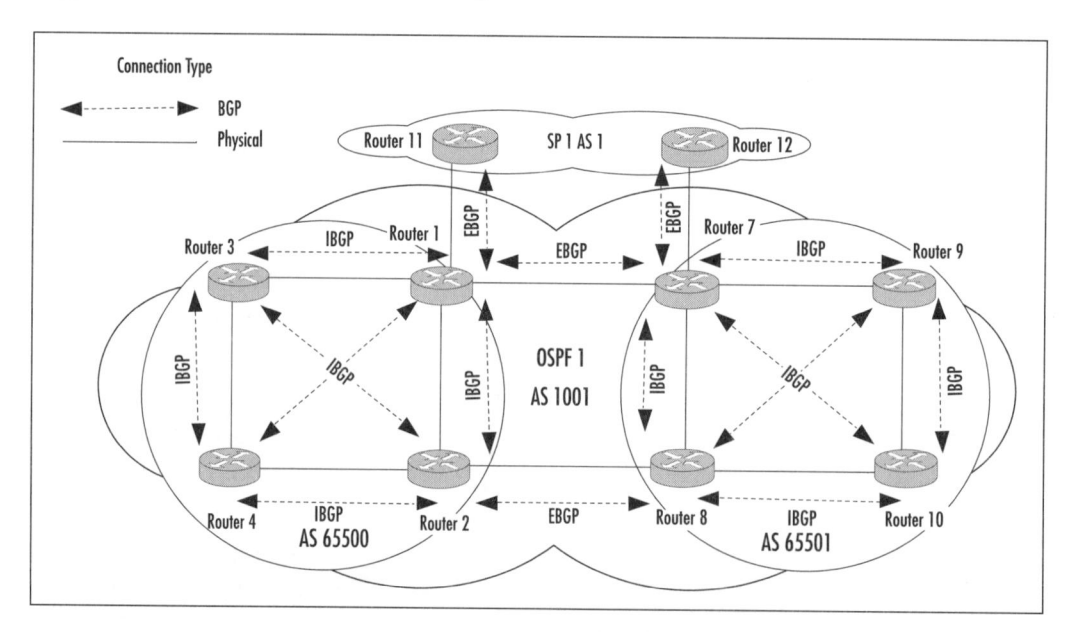

Advanced BGP Network Design

In this section, we discuss some of the advanced BGP design topics. There is no real magic about these topics, but some of the design concepts require thinking through the IP address structure and how the various address blocks appear to the different parts of the network. The key topic we discuss is redundancy in the network from the access LAN to the Internet point of presence (POP). We will also identify some common design methodologies used in redundant and high availability networks.

Building Network Redundancy

Network redundancy is the primary item that can either cause a network to run effectively or lead to numerous problems. The key is to keep the configuration simple by providing a stable physical topology and a stable software configuration. Your goal in building redundancy is not to see how complex a network you can build. The goal is to build a high availability data network that will provide the 99.999 per cent up time experienced with other networks. Remember, problems will occur and you will be trouble-shooting the problems quickly. You should also be aware of the weak points of the network design. Furthermore, we always put a lot of effort into designing the physical layer redundancy, but often forget the software components. To address this problem, ask yourself the following questions:

- Have you ever experienced a problem in your network after upgrading the network software?

- Have you ever had an IP routing problem that affected the entire network?

- Have you ever had an IP routing problem that rendered the redundancy useless?

Keeping these issues in mind will help you formulate a stable software design that prevents user problems and provides the high availability network your customers want. Also, remember that each time we raise the service level in the network, our customers also raise their service expectations. Figure 10.22 depicts a typical redundant network configuration involving dual Internet connections, multiple BGP ASs, physical redundancy, and a means to get software redundancy. This figure depicts two BGP peering connections using a public AS of 1001. In this example, AS 1001 serves as a proxy AS for the private ASs located within the network. To accomplish this, Router 3 and Router 4 will strip the private AS information from the AS path of all network prefixes located in AS 65000, AS 65001, AS 65501, and AS 65502 before advertising them to Router 1 and Router 2. Furthermore, AS 1001 is a transit AS in relation to AS 65000, AS 65001, and the Internet.

The routing policy that we enforce will determine whether AS 1001 will serve as a transit AS between AS 65000 and AS 65001. Since these two ASs have a direct EBGP link between Router 6 and Router 7, it is preferred that the transit functions between these ASs occur at this level instead of at the Internet Peering layer. Direct EBGP connections at the Core layer between all Core routers may be cost prohibitive. In this case, AS 1001 could provide the redundant connection between AS 6500 and AS 65001.

The Distribution layer gains its redundancy through cross connects to the Core layer networks. In this example, we see AS 65501 connected to both AS 65000 and AS 65001. Also, AS 65502 has connectivity to both AS 65000 and AS 65001. These are two examples of multihomed ASs connecting to different service providers. Interconnecting the Distribution layers will add additional redundancy, but it will also add a tremendous amount of complexity to the network configuration.

The Access layer has redundancy in the form of two routers and two circuits. Although not depicted here, we could also have redundancy in the LAN segment electronics and dual cabling to the workstations. As well, the circuits depicted could be leaving the building via a separate path to a different serving central office (CO).

Finally, we need to evaluate our software redundancy requirements in regards to an acceptable failure domain. In this example, you can see that it would be very easy to run different software versions in the Core layer, and that we have a different instance of an IGP and BGP on the two ASs. We could push this separation down to the LAN segment with some creative solutions. However, this would add a degree of complexity, would be more difficult to manage, and might have more redundancy than necessary.

Figure 10.22 Redundant BGP Design

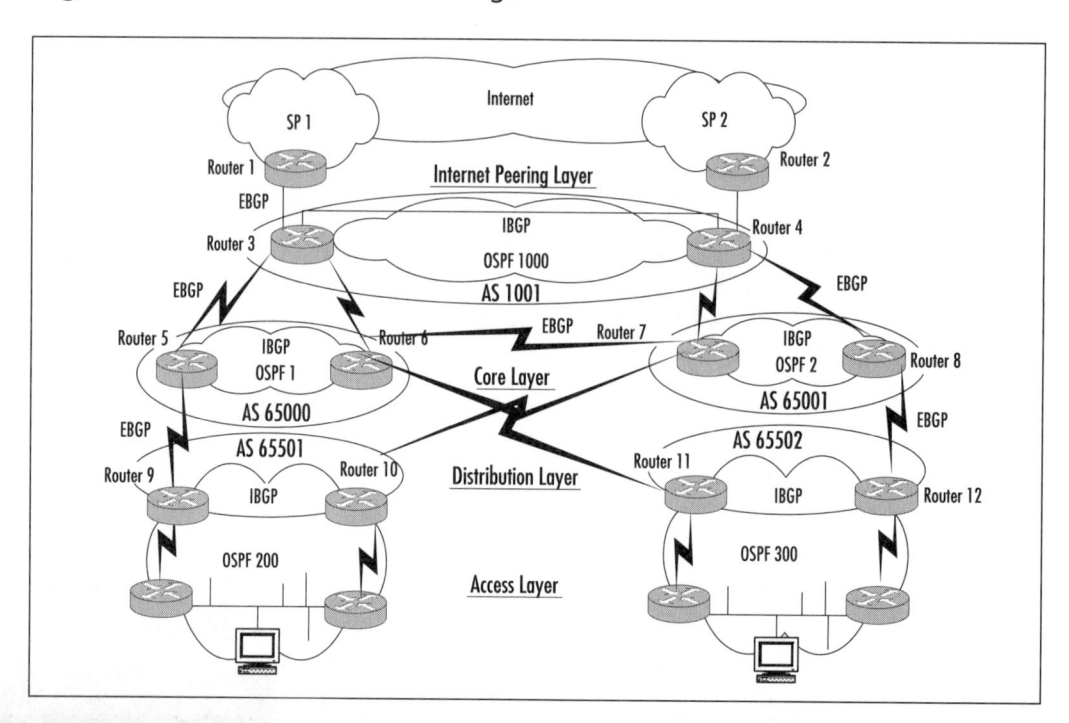

Common Design Methodologies

The methodologies for designing a BGP 4 network follow the guidelines for building a stable IGP network. Thus, BGP 4 demands as much attention to detail for a stable network design as is required for a stable IGP design. After all, we also use an IGP within the AS to carry the next hop routing information.

- Avoid single points of failure throughout the network.
    - Evaluate geographic failure zones.
    - Evaluate power sources.
    - Consider alternate service providers.
    - Evaluate the service level that is expected and funded.
- Carefully plan the IP network CIDR boundaries down to the lowest summarization level.
- Always plan for optimum IP network summarization along CIDR boundaries.
- Use a physical layer hierarchy that supports the network address summarization plans.
- Do not use backdoor connections between access layer segments.
- Use BGP 4 to solve the scaling problems of an IGP; you cannot use it in place of an IGP.
- Use Route Reflectors or Confederations to assist full mesh peering if necessary within an AS. Route Reflectors must follow the physical topology path or routing loops will occur.
- Design EBGP connections around stable network connections.
- Use a loopback interface for peering between IBGP neighbors. Loopback interfaces will not go down because of a link failure.
- Try to build a redundant network that facilitates software redundancy.
    - Can the software version on one side of the network be different for a transition period?
    - Will an IGP failure affect the entire network?
- Plan for multiple Internet connections to different ISPs. Even if you do not need them now, a future project will likely demand this service level.

Summary

In this chapter, we discussed the fundamentals of EGP and the improvements that eventually brought about the existence of BGP 4 as we know it today. We saw the limitations presented by EGP, and how creative solutions were developed to solve some of these problems. We learned how the CIDR capabilities of BGP 4 help slow down the logarithmic growth in Internet database sizes.

Also, we discussed in detail the four types of BGP messages and how they are used to exchange information about the BGP session. We learned the process that BGP speakers use to establish the BGP session, and how the Finite State Machine maintains the BGP session.

We discussed the various aspects of EBGP and IBGP and how they work in harmony with each other. We also discussed the various options for full mesh IBGP peering. Thus, we learned that Route Reflectors and Confederations are both solutions to the IBGP full mesh problem. We identified the limitations of these configurations and the key components that cannot be eliminated.

Finally, we discussed advanced design issues, building redundant networks, and some common design methodologies. This information provides a sound foundation for the next chapter, which covers the specifics of BGP configuration. If you need additional information, the References sidebar lists several sources for further study and investigation. Also, you should review the RFCs on BGP and understand the functionality that they specify, before starting a network configuration. This resource is unfortunately often the last place we look for answers. Be proactive and read the RFCs first to avoid misunderstanding the capabilities of the protocol.

References for Further Study

RFC 1771, "A Border Gateway Protocol 4 (BGP-4),"
www.faqs.org/rfcs/rfc1771.html

RFC 1772, "Application of the Border Gateway Protocol in the Internet," www.faqs.org/rfcs/rfc1772.html

RFC 1654, "A Border Gateway Protocol 4,"
www.faqs.org/rfcs/rfc1654.html

Continued

RFC 1267, "A Border Gateway Protocol 3 (BGP-3),"
www.faqs.org/rfcs/rfc1267.html

RFC 1092, "EGP and Policy Based Routing in the New NSFNET Backbone," www.faqs.org/rfcs/rfc1092.html

RFC 1519, "Classless Inter-Domain Routing (CIDR): an Address Assignment and Aggregation Strategy," www.faqs.org/rfcs/rfc1519.html

RFC 904, "Exterior Gateway Protocol Formal Specification," www.faqs.org/rfcs/rfc904.html

Halabi, Sam. Internet Routing Architectures, Second Edition

Raza, Khalid. Large-Scale IP Network Solutions

Cisco Documentation. "Border Gateway Protocol," www.cisco.com/univercd/cc/td/doc/cisintwk/ito_doc/bgp.htm

Cisco Systems Technical Notes. "BGP Best Path Selection Algorithm," www.cisco.com/warp/public/459/25.shtml

Ferguson, Paul. "Introduction to the Border Gateway Protocol (BGP)," www.academ.com/nanog/feb1997/BGPTutorial/index.htm

FAQs

Visit **www.syngress.com/solutions** to have your questions about this chapter answered by the author.

Q: A network prefix is in the BGP table, and not in the routing table, in a transit AS network running OSPF as the IGP. What is happening?

A: This is probably a BGP synchronization problem. Synchronization is on by default in Cisco IOS software. In this case, there must be a match for the prefix in the IP routing table to consider an internal BGP (IBGP) as a valid path. If the matching route is learned from an OSPF neighbor, its OSPF router ID must also match the BGP router ID of the IBGP neighbor. This might be a case where you should disable synchronization using the **no synchronization** BGP subcommand, or check to see that the BGP router ID and the OSPF router ID match.

Q: Since BGP is a "hop-by-hop" protocol, does this mean that BGP uses hop count to determine the best path?

A: No, BGP uses the AS path length as one selection criteria, and the shortest AS path is usually selected as the best route. However, there are other factors in path selection that could override this variable. In any case, this is not the same as an IGP's hop count metric, and it is not the sole means for determining the best path for a given network.

Q: Has all routing information been exchanged once the BGP session indicates a status of "established?"

A: The answer is no. The exchange of routing information cannot occur until both BGP neighbors agree on all parameters. At this point, the session is established and both peers exchange the complete BGP table.

Q: Can an EBGP neighbor be located farther away than a connected interface? In other words, I cannot connect to a local interface on two EBGP neighbors. Is this a valid configuration?

A: The answer is yes. However, you must configure BGP multihop on both EBGP neighbors. Although this configuration works, it is not preferred since there are IGP problems that can lead to BGP instability and connectivity problems.

Q: How do you handle CIDR routing situations where a network within the CIDR block is located in a different geographical location than the CIDR block? Does this section have to be readdressed?

A: The answer is that you have to inject a longer prefix for the exception network. The rule of IP routing is that the longest prefix, or the most bits identifying the network, will always override the shorter prefix of a CIDR block. Also, remember to establish a routing "bit bucket" at the location generating the CIDR advertisement. The "bit bucket" is created with a static route for the CIDR block that points it to a Null Interface. If the corporate policy is to minimize routing tables with CIDR, then the exception group should be readdressed to follow the policies. Otherwise, one exception leads to two or three, and eventually, you end up with a network of exceptions.

Chapter 11

Configuring Border Gateway Protocol

Solutions in this chapter:

- Relevant RFCs
- Enabling BGP Routing
- Configuring EBGP Neighbors
- Configuring IBGP Neighbors
- Configuring Route Reflectors
- Configuring Confederations
- Weight, MED, LOCAL PREF, and Other Advanced Options

Introduction

Many highly skilled network engineers who are completely confident trying out new features with ISDN, Frame Relay, EIGRP, OSPF, and so forth are intimidated by the complexity of BGP. However, although advanced BGP configurations on the Internet backbone can be extremely complex, the basic setup of BGP for the majority of enterprise and small provider environments is really not that complicated.

In this chapter, we show you some of the most common configurations for forming basic BGP neighbor relationships, influencing route selection, and redistributing certain BGP routes into your IGP. This will give you the skill and confidence to properly configure BGP, even including some of the more advanced options.

This chapter does not delve into the more advanced configurations on the Internet backbone. For configurations not discussed in this chapter, an excellent resource is Cisco's Web site (www.cisco.com).

Relevant RFCs

The following bulleted items are Internet Request For Comments (RFCs) documents that describe most of the important policies and protocols concerning the Border Gateway Protocol (BGP).

- **RFC 1403** BGP OSPF Interaction
- **RFC 1657** Definitions of Managed Objects in BGPv4
- **RFC 1745** BGPv4/IDRP for IP—OSPF Interaction
- **RFC 1771** A Border Gateway Protocol 4 (BGPv4)
- **RFC 1772** Application of BGP in the Internet
- **RFC 1965** Autonomous System Confederations for BGP
- **RFC 1966** BGP Route Reflection
- **RFC 1997** BGP Communities Attribute
- **RFC 2283** Multiprotocol Extensions for BGP (MBGP)
- **RFC 2385** Protection of BGP sessions via the TCP MD5 Signature Option

- **RFC 2439** BGP Route Flap Dampening
- **RFC 2545** Use of BGPv4 Multiprotocol Extensions for IPv6 Interdomain Routing

Before we begin our discussion of BGPv4, let us review a very important issue concerning how BGP works. When a routing table lookup is executed for a particular destination address, BGP informs us that to get to that particular destination address, we must go to the next-hop address. Then, a second (or "recursive") routing table lookup must be performed in order to determine if this next-hop address is reachable. If the next-hop address is not reachable, BGP will be broken.

Enabling BGP Routing

We begin our discussion of configuring BGP with a simple configuration that leads us through some basic configuration commands. After we have mastered simple configurations, we will move on to more complex examples and configurations.

Before we can start configuring BGP, we need to gather some fundamental information about the task at hand and make some basic decisions that demonstrate the differences between external BGP (EBGP) and internal BGP (IBGP) speakers.

The fundamental information that we will need for each router is as follows:

- Connected interfaces and their IP addresses
- Loopback interfaces and their IP addresses
- Interior Gateway Protocols (IGP) and their associated AS or process IDs (such as EIGRP and OSPF) that are to be redistributed into BGP

Basic decisions that we need to make that demonstrate the differences between EBGP speakers and IBGP speakers include what interface and IP address we will use to establish BGP neighbor relationships:

- What AS numbers will be used for configuring BGP
- What IP addresses will be used for configuring BGP
    - For EBGP neighbors, use the IP address of the directly connected interface. The use of loopback interfaces, or the ebgp-multihop command, is not recommended for EBGP as this could cause suboptimal routing when there are multiple paths to the loopback interface.
    - For IBGP neighbors, use the IP address of a loopback interface configured on the routers.

When configuring BGP for a network that is not connected to the Internet, the BGP AS number can be completely arbitrary within the accepted range (1 to 65535). The same is true when connecting two networks that are also not connected to the Internet. However, it is recommended to use the private AS number range to avoid any conflicts or configuration issues in the future.

If a network is serving as a transit network between two public ASs, we must either use a public AS number or ensure that the respective upstream ASs strip the private AS number or numbers before communicating with the Internet.

An example of stripping private AS numbers from the AS_Path will be given later in this chapter.

The IP address selection is recommended because most EBGP relationships are dependent on directly connected interfaces; thus, the IP address of the adjacent router interface involved in the connection is used to configure the neighbor relationship. Most IBGP routers will probably have redundant connections, so they can benefit from not having to depend on the status of a single physical interface to maintain their neighbor relationships.

Defining BGP for an Autonomous System

In order to configure BGP, we must examine the topology of our network and determine how many autonomous systems we need. This process is usually straightforward, in that each autonomous system should correspond to a network with a different administrative entity.

If we are interconnecting three different networks from three different companies, we may want to have three different autonomous systems.

If we then connect those three networks to the Internet, we could create another AS using a publicly registered AS number, rather than having to obtain three different public AS numbers. We, or our Service Provider, would strip the private AS numbers from the AS_Path so that we could connect to the Internet.

BGP autonomous system numbers are distinct from the autonomous system numbers of Interior Gateway Protocols (IGP), such as EIGRP, or the area numbers of OSPF. There are no intended relationships between IGP autonomous system numbers and EGP autonomous system numbers. Whether you use the same number values for your BGP ASs, your OSPF areas, or EIGRP ASs is completely arbitrary.

For example, consider the case where Company A takes over Company B and needs to connect the networks of the two companies (see Figure 11.1). We have added a new router to each company's core site, Router 1 and Router 2, respectively, in order to connect the two networks. The private IP addresses (172.168.x.x) are already in use by each respective company.

Figure 11.1 Network Configuration Example

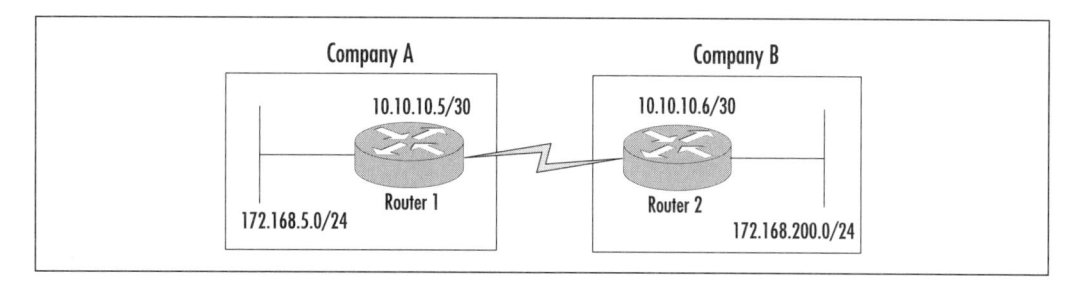

We have decided to use the 10.x.x.x private IP address with a 30-bit mask (a mask commonly used for point-to-point connections) to configure the two serial interfaces of Router 1 and Router 2. Since we are going to configure EBGP between the two networks, we will use the IP addresses of the directly connected interfaces.

Company A is using EIGRP as the IGP with EIGRP AS number 1 within its network, whereas Company 2 is using EIGRP as the IGP with EIGRP AS number 2 within its network.

Before we select the AS number for our local network, we need to discuss two other issues: how to define the remote AS, and whether we should use a public AS number or a private AS number.

Defining the Remote AS

The remote AS number will often be defined by the administrative entity whose network you are connecting to. When connecting networks, make sure that the AS numbers, if there are several, are unique within the resulting connected network. Any duplicate AS numbers should be removed.

In this example, we will define two private BGP autonomous systems (AS)—one for each company. The reason we have decided to use two AS networks is to maintain the distinctness of each network while providing connectivity and enhancing manageability.

The interconnecting routers between the two AS networks will be running EBGP. This will provide a new level of stability and administration to our network. It will also assist us in isolating inherent problems within each network and provide overall stability and reliability for the new larger network as a whole. For example, since we will not be redistributing the EIGRP AS from one network into the EIGRP AS of the other, we can ensure that the EIGRP query range is no larger than the two respective EIGRP ASs. The EIGRP query range is the area of EIGRP speaking routers that is queried for paths to destination networks when a failure has occurred to that destination network. The smaller the EIGRP query range, the shorter the time of convergence and the more inherent stability in a network.

Public versus Private Autonomous Systems

Public autonomous systems are those networks that communicate with other networks using the Internet. Given the interconnection among the autonomous system networks, the AS numbers must be globally unique. Thus, these networks must obtain an official AS number from the American Registry for Internet Numbers (ARIN).

ARIN charges a first time fee of $500.00 to register an AS number. Thereafter, ISPs that did not receive their IP address space from ARIN will be charged an annual $30.00 maintenance fee. ARIN has a Web site located at www.arin.net. The specific template for requesting a public AS number can be found at www.arin.net/regserv/templates/asntemplate.txt.

Public AS numbers are in the range of 1 to 64511, whereas private AS numbers are in the range of 64512 to 65535. We may use any AS number within the valid range of AS numbers (1 to 65635) to configure BGP, as long as any private AS number is dealt with in respect to connectivity with the Internet.

We will use private AS numbers in the following example to facilitate any possible future connectivity to the Internet. Having made the choice to use private AS numbers, we are free to choose any two numbers between the values of 64512 and 65535. For simplicity and ease of memory, we will make the following AS assignments:

Company A will be assigned AS 65001

Company B will be assigned AS 65002

Now that we have decided to use two ASs and have assigned an AS number to each system, we can proceed to enable BGP routing.

Enabling BGP Routing

To enable BGP routing, we need to enter the following Cisco IOS command while in privileged mode.

```
hostname(config#)router bgp <AS number>
```

To enable BGP routing in our example involving Company A and Company B, we would thus enter the following commands in each respective router:

```
router1(config#)router bgp 65001
```

```
router2(config#)router bgp 65002
```

Enabling BGP is as simple as that! Now, we will proceed to configure EBGP neighbors and move on to more complex configurations involving IBGP and path selection.

Configuring EBGP Neighbors

After enabling BGP routing, we next need to configure EBGP neighbors. EBGP speakers must establish neighbor relationships before they can exchange EBGP routing information. EBGP neighbors do not have to be directly connected, because BGP uses TCP port 179 to communicate "through" non-BGP speakers. In order for EBGP speakers to communicate without being directly connected, we must use the "ebgp-multihop" command, explained later in this chapter.

When configuring EBGP neighbor relationships, the AS number of the remote AS is configured in the local router using the following syntax:

```
hostname(config-router)#neighbor <ip address> remote-as <remote AS number>
```

We will use the IP address of the directly connected interfaces in order to enter the neighbor command syntax in each respective router (see Figure 11.2). The reason we use the IP address of the directly connected interface rather than the IP address of a loopback interface is that it will give us a route to the peer without the need to depend on an IGP like OSPF or a configured static route.

For Company A, the syntax is as follows:

```
router1(config)#router bgp 65001
```

```
router1(config-router)#neighbor 10.10.10.6 remote-as 65002
```

For Company B, it looks like this:

```
router2(config)#router bgp 65002
```

```
router2(config-router)#neighbor 10.10.10.5 remote-as 65001
```

Figure 11.2 Configuring EBGP Neighbors

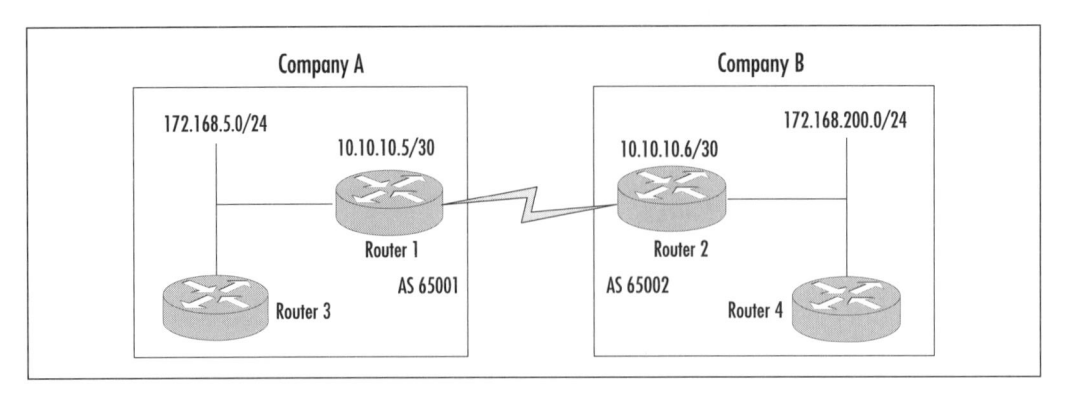

It is important when configuring EBGP relationships that we double-check our work to make sure we have configured the correct AS number on each router. For EBGP speakers, the AS number entered using the neighbor command should be the AS number of the opposite EBGP peer router, that is, the one whose IP address you also used in the neighbor command. For example, here is part of the configuration file of Router 2:

```
hostname router2
!
router bgp 65002
neighbor 10.10.10.5 remote-as 65001
```

Note that the AS number on the neighbor command line is the AS number belonging to Router 1 (AS 65001), *not* the AS number belonging to Router 2 (AS 65002).

To allow BGP sessions between routers that are not directly connected, we need to use the EBGP multihop command. The EBGP multihop command allows neighbor relationships to be established only when there is a specific path to the EBGP peer in question. That is, the default gateway route will not be used by EBGP to establish multihop neighbor relationships.

The syntax for the EBGP multihop command is as follows:

neighbor <ip address | peer group name> **ebgp-multihop**

Defining the Remote Version

BGP defaults to the current version of BGP (BGPv4) when attempting to establish relationships with its neighbors. If BGP, version 4, cannot be agreed on, negotiation will continue using lower versions until a version can be agreed on. *All* connections to the Internet use BGP, version 4.

We can force BGP to use a certain version when necessary by using the BGP version parameter of the neighbor command. Supported versions are 2, 3, and 4.

The syntax of the BGP version command follows. It must be entered while we are in router configuration mode:

neighbor <ip address> **version** <version number>

For example, to force Router 2 in Figure 11.2 to use BGP, version 2, when communicating with its neighbor, Router 1, we would enter the following commands:

router2(config)# **router bgp 65002**
router2(config-router)# neighbor 10.10.10.5 version 2

You should be cautious about setting the BGP version to anything less than the current version of BGPv4, especially given the fact that the Internet uses BGPv4.

Removing Private AS Numbers

Before we can have full connectivity with the Internet using EBGP, any private AS numbers must be stripped from the AS_Path in the BGP updates.

Using the **remove-private-as** parameter of the BGP neighbor command on an individual neighbor basis can do this. This parameter strips the private AS numbers of outbound EBGP updates to the specified peers.

The syntax of this command is as follows:

neighbor <ip address> **remove-private-as**

There are considerations that guide us in the use of this command.

This command will work only if all the AS numbers in the AS_Path are private, and it removes *all* such private AS numbers. If the AS_Path is a mix of public and private AS numbers, the command will be viewed as an error, and the private AS numbers will not be removed. This implies that private AS numbers should be stripped by the first public AS that encounters them.

An example of removing two private AS numbers is given in Figure 11.3.

Figure 11.3 Removing Private AS Numbers

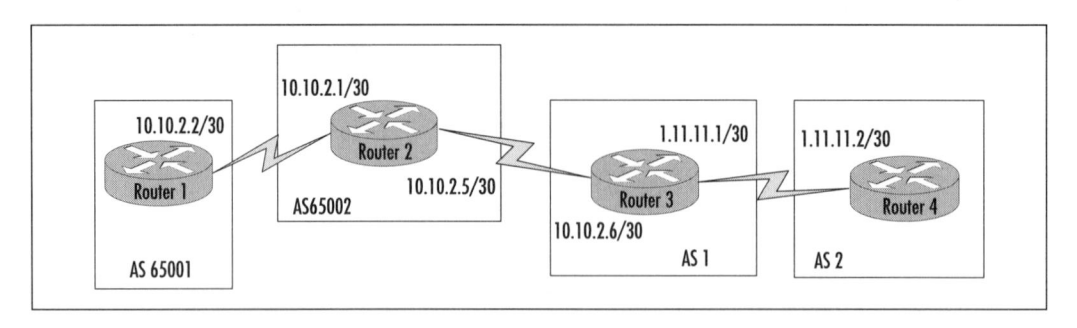

The relevant lines from the configuration files for these routers would be as follows:

```
hostname router1
!
interface serial 0
ip address 10.10.2.2 255.255.255.252
!
router bgp 65001
neighbor 10.10.2.1 remote-as 65002
!


hostname router2
!
interface serial 0
ip address 10.10.2.1 255.255.255.252
!
interface serial 1
ip address 10.10.2.5 255.255.255.252
!
router bgp 65002
neighbor 10.10.2.2 remote-as 65001
neighbor 10.10.2.6 remote-as 1
!
```

```
hostname router3
!
interface serial 0
ip address 10.10.2.6 255.255.255.252
!
interface serial 1
ip address 1.11.11.1 255.255.255.252
!
router bgp 1
neighbor 10.10.2.5 remote-as 65002
neighbor 1.11.11.2 remote-as 2
neighbor 1.11.11.2 remove-private-as
!


hostname router4
!
interface serial 0
ip address 1.11.11.2 255.255.255.252
!
router bgp 2
neighbor 1.11.11.1 remote-as 1
!
```

The effect of the **remove-private-as** command is to strip both AS 65001 and AS 65002 from the AS_Path on the outbound update from Router 3 to Router 4. Thus, Router 4 will view any networks learned from AS 65001 or AS 65002 as having only AS 1 in the AS_Path.

There are a number of recommendations for Service Providers (SPs) in terms of filters that should be applied when connecting new ASs to the Internet. These recommendations can be found on the North American Network Operator's Group (NANOG) Web site at www.nanog.org/resources.html.

Configuring IBGP Neighbors

Configuring IBGP speakers to establish neighbor relationships is a simple and straightforward process, once we understand a very important point about the way IBGP peers communicate. When an IBGP peer learns a network from another IBGP peer, it cannot advertise that network to other IBGP peers in order to avoid routing loops. Thus, all IBGP peers must be fully meshed, either literally, or by using techniques that will be discussed later, so that they can learn about networks first-hand.

Since all IBGP peers must be fully meshed, there is no "ibgp-multihop" command as there is for EBGP.

Peering to Loopback Interfaces

The fully meshed nature of IBGP peers lends itself to the use of loopback interfaces for configuring neighbor relationships. When the physical or logical interface of a direct connection goes down, any BGP sessions that were using the IP address of that interface will be closed. This will affect the reliability of your network.

Loopback interfaces are virtual interfaces that are always "up" unless the loopback interface has been administratively shut down, or the router itself is down. This means that if a router has multiple connections to an IBGP peer based upon the IP address of the loopback interface, the BGP sessions will remain open as long as a convergent secondary path remains up. Thus, it is highly recommended that you create and use loopback interfaces on all the routers that will be members of an AS.

Figure 11.4 shows an example of a fully meshed IBGP network using loopback interfaces for the peer relationships. The relevant sections of the three routers' configuration files follow.

Figure 11.4 Using Loopback Interfaces for IBGP Peers

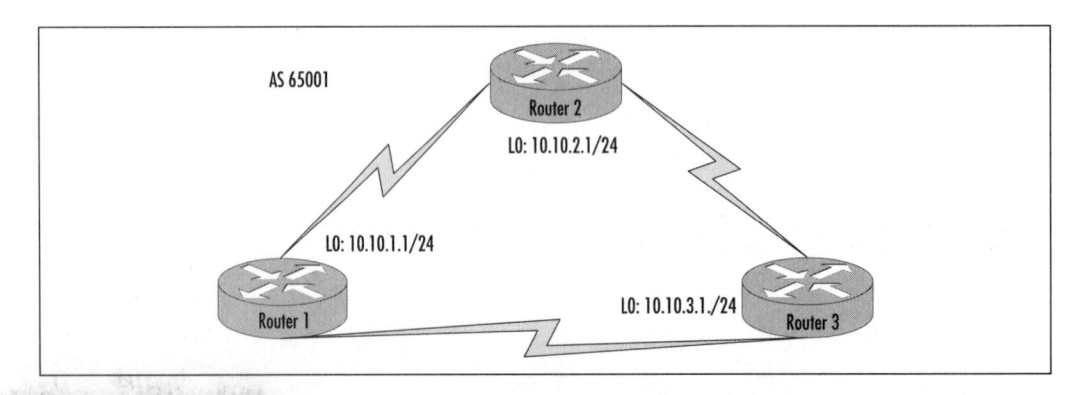

This is the code for Router 1:

```
!
interface loopback 0
ip address 10.10.1.1 255.255.255.0
!
router bgp 65001
neighbor 10.10.2.1 remote-as 65001
neighbor 10.10.3.1 remote-as 65001
!
```

Here is the code for Router 2:

```
interface loopback 0
ip address 10.10.2.1 255.255.255.0
!
router bgp 65001
neighbor 10.10.1.1 remote-as 65001
neighbor 10.10.3.1 remote-as 65001
!
```

Router 3's code is like this:

```
interface loopback 0
ip address 10.10.3.1 255.255.255.0
!
router bgp 65001
neighbor 10.10.1.1 remote-as 65001
neighbor 10.10.2.1 remote-as 65001
!
```

As this example of just three fully meshed routers demonstrates, it can be very cumbersome, expensive, complicated, and difficult to maintain a large network of IBGP speakers that are fully meshed. Fortunately, we have assistance in the form of Route Reflectors (RR) and Confederations.

Configuring Route Reflectors

Contrary to our understanding that IBGP routers cannot receive updates from other IBGP peers, Route Reflectors (RRs) work by forwarding IBGP learned updates to other IBGP peers. Route Reflectors thus provide a very important function.

Without RRs, IBGP would not be very scalable. RRs also allow for easy migration, as only the routers that are acting as RR Servers need to be modified. Additionally, we can build redundant RR Servers to ensure network reliability.

Before we can implement RRs in our network, we must decide which IBGP router or routers will act as our route reflectors. For discussion purposes, we will call these routers our "RR Servers." The RR Servers need only a single connection to their "client" routers (RR Clients), but they must be fully meshed to one another. The RR Clients, however, do not need to be fully meshed with one another. Together, the RR Clients will form a cluster that will receive IBGP updates from the RR Server.

Any other routers in the AS network that are not RR Clients must be fully meshed in order to meet the IBGP update requirements. For these non-client routers, all the IBGP rules about updates still apply.

The syntax for the Route Reflector command is straightforward:

```
neighbor <ip_address> route-reflector-client
```

Using the example in Figure 11.5, we would configure Router 1 to be the RR for AS 65001 with the following commands.

Figure 11.5 Configuring a Route Reflector Server for AS 65001

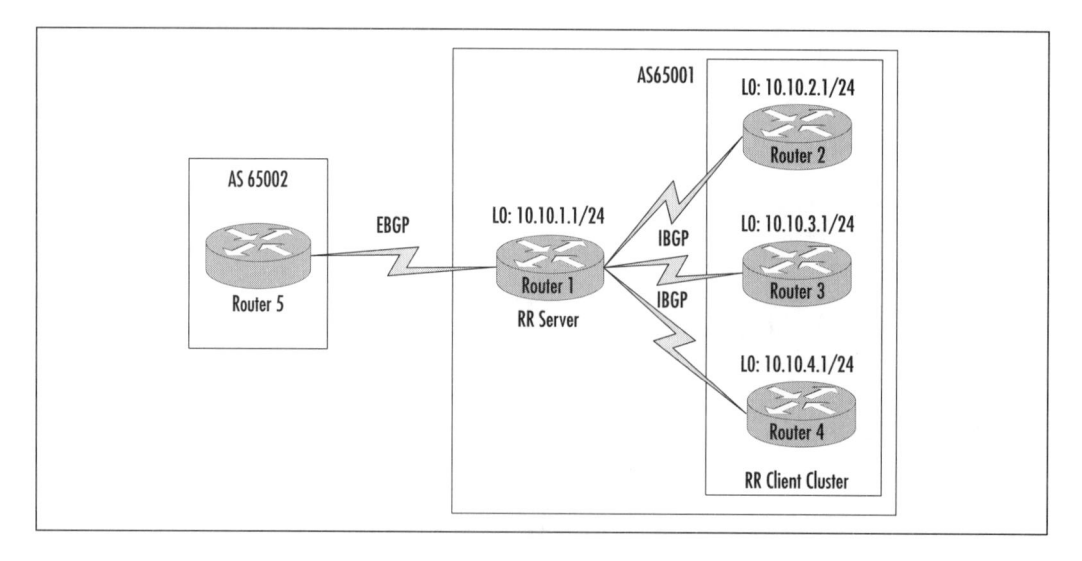

```
router1(config)#router bgp 65001
router1(config-router)#neighbor 10.10.2.1 route-reflector-client
router1(config-router)#neighbor 10.10.3.1 route-reflector-client
router1(config-router)#neighbor 10.10.4.1 route-reflector-client
```

The relevant portions of the configuration files for the other three routers would be as follows:

```
hostname router2
!
interface loopback 0
ip address 10.10.2.1 255.255.255.0
!
router bgp 65001
neighbor 10.10.1.1 remote-as 65001
!

hostname router3
!
interface loopback 0
ip address 10.10.3.1 255.255.255.0
!
router bgp 65001
neighbor 10.10.1.1 remote-as 65001
!

hostname router4
!
interface loopback 0
ip address 10.10.4.1 255.255.255.0
!
router bgp 65001
neighbor 10.10.1.1 remote-as 65001
!
!
```

Figure 11.5 shows that configuring Router 1 as a RR Server alleviated the need for Router 2, Router 3, and Router 4 to be fully meshed IBGP speakers. Using IBGP, Router 1 will advertise to all of its clients any routes it learns via EBGP from Router 5. A route from one RR Client, for example, Router 4, will be advertised to all the other RR Clients in the cluster.

If there were any non-RR Client routers in AS 65001 connected to the RR Server (Router 1), any routes learned by Router 1 from these routers would be advertised to the RR Clients. Conversely, Router 1 would advertise any routes learned from its clients to this non-client router.

Remember that *all* non-RR Client routers and *all* RR Servers must be fully meshed in order for IBGP to work correctly.

Configuring Confederations

Confederations are used to segment an AS into smaller fully meshed pieces that are visible to the outside world as a single AS. You can use Confederations and Route Reflectors within the same network.

The syntax for the confederation command is more complex than that of the RR, but still straightforward:

```
bgp confederation identifier <AS number>
bgp confederation peers <Sub AS number1><Sub AS number2> …
```

In Figure 11.6, we have identified two sub-AS numbers (64901 and 64902) that will be seen as a single AS (649) by the outside world. Router 1 is directly connected to AS 650 and is exchanging EBPG updates with that router (Router 7). The relevant configuration commands for each router are as follows.

This is the configuration for Router 1:

```
router1(config)#router bgp 64901
router1(config-router)#bgp confederation identifier 649
router1(config-router)#bgp confederation peers 64902
router1(config-router)#neighbor 10.10.1.1 remote-as 64901
router1(config-router)#neighbor 10.10.2.1 remote-as 64901
router1(config-router)#neighbor 10.10.3.1 remote-as 64901
router1(config-router)#neighbor 10.11.6.1 remote-as 64902
router1(config-router)#neighbor 192.168.17.2 remote-as 650
```

Figure 11.6 Configuring Confederations

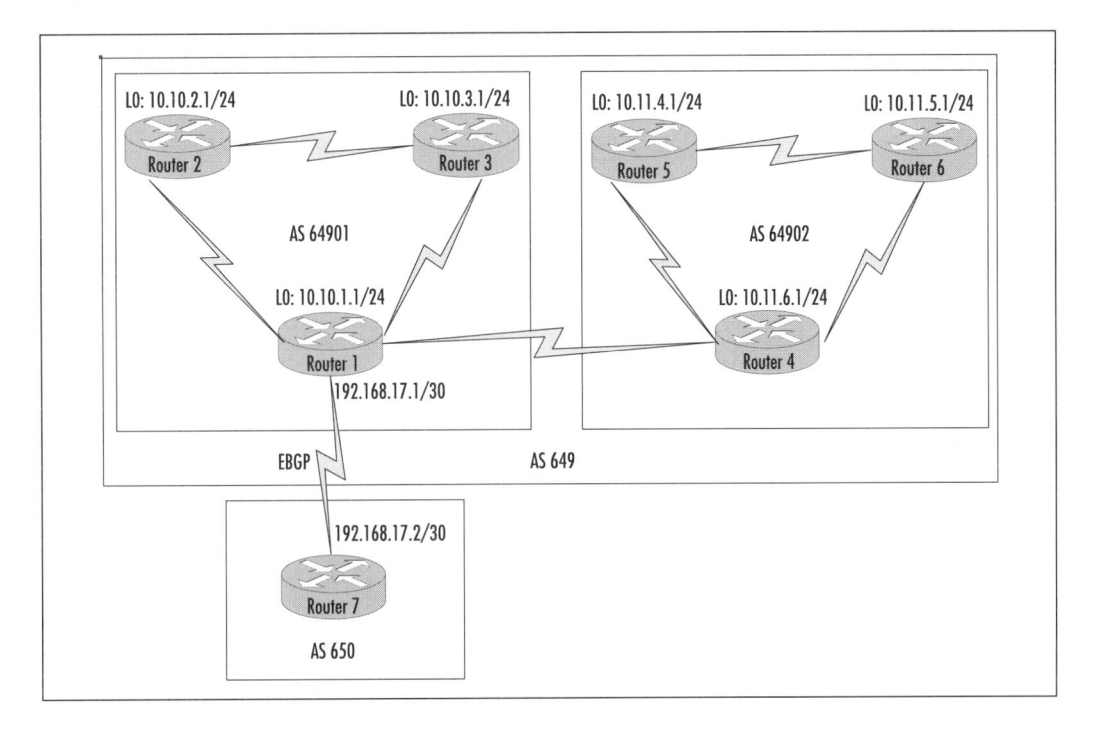

[Figure 11.6: Network diagram showing AS 649 containing two sub-autonomous systems: AS 64901 (Router 1 with LO: 10.10.1.1/24, Router 2 with LO: 10.10.2.1/24, Router 3 with LO: 10.10.3.1/24) and AS 64902 (Router 4 with LO: 10.11.6.1/24, Router 5 with LO: 10.11.4.1/24, Router 6 with LO: 10.11.5.1/24). Router 1 connects via EBGP (192.168.17.1/30) to Router 7 (192.168.17.2/30) in AS 650.]

Here are the commands for Router 2:

```
router2(config)#router bgp 64901
router2(config-router)#bgp confederation identifier 649
router2(config-router)#neighbor 10.10.2.1 remote-as 64901
router2(config-router)#neighbor 10.10.1.1 remote-as 64901
router2(config-router)#neighbor 10.10.3.1 remote-as 64901
```

This is what Router 3 looks like:

```
router3(config)#router bgp 64901
router3(config-router)#bgp confederation identifier 649
router3(config-router)#neighbor 10.10.3.1 remote-as 64901
router3(config-router)#neighbor 10.10.1.1 remote-as 64901
router3(config-router)#neighbor 10.10.2.1 remote-as 64901
```

These are the commands for Router 4:

```
router4(config)#router bgp 64902
router4(config-router)#bgp confederation identifier 649
```

```
router4(config-router)#bgp confederation peers 64901
router4(config-router)#neighbor 10.11.4.1 remote-as 64902
router4(config-router)#neighbor 10.11.5.1 remote-as 64902
router4(config-router)#neighbor 10.10.6.1 remote-as 64902
router4(config-router)#neighbor 10.10.1.1 remote-as 64901
```

Here is the Router 5 configuration:

```
router5(config)#router bgp 64902
router5(config-router)#bgp confederation identifier 649
router5(config-router)#neighbor 10.11.5.1 remote-as 64902
router5(config-router)#neighbor 10.11.4.1 remote-as 64902
router5(config-router)#neighbor 10.11.6.1 remote-as 64902
```

The following configuration is for Router 6:

```
router6(config)#router bgp 64902
router6(config-router)#bgp confederation identifier 649
router6(config-router)#neighbor 10.11.6.1 remote-as 64902
router6(config-router)#neighbor 10.11.4.1 remote-as 64902
router6(config-router)#neighbor 10.11.5.1 remote-as 64902
```

And here is Router 7's configuration:

```
router1(config)#router bgp 650
router1(config-router)#neighbor 192.168.17.1 remote-as 649
```

When Do I Need Route Reflectors and Confederations?

You should use Route Reflectors and Confederations to minimize the expenses, administrative overhead, and complexity associated with fully meshed IBGP networks. In networking, we often speak of the seven layers of the OSI model: Layer 1–Physical, Layer 2–Data-Link, and so on up to Layer 7–Application. However, it is usually the undocumented layers that affect us the most. These layers are known as Layer 8–Finance, and Layer 9–Politics.

Fully meshed networks are expensive to build and difficult to maintain. Reliability can be affected by routing flaps associated with unstable links, inefficient IP addressing schemes, large routing tables, and interruption of services caused by Service Provider error. Figure 11.7 shows the connections that would be required to implement the Confederation example of Figure 11.6 using a fully meshed network.

Figure 11.7 A Fully Meshed IBGP Network (AS 649)

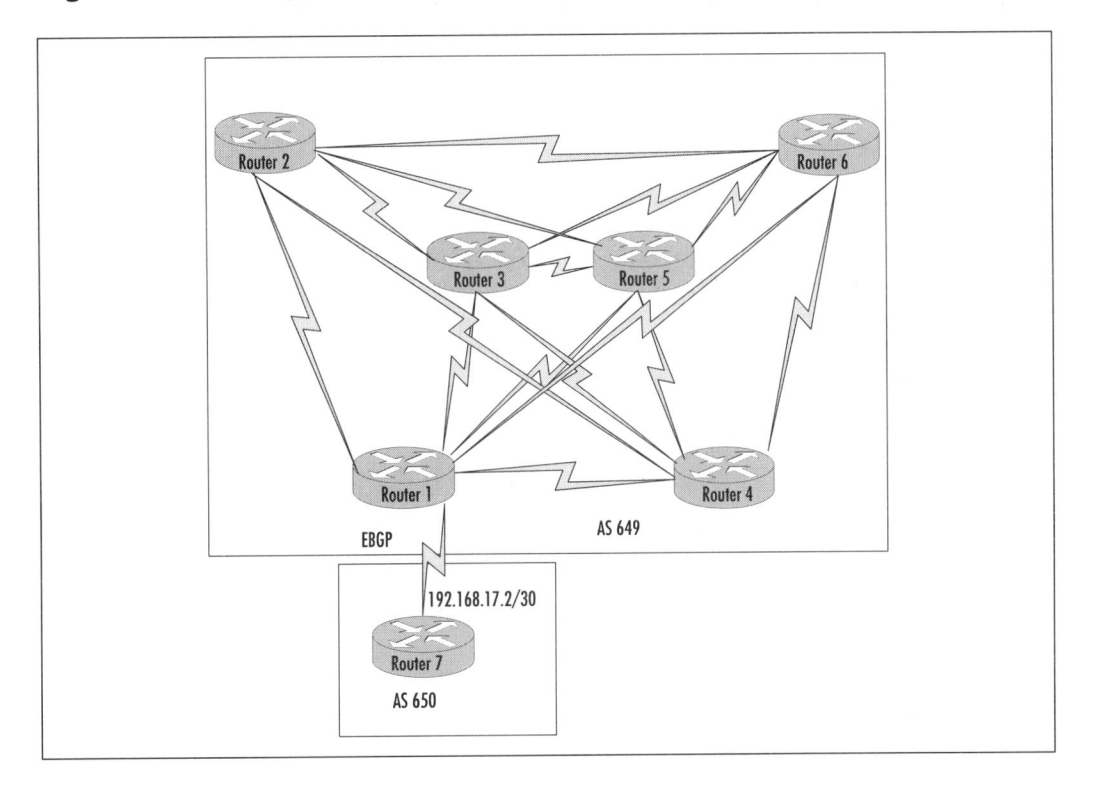

This network would be expensive in terms of the number of circuits required to create the full mesh, the amount of time necessary to maintain the network, and the unreliability inherent in such configurations (route flapping, slow convergence, and so on). We can use Route Reflectors and Confederations to mitigate the influences of Layers 8 and 9, or to compensate when circuits have not been delivered to complete the mesh of a remote site when required.

Weight, MED, LOCAL PREF, and Other Advanced Options

BGP provides many advanced configuration options that allow network administrators to implement path selection policies. These configuration options guide BGP speakers in determining and selecting a specific path, the best path, from among multiple paths to a network destination. Once the BGP speaker has determined the best path to a destination network, it advertises its selection to its neighbors.

Following are the attributes most often used by network administrators to configure routers for best path determination:

- Weight attribute
- Multiexit Discriminate (MED) attribute
- Local Preference attribute

There are several other attributes that are involved in path selection:

- AS_Path attribute
- Origin attribute
- Next_Hop attribute

BGP goes through a multistep decision process to select the best path to a destination network. It examines BGP attributes in the following order to determine this path.

1. **Next Hop** If next hop is unreachable, the path is discarded.
2. **Weight** From existing paths, select the path with the largest weight attribute.
3. **Local Preference** If multiple paths exist with equal weights, select the path with the largest local-preference value.
4. **Originated Locally** If everything so far is equal, select the path originated locally.
5. **AS_Path** If everything so far is equal, select the path with the shortest AS_Path field. The advertisement that passes through fewer ASs may be assumed to be the best.
6. **Origin Type** All thus far being equal, select the lowest origin type.
7. **MED** If everything so far is equal, select the path with the lowest MED value.
8. **External Path** If everything so far is equal, select external paths over internal paths.
9. **Nearest IGP Neighbor** All thus far being equal, select the path with the closest Internal Gateway Protocol (IGP) neighbor.

10. **Lowest BGP router identifier** If everything else is equal, the router with the lowest BGP identifier is chosen as the best path.

This list shows the granularity network administrators have in influencing the best-path decision making process of BGP. However, with such granularity comes the complexity that BGP is known for.

Route-Map, Match, and Set Commands

In many instances, we may want to use route maps for a more granular approach to setting the BGP attributes. The following is a general guide to using route-map, match, and set statements, including specific examples of setting some of the BGP attributes.

Using EIGRP as an example of an IGP used for redistribution, the command syntax of route-map statements for BGP is as follows. You can use either the first two commands or the neighbor statement along with the route-map, match, and set commands that follow:

```
router eigrp 1
redistribute bgp <AS number> route-map <map tag>
```

or **neighbor** <ip address> **route-map** <map tag> [**in**|**out**]

used with **route-map** <map tag> [**permit**|**deny**] <sequence number>
match <condition to be matched>
set <attribute to set> <attribute value>

Table 11.1 shows match and set conditions.

Table 11.1 Match and Set Conditions

Match	Set
as-path	as-path
metric	weight
ip next hop	local preference
ip address	origin
tag	metric
	interface
	ip address
	ip precedence

The network administrator's ability to master route map configurations to set the BGP attributes will determine his ability to scale and granularize BGP.

Weight Attribute

The Weight attribute is used to give preference to one BGP path over another when multiple paths exist to the same destination network. It has only local significance, that is, it is not sent in routing updates to other BGP speakers, and a higher weight has precedence over other lower weighted paths to the destination network. The value of the weight attribute is 32768 for self-originated paths, and 0 for paths originated by other routers.

There are three ways to configure the weight metric:

- Using the neighbor/weight command
- Using a route-map statement
- Using an access list

To illustrate the three different techniques for configuring the weight attribute, we return to our example of the problem with four autonomous systems. We want to force Router 4 to use the path it has learned from Router 3 to reach AS 65002.

Setting the Weight Attribute Using the Neighbor Statement

The neighbor/weight command is an "all or nothing" parameter that sets the weight on a per peer basis for all the routing updates coming from that peer. Here is the syntax of the neighbor/weight command:

neighbor <ip address> **weight** <weight value>

Using the illustration in Figure 11.8, we would add the following commands to Router 4:

Router4(config)#**router bgp 65004**
router4(config-router)#**neighbor 10.10.1.6 weight 300**
router4(config-router)#neighbor 10.10.1.2 weight 100

The effect of this command is that *all* routing updates from Router 3 are given a weight of 300, and *all* routing updates from Router 1 are given the lower preference weight of 100. Thus, the weight attribute is very definitive for configuring path selection, in that it does not distinguish one route from another coming from a single neighbor.

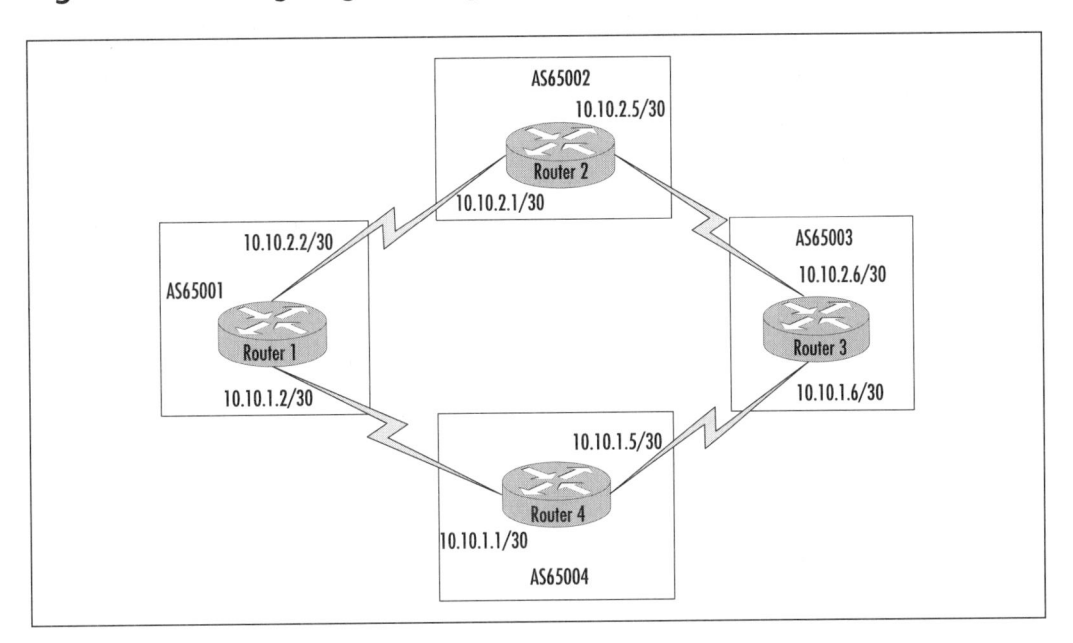

Figure 11.8 Configuring the Weight Attribute

[Figure 11.8: Network diagram showing four routers. Router 1 in AS65001 (interfaces 10.10.2.2/30 and 10.10.1.2/30), Router 2 in AS65002 (interfaces 10.10.2.1/30 and 10.10.2.5/30), Router 3 in AS65003 (interfaces 10.10.2.6/30 and 10.10.1.6/30), Router 4 in AS65004 (interfaces 10.10.1.5/30 and 10.10.1.1/30).]

Setting the Weight Attribute Using Access lists

The access list command allows us to set the path selection precedence by AS number. There are two commands that need to be entered in order to configure the router. The syntax of the two access list commands follows:

neighbor <ip address> **filter-list** <list number> **weight** <weight value>
ip as-path access-list <list number> [permit|deny] <AS number>

Using the illustration in Figure 11.8, we would add the following commands to Router 4:

router4(config)#**router bgp 65004**
router4(config-router)#**neighbor 10.10.1.6 filter-list 1 weight 300**
router4(config-router)#**neighbor 10.10.1.2 filter-list 2 weight 100**
router4(config)#**ip as-path access-list 1 permit ^65003**
router4(config)#ip as-path access-list 2 permit ^65001

The effect of these commands is to assign the weight of 300 to the routing updates received from AS65003, and 100 to the routing updates received from AS65001. The updates from AS65003 are thus the preferred paths.

Setting the Weight Attribute Using Route Maps

We can also use route maps with the weight attribute to set the path selection precedence. Again, considering the illustration in Figure 11.8, we enter the following commands in Router 4.

```
router4(config)#router bgp 65004
router4(config-router)#neighbor 10.10.1.6 route-map set-hiwght in
router4(config-router)#neighbor 10.10.1.2 route-map set-lowght in
router4(config-router)#exit
router4(config)route-map set-hiwght permit 10
router4(config)#match as-path 1
router4(config)#set weight 300
router4(config)#route-map set-lowght permit 20
router4(config)#match as-path 2
router4(config)#set weight 100
router4(config)#ip as-path access-list 1 permit ^65003
router4(config)#ip as-path access-list 2 permit ^65001
```

Multiexit Discriminate (MED) Attribute

Multiexit Discriminate (MED) is used to influence inbound traffic when there are several entry points into an AS. The MED metric is exchanged between ASs, and the lower value is the preferred route into the AS, the default being 0. You can set the MED attribute using the following commands:

- **Set metric** Used with route-map statements.
- **Default-metric** Used when redistributing one routing protocol into another.

For example, consider the network illustrated in Figure 11.9. In this illustration there are redundant connections to the AS (65002), and we want BGP to select Router 2 as the best path to network 192.168.10.0/24. We would thus want Router 2 to have a lower MED value than Router 3, all other BGP metrics being equal.

Figure 11.9 Configuring the MED Attribute

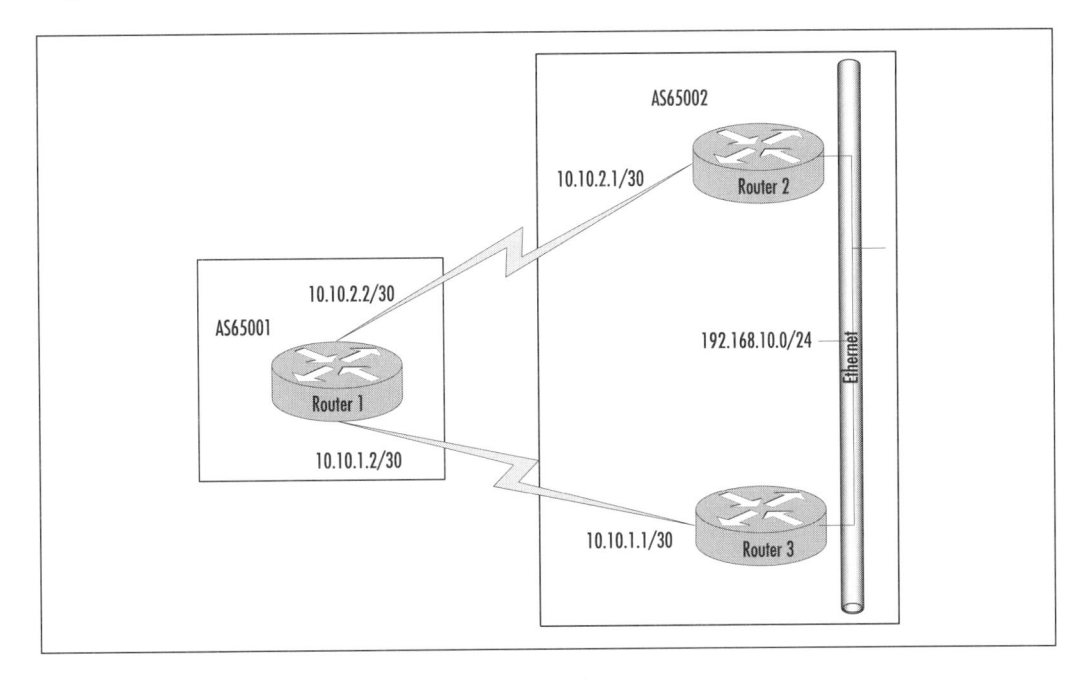

Setting the MED Attribute Using the Set Metric Command

To use the **set metric** command and a route map to modify the MED attribute, we would use the following command syntax:

set metric <metric-value>

The syntax for the route map command is as follows:

route-map <map-tag> [**permit**|**deny**] <sequence-number>
[conditions]

In our example in Figure 11.9, we would enter the following commands in privileged mode.

These commands would be entered in Router 2:

router2(config)#**router bgp 65002**
router2(config-router)#**neighbor 10.10.1.2 route-map setmed out**
router2(config-router)#**exit**
router2(config)#**route-map setmed permit 10**
router2(config)#**set metric 100**

And in Router 3, we would add these commands:

```
router3(config)#router bgp 65002
router3(config-router)#neighbor 10.10.2.2 route-map setmed out
router3(config-router)#exit
router3(config)#route-map setmed permit 10
router3(config)#set metric 150
```

Setting the MED Attribute with the Default-Metric Command

To modify the MED attribute using the **default-metric** command for redistributed routes, we use the following command syntax in router configuration mode:

```
default-metric <metric value>
```

For our example in Figure 11.9, if network 192.168.10.0/24 were learned via EIGRP, we would enter the following commands in privilege router configuration mode.

In Router 2, we add these commands:

```
router2(config)#router bgp 65002
router2(config-router)#redistribute EIGRP 10
router2(config-router)#default-metric 100
```

And here are the commands we would add in Router 3:

```
router3(config)#router bgp 65002
router3(config-router)#redistribute EIGRP 10
router3(config-router)#default-metric 150
```

Local Preference Attribute

The **local-preference** command is used to set the preferred route out of the autonomous system, and it is distributed within the autonomous system via routing updates. Use this attribute to select the best path out of an AS to a destination network where multiple paths exist to that destination network. The default value is 100.

Setting Local Preference with the Default Local-Preference Command

To use the **default local-preference** command to set the preferred path out of an AS, we use the following command syntax in router configuration mode:

`bgp default local-preference` <preference value>

This command sets the local preference value for *all* routing updates received by the configured router.

Consider the network illustrated in Figure 11.10, where there are two paths from AS65001 to network 192.168.20.0/24. The routers involved need to have the proper BGP neighbor statements configured for both EBGP and IBGP. We want to force BGP to select the path via Router 4.

Figure 11.10 Configuring Local Preference

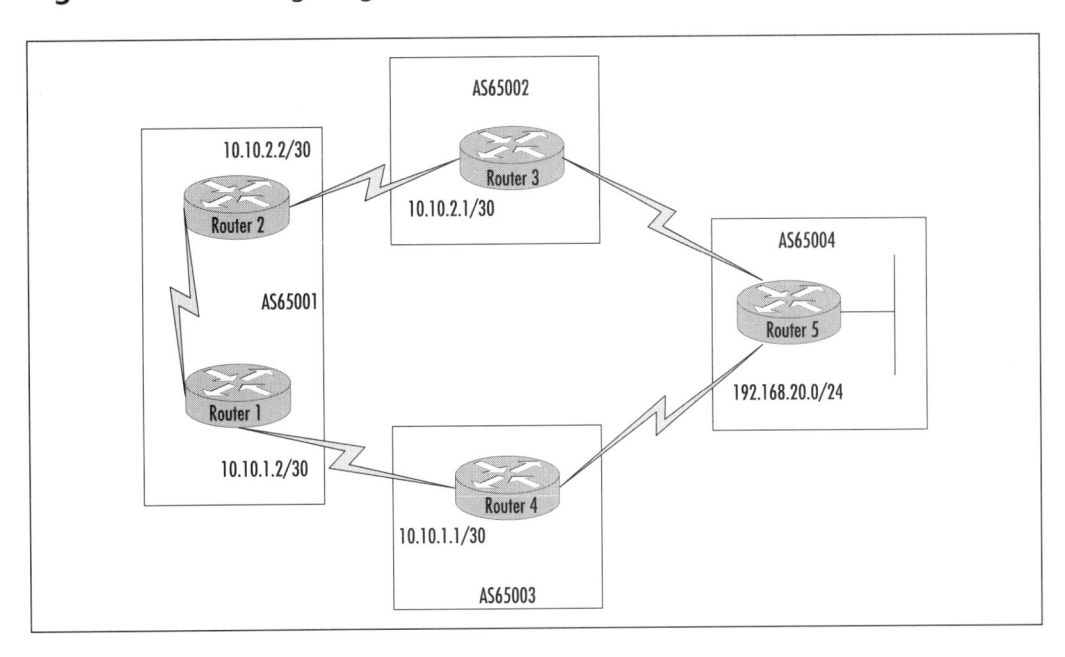

In Router 1, we would add the following commands:

```
Router1(config)#router bgp 65001
Router1(config-router)#bgp default local-preference 200
```

Since the default local preference value for Router 3 will be 100, the path through Router 4 will be selected as the best path, all other BGP attributes being equal.

The following are pertinent commands from the configuration file of Router 1 which also show the configuration of the BGP neighbor relationships:

```
router bgp 65001
neighbor 10.10.1.6 remote-as 65001
neighbor 10.10.1.1 remote-as 65003
bgp default local-preference 200
```

Setting the Local Preference Attribute with the Set Local-Preference Command

The local preference can also be set using route-map commands. Using route-map statements instead of the default local-preference command gives us more granular control over setting the preference values. For example, we can set the local preference values for specific AS numbers.

To use the route-map form of the local preference command in relation to our example in Figure 11.10, we enter the following commands in Router 1:

```
router1(config)#router bgp 65001
router1(config-router)#route-map localpref in
router1(config-router)#exit
router1(config)#ip as-path 5 permit ^65003$
router1(config)#route-map localpref permit 10
router1(config)#match as-path 5
router1(config)#set local-preference 200
```

The result of this approach is that only the updates from AS 65003 will have their local preference set to 200, as opposed to all the updates received by Router 1, as was the case with using the **default local-preference** command.

AS_Path Attribute

The AS_Path attribute contains a list of AS systems that the routing update has passed through on its journey to the receiving router. As the routing update passes through each EBGP speaker, the EBGP speaker examines the list to make sure that its AS number is not already contained within the attribute. If its AS number were already in the list, this would indicate a routing loop, and the update would be discarded. On the other hand, if the EBGP speaker does not find its own AS number within the list, it appends the number to the update and proceeds as normal. IBGP speakers do not append their AS numbers to the list; this would always be considered a routing loop, since all IBGP speakers are in the same AS.

Origin Attribute

The origin attribute indicates the origination of the routing update. It may be one of three values, listed here in order of preference:

- IGP
- EGP
- Incomplete

This attribute is not normally used in the best path selection process.

Next_Hop Attribute

The Next_Hop attribute is used to identify the next hop for NLRI. NLRI is a list of IP address prefixes used to distinguish networks, default routes, and hosts from each other. The Next_Hop attribute is not modified between IBGP neighbors unless a network administrator manually configures it.

We can force the Next_Hop attribute to reflect the address of the current IBGP peer by using the following command:

`Neighbor <ip address|peer group name> next-hop-self`

> ### Using Prefix Lists
>
> Special lists called "prefix lists" can be used instead of access lists to implement many BGP route filtering options. Although the use of prefix lists is beyond the scope of this chapter, these lists are invaluable to administrators who must support large and complex BGP networks.

Other Advanced Options: BGP Multiprotocol Extensions

One of the strengths of BGP is its capacity to implement specific administrative policies and routing enhancements when required on a peer-by-peer basis or to a group of routers that form a BGP peer group. Some of the more common options are discussed to show how to enable support for multicasting, how to enable authentication, how to adjust timing parameters, and how to create peer groups for ease of administration.

A word of caution: as with anything, the simpler the design and the configuration, usually the more reliable the end result. Be very careful when "tweaking" BGP or any other routing protocol, especially in a production network. If possible, make your changes in a laboratory environment, and test their functionality and impact before implementing them in your network. If this is not possible, implement your changes in the least intrusive manner possible and to the smallest range of affected routers or networks as possible. Always have a fallback plan, including saving configuration files to TFTP servers, or to your laptop or desktop, before making changes to your network.

BGP peers use configurable community attributes and multiprotocol extensions to validate relationships and enforce policies. Such extensions include support for Virtual Private Networks (VPNs) and Multicast BGP (MBGP). Here we give a brief overview of the MBGP extension.

Multicast BGP (MBGP)

The MBGP extension enables routers to support multicasting, while giving administrators the ability to create policies that are specific to multicast traffic within interconnected BGP routers. For example, network administrators can construct separate paths for multicast traffic and unicast traffic.

Networks that are constructed with separate paths for unicast and multicast traffic are often referred to as "incongruent" networks. That is, if we were to take a network diagram and lay the path of the multicast traffic over the unicast traffic, the two paths would diverge at one or several points.

A bonus is that everything we learned about unicast policies of BGP can also be applied to MBGP. So, we can use the same granular approach as needed to create policies within our ASs that are running MBGP, including building multicast Route Reflectors (RR).

Unlike IOS versions 11.1(20)CC and 12.0(2)S, Cisco IOS version 12.1 and later does not support the use of the **nlri** keywords to enable multicast BGP).

Instead, Cisco uses separate address families to enable multicast over BGP. For those who upgrade their IOS from a previous version to Cisco IOS 12.1, the nlri keywords in the configuration will automatically be converted to the family address configuration.

To enable MBGP in a peer, we enter the following commands in privileged mode:

`router1(config)#`**`router bgp`** `<as number>`

`router1(config-router)#`**`neighbor`** `<ip address|peer group>` **`remote-as`** `<as number>`

`router1(config-router)#`**`address-family ipv4 multicast`**

`router1(config-router)#`**`neighbor`** `<ip address|peer group name>` **`activate`**

Next, we need to inject the source of the MBGP traffic into the multicast Routing Information Base (RIB) of our router:

`router1(config-router)#`**`network`** `<network number> <mask>`

Complex configurations for MBGP are beyond the scope of this book, but for more information on how to create advanced MBGP configurations, visit the Cisco Systems Web site at www.cisco.com.

Configuring BGP Authentication

Network security can be enhanced for BGP peers by invoking a hashing algorithm known as Message Digest 5 (MD5). MD5 authentication can be configured between two BGP peers, or on a BGP peer group basis.

MD5 works by executing a mathematical algorithm on the user configurable password to create a 128-bit output known as the "message digest." The message digest output will be exactly the same, given the identical input, no matter how many times the algorithm is executed.

To configure MD5 authentication for BGP, the same password must be configured on each router taking part in the authentication process. The identical password must be used because the receiving BGP peer will compare the results of its calculated message digest with the incoming message digest from its BGP authentication peer or peers. The incoming messages that match will be authenticated; those that do not will be denied BGP sessions.

To enable MD5 authentication to check the segment of TCP connection between BGP peers, perform the following command in router configuration mode:

`neighbor` `<ip address| peer group name>` **`password`** `<password>`

For example, to configure MD5 between the two BGP peers in Figure 11.11, enter the following commands:

```
router1(config)#router bgp 65001
router1(config-router)#neighbor 10.10.1.2 password Not4u2know

router2(config)#router bgp 65001
router2(config-router)#neighbor 10.10.1.1 password Not4u2know
```

Figure 11.11 Configuring BGP Authentication

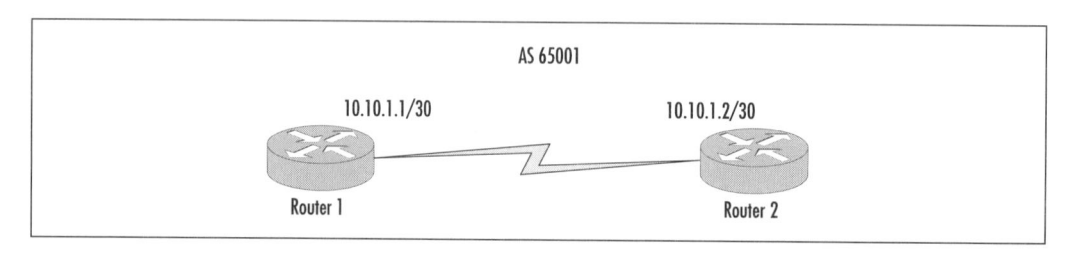

[Diagram: AS 65001 containing Router 1 (10.10.1.1/30) connected to Router 2 (10.10.1.2/30)]

The password can be up to 80 characters long, it can contain any alphanumeric characters, including spaces, as long as it does not start with a number, and it is case sensitive.

Troubleshooting BGP Authentication

Most authentication failures are caused by different passwords being configured in the BGP peers, usually by typographical error). Cisco routers will give a "Invalid MD5 digest from..." message when this occurs. It is recommended that authentication passwords be copied and pasted into the routers using an application such as Microsoft Notepad to avoid such problems.

Route Dampening

One of the most common problems associated with large networks is "route flapping." Route flapping is characterized by a connection to a destination network continuously going up or down over a relatively short period of time. The effect of this "flapping" is to prevent the convergence of the affected part of the network. If OSPF is the IGP being used, the entire area may become unstable, and with EIGRP, the query range will become unstable.

BGP allows you to mitigate, or "dampen," the effect of flapping routes by configuring EBGP peers to ignore route flapping from other peers.

The command syntax for route dampening is entered in router configuration mode as follows:

```
bgp dampening
```

There are five associated parameters, the default values being shown in parentheses:

- **Penalty (1000)** Penalty applied to the route each time it flaps.
- **Suppress Limit (2000)** The upper limit the penalty can reach before the route is dampened.
- **Reuse Limit (750)** The penalty must fall below this value before it is readvertised.
- **Half-Life (15 minutes)** For each half-life period that passes, the penalty is cut in half.
- **Maximum Suppress Limit (4 Half-Life)** The maximum amount of half-life the route can be ignored.

Adjusting BGP Timers

BGP uses timers to control the sending of keepalive messages. The default value is 60 seconds, and the holddown timer is three times that value, or 180 seconds. There may be occasions when you need to change the value of the keepalive timers. This can be done to all neighbors at once, or to a specific neighbor, using the following respective commands:

```
timers bgp <keep-alive> <hold-down>  (changes all neighbors)
```

```
neighbor <ip address|peer group name> timers <keep-alive> <hold-down>
```

When BGP connections are initiated, the timers are negotiated. When both commands are configured, the specific neighbor command will override the command for all neighbors.

Configuring BGP Peer Groups

If BGP neighbors share the same administrative policies, such as distribute lists, update sources, and so on, , they can be placed into groups to simplify configuration and support.

First, we must create a BGP peer group. Then we can use the peer-group name in the BGP configuration options, as discussed earlier in this chapter. Lastly, we can add neighbors to the peer group.

To create a BGP peer group, use the following command:

`neighbor <peer group name> peer-group`

To add a neighbor to the peer group, use this command:

`neighbor <ip address> peer-group <peer group name>`

To disable a BGP peer group or neighbor, use the following command:

`neighbor <ip address|peer group name> shutdown`

Summary

This chapter covered many of the most commonly used BGP configuration commands. We saw that BGP obtains its granularity and scalability from the attributes associated with its path selection, as well as some of the advanced configuration options such as route dampening.

As the examples demonstrated, configuring BGP for enterprise and small service providers is not as complex as it appears. Most configurations use neighbor statements to set up EBGP speakers between two different networks. When configuring EBGP speakers, the IP address of the directly connected peer interface should be used, whereas with IBGP, the IP address of a loopback interface should be used.

We also learned that there are significant topology differences between EBGP systems and IBGP systems. Although EBGP speakers can operate well with a single connection to another EBGP speaker, even when they are not directly connected, IBGP speakers must be either fully meshed, or supported by Route Reflectors or Confederations to ensure end-to-end connectivity.

Finally, we saw that we can change BGP attributes to select the best path between networks, or to stabilize the network. Such attributes may be changed either en masse, or individually and specifically using route-map statements.

The benefits of BGP make it a superior External Gateway Protocol and are the reasons that it remains very popular among Internet Service Providers of medium to large enterprises as a method to interconnect networks and provide a stable operating core.

FAQs

Visit www.syngress.com/solutions to have your questions about this chapter answered by the author.

Q: What is the range of numbers for autonomous systems (ASs)?

A: The valid range is from 1 to 65355. The subset of 64512 to 65355 represents the private AS numbers.

Q: Do I have to use a registered AS number in order to communicate with the Internet using BGP?

A: Often your ISP will provide a private AS number for you to use when you communicate with them. However, if you want to have a public AS number, there are certain guidelines that your network must meet. Further details can be obtained from the ARIN web site at www.arin.org.

Q: How large does my network need to be in order to use BGP?

A: Generally speaking, OSPF, IS-IS, and EIGRP can scale in networks to several thousand routers if the OSPF areas are properly defined, the EIGRP query range is sufficiently bound, and your IP address summarization is sufficient. It is becoming more of a common practice to use BGP in the core of large networks in order to segment the network into several IGP domains to enhance network reliability. BGP should not be used as a tourniquet to heal routing problems in a network where OSPF, IS-IS, EIGRP, or the IP address space has not been designed properly.

Q: Can BGP be used for load balancing?

A: In some circumstances, it can. For the inbound side, we can set outbound attributes such as MED and communities, or append entries to the AS path. For the outbound side, we can use default routes and select specific routes out.

Q: What does it mean when BGP neighbors cycle through the Idle, Connect, and Active states?

A: Usually this means there is no IP path between the two neighbors. Check your IP configurations between the routers, and make sure your addressing scheme is correct.

Chapter 12

Multiprotocol Label Switching (MPLS)

Solutions in this chapter:

- **Understanding MPLS**
- **Integrating MPLS into QoS**
- **Standardizing MPLS for Maximum Efficiency**
- **Controlling MPLS Traffic Using Traffic Engineering**
- **Integrating MPLS and Virtual Private Networking (VPN)**

Introduction

Multiprotocol Label Switching is designed to forward packets through a network with extremely high performance by adding a label to packets as they enter the network at edge routers. Normally, every router along the packet's path looks at each individual piece of the IP header. However, since MPLS applies a fairly simple label to each packet that includes all of the information needed to route the packet, the overhead created by each router looking through the packet's header is greatly reduced, and the packet forwarding capabilities of each router are enhanced.

This chapter, unlike earlier chapters, both introduces MPLS and shows some configuration examples. Since the basic theory of MPLS is fairly simple, separate chapters are not required to discuss theory and implementation. Relatively speaking, MPLS is a new technology, and there are many enhancements, such as the capability to use RSVP with MPLS to request labels, that are being developed but are not yet fully deployable. This chapter focuses on the current RFCs pertaining to MPLS and does not discuss features that may not make it to full implementation.

Understanding MPLS

MPLS is the standardized version of Cisco Systems Tag Switching technology that integrates the flexibility and scalability of Layer 3 routing with the high performance and traffic-engineering capabilities of Layer 2 switching. MPLS is based on the concept of label swapping, in which packets or cells are assigned short, fixed-length labels that tell high-speed switching nodes how data should be forwarded.

The key to understanding MPLS is to first identify the roles of each MPLS component. The main components are listed below, and you can see an illustration of specific MPLS components in Figure 12.1.

- **Label** A constant width identifier used to select how to forward a packet. Labels are also known as "*Tags.*" These labels are typically 32 bits in length unless MPLS is running over ATM. When MPLS is operating over an ATM infrastructure, the label size is an aggregate of the ATM VPI/VCI fields.

- **Edge Label Switch Routers or Label Edge Routers (LERs)** Label edge routers are network layer routing devices located at the edges of a MPLS network. The primary function of the label edge routers is to apply labels, or tags, to packets entering the MPLS network, and remove labels from packets leaving the MPLS network.

Figure 12.1 MPLS Components

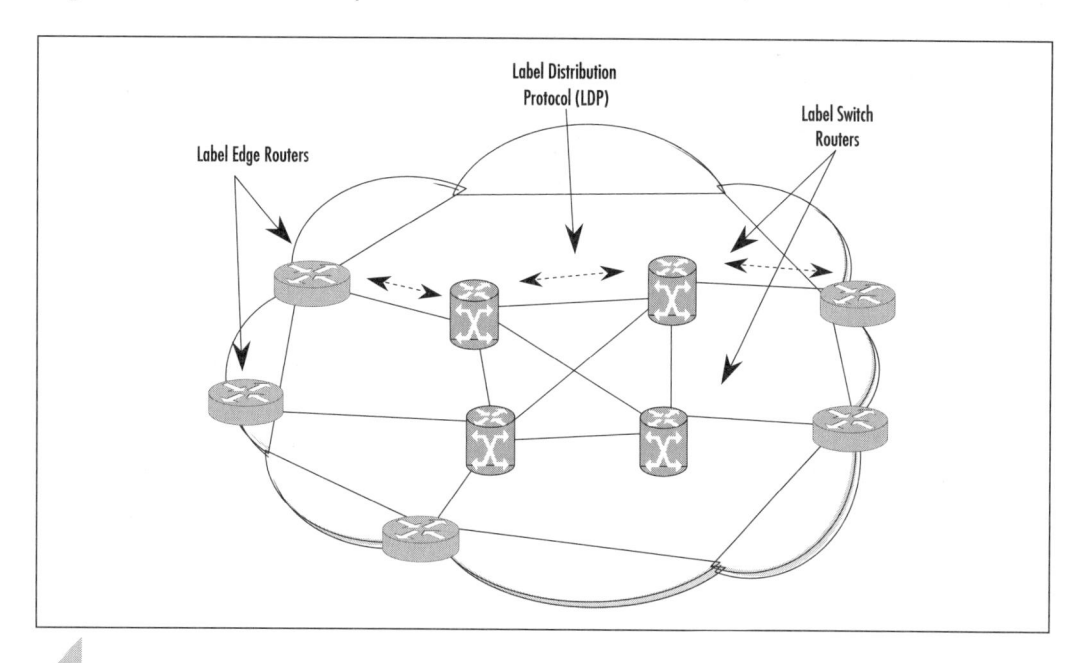

> **NOTE**
>
> Label edge routers examine incoming packets from traditional routed environments and perform the appropriate security, accounting, and quality of service classifications. LERs run traditional routing protocols to determine network reachability information such as OSPF and IS-IS. Then, they apply the proper label to the packet and forward the packet to its next hop.

- **Label Switch Routers (LSR)** Label switch routers are high-speed switching nodes whose main purpose is to forward packets at very high speeds. Label switch routers typically form the core of the network and run traditional IP routing protocols in order to gain knowledge of network layer reachability information. These devices are usually either high-speed routers or ATM switches.
- **Label Distribution Protocol (LDP)** This protocol is used to dynamically distribute labels among MPLS network elements. Labels are considered locally significant and must be unique on a per interface basis.

> **NOTE**
>
> LDP uses UDP port 711 for neighbor discovery, and TCP port 711 to reliably exchange label information among MPLS devices.

- **Label Switched Path (LSP)** This is a communications channel used to forward MPLS traffic between two MPLS enabled network elements. LSPs can be either dynamically created via label distribution protocol (LDP) or statically defined by the network administrator.
- **Label Information Base (LIB)** This is the set of all labels learned from neighbor routers. LIB is populated via LDP.
- **Label Forwarding Information Base (LFIB)** This is the set of labels that are actually used to forward packets. LFIB is derived from LIB.

MPLS exercises a label-based forwarding mechanism in which labels are used to indicate both routes and service attributes. The ingress edge label switch router processes incoming packets and assigns a label to each packet. These packets are forwarded based on label toward the next hop router. The next hop routers simply read the labels and forward packets based on these labels. The key is to understand that processor-intensive analysis, classification, and filtering occur only once, at the ingress edge label switch router. Label switch routers in the core do not interrogate each packet; they merely switch each packet based solely on the assigned label. At the egress edge label switch router, labels are removed, and packets are forwarded to their final destination based on traditional routing methods.

Label Switching Basics

In a traditional router network, each router must process every packet to determine the next hop that the packet must take to reach its final destination (see Figure 12.2). This action is repeated hop-by-hop, resulting in variable latencies through each router. This can adversely affect real-time applications that must maintain a low end-to-end delay.

In contrast, in an MPLS network, only the label edge routers fully process each packet. Label switches within the network simply forward packets based on the label. This decreases the latency experienced by traditional routed networks performing standard IP routing. There are, of course, other reasons to deploy

MPLS, such as traffic engineering and VPNs. The other major difference between regular IP routing and label switching is the separation of the control and data planes–an essential concept for MPLS over ATM as well as TE.

Figure 12.2 Traditional IP Routing Illustration

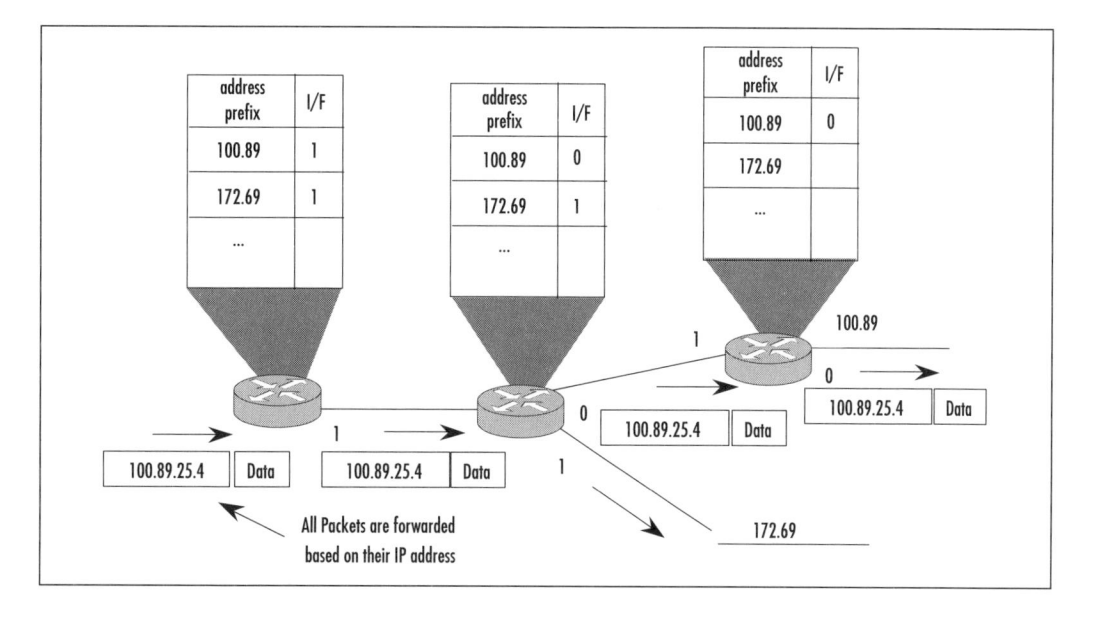

We can now proceed to discuss MPLS operation in more detail. The following steps illustrate how packets are forwarded across an MPLS network. Refer to Figure 12.3 for illustrations of each step.

1. We begin with a group of routers running a traditional routing protocol such as OSPF or IS-IS. These routers are MPLS enabled and have established adjacencies with their neighbors.

2. After the routing tables have been populated, label distribution protocol dynamically binds labels to each IP route in the routing table, and by default advertises these label bindings to all neighbors.

3. As unlabeled IP packets enter the MPLS LER, the router queries its IP routing table and forwarding information base. The router determines which interface the packet should be forwarded through, and what label should be assigned to each packet. The decision of which interface to forward the packet through need not be made purely on the basis of destination prefix; therefore, an FEC (forwarding equivalence class) may represent a prefix but could also represent a type of packet or level of

precedence. The router performs a label imposition to attach the label to the packet, and forwards the packet out the appropriate interface toward the next hop router. See Figure 12.4.

Figure 12.3 MPLS Conceptual Network

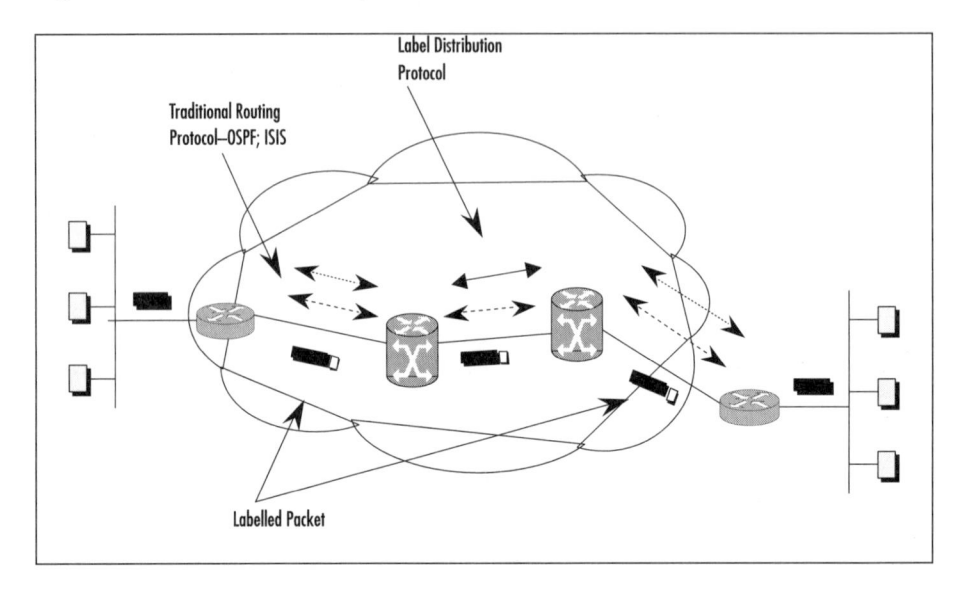

Figure 12.4 MPLS Packet Flow

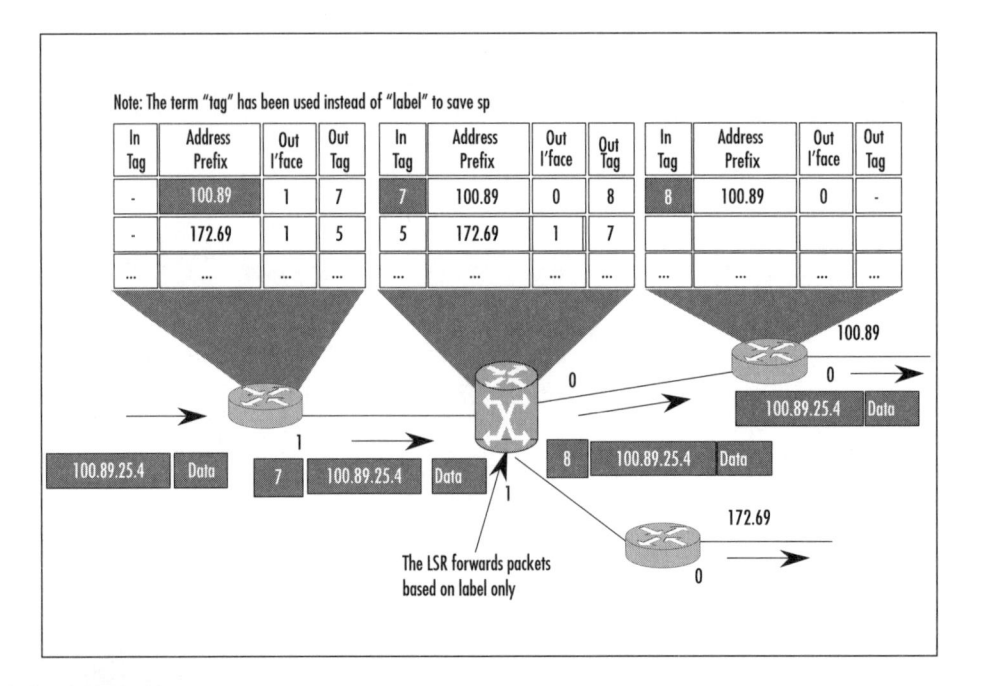

4. When a label switch router receives a labeled packet, the switch reads the label value of the incoming packet. Using the incoming label value as the index, the switch checks its label forwarding information base (FIB) to determine the outgoing label value and the outgoing interface. The incoming label value is replaced with the outgoing label value, and the packet is switched out the appropriate interface toward its next hop.

5. Packets are forwarded through the MPLS network in this manner hop by hop until they reach the egress label edge router. The label edge router performs a lookup of the incoming label in the forwarding information base and determines that there is no outgoing label. The router then strips off the label and forwards the packet as a traditional IP packet.

That Sounds a Lot Like Routing!

The separation of control and data planes allows additional Layer 3 routing services to be implemented without having to change the forwarding decision engine. Engineers who are used to configuring Cisco routers via IOS will feel comfortable configuring MPLS. Figure 12.5 illustrates a simple MPLS network. The configuration files are also provided for reference.

Figure 12.5 MPLS Network Example Configuration

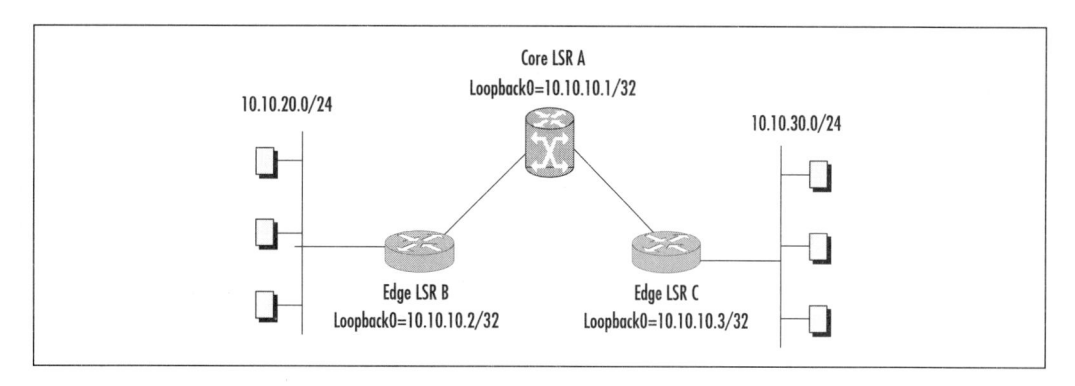

The following is the output from the CORE LSR A Router.

```
!
version 12.1
!
hostname Core-LSR-A
```

```
!
ip subnet-zero
ip cef
!
interface Loopback0
 ip address 10.10.10.1 255.255.255.255
 no ip directed-broadcast
!
interface Ethernet1/0
 no ip address
 no ip directed-broadcast
 shutdown
 no cdp enable
!
interface Ethernet1/1
 no ip address
 no ip directed-broadcast
 shutdown
 no cdp enable
!
interface Ethernet1/2
 no ip address
 no ip directed-broadcast
 shutdown
 no cdp enable
!
interface Ethernet1/3
 no ip address
 no ip directed-broadcast
 shutdown
 no cdp enable
!
interface FastEthernet2/0
 IP unnumbered loopback0
```

```
  tag-switching ip
!
interface FastEthernet2/1
 IP unnumbered loopback0
 tag-switching ip
!
!
router ospf 10
 network 10.0.0.0 0.255.255.255 area 0
!
ip classless
no ip http server
!
no cdp run
!
line con 0
 exec-timeout 0 0
 transport input none
line aux 0
line vty 0 4
 password cisco
 no login
!
end
```

The following is the output of the EDGE LSR B Router.

```
!
version 12.1
!
hostname Edge-LSR-B
!
ip subnet-zero
ip cef
!
interface Loopback0
```

```
 ip address 10.10.10.2 255.255.255.255
!
interface Ethernet1/0
ip address 10.10.20.1 255.255.255.0
!
interface Ethernet1/1
 no ip address
 no ip directed-broadcast
 shutdown
 no cdp enable
!
interface Ethernet1/2
 no ip address
 no ip directed-broadcast
 shutdown
 no cdp enable
!
interface Ethernet1/3
 no ip address
 no ip directed-broadcast
 shutdown
 no cdp enable
!
interface FastEthernet2/0
 IP unnumbered loopback0
 tag-switching ip
!
interface FastEthernet2/1
 no ip address
 no ip directed-broadcast
 shutdown
 no cdp enable
!
router ospf 10
 network 10.0.0.0 0.255.255.255 area 0
```

```
!
ip classless
no ip http server
!
no cdp run
!
line con 0
 exec-timeout 0 0
 transport input none
line aux 0
line vty 0 4
 password cisco
 no login
!
end
```

The following output is from the EDGE LSR C Router.

```
!
version 12.1
!
hostname Edge-LSR-C
!
ip subnet-zero
ip cef
!
interface Loopback0
 ip address 10.10.10.3 255.255.255.255
!
interface Ethernet1/0
ip address 10.10.30.1 255.255.255.0
!
interface Ethernet1/1
 no ip address
 no ip directed-broadcast
 shutdown
```

```
  no cdp enable
 !
 interface Ethernet1/2
  no ip address
  no ip directed-broadcast
  shutdown
  no cdp enable
 !
 interface Ethernet1/3
  no ip address
  no ip directed-broadcast
  shutdown
  no cdp enable
 !
 interface FastEthernet2/0
  IP unnumbered loopback0
  tag-switching ip
 !
 interface FastEthernet2/1
  no ip address
  no ip directed-broadcast
  shutdown
  no cdp enable
 !
 router ospf 10
  network 10.0.0.0 0.255.255.255 area 0
 !
 ip classless
 no ip http server
 !
 no cdp run
 !
 line con 0
  exec-timeout 0 0
  transport input none
```

```
line aux 0
line vty 0 4
 password cisco
 no login
!
end
```

Understanding Labels

The key to understanding MPLS is the concept that each packet is assigned a short fixed-length label. The MPLS hardware is optimized to read these labels and use them as a basis for forwarding packets. Labels are assigned to each packet in order to identify the destination, precedence, VPN membership, quality of service characteristics, and, potentially, any traffic-engineered routes that the packet should utilize. Labels are locally significant; this means that the label must be unique only on a per interface basis.

Figure 12.6 illustrates where the packet label header resides when using MPLS with SONET, LAN 802.3, and ATM cell or frame formats.

The label is typically placed between the Layer 2 and Layer 3 portions of the packet. When MPLS is used over ATM networks, the ATM VPI/VCI fields are used by MPLS to assign the appropriate label to the packet.

Figure 12.6 Frame Formats

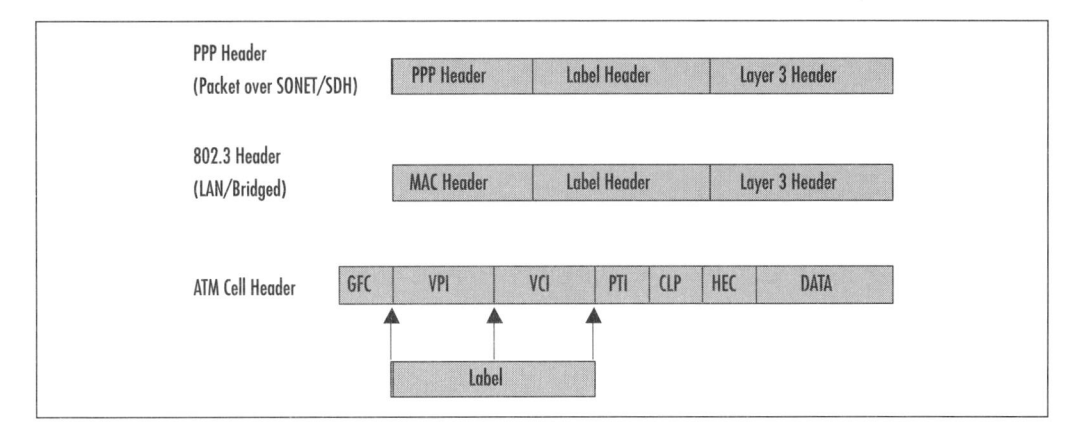

Integrating MPLS into QoS

MPLS technology satisfies the requirements of bringing Quality of Service (QoS), privacy, high availability, and scalability to large networks. MPLS reduces the costs and complexity of provisioning from a service provider perspective, resulting in lower costs and faster turn up of services to the subscriber.

Many large IP routed networks overlay IP on ATM to deliver QoS, privacy, and traffic engineering. MPLS can be used to integrate IP and ATM functionality in order to add IP intelligence to ATM network elements. This IP awareness transforms the ATM switch into a high-speed IP router capable of performing the same level of QoS, privacy, and availability as the overlay model. This transformation regularly reduces the number of router adjacencies and virtual circuits, as well as the processing power required to operate the network, at the same time increasing the scalability of the network (see Figure 12.7).

Figure 12.7 Adjacency Reduction

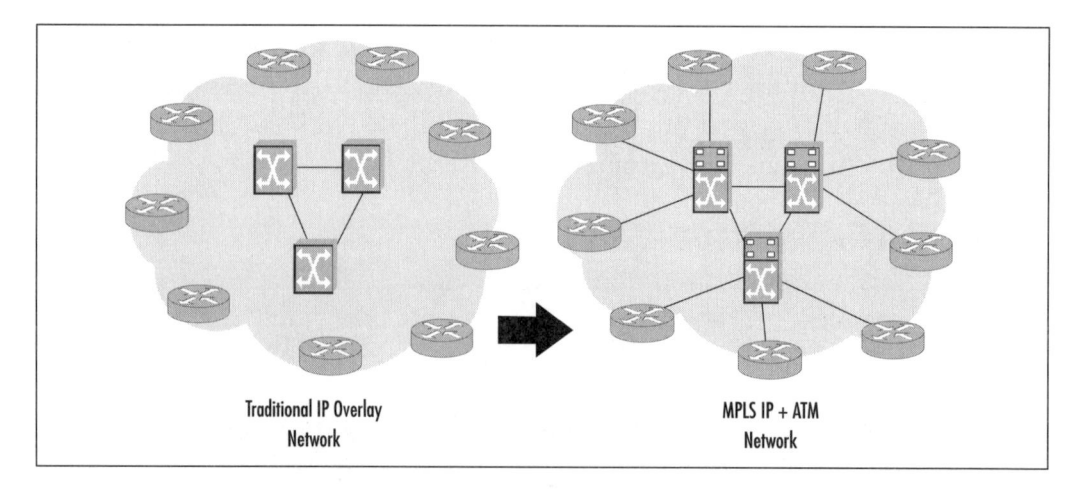

Ensuring MPLS Is Efficient and Reliable

MPLS can be more efficient and reliable than other approaches to IP routing. Since MPLS packet forwarding is based on a fixed-length label, IP routers can more efficiently process packets at higher forwarding rates. MPLS networks can prioritize real-time traffic and reduce the end-to-end latency encountered in traditional IP networks. This is because packets are routed only once at the edge of the network and switched to their final destination.

Network reliability and survivability can be enhanced via a fully redundant architecture capable of achieving 99.999 percent availability. Since MPLS is not media dependent, it can leverage automatic protection switching available via SONET, while still using other technologies such as Ethernet, Frame Relay, and ATM to provide the versatility of any-to-any connectivity.

MPLS networks use mature IP routing protocols that can dynamically load balance and re-route traffic in the event of a link failure.

Integrating ATM Classes of Service (CoS) with MPLS

MPLS can also leverage ATM switching as a transport technology. In some cases, it may be more cost effective to interconnect MPLS network elements via a public ATM network. This is accomplished by ordering an ATM permanent virtual path (PVP) from an ATM service provider. A permanent virtual path connection (PVPC) is an ATM connection in which switching is performed on the VPI field only of each ATM cell. This enables the terminating ATM end points or MPLS switching elements to dynamically assign the VCI values to the path on an as-needed basis. These VCI values serve as labels from an MPLS perspective.

The permanent virtual path connection must be ordered with a specific ATM class of service. The following reference list shows the ATM classes of service defined by the ATM Forum along with their common applications.

- **Constant Bit Rate Service (CBR)** This traffic class is usually provisioned to support circuit emulation, uncompressed voice, and video.

- **Variable Bit Rate Real Time (VBR-rt)** This traffic class is used to support bursty real-time traffic such as compressed voice and video.

- **Variable Bit Rate Non-real Time (VBR-nrt)** This traffic class can be used to support bursty data applications such as Frame Relay over ATM.

- **Available Bit Rate (ABR)** This is primarily used for most data applications. ABR service implements flow control mechanisms that manage congestion. In addition, ABR can guarantee a minimum cell rate and allow subscribers to sustain bursts up to their peak cell rate, as long as there is enough capacity in the network.

- **Unspecified Bit Rate (UBR)** This traffic class is used for bursty data applications. UBR service does not guarantee any quality of service. Traffic is delivered on a best-effort basis.

Commonly, network architects will order either CBR or VBR ATM services for MPLS applications. Cost is always a driving factor, so in practice, make certain that you price both CBR and VBR services from multiple providers before processing your circuit order. Pricing can vary greatly among providers, and you may also find that you can get twice as much guaranteed bandwidth from a VBR service as from a CBR service for approximately the same cost. If you choose this option, verify that the end-to-end latency guaranteed by the provider is within tolerances to support any real-time applications on your network.

Reducing Congestion with Traffic Engineering and VPN

Traffic engineering enables network architects to reduce congestion and maximize the use of bandwidth in their networks. IP networks have traditionally used both static and dynamic routing protocols to determine the best path from location "A" to location "Z". IP routers calculate the best path on a per hop basis and forward traffic accordingly. Traffic engineering can override path selection in order to forward specific traffic via alternate paths. Typically, traffic engineering is used to steer traffic so that it flows over underutilized links, low latency paths, or high capacity circuits.

A VPN is a network in which subscriber connectivity between sites is provisioned across a shared infrastructure in a secure manner. MPLS-based VPNs distribute traffic among all members of each individual VPN, while guaranteeing quality of service and confidentiality. As new sites are added to a VPN, provisioning occurs only once at the access point of presence (POP). It is not necessary to configure the VPN service end to end; the MPLS network automatically exchanges reachability information among all members of the VPN. The result is a decrease in the time it takes to provision additional VPN subscribers, and a reduction in operational costs caused by the increased speed of provisioning.

MPLS-based VPNs do not require any changes to their subscribers' IP addressing plans. More specifically, the VPN architecture can support subscribers with overlapping address space as long as they are in separate VPNs. This is a key differentiator between this and other VPN solutions.

VPNs will be discussed in further detail in the sections that follow.

Standardizing MPLS for Maximum Efficiency

The standardization of MPLS ensures that there will be full vendor interoperability as the technology matures. This will enable network managers to select the best products to meet their needs without being locked into a single vendor's solution or feature set.

MPLS natively support the following Quality of Service features:

- **Packet Classification and Marking** Packet classification allows traffic to be partitioned into multiple priority levels or classes of service. The IP packet type of service bits directly map to the MPLS class of service field to maintain the correct packet priority indicators.

- **Congestion Avoidance** Congestion avoidance is provided via a weighted random early detection (WRED) algorithm enabled on network interfaces to provide buffer management.

- **Congestion Management** When a network interface becomes congested, queuing techniques are necessary to ensure that the critical applications get priority over non-critical traffic. Some examples of these queuing methods are priority queuing, custom queuing, weighted fair queuing, and class-based weighted fair queuing.

- **Traffic Conditioning** Using traffic shaping or policing can condition traffic entering a network. Shaping smoothes the traffic flow to a specified rate by using buffers, whereas policing enforces a rate-limit. An example of traffic shaping is Frame Relay Traffic Shaping (FRTS), and an example of policing would be committed access rate (CAR).

- **Signaling** Resource Reservation Protocol (RSVP) is the primary mechanism to perform Admission Control for flows in a network. RSVP can request resources from a network that meet the requirements of a specific traffic flow across a given network.

Deploying Link State Protocol Support

Service providers typically deploy MPLS using a link state Interior Gateway Protocol such as IS-IS or OSPF to interconnect MPLS network elements. Distance vectors protocols such as RIP and EIGRP are not supported. The provider edge routers use BGP 4 to communicate VPN information with one another across the MPLS network.

The MPLS devices from the provider network must also interface with subscriber routers, otherwise known as customer edge routers (CERs). Customer edge routers can exchange routing updates with MPLS provider edge routers via BGP 4, RIP, OSPF, IS-IS, or static routes. This enables nearly any-to-any connectivity between the provider and the customer premise.

Integrating VPNs with BGP

MPLS VPNs use BGP multiprotocol extensions to distribute VPN information among MPLS network elements. VPN IP version 4 Address Families are used to create separate IP forwarding tables for each individual VPN defined. These tables contain the data necessary to maintain multiple routing instances on a per VPN basis. More MPLS VPN mechanics are discussed in the MPLS VPN section of this chapter.

Controlling MPLS Traffic Using Traffic Engineering

Traffic engineering is a term referring to the process of measuring, modeling, and controlling traffic. Network engineers employ traffic-engineering techniques to improve link utilization by explicitly routing traffic over underutilized links.

Standards-based routing protocols have been designed to forward traffic down a path that is considered the best metric, or shortest distance, between the source and destination, without taking into account any network conditions such as congestion, available bandwidth, or delay. Traffic engineering enables you redistribute traffic more evenly in order to achieve a more uniform utilization across all transmission paths. The traffic-engineered path may not be the shortest path between two points, but it may offer other benefits such as additional capacity or lower latency. This enables service providers to meet the requirements of the most stringent service-level agreements (SLAs).

Traditional IP networks can perform policy routing, a rather primitive approach to traffic engineering. Policy routing can be used to manually assign the path that traffic should follow. One deficiency of policy routing is that it impacts the performance of the router at each hop. In contrast, MPLS traffic engineering creates a label switch path across the route defined via traffic engineering without any performance impact on the MPLS hardware, and with no additional end-to-end latency.

It is important to understand that traffic engineering can be based not only on network policies, but also on current congestion and link availability throughout the network. This method of traffic engineering is known as routing for resource reservation (RRR). RRR permits network architects to dynamically apply traffic-engineering rules that override the traditional IP forwarding mechanisms. RRR creates one or more explicit paths with bandwidth guarantees for each link in the network. It takes into consideration the policy constraints associated with links, physical transmission resources, and network topology. This results in a forwarding paradigm based on packets being routed according to resource availability and traffic classification policy. The signaling protocol used in RRR is RSVP.

Resource Reservation Protocol (RSVP) is used to automatically establish and maintain LSP tunnels across the MPLS network. RSVP selects the traffic-engineered physical path based on the tunnel resource requirements and the available bandwidth in the network. A tunnel can dynamically increase or decrease its resource reservations based on changing network conditions.

MPLS traffic-engineered paths are configured at the edge label switch router by specifying a sequence of hops that the path must traverse. MPLS control messages flow across the path, setting up the necessary label-forwarding information for each LSR along the path. The network operator can specify a policy regarding which packets are to use a specific path. In other words, the network operator classifies which packets or applications are to use the traffic-engineered routes.

Deploying MPLS Using Cisco Express Forwarding

When deploying MPLS with Cisco Systems hardware, it is necessary to use Cisco express forwarding (CEF). Cisco express forwarding is a Cisco proprietary IP switching technology. CEF is based on a full topology-driven architecture that exercises all the available routing information to build an optimized IP forwarding information base (FIB). The FIB is a mirror image of the IP routing table. The FIB is used in conjunction with an adjacency table that maintains the Layer 2 next hop addresses for entries in the forwarding information base. CEF technology queries both of these tables in order to switch packets.

CEF is different from other switching architectures that use the first packet in a flow to build an IP destination route cache, which is then used by subsequent packets to the same destination. Since the CEF FIB contains a full copy of the routing table, there can never be any route cache misses. A route cache miss occurs when there is no current route stored in cache, resulting in a query to the main CPU which causes that first packet to be process switch, thus impacting performance.

Cisco express forwarding offers the following benefits:

- **Increased Performance** Because of the simplistic architecture of CEF, it is less CPU intensive than other Layer 3 switching mechanisms. The additional CPU cycles gained from using CEF can be used to increase packet-forwarding performance and support other router features such as QoS and encryption.

- **Scalability** The technology has been designed to support very large networks with thousands of routes, and it supports a distributed hardware environment.

- **Resiliency** CEF is more stable and accurate than other switching mechanisms that use route-caching technologies. For example, there are no cache misses.

CEF can be deployed in either distributed or centralized modes. In centralized mode, all packet processing occurs at the main CPU. In distributed mode, packet processing is dispersed between the main CPU and versatile interface processors on the 7500, or between the main CPU and the line cards on a Cisco Gigabit Switch Router (GSR). When running in distributed mode, CEF employs the reliable interprocess communication (IPC) mechanism to synchronize all FIBs to the master copy running on the main CPU.

> **NOTE**
>
> Distributed Cisco express forwarding (DCEF) is the only forwarding method available on the GSR 12000. Disabling this feature will impair packet forwarding.

Unequal Cost Load Balancing

When performing traffic engineering, it is common to encounter situations in which there is a substantial amount of traffic that needs to flow from location "A" to location "Z". The problem is that these locations are geographically dispersed and the dynamic routing protocol selected, for example, IS-IS or OSPF, has calculated a single path between these locations, when, in fact, there are actually four different paths the traffic could follow to deliver the data. By leveraging the features of both Cisco express forwarding and MPLS traffic engineering, four separate tunnels can be built between these locations to leverage the alternate paths to the destination.

Let us assume that we have built four tunnels to use these alternate paths. We now have the option of load balancing the traffic evenly or unevenly. If the traffic is being load balanced evenly among the tunnels, 25 percent of the traffic is flowing across each tunnel. Based on resource requirements, availability, and topology, it may be more beneficial to provide an unequal distribution of the load. For instance, if one of the tunnels flows over three router hops interconnected via OC12 circuits, this path is significantly underutilized. Therefore, we may choose to deliver 55 percent of the traffic between these sites over this specific tunnel, and 15 percent of the traffic flow over the other three traffic-engineered tunnels.

In order to accurately create and size the traffic-engineered tunnels to be used in traffic engineering, it is recommended that a detailed traffic study be completed. This will ensure that all mission-critical and low latency applications are serviced correctly, that traffic patterns are identified, and that link utilizations are considered during peak and off-peak hours. A traffic study will empower traffic engineers with the information necessary to properly engineer the network.

Configuring Loopback Interfaces

A loopback interface is a logical interface on a router. Loopback interfaces are not bound to any physical port and can never enter a down state. This capability to always remain up and active is used to increase the stability and scalability of large IP routed networks. Cisco routers also use the loopback interface address as their router ID when using protocols such as OSPF.

By default, OSPF makes use of the highest IP address configured on a router's interfaces as its router ID. If the interface associated with this IP address is ever disabled, or if the address is deleted, the OSPF routing process must recalculate a new router ID and retransmit all of its routing information to its neighbors.

However, if the loopback interface were configured with an IP address, the router would select this IP address as its router ID. This is because the loopback interface is given precedence over all other interfaces. Once the loopback interface has an IP address, it will be used for router ID selection, regardless if any other interfaces are configured with a higher IP address.

Here is a loopback interface configuration example.

```
Router# conf t
Enter configuration commands, one per line. End with CNTL/Z.
Router(config)# interface loopback 0
Router(config-if)# ip address 10.10.10.1 255.255.255.255
Router(config-if)# description OSPF Router ID
```

Integrating MPLS and Virtual Private Networking (VPN)

MPLS virtual private networking is the most scalable VPN solution ever developed. Border Gateway Protocol (BGP) is used to distribute VPN information across the MPLS network. An IGP, such as OSPF or IS-IS, is employed to distribute routing information among MPLS network elements. MPLS label bindings are distributed among other MPLS peers via label distribution protocol (LDP), whereas BGP is used to distribute label bindings for external routes, such as those within each VPN.

MPLS requires separate VPN routing and forwarding (VRF) tables or route-forwarding instances for each VPN provisioned. Separate forwarding tables ensure that subscribers of a specific VPN cannot reach destinations outside their VPN. These VPN-specific forwarding tables are created using BGP multiprotocol extensions. MPLS VPNs use VPN IP version 4 (IPv4) Address Families, consisting of an 8-byte route distinguisher and ending with a 4-byte IPv4 address, to forward VPN information among BGP peers.

VPN membership is statically configured on a per port or per interface basis. Each interface or sub-interface on the label edge router is configured with a unique route distinguisher. The purpose of the route distinguisher is to allow the system to create distinct routes to IPv4 address prefixes. The route distinguishers are known only to the MPLS network elements and are unknown to the customer edge router or routers.

A route distinguisher can be up to 8 bytes long. The 8-byte field is comprised of a 4-byte autonomous system number and a 4-byte subscriber number that is assigned by the provider.

When a subscriber router sends a packet to the MPLS LER, the LER verifies which interface the packet was received on and performs a lookup in the VPN-specific forwarding information base. The forwarding information base supplies the outgoing interface and two labels. The first label is used to reach the destination

LER in the MPLS network, and the second label is used to determine how to handle the packet at the egress LER. More specifically, the second label is used to determine how to forward the packet to the correct outgoing VPN interface at the MPLS network egress.

An MPLS VPN is a lot easier to configure than it looks. Table 12.1 reviews the VPN portion of a sample IOS configuration from a MPLS provider edge LSR, and explains the command syntax.

Table 12.1 MPLS VPN Configuration and Explanation

Configuration	Explanation
	Log in to router
Enable <password>	Enter enable mode
!	
Configure Terminal	Enter global configuration mode
!	
ip vrf Red	Creates a new VPN routing table called Red
rd 65050:1	Creates the route distinguisher (AS number: ID) that is bound to the VPN routing table Red
route-target export 65050:1	Exports routing information to the target MPLS VPN extended community
route-target import 65050:1	Imports routing information from the target MPLS VPN extended community
!	
!	
ip vrf Blue	Creates a new VPN routing table called Blue
rd 65051:1	Creates the route distinguisher (AS number: ID) that is bound to the VPN routing table Blue
route-target export 65051:1	Exports routing information to the target MPLS VPN extended community

Continued

Table 12.1 Continued

Configuration	Explanation
route-target import 65051:1 ! ! !	Imports routing information from the target MPLS VPN extended community
interface FastEthernet2/0	Fast Ethernet Interface
ip vrf forwarding Red	Associates interface with the Red VPN
ip address x.x.x.x y.y.y.y !	IP address and mask
interface FastEthernet2/1	Fast Ethernet Interface
ip vrf forwarding Blue	Associates interface with the Blue VPN
ip address x.x.x.x y.y.y.y !	IP address and mask
router ospf 100	Enables OSPF routing process 100
network a.a.a.a m.m.m.m area 0	Specifies the networks directly connected to the router and identifies OSPF area membership
! router ospf 17 vrf Red	Enables OSPF routing process 17 for the Red VPN
network a.a.a.a .m.m.m.m area 0	Specifies the networks directly connected to the router and identifies OSPF area membership
redistribute bgp 65500 metric-type 1 subnets	Redistributes BGP routes and Injects BGP routes into OSPF as type 1 routes
! router bgp 65500	Enables BGP routing for autonomous system 65500

Continued

Table 12.1 Continued

Configuration	Explanation
no synchronization	Since all MPLS routers are running BGP, synchronization is disabled, resulting in the network converging more quickly.
no bgp default ipv4-unicast	Specifies the IBGP neighbor and autonomous system number
neighbor z.z.z.z remote-as 65500	
neighbor z.z.z.z update-source loopback 0 !	Forces the router to use the IP address assigned to loopback 0 as the source address for BGP packets
address-family ipv4 vrf Red	Configures the address family for VRF Red
redistribute ospf 17	Redistributes routes from ospf to BGP Red VPN routing table
No autosummary	Disables summarization
exit-address-family !	Exits address family configuration mode
address-family ipv4 vrf Blue	Configures the address family for VRF Blue
redistribute static	Redistributes static routes
redistribute static connected	Redistributes connected routes
exit-address-family !	Exits address family configuration mode
address-family vpnv4	Configures the address family using VPN IPv4 prefixes
neighbor a.a.a.a activate	Activates IBGP neighbor
neighbor a.a.a.a send-community extended	Forward VPN extended attributes

In order to understand the information in Table 12.1, consider the following example of a real world MPLS application. A service provider needs to provide virtual private networking services to two local Intranets via MPLS. One Intranet, known as the RED VPN, will have a 10MB Ethernet connection to the provider. This subscriber owns a router and plans to use the provider as the default gateway to their HQ facility. The other Intranet, known as the BLUE VPN, will have a 100MB connection to the provider. This subscriber is running OSPF and plans to use the provider to form Area 0.

The subscribers and the provider are using overlapping private address space. This is allowed because once an interface is configured as part of a VPN, it is removed from the global routing table. Each VPN will have its own virtual route-forwarding instance, resulting in secure transport across the MPLS cloud.

Multiple OSPF routing processes are required in order to exchange topology information between the subscriber and the provider. The provider runs an internal OSPF routing process to exchange reachability information among other MPLS peers. The details of this example are depicted in Figure 12.8.

Figure 12.8 MPLS VPN Configuration Example

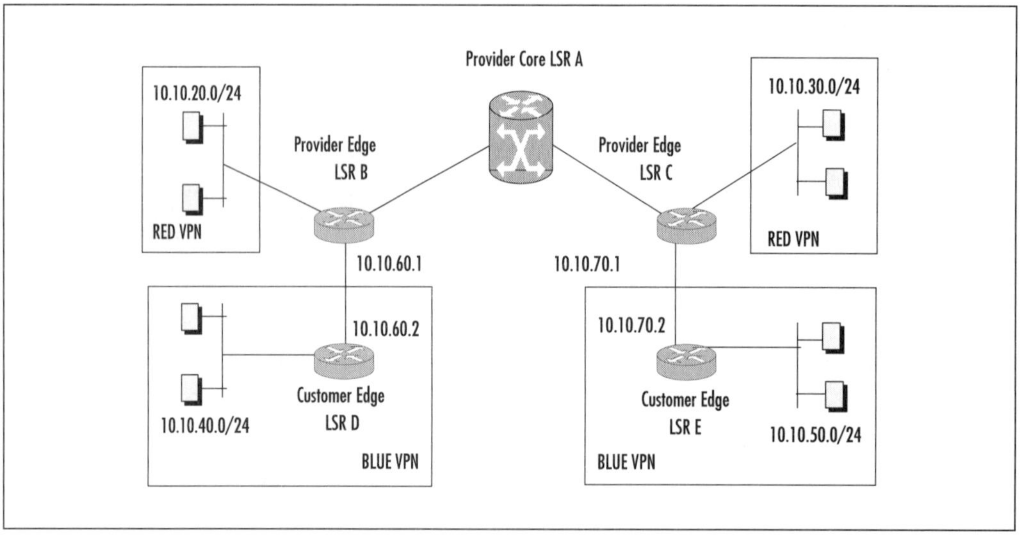

The following is the configuration for PC LSR A.

```
!
version 12.1
!
```

```
hostname LSR-A
!
ip subnet-zero
ip cef
!
interface Loopback0
 ip address 10.10.10.1 255.255.255.255
 no ip directed-broadcast
!
interface Ethernet1/0
 no ip address
 no ip directed-broadcast
 shutdown
 no cdp enable
!
interface Ethernet1/1
 no ip address
 no ip directed-broadcast
 shutdown
 no cdp enable
!
interface Ethernet1/2
 no ip address
 no ip directed-broadcast
 shutdown
 no cdp enable
!
interface Ethernet1/3
 no ip address
 no ip directed-broadcast
 shutdown
 no cdp enable
!
interface FastEthernet2/0
 IP unnumbered loopback0
```

```
  tag-switching ip
!
interface FastEthernet2/1
 IP unnumbered loopback0
 tag-switching ip
!
!
router ospf 10
 network 10.0.0.0 0.255.255.255 area 0
!
ip classless
no ip http server
!
no cdp run
!
line con 0
 exec-timeout 0 0
 transport input none
line aux 0
line vty 0 4
 password cisco
 no login
!
end
```

The following is the configuration for PE LSR B.

```
!
version 12.1
!
hostname LSR-B
!
ip subnet-zero
ip cef
!
ip vrf RED
```

```
 rd 65050:1
 route-target export 65050:1
 route-target import 65050:1
!
ip vrf BLUE
 rd 65051:1
 route-target export 65051:1
 route-target import 65051:1
!
interface Loopback0
 ip address 10.10.10.2 255.255.255.255
!
interface Ethernet1/0
 ip vrf forwarding RED
 ip address 10.10.20.1 255.255.255.0
!
interface Ethernet1/1
 no ip address
 no ip directed-broadcast
 shutdown
 no cdp enable
!
interface Ethernet1/2
 no ip address
 no ip directed-broadcast
 shutdown
 no cdp enable
!
interface Ethernet1/3
 no ip address
 no ip directed-broadcast
 shutdown
 no cdp enable
!
interface FastEthernet2/0
```

```
  IP unnumbered loopback0
  tag-switching ip
!
interface FastEthernet2/1
  ip vrf forwarding BLUE
  ip address 10.10.60.1 255.255.255.0
!
router ospf 10
  network 10.0.0.0 0.255.255.255 area 0
!
router ospf 20 vrf BLUE
  network 10.0.0.0  0.255.255.255 area 0
  redistribute bgp 65500 metric-type 1 subnets
!
router bgp 65500
 no synchronization
 no bgp default ipv4-unicast
 neighbor 10.10.10.3 remote-as 65500
 neighbor 10.10.10.3 update-source loopback 0
!
  address-family ipv4 vrf BLUE
   redistribute ospf 20
   no autosummary
   exit-address-family
  !
  address-family ipv4 vrf RED
   redistribute static
   redistribute static connected
   exit-address-family
  !
  address-family vpnv4
  neighbor 10.10.10.3 activate
  neighbor 10.10.10.3 send-community extended
 !
 ip classless
```

```
no ip http server
!
no cdp run
!
line con 0
 exec-timeout 0 0
 transport input none
line aux 0
line vty 0 4
 password cisco
 no login
!
end
```

The following is the configuration for PE LSR C.

```
!
version 12.1
!
hostname Edge-LSR-C
!
ip subnet-zero
ip cef
!
ip vrf RED
 rd 65050:1
 route-target export 65050:1
 route-target import 65050:1
!
ip vrf BLUE
 rd 65051:1
 route-target export 65051:1
 route-target import 65051:1
!
interface Loopback0
 ip address 10.10.10.3 255.255.255.255
```

```
!
interface Ethernet1/0
 ip vrf forwarding Red
 ip address 10.10.30.1 255.255.255.0
!
interface Ethernet1/1
 no ip address
 no ip directed-broadcast
 shutdown
 no cdp enable
!
interface Ethernet1/2
 no ip address
 no ip directed-broadcast
 shutdown
 no cdp enable
!
interface Ethernet1/3
 no ip address
 no ip directed-broadcast
 shutdown
 no cdp enable
!
interface FastEthernet2/0
 IP unnumbered loopback0
 tag-switching ip
!
interface FastEthernet2/1
 ip vrf forwarding BLUE
 ip address 10.10.70.1 255.255.255.0
!
router ospf 10
 network 10.0.0.0 0.255.255.255 area 0
!
router ospf 20 vrf BLUE
```

```
  network 10.0.0.0  0.255.255.255 area 0
  redistribute bgp 65500 metric-type 1 subnets
 !
router bgp 65500
 no synchronization
 no bgp default ipv4-unicast
 neighbor 10.10.10.2 remote-as 65500
 neighbor 10.10.10.2 update-source loopback 0
 !
 address-family ipv4 vrf BLUE
  redistribute ospf 20
  no autosummary
  exit-address-family
 !
 address-family ipv4 vrf RED
  redistribute static
  redistribute static connected
  exit-address-family
 !
 address-family vpnv4
 neighbor 10.10.10.2 activate
 neighbor 10.10.10.2 send-community extended
!
!
ip classless
no ip http server
!
no cdp run
!
line con 0
 exec-timeout 0 0
 transport input none
line aux 0
line vty 0 4
 password cisco
```

```
 no login
!
end
```

The following configuration is for CE LSR D.

```
!
version 12.1
!
hostname LSR-D
!
ip subnet-zero
ip cef
!
interface Ethernet1/0
 ip address 10.10.40.1 255.255.255.0
!
interface Ethernet1/1
 no ip address
 no ip directed-broadcast
 shutdown
 no cdp enable
!
interface Ethernet1/2
 no ip address
 no ip directed-broadcast
 shutdown
 no cdp enable
!
interface Ethernet1/3
 no ip address
 no ip directed-broadcast
 shutdown
 no cdp enable
!
interface FastEthernet2/0
```

```
  ip address 10.10.60.2 255.255.255.0
 !
 interface FastEthernet2/1
  no ip address
  no ip directed-broadcast
  shutdown
  no cdp enable
 !
 !
 router ospf 20
  network 10.0.0.0 0.255.255.255 area 0
 !
 ip classless
 no ip http server
 !
 no cdp run
 !
 line con 0
  exec-timeout 0 0
  transport input none
 line aux 0
 line vty 0 4
  password cisco
  no login
 !
 end
```

The following is the configuration for CE LSR E.

```
!
version 12.1
!
hostname LSR-D
!
ip subnet-zero
ip cef
```

```
!
interface Ethernet1/0
ip address 10.10.50.1 255.255.255.0
!
interface Ethernet1/1
 no ip address
 no ip directed-broadcast
 shutdown
 no cdp enable
!
interface Ethernet1/2
 no ip address
 no ip directed-broadcast
 shutdown
 no cdp enable
!
interface Ethernet1/3
 no ip address
 no ip directed-broadcast
 shutdown
 no cdp enable
!
interface FastEthernet2/0
ip address 10.10.70.2 255.255.255.0
!
interface FastEthernet2/1
 no ip address
 no ip directed-broadcast
 shutdown
 no cdp enable
!
!
router ospf 20
 network 10.0.0.0 0.255.255.255 area 0
!
```

```
ip classless
no ip http server
!
no cdp run
!
line con 0
 exec-timeout 0 0
 transport input none
line aux 0
line vty 0 4
 password cisco
 no login
!
end
```

VPN Scalability

VPN scalability is a critical issue for most service providers. In Cisco's case, IOS releases after 12.0(5) can support one million VPN sites. One million sites can be broken down as 1,000 VPNs with 1,000 sites each, or 10,000 VPNs with 100 sites each.

Reducing the Load on Network Cores

Cisco's architecture is based on the peer-to-peer model and does not require that all routers in network know about every VPN configured on the network. An MPLS router must know only about the VPNs that are directly connected. LSRs in the core do not need to know anything about the VPNs provisioned in the network, as long as there are no VPN subscribers directly connected to them.

Summary

MPLS has truly married high-speed routing and Layer 2 switching, maintaining the best attributes of each. In the years ahead, MPLS will continue to evolve to meet the requirements of both service providers and subscribers. As the deployment of MPLS networks continues, the end user will significantly benefit from the technology in terms of lower network costs and guaranteed service levels.

Virtual private networking advances will continue to lure both service providers and subscribers into investigating the MPLS solution. Simplicity and scalability are vital to both market segments. MPLS technology can be used in tandem with other security mechanisms such as IPSec to meet the tightest security concerns.

The demand for traffic engineering is growing as service providers struggle to meet the most hardened service-level agreements. A network that is properly traffic engineered can meet and exceed all service-level agreements. Network architects typically must traffic engineer their networks to sustain subscriber service levels even under failure conditions. This is where a solid network design and traffic-engineering plan can make internal network issues transparent to subscribers and end users. Traffic engineered paths can dynamically calculate which route meets traffic requirements based on all available network resources to ensure that the subscriber traffic is delivered on time and error free.

FAQs

Visit www.syngress.com/solutions to have your questions about this chapter answered by the author.

Q: When using a Cisco IP plus ATM solution, can the label switch controller act as a label edge router?

A: Yes, but this is not recommended. Packets are process switched when traffic flows from an edge interface across the BPX VSI interface. In addition, the 7200 series ATM port adaptor has limitations regarding the number of label virtual circuits that can be supported. The ATM port adaptor A1 can support only 2048 LVCs, and the enhanced ATM port A3 can support 4096 LVCs.

Q: What version of code should I be looking at for MPLS?

A: It depends on the features required and software bugs reported. Starting at 12.1.5T or later would take advantage of both traffic engineering and MPLS VPNs.

Q: How do I display the IP routing table for a specific VPN?

A: Enter the command **show ip route VRF <VPN Name>**.

Q: Can traffic engineering be used across OSPF areas?

A: Currently, as of version 12.1.5T, traffic engineering cannot be implemented across area boundaries.

Q: When should an IP plus ATM solution be considered?

A: IP plus ATM should be considered when there is a requirement for ATM/Frame Relay switching or when there is an existing ATM infrastructure installed that needs to support new IP based products and services. An IP plus ATM solution allows corporations to add IP functionality to ATM hardware, thus providing a greater return on investment.

Index

1 Idle, 381
2 Connect, 381
3 Active, 381
4 OpenSent, 381–382
5 OpenConfirm, 382
6 Established, 382
10Base T Ethernet, 218
7500 routers (Cisco), 196
7513 routers (Cisco), 198

A

AAL5-MUX, 309
AAL5-NLPID, 309
ABR. *See* Adaptive Bit Rate; Available bit rate
Access Control List (ACL), 182, 183, 207. *See also* Extended Access Control Lists; Internet Protocol; Standard Access Control Lists
  configuration, examples, 25
  usage, 285, 301, 303. *See also* Network Address Translation
Access lists, usage. *See* Rate limiting; Weight
Access routers, 88
Access-group command, 33
Acknowledgement (ACK), 227
  numbers, 66
ACL. *See* Access Control List
Active. *See* 3 Active
Active timer, 108
Adaptive Bit Rate (ABR), 148
Addresses. *See* Transmission Control Protocol/Internet Protocol
  summarization, 80. *See also* Enhanced IGRP
  translation. *See* Destination Address Rotary Translation; Dynamic Source Address Translation; Port Address Translation; Static Address Translation
Addressing
  scheme. *See* Transmission Control Protocol/Internet Protocol
  usage. *See* Classless addressing
Adjancencies, 58
Admission
  control, 283
  failure, 159
  requirements. *See* Integrated Service
Adspec, 158

497

Advanced BGP network design, 414–417
Advanced EIGRP, configuration, 87–97
Advanced QoS
  configuration, 321
  FAQs, 318–319, 372–374
  overview, 271
Aggregation, 88–90
Ambiguous path, 159
ANDing, 4, 17, 18, 23
AppleTalk, 57, 139
  traffic, 253
  usage, 235
Application, 183
Application aware classification, 169–176
APPN, 137
ARP. *See* Proxy ARP
AS. *See* Autonomous System
ASBR. *See* Autonomous System Boundary Router
ASP, 168
Asynchronous Transfer Mode (ATM), 125, 166–168, 301
  classes of service, integration. *See* Multiprotocol Label Switching
  interfaces, 187
  networks, 153
  usage, 152
ATM. *See* Asynchronous Transfer Mode
Attribute flags, 389
Attribute type code, 389
Authentication. *See* Border Gateway Protocol
Autonomous System (AS), 13, 386, 423
  AS_Path, 440
    attribute, 448–449
  BGP, defining, 424–425
  contrast. *See* Public AS
  defining. *See* Remote AS

definition, 395–401
numbers, 423
numbers, removal. *See* Private AS
paths, usage. *See* Border Gateway Protocol
Autonomous System Boundary Router (ASBR), 98
Auto-summarization, 88, 109–110
  troubleshooting, 115–117
Auto-summary, 96
Available bit rate (ABR), 471
AVAILABLE_PATH_BANDWIDTH, 154
Average rate. *See* Traffic

B

Backbone connections, 155
Backward explicit congestion notification (BECN), 145
  messages, 301
  process, explanation, 302–303
  support, 188, 303
Bad flow specification, 159
Bandwidth (BW), 13, 52, 68–69
  allocation, 292–294
  guaranteed minimum, 307
  manager. *See* Subnetwork
  monopolization, 24
  protection/policing, 170
  statement, 84
  throttling, 301
  unavailability, 159
  usage, 49
bandwidth (command), 330, 331
Bc. *See* Committed Burst
Be. *See* Excess Burst
BECN. *See* Backward explicit congestion notification
Bellman-Ford algorithms, 50

Berkley Standard Distribution (BSD), 37
Best practice network design. *See* Integrated Service
Best-effort delivery system, 167
Best-effort QoS, 189
Best-effort service, 127
BGP. *See* Border Gateway Protocol
BGP 4 KEEPALIVE (message). *See* Border Gateway Protocol
BGP 4 NOTIFICATION (message). *See* Border Gateway Protocol
BGP 4 OPEN (message). *See* Border Gateway Protocol
BGP 4 UPDATE (message). *See* Border Gateway Protocol (BGP)
Bit-level addressing, 91
Bit-rate service, 157
Border Gateway Protocol (BGP). *See* External BGP; Internal BGP; Multicast BGP
  advanced options, 439–454
  authentication
    configuration, 451–452
    troubleshooting, 452
  BGP 4 KEEPALIVE (message), 393
  BGP 4 NOTIFICATION (message), 391–393
  BGP 4 OPEN (message), 385–387
  BGP 4 UPDATE (message), 387–391
  configuration, 421, 423
  defining. *See* Autonomous System; Internal BGP
  FAQs, 419–420, 455–456
  finite state machine logic, 381–383
  functionality, maximization, 380–393
  history, 376–380
  hop count, usage, 397
  identifier, 386
  messages, types, 384
  metric, 400
  movement, 398–399
  multiprotocol extensions, 450–454
  neighbors, configuration. *See* External BGP; Internal BGP
  network design. *See* Advanced BGP network design
    methodologies, 417
  optional length, 386
  optional parameters, 387
  original implementation, 377–380
  overview, 375
  packets, format, 384–393
  path selection
    example, 403–407
    process, 402–408
  AS paths, usage, 397
  peer groups, configuration, 454
  redistribution. *See* Interior Gateway Protocol
  remote version, defining, 428–429
  route identifier, 441
  routing
    enabling, 423, 426–427
    process, 380–393
  session, 382
  synchronization, 410–411
  timers, adjustment, 453
  usage, 285
  version, 386
  VPN, integration, 474
  weight, 397–398
BSD. *See* Berkley Standard Distribution
Bucket. *See* Leaky bucket; Token bucket
Burst. *See* Normal burst
  size, 300. *See also* Excess burst size
BW. *See* Bandwidth
Byte count, adjustment, 254

C

Caching, 307
CAR. *See* Committed Access Rate
CBR. *See* Constant bit rate
CBT. *See* Core-Based Tree
CBWFQ. *See* Class-based Weighted Fair Queuing
CDP. *See* Cisco Discovery Protocol
CEF. *See* Cisco Express Forwarding
CIDR. *See* Classless Interdomain Routing
CIR. *See* Committed Information Rate
Cisco. *See* Content Networking; Foresight congestion notification; Internetwork Operating System; Network Based Application Recognition
   routers, 13, 21
Cisco Discovery Protocol (CDP), 251
Cisco Express Forwarding (CEF), 169, 187, 307, 350. *See also* Distributed Cisco Express Forwarding
   enabling, 197–198
   monitoring, 198–200
   troubleshooting, caveats/bugs, 200–201
   usage. *See* Multiprotocol Label Switching
Cisco Express Forwarding (CEF), configuration, 196–201
Citrix classification, 170
Citrix Independent Computing Architecture Traffic, 170
Citrix traffic, classification, 204
Class A, 5–8
   address, 21
      range, 19
Class B, 5–8
Class C, 5–8
   address, 19, 21
   subnet mask, 21
Class D addresses, 8–10

Class map
   creation. *See* Network Based Application Recognition
   defining, 328–330
   usage. *See* Network Based Application Recognition
Class of Service (CoS), 211
   mapping. *See* Internet Protocol
Class policy, configuration. *See* Policy map
Class-based Weighted Fair Queuing (CBWFQ), 174, 201, 304. *See also* Distributed Class-based Weighted Fair Queuing
   case studies, 288–290
   configuration, verification, 334–336
   default class, treatment, 332–333
   enabling, 328–334
   NBAR, integration, 206–209
   need, explanation. *See* Network
   process, explanation, 284–286
   RSVP, relationship, 290–291
   troubleshooting, 328, 336
   usage, 284–291. *See also* Differentiated Service
   verification, 328
Classes of service, integration. *See* Multiprotocol Label Switching
Classful behavior, 110
Classful IP routing, 2–16
Classification. *See* Application aware classification; Citrix classification; HyperText Transfer Protocol; Integrated Service; Packet
   disadvantages, 166
   examination. *See* Protocol
   process, considerations, 246
   usage. *See* Intelligent network
Classless addressing, usage, 21

Classless Interdomain Routing (CIDR), 7, 379–380
  boundaries, 417
class-map match-all (command), 329
class-map match-any (command), 329
Cleanup timeout interval, 278
Coloring. *See* Packet
Committed Access Rate (CAR), 306, 307, 359
  configuration. *See* Distributed CAR
  definition, 185–188
  effect. *See* Internet Protocol
  monitoring, 196
  multilevels, marking/transmitting, 190–191
  statements, 186
  usage. *See* MAC addresses
Committed Burst (Bc), 350
Committed Information Rate (CIR), 145, 300, 301, 349. *See also* Minimum CIR
Complex NBAR, configuration, 204–206
Complicated cores, 227
Compressed RTP (CRTP), 293, 308, 314
Compression. *See* Hardware compression; RTP header compression; Software compression
Confederations, 413–414
  configuration, 436–439
  defining, 411–414
  usage, 417
    timing, 438–439
Confirmation messages, 159
Congestion avoidance, 307, 473
  advantages/disadvantages, 142–143
  configuration, 239
  FAQs, 236–238, 268–269
  overview, 217
  understanding, 141–143
  usage, 142–143

Weighted Random Early Detection, usage, 174
Congestion management, 473
  understanding, 129–130
Congestion reduction
  traffic engineering, usage, 472
  VPN, usage, 472
Connect. *See* 2 Connect
Connected interfaces, 423
Constant bit rate (CBR), 471
Content Network, design guidelines. *See* Network Based Application Recognition
Content Networking (Cisco), 168–176
Controlled-load servers, 280
Core router, 97
Core-Based Tree (CBT) protocol, 9, 10
Cores. *See* Complicated cores
CoS. *See* Class of Service
CPU cycles, 228, 282
CPU utilization, 114, 201
CQ. *See* Custom queuing
Credit manager, 299
Critical precedence, 136
CRTP. *See* Compressed RTP
CSCdr56112, 200
CSCdr68372, 200
CSCdr97427, 201
CSCds21333, 201
CSCds53550, 201
Cu-SEEME traffic, classification, 204
Custom queuing (CQ), 129, 139–141, 224–228, 252–259, 304. *See also* RSP-based custom queuing
  configuration
    application. *See* Interfaces
    verification, 255–257
  enabling, 252–254
  need, explanation, 227–228

process, explanation, 224–228
protocol interactions, 226–227
troubleshooting, 257–259

D

Data (field), 392
Data Link Channel Identifier (DLCI), 145, 213
Data Link Switching (DLSW), 138–139
Data-rate mismatches, 301
DCAR. *See* Distributed CAR
DCBWFQ. *See* Distributed Class-based Weighted Fair Queuing
DCEF. *See* Distributed Cisco Express Forwarding
debug (commands), usage, 258
Default class, treatment. *See* Class-based Weighted Fair Queuing
Default local-preference (command), usage. *See* Local preference
Default route, 83
  redistribution, 409–411
Default-metric (command), 101, 444
  usage. *See* Multiexit Discriminator
default-metric (command), 99
Deficit round robin (DRR), 359. *See also* Modified deficit round robin
Delay (DLY), 13, 68. *See also* End-to-end delay; Low-volume delay
Delay-sensitive applications, 138
  performance increase, 126
Denial of Service (DoS) attack, 33–35
Dense wave division multiplexing (DWDM), 155, 167
Destination Address Rotary Translation, 37–38
Destination host address, 18
Destination IP address, 136
Destination port, 136

Differentiated Service Code Point (DSCP), 148, 162–168
Differentiated Service (DiffServ), 128
  architectures, 174
  functionality, 164–165
  introduction, 161–168
  model, CBWFQ usage, 289–290
Diffserv. *See* Differentiated Service
Diffusing Update Algorithm (DUAL) finite state machine, establishing, 59–63
Distance Vector Multicast Routing Protocol (DVMRP), 9
Distance vectors, usage. *See* Path selection
Distance-vector routing, 50
Distinct reservation, 280
Distributed CAR (DCAR), configuration, 188
Distributed Cisco Express Forwarding (DCEF), 360
Distributed Class-based Weighted Fair Queuing (DCBWFQ), 307
Distributed mode
  features, 307–308
  operational differences, 308
  restrictions, 308–309
  running, 307–309
Distributed RSVP, 283
Distributed technologies, explanation, 359–361
Distributed Update Algorithm (DUAL), configuration, 64–75
Distributed Weighted Fair Queuing (DWFQ), 307, 309
Distributed Weighted Random Early Detection (DWRED), 142, 307, 360–361
  configuration, 309
distribute-list (command), 100–101
Distribution routers, 88
DLCI. *See* Data Link Channel Identifier

DLSW. *See* Data Link Switching
DLSw+, 137, 211, 213
DLY. *See* Delay
DoS. *See* Denial of Service
Drop rate, 349
DRR. *See* Deficit round robin
DSCP. *See* Differentiated Service Code Point
DTS, 307
DUAL. *See* Diffusing Update Algorithm; Distributed Update Algorithm
DVMRP. *See* Distance Vector Multicast Routing Protocol
DWDM. *See* Dense wave division multiplexing
DWFQ. *See* Distributed Weighted Fair Queuing
DWRED. *See* Distributed Weighted Random Early Detection
Dynamic Source Address Translation, 37
Dynamic translation, static translation contrast, 39

E

E1 links, 153
EBGP. *See* External BGP
Edge label switch routers, 458
EGP. *See* Exterior Gateway Protocol
EIGRP. *See* Enhanced IGRP
End-to-end delay, 154
End-to-end network transport functions, 313
End-to-end QoS, 127
End-users, 127
  segment, 75
Enhanced IGRP (EIGRP), 26, 48, 423
  addresses, summarization, 88–97
  basic concepts, review, 48–57
  caveats, recognition, 108–110
  components, defining, 57–60
  configuration, 75–86. *See also* Advanced EIGRP
  FAQs, 120–121
  legacy networks, relationship, 58
  optimum path, selection, 50–57
  process, explanation, 50–57
  queries/replies, 49
  redistribution, 97–108
  scalability, 49
  troubleshooting, 110–119
  usage, 285
Enhanced queuing support, 303
Equal-cost paths, 78
Error, 392
  subcode, 392
Error messages, 159
Established. *See* 6 Established
EtherChannel, 187
Ethernet, 124
  segment, 226
Ethernet 0/0, 245
Excess Burst (Be), 350
Excess burst size, 186
Express Forwarding. *See* Cisco Express Forwarding
Extended Access Control Lists, 25–35
  benefits, 30–35
  configuration, examples, 32–35
  ports, usage, 30–32
Extended access list, 139
Exterior Gateway Protocol (EGP), 376–377
External BGP (EBGP), 393–401, 423
  information sources, 407–408
  neighbors, configuration, 427–431
External path, 440

F

Failure. *See* Admission; Single-link failures
  handling, 72–75
  points, avoidance. *See* Network
  zones, evaluation. *See* Geographic failure zones
Fair queuing, 136–137. *See also* Weighted Fair Queuing
Fast EtherChannel, 307
FastEthernet LAN interface, 131
FC. *See* Feasibility condition
FD. *See* Feasible distance
FDDI, 194
Feasibility condition (FC), 70
Feasible condition, 71
Feasible distance (FD), 69, 71
Feedback, providing. *See* Receivers
FF. *See* Fixed-Filter
FIB. *See* Forwarding Information Base
FIFO. *See* First In First Out
File Transfer Protocol (FTP), 125, 127, 136, 154
  traffic, 144, 191
  usage, 219, 223
Filtering. *See* Traffic
Finite state machine
  establishing. *See* Diffusing Update Algorithm
  logic. *See* Border Gateway Protocol
First In First Out (FIFO), 145, 218–221, 240–244
  enabling, 240–242
  operations, verification, 242–243
  queuing, 129, 134–135, 286
  RED, usage, 243–244
  usage. *See* Quality of Service
  timing, 220–221

Fixed-Filter (FF) style, 281
Flags, 148. *See also* Attribute flags
Flash precedence, 136
Flash-override precedence, 136
Flow descriptor, 281
Flow spec, 158
Flow timer. *See* Multicast
Flow-based, definition, 231–232
Flow-based Random Early Detection (FRED), 299
Flow-based Weighted Fair Queuing, 174
Flow-based WRED (FRED), 342
Flows, merging, 280–282
Flowspec, 281
Flush timer, 56
Ford-Fulkerson algorithms, 50
Foresight congestion notification (Cisco), support, 303
Forward explicit congestion notification (FECN)
  process, explanation, 302–303
  support, 188
Forward VPN, extended attributes, 482–493
Forwarding Information Base (FIB), 196
  information, 199
Fourth octet, 389
Fraggle attack, 34, 35
Fragmentation. *See* Internet Protocol
Frame Relay, 124, 153
  interface, map class application, 357
  relationship. *See* Link fragmentation and interleaving
  usage, 188
Frame Relay Forum 12 (FRF12), 313
Frame Relay Traffic Shaping (FRTS), 144, 145
  configuration, 349, 354–357
    verification, 357–359
  enabling. *See* Interfaces

need, explanation. *See* Network
process, explanation, 303–305
usage, 299–306
verification, 354
frame-relay adaptive-shaping (command), 356
frame-relay Bc (command), 356
frame-relay Be (command), 356
frame-relay CIR (command), 356
frame-relay mincir (value), 356
frame-relay traffic-rate (command), 355
FRED. *See* Flow-based Random Early Detection; Flow-based WRED
FRF 12. *See* Frame Relay Forum 12
FRTS. *See* Frame Relay Traffic Shaping
FTP. *See* File Transfer Protocol

G

G.729 codec, 293
Gateway Routing Protocol. *See* Interior Gateway Routing Protocol
Generic routing encapsulation (GRE), 26, 230
tunnels, 307
Generic Traffic Shaping (GTS), 144, 145
configuration, 349–351
verification, 352–354
need, explanation. *See* Network
process, explanation, 301
usage, 299–306
verification, 349
Geographic failure zones, evaluation, 417
Gigabit Ethernet, 126
Global synchronization, 132, 234, 302
GRE. *See* Generic routing encapsulation
GTS. *See* Generic Traffic Shaping

H

Half-life, 453
Hardware compression, 307
HDLC, 125
Hello interval, 58
Hello packet, 59
Hellos, 108, 109
High-speed links, low-speed links contrast, 220
Hold time, 386
Hold-down timers, 55, 56, 58
Hop. *See* Next hop
Hop count, 50
movement, 398–399
usage. *See* Border Gateway Protocol
Hop-by-hop protocol, 110
HTTP. *See* HyperText Transfer Protocol
Hub-and-spoke network, 83
HyperText Transfer Protocol (HTTP), 127, 166, 223
classification, 169–170
requests, 169
traffic, 154, 184

I

IANA. *See* Internet Assigned Numbers Authority
IBGP. *See* Internal BGP
ICMP, 26
Idle. *See* 1 Idle
IETF. *See* Internet Engineering Task Force
IGMP. *See* Internet Group Management Protocol
IGP. *See* Interior Gateway Protocol
IGRP. *See* Interior Gateway Routing Protocol

Immediate precedence, 137
In-band signaling protocol, 274
INIT flag, 65, 66
Inserv, 160
Integrated Service (IntServ), 127–128
 admission requirements, 153, 155–156
 architectures, 174
 best practice network design, 165
 classification, 153
 explanation, 152–154
 scaling, 160–161
 scheduling, 154
Integrated Services Digital Network (ISDN), 153
 connections, 160
 PRI interfaces, 187
Integrated Services Model, 161
Intelligent network
 classification, usage, 168
 devices, 168
Intelligent policy management, 168
Interfaces. See Connected interfaces; Subinterface; Tunnels
 blocking, 82
 CQ configuration, application, 254–259
 FRTS, enabling, 354
 map class, application. See Frame Relay policy
  attachment, 208–209, 334
  map application, 203
 priority list, application, 247–252
 queuing, 130
 usage. See Loopback interfaces; Packet
Interior Gateway Protocol (IGP), 376, 423
 BGP, redistribution, 408–411
Interior Gateway Routing Protocol (IGRP), 10, 13–16, 21, 26, 50–54. See also Enhanced IGRP

Internal BGP (IBGP), 412–414, 423
 defining, 411–414
 neighbors, 440
  configuration, 432–433
Internet, 393–401
 control precedence, 136
 firewall, 204
 information sources, 407–408
Internet Assigned Numbers Authority (IANA), 9
Internet Engineering Task Force (IETF), 128, 272
 1994b, 152
 1997F, 156
 1997g, 154
Internet Group Management Protocol (IGMP), 26, 157, 274
 request, 278
Internet Protocol (IP), 26, 139
 ACLs, 23
 addresses, 117, 118, 423. See also Destination IP address; Source IP address
  classes, 2–16
 addressing, 75
 conflict, 287
 datagrams, 155, 158
 fragment, 139
 fragmentation, 307
 network summarization, 417
 precedence, 185
  levels, definition, 151–152
  WRED relationship, 296–297
 protocol, 136
 routing. See Classful IP routing
  problem, 415
 ToS, SNA CoS mapping, 211–212
 traffic, 252. See also Non-IP traffic
  CAR effect, 187

Internet Protocol Security (IPSec), 307
Internet Service Provider (ISP),
    marking/rate limiting, 191–196
Internetwork Operating System (IOS)
    [Cisco], 129, 132, 140, 164
  code, 304
  FAQs, 44–45
  feature review, 1
  Release 12.1(3)T, 201
  usage, 220, 242
  versions, 308
Interoperability, 283
IP. *See* Internet Protocol
IPINIP, 26
IPSec. *See* Internet Protocol Security
IPX, 57, 58, 139
  traffic, 253
  usage, 235
ISDN. *See* Integrated Services Digital
    Network
ISP. *See* Internet Service Provider

K

KEEPALIVE (message), 384, 385. *See also*
    Border Gateway Protocol

L

L2/L3/L4 Headers, 169
Label Distribution Protocol (LDP), 459–460
Label edge routers (LERs), 458–459
Label Forwarding Information Base (LFIB),
    460
Label Information Base (LIB), 460
Label switch router (LSR), 459
Label Switched Path (LSP), 460
Label switching, basics, 460–469

Labels, 458
  understanding, 469
LAN. *See* Local Area Network
LDP. *See* Label Distribution Protocol
Leaky bucket, 131–132, 218
Legacy networks, relationship. *See* Enhanced
    IGRP
Legacy traffic, 169
LERs. *See* Label edge routers
LFI, 304. *See* Link fragmentation and
    interleaving
LFIB. *See* Label Forwarding Information
    Base
LIB. *See* Label Information Base
Link fragmentation and interleaving (LFI),
    200. *See also* Multilink PPP with link
    fragmentation and interleaving
  configuration, 362–364
    verification, 365–366
  Frame Relay, relationship, 364
  process, explanation, 311–313
  troubleshooting, 362
  usage, 309–313
  usefulness. *See* Network
  verification, 362
Link state protocol support, deploying,
    473–474
LLQ. *See* Low latency queuing
Load, 13
Load balancing, 307. *See also* Unequal cost
    load balancing
Local Area Network (LAN)
  environment, 288
  interface. *See* FastEthernet LAN interface
Local preference, 401, 439, 440
  attribute, 446–448
  setting
    default local-preference command,
      usage, 447–448

set local-preference command, usage, 448
Logging, 26
Loop avoidance, configuration, 54–57
Loopback interfaces, 423
 configuration, 477–478
 peering, 432–433
 usage, 417
Low latency queuing (LLQ), 174, 304, 307
 configuration, 337–338
 limitations/caveats, 294
 need, explanation. *See* Network
 process, explanation, 291–294
 troubleshooting, 337, 339
 usage, 291–295
 verification, 337–339
Lowest-cost path, 53
Low-speed links, contrast. *See* High-speed links
Low-volume delay, 136
LSP. *See* Label Switched Path
LSR. *See* Label switch router

M

MAC addresses, 190
 matching/limiting, CAR usage, 194–195
Map class, application. *See* Frame Relay
Marker, 384
Marking. *See* Committed Access Rate; Internet Service Provider; Packet; Traffic; World Wide Web
match (command), 40, 42, 441–442
match input-interface (command), 329
match protocol (command), 329
Maximum suppress limit, 453
Maximum transmission unit (MTU), 13, 48, 68, 98, 292

size, 311
max-reserved bandwidth (command), 331
MBGP. *See* Multicast BGP
MDRR. *See* Modified deficit round robin
Mean rate, 300
MED. *See* Multiexit Discriminator
Messages. *See* Confirmation messages; Error messages; Path; Reservation-Request messages; Resource Reservation Protocol; Teardown
 types. *See* Border Gateway Protocol
Metric, 50
Mincir. *See* Minimum CIR
Minimum CIR (Mincir), 350
MINIMUM_PATH_LATENCY, 154
Mission critical applications, priority, 126
MLP. *See* Multilink PPP
MLP/LFI. *See* Multilink PPP with link fragmentation and interleaving
Modified deficit round robin (MDRR), 359
MOSPF. *See* Multicast Open Shortest Path First
MPLS. *See* Multiprotocol Label Switching
MSFC configuration, 184
MTU. *See* Maximum transmission unit
Multicast, 8–10, 64–65. *See also* Reliable multicast
 distributed switching, 307
 flow timer, 59
 services, 313
Multicast BGP (MBGP), 450–451
Multicast Open Shortest Path First (MOSPF), 9
Multicasting, 72
Multiexit Discriminator (MED), 400, 439, 440
 attribute, 444–446
 setting, default-metric command usage, 446

Index

setting, set metric command usage, 445–446
Multilink PPP (MLP), 200, 362–364
   troubleshooting, 366–367
Multilink PPP with link fragmentation and interleaving (MLP/LFI), 307, 312–313
Multiprotocol extensions. *See* Border Gateway Protocol
Multiprotocol Label Switching (MPLS), 457
   ATM classes of service, integration, 471–472
   components, 458–460
   deployment, CEF usage, 475–478
   efficiency/reliability, ensuring, 470–472
   FAQs, 494–495
   integration. *See* Quality of Service
   performance increase, 476
   reliability, 476
   scalability, 476
   standardization, 473–474
   traffic control, traffic engineering usage, 474–478
   understanding, 458–469
   VPN, integration, 478–493
Multiservice, 307

N

Napster, 126, 174
NAT. *See* Network Address Translation
NBAR. *See* Network Based Application Recognition
Neighbors, 48, 98. *See also* Upstream
   discovery/recovery, establishing, 58–59
   statement, usage. *See* Weight
   table, 58
Netflow, 350
NetFlow export, 307

Network. *See* Asynchronous Transfer Mode; Hub-and-spoke network; Transmission Control Protocol/Internet Protocol
   address space, 96
   CBWFQ need, explanation, 286–290
   classification, usage. *See* Intelligent network
   control precedence, 136
   design. *See* Advanced BGP network design; Integrated Service
   devices. *See* Intelligent network
   failure points, avoidance, 417
   FRTS need, explanation, 305–306
   growth, 75
   GTS need, explanation, 301–303
   independence/flexibility, 283
   investment usage, maximization, 126
   layer reachability information, 389
   LFI, usefulness, 313
   LLQ need, explanation, 294–295
   RED need, explanation, 235
   redundancy, building, 415–417
   RSVP need, explanation, 282–283
   software, upgrading problems, 415
   traffic, 21
      flows, change/response, 126
   WRED need, explanation, 298–299
Network Address Translation (NAT), 2, 35–40
   configuration, example, 40
   control, ACL usage, 39–40
Network Based Application Recognition (NBAR) [Cisco], 148, 169–176, 196, 307
   class map, creation, 202–203
   configuration, 201–203. *See also* Complex NBAR
      Random Early Detection, usage, 209–211

Content Network design guidelines, 175–176
identification, class map usage, 207
integration. See Class-based Weighted Fair Queuing
supported protocols, 170–174
supported QoS services, 174
usage, 170
Next hop, 440
Next_Hop attribute, 449–454
Next-hop TCP/IP addresses, 41
NLSP, 57
no auto-summary (command), 77, 116
no ip address (command), 363
Non-adaptive flows, 298
Non-blocking, 165
Non-IP traffic, 187
NON_IS_HOP, 154–155
Non-RSVP request, 278
Non-sharing mode, 170
Non-TCP protocols, 143
Non-VIP, 201
Normal burst, 186
NOS, 26
NOTIFICATION (message), 384, 385. See also Border Gateway Protocol
not-on-common-subnet, troubleshooting, 117–119
Novadigm, 174
NUMBER_OF_IS_HOPS, 155

O

OC3 speeds, 165
Octets, 3. See also Fourth octet; Third octet
One-to-all hosts, 8
One-to-many hosts, 8
OPcode, 61
OPEN (message), 384, 385. See also Border Gateway Protocol
Open Shortest Path First (OSPF), 9, 26, 64, 423. See also Multicast Open Shortest Path First
redistribution, 97–108
usage, 285
OpenConfirm. See 5 OpenConfirm
OpenSent. See 4 OpenSent
Optical Networking, 126
OR operation, 23, 26
Origin
attribute, 449
type, 440
Originated locally, 440
OSI model, 221, 284
OSPF. See Open Shortest Path First
Out-of-band signaling protocol, 273

P

Packet
arrival, interface usage, 139
classification, 156, 473
coloring, 174
dropping, 186
marking, 174, 473
scheduling, 156
size, 183
minimum, 155
transmitting, 186
types
implementation, 60–75
PBR usage. See Route
Packet Description Language Module (PDLM), 174–176
Parameters. See Border Gateway Protocol
type/length/value, 387

PAT. *See* Port Address Translation
Path. *See* Ambiguous path; Equal-cost paths; External path; Lowest-cost path
   messages, 158
Path attribute, 388–389
   length. *See* Total path attribute length
Path selection. *See* Enhanced IGRP
   choice, 64–72
   distance vectors usage, 50–57
   process. *See* Border Gateway Protocol
PATH_MTU, 155
PBR. *See* Policy-based Routing
PcAnywhere traffic, 202
PDLM. *See* Packet Description Language Module
Peer groups, configuration. *See* Border Gateway Protocol
Peering. *See* Loopback interfaces
Penalty, 453
Per Hop Behavior (PHB), 163–165
Per interface rate control (PIRC), 359
Per-flow state, 128
Per-packet resources, 155
PHB. *See* Per Hop Behavior
Physical layer hierarchy, 417
PIM. *See* Protocol Independent Multicast
PIRC. *See* Per interface rate control
PointCast, 126
Point-to-Point Protocol (PPP), 124. *See also* Multilink PPP; Multilink PPP with link fragmentation and interleaving
Policed unit, minimum, 155
Policing. *See* Traffic
   techniques, 144
   understanding, 143–145
Policy
   attachment. *See* Interfaces
   creation, 330–334

   management. *See* Intelligent policy management
Policy map
   application. *See* Interfaces
   class policy, configuration, 207–208
   creation, 203
Policy-based routing (PBR), 203
   configuration, 182–185
   usage. *See* Route
Port Address Translation (PAT), 36, 37
Ports. *See* Destination port; Source port
   number. *See* Transmission Control Protocol; User Datagram Protocol
   traffic. *See* Transmission Control Protocol; User Datagram Protocol
   usage. *See* Extended Access Control Lists
Power sources, evaluation, 417
PPP. *See* Point-to-Point Protocol
ppp multilink interleave (command), 363
PQ. *See* Priority Queuing
Precedence. *See* Critical precedence; Flash precedence; Flash-override precedence; Immediate precedence; Internet; Network; Priority; Routine precedence
   bit, remarking, 189–190
   levels, 190
      definition. *See* Internet Protocol
   setting, 186
Preference. *See* Local preference
Prefix Exceeded, 382
PRI. *See* Primary Rate Interface
Primary Rate Interface (PRI), interfaces. *See* Integrated Services Digital Network
Priority
   classes, 349
   list, application. *See* Interfaces
   precedence, 137
   traffic, classification, 292

Priority Queuing (PQ), 129, 138–139,
        221–223, 244–252, 304
    configuration, verification, 248–250
    enabling, 244–247
    mechanisms, 156
    need, reasons, 222–223
    priorities, 221
    process, explanation, 221–223
    troubleshooting, 250–252
Private AS
    contrast. *See* Public AS
    numbers, removal, 429–431
Process IDs, 423
Protocol, 183
    classification, examination, 245–247
    interactions. *See* Custom queuing
    port traffic. *See* Transmission Control
        Protocol; User Datagram Protocol
    type, 139
Protocol Independent Multicast (PIM), 10
Protocol-dependent modules, establishing,
        57–58
Protocol-discovery interface, 202
Proxy ARP, 20
Public AS, Private AS contrast, 426
PVC configuration mode, 193

Q

QoS. *See* Quality of Service
Quality of Service (QoS), 307. *See also* Best-
        effort QoS; End-to-end QoS
    amount, 186
    applications, 126–128
    classes, 167
    defining, 124–128
    definition, 125–126
    expansion, 168–176
    FAQs, 146
    FIFO, usage, 221
    group, setting, 187
    introduction, 123
    levels, 127–128
    mechanisms, 157
    MPLS, integration, 470–472
    origin, 166–168
    overview. *See* Advanced QoS
    parameters, definition, 153–156
    request, RSVP usage, 279–280
    requirements, 231
    reservation state, 159
    services, 155
    supported services. *See* Network Based
        Application Recognition
Queries/replies. *See* Enhanced IGRP
Query boundary, 88
Queue
    limits, configuration, 247–248
    size, 222, 226
        adjustment, 254
    starvation, 138, 223
Queue 0, explanation, 228
queue-limit (command), 330
Queuing. *See* Interfaces
    concepts, defining, 130–141
    configuration. *See* VC
    mechanisms, RED usage, 264–266
    support. *See* Enhanced queuing support
Queuing avoidance
    congestion, 239
    FAQs, 236–238, 268–269
    overview, 217

R

Random Early Detection (RED), 148,
        232–235, 263–267. *See also*
        Distributed Weighted Random Early

Detection; Flow-based Random Early
  Detection; Flow-based WRED;
  Weighted Random Early Detection
 configuration, verification, 266–267
 enabling, 263–267
 need, explanation. See Network
 process, explanation, 232–235
 troubleshooting, 267
 usage, 132, 141. See also First In First Out;
  Network Based Application
  Recognition; Queuing
random-detect (command), 330, 340
random-detect precedence (command), 297
Rate enforcement, 301, 303
Rate limiting. See Internet Service Provider
 access list, usage, 193–194
RD. See Reported Distance
RDP traffic, 184, 185
Real Time Protocol (RTP), 200
Real-time applications, 153, 282. See also
  Tolerant real-time applications
Real-time conferencing, 313
Receivers, feedback (providing), 313
Reconvergence, 56
Recovery
 establishing. See Neighbors
 handling, 72–75
RED. See Random Early Detection
redistribute (command), 99, 100
Redundancy, 75
 building. See Network
Reliable multicast, 59
Reliable Transport Protocol (RTP),
  management, 59
Remarking. See Precedence
Remote AS, defining, 425–426
Remote Source Route Bridging (RSRB),
  139
Reported Distance (RD), 68, 70

Request For Comment (RFC)
 791, 149, 150
 1058, 11
 1403, 422
 1657, 422
 1723, 11
 1745, 422
 1771/1772, 422
 1918, 36
 1965-1967, 422
 2201, 9
 2205/2208, 272
 2283, 422
 2385, 422
 2439, 423
 2474/2475, 162, 163
 2545, 423
 2597, 164
 2598, 163
 2744, 163
 current usage, 378–379
Reservation styles, 280–282
Reservation-Request messages, 158
Resource Reservation Protocol (RSVP),
  128, 154, 156, 231. See also
  Distributed RSVP
 configuration, verification, 324–327
 definition, 273–275
 enabling, 322–324
 introduction, 156–161
 messages, 158–161
 need, explanation. See Network
 operation, 157
 process, explanation, 275–282
 proxy, 326–327
 relationship. See Class-based Weighted Fair
  Queuing
 scaling, 160–161

service support, 159
setup time, 283
traffic types, 157
troubleshooting, 322, 327
usage, 272–283. *See also* Quality of Service
   advantages/disadvantages, 283
verification, 322
WRED, relationship, 297
Resource reservation requirements, 156
Resvconf, 159
Resverr, 159
Retransmission timeout (RTO), 59, 66
Reuse limit, 453
RFC. *See* Request For Comment
RIP. *See* Routing Information Protocol
Round-robin fashion, 229
Round-robin procedure, 37
Route. *See* Withdrawn route
   dampening, 452–453
   identifier. *See* Border Gateway Protocol
   length. *See* Unfeasible route length
   poisoning, 55
   redistribution. *See* Default route
   selection/stability, 283
   specific packet types, PBR usage, 184–185
   troubleshooting. *See* Stuck-In-Active
Route maps, 40–43, 100
   configuration, example, 41–43
   usage. *See* Traffic; Weight
      location, 41–43
Route reflectors, 412–413
   configuration, 433–436
   defining, 411–414
   usage, 417
      timing, 438–439
Route-map (command), 441–442
route-map (command), 40–41
Router. *See* Access routers; Cisco;
   Distribution routers; Edge label switch

routers; Label edge routers; Label
   switch router
configuration, 205–206
Route/Switch Processor (RSP), 307
Routine precedence, 137
Routing. *See* Classful IP routing;
   Distance-vector routing
   amount, 463–469
   decisions, 397
   loop, 15, 16
   problem. *See* Internet Protocol
   process. *See* Border Gateway Protocol
   protocol, 75
Routing by rumor, 10, 50
Routing Information Protocol (RIPv1),
   9–13, 48
RSP. *See* Route/Switch Processor
RSP4, 197
RSP-based custom queuing, 309
RSRB. *See* Remote Source Route Bridging
RSVP. *See* Resource Reservation Protocol
RTO. *See* Retransmission timeout
RTP. *See* Real Time Protocol; Reliable
   Transport Protocol
RTP header compression, 307
   configuration, 367, 368
      verification, 368–369
   explanation, 313–315
   process, explanation, 314–315
   troubleshooting, 367, 369–370
   usage, timing, 315
   verification, 367
RTP priority, 304

S

SBM. *See* Subnetwork Bandwidth Manager
Scalability. *See* Enhanced IGRP

Scaling. *See* Integrated Service; Resource Reservation Protocol
  issues, 283
Scheduling. *See* Integrated Service; Packet
SE. *See* Shared-Explicit
Serial Tunneling (STUN), 138
Serial/hssi interfaces, 201
Service profile. *See* Type of Service
Service providers, alternate considerations, 417
Sessions
  maintenance, 278–279
  startup, 276–278
  teardown, 278–279
Set (command), 441–478
Set local-preference (command), usage. *See* Local preference
Set metric (command), 444
  usage. *See* Multiexit Discriminator
set-prec-con, 188
set-prec-trans, 188
Setup time. *See* Resource Reservation Protocol
Shaping. *See* Traffic shaping
  techniques, 144
Shared reservation, 280
Shared-Explicit (SE) style, 281
Shortest path first, 64. *See also* Open Shortest Path First
show eigrp topology (command), 86
show interface (command), 266
show ip eigrp traffic (command), 86
show ip interfaces (command), 350
show log (command), 34
show running-config (command), 14
show traffic-shaping (command), 352
Shutdown, 382
SIA. *See* Stuck-In-Active
Signaling, 473

Single-link failures, 78
Sliding window, 132. *See also* Transmission Control Protocol; Transmission Control Protocol/Internet Protocol
Slow LAN link, SQL application usage, 288–289
SMDS. *See* Switched Multimegabit Data Service
Smooth round-trip time (SRTT), 59
SNA. *See* System Network Architecture
Soft states, 279
Software compression, 307
SONET, 125
Source IP address, 136
Source port, 136
Source system address, 183
Split horizon, 54, 72
Split-horizon updates, 16
SQL application, usage. *See* Slow LAN link
SQL traffic, classification, 204
SRTT. *See* Smooth round-trip time
Standard Access Control Lists, 21–25
Standard access list, 139
Static Address Translation, 36–37
Static translation, contrast. *See* Dynamic translation
StrataCom, 304
Stuck-In-Active (SIA), 108–109
  routes, 85
  troubleshooting, 110–115
STUN. *See* Serial Tunneling
Subcode. *See* Error
Subinterface, 301
Subnet, 18
  mask, 5, 54. *See also* Class C; Variable-length subnet mask
Subnetting, uses, 20–21
Subnetwork, bandwidth manager, 282

Subnetwork Bandwidth Manager (SBM), 282
Sub-protocol types, 224
Successor, 69
   route, 109
Summarization, 94. *See also* Auto-summarization; Enhanced IGRP
Suppress limit, 453. *See also* Maximum suppress limit
Switched Multimegabit Data Service (SMDS), 301
Switching. *See* Multicast distributed switching
Synchronization. *See* Border Gateway Protocol
System Network Architecture (SNA), 125, 137, 138, 169
   CoS, mapping. *See* Internet Protocol
   traffic, 126
      prioritization, 211–213
      usage, 222
System Network Architecture (SNA) ToS configuration, 211–213

T

T1 circuit, 286
T1 frame relay, 160
T1 links, 153
T1 WAN circuit, 131
T3 interface, 220
T3 speeds, 165
Tail drop, 132–133, 349
Tc. *See* Time interval
TCP/IP. *See* Transmission Control Protocol/Internet Protocol
TDM. *See* Time-division multiplexing
Teardown. *See* Sessions
   messages, 159, 279

Telnet, 154
   packets, 246
   traffic, 166
Third octet, 389
Time interval (Tc), 300, 350
Time stamping, 313
Time-division multiplexing (TDM), 303
Timers, adjustment. *See* Border Gateway Protocol
TLV. *See* Type/Length/Value
TN3270, 166
Token bucket, 133–134, 299–301
   depth, 155
   model, 156
Token rate, 155
Token Ring, 124
TOKEN_BUCKET_TSPEC, 155
Tolerant real-time applications, 280
Topology table, 54, 67
ToS. *See* Type of Service
Total path attribute length, 388
Total traffic classification, 289–290
Traffic. *See* File Transfer Protocol; HyperText Transfer Protocol; Internet Protocol
   average rate, 186
   conditioning, 473
   control. *See* Multiprotocol Label Switching
      route maps, usage, 41
   engineering, usage. *See* Congestion reduction; Multiprotocol Label Switching
   filtering, 24
   marking, 349
   policing, 174
   selection, 301, 303
   types. *See* Resource Reservation Protocol
Traffic classification. *See* Priority; Total traffic classification

configuration examples, 181
FAQs, 178–179, 215
overview, 147
Traffic shaping, 174, 307
parameters, configuration, 354–356
understanding, 143–145
Transmission Control Protocol (TCP), 26
connection, 34
port
information, 41
number, 139
translation, 37
protocol. *See* Non-TCP protocol
port traffic, 25
retransmissions, 288
sliding window, 148
stream, 170
TCP-based environments, 143
Transmission Control Protocol/Internet Protocol (TCP/IP), 2
addresses, 4, 5, 17, 33, 39. *See also* Next-hop TCP/IP addresses; Unregistered TCP/IP address
addressing, 5, 6
scheme, 3
conversations, 133
network, 20
sliding window, 233–235
Transparency, 283
Triggered updates, 55
Tspec, 158
parameter, 157
Tunnels. *See* Generic routing encapsulation interfaces, 187
Type of Service (ToS), 26, 52. *See also* Internet Protocol
bit, 148
byte, 137

configuration. *See* System Network Architecture
field, 136, 149, 151
introduction, 148–152
service profile, 150–151
Type/Length/Value (TLV), 61–63

U

UBR. *See* Unspecified bit rate
UDP. *See* User Datagram Protocol
Unequal cost load balancing, 103–108, 476–477
Unfeasible route length, 388
Unicast, 66
services, 313
Unregistered TCP/IP address, 35
Unspecified bit rate (UBR), 471
UPDATE (message), 384, 385. *See also* Border Gateway Protocol
Upstream, 50
neighbors, 74
User Datagram Protocol (UDP), 26, 287
connection, 37
echo requests, 34, 35
port
information, 41
number, 139, 246
translation, 37
protocol port traffic, 25
stream, 294
traffic, 233

V

Variable bit rate non-real time (VBR-nrt), 471
Variable bit rate real time (VBR-rt), 471

Variable-length subnet mask (VLSM), 5, 7, 17–21
  need, explanation, 19–21
  usage, 48, 88
VBR-nrt. *See* Variable bit rate non-real time
VBR-rt. *See* Variable bit rate real time
VC. *See* Virtual circuit
VC, queuing configuration, 356–357
Vector metric, 68
Versatile Interface Processor (VIP), 201, 228. *See also* Non-VIP
Video/audio streams, synchronization, 313
VIP. *See* Versatile Interface Processor; Virtual Interface Processor
VIP-based platform, 186
Virtual circuit (VC), 305
Virtual Interface Processor (VIP), 141
  card, 142
Virtual Private Network (VPN), 307
  extended attributes. *See* Forward VPN
  integration. *See* Border Gateway Protocol; Multiprotocol Label Switching
  usage. *See* Congestion reduction
VLSM. *See* Variable-length subnet mask
Voice over Internet Protocol (VoIP), 127, 160
  dial peers, 275
Voice over IP over Frame Relay (VoIPoFR), 200
VoIP. *See* Voice over Internet Protocol
VoIPoFR. *See* Voice over IP over Frame Relay
VPN. *See* Virtual Private Network

W

WAN. *See* Wide Area Network
WCCP, 307
Web. *See* World Wide Web

Weight, 439, 440. *See also* Border Gateway Protocol
  attribute, 442–444
    setting, access lists usage, 443
    setting, neighbor statement usage, 442–443
    setting, route maps usage, 444
  factor, usage, 230–231
Weighted Fair Queuing (WFQ), 129, 174, 228–232, 259–263. *See also* Class-based Weighted Fair Queuing; Distributed Weighted Fair Queuing; Flow-based Weighted Fair Queuing
  configuration, verification, 260–261
  enabling, 259–263
  need, explanation, 231–232
  process, explanation, 228–232
  support, 301
  troubleshooting, 262–263
  usage, 136, 137
  versions, 135
Weighted Random Early Detection (WRED), 128, 132, 359. *See also* Distributed Weighted Random Early Detection; Flow-based WRED
  algorithm, 297–298
  configuration, 340–342
    verification, 340, 343–348
  functions, 142
  need, explanation. *See* Network
  process, explanation, 295–298
  relationship. *See* Internet Protocol; Resource Reservation Protocol
  troubleshooting, 340, 348–349
  usage, 141, 295–299. *See also* Class-based Weighted Fair Queuing
WF. *See* Wildcard-Filter
Wide Area Network (WAN), 220
  circuit, 143. *See* T1 WAN circuit

connections, 184
links, 103–105, 109, 113, 204. *See also* Slow WAN link
Wildcard, usage, 280
Wildcard-Filter (WF) style, 281
Withdrawn routes, 388
World Wide Web (WWW / Web), 126
  browsing, 288
  traffic, 169
    classification, 204
marking/transmitting, 188–191
WRED. *See* Weighted Random Early Detection

X

X Windows, 204
X Windows traffic, classification, 204
X.25, 125, 153
Xmit Queue Un/Reliable, 85

The Global Knowledge Advantage

Global Knowledge has a global delivery system for its products and services. The company has 28 subsidiaries, and offers its programs through a total of 60+ locations. No other vendor can provide consistent services across a geographic area this large. Global Knowledge is the largest independent information technology education provider, offering programs on a variety of platforms. This enables our multi-platform and multi-national customers to obtain all of their programs from a single vendor. The company has developed the unique CompetusTM Framework software tool and methodology which can quickly reconfigure courseware to the proficiency level of a student on an interactive basis. Combined with self-paced and on-line programs, this technology can reduce the time required for training by prescribing content in only the deficient skills areas. The company has fully automated every aspect of the education process, from registration and follow-up, to "just-in-time" production of courseware. Global Knowledge through its Enterprise Services Consultancy, can customize programs and products to suit the needs of an individual customer.

Global Knowledge Classroom Education Programs

The backbone of our delivery options is classroom-based education. Our modern, well-equipped facilities staffed with the finest instructors offer programs in a wide variety of information technology topics, many of which lead to professional certifications.

Custom Learning Solutions

This delivery option has been created for companies and governments that value customized learning solutions. For them, our consultancy-based approach of developing targeted education solutions is most effective at helping them meet specific objectives.

Self-Paced and Multimedia Products

This delivery option offers self-paced program titles in interactive CD-ROM, videotape and audio tape programs. In addition, we offer custom development of interactive multimedia courseware to customers and partners. Call us at 1-888-427-4228.

Electronic Delivery of Training

Our network-based training service delivers efficient competency-based, interactive training via the World Wide Web and organizational intranets. This leading-edge delivery option provides a custom learning path and "just-in-time" training for maximum convenience to students.

Global Knowledge Courses Available

Microsoft
- Windows 2000 Deployment Strategies
- Introduction to Directory Services
- Windows 2000 Client Administration
- Windows 2000 Server
- Windows 2000 Update
- MCSE Bootcamp
- Microsoft Networking Essentials
- Windows NT 4.0 Workstation
- Windows NT 4.0 Server
- Windows NT Troubleshooting
- Windows NT 4.0 Security
- Windows 2000 Security
- Introduction to Microsoft Web Tools

Management Skills
- Project Management for IT Professionals
- Microsoft Project Workshop
- Management Skills for IT Professionals

Network Fundamentals
- Understanding Computer Networks
- Telecommunications Fundamentals I
- Telecommunications Fundamentals II
- Understanding Networking Fundamentals
- Upgrading and Repairing PCs
- DOS/Windows A+ Preparation
- Network Cabling Systems

WAN Networking and Telephony
- Building Broadband Networks
- Frame Relay Internetworking
- Converging Voice and Data Networks
- Introduction to Voice Over IP
- Understanding Digital Subscriber Line (xDSL)

Internetworking
- ATM Essentials
- ATM Internetworking
- ATM Troubleshooting
- Understanding Networking Protocols
- Internetworking Routers and Switches
- Network Troubleshooting
- Internetworking with TCP/IP
- Troubleshooting TCP/IP Networks
- Network Management
- Network Security Administration
- Virtual Private Networks
- Storage Area Networks
- Cisco OSPF Design and Configuration
- Cisco Border Gateway Protocol (BGP) Configuration

Web Site Management and Development
- Advanced Web Site Design
- Introduction to XML
- Building a Web Site
- Introduction to JavaScript
- Web Development Fundamentals
- Introduction to Web Databases

PERL, UNIX, and Linux
- PERL Scripting
- PERL with CGI for the Web
- UNIX Level I
- UNIX Level II
- Introduction to Linux for New Users
- Linux Installation, Configuration, and Maintenance

Authorized Vendor Training
Red Hat
- Introduction to Red Hat Linux
- Red Hat Linux Systems Administration
- Red Hat Linux Network and Security Administration
- RHCE Rapid Track Certification

Cisco Systems
- Interconnecting Cisco Network Devices
- Advanced Cisco Router Configuration
- Installation and Maintenance of Cisco Routers
- Cisco Internetwork Troubleshooting
- Designing Cisco Networks
- Cisco Internetwork Design
- Configuring Cisco Catalyst Switches
- Cisco Campus ATM Solutions
- Cisco Voice Over Frame Relay, ATM, and IP
- Configuring for Selsius IP Phones
- Building Cisco Remote Access Networks
- Managing Cisco Network Security
- Cisco Enterprise Management Solutions

Nortel Networks
- Nortel Networks Accelerated Router Configuration
- Nortel Networks Advanced IP Routing
- Nortel Networks WAN Protocols
- Nortel Networks Frame Switching
- Nortel Networks Accelar 1000
- Comprehensive Configuration
- Nortel Networks Centillion Switching
- Network Management with Optivity for Windows

Oracle Training
- Introduction to Oracle8 and PL/SQL
- Oracle8 Database Administration

Custom Corporate Network Training

Train on Cutting Edge Technology
We can bring the best in skill-based training to your facility to create a real-world hands-on training experience. Global Knowledge has invested millions of dollars in network hardware and software to train our students on the same equipment they will work with on the job. Our relationships with vendors allow us to incorporate the latest equipment and platforms into your on-site labs.

Maximize Your Training Budget
Global Knowledge provides experienced instructors, comprehensive course materials, and all the networking equipment needed to deliver high quality training. You provide the students; we provide the knowledge.

Avoid Travel Expenses
On-site courses allow you to schedule technical training at your convenience, saving time, expense, and the opportunity cost of travel away from the workplace.

Discuss Confidential Topics
Private on-site training permits the open discussion of sensitive issues such as security, access, and network design. We can work with your existing network's proprietary files while demonstrating the latest technologies.

Customize Course Content
Global Knowledge can tailor your courses to include the technologies and the topics which have the greatest impact on your business. We can complement your internal training efforts or provide a total solution to your training needs.

Corporate Pass
The Corporate Pass Discount Program rewards our best network training customers with preferred pricing on public courses, discounts on multimedia training packages, and an array of career planning services.

Global Knowledge Training Lifecycle
Supporting the Dynamic and Specialized Training Requirements of Information Technology Professionals:

- Define Profile
- Assess Skills
- Design Training
- Deliver Training
- Test Knowledge
- Update Profile
- Use New Skills

Global Knowledge

Global Knowledge programs are developed and presented by industry professionals with "real-world" experience. Designed to help professionals meet today's interconnectivity and interoperability challenges, most of our programs feature hands-on labs that incorporate state-of-the-art communication components and equipment.

ON-SITE TEAM TRAINING

Bring Global Knowledge's powerful training programs to your company. At Global Knowledge, we will custom design courses to meet your specific network requirements. Call (919)-461-8686 for more information.

YOUR GUARANTEE

Global Knowledge believes its courses offer the best possible training in this field. If during the first day you are not satisfied and wish to withdraw from the course, simply notify the instructor, return all course materials and receive a 100% refund.

REGISTRATION INFORMATION

In the US:
call: (888) 762–4442
fax: (919) 469–7070
visit our Web site:
www.globalknowledge.com

Get More at access.globalknowledge

The premier online information source for IT professionals

You've gained access to a Global Knowledge information portal designed to inform, educate and update visitors on issues regarding IT and IT education.

Get what you want when you want it at the access.globalknowledge site:

Choose personalized technology articles related to *your* interests. Access a new article, review, or tutorial regularly throughout the week customized to what you want to see.

Keep learning in between Global courses by taking advantage of chat sessions with other users or instructors. Get the tips, tricks and advice that you need today!

Make your point in the Access.Globalknowledge community with threaded discussion groups related to technologies and certification.

Get instant course information at your fingertips. Customized course calendars showing you the courses you want when and where you want them.

Get the resources you need with online tools, trivia, skills assessment and more!

All this and more is available now on the Web at access.globalknowledge. VISIT TODAY!

Access
global knowledge

http://access.globalknowledge.com

Syngress Publishing's Sweepstake Terms

OFFICIAL RULES - NO PURCHASE NECESSARY

1) TIMING

The contest (the "Contest") begins March 1, 2001 at 9:00 a.m. EST and ends November 30, 2001 at 11:59 p.m. EST (the "Entry Period"). You must enter the contest during the Entry Period.

2) THE PRIZES

Three (3) prizes will be awarded: (a) a Sony DVD Player ("1st Prize"); (b) a Palm Pilot V ("2nd Prize"); and (c) a Rio MP3 Player ("3rd Prize"). One of each prize will be awarded. The approximate retail value of the three prizes is as follows: (a) the Sony DVD Player is approximately $595; (b) the Palm Pilot V is approximately $399; and (c) the Rio MP3 Player is approximately $299.

Sponsors make no warranty, guaranty or representation of any kind concerning any prize. Prize values are subject to change.

3) ELIGIBILITY REQUIREMENTS

No purchase is necessary. Contest is void in Puerto Rico, and where prohibited by law. Employees of Syngress Publishing, Inc. (the "Sponsor") and their affiliates, subsidiaries, officers, agents or any other person or entity directly associated with the contest (the "Contest Entities") and the immediate family members and/or persons living in the same household as such persons are not eligible to enter the Contest.

This contest is open only to people that meet the following requirements:

- legal residents of the United States
- Must be at least 21 years of age or older at the time of winning
- Must own a major credit card

4) HOW TO ENTER:

No purchase is necessary to enter. Contestants can enter by mail (see below) or may enter on the Syngress website located at: www.syngress.com/sweepstake.html. ONLY ONE ENTRY PER PERSON OR E-MAIL ADDRESS PER HOUSEHOLD WILL BE ACCEPTED.

No purchase is necessary to enter. To enter by mail, print your name, address, daytime telephone number, email address and age. Mail this in a hand-addressed envelope to: **Syngress Publishing Contest, Syngress Publishing, Inc., 800 Hingham Street, Rockland, MA 02370**. All mail entries must be postmarked before November 15, 2001.

Sponsor assumes no responsibility for lost, late, or misdirected entries or for any computer, online, telephone, or human error or technical malfunctions that may occur. Incomplete mail entries are void. All entries become the property of Sponsor and will not be returned.

If a prize notification or prize is returned to Sponsor or its fulfillment companies as undeliverable for any reason, it will be awarded to an alternate. If necessary, due to unavailability, a prize of equal or great value will be awarded at the discretion of the Sponsor. Prizes are not transferable, assignable or redeemable for cash.

By entering the Contest on the Sponsor Internet site, you may occasionally receive promotion announcements from Sponsor through e-mail. If you no longer wish to receive these e-mails, you may cease your participation in such promotions by sending an e-mail to promotions@syngress.com with your First Name, Last Name, and your e-mail address.

5) WINNER SELECTION/DEADLINE DATES: Random drawings will be conducted by the Sponsor from among all eligible entries. Odds of winning the prize depend on the number of eligible entries received. The first drawing will be for the winner of the 1st Prize, then a drawing will be held from all remaining eligible entries for the winner of the 2nd Prize and finally a drawing will be held from all remaining eligible entries for the winner of the 3rd Prize. These drawings will occur on December 1, 2001, at the offices of Syngress Publishing, Inc., 800 Hingham Street, Rockland, MA 02370. The decisions by the Sponsor shall be final and binding in all respects.

6) GENERAL CONDITIONS: Contest entrants agree to be bound by the terms of these official rules. The laws of the Commonwealth of Massachusetts and the United States govern this Contest, and the state and federal courts located in Suffolk and Middlesex Counties in the Commonwealth of Massachusetts shall be the sole jurisdiction for any disputes related to the Contest. All federal, state, and local laws and regulations apply. Winners will be notified via e-mail and/or U.S. Mail within two (2) weeks of prize drawing. Winners will be required to execute and return an Affidavit of Eligibility and Release of Liability and where legal, Publicity Release within 14 days following the date of issuance of notification. Non-compliance within this time period or return of any prize/prize notification as undeliverable may result in disqualification and selection of an alternate winner. Acceptance of prize constitutes permission for Sponsor to use winner's name and likeness for advertising and promotional purposes without additional compensation unless prohibited by law. BY ENTERING, PARTICIPANTS RELEASE AND HOLD HARMLESS SYNGRESS PUBLISHING, INC., AND ITS RESPECTIVE PARENT CORPORATIONS, SUBSIDIARIES, AFFILIATES, DIRECTORS, OFFICERS, PRIZE SUPPLIERS, EMPLOYEES AND AGENTS FROM ANY AND ALL LIABILITY OR ANY INJURIES, LOSS OR DAMAGE OF ANY KIND ARISING FROM OR IN CONNECTION WITH THE CONTEST OR ACCEPTANCE OR USE OF THE PRIZES WON.

7) INTERNET: If for any reason this contest is not capable of running as planned due to infection by computer virus, bugs, tampering, unauthorized intervention, fraud, technical failures, or any other causes beyond the control of the Sponsor which corrupt or affect the administration, security, fairness, integrity, or proper conduct of this contest, the Sponsor reserves the right, at its sole discretion, to disqualify any individual who tampers with the entry process, and to cancel, terminate, modify, or suspend the online portion of the contest. The Sponsor assumes no responsibility for any error, omission, interruption, deletion, defect, delay in operation or transmission, communications line failure, theft or destruction or unauthorized access to, or alteration of, entries. Sponsor is not responsible for any problems or technical malfunction of any telephone network or telephone lines, computer on-line systems, servers, or providers, computer equipment, software, failure of any e-mail or entry to be received by Sponsor on account of technical problems, human error or traffic congestion on the Internet or at any Web site, or any combination thereof, including any injury or damage to participant's or any other person's computer relating to or resulting from participation in the Contest or downloading any materials in the Contest. CAUTION: ANY ATTEMPT TO DELIBERATELY DAMAGE ANY WEB SITE OR UNDERMINE THE LEGITIMATE OPERATION OF THE CONTEST IS A VIOLATION OF CRIMINAL AND CIVIL LAWS AND SHOULD SUCH AN ATTEMPT BE MADE, SPONSOR RESERVES THE RIGHT TO SEEK DAMAGES OR OTHER REMEDIES FROM ANY SUCH PERSON (S) RESPONSIBLE FOR THE ATTEMPT TO THE FULLEST EXTENT PERMITTED BY LAW. In the event of a dispute as to the identity of a winner based on an e-mail address, the winning entry will be declared made by the authorized account holder of the e-mail address submitted at time of entry. "Authorized account holder" is defined as the natural person who is assigned to an e-mail address by an Internet access provider, on-line service provider, or other organization (e.g., business, educational, institution, etc.) that is responsible for assigning e-mail addresses for the domain associated with the submitted e-mail address.

8) WHO WON: Winners who enter on the web site will be notified by e-mail and winners who had entered via mail will be notified by mail. The winners will also be posted on our web site. Alternatively, to receive the names of the winners please send a self addressed stamped envelope to: Syngress Publishing Contest, care of Syngress Publishing, Inc., 800 Hingham Street, Rockland, MA 02370.

The Sponsor of this sweepstakes is Syngress Publishing, Inc., 800 Hingham Street, Rockland, MA 02370.

SYNGRESS SOLUTIONS...

AVAILABLE NOW!
ORDER at
www.syngress.com

Configuring Cisco AVVID

AVVID (Architecture for Voice, Video, and Integrated Data) is a network architecture made up of hardware and software that transmits a company's data such as e-mail, web traffic, file transfers, voice traffic, and video traffic over the same physical computer network. *Configuring Cisco AVVID* will introduce you to the new AVVID components from Cisco that can save hard dollars and increase a company's overall performance. This book will give IT professionals, ISPs, and engineers the first insight into how each piece of hardware and each software application function independently, as well as how they interoperate, forming a completely converged solution. It covers the many components of AVVID, including Cisco Routers, Cisco Catalyst Switches, Cisco IP Telephones, Cisco CallManager Servers, Analog and Digital Gateways, Voice Trunks, Voice Modules, CallManager 3.0, SoftPhone, WebAttendant, and Active Voice.

ISBN: 1-928994-14-8
Price: $59.95

AVAILABLE NOW!
ORDER at
www.syngress.com

MANAGING CISCO NETWORK SECURITY

Developed for IT professionals, *Managing Cisco Network Security* details the strategies, tactics, and methods for designing, configuring, and maintaining CiscoSecure networks. It includes thorough discussions on hot topics ranging from secure VPNs and intranets, to protected LANs and WANs. It also covers the full range of CiscoSecure hardware and software solutions, including PIX Firewall, Intrusion Detection System, Access Client/Server (ACS) software, and Authentication Agent.

ISBN: 1-928994-17-2
$59.95

AVAILABLE NOW!
ORDER at
www.syngress.com

BUILDING CISCO REMOTE ACCESS NETWORKS

Building Cisco Remote Access Networks (BCRAN) covers the key technology area of remote access. Cisco is a dominant force in this Internet economy and BCRAN is more than a product line; it is a technology delivery platform of products. This book covers the key protocols involved, as well as technical connectivity considerations. It provides the reader with instruction on interconnecting central sites to branch offices, and supporting home office workers and telecommuters. BCRAN is about technological empowerment. This book will help you grow technically, expand your career opportunities, and enhance your experience of the Internet Revolution.

ISBN: 1-928994-13-X
Price: $49.95

solutions@syngress.com

SYNGRESS®